Human Families

Social Change in Global Perspective

Mark Selden, *Series Editor*

Exploring the relationship between social change and social structures, this series considers the theory, praxis, promise, and pitfalls of movements in global and comparative perspective. The historical and contemporary social movements considered here challenge patterns of hierarchy and inequality of race, gender, nationality, ethnicity, class, and culture. The series will emphasize textbooks and broadly interpretive synthetic works.

Human Families, STEVAN HARRELL

African Women: A Modern History, CATHERINE COQUERY-VIDROVITCH, translated by BETH GILLIAN RAPS

Portraits of the Japanese Workplace: Labor Movements, Workers, and Managers, KUMAZAWA MAKOTO, translated by MIKISO HANE

Capital, the State, and Late Industrialization: Comparative Perspectives on the Pacific Rim, edited by JOHN BORREGO, ALEJANDRO ALVAREZ BEJAR, and JOMO K.S.

Power Restructuring in China and Russia, MARK LUPHER

The Challenge of Local Feminisms: Women's Movements in Global Perspective, edited by AMRITA BASU, with the assistance of C. ELIZABETH MCGRORY

The Transformation of Communist Systems: Economic Reform Since the 1950s, BERNARD CHAVANCE

Human Families

Stevan Harrell

WestviewPress

A Division of HarperCollins*Publishers*

306.85
H29h

Social Change in Global Perspective

Published in 1997 in the United States of America by Westview Press, 5500 Central Avenue, Boulder, Colorado 80301-2877, and in the United Kingdom by Westview Press, 12 Hid's Copse Road, Cumnor Hill, Oxford OX2 9JJ

Library of Congress Cataloging-in-Publication Data
Harrell, Stevan.
  Human families / Stevan Harrell.
    p.   cm. — (Social change in global perspective)
  Includes bibliographical references and index.
  ISBN 0-8133-2728-8 (hc.)
    1. Family—Cross-cultural studies.   2. Kinship—Cross-cultural
studies.   3. Social structure—Cross-cultural studies.   I. Title.
II. Series.
GN480.H37   1997
306.85—dc20
                                                                        96-44887
                                                                        CIP

The paper used in this publication meets the requirements of the American National Standard for Permanence of Paper for Printed Library Materials Z39.48-1984.

10   9   8   7   6   5   4   3   2   1

In memory

of a dear friend, who practiced anthropology with

Joy
Rigor
InnovAtion

Contents

PART SEVEN
THE M-CLUSTER: FAMILIES IN MODERN SOCIETY

Figures and Tables

Tables

Maps

Preface

I began this book in the summer of 1979 because of my own family. My wife was a medical student, our children were small, and there was thus no immediate prospect of fieldwork. I had been teaching a course called "Comparative Family Organization" for several years, and in looking for teaching materials for that course had read Jack Goody's *Production and Reproduction*. I considered Goody's book a challenge; it contrasted the family systems of Eurasia and Sub-Saharan Africa on a materialist basis, but said little about the variation within Eurasia or within Africa. I set out to document the Eurasian variation, and that summer I wrote a draft of what would become Part Six of the present book. I sent the draft "monograph" to Professor Goody, who was helpful and encouraging. I thought maybe I ought to document the variation within Africa as well, and before long I had conceived the present structure, looking at the history of human family organization over the three great transformations of history—sedentarization, the development of social classes, and the industrial/scientific revolution. I thought the project would take two or three years.

It is now the winter of 1996. My wife has been in medical practice for over a decade and is about to retire, our children are grown, I have done fieldwork four times in the interim. I have been ready many times to abandon this project as outmoded and unwieldy, but friends have urged me to bring it to completion, and I owe it to all my family to demonstrate that this strange and episodic obsession indeed has an endpoint.

This I have done, but much has changed in the meantime besides the inevitable rolling of my own family's developmental cycle. The discipline of cultural anthropology is at present little interested in the problem that spurred this book in the first place—the problem of explaining human diversity. The very concepts with which my generation learned the field— societies, cultures, ethnographic reporting itself—are now objects of critical inquiry rather than the given conceptual tools of the time of our collective innocence. Why, then, present such a comparative book at such a critical period? I think there are three reasons.

First, the intellectual challenge is still there. It is the same challenge faced by Morgan, Engels, Westermarck, Lévi-Strauss, and G.P. Murdock as well as more recent synthesizers using the perspectives of feminism, sociobiology, or historical demography. It is the challenge to make sense, to make order, out of a wide but not infinite variety of human social systems that have changed over the course of history but, we believe, neither in random, exclusively culturally determined ways nor entirely according to the dictates of material conditions.

Second and perhaps most importantly, questions of family continue to occupy a salient place in political and social debates all over the world, and nowhere more prominently than in the United States. The decline of the American family has been decried now for approximately 120 years, but the velocity of the discourse, if not of the decline itself, has accelerated in the last few years with public debates about single motherhood, same-sex partner medical benefits, and how to care for us baby-boomers when one more turn of the cycle makes us old and dependent. A comparative analysis can give us perspective on current social issues; we can set the questions about the current direction of the family into the context of the full range of human possibilities and experiences.

Finally, the theoretical pendulum will swing again. Anthropology has already experienced at least two full swings from comparative, evolutionary approaches to particularistic, cultural ones; the violence done to the particular by comparativism balances the trivialization of the whole by particularism, and so the center cannot hold. The approach of this book is a once-and-future anthropology, and in another half-century it will be dated and irrelevant for the second time.

Still, I do not wish to present this account in stubborn ignorance of recent turns in anthropology, particularly the critique of ethnographic writing and authority (the canonical sources are now Clifford and Marcus 1986 and Marcus and Fischer 1986). In order to formulate a comparativist account such as this one, a writer has to make judgments as to the validity of what he finds in the numerous ethnographic accounts, most of them published before anthropological criticism became very sophisticated. But this is about all a writer can do—he cannot subject every account to an analysis of the rhetorical and/or scientific sources of its authority. Some accounts can be dismissed as fantasies or total misconstruals (Linton 1940 on the Marquesas is a famous example); in other cases seemingly contradictory accounts must be reconciled (Mead 1928 and Freeman 1983 provide a well-known instance). Many times, as with the British Social Anthropology accounts of Africa, written from the 1940s to the 1960s, a particular static, functional bias must be taken into account. And often, of course, terminologies and conceptual frameworks (particularly those that ignore the dynamics of the developmental cycle) must be adjusted to the writer's own standards. But if one is to write a comparative book at all, one must have something to compare, and these objects of comparison must be the family systems of various communities as read through the writer's own lens from the accounts in the ethnographic and other literatures. There are, in turn, two ways to read the web of systems that I have constructed in this account.

The first is to take the systems as somehow real, allowing that some of the descriptions may be biased or even mistaken. The book then becomes a history of the family. The second is to take the systems as "raw structures" in Lévi-Strauss's sense, whose relation to physical reality is less important than their relation to one another. The book then becomes an exercise in logic. I prefer the former reading, but I realize the latter is possible.

In the preparation of this work, editors Susan McEachern, formerly of Westview Press, and Lynn Arts and Carol Jones, now of Westview, have been ever patient and constructive. Gabrielle O'Malley has been invaluable—typesetting, formatting, indexing, and (usually gently) coaxing me to stay on task in the midst of a hundred other projects. Jennifer Leehey has been an able proofreader.

Many friends, colleagues, and students have read part or all of this book at various draft and manuscript stages and provided helpful comments, suggestions, and bibliography. They include John Atkins, Alan Barnard, Crisca Bierwert, Debra Connelly, Nancy Donnelly, Maria Duryea, Larry Epstein, Jack Goody, Margaret Hollenbeck, Charles Keyes, Patrick Kirch, Barbara Knox-Seith, Donna Leonetti, Leslie Morris, James Nason, Harley Schreck, Mark Selden, John Shepherd, Eric Smith, Theresa Smith, Clark Sorensen, David Spain, Danette Swanson, Peter Whitely, Nancy Williams, Edgar Winans, Diane Wolf, and Shusuke Yagi. It is ironic that the one I wanted most to read it is the only one who has died while I have fiddled. I have dedicated it to his memory.

Stevan Harrell

Credits

PART ONE

Concepts and Methods

1

Introduction

The family has existed nearly always and nearly everywhere in human history. That is, nearly always and nearly everywhere, people have cooperated more closely with certain close blood or marital relatives than with other people in the activities that produce and reproduce their daily existence. But the activities in which they cooperate, and the precise relationships between people who cooperate in carrying out these activities, vary through time and space. For example, at a particular time and place, the family may be important as a residential group, as a group for the division between income-producing and domestic labor, as a legal unit for the payment of taxes, as a group that cares for the disabled and the feeble aged, as a regulator of sexual mores, or for any number of other activities. Somewhere else, or at another time, people may relegate all these activities to some group other than the family. They may live primarily in age villages or dormitories, division of labor may be carried out at the level of the foraging band or the agricultural producers' cooperative, taxes may be based on individual income or value added, the disabled may be relegated to sanitoria and the aged to old-folks homes, sexual mores may be regulated by clans or mens' and women's secret societies, and so on. Or some of these activities—taxation, for example—may be absent altogether in a particular society. In other words it becomes a practical impossibility to define the family in terms of its *functions*—some are important in one place, some in another; some are widespread and some rare; but none is universal or necessary and sufficient to define a family.

Similarly, the group of relatives that cooperates in family activities also varies widely. Small children usually live with their biological parents, but the rate of adoption can approach one-third or higher in some places, or mother and father may not customarily live together. Married couples may take up residence with the husband's parents, the wife's parents, or the husband's mother's brother, or they may set up a new household on their own. Married siblings may or may not be allowed or expected to cooperate in residence, production, consumption, or ritual. Marriage may be monogamous, polygynous, or occasionally involve some other combination of husbands and wives. Young married couples may cooperate with one set of parents in certain activities throughout the parents' lives, or they may be expected to become independent in residence, production, taxation or ritual, upon the marriage of a younger sibling, upon the retirement of the father, or at some other specified time. In other words, it becomes a practical impossibility to define the family according to its *structure*. Some relationships may be more likely to fall within its compass than others, but there is always an exception to be found. As in the case of function, no structure, no particular relationship, is necessary and sufficient in defining the family.

Despite this difficulty in pinning it down, however, almost everyone would agree with my initial statement that the family has existed almost always and almost everywhere, and with the descriptive passages that show there is wide variation both in how the family is organized and in what it is organized for. The task of this book is to explain that variation.

This comparative task is, unlike many global, cross-cultural comparative projects in anthropology, a feasible one. Culture, in many of its aspects, can display almost infinite variation. Technology, for example, while limited by the availability of materials and the tasks it must perform, can display wide variation because it is capable of influencing the social process of production to create new needs, new tasks, even new materials which can, in turn, foster its own further expansion. Art and religion are limited only by the cognitive and aesthetic properties of the human imagination—limits we do not know and perhaps can never hope to know. The family, on the contrary, is limited by the basic need of human beings to reproduce themselves—reproduce in the widest sense of re-creating the means of their own biological and social existence. (Insofar as there are social groups that are not organized to allow their members to reproduce themselves, these groups are the primary exception to the generalization that the family exists everywhere.) The nature of what has to be reproduced may vary, but the variation is not unlimited—children must be borne and raised and socialized; adults must be provided with the means of physical and social existence; old people must be cared for when they can no longer meet their own needs. The reasons why people organize the family, the activities in which family members cooperate,[1] thus vary over time and space, but they can be analyzed and compared in a reasonably systematic manner.

The structure of the family is similarly delimited, and by three factors: the fact of sexual reproduction, the length of the human lifespan and of its dependent segments, and the activities people engage in as members of families. Two sexes means that marriage, or something closely equivalent to it, will involve a limited number of possibilities for singular and plural unions. The human lifespan and generational span mean that there are usually two, but seldom more than two adult generations alive at any one time, a fact with universal but usually unrecognized significance for family organization. And the activities for which a family is organized in a particular social context limit the nature of the structures a family can have and still be organized for those activities. The activities do not create or determine the structures, because a certain activity usually can be organized in more than one way. But they do constrain the possibilities, and this can be used to account for much of the variation in family systems.

It should be made clear from the beginning that this is not a book about kinship in general, and that it treats extended kinship groups (larger than family) only insofar as they are relevant to understanding family organization. Kinship is a set of principles, while the family is a type of group. If kinship is a way of organizing social relationships on the basis of parent-child and husband-wife links, then the family, by definition, is organized along kinship principles. But kinship principles have ramifications beyond the family, whether in ego-centered networks, unilineal descent groups, or other extended kinship organizations. The family is a special type of kinship group, one consisting of close relatives in close cooperation in daily life. In many cases, the principles of family organization, or the activities of the family, are not the principles of organization or the activities of the larger kin groups in which families are embedded. In such cases, we must be careful not to confuse the family with other kinship groups.

At the same time, this book argues that the family in any community cannot be understood only paradigmatically, in comparison to families in other communities, but must also be understood syntagmatically, in relation to other groups in which its members participate. These other groups include extended kin groups, and the existence, for example, of corporate matrilineages in a particular community may be extremely important for the family in that community. But so may the existence of groups not organized according to a kinship principle, such as age-sets, castes, or daycare cooperatives. Once again, the emphasis is on the family as a group of people that do certain things with, for, or to each other, rather than on kinship as a principle that organizes groups.

Notes

1. A shorthand way to refer to these activities would be to call them "the functions of the family." I have in fact done that in previous drafts of this book. The problem with this terminology is that for many readers, the term "functions" implies some sort of logic in which the effects of a phenomenon are assumed to be its cause, in a mechanical way that leaves out the intermediate variable of human intentions. For example, if I say that people in a particular community cooperate with family members to harvest corn, I convey an awareness of human intention. If I say that the family functions to get the corn harvest in, I am describing the same activities, but in a way that transfers intentionality to a group. In order to avoid this misunderstanding, I have sacrificed eloquence for clarity and eliminated the idea of "functions." For a thorough, difficult discussion of functionalist vs. intentionalist logics of explanation, see Elster 1983: 49-89.

2

Describing Variation: The Family Developmental Cycle

In order to explain the variation in family activities and family structure, we must see the family not as a static entity, a group of people frozen in time, but as the process a group with changing membership goes through as its members reproduce it. This process is manifested both in the activities of the members as a family and in the composition of the family group. The particular tasks in which family members cooperate change as members enter and leave the family and change status within it, and the family form changes as members are added subtracted, as it divides into several families or combines with others to form a single family. This elementary fact was first pointed out in an ethnographic case study by Meyer Fortes (1949), who elaborated it later in a short programmatic essay (1958).[1] Unfortunately, that essay was narrow in its conception, dividing the developmental, or generational, cycle of the family into three rather rigid phases based on nuclear family organization, and the developmental cycle has not, for that reason, become the basic assumption of anthropological family studies that it really ought to be. But if we remove the narrow focus on a particular kind of family structure and the specific phases of its generational cycle, and apply the concept of a developmental cycle in each generation to whatever family structure we might find in a particular case, we find that the concept is absolutely necessary to understanding family organization. Static or synchronic descriptions or comparisons of families are virtually meaningless, because they do not tell us how family members that occupy certain statuses at a certain time acquired those statuses, or what is likely to happen to those people in the following decades. Such a

7

concentration on synchronic comparisons or census statistics has often misled students of the family.

For example, Ward Goodenough and John Fisher (Goodenough, 1956; Fisher, 1958), in independent censuses of the population of the same Trukese island taken three years apart, found widely differing percentages of various categories of marital residence. These disparities were not resolved until they were examined, not from the standpoint of who was living with whom at the time of the census, but through looking at the history of how each couple, as a part of the family developmental process, came to be living in its current household.

In another telling example, Peter Laslett (1972, 1978) has devoted a great amount of energy in a very productive career to a misguided effort to try to disprove the importance of the three-generation, stem family in pre-modern and early modern England. He has shown conclusively that only a small portion, varying from 6 to 19%, of families in any one village sample took on the stem form (Laslett 1972:61). But it has been convincingly shown for similar populations by Berkner (1976) and others, that a stem- family cycle, in which people always lived in stem families between the time of the marriage of the single successor and the death of the holding parents, would produce a synchronic population in which only a small percentage of families actually took the stem form *at any one time*, but where nearly every family spent some time in the stem phase of its developmental cycle in each generation.

The same kind of problem arose with studies of Chinese joint families. Early Western-trained anthropologists, entering the Chinese field and expecting great multi-generation joint family compounds reminiscent of the Jia family in the social novel *Dream of the Red Chamber*, were disillusioned to find very small percentages of joint families in the rural communities they studied (Gamble 1954:84, Fei 1939:28-29). But a closer examination has revealed that, given the vagaries of fertility and mortality, many families would not produce the requisite two or more sons to form a joint family at all in each generational cycle, and even those who had more than one son usually remained in the joint phase for only a small portion of the time span of each generation (Wolf and Huang 1980; Wolf 1984; Harrell and Pullum 1995). A synchronic census of such a population would thus reveal only a small number of joint families in a population whose members were, paradoxically, practicing a joint family system.

Examples could be multiplied, but the point is clear: synchronic description of families can never yield a family system, unless these synchronic descriptions are projected onto a cyclical process of family social reproduction. Similarly, when we go about comparing family systems, we must compare them in terms of the series of processes that form their developmental cycle in each generation. These processes will not necessarily occur in the same order in every family in every generation. For example, the death of a father may come before or after his son's marriage. Similarly, not exactly the same series of processes will occur in every family. For example, a patrilocal family with one son will not divide when that son's parents die, as a family with two sons might. Freed and Freed (1983), in observing these irregularities in the family processes in an Indian village, have suggested that the concept of developmental cycle is therefore too rigid to portray the complex reality of families in an actual community. They observe, and rightly so, that in no community is there a single sequence of family types or of events that mark transitions from one type to another. But what they fail to emphasize is that in a single community, there are a set of principles according to which family events are structured—these principles include, for example, place of marital residence, inclusiveness or restrictiveness of offspring as family members, and so forth. Members of a community who follow one set of principles will produce a set of sequences of family events, whether or not every event occurs in every generation and regardless of the exact order in which events occur. It is in this sense that we can talk of the developmental cycle in a particular community.

Comparison, Classification, and Variation

Before embarking on the detailed work of comparison, it is imperative that we state clearly exactly what we are comparing. Recent rethinking of anthropological assumptions has shed necessary doubt on the idea of "a society," for example, pointing out that the boundaries of a society, culture, or people have often been as much the creation of administrators or even anthropologists as perceptions that rule the lives of community members. What I want to avoid here is what Abu-Lughod (1991:146) calls the tendency to "freeze differences," to identify, in a sort of holistic and mechanical way, a place, a people, and a way of doing things. What I am comparing here is family systems, particular ways of organizing closely related people to cooperate in certain activities. Insofar as a collection of people share the same assumptions and rules about how to organize their family lives, they share a family system. It is immaterial, however, whether this collection of people is composed of all the people on an island, all the people that speak the same language, a fuzzily bounded group of people who consider themselves a nationality, or members of a particular (equally fuzzily bounded) social class. So when I speak of a Sicilian (or a Gonja or a Puget Salish) system, for the purposes of this analysis the term "Sicilian" refers to this system and "Sicilians" to those who practice it, without any implication that everyone on the island of Sicily does so. In comparing the family systems themselves and the circumstances under which they develop and persist, social factors are always important, since both information about how things are done and coercion that compels people to do things a certain way tend to travel within certain customary channels. But I am not comparing societies; I am comparing family systems.

In order to account for the variation in the developmental cycles of various family systems, we must find a way to describe this variation accurately. If we were comparing only two systems, we could simply give as complete as possible a description of each, and proceed to describe how the two systems differed and why. But when we compare more than two systems, we want to be able to talk about *patterns* of variation—how certain family systems are like each other and different from other systems. One way to talk about patterns is to classify family systems into types—to take a group of family systems that are alike in certain ways, call them a type, and contrast the characteristics of that type with those of some other similar group of systems, referred to as another type. We would then end up with a classification, or typology, of family systems, and would be able to compare and contrast systems that fall into various places in the typology. This has been done with some success, for example by Hammel and Laslett (1974) in regard to formal models of household structure, and by Goldschmidt and Kunkel in a survey of peasant family systems (1971).

But there are problems with typologies—there are usually systems that do not fit, that are intermediate between two or more types. There are two solutions to this problem, neither of them particularly satisfactory. One is the lumping solution, drawing precise boundaries between types and classifying "atypical" systems in the type that they approximate most closely. The second is the splitting solution, taking "atypical" systems to constitute an additional type. In either case, further comparison is needed to account for the "atypical" system, either in the form of intra-type comparison in the lumping case, or in the form of additional comparisons between types in the splitting case. Since the variation in family systems is bounded, and the number of known systems is finite, the task is theoretically possible, but only if we make an unwieldy number of comparisons. As an alternative, inconvenient types can be left out altogether, an honest procedure if admitted, but ultimately an unsatisfying one.

There is, however, a more satisfactory way out. We can treat differences, not as classification, but as the conjunction of values along a number of dimensions of variation. We can then, instead of asking "what makes Type A family systems different from Type B systems?", ask rather "what causes various family systems to have higher or lower values of particular variable dimensions?", and thus avoid the problem of having to place a system somewhere in a typology in order to describe it or to contrast it with other systems. We will, most likely, find that large numbers of systems tend to cluster in various narrow regions in the n-dimensional matrix of variation, and such clusters can be conveniently referred to as types. But the types become empirical constructs, not part of the logical basis of the comparative analysis. Then when we find systems that have few close neighbors in the matrix, they become less the atypical or problem societies, but simply more cases to be explained in terms of variation on the same series of dimensions. Types thus become Weberian "ideal types" (Gerth and Mills 1946:59-60), heuristic devices around which to organize discussion. But intermediate or atypical societies no longer need be treated as anomalies. In the following sections of this introduction, and in the later chapters of the book, I organize family systems according to certain kinds of variation along certain dimensions. In particular cases, of course, these variables may be non-continuous, even (rarely) dichotomous. But continuous variables need not be treated as if they were non-continuous, and even non-continuous variables can still be seen as dimensions of variation, with intermediate values simply not occupied by empirical cases.

What this book is doing, then, is tracing patterns of variation in the developmental cycle of human families. In order to do so, we have to consider two aspects of that variation:

First, *what do people do* as members of families? What activities are organized by and for family members at various stages of the developmental cycle?

Second, *who does these things with and for whom*? What are the rules by which people enter and exit the family group as the developmental cycle progresses?

What People Do in Families

To understand why a particular family system works the way it does in any particular generation we must see it as a product of two factors: (1) the system practiced by that family's members in the previous generation and (2) any pressures that will tend to change the activities people perform as members of family groups. This formulation is based on two assumptions. First, people organize families in order to reproduce themselves socially, and in order to do so, they have to perform certain activities with, for, or to other family members. Second, in the absence of pressure to change the way they organize these activities, people will tend to organize their families in the manner they have learned from growing up among other people who organize their families that way. In order to explain variation among family systems, then, we first have to understand the activities for which families are organized. The activities organized in the family, though varying widely in the expression and in the way they are performed, fall into a very limited number of categories:

1. Division of labor in *procuring* material goods necessary for subsistence or luxury consumption. Because of the universally present sexual division of labor, and because of the presence of dependents (young, old, permanently or temporarily disabled) as part of family groups, every family system will include the expectation that family members will share with other members some of the goods they procure through hunting, gathering, cultivation, purchase, or whatever other means. In general, people share such goods within the family on the basis of what Sahlins (1965:193) has called generalized reciprocity: they give freely with no accounting of requital or return, though they expect that others will share, equally freely, when they have something to share.

2. Division of labor involved in *processing* goods procured by family members for consumption by family members. This occurs for the same reasons as the division of labor in procuring goods—there are those within the family who, by reason of youth, age, disability, or another part in the division of labor, depend on the services of other members for processing of consumption goods. Again, they usually share on the basis of generalized reciprocity. There is a general tendency for the sexual division of labor to emphasize males as procurers and females as processors of goods to be consumed. There are, however, other possible and empirically observed arrangements.

3. Providing and limiting access to *sexual* partners. In practically every family group, there are both people who are expected to have sexual relations with each other and people who are prohibited from doing so. Family systems also vary in the extent to which sexuality outside the family group is permitted, discouraged, encouraged, or forbidden.

4. *Socialization* of children. In every system at least some, and frequently the greater part, of the duties of enculturating children fall to family members. These duties, in fact, are of two kinds: the *care* of very young children, and the *education* of both younger and older children.

5. *Management* of property and offices and their transmission to the next generation through inheritance and succession. This is not important in all family systems—in some societies there is nothing to succeed to or to inherit. But where it does exist, it becomes important, especially since household membership is usually transmitted from one generation to the next through the same or a similar pattern of routes of transmission.

6. *Representation* of the family in the public activities of politics or community ritual. Again, this is not relevant everywhere. But in those communities that are part of societies where there is a sphere of activities that is clearly public, as opposed to domestic (see below), that public sphere often

involves every member of society as an object of activity (as a head to be taxed, or as a potential beneficiary of ritual, for example), but involves only certain members as active participants. Where this occurs, active participants perform these public activities at least partially on behalf of those members of their families who do not participate actively.

7. *Enabling* the participation of certain family members in public activities of economic exchange, politics, and ritual. Where these activities are important, it is through the mobilization of family labor or family goods that an individual is enabled to participate and/or succeed in such public activities. For example, family wealth may enable participation in political elections, or family labor may produce some of the goods used in large-scale, prestige-building ceremonial exchanges.

8. Providing *emotional* warmth, support, and comfort for family members. Of all the possible family activities enumerated here, this is the most difficult to describe and analyze, yet it may be one of the most important. Some family relationships, everywhere, are expected to be emotionally close in this way. The configuration of which relationships are expected to have what content varies widely. In some communities such closeness is expected almost entirely within the family group; in others, people typically look outside the family for such support and companionship.

The exact nature of this kind of list of activities is something we can argue about. Netting and Wilk, for example (1984:5), posit a five-item list: production, distribution, transmission, reproduction, and coresidence. Carter, in another article in the same volume (1984:52) gives us a somewhat different list: provision of food, shelter, clothing, and health care, as well as socialization. I think any carefully thought-out list will do; I also think that a list that does not include enabling is severely weakened in its explanatory power.

Who Are Family Members?

Having talked about what people do as members of families, we can now consider who is doing these things with, for, or to whom.

To begin with, we must remember that the possibilities for the structure of the family developmental cycle are constrained by two human universals. The first is the fact of two sexes and two aspects of their usual relations—their propensity to form long-lasting, relatively exclusive sexual partnerships, and their participation in a sexual division of labor.[2] Long lasting does not mean permanent—divorce and remarriage, sometimes several times, are the norm in many places, and exclusive does not mean rigorously one-to-one—at most times and places there are either plural unions or some degree of sexual freedom before, between, or during the periods when stable unions are operating. But long-lasting does mean more than casual, and exclusive means that there are people with whom sexual relations are prohibited or strongly discouraged, a category that may include everyone except a current spouse, or a category that may be much more restricted. Pairing, then, in the sense used long ago by Morgan (1877) and Engels (1883) seems to be a nearly universal fact in communities where people reproduce,[3] often allowing for the possibility of certain people participating in more than one pair at a time. The nature of pairing is also limited by the nearly universal prohibition on sexual pairing between siblings or parent and child. I accept these tendencies as given; my purpose here is not to explain them but to describe their effects on family organization.

The sexual division of labor is, similarly, a virtual universal, based *primarily* on the roles of the two sexes in biological reproduction. In general, certain activities that require prolonged travel or prolonged, strenuous moving around are incompatible with advanced pregnancy or with breastfeeding, and have tended across most of history to become male activities. Other activities, which may require as much strength or stamina, but not as much mobility, have tended to be seen as women's work.[4] Families contain members of both sexes not just as sexual pairs, but also as partners in an equal or unequal sharing of the tasks of production and of both biological and social reproduction necessary to the livelihood and continuance of the family and society.

The second universal is the aforementioned life span and generational span. The physiological human life-span, in any society, seems to be between 90 and 100 years on the average (Weiss 1981),[5] but very few people actually live that long anywhere, and the practical life-span seems to hover around seventy years or so. The generational span varies, and tends to be shorter from mother to offspring than from father to offspring, but twenty to thirty years seems to be the average. The ratio of life-span to generational span thus approximates 3:1. This means that, even in where the likelihood of living to old age is high, very few people spend much time alive at the same time as their great-grandparents or great-grandchildren or, to put it another way, grandparents and grandchildren are seldom adult for very long at the same time. For all practical purposes, then, this means that there will be either one or two adult generations alive at any one time. Most people who live past early childhood can expect to see their children grow to adulthood, and to see their grandchildren born. It is rare that there are no adult generations alive; it is also rare that there are three, and when there are, the eldest is usually old and dependent. Together with the facts of pairing and the sexual division of labor this means that an ordinary family in whatever system at any one time will contain both sexes and a maximum of one immature and two adult generations, or that the developmental cycle in any system will consist of an alternation between two and three generations alive at once, of which only the oldest one or two will consist of people in marital pairs. We need not worry about large-scale group sex, about dominance hierarchies and sexual access (except as filtered through systems of polygyny and hypergamy, which are forms of pairing), about the relationship between young adults and their great-great grandparents, or about six-generation extended families. The limits to the family cycle are set, and they are fairly rigid limits.

Within these limits, there are several dimensions of variation. The major ones are the (1) direction of connections between the elder and younger generations in a family group, (2) the inclusiveness or restriction of inclusion of junior adults in the family group, (3) the limits of individual participation in marital pairs, and (4) the time of transfer of statuses and their attendant rights and responsibilities from senior generations to junior.

I will discuss each of these dimensions of variation in detail, but first I must detour to introduce a graphic notation for representing family systems that will be used, with slight variation, throughout the book. This notation allows us to compare systems with one another and to highlight the salient features of each cluster of systems treated in individual chapters.

In this notation, the family into which daughters and sons are born is represented by a boundary (in the simplest case, a square), with sons on the left and daughters on the right, elder siblings at the top and younger siblings at the bottom (Figure 2-1).[6]

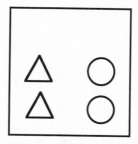

FIGURE 2-1: The Basic Family Configuration

What the square itself represents depends on the type of family system we are portraying. It might, as in the complex-society systems discussed in Chapters 17-20, represent a solidary household, which cooperates in all or almost all of the activities usually organized on a family basis. In other cases (detailed below) there may be more than one boundary (represented, for example, by a square in a circle), as in the family and the band in hunting and gathering bands (Chapters 4-5) or the small family and the household, as in the families of the Northwest Coast (Chapters 14-16).

The parents, if necessary, can be represented by conventional male and female symbol (Figure 2-2). In most cases, however, this is not necessary, and the parents are implied.

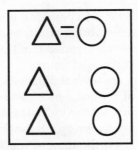

FIGURE 2-2: Family Configuration with Parents

A single copy of this diagram, with a boundary and some circles and triangles, represents a family at only one stage in the developmental cycle. If we are to illustrate the developmental cycle as a whole, we need to show the family on both sides of any transition that is crucial in determining the form of the cycle. In most cases, the form of the developmental cycle is determined primarily by a single transition—what happens when the younger generation reaches adulthood. A sufficiently complete represen-tation of the developmental cycle will thus consist of two copies of the diagram—one showing the children before they reach adulthood and marry, and the other afterward (Figure 2-3).

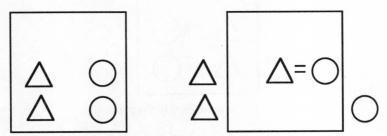

FIGURE 2-3: Two Stages in the Developmental Cycle

In this case, we see from the second diagram that the eldest daughter remains in the family upon marriage; the other daughters and all the sons leave. But if we think about it for a moment, the first diagram in the series will look almost exactly the same for any family system—all the children will be in the group headed by their parents. We can thus dispense with the first diagram in most cases, and just look at the second copy, which shows what happens *after* the children reach adulthood, which is what differentiates one family system from another. We always understand that the absent first diagram is implied.

In our example, we illustrate the fact that the eldest daughter, remaining in the household, takes in a husband, by attaching a triangle to her by a conventional marriage sign; a son taking in a wife would be indicated by a circle similarly placed. (We know in our example that this is a daughter taking in a husband, not a son taking in a wife, because the circle remains in its original position in the upper-right hand corner of the space enclosed by the boundary). But in most cases, we can also dispense with the indication of a spouse, since children remaining to adulthood in their parents houses ordinarily bring in a spouse. We can use these diagrams to represent any aspect of the rights and duties of family membership passed on to the next generation. When we consider the particular activities associated with the family in particular clusters of societies, we will introduce special symbols that will highlight the nature of and variation in family organization in those particular societies.

The Direction of Connections Between the Elder and Younger Generations

The family, of course, includes elder and younger generations. But as children grow to adulthood, not all of them continue to participate in all the activities of a family containing their parents. In any sphere of activity organized in and for a family, the fact of marriage means that there are several possibilities as to which children the parents will remain connected to after the children are married or, in some cases, even earlier. If spouses are going to live together (with cooperation in whatever activities this implies in a particular system) they cannot systematically live with the parents of both. This forces the parents to retain some children in, and expel others from, the group that lives in a house and cooperates in certain spheres of activity—will they retain their sons and sons' wives, their daughters and daughters' husbands, or whom? The same is true of succession to office—ordinarily only one child can succeed one parent. Descent and inheritance do not force such a course—they can be bilateral, with every child inheriting and descending from both parents automatically. But in practice, in many places descent and inheritance are directional, including children of one sex and excluding those of the other (unilineal descent and inheritance) or forcing the parents and children to make a choice of one direction or the other in the case of each specific marriage (ambilineal descent and inheritance). In practice, there is a strong tendency for certain directions of transmission of rights and duties (succession to office, descent, and inheritance) to be associated with corresponding systems of residence, so that those in line to inherit or succeed live with those they expect to inherit from or succeed to. This correlation, of course, is not an exact one, and everyone can point to a "disharmonious" system (Levi-Strauss 1969:323-324) in which residence rules do not keep property holder and heir, or office holder and successor, together, but these disharmonious systems are in the minority.

The logical possibilities for the directionality of transmission of rights and duties are, as Fox (1967:141) has pointed out, quite numerous. It is conceivable, for example, that rights and duties connected with descent-group membership might be passed from mother to son and from father to daughter. Mead (1935, chs 10,11), in fact has reported just such a system among the Mundugumor. Or a mother's rights might pass to all her children, and father's to nobody at all. But these are empirically very rare or non-existent, and we do not need to spend much time in the kind of logical fantasies that rapidly lead us to impractical solutions. In practice, systems of transmission of rights and duties take five different values on the dimension of directionality:

1. matrilineal—transmission through mother
2. patrilineal—transmission through father
3. ambilineal—transmission through the mother *or* father, but not both
4. dual unilineal—transmission of *some* rights and duties through the mother, and *other, distinct* rights and duties through the father
5. bilateral—transmission *indiscriminately* through the mother and father

It is important to realize that the same people can use different routes to transmit different kinds of rights and duties. In fact, ambilineal and dual-unilineal systems are simply those in which people *commonly* use more than one route. It is also necessary to remember that matrilineal transmission can occur from female to female (mother to daughter) or from male to male (senior to junior male within a matrilineal group, commonly referred to as "mother's brother to sister's son," using those terms in a classificatory sense). It is also possible for patrilineal transmission to occur between females, but this is much less common.

One special form of connection between generations is residential connection—so special that anthropologists usually relegate "residence" to a category separate from that of connections of transmission of rights and duties, and employ a separate terminology. For our purposes, though we can continue to employ this terminology, it is convenient to consider residence with members of the adjacent generation as simply one more aspect of the dimension of variation in direction of connection—as a form of passing on household or neighborhood membership. And household or neighborhood membership is defined less by just living in the same building (lodgers in a flophouse do that), than by cooperating in the activities normally shared by members of a family group—procuring, processing, sex, socialization, etc. In this case, matrilocal residence (residence of the married couple with or near the wife's parents) becomes matrilineal transmission of household membership (and the activities which household membership embodies) between females. A system of matrilocal residence can be diagrammed like this (Figure 2-4):

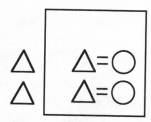

FIGURE 2-4: Matrilocal Residence

Similarly, avunculocal residence, of the married couple with or near the husband's mother's brother, is matrilineal transmission of household membership from senior to junior matrilineally related male.[7] And so on—neolocal residence is the lack of transmission of family membership, in respect to residence, from one generation to the next; it is comparable, for example, to the lack of kin-based succession to political offices in modern capitalist and socialist republics. Duolocal residence (husband and wife living with their own natal families) is comparable to "parallel inheritance" of men's goods patrilineally and women's goods matrilineally.

We thus have a congeries of rights and duties that are transmitted from one generation to another, including descent, succession, inheritance, and household membership, each of which can sometimes be broken up into smaller units, such as inheritance of land and inheritance of tools, or succession to secular office and to sacred office. In any system, people will transmit certain of these rights and duties by one route—patrilineal, matrilineal, or bilateral, and others by other routes. If there is a predominant route, we usually use a convenient shorthand and describe the family system and/or the total kinship system as bilateral or matrilineal or patrilineal; if there is an obvious mixture of routes, we may describe the system as double-unilineal or ambilineal.

It should also be remembered that this dimension—the direction of transmission—is a non-continuous dimension only for the transmission of a particular right or duty. There is no assumption that in a system where people transmit some family rights and duties patrilineally, they will necessarily transmit others by the same route, nor is there any implication that those aspects of the kinship organization that lie outside the family system will operate in the same directions of transmission in which the family system operates.

The Inclusion or Restriction of Junior Adults

The direction of transmission of rights and duties does not tell us everything about who receives these rights and duties in the junior generation. For it is possible to pass on a certain right or duty to only one member of the junior generation, to pass it in varying amounts to several members, or to pass it equally to all members. For a patrilineally transmitted right, for example, this can mean that only one son receives that right (and he, in turn, can be specified as the eldest, the youngest, or left unspecified) (Figure 2-5); it can mean that all sons receive the right to some degree, but that some son or sons receive more than the others (and again, the favored son or sons may come anywhere in the sibling order) (Figure 2-6); or it can mean that all sons receive the right equally (Figure 2-7).

Eldest Son   Youngest Son   Unspecified Son

FIGURE 2-5: Impartible Patrilineal Inheritance

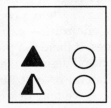   

FIGURE 2-6:   FIGURE 2-7:
Unequal Transmission   Equal Patrilineal Transmission

The same range of variation is possible with sisters' sons, or with daughters, in a matrilineal system, or with children in general in an ambilineal or bilateral system.

This dimension of variation is important for inheritance, succession, and residence. In terms of inheritance, scholars have usually dichotomized this dimension into impartible (only one child inheriting) or partible (more than one inheriting), but it becomes clear upon examination of the ethnographic record that there is continuous variation from nearly absolute exclusion of all but the chosen heir, though various unequal combinations, to almost absolutely equally parted inheritance (see detailed discussion in Chapters 19-20). In terms of succession, if we think of succession to political office as a model, it would seem that single succession would be the rule, and it does predominate. (There is, however, a well-documented case, that of certain Nyakyusa chiefdoms in the 19th and 20th centuries, in which an expanding population passed on the chiefship to *two* sons of each previous chief in each generation [Wilson 1951:22-23]). And succession to family headship is not simple either; it is possible for a single successor to take over the headship of a continuing family corporation, or for the corporation to split in each generation, with each included member of the junior generation taking over the headship of one of the family units resulting from the split.

Turning to residence, we find that, in general, this too has been looked upon as a dichotomous variable; among those systems that transmit household membership to junior adults at all (neolocal systems are, of course, outside this dimension altogether), there is usually a division made between stem systems, in which only one child remains with the parents, and joint systems, in which all members of the inheriting or succeeding sex (or half the children of both sexes, in an ambilineal system) remain with the parents until the latter die. But in fact, even here there are intermediate cases: in many systems, a specified son or daughter will succeed to household headship, but other sons or daughters may have some rights to remain in the household for a limited time, or with limited rights, or perhaps as long as they do not marry. So this too, is a continuous variable.

It should be noted that household membership, if it is not totally restrictive, involves at some point a process of household division. Except in polyandrous, or sharing, marriage systems (see Chapter 19), an inclusive system of transmission of household membership implies that, if there are two or more juniors to be included, those juniors will not stay together forever, but will eventually split the household to form a series of new units with themselves at the respective heads. In this sense, then, restrictive household membership means household continuity, while inclusive membership means the destruction and re-emergence of the household in each generation.

It is possible, at the same time, that household membership is not passed on at all—that the marital residence is neolocal and each couple sets up an independent household upon marriage (Figure 2-8).

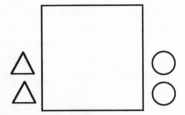

FIGURE 2-8: Neolocal Residence

This can be seen as even more restrictive than the stem-family or single transmission of household membership, but it tends to correlate with in-clusiveness of inheritance and of succession to household headship, both of which are associated with *either* joint or nuclear family systems. The crucial difference here is in the time of formation of the independent house-holds headed by the junior generation, a variable that will be treated in the section on time of transmission.

Individual Participation in Marital Pairs

In different family systems, people may have only one spouse in their lives, or only one spouse at once, or several at once. Most introductory treatments of kinship see three possibilities in either the synchronic or the diachronic dimension—monogamy, polygyny, or polyandry, and some add a fourth, called something like polygynandry (Berreman 1975:130). Logi-cally, this is of course correct, but here I think a too-rigorous logic runs against the true nature of the variation on this dimension. Because almost all cases of polyandry are fraternal (the sole ethnographic exception, the Marquesas Islands in the 18th and 19th centuries, is probably not a case of multiple marital pairing at all; for further discussion see below, chapter 16), the best way to look at this dimension is in terms of how many wives a man can have, and the consequent opportunities he has to reproduce. At the low end of this dimension, we have so-called polyandrous systems, in which a man gets one wife or less—these systems are designed to maintain undivided, patrilineally transmitted estates while allowing all brothers to marry. (This, of course, prevents many women from marrying). In the middle of the dimension come the monogamous systems, in which a man can have one wife, and then come the polygynous ones, in which a man can have one or more wives.

The implications of sharing, singular, and plural unions go beyond the sphere of marital relations themselves and affect the organization of the first two dimensions mentioned, particularly the inclusive-restrictive dimension. *Polyandrous* or sharing unions, merging the rights and duties held by two or more brothers into a single line, but allowing all sons of that line to receive the rights and duties, are always inclusive, but without the expanding characteristics of other, monogamous or polygynous inclusive systems. Monogamous and polygynous systems alike can be either inclusive or restrictive, but polygyny adds another way in which the restriction or partial inclusion can be organized. In monogamous systems, the distinctions made are those between siblings, but in polygynous systems half-siblings, or in some cases various kinds of half-siblings (Gluckman 1950:195-96; Wilson 1950:132) are treated differently. Rather than simply distinguishing among children of different birth-orders, such systems can distinguish among children of different wives, and in various ways.

The Time of Transfer of Statuses from Senior to Junior Generation

People do not transfer rights and duties from one generation to another in some universal, automatic way, but rather by culturally specific processes. The timing of these processes is a continuous dimension, ranging from the time when members of the receiving generation are born, at the earliest, through the time when they marry, to the time when members of the older generation die, at the latest. In practice, of course, the elders may die, for example, before any or all members of the next generation are married, but the normative order is the other way around, and we can thus compare systems on the basis of this normative order, realizing that the vagaries of demography sometimes force an *ad hoc* adaptation to particular circumstances.

As in the other dimensions described, particular bundles of rights and duties are logically independent of each other in their time of transfer. For example, in many neolocal systems, characteristic of the early 20th-century European peasantry, though a young married couple was expected to set up a new household on its own at the time of marriage, neither of the young people received title to any property until their parents died. Similarly, in many dowry systems, a woman receives her share of her parents' estate at marriage, while her husband has to wait for his parents to die to claim his own inheritance (Harrell & Dickey 1985). On the whole, there is a much greater than random association between the transfer of one right or duty and that of another, but the empirical variation between those systems that do transmit at the same time and those that do not is also a subject for comparative study.

The structure of the developmental cycle, of the process of social reproduction of the family unit, can be described for any system in terms of variation along the four dimensions mentioned above. There is little, if any, structural variation that falls outside this four-dimensional matrix.

Notes

1. Alexander Spoehr used a kind of developmental cycle analysis in his work on social organization in Majuro in the Marshall Islands, published about the same time as Fortes's work (Spoehr 1949). But Spoehr's analysis seems not to have led to any further theoretical developments.

2. There is a considerable literature about cultures in which there is a category of a third gender, not quite male or female socially (Herdt 1994). As far as I know, third-gender persons usually live outside the ordinary patterns of a family system, and are thus not germane to this analysis.

3. I know of only one community where there was a concerted effort to prevent any kind of pairing while still permitting sexual relations and, at some times, the birth of offspring. This was the Oneida Community of New York in the late 19th century, described in Chapter 24.

4. The myriad cultural variations and elaborations on this common theme have themselves become a major topic for anthropological inquiry, and the nature of the variations interact in diverse ways with other aspects of family organization, as will be demonstrated repeatedly in the later chapters of this book. But even in industrial situations where the sexual division of labor is no longer readily explicable in terms of the compatibility between reproductive and other roles, the fact of its existence can always be traced back historically to the basic nature of reproductive roles. A recent article by Peacock (1991) reminds us that the constraints imposed by women's reproductive roles are not rigid, and take different forms in different places; certainly no single type of activity is either enjoined or precluded absolutely. But even in the case of the Efe, where Peacock describes women engaging in long-distance travel, for example, camps tend to be located so that women have to travel somewhat shorter distances than men. In addition, women's tasks are still on the whole less dangerous than those performed by men.

5. Life span, the time it takes the human body to run down and wear out, must not be confused with life expectancy, the mean age of death. This latter is, of course, highly variable because of extrinsic causes of mortality. But since infant mortality is the factor that has the strongest shortening effect on life expectancy in most situations, adults can expect to live out more of their life span than a quick glance at a life expectancy figure would lead one to believe.

6. The original geometric concept for this kind of diagram was suggested by John Atkins, to whose memory this book is dedicated. Danette Swanson spent considerable time thinking about initial refinements.

7. Complex combinations such as avunculocal residence and bilateral inheritance can be diagrammed in our system, but they will be illustrated only when they occur in the discussion of actual cases.

3

Explaining Family Variation

The Relationship Between Activities and Personnel

In order for people to reproduce their families, the families must be useful to them by providing a way of organizing the activities they need to carry out in the cultural community to which they belong. This means, of course, that some of these activities are important everywhere, and some only at certain times and places. Where livelihood depends on families' owning and working small pieces of land, for example, the family must be organized for the division of labor in working the land and processing its products for consumption or sale. This may dictate or, more likely, at least influence, the form that the developmental cycle can take in that family system. Somewhere else, in a hunting and gathering band, for example, such desiderata as providing for the transfer of property and offices from one generation to the next may be irrelevant, because private property is personally destroyed at death, or is otherwise not inherited, and there are no formal offices to succeed to, or those offices are not passed on within the family group. What I have listed in Chapter 2, then, is an expansive list of the possible activities organized in families, not a list of its universally necessary ones.

But to return to the problem of explanations, we need to ask two questions: why do people need to organize certain activities on a family basis in certain places, and to what extent does the need to organize these activities determine family structure? First, we must recognize that people adapt their family systems to the environment, and that in this adaptational process, family systems are by and large the dependent variable. Families, as small groups with little wide political or social influence individually, are

part of societies, that is, of collections of people who participate in relationships of power and exchange.[1] As such, people are required to adapt their
family organization to the social organization of which they are a part.
There is, of course, the possibility of influence in the other direction—social change may come about as a result of certain changes in the family
system. But on the whole, it is change in the larger social organization that
brings about family change, rather than the other way around. This means
that the needs to organize a family system to carry out certain activities are
set by the nature of the social system in which the family system is embedded, though the family system may play a small part in determining the
nature of that larger social system. This leads to the approach, explained in
more detail below, of analyzing family systems as part of a·process of the
evolution of social systems. It does not lead, however, to the assumption
that there is a one-to-one correlation between a family system and a social
system. Variation within societies, by class, caste, or ethnic group, is frequent and important, and is treated in detail in our discussions of both
Oceanic family systems (Chapters 11-13), and family systems in complex
societies (Chapters 17-24).

But once the organizational needs are determined, to what extent do
they determine the structure of the developmental cycle? In other words,
to what extent is family process *constrained* or *dictated* by the nature of the
activities for which people need to organize? The answer is that the ecological and social environment set limits on family structure, but can rarely
determine it absolutely. In old-fashioned language, there are various "functional alternatives." If the ruling classes of a society practicing intensive
agriculture, with a social class system based on expropriation of surplus
peasant labor as rent, demand that families organize for management and
transmission of property, for political representation by family heads, and
for ritual representation of families in community rituals, among other
things, they do not thus automatically demand that the family organize for
these things along a patrilineal, patrilocal, joint family cycle, or a bilateral,
neolocal, nuclear family cycle, or any other kind of cycle *in particular*. The
dictates of such ruling classes, however, do influence family organization
in certain directions. It seems, for example, very difficult (though not impossible) for matrilineal organization to exist under such circumstances as
described above. The social organization, as it develops historically, seems
to influence a family system in such circumstances away from the
matrilineal toward the bilateral or patrilineal, away from the polygynous
toward the monogamous pole of the relevant dimensions of structural variation.

But as I said, the nature of activities in which people cooperate as families only sets limits and influences structure in particular directions, that is,
in the directions of the various alternative ways of organizing those activi-

ties. And they do not act, as they develop and change, on cultureless animals, but upon human beings who already carry with them ideas and models for organizing their families—their learned culture of family organization. If some aspect of transmission of rights and duties in a family system practiced by people belonging to a pre-complex society is, for example, patrilineal, this cultural heritage, along with the changing nature of social activities, will act to shape the form the family cycle takes as the society moves from pre-complex to complex, with concomitant changes in property relations, methods of cultivation, systems of social and economic exchange, and so on. And how did the family system come to be patrilineal in the pre-stratified society? We would have to look, once more, at the history of its development, keeping in mind the interaction between the culture of family organization existing in a more remote past, and the changes in the nature of the activities family members might need to perform as the society itself evolves.

It is doubtful if we will ever get to the bottom of this—to do so would be to trace all known family systems back through long series of previous forms to our proto-human ancestors, a task made impossible by the lack of historical evidence. (It seems to me that the gap between living apes and the earliest possible reconstructions of *family systems* is so great as to be bridgeable only by spectacular flights of speculative fancy. These are fun, but not useful; see Cucchiari 1982.) I also think that the same reasons that prohibit us from investigating the origin of the family, or the precise origin of all but very recent family systems, also work to make cross-cultural statistical comparisons of family systems so unsatisfying. This is amply demonstrated, for example, in the first few chapters of Goody's *Production and Reproduction*. Goody tries to suggest, by means of the *Ethnographic Atlas* materials and some sophisticated numerical techniques, certain correlations between complex societies and certain kinds of family systems. The correlations and other measures of association are statistically significant, and indeed suggestive of more hypotheses than Goody has time to consider in his short book. But they remain unsatisfying, because of the number of anomalous cases that do not conform to the predicted associations. The answer to such anomalous cases may lie in more precise environmental variables or even in better ethnographic reporting, but I doubt the entire answer lies there—some systems have at least partially resisted the pressures exerted by changes in economy and society, and have retained, as sometimes quite awkward alternatives, some aspects of historically inherited, formerly perhaps better adapted systems. As long as, in Sahlins' words, "historical analyses begin with a culture already there" (1976:15) we will never find an exact fit between why people organize and how they organize, only limits and influences.

This brings up another difficult question—if culture or historical contingency always provides an out, if such differences can never be ignored when comparing family systems across societies, or especially across broad geographic regions, how do we demonstrate the effect of the socially determined nature of family organized activities at all? How can we rule out cultural variation as the explanation for everything? I think there are two things that can help us here. One are the very cross-cultural statistical comparisons mentioned above as unsatisfying. Unsatisfying, yes, but also suggestive. If the effects of a common historical origin of two or more systems are minimized, and certain environmental variables can be shown to be associated with even a strong statistical tendency toward uniformity in family systems existing in similar environments worldwide, then this is strong evidence that the need for adaptation has an effect. The other, perhaps stronger kind of evidence for the effect of the necessity to adapt to the nature of the larger social system lies in intra-societal comparison. If family systems that exist in the same society, and partake of the same history and cultural traditions, nevertheless show significant variation in their family developmental cycles, and this variation can be shown to covary with certain environmental factors that would be expected to influence family organization, then we have strong evidence. The evidence becomes even stronger if we can show the same kind of variation internal to more than one social system. For example, if the difference between Japanese farmers and fishers is parallel to the difference between Portuguese farmers and fishers, we can confidently attribute this difference to the nature of adaptation of family systems to farming and fishing economies.

Evolution, History, and the Great Transformations

So far, I have discussed only the way in which the content of family-based activities can influence family organization, and how we can sort out this influence from that of historical contingency or cultural tradition. There is, however, another, much broader connection between what a family does and how it is organized. I have mentioned already that people need to organize their families to adapt to the nature of the larger social system in which they reproduce their families, and I think that we can find some order in family systems if we recognize that these social systems are not randomly distributed geographically or historically, but that there has occurred in the past several millenia a definite and fairly uniform (though, in Steward's terms, certainly "multilinear" [1955:11-29]), phenomenon of social evolution from less to more complex societies.

This phenomenon of social history has been evolutionary in both the conventional senses of the term (Rambo 1991:24). It is an evolutionary sequence in that there has been a progression from smaller to larger societies and cultural communities, from less to more complex division of labor, from less to more complex technology. But as many critics of "cultural evolution" have pointed out, an evolutionary sequence of this sort is not a mechanism (Sahlins and Service 1960:33; Rambo 1991). Any general trend of this sort must be the result of an evolutionary process, a mechanism in which fitter or more viable forms win out in competition with less fit or less viable forms. In biological evolution, this process is accomplished by genetic variation and natural selection, and the process by which social forms evolve is in many ways analogous. In most social environments, larger groups with more complex divisions of labor and technologies can reproduce themselves at faster rates than can smaller, less complex groups. There are several reasons for this. First, in direct competition such as warfare, both group size and more complex technology confer advantages. The displacement of the rank societies of native North America with the complex and emerging modern societies of Euro-Americans is a morally tragic but evolutionarily comprehensible and well-known example. Second, more complex technologies and divisions of labor often confer an advantage in reproductive rates themselves. Sedentarization of nomadic populations reduces birth intervals and thus increases total fertility (R.B. Lee 1979:318-325), creating both an imbalance in population between settled cultivators and their nomadic, foraging neighbors and further chances of direct competition as expanding sedentary populations require further resources. Finally (and this is where social evolution diverges from the model set by biological evolution), members of populations whose social and technical systems put them at an evolutionary disadvantage can often perceive the disadvantage and "convert" to the cultural and social norms of the evolutionarily advantaged group, adding a Lamarckian process to the Darwinian factors of direct competition and reproductive advantage (Boyd and Richerson 1992:62).

There is another important parallel between social evolution and biological evolution, at least as conceived of by theorists S. J. Gould and Niles Eldredge (1977). This is the idea that evolution, in this case history, proceeds most importantly not by slow, incremental change, but by major, qualitative leaps. This idea of punctuated equilibria is in fact paralleled in some ways by Polanyi's vision of "The Great Transformation" and by Marx's idea of revolution (Polanyi 1957; Marx 1970:21). I am proposing here a vision of history that is similar to all these models, an idea that human societies have undergone a series of revolutions or transformations (I prefer the latter term, since its political connotations are relatively neutral), each of them altering the fundamental conditions of existence and shaping the fundamental principles which guide human agents in setting and pursuing their life goals. There have been three of these transformations, producing four major stages in human history so far: nomadic bands were transformed into rank societies by the sedentarization transformation; rank societies became complex societies by the class transformation; and complex societies became modern societies by the industrial (or, more accurately, the industrial/scientific) transformation. Each transformation yields societies that are larger, socially and culturally more complex, and in most cases evolutionarily favored over societies that have not yet undergone that particular transformation.

Because the sequence of evolution is merely the sum of many events in the process evolution, and because those events of specific evolution depend on adaptive advantage in particular environments, the sequence of evolution is not uniform or general. The Three Great Transformations have not taken place at the same time in all places. In the absence of the particular environments that confer advantage on larger and more complex groups, groups at a simpler stage may remain for a long time (as some nomadic foragers who existed, despite contact with more advanced groups, into the 1960s), or even replace a more advanced with a simpler social formation (Rambo 1991:45-47). In environments, for example, where sedentarization on the basis of agriculture is impossible, foraging has persisted into the twentieth century. In sparsely populated areas, direct competition may never occur. Finally, in isolation or in circumstances where neither direct competition nor reproductive advantage is perceptible, there will be no incentive to "convert" to more complex social or cultural forms. As a result, the general trend toward greater complexity has not been a uniform one, and societies at all levels of complexity have coexisted for centuries.

Nevertheless, there has been a general trend for societies to undergo the three great transformations, each to a new level of complexity, and at each level of complexity, the reasons why people cooperate as members of a family make for a pattern of family systems that is fundamentally different. This kind of assumption lies behind Goody's aforementioned *Production and Reproduction*, where he shows that the family in the unstratified, hoe-agricultural societies of sub-Saharan Africa is fundamentally different from the family in the stratified, plough-agricultural societies of Eurasia. He even goes so far as to suggest, with caveats to be sure, that African societies may be representative of non-stratified societies in general, and Eurasian societies of stratified ones. I think these speculations are insufficiently founded in the ethnographic record, but that they are a fruitful basis for constructing a more comprehensive model of family systems.

The most important thing to remember here is that the *social formations are more basic than the family systems*. If we want to understand how the family has evolved through the course of human history, it is futile and sterile to posit an evolutionary sequence (or even a multilinear set of sequences) of structural types. What has evolved most consistently as human societies have transformed themselves into larger, more complex, and more technologically sophisticated forms is the nature of the activities family members are called upon the perform (see Netting and Wilk 1984:20). Because people can use a variety of structural arrangements to perform the necessary activities in any particular situation, there will be a variety of family systems found at any level of social complexity. But the variety will not be infinite, because some family forms are clearly incompatible or extremely awkward for carrying out some constellations of activities. There will be a pattern. Because members of bands do not have to worry about succession to political office, because villagers in ranked island societies do have to worry about the relation between expanding populations and finite land areas, because landlords have to worry about providing for all their children without dividing their estates too minutely, and so on, there will be certain kinds of family organization that will characterize bands, islanders, or the landed classes in complex stratified societies. Or to put it another way, the family systems found in each of these particular groups of societies will tend to cluster in certain regions of the four dimensional matrix of family structural variation. Within each cluster, we should be able to test the effect of smaller variations in family activities by looking at intra-society or even intra-community variation, but at the same time we will never be able to explain all the variation within a cluster, because of the different cultural traditions to which the family systems in the cluster belong.

Family Activities, Family Strategies, and the Great Transformations

In any family system there are three possibilities for any of the enumerated activities performed in or for family groups:

1. It may not exist at all in that system. Five of the listed sets of activities—both kinds of division of labor, regulation of sexuality, socialization, and emotional warmth are basic human requisites that exist regardless of the particular nature of a social environment in which a family systems exists. The other three, however—representation, enabling, and the management and transmissal of property and offices— simply do not exist in certain kinds of societies. Where they are not necessary at all, they will not impinge upon the structure of the family system.
2. It may exist, and be a requisite for social reproduction, but be performed wholly or primarily in and for a group other than the family.

For example, in many bands, the division of labor for the procuring of subsistence goods, particularly animal products, may be at the level of the band or other local group, rather than at the level of the family. Or in modern republics, political offices exist and are transmitted, but by an electorate, a junta, a central committee—something other than a family. Even sexuality shows a wide variation in the extent to which it is restricted to family members—that is, married couples. Where a particular activity exists in a particular social environment, but is performed primarily in and for a group other than the family, it still may impinge on family organization because the necessity for some members to participate in the group that performs this activity will affect the way in which these members relate to other members of their families. But the family itself will not have to organize for the performance of this activity.

3. It may exist and be performed by the family. In this case the family organization will have to be compatible with the family's carrying out this activity.

The structure of the family is thus limited and influenced by the varying nature of the activities that either need to be performed in and for the family or shape the participation of family members in wider spheres of social activity. In particular, the activities people ordinarily perform as a family will influence what I call people's "family strategy": the way in which people who hold power in a certain family system attempt to regulate family membership in order to bring about the most advantageous possible performance of the activities at hand. In making decisions that add to or subtract from a family's membership—decisions of marriage, childbearing, contraception, abortion, divorce, adoption, family division, and so on, people will be influenced by the prospective effect that such decisions will have on a family's ability to carry out certain activities to its members' advantage. Depending on which sets of activities are relevant in a particular family system, the guiding principle behind family strategies will differ. And it is important to remember that family strategies are strategies pursued by individuals: families are not actors and do not have strategies; rather individuals as members of families pursue strategies that either benefit the family or benefit their own personal interests within the family.[2]

There are three basic principles that lie behind virtually all family strategies:

1. The *adjustive* principle. An adjustive strategy is one that seeks to maintain the family balance between available productive resources and consumption needs. This will involve attempts to both add and subtract family members, depending on whether the resources in shorter

supply are land and capital or labor. This kind of principle is likely to be paramount when enabling is non-existent or at least unimportant, and is a factor in women's family strategies almost everywhere.

2. An *accretive* strategy is one that seeks to make a family as large as possible. It tends to predominate in situations where access to productive resources other than labor is not problematical, and where enabling is of paramount concern. It involves maximal fertility, polygyny, clientage, and other structural features that enable an ambitious family head to amass a large number of followers in the family group. The accretive strategy may exist alongside the adjustive strategy: in sub-Saharan Africa, for example, men's strategies tended to be much more accretive than women's; in Polynesia, aristocrats often pursued accretive strategies while commoners, who were excluded from status competition, were content with adjustive family patterns.

3. The *exclusive* principle. An exclusive family strategy is one that seeks to limit a family's membership in such a way that the family's status position in the community or society is preserved or enhanced. Exclusive strategies tend to emphasize better marriages rather than more marriages, and thus to involve the strict regulation of premarital and extramarital sexuality. The exclusive principle may act in concert with either or both of the others, but it operates only in those situations in which the enabling connection between the domestic and public spheres of activity is complemented by the allocative connection, in which a family member's position in the public sphere partially or wholly determines that person's family's access to resources. The exclusive strategy thus tends to be most important in complex, stratified societies, although it can also be found, for example, in the aristocracies of both Oceanic and Northwest Coast societies.

As we follow the process of evolution across the great transformations from simpler to more complex forms of social organization then, we find that there are changes in the nature of the activities that family members are called upon to perform, and that these changes in turn bring about changes in the nature of the strategies of family-building that people will have to follow in order to adapt their family structure to the particular social forms.

This book attempts to illustrate the relationship between wider social organization, family activities, and family strategies for four broad stages in an evolutionary sequence of human societies: band societies, rank societies, pre-modern complex societies, and modern societies. Each of these stages is separated from the last one and the next one by a Great Transformation, a fundamental shift in the nature of social and political relations from one stage to the next.[3]

Band Societies (B-Cluster Systems)

This is Service's term (1962), but seems to be practically coterminous with Fried's category of "egalitarian societies" (1967). These societies are almost inevitably foragers or hunters and gathers (though the organization of a few societies of shifting cultivators with very low population density seems to approach the band model quite closely). Not all societies depending on a foraging technology are bands; the standard exception in ethnographic times is the Northwest Coast of North America, though there were almost certainly other societies in the past that evolved more complex forms of social organization on a foraging base. The nature of hunting and gathering in most environments, however, has placed certain limits and requirements on social organization. First, population density is low and local groups are small. Most environments will simply not support high densities over prolonged periods, and groups must be small enough that they can cover the territory necessary to sustain them without too many or too frequent trips away from camp overnight. Second, local group membership tends to be flexible, with individuals and families often changing groups at fairly frequent intervals (see Silberbauer 1981:185ff). This has been seen as an efficient mechanism for distributing population with respect to material resources. Third, concepts of property in subsistence goods are weakly developed. Land is ordinarily not owned in the sense of its being a disposable possession of an individual or family; even local groups' rights to land tend to be tenuous and violable with permission. The same is true of animal and plant resources on the land. Fourth, and closely connected to this, there tends to be an ethic of generalized reciprocity among members of a local group and sometimes beyond. In an unpredictable, basically unmodified natural environment, it makes more sense to share surplus with the expectation of getting a share of someone else's some other time than it does to hoard resources that one can neither consume nor carry very far in the group's frequent migrations (see Dyson-Hudson and Smith 1978).

All these characteristics of the natural and social environment directly influence the activities that people will perform in families in band societies. First, the activities of management and transmission, representation in public activities and enabling public participation are absent or irrelevant for family organization. If there is no property to pass down and no formal offices to hold, these do not have to be managed or transmitted. But most significantly, there is little separation in such social systems between the domestic and the public spheres of activity. The domestic sphere, the provision of the daily necessities of life, and hence of the family's social reproduction, is not clearly cut off from the public sphere of the management of the political and ritual affairs of the entire group. Hence there need be no formal representation, and any able-bodied adult is automatically enabled to participate in public activities. This, in turn, is because division of labor, particularly in the provision of goods, is usually not at the family but at the local group level. Group hunts, rules for sharing the kill, the desirability of sharing even vegetable foods, and the aforementioned ethic of generalized reciprocity within the local group all weaken the distinction between the family and the larger, local group of which it is a part.

With regard to the regulation of sexuality, the evidence is not crystal clear, but seems to point to generally rather loose restrictions for both sexes, though there remains the institution of pairing and the means of determining parenthood of children. These children, however, often tend to be socialized as much by the local group as a whole as by their individual families. And emotional closeness is found both with family members and with others.

In sum (and these characteristics are documented carefully in Chapters 4-5), the requirements of a nomadic, foraging existence in small bands have created a particular kind of relationship between the family (the domestic sphere) and the larger community and society in which it is embedded (the public sphere): one of indistinct boundaries, in which participation in one is implicitly and usually without distinction participation in the other, where it is difficult, in the end, to decide what, in such a community, constitutes a family at all. With the concerns of both men and women in band societies being directed at fulfilling the five universal groups of activities, and with no concern toward enabling prestige competition in the public sphere (because there is no separate public sphere), the family strategies pursued by both men and women in band societies tend to be almost entirely of an adjustive nature.

By portraying the separation between domestic and public spheres of activity as blurry here, I hope to address an important caution brought up by Michelle Rosaldo in one of her last published works: the concept of a domestic/public dichotomy must be approached cautiously, in order to avoid the gender-based equivalent of what Abu-Lughod, writing about culture, called "freezing differences" (1991:146) To begin with the *a priori* assumption that the domestic-public distinction explains gender denies us the opportunity to explore the way in which gender differences, like family systems, are adaptations to particular natural and social environments, and are embedded in larger social formations (Rosaldo 1980:409). Chapters 4 and 5 explore the nature of family systems in band societies in detail: I discuss the general characteristics and attempt to account for the variation in this group of societies. Since they are clustered at a particular values in some of the four dimensions of family structure, and since band organization is characteristic of their social organization, I call these B- (for band) cluster family systems.

Family Systems in Rank Societies

Band organization has its evolutionary limits. Foraging technologies can support only very low population densities, and even the gradual increase in population that seems to characterize societies at this level eventually mandates either geographical expansion, which is often limited by direct competition, or, eventually, leads to the first great transformation: sedentarization,[4] conversion to a more resource-intensive mode of production, and an increase in the size of the local settlement. This creates problems of social control in the absence of hierarchy, and leads people to adopt formal leadership and hierarchy as means of social organization and control. Chagnon's work on the Yanomamö (1979:91-98), a society where elements of band organization still existed in the 1960s in spite of a larger local social group, seems to indicate that hierarchy begins to emerge when local group sizes reach much over 100 people for extended periods of time. In places like Yanomamö, where hierarchy is not firmly established, the social situation seems rather unstable, but in most of the societies of sub-Saharan Africa, Oceania, and the Northwest Coast of North America, treated in Parts 3, 4, and 5 of this book, relatively stable social systems embodying the hierarchy characterized by Fried (1967) as rank had emerged before the 18th century for sure, and probably (though we lack documentation) many centuries before that. Once rank has emerged, rank societies seem to have an advantage both in direct competition and in reproductive rates over and against band societies; consequently, for the last ten or twelve millennia band societies have been shrinking until, at the end of the twentieth century, they have practically disappeared from the Earth. The first sort of societies to replace band societies were rank societies.

Rank societies, in a paraphrase of Fried's formal definition, are those where not every position in the public sphere is available to every member of the appropriate sex who reaches a certain age (here these societies contrast with egalitarian, or band societies), but where the inequalities do not amount to restricting the access of any families to the basic goods necessary for social reproduction (here these societies contrast with stratified, or complex, societies) (Fried 1967). This type of social and political organization also tends to be associated with certain other variables. Technologically, people living in such societies tend to depend on swidden agriculture or intensive gardening, combined with livestock raising, hunting wild game, fishing, or some combination of the three. A few societies (on the Northwest Coast) have reached this level of scale and organization on the basis of a foraging economy, but they are rare, and it is also very rare that people in such societies employ the plough in agriculture.

Population density tends to be somewhat higher here, and local groups, usually living in permanent or semi-permanent settlements, are larger, ranging up to a few hundred persons. Concepts of property begin to occur, with land or other resources commonly belonging to a kin group or sometimes a family group, but without the possibility of purchase and sale of land or other basic resources. With attachment of particular groups of people to particular pieces of land or other productive property, group membership tends to be more permanent, or if there are frequent transfers, they are not casual but must be recognized formally by the groups involved. Ranking implies offices, or at least prestigious positions attainable by only some members of a particular gender and age, and the problems of access to productive resources and to public positions necessitate a more formal, more highly organized group structure. In a great number of cases, this means an elaborated system of descent and alliance, a system not just of kin-reckoning, which exists everywhere, but of formal kin groups and kinship relations, both consanguineal and affinal. It should be stressed, however, that both the principle of kinship and that of locality are used to organize formal social relations in these societies.

These basic aspects of rank society organization mean that family members tend to organize for a quite different set of activities than in B-cluster systems. The division of labor in procuring and in processing goods is now more likely to be organized in and for discrete, definable family groups. There may be extensive cooperation between members of such groups, and there may be frequent and prescribed exchanges of subsistence or other goods. But there is now a clearer line between the division of labor within the family, still based on generalized reciprocity, and exchange or cooperation among families, where the ethic is now one of balanced reciprocity, the immediate or delayed exchange of equivalent values (Sahlins 1965:194-95). This marks the beginning of the clear division between family and society, and between domestic and public spheres of activity. With the creation of concepts of property in subsistence goods attached to particular families, either directly or through their membership in extended kin groups, comes the necessity of transmitting property from one generation to another—we have inheritance as an important concern in family organization. Similarly, offices can mean succession, though there is considerable variation within the broad range of rank societies as to whether offices are succeeded to in regular, kin-based patterns. And with the formation of kin groups comes the importance of reckoning descent. In general, then, it is at the rank level that the family becomes a group within which people manage and transmit property and offices.

In rank societies, there also seems to be a tendency toward the greater restriction of sexuality, if not premaritally, then at least extramaritally, because the consequences of an improper pregnancy are much greater in a system based primarily on kinship organization. Similarly, at this stage family members tend to take a more predominant part in the socialization and education of their own children, who belong to particular families in these cases, not to the society or local group as a whole.

In rank societies too, the relationship between the now-separate domestic and public spheres becomes important for understanding the role of the family in society. The relationship, however, is not uniform across the whole range of rank societies: it differs in the emphasis given to two kinds of connections between the two spheres of activity. The first is the *enabling* connection, in which family goods and products of family labor enable members of a family to take prominent roles in the public sphere. The second is the *allocation* connection, in which certain prominent people or institutions in the public sphere allocate to families certain rights in land, property, and sometimes offices. Different combinations of the enabling and allocation connections between domestic and public spheres make for very different kinds of family organization, even within the broad category of rank societies. In this work, I examine three clusters of family systems within the broad category of rank societies. Each cluster is both a geographic unit and a group of similar family systems. The most salient factor that distinguishes one cluster from another is the nature of domestic-public relationships.

The A- (African) Cluster

The first of these three I will call the A- (for African) cluster, characteristic of most of sub-Saharan Africa in the immediate pre-colonial and early colonial periods. This is the type that Goody has investigated and contrasted with family systems in complex societies (1973, 1976). In this cluster, we can easily see the separate spheres of domestic and public activity. But the connection between the spheres is one-directional. In most sub-Saharan African systems, actors in the public sphere play little role in allocating rights to goods for use in the domestic economy—this seems to be because, in most of pre-colonial Africa, there was little scarcity of such goods, and subsistence was unproblematical, except in famines, when everyone suffered. In a word, the ecological context was a relatively open one, limited more by labor than by land availability. Exceptions to this generalization seem to have occurred in places where African societies were beginning, under pressure of population and competition, the Second Great Transformation toward complex, stratified organization.

The enabling connection, on the other hand, was much more important.

In most parts of Africa, a prominent man (or in some western and southern African communities, occasionally a prominent woman) was aided in his prominence by having a large household and many followers, and there seems to have been a mutually reinforcing effect between such large followings and the prominence they enabled. Also, these followers seem to have been necessary for political and military exploits, and for cementing alliances through marriage, not exclusively for the labor power that they provided to the family head. We can thus say that, while definite domestic and political spheres were at work in A-cluster systems, their connection was one-way, and concerned with men building followings, enabling them to participate prominently in the public sphere.

In the A-cluster, with its strong emphasis on building a following and on accumulating rights over persons, the family strategies of men, who are the great majority of competitors in the public spheres, tended to be strongly accretive. Women, on the other hand, excluded in most cases from prestige competition in their own right, were more concerned with security, and with the balancing of subsistence resources, particularly labor, against the consumption needs of themselves and their children. Women's strategies were thus adjustive in the main. At the same time, however, there were certain societies in which important portions of the public sphere were dominated by women—as with many markets and some dualistic political systems in West Africa, and others where women in special circumstances could assume public roles ordinarily reserved for men. The *predominantly* domestic role of women, nevertheless, had important ramifications for many of the aspects of African family organization discussed by Goody (1973, 1976) and others; these will be treated in detail in Part III.

The O- (Oceanic) Cluster

In the inevitably more closed ecological environment of the Micronesian and Polynesian islands of the Pacific Ocean, we find a much more complex pattern of domestic-public connection, and a much greater variation in the use of adjustive, accretive, and exclusive family strategies. On the smallest and resource-poorest islands, including many coral atolls, there was usually population pressure against resources, combined with hereditary differences in social status. These two factors together meant that the allocation connection was more important than the enabling connection; the ability of chiefs and councils to determine access to land was one of the crucial activities of the public sphere, but since wealth differences were minimal and status basically hereditary, there was little prestige competition for people to engage in or for families to enable their members to engage in. And family strategies were almost purely adjustive—people were always working, particularly through adoption and through the creation of property rights in multiple groups, to adjust the balance between people and the ever scarce resource, land.

On larger, better endowed islands, however, we find the enabling connection to have been more important, at least to those who could claim some sort of hereditary high status. Since high status here meant control over followers and over distribution networks of ritual and other goods, hereditary status was not enough; rather family labor and the building of a following were necessary to make hereditary high status count for something. Thus among the aristocracy of such islands, the enabling connection was strong and the family strategy strongly accretive. For commoners, on the other hand, the connection between the public and domestic spheres was much weaker; as subjects of a local ruler, commoners might in theory depend on that ruler for allocation of land, but in fact it could not often be denied them, and since they were excluded from most kinds of status competition, the enabling connection was not important for them, and their family strategies remained basically adjustive.

On some of the largest islands, with the most developed systems of aristocratic privilege and status differentiation, enabling and accretion faded into the background as the high-ranking aristocrats pursued strategies of family exclusion, with the object of restricting access to the prerogatives of high status to the few highest-born, through stratum endogamy, arranged marriage, and even marriage with close kin, as in Hawai'i. In these highly differentiated systems, commoners continued to pursue basically adjustive strategies, dependent to a degree on the aristocracy for the allocation of goods, but excluded from prestige competition and thus not concerned with the enabling function of the family. I describe O-cluster systems in detail in Part IV.

The N- (Northwest Coast) Cluster

As a final example of a geographic cluster of rank societies, I will consider the Northwest Coast of North America (the N-cluster), in which we find a third pattern of domestic-public relationships. Here the allocation connection was not particularly important. In some places, resources were individually or family-owned and jealously guarded (though provided even to strangers in times of need); in others, resources were free for the taking; in still others, important men had rights of overlordship, but since resources were abundant, they found it difficult to use allocation of resources as a way of attracting followers.

The enabling connection, by contrast, was crucial. Positions of prominence on the Coast were gained through a process I have called "heredi-

tary achievement"; in some places high birth had to be validated by acquisition and redistribution of wealth; in others the ability to acquire and redistribute wealth was rationalized in terms of high birth. But in either case,
the accumulation of wealth necessary to hold the potlatch or other large
redistribution could only be gained by mobilizing the labor of family members and by marrying advantageously to create allies. This meant that the
family strategies pursued by ordinary people were primarily adjustive, but
that those pursued by prominent leaders were both accretive (in that more
labor in the household meant a more effective organization for production
and distribution) and exclusive (in that better marriages meant better allies). The difference between the African and Northwest Coast systems lies
in the nature of the goal: in Africa, wealth was a way to a following, while
on the Northwest Coast, a following was the way to wealth.

These three clusters include only a large minority of the rank societies
existing on earth in the eighteenth through the early twentieth centuries;
there are undoubtedly other possible patterns of domestic-public connection and associated family strategies in other areas and other forms of rank
societies, and the reader may be thankful that this book only has room for
three.[5] It should be emphasized again, though, that in terms of the family
activities of division of labor (both kinds), child rearing, regulation of sexuality, and transmission of property and offices, rank societies have much in
common that tends to separate them as a whole (a super-cluster) from societies both less and more complex than they. And they also have in common that here, for the first time, we can distinguish clearly domestic from
public, family from society. But at the same time, we often find a lack of
coincidence between the family as constituted for the performance of one
set of activities and as constituted for the performance of another. There
may be one group that owns and shares land, another with a common
hearth, a third with a common residence, and so on—this appears equally
true in the A-, O-, and N-cluster systems we will investigate. It is in the
nature of the domestic-public connection that the three clusters differ radically, and this difference seems to be attributable to the particular interaction between environment and history that produced public societies of
the kind found in the three regions.

The C-Cluster: Family Systems
in Pre-modern Complex Societies

The development of inequality, from hierarchy as a basis of social order
to social class as an unequal division of labor, is the most important aspect
of the Second Great Transformation: from rank to complex societies. As in
the transition from band to rank societies, the transition from rank to complex societies seems to have been propelled in the first instance by a prob-

lem of the supply of subsistence resources. At the rank level, luxury goods and legal or political privileges have ordinarily distinguished one rank from another, but subsistence resources have been available to everyone. When further population growth and expansion make access to subsistence resources problematical, high-ranking members of societies begin to assert prerogatives of differential control over those subsistence resources, leading to a division of labor between those who own land, livestock, commercial goods, etc. and those whose access is dependent on subordinating themselves to the owners. Resistance to the transition from those ranked lower in the hierarchy, along with often violent repression from the high-ranked who are in the process of becoming the high-class, usually marks this transition;[6] when the transition is complete we have a complex society. Once again, complex societies in most environments where they have developed have had an evolutionary advantage in direct competition particularly, but also in reproductive rates, against neighboring rank societies, which they have tended to conquer, absorb, convert, or a combination of the three.

We can define complex societies as those in which the division of labor by criteria other than age and sex results in differential access to the means of subsistence or, in simpler language, societies with social classes or social stratification. (Class I take to be the dynamic, and stratification, the static aspect of this kind of division of labor.) The technological base of such a social system must allow for the production of a surplus to supply the needs of non-producing classes; it usually involves plough agriculture and allows for very dense concentration of population including cities consisting primarily of non-producers and craft specialists.

Social stratification, differential access to the means of social reproduction, must be based on the concept of property rights belonging differentially to individuals, families, or occasionally other groups in a society. It is by restricting access to these basic goods that the inequalities of social class are created and maintained. In terms of family activities, it means that they are conditioned by a two-way connection between the activities of the domestic and the public sphere. The allocation connection is paramount—it is through the laws and other control mechanisms of the state (necessary to maintain social classes—see Fried 1967) that property rights, and thus differential access to means of social reproduction, are maintained. A family's economic standing is thus based on the protection or prevention of its rights to certain kinds of property, backed by the state. At the same time, the enabling connection is important also, since the products of family property and labor determine the status that a family can have in the public sphere. (This does not deny that status may be ascribed in many complex societies. But this status, as well as any status based on accumulation of resources, is protected by the public sphere and necessary for certain kinds of public participation. Thus the double connection between domestic and public operates whether status is achieved, ascribed, or a combination of the two.)

The paradox of the double domestic-public connection is that, in making family production so crucial for public status (status that means differential access to basic goods, not just differential prestige), this isolates families from each other, because every family is in competition with every other for the social status that is at least partially determined by that family's success or failure in managing its own resources for its own advantage. And it is this competitiveness and isolation that, in spite of the two-way connection of the domestic and public spheres, distinguishes the domestic from the public more clearly here than in other stages of social evolution. Especially in those social classes that depend for their livelihood on some kind of rights to property (and these are the majority, if we include tenancy, customary *jajmani* payments, etc.), all the enumerated activities of the family are important and tend to be concentrated in a single type of family group.[7]

Take to begin with the division of labor. Since all members of a family are working primarily or exclusively for the family's benefit, exchanges of labor or goods with other families will be on a strict basis of balanced reciprocity; the only division of labor in which people give freely to others of the fruits of their labor is within the family itself, and the family becomes a clearly bounded group within which people share tasks of both procurement and processing of all consumer goods.

The family as a group within which people manage and transmit property and offices also becomes crucially important here, because access to property and offices determines not only the material well-being and social standing of the family at any particular time, but also the access to social status and its requisites for members of the next generation. This means that adults will act to maximize their own chances and those of their children in the game of competition for social status. This is the origin of the complex family structural features subsumed under "diverging devolution" by Goody (1976).[8]

With the necessity that people manage their family resources in this way, determination of family membership becomes extremely important, for it decides where a child will end up as an adult in the society's system of social inequality. This, in turn, leads to the strict regulation of sexuality to the confines of the family, usually entailing bans or at least strong discouragement of sex both before and outside marriage. A wrong pregnancy, while generally embarrassing in many rank societies, is a potential disaster in stratified societies, and the ban on sex outside marriage is an attempt to control physiological reproduction in a way that will allow it to fit in harmoniously with the society's system of social reproduction.

Similarly, here the family takes more nearly exclusive charge of the socialization of its own children, at least in the case of the majority of people, who have no access to formal, literate education. Those who do have such access give over much responsibility to teachers who are specialists acting in the public sphere, but it is noteworthy that the curricula of schools in many such societies emphasize family-centered values—the public sphere provides education to members of privileged families in the virtues of family-centered ethics and behavior.

Representation is also at its most important here. Only certain members of families typically participate in public-sphere activities, and those activities are so closely tied in with the welfare of the family that they hold great importance for the family members who do not participate, i.e. those who are represented. Politics, business, law, warfare, all are areas of action that are important both because they control families' access to goods and because participation in them enables family members to gain or maintain status and prestige.

It is in C-cluster systems, then, that the family becomes most discernible as a discrete group, that it performs all of its enumerated activities, and that the groups in and for which people perform the various activities tend to coincide most closely with each other (though even here the fit is seldom perfect). The family is the basic unit of society, closely embedded in the larger social system, but the nature of its embeddedness turns its members inward toward the protection of their own exclusive interests in preserving and enhancing its own status in that larger society. Because of these rather stringent tasks encompassed in the family in such a social system, the variation in family systems is limited to a quite narrow range—in premodern complex societies across the world, we find family systems so similar that there is no need to divide them for analytical purposes into geographic or other clusters.

It should be remembered, however, that the very nature of complex societies means that the larger social system places different constraints on the families of people at different places in the system of social inequality, or to put it another way, that there is much variation according to occupation, locality, or class among communities within the society. The typecase complex society family, described above, is most typical of propertyholding or at least property-access holding classes. Those who work for wages, who have no close connection or access to property as a means of livelihood, have fewer constraints than do those who have property, and thus tend to blur the boundaries of the family as an insulated group in competition with all other families. This, in turn, often leads to loosening of the restrictions on sex outside marriage, a lack of senior generation control over young adults to whom they will not transmit property, office, or good name, and often a more tolerant attitude toward deviance from the family norms in general. It seems to be interests in a common estate that, above all, hold families together in the type-case form; when these are absent, family structure once again resembles more closely that in rank societies. We will see several examples of this in Part VI, which deals with C-cluster family systems.

The M-Cluster: Modern Family Systems

Modern societies evolved out of pre-modern complex societies because of the evolutionary advantage of industrial technology, which in turn led the process of the Third Great Transformation, whose social and cultural aspects have included the concentration of the means of production in a few hands, public or private; the concentration of population in cities; occupational, social, and class mobility; and moral and legal emphasis on the rights and responsibilities of the individual. The industrial order and its accompanying informational/communications order have an evolutionary advantage over the older agrarian technologies of production and communication; the perceived advantages of industrialization are apparent to those who come in contact with the modern order. Thus world industrialization continues apace, not only displacing the agrarian order but bringing to a virtual end those remnants of both band and rank societies that managed to survive into the late twentieth century.

The structural difference in property-holding aspects of family systems between pre-complex modern societies and modern societies is not so much one of kind as one of proportion. In the C-cluster societies, the majority lives from property or some sort of customary rights to the income from property. In modern societies, the majority lives from the sale of labor, in some ways similar to the lowest classes of premodern societies. What this means in terms of the activities normally performed in and for families is that the wealthiest classes, the propertied classes of modern societies, will tend to retain much of the C-cluster family organization of their societies' pre-modern phases, because their economic base, though larger, is similar in structure. This will also be true, to a lesser extent, of small property-holders such as small merchants and shopkeepers. The great majority, however, the salaried middle-class and the working class, will have their family organization influenced in other directions. For most of these people, the enabling connection becomes much weaker because it is through individual skill and initiative, rather than through access to family property, that people gain access to the jobs that will be their means of livelihood. The place, in fact, where the enabling function remains the strongest is in education, where a family of good means can enable its members to be educated and thus qualified for positions that will enhance their social standing. The allocation connection is still strong, in that the legal and coercive apparatus of the state still protects property rights, but is weakened in that these property rights are less crucial and in that the allocation of social status that still flows from the public sphere in modern societies flows more to the individual, only loosely connected to the family group because of the declining importance of the family estate.

With both the enabling and the allocation connections weakened, families modern societies mostly cease to be the sole, discretely bounded arenas for the division of labor, especially between adults. While family groups contain children, the division of labor within the family is vital for these children's support and care, but the division of labor is less necessary for adults, since most adults have direct access to resources from the public sphere through the sale of their labor. At the same time, technological change in the form of improved public health has lowered infant mortality rates in modern societies to the point where only a few children need to be born to reproduce the parents biologically and socially, and even these children are not absolutely necessary, because dependent elders in such a society can be cared for by the state or from their own savings. So while division of labor within families is important for people with children, families with children are themselves taking up a smaller and smaller proportion of the life cycle of the individual. The declining dependence on property, along with the virtual elimination of the kin-based succession to offices, means that the family as steward and transmitter of property and office is much less important in modern society than previously, and this makes for a great alteration in the power of parents over children and in the relationships between senior and junior generations. This is, of course, connected with the declining disastrousness of an unwanted pregnancy, which combined with the invention of cheap, reliable contraceptive methods has meant a pressure toward the loosening of strictures on sex outside marriage.

In sum, modern societies have seen a blurring of the boundaries and a weakening of the activities performed in and for the family group from what they were in pre-modern complex societies. This has, in turn, allowed considerable conscious experimentation with family and local-group living arrangements, in attempts to satisfy both universal and socially determined needs through the organization of other kinds of groups. Communal experimenters in a wide range of social and ideological contexts have taken advantage of the declining necessity for *families* to fulfill these needs, and have tried to eliminate what their originators have seen as the unfortunate consequences of the family as it has "traditionally" (in pre-modern and modern complex societies) operated.

Incidentally, both C- and M-cluster systems provide us with the best material for testing the effects of social environments on family organization. This is because in such societies, usually ruling classes are reasonably successful in imposing their ideology on the ruled, in family matters as well as in other things. When we find, then, members of different social classes in a single society whose family systems differ according to what would be expected from the differences in the activities they perform, we can be reasonably sure that these differences are related to the nature of the activities themselves, and not simply due to differing cultural traditions.

The primary characteristics of the family systems of the society clusters described in this book are set out in Table 3-1.

TABLE 3-1: Basic Characteristics of Clusters of Family Systems

Cluster/Location	Important Family Activities	Domestic-Public Connection	Family Strategies
B/Worldwide	Procuring, Processing, Sex, Socialization, Emotion	Not clearly distinguished	Adjustive
First Great Transformation—Sedentarization			
A/Subsaharan Africa	Above plus M & T, Representation, **Enabling**	Enabling	Women Adjustive Men Accretive
O/Polynesia-Micronesia	Same	Enabling/ Allocation	CommonerAdjustive Noble Accretive/ Exclusive
N/Northwest Coast	Same	Enabling	Adjustive/Accretive
Second Great Transformation—Development of Social Classes			
C/Worldwide	Same	Two-Way	Adjustive/Exclusive
Third Great Transformation—Industrialization (Still Incomplete)			
M/Worldwide	Procuring, Processing, Sex, **Socialization, Emotion**, Enabling	Weak	Adjustive/Exclusive

So far I have not said anything about the actual form of particular family systems—that is the task of the remainder to this book. Now that we have seen how the reasons for acting as a family have changed over the course of the three great transformations, we can look carefully at each cluster of societies and the variation among family systems within it, to try to discover how well the various structures provide family members with the means to perform these activities, and combining this with knowledge of the cultural traditions of the societies involved, can begin to explain the variation in developmental cycle from one family system to another. When we understand the variation in developmental cycles—who is part of a particular family group at a particular time—and the nature of the activities that each family member performs with, for, or to the others, we can begin to explain the content of family relationships. The systematic treatment of this content is reserved for another work, but this one ought to at least provide a basis, combined perhaps with the insights gained from developmental psychology, for understanding that content systematically.

Notes

1. The difference between the terms cultural community and society should thus become clear. I use cultural community to refer to a collection of people who follow the same rules and precepts; I use society to refer to a collection of people bound in a particular web of exchange and power relationships. A social class, for example, can be a cultural community, but it is only part of a society.

2. Becker (1991:296-303) discusses in formal economic terms the conditions under which parents will behave altruistically, and their preferences will benefit the family as a whole, in contrast to conditions in which the preferences of parents and children will conflict. He reaches, on logical grounds, the conclusion that altruism usually dominates family behavior, a conclusion that seems empirically doubtful, or at least uninformed by any idea of the importance of crises and transformations in the developmental cycle. On the other hand, he is not dogmatic, and does allow for selfishness in the family in certain situations.

3. In a work on the family, which is not a work on the theory of social evolution, I do not have time to go into the nature of the relationship between technological, demographic, and political changes as motive forces in the process of social evolution (Rambo 1991:47-52). Suffice it to say that my classificatory criteria are social and political, rather than technological, though I incline toward technological changes as explanatory mechanisms.

Another important issue to which I cannot give full attention here is the relationship between the band and rank societies observed by ethnographers and other students of social organization in the last few centuries, societies already influenced to some degree or other by contact with more advanced forms, and such band or rank socities as may have existed before the Second Great Transformation produced class societies. The best I can offer here is an assumption that aspects of family life in recent band and rank societies tell us at least something about what it was like before "contact," and a watchful eye for those aspects that may have been influenced directly by colonial or other outside influences.

4. Some rank societies, and even some geographically peripheral communities in stratified societies, are nomadic, following herds. But it now seems more likely that these kinds of nomadism did not grow directly out of nomadic band organization, but rather are a secondary adaptation to agriculturally marginal environments after the establishment of rank or stratified societies. The putative succession hunters-herders-farmers-merchants, so beloved of both Marx and Adam Smith, was a misunderstanding of this process.

5. Other areas that might be explored profitably here would be Melanesia-New Guinea, the Amazonian Basin, the North American East, and the uplands of Southeast Asia and South China. I first chose Africa because it was Goody's example in contrasting non-class with class societies, then seized on Polynesia/Micronesia and the Northwest Coast as offering obvious contrasts with the African pattern. Then I figured I had enough.

6. Examples of the transition rather far advanced but not complete can be seen in the 17th-19th century history of some of the West African states discussed in Chapter 10. Examples of places where the transition was less advanced but clearly in progress come from the immediate pre-contact history of some of the larger Polynesian island groups, such as Hawai'i and the Society Islands, discussed in Chapters 11-13.

7. It is in referring to this single, bounded, multi-activity group that I believe the term "household" is best employed.

8. At the same time, it is important to point out that the inheritance and succession systems of the O- and N- clusters are much closer structurally to the "diverging devolution" of the C-cluster complex societies than to the "homogeneous transmission" found in Africa. This simply illustrates the point that the basic evolutionary sequence is one of activities and strategies, not of structures.

PART TWO

The B-Cluster:
Nomadic Foraging Bands

Prelude: Children in an Mbuti Camp

Colin Turnbull discusses the relations between adults and children at a camp in the Ituri Forest, Central Africa:

> ...It is no accident that a child calls everyone in the same age group as his parents "father" or "mother"; those still older are called "grandparent." Those of the same age as himself he refers to by a term which could be translated as either "brother" or "sister," and anyone younger is "child," though more often than that they are just called by name...

> ...The Pygmies have learned from the animals around them to doze with one eye open, and a sleepy midday camp can become filled in a minute with shouts and yells and tearful protestations as a baby, crawling around this warm, friendly world, gets into a bed of hot ashes, or a column of army ants. In a moment he will be surrounded by angry adults and given a sound slapping, then carried unceremoniously back to the safety of a hut. It does not matter much which hut, because as far as the child is concerned all adults are his parents or grandparents. They are all equally likely to slap him for doing wrong, or fondle him and feed him with delicacies if he is quiet and gives them no trouble. He knows his real mother and father, of course, and has a special affection for them and they for him, but from an early age he learns that he is the child of them all, for they are all children of the forest.

> When a hunting party goes off there are always people left in the camp—usually some of the older men and women, some children, and perhaps one or two younger men and women. The children always have their own playground, called *bopi*, a few yards off from the main camp. At Apa Lelo it was on the shore where the river twisted around an island...The water was fairly shallow there, and all day long the children splashed and wallowed about to their heart's content. If they tired of that, they had a couple of vine swings in their *bopi*; one was a small one for younger children, and the other was hung from two tall trees. Infants watched with envy as the older children swung wildly about, climbing high up on the vine strands and performing all sorts of acrobatics.

> ...Like children everywhere, Pygmy children love to imitate their adult idols. This is the beginning of their schooling, for the adults will always encourage and help them. What else is there for

53

them to learn except to grow into good adults? So a fond father will make a tiny bow for his son, and arrows of soft wood with blunt points. He may also give him a strip of a hunting net. A mother will delight herself and her daughter by weaving a miniature carrying basket. At an early age boys and girls are "playing house." They solemnly collect the sticks and leaves, and while the girl is building a miniature house the boy prowls around with his bow and arrow. He will eventually find a stray plantain or an ear of corn which he will shoot at and proudly carry back. With equal solemnity it is cooked and eaten, and the two may even sleep the sleep of innocence in the hut they have made.

They will also play at hunting, the boys stretching out their little bits of net while the girls beat the ground with bunches of leaves and drive some poor tired old frog in toward the boys. If they can't find a frog they go and awaken one of their grandparents and ask him to play at being an antelope. He is then pursued all over the camp, twisting and dodging among the huts and trees, until finally the young hunters trap their quarry in the net, and with shouts of delight pounce on him, beating him lovingly with their little fists. Then they roll over and over in a tangle with the net until they are exhausted.

Colin Turnbull, *The Forest People* (New York: Simon and Schuster, 1961), pp. 126-29. Reprinted by permission.

4

Band Societies: The Family and the Larger Community

Family organization in band societies was remarkably uniform. The dedicated ethnologist can find more variation in structure in a single complex society, such as Greece or Spain, than in all the hunting and gathering bands known to modern ethnography. Since there was wide variation in other aspects of band-level cultures, such as religion and ritual or even extended kinship organization, we must ask ourselves what there is about the ecological relations under which bands lived that shaped all their family organizations in such a similar way. Since family systems everywhere involve adaptation to the nature of the larger social systems in which they are embedded, let us first look at band organization and its relation to economic necessity.

With rare exceptions, people living in bands had no domesticated food plants or animals, and were thus dependent on hunting, fishing, and collecting to secure their material means of subsistence. In certain places and at certain times, resources available in the natural environment have been rich enough to allow people without agriculture or animal husbandry to settle permanently in villages of several hundred, and thus to develop social organization considerably more complex than that we usually characterize as the band. The Northwest Coast of North America is the example usually cited (see Chapters 14-16), but there are other places where a sedentary pattern of settlement and relatively large aggregations of people have been built on a hunting-and-gathering subsistence base—many Western Alaskan Eskimos, for example, as well as the Ainu of Hokkaido probably fit into this category (Watanabe 1968). In addition, the hunters and gatherers we have known for the past few centuries of contact have all lived in relatively marginal environments. While doubt has been shed on

55

the previous notion that these are refugee groups (Lee 1969:76; Oswalt 1967), it is nevertheless true that by the 18th century there were few hunters and gatherers left in environments that could support social structures more complex than the band on the basis of a hunting-gathering subsistence economy. My opinion is that over the course of human history there must have been a lot of such groups, that the Northwest Coast peoples were merely a remnant of what once must have been a widespread hunting-gathering/rank (as opposed to egalitarian band) type. But the great majority of hunters and gatherers whose social systems are known to us have lived in bands, and it is on bands that this chapter concentrates.

The Nature of Bands and Their Relationship to the Environment

There are several characteristics of band organization that can be tied directly to the requirements of subsistence production in marginal environments.

Low Population Density

Hunting-gathering groups had to remain sparsely enough distributed on the land that even in bad years, when normal resources failed, there were enough food, water, and other subsistence goods available in the environment to sustain the group through the season of scarcity. This maximum safe density of course varied from one environment to another; in band societies it seems to have ranged from about one per square mile in such places as coastal Arnhem Land (Yengoyan 1968:190) to one per 50 or more square miles in such truly sparsely populated areas as the Central Arctic (Damas 1969:120-21). There are, of course, environments that would have supported a denser population of hunters and gatherers, but in these environments the people are likely to have organized themselves into structures more complex than bands.

Small Camp Size

For hunters and gatherers, living off the land, with few facilities for long-term storage of consumables such as food, the size of the camp was determined by the population density that could exist in the particular environment. If it took S square kilometers to support one person at a particular season of the year (and this will vary from season to season and from year to year), then a group of N persons will have needed an area of NS square kilometers to which it had the exclusive or at least prior rights to food resources, and it needed to be able to send some of its members, some of the time, to the edges of this area in search of resources. The bigger the area, the farther certain group members had to travel on their daily quest or, alternatively, the more often and over the greater distance the whole group had to move camp. So whereas seasonal accumulations of several hundred people are reported for short periods among band societies as distant from each other as Australia (Myers 1982:178; Kaberry 1939:30) and the Eastern Subarctic of North America (Leacock 1969:10-12), these gatherings were always short-lived, and usually depended on the amount of stored food the participants could carry to the mass camping site. At other times of the year, the functional group size might be as large as a hundred persons, as in Netsilik, Copper, and Iglulik Eskimo winter sealing camps (Damas 1969), or dry-season water-hole camps among the !Kung in the relatively lush part of the Kalahari (Lee 1979:356-60), or it might be as small as single nuclear families, as was the case during most of the yearly round for many of the Great Basin Shoshoni, or for short periods among the G/wi Bushmen and certain Western Desert Australian groups (Steward 1939:231; Silberbauer 1981:105-5; Meggitt 1962:80).

Flexibility of Local Group Membership

Not only did the local group have to be fairly small; it also had to be flexible in its composition. This flexibility had two forms—seasonal flexibility and long term flexibility. In practically any environment, the ideal size of local groups varied from season to season, depending on the particular distribution of resources at those seasons. Thus the Netsilik Eskimo gathered in aggregations of up to a hundred for breathing-hole sealing in the winter (Balikci 1970:57-58), but dispersed into groups consisting of just a few closely related nuclear families for caribou hunting in late summer. Similarly, the G/wi Bushmen of the Central Kalahari dispersed in the dry season into individual families, and came together as entire bands of 25-85 people in the wet season (Silberbauer 1981:138). There are many other examples.

Even more germane to family organization is long-term flexibility. Since people in band societies had very little control over either their environment or their own demographic increase or decline, a group might find

itself either too large to live comfortably off its accustomed area of foraging, or too small to exploit its resources effectively. Neighboring groups
might have the opposite problem. In such situations, it made sense for families to be able to move from one band to another, attaching themselves
according to kin or other ties with other members of the respective bands.

Permeability of Boundaries

In almost all band societies, individual bands had clearly recognized
associations with certain areas or "countries." In some cases, such as the
BaMbuti pygmies (Turnbull 1965a:27), and many Australian groups (Hiatt
1982:101; Williams 1982:15) the boundaries of these areas were clearly demarcated. But almost nowhere did the ownership of an area by a band
allow that band to use its area exclusively. Permission was often required
to hunt or gather on another band's territory, but in places where it was
required, it was almost always granted if asked (Williams 1982:146-48;
Myers 1982:184-85; Marshall 1976:190). This characteristic of band organization, together with the flexibility of band membership, mentioned above,
means that it was possible for families to live on and exploit the area belonging to a band that either the husband or wife, or sometimes neither,
was born into.

There were cases in which foragers defended territory (Dyson-Hudson
and Smith 1978); most of these occurred in situations where resources were
relatively stable, predictable, and defensible. Most people, however, living
in areas of less stable resources, tended to regulate access by reciprocal
permission to forage, rather than by defending the boundaries of territories (Cashdan 1983).

Mobility and Its Restriction on Material Possessions

It is clear by now that no band society was "primitively communistic"
in the sense that all kinds of goods belonged to everyone equally. Everywhere, in fact, certain things were owned by bands, families, or individuals. But with the seasonal and irregular mobility required to forage in most
environments, the number of personal possessions was limited to what
one could carry or, occasionally, drag on some kind of sledge, as among
certain Eskimo groups. This meant that accumulations of material goods
quickly became more bothersome than useful, so that competition for material goods between individuals or between families was everywhere discouraged and in some places apparently very rare.

A Particular Kind of Sexual Division of Labor

Since women had not only to bear but also to breastfeed and care for young children (and breastfeeding in band societies often lasted three or four years), they were ordinarily unable to range far from camp for the strenuous pursuit of large game. This meant that everywhere the hunting of large game was primarily the duty of the men. In areas where relatively immobile foods predominated, or at least formed a significant portion of the diet, the gathering of such foods was usually primarily the province of the women, though nearly everywhere men would gather plant foods for themselves and in some places for their families as well (Turnbull 1965a:167). In most northerly climes, where animal foods composed all or almost all the diet, the men were still the hunters of large game, and the women's role in getting subsistence goods either concerned hunting small animals, as among the northern forest Mistassini Cree (Rogers 1972:109), or was negligible, with women's attention concentrated on the processing of those goods brought in by the men. It is noteworthy that such processing, including importantly the sewing of winter clothes, as among most Eskimo groups (Balikci 1970:52-55) was a much bigger job than it was in tropical environments; it is conceivable that women in northern hunting-gathering societies spent as much time scraping and sewing as !Kung or Australian women spent gathering.

An Ethic of Sharing

Where the availability of resources was variable and unpredictable, and where accumulation led to encumbrance or plain wastage, it made sense to perceive an advantage in sharing resources with other people. Not only did this prevent the resources from going to waste, it also provided insurance against unequal access to resources. If I share with you when I have an abundance of something, I can thus expect you to reciprocate when you have a lot and I am short. This does not mean that members of band societies were not covetous or greedy—many of them were, and disputes caused by failure to share, for example, are recorded from Bushmen (Marshall 1976:312; Lee 1979), Pygmies (Turnbull 1965a:197-8) and other groups. Graburn (1968) reports Eskimos to have been fiercely competitive for women and prestige. But ethics concerning material resources nearly always declared that sharing was desirable or even pleasing to the spirits, as among the Central Eskimo (Guemple 1979:32), because people realized that however much they wanted to have their food or property to themselves, it was generally to their long-term advantage to share it.

Egalitarianism

That hunting-gathering societies tended to be egalitarian is asserted both by theorists (Fried 1967:54) and by ethnographers discussing particular cases. Egalitarianism, of course, does not mean the absence of distinctions based on age or sex, nor does it preclude the recognition of people with special virtues or abilities. But it does mean that people of the same age and sex were not given formal authority or power over others. Indeed, it is difficult to see how such power would have been maintained in a band, since the subsistence quest was open to all, without property or other restrictions, and there were no resources to which one could withhold access by others.

Activities Organized by the Band and by the Family in Band Societies

Keeping in mind these characteristics of band social organization, we can now examine the possible activities organized by and for the family, as outlined in Chapter One, and look at which activities are likely to have been organized at the band level, and thus did not need to be performed by the family, which activities did need to be performed in and for the family, and which were simply nonexistent in band societies.

Procuring Subsistence Goods

Hunting was important everywhere in band societies. Although in some places, notably in the tropics, products of the hunt constituted a minority of the food resources of the groups (Lee 1968:43), such groups nevertheless valued them highly (Marshall 1976:93; Lee 1979:205; Woodburn 1968:52). In the north, where vegetable foods were scarcer or nonexistent, and where even small animals took a back seat to big game as food source, hunting was not only important but all-important.

Although there were exceptions, most hunting of large game had to be done cooperatively by members of more than one family. There were several reasons for this. First, many kinds of hunting technology required cooperation of more than one hunter. When Eskimos hunted seals at their winter breathing-holes on the polar ice, for example, there was no way to know which of its several breathing holes a seal was going to use at a particular time. So several hunters were necessary to cover the contingencies of the various holes; three seems to have been the optimum number, and it was rare that a family had three adult male hunters (Balikci 1970:57; Nelson 1969:240; E.A. Smith 1991:323-330). Similarly, the net-hunts of such widely separated peoples as the Mbuti in central Africa (Turnbull 1965a:153-61) or the Birhor of Bihar (Sinha 1972:376) were accomplished by a number of men, perhaps 6 to 30, lining up their nets in a semicircle and having beaters drive the animals into the nets where they could be speared. If the semicircle was too small, if it consisted of only one net, for example, the animals could escape. Even the Shoshoni, who foraged alone in nuclear family groups most of the year, required large aggregations of hunters for the fall rabbit-drives, where the animals were driven into a sagebrush enclosure and then killed at close range (Steward 1938:82-83).

These hunts, however, did not simply require the cooperation of more than one person. They generally also required the cooperation of members of more than one family, because, for reasons suggested above, it was usually infeasible for any but adult males to take part in long-distance hunting, and those forms of hunting that did depend on female as well as male participation were often very large-scale affairs such as net hunts and rabbit drives, which required more than one family's worth of people even if women participated.

But there was another, perhaps more important way in which hunting had to be cooperative, and that is in the distribution of the product in order to reduce risk. Hunting is a matter of luck as much as of skill. Though people such as the !Kung and Hadza recognized that some men were more skilled at hunting than others, and that these men would, over the long haul, bring in more game than their less skilled or lazier colleagues, in the short run, there would be wild fluctuations of hunting success. The ethic of sharing thus had to extend to several hunters, in order to even out the distribution of valued resources, and to provide insurance for the unlucky hunters and their families. This meant that most band groups had more or less detailed rules for the distribution of the meat from a large kill among the families in a camp. Sometimes kinship was the important factor, as among the Australian Tiwi, where a hunter, male or female, was required to share first with the spouse, parents, children (and, for a male hunter, the wife's mother), then with real and close classificatory siblings, and then with mother's relatives (Goodale 1971:171). In other cases, sharing might be based primarily on non-kin partnerships, as among the Copper and Netsilik Eskimo, who gave every boy at birth a series of seal-partners, with whom he shared specific parts of any seal he caught, keeping very little for himself (Damas 1972:24; Balikci 1970:134-35). In still other cases, more than one principle might be employed: the !Kung San determined shares of a kill by who owned the fatal arrow, who participated in the hunt, and who was related to whom (Marshall 1976:295-98).

The lesson of all this is that products of a chancy process such as long-distance hunting could not be kept by the hunter and his family, that the procuring and distribution of hunted goods took place at the band level, not the level of the family. Only after the hunter had distributed parts of the kill among those to whom he was obligated was meat then further distributed to the families of those who received shares in the first division.

When we look at the other major aspect of the subsistence quest, the collecting of relatively immobile foods, primarily by women, we find a different picture altogether. The collection of such foods ordinarily entailed neither large-scale cooperation nor much risk. The work may have been arduous; it may have required intimate knowledge of the natural environment; it may sometimes have failed for climatic or other reasons in certain seasons or certain years. But if the resources were available at all, they would be available to any woman (or man) who had the requisite knowledge and skills to be able to go get them. For this reason, we find that the gathering and distribution of relatively immobile foods was usually organized on a family basis. This was true, for example among !Kung and G/wi Bushmen (Marshall 1976:97; Silberbauer 1981:153), among the African Hadza (Woodburn 1968a:51) and among nearly all Australian Groups (see for example, C. Berndt 1970:41; Kaberry 1939:37). A woman, sometimes with the assistance of men or children, gathered the foods needed for her own family, and was rarely obligated to share them among other members of the band.

This does not mean, or course, that gathering was a solitary activity, nor does it imply that gathered food products were exempt from the general ethic of sharing in band societies. Women in most places usually gathered together with kinswomen or friends, because the work was more enjoyable and less drudgerous that way. Marshall, for example, says of the !Kung that "The women form gathering parties together. The !Kung do not like to be alone" (1976:98). Similarly, Mbuti women, gathering on the way to and from the communal net-hunt for which they acted as beaters, went off to gather forest plants in twos and threes. Rogers (1972:121) states that among the Mistassini Cree, female cooperation was mainly for sociability. But this does not mean that the food had to be shared, only that people would rather work in groups when possible. At the same time, however, while there was rarely any compulsory sharing of gathered foods in ordinary circumstances, let alone strict rules for their distribution, it was still expected that women would share some of the food they gathered with people other than family members, simply out of good mannerliness and the general idea, pervasive in band societies, that sharing in its own right is a good thing.

Elizabeth Marshall Thomas provides perhaps the classic example of this kind of sharing in her story of the !Kung women standing by the Marshalls' jeep, passing identical bagfuls of tsi nuts back and forth (1958:214-15). But similar behavior, the voluntary sharing of gathered resources, is reported from such widely scattered groups as the Mbuti (Turnbull 1965a:167), Walbiri (Meggitt 1962:82), and Shoshoni (Steward 1938:231). In addition, in times of shortage, it was almost everywhere expected that people would share any surplus with those less fortunate than they. Silberbauer, for example, reports that among the G/wi, plant foods were not ordinarily shared, except in time of shortage, when sharing was expected (1981:153). And Leacock, writing about a very different part of the world, speaks of the unquestioned generosity with which a Naskapi man would share his resources with someone in need, even though they were members of different bands and in spite of the fact that his sharing meant reducing his possible fur catch (1969:13-14). That gathered foods belonged to the family and were ordinarily not shared beyond its limits in any regular fashion seems more than anything else to be a matter of convenience, and perhaps an incentive to work hard and not take free rides on other, more diligent gatherers. It did not mean that a family could gain much advantage from gathering more.

The Processing of Hunted and Gathered Goods

The importance and arduousness of processing labor varied greatly according to environments. In the more northern climes, where hides had to be cured, scraped, and sewn to make winter garments, where shelter from the elements was really necessary, and where, in some cases, storage was necessary for the unproductive winter season, processing labor was much more important than it was in warmer areas where garments were minimal, where shelter was rudimentary or, at some seasons, even absent, and where the environment provided something to eat the year around. But whatever amount of processing labor was necessary, it *tended* to be organized on a family basis. (Exceptions usually concern tasks too large to be done by a single family, such as butchering whales or elephants.)

The reason for this is closely related to the reason why gathering was similarly organized. In general, the supply of raw, unprocessed goods to any family was already secured, in the case of gathering by the family's own rights to what its members collected, and in the case of hunting by the family's link to the systems of meat and hide distribution that assured that every family received some share of the cooperative kill. Once the products were in hand, there was no particular need to cooperate, and certainly no risk involved, in their processing. So, for example, the Netsilk woman did all the skin work for her own family—"She scraped, cut, dried, cleaned, and washed the various kinds of skins, sewed all clothes and boots, made tents and skin containers, covered kayaks. This work was considered essential to the survival *of the family*" (emphasis added) (Balikci 1970:104). Kjellström (1973:26) reports a similar pattern as general among Eskimo groups. Even in areas where processing labor was much less arduous and time consuming, it generally was performed on a family basis: Australian women made fires for their families; both men and women then cooked what they brought in (Kaberry 1939:32; Meggitt 1962:92, etc.). Among the Bambuti, Turnbull tells us, mealtime was the only time when there was a definite emphasis on the nuclear family (1965a:123), and men were often much more concerned about their wives' cooking ability than about their sexual fidelity (1961:216; 1965a:122).

Regulation of Sexuality

At issue here is not the nature of sexual relations between husband and wife, about which it is difficult to gain any precise or accurate knowledge, but the degree to which sexual relations, ideally and in practice, were confined to married couples, and if there were strictures against pre- or extramarital sex, what were the consequences of breaking them. In general, the answer to these questions is that in band societies, attitudes toward premarital sex were almost always approving, and even extramarital sex often did not receive severe opprobrium.

For some groups, the notion of premarital sex, that is, where both partners were as yet unmarried, never came about. In most San groups (Marshall 1976:280-81; Silberbauer 1981:149), as well as in most of Australia (Kaberry 1939:84; Goodale 1971:44; Meggitt 1962:57), girls were married and had their husbands living and working with them as early as eight or ten years old, certainly well before puberty and usually before they began any kind of sexual relations. But in other places, particularly in the more northerly groups, where acquiring the subsistence skills to qualify one for marriage took considerably longer, both boys and girls had opportunities for premarital sex. For Eskimos at least, premarital sexual relations, and even sexually oriented games from a very early age, were assumed and even encouraged (Kjellström 1973:25; Guemple 1979:31; Balikci 1970:160). Similarly, among the Mbuti, who did not marry until a few years after puberty, premarital sex was one of the prime recreational interests of adolescent boys and girls (Turnbull 1965a:121; 1961:121).

When we turn to extramarital sex, the situation is a bit more diverse, ranging from societies like the !Kung, where marital fidelity was expected for both sexes, though certainly violated sometimes (Marshall 1976:279; Shostak 1981:266-68); to the Mbuti at the other end of the spectrum, where Turnbull states that he knows of no occasion when extramarital sexual relations, as common as they were, were ever cause for any kind of dispute (1965a:122). In general, the pattern seems to have been that both men and women were jealous of their spouses' sexuality, and extramarital sex, because it led to disputes, was discouraged, but happened all the time anyway. For example, this kind of situation is stated to have been the case in Australia, in the Western Desert (Meggitt 1962:81), in the Kimberly mountains (Kaberry 1939:102), and in northeastern Arnhem land (Warner 1958:68). A representative attitude about adultery (extramarital sex without the consent of the excluded spouse) in many band societies is expressed by Balikci's remark concerning the Netsilik: that even though homicide was very common in this society, adultery never led to killing: "It was simply not considered important enough" (1970:161).

In addition to adultery, there was another form of extramarital sex in many foraging societies: formalized spouse exchange partnership. This is best known from the Eskimo groups (Damas 1969:129; Kjellström 1973:150), but also occurred among the !Kung (Marshall 1976:279) and in some places in Australia (Meggitt 1962:50, 104). In some areas, such exchanges were based on kinship; in others, on non-kin ritual partnerships. In nearly all such cases, males predominated in arranging the exchanges, but could rarely prevail on their wives to make the swap if the wives were unwilling. Children always remained children of the spouse, even if born as a result of a spouse-exchange; indeed, among some Eskimo groups a barren marriage was thought a good reason to try a switch (Guemple 1979:32).

So we have a general picture of relative sexual freedom in most band societies—certainly the freedom of extramarital relationships seems unusual when compared with human societies at other stages of social evolution. The reason for this, I think, is to be sought in the consequences of such sexual activity—in band societies, it rarely harmed people's long-term interest in rights to spouses' reproductive or labor services. Premarital conception could simply lead to marriage, no problem in the great majority of band societies that did not have prescriptive marriage rules. (In Australia, where such rules were always important, girls were married well before they started having sexual relations.) Since marriage commonly involved little or no exchange of wealth, or when it did, this wealth was symbolically important but did not require much effort to produce or assemble, a marriage could easily be made if it was necessary. The rather casual attitude to adultery is such societies can be viewed in the same way. If an affair resulted in a pregnancy, the child belonged to the woman's husband anyway, and he was often glad to have it. I think, too, that the key to understanding the role of adultery in band societies lies in the common assertion that adultery was accepted in most bands as long as it was kept discreet and did not become a public issue (Silberbauer 1981:156; Meggitt 1962:98-99; Goodale 1971:131).

This formulation helps us, I think, to reconcile this view, expressed by many ethnographers, with that outlined by Jane Collier in her analysis of what she calls "brideservice societies," a category that includes my category of bands (1988:15). Collier asserts that in such societies, "adultery and wife stealing are the most commonly mentioned reasons for fights among men" (1988:45), and goes on to explain this by the fact that a man in a brideservice society validates his status as a responsible adult by having a wife, from whom he can receive sexual and domestic services. In her analysis, Collier is focusing on those cases where adultery becomes a threat to a man's position as husband, which it does when his wife deserts him for another man, and here serious conflict can and does occur. Where adultery seems to be mere flirtation without threat of breakup of the marriage, or if the husband has other wives, as do the elders in some of the societies Collier discusses, particularly in Australia (1988:35-36), men can tolerate some extramarital activity on their wives' part without their status as adults being threatened.

We can look at formal spouse-exchange in the same light—since all parties supposedly agreed on the exchange before it happened, the main cause of disputes over extramarital sex—the jealousy of the adulterer's spouse—was guarded against, if not totally eliminated, at the outset. (There are cases recorded in the Eskimo literature where spouse exchange led to alienation of affection, and thus threatened the husband's position [Balikci 1970:143-44].) But in general, the consequences were slight, and some Eskimos stated in fact that spouse exchange was pleasing to the spirits, precisely because it was a form of sharing, and sharing, as mentioned earlier, was a good thing in itself (Guemple 1979:32). Thus the positive advantages of such exchanges, in increasing the number of people with mutual obligations, as well as in increasing sexual variety, were not contradicted by serious negative consequences.

In sum, people in all band societies formed long-lasting, ideally permanent sexual unions, and they usually had some feeling that it was wrong, or at least undesirable, to have sex outside these unions once one entered into them. But the infraction thus committed was usually not a serious one, because the consequences were usually not great. When it threatened to lead to permanent separation, it might be the cause of serious fighting.

Socialization of Children

The question of the extent to which the socialization and care of children was a organized in families or in wider groups is a complex one—we must consider the care of very young children (which did not involve much discipline or training in band societies) separately from the training or education of older girls and boys, who needed less care but had to learn the techniques of survival, and sometimes other kinds of knowledge, before they reached adulthood.

Let us first consider the care of very young children. In nearly all foraging societies, the breastfeeding period was long, even by non-Western standards. Three to four years seems to have been the most common duration of breastfeeding (Damas 1972:41; Goodale 1971:34; Kaberry 1939:50; Marshall 1976:102); the shortest period reported is "over two years" for the Western Desert Pitjandjara (Tindale 1972:259). During this period, unless the infant was adopted out, it would perforce spend much or perhaps almost all of its time in the company of the mother, accompanying her on gathering trips as well as around camp. Wet-nursing was of course a possibility; it is reported for some Australian groups (Goodale 1981:28; Warner 1958:85), as well as for the Mbuti pygmies (Turnbull 1965a:26). In other areas, however, wet-nursing was not practiced: among the G/wi only the mother nursed (Silberbauer 1981:163), and among most Eskimo groups, only co-wives nursed each other's babies (Kjellström 1973:390). In fact Eskimos, who generally preferred to adopt children at birth if possible, often delayed the adoption if the adoptive mother did not have milk: it was felt that wet-nursing would not be advisable because the mother-child bond formed in nursing was the social basis of the whole mother-child relationship (Guemple 1979:13). And in many cases where wet-nursing was practiced, it seems clear that the mother always remained the predominant feeder of the child—even among the Pygmies, Turnbull states that "a mother will *let* others nurse her baby" (1965a:26, emphasis added).

Besides nursing them, mothers in most band societies spent most of their time with their very young children, and often slept beside them until they were weaned. The role of other caretakers thus always seems subordinate at this period of the child's life. Fathers often took a role, at least in entertaining the child—Balikci reports this for the Netsilik (1970:106); Helm, for the Athapaskan Dogrib (1972:35), Leacock, for the Naskapi (1972:39), and Meggitt, for the Walbiri (1962:116), among others. Often the mother's sisters or co-wives also helped out with the care of infants and very small children: Steward reported that among the Shoshoni, one of the primary roles of people too old to go on long foraging expeditions was to care for toddlers while the parents were out procuring food (1938:240, 243). But the mother's role was always predominant at this age, and I think we need go no further than the apparently universal human mother-infant bond to explain this.[1]

When we turn to the education of older children, the situation becomes somewhat more complex, but in general we can say that such children almost always learned their life skills from role models of the same sex, and that the parents might or might not have been the predominant role models in any particular case. For example, Silberbauer reports that, among the G/wi, the training of older children was a group effort, in which neither parent was especially predominant (1981:163). Similarly, a Walbiri boy gained as much training from his sister's husband (likely to be much older than he because of the great age-differential at marriage), or from his mother's mother's brother as from his father, and a girl from her elder sister or her mother's mother as from her own mother (Meggitt 1962:82). Mbuti boys learned their hunting skills primarily from their fathers, and were expected to assist at their own fathers' nets before they married and acquired their own nets. But even here, other senior men played a significant part in the boys' training (Turnbull 1965a:109). This diffusion of responsibility for child-training does, of course, reflect the general emphasis on cooperation in economic life, particularly hunting. But this is not the whole explanation. With extended family organization so weak in most of these societies, children were being trained for their roles as adult members of society, rather than as continuing representatives of particular families. They might have been expected to support their parents or parents-in-law when the latter became old and dependent, but they rarely joined with them in a common corporate unit. So there was no overriding interest in the socialization of one's own children to the exclusion of others'. It is noteworthy in this respect that among the Netsilik Eskimo, where patrilocal extended families were cooperative and food sharing units during certain seasons of the year, the socialization of young hunters seems to have been almost exclusively in the hands of their own fathers (Balikci 1970:105).

Finally, with regard to the routine care of children past weaning, as opposed to their explicit training, I get the general impression that in most band societies this was not of much concern to people. /Du/da area !Kung children, for example, spent much time in close association with a variety of adults (Draper 1976:202), and Mbuti children, as indicated in the Prelude to this Part, are said to have been the responsibility of the band as a whole (see also Turnbull 1965a:113). This probably can be explained by the public nature of life in hunting-and-gathering camps. As Draper has expressed this, "We Westerners combine intensively private domestic lives (shared with five or fewer individuals) with daily exposure to hundreds or thousands of total strangers. The !Kung conduct their daily domestic life in full view of thirty or forty relatives and rarely see a stranger (1976:200)." The sharing of child care and child training responsibilities was a natural consequence of the sharing of almost all the interaction of daily life in a band society. The exclusive role of the family in child socialization was thus limited to maternal care and feeding of the very young, and sometimes a predominance of the parents in the training, but not the routine care of older children.

The activities I have discussed so far—the procuring and processing of necessary material goods, the satisfaction of sexual needs, and the care and training of children, can be seen as only weakly attached to the family in band societies. As we have seen, people organized a lot of these activities at the band level. But the activities were still there, and were necessary for social reproduction in every single band society—if they were not organized in and for the family, they were organized in and for larger social groups. When we turn to the next three activities on our list—the management and transmission of property and offices, the representation in political or ritual bodies, and the enabling of public participation on the basis of family resources, we run into a somewhat different situation. These activities, because of the nature of band societies, did not even always exist in band-level societies. Let us look at each of them in turn, along with the probable reasons why they assume such minor importance in the life of hunting-gathering bands.

The Management and Transmission of Property and Offices

In most band societies, property, the rights and duties people held in relationship to significant material things, was not a unified concept. We can divide ideas of property into three spheres—land or territory; permanent movable goods, such as implements, tools, or clothing; and food.

In thinking about almost any band society, it is better to conceive of people belonging to the land than of the land belonging to people. Land in band societies was associated with groups larger than the family, and these groups could be structured in various ways. For example, almost all Australian groups conceived of land divided into "countries," each country belonging to what amounted to a patrilineal descent group, usually of a totemic nature. Such groups were associated with particular areas of land primarily for mystical reasons—their totemic ancestors lived there; certain sites within the country were sacred for ritual purposes; it was from certain parts of the country that spirit children emerged to enter the mother's womb and create the animated being that was a child, a member of the totemic patriclan (Kaberry 1939:42). And in fact, in many Australian groups, male members of a patriclan might often, even usually, live and hunt in their own clan's country. But in contrast to what was thought about Australian local organization by early ethnographers, it appears that, in actual practice, the members of Australian totemic clans neither resided and hunted exclusively on their own clan land nor excluded members of other clans from crossing into their own territory, either to hunt temporarily or to join a band living on the clan's country. For example, Hiatt says of the Gidjingali of Arnhem Land that the patriclans did not hold exclusive rights to their territories, and that local groups, each of which exploited areas considered the totemic territory of more than one clan, typically included members of from two to twelve patriclans. Furthermore, members of other clans, living in other local groups, could use a clan group's territory by asking permission (Hiatt 1968:100). Kaberry tells us that among the peoples of the Kimberly district, those who did or did not "belong to the country" had the same rights to the food found in the country (1939:22). Peterson sums this up neatly in a continent-wide survey, stating that the patrilineal, patrilocal band "does not appear as an actual residential group" in aboriginal Australia (1970:9). Almost everywhere in Australia, it seems, permission to use another group's resources had to be asked; almost everywhere, it was routinely granted. The association between the people and the land was a ritual one and a strong emotional one (Hiatt 1968:102); in addition, it has been suggested that people gained a sense of autonomy or personal prestige from knowing that they were the ones who were in charge in a particular area (Myers 1982:188), even if being in charge did not bring with it the right to exclude others.

In other parts of the world, the relation to territory seems to have been basically the same, though it often lacked the explicit ideological attachment of people to land found in Australia. !Kung territories were owned not by patriclans, but by core groups of siblings and children of siblings of both sexes (Lee 1972:351; Marshall 1976:184-87), but the same kinds of rules of flexible residence, requiring permission of outsiders, and sharing or generosity in granting that permission, tended to prevail. The same can be said for many Canadian forest groups—in fact Helm goes so far as to state that, in terms of membership in local groupings, "!Kung and Athapaskan band composition is indistinguishable." So, apparently, was the conception of allowing access to outsiders (Leacock 1972:19-20; Rogers 1969:29). The Hadza of Tanzania probably reached an extreme in this regard—no Hadza group asserted even residual rights over any particular piece of land, and people could live wherever they liked. By contrast, the Mbuti pygmies seem to have maintained rather more rigid territorial boundaries between bands, but perhaps they compensated for this by an extreme rate of mobility between bands for individual families (Turnbull 1965a:96, 175), and even they did permit trespass under certain circumstances, such as the pursuit of wounded elephants (Turnbull 1965a:96).

This lack of rigid territorial rights can be explained easily enough by the aforementioned need for flexibility of residence and aggregation in relationship to resources, but it is important for explaining why members of band societies did not transmit rights to land along family lines. In respect to land, it was membership in a landowning group that was passed on, through whatever kinship route, from one generation to the next. Such membership was passed on—its route of passage was most evident among the patrilineal Australians—but it did not confer, in any part of the world, exclusive rights to support one's family off that particular group's piece of land.

Turning to the second sort of property—permanent movable items—we find that inheritance of these was of so little consequence in most band societies that ethnographers almost never mention it in their discussions of family or kinship organization. People simply did not own enough that was durable enough to worry about passing it down to the next generation.

Property rights in food are also irrelevant to our discussion. Food, of course, belonged to the family of the gatherer or to the family of the person who stood in a particular relationship to the hunter, but it is of its nature perishable, and one speaks no more of inheriting mongongo nuts or seal blubber in band societies than one speaks of inheriting banana splits in ours.

In sum, if there was inheritance in band societies, it was not inheritance of specific goods, but at most inheritance of rights to associate with particular territorial resources. But these resources never belonged to a family corporation in the first place—they belonged either to a unilineal descent group or to a vaguely defined group of siblings. Inheritance was no concern of the family in band societies, and it was not a pressing economic concern for larger groups either, though it may have been of extreme ritual and emotional significance, at least in Australia.

Representation in Politics and/or Ritual

Representation of this sort implies a prohibition on certain family members' participation in the political or ritual activities in question, and other members' participation on their behalf. Formal political councils were absent in the basically egalitarian organization of band societies, and rituals that excluded people of a certain social status from any kind of participation were rare in most parts of the world. Australian aborigines are, of course, known for their secret men's and women's ceremonies, many of them done for the benefit of the entire community. But men participated in these ceremonies not as representatives of the family, but as adult males, a solidary group with reference to the entire remaining population of women and uninitiated boys.

Enabling Participation in the Public Sphere

This was likewise not important in band societies. As should be abundantly clear by now, the blurring of distinctions between the family and larger groups in band societies meant in the end that there was no great distinction between domestic and public spheres of activity. A person who was prominent in a hunting-gathering band society gained such prominence from personal ability of some kind or other—in economic pursuits, in ritual or shamanic activity, or in respected judgment and wisdom. None of these ever stemmed from the enabling labor or property of other family members.

Providing Personal Warmth and Affection

For one used to dealing with the emotional ambivalence of family interrelationships in propertied societies, with the strong attachments and equally strong resentments that form a highly structured network in these family systems, both the general warmth and affection reported of family relationships in band societies and the lack of structure to these relationships are striking. In general, people in band societies seem to have gotten along about as well as people anywhere else. They formed deep and lasting emotional attachments with various relatives, and they also had long-lasting differences, not a few of which broke out into open bickering or worse. But it is the generality and randomness of these feelings, their failure to follow clear lines of social cleavage, that perhaps distinguishes emotional family relations in band societies from those elsewhere.

Most reports of emotional ties in band societies concentrate on the bond between spouses, something that probably reflects the extraordinary concern with the "quality of marriages" in the Euro-American society to which the ethnographers belong. But the uniformity and consistency of these reports is nevertheless striking. We find reports of a strong bond of affection, usually growing with age, among such widely dispersed peoples as the Netsilik (Balikci 1970:103), the Mistassini Cree (Rogers 1972:119); the Walbiri (Meggitt 1962:86), the Kimberly district peoples (Kaberry 1939:154), the G/wi (Silberbauer 1981:161) and the Mbuti (Turnbull 1965a:14). It seems virtually universal that spouses cared strongly for each other, and that there were few if any structural strains in the marital relationship: when spouses did not get along it was because of personal incompatibilities, not because of anything in the nature of the marriage institution.

For other close familial relationships, the data are much sparser, but a similar pattern emerges—ties between parents and children (Meggitt 1962:116), between siblings (Silberbauer 1981:165-6; Balikci 1970:107), even between co-wives (Balikci 1970:156; Meggitt 1962:109) are all reported to have been usually amiable. We find very little of a structural nature to grasp onto here, only the general assertion that people felt close to their immediate family members, and that their conflicts had more to do with individual personality than with position in the family system.

The evidence is fragmentary, to be sure, but insofar as it points this direction, I think it can be explained by the quite limited power of people in certain kinship positions over adults in other positions. Lee's statement that among the !Kung, not even the senior man in a large extended family could tell his sons what to do when they were adults (1972:347) would seem to be representative of many band societies. And this lack of authority, of course, went along with the fact that fathers lacked property or other means to force their grown children to comply. With the lack of authority went the lack of a source for resentment. Between husband and wife, there was often authority: frequently the husband was the senior partner in the marriage (see below). But even here, ethnographers agree that this authority was not absolute and usually not particularly harsh. So again there was no source for systematically occurring resentment.

Given this rather loose, vague structure to interpersonal relations, it is instructive to examine those cases in which structurally based resentment is reported. For example, in Eskimo societies, the co-husbands in a polyandrous marriage are always reported to have been in constant and jealous conflict with each other (Kjellström 1973:143; Balikci 1970:156-7). Brothers in Australia, as potential sexual rivals for the same woman, also lived in an atmosphere of distrust (Meggitt 1962:130). Among the Mbuti, the only relationship in which Turnbull reports a systematic pattern of friction was that between father and young adult son, when the latter had to help his father at the net in the collective hunt. In all these situations, unlike the normal spouse relationship in band societies, there was a potential source of conflict over sex or over authority. This seems to confirm the notion that where there was no specific, visible source of conflict (and there was not, where property management, political representation, and enabling were weak or absent from the family relationships), then patterns of conflict had much more to do with individual personalities, likes and dislikes, than with relative positions in the social organization. The family was a source of warmth and affection in band societies, and usually in a much more general and less structured pattern than was the case elsewhere.

In sum, the family in band societies was the locus of only some of the types of family activities listed in Chapter one. The labor of procuring subsistence goods was divided between the band, in the case of hunting large animals, and the family, in the case of gathering small and immobile food items. Processing labor was confined within the family. The family was everywhere the ideal arena for sexual activity, at least for married people, but they had considerable leeway outside. Socialization was performed within the family for very young children, but in most cases tended to be a more diffused responsibility when the children got older. Property rights in territory connected with the band; other property rights were insignificant. Representation and enabling had to wait for the establishment of a separate public sphere of activity. And emotional warmth did come from family members, among others, though in a quite diffuse way.

The Boundaries of the Family in Band Societies

We might, then, characterize the family as being only roughly delineated in band societies—in a sense there was no clear division between the domestic sphere, the affairs of the family, and the public sphere, the affairs of the band and occasionally relationships between bands. People were on intimate terms with a large number of people, in economic, socialization, often sexual, and certainly emotional spheres. The intimacy was perhaps thicker within the family group, but it did not end there—the boundaries of the family were blurry.

If the family boundaries in band societies were everywhere blurry, in some places and under some circumstances they blurred more than in others. Steward, for example, in a famous and disputed chapter (1963:101-121), described the Shoshoni as living as "a family level of organization," where there was no effective political group above the level of the family. I think, in fact, that Steward has been misread in this—he never denied cooperation between families, but not understanding the dynamics of band organization, denied that there was such a thing as a "band" in Shoshoni society because the local groups that did come together in certain seasons had no institutionalized leadership. Nevertheless, we can look at the Shoshoni as an extreme example of clear boundaries of the family. On the other extreme, we might take the Mbuti pygmy net-hunters, in whose society every single function of the family was taken up in some part by the larger group, and where families were almost invisible to the casual observer (Turnbull 1965a:118). In between we find various degrees of blurring of boundaries. What accounts for variation along this dimension?

This will become clearer, I think, if we look at a few cases in more detail. In each case, it is possible to contrast a pair of closely related groups, one with much more distinct family boundaries than the other, thus minimizing the effect of cultural-historical variation and bringing the effects of certain adaptive necessities into sharper relief. Let us begin with the famous Western Shoshoni and their close linguistic and geographical neighbors, the Owens Valley Paiute. The Western Shoshoni, living in perhaps the least hospitable territory in temperate North America, were nomadic foragers most of the year. During all but the late fall and winter seasons, individual nuclear families, sometimes with attached members of a senior generation, ranged widely and in no predetermined pattern in search of seasonally and irregularly available resources, particularly pine nuts (Steward 1938:27-8). For the Western Shoshoni, then, families lived an almost independent existence, and did so out of ecological necessity: resources were so sparse and unpredictable that it was rare for large encampments to be possible. People did gather in larger groups, however, on three kinds of occasions. First, in the wintertime, when nothing was growing, people lived in villages of a few houses, and subsisted mainly on stored foods (Steward 1938:20). The village was not a corporate unit—it was unsure from one year to the next which village a particular family would choose to settle in for the winter. But when people were living together, they did cooperate, out of a feeling of neighborliness if nothing else. Women frequently shared seeds with relatives and neighbors, for example, though they were under no obligation to do so (Steward 1938:231). And in times of dire need, families shared with each other. But this does not amount to much blurring of the economic boundaries of the family.

These boundaries were blurred a bit more in the case of two kinds of communal hunts. Antelope drives, which the environment would only support once every few years in a given area, were conducted cooperatively, under the leadership of a shaman (Steward 1938:34). And rabbit drives, a regular feature of late fall life in the villages, were conducted cooperatively by six to eight families, each of which owned a hunting net. The associations of families were not, however, regular in their formation—a family might hunt rabbits with one group and antelope with another, and only large game was shared beyond the family (Steward 1938:231).

The relative independence of the family among the Western Shoshoni was emphasized by the lack of property rights in resources on the land. The Shoshoni considered nothing to be privately owned (except eagles' nests—I have no idea why) until it had been collected or transformed by human effort (Steward:253). Thus any family in practice had rights to hunt or gather at any location, and did so, following the irregular pattern of ripening of pine nuts and other seeds.

When we look at the Owens Valley Paiute, by contrast, we find a very different pattern. Here the environment was better watered, permitting permanent settlement, irrigation of naturally occurring plants, and some incipient horticulture (Steward 1938:233-5). In this area, bands were considered to own certain tracts of land, which their members had a right to farm. The same groups of people cooperated for hunting and irrigation on a regular basis, thus embedding the family much more closely in the structure of larger groups.

The same kind of contrast can be made in Australia where, according to Sutton and Rigsby, "Western Desert Aboriginal People display a more flexible, individualistic, and religion-cast approach to invoking attachment to land than do their more sedentary, clannish, and secular counterparts on the coasts and in the uplands" (1982:158). There seem to have been good ecological reasons for this. In many parts of the Western Desert, the effective local unit in at least some seasons was a nuclear family group, perhaps augmented by some older relatives (Meggitt 1962:50), or at most a group of ten to twenty persons, ranging widely in the months of scarcity (Tindale 1972:235-6). In such groups, although people were expected to share food outside the family, they were not expected to do so according to a rigid set of rules, or to include the entire camp (Meggitt 1962:11-126, passim). On the other hand, in Arnhem Land, a much richer environment with a higher population density and not nearly such wide-ranging hunting practices, there tended to be mechanisms for distribution of meat to the whole camp (Warner 1958:129); the same appears to be true for the Tiwi on neighboring Melville and Bathurst Islands, who had a strict system of obligations to kin, which ended up, in the case of large animals, with everyone in camp getting some (Goodale 1971:171-2). Data on other family activities are not so clear for Australia, but we see that, at least in economic terms, the family tended to be more independent in arid regions, and more embedded in the band in areas of richer resources and higher population density.[2]

Moving to the Kalahari, we can see another case of such differences in family independence between two San groups, the !Kung and the G/wi. The !Kung lived in an environment where, even in the face of seasonable variability, they could remain in bands all year long. The bands were, in turn, organized into families, but families as economic units were discouraged in two ways. First, in the case of hunting, as Marshall says, "society seems to want to extinguish the concept of meat belonging to the hunter" (1976:297). There was a complex and fairly rigid set of rules for distribution of the meat, rules which specified certain *individuals* (not families) to which the meat was given, with the consequence that meat never became family property (Marshall 1976:302). Even in the case of vegetable foods, which were theoretically family property, there was a lot of informal sharing between families (Lee 1972:348). It is as if any tendency toward family self-sufficiency in the food quest was suppressed both by formal rules and by more general ideas about the desirability of sharing.

Among the G/wi, however, the situation was somewhat different. The central Kalahari where the G/wi lived is a much harsher environment than the area inhabited by the !Kung, and at least in the dry season of every year, the bands split up into family groups—sometimes nuclear families, sometimes a couple with their children and the husband of a daughter—for several months of independent foraging. During this phase, it goes without saying that the family, nuclear or lineally extended, was the group that shared food resources. But even during the greater part of the year, when the G/wi were living together in bands of 25-85 people, they shared food and other resources much less than did the !Kung. Meat was shared in what eventually amounted to a nearly general distribution, but there were no strict rules, and as often as not meat was given to a person to whom the hunter or arrow owner owed something from a previous exchange—a nudge in the direction of balanced, rather than generalized reciprocity outside the family unit (Silberbauer 1981:233-5; 253-4). And vegetable foods were almost never shared, except in times of shortages (Silberbauer 1981:153). Even co-wives, who usually built adjacent shelters in the camp, did not ordinarily share food (Silberbauer 1981:156). And mother and daughter, who cooperated in processing labor during the initial phase of the daughter's marriage, while she was still a young girl, still did not share vegetable foods. This is a picture of considerably greater economic autonomy for the family.

Finally, let us briefly look at Colin Turnbull's contrast between two groups of Mbuti Pygmies—the Sua net hunters, subject of most of Turnbull's own ethnographic work, and the Efe archers, a related group with a different hunting technology, living in the eastern part of the Ituri Forest. Among the net-hunters, we probably find the greatest degree of submersion of the family in the band of any carefully described band society—almost every social activity that existed at all was organized to major extent by the band. For example, not only was hunting itself cooperative—men tied their nets end to end and stood in wait for the game beaten into the nets by the women and children—but the explicit rules for the division of the kill not only covered the entire band but ignored family and kinship considerations in doing so. Parts of the kill were awarded to the hunter and his helpers at the net, but further shares were divided according to categories of sex and age grades, explicitly not according to kinship (Turnbull 1965a:158). With regard to gathered produce, most of what a woman gathered was considered to belong to her and her family, but there was frequent sharing, explicitly to emphasize that rights to forest produce were held communally by the band (Turnbull 1965:113). Even old people, when they could no longer forage for themselves, were supported by the rest of the band in general, regardless of any kinship connections (Turnbull 1965:152).

Turning to sex, I already mentioned that the Mbuti had what seems to have been one of the most open attitudes toward extramarital sex of any known society (Turnbull 1965 122). Socialization of children beyond weaning was likewise the responsibility of the band as a whole, particularly of those older people who stayed in camp when the young and middle-aged adults were out on the food quest (Turnbull 1965:113). This was also facilitated by the building of the *bopi* playground described in the Prelude to Part II, where children spent much of their time in the company of peers, rather than of adults (Turnbull 1965a:124). Even here, emotional attachments were often strongest among members of nuclear families, but this can be viewed as existing in spite of, not because of, any aspects of band structure.

Lest we think this submersion of the family a general Mbuti characteristic, however, we have evidence of a much more important family group among the neighboring Efe archers, also an Mbuti group. These people spent the better part of their year in individual families, often patrilineally and patrilocally organized, or in groups of two or three closely related families. We have no details of their sharing arrangements or sexual life, but we hear of an increased prominence of men over women, an exclusion of women from the hunt, and in general a higher degree of family and kinship organization. This organization apparently prevailed even when, during the honey season, Efe families came together in larger band camps (Turnbull 1965b:244-6).

In all four of these cases, we find a greater emphasis on the family in those areas where it was economically more independent, where it had to hunt for itself. In the San, Australian, and Great Basin cases, this was a direct result of ecological adaptation—for a great part of the year in the more arid parts of all three of these areas, the family had to subsist on its own, and its self sufficiency at these times of year was transformed into a greater autonomy within the band during times when the whole band camped together. Among the Mbuti, it was not any particular ecological difference (the Sua and Efe habitats appear to be identical) but simply a technological difference that gave the family greater economic independence among the Efe than among the Sua, but the result was the same. The same activities organized in and for the family among the Efe were generally assumed by the band in neighboring Sua groups, who had larger settlements.

Notes

1. Scheper-Hughes (1987) has challenged the universality of mother-infant bonding on the basis of her observation that mothers in a Brazilian shantytown selectively neglect some of their children as a rational strategy, and protect themselves emotionally by adopting an attitude of distance toward infants until they are fairly confident the infants will survive. An alternative explanation of this is that it does not question the biological nature of mother-infant bonding, but describes a case of social pathology, born of poverty and desperation, in which a strong biological instinct can be overcome.

2. It is important to remember, however, that we are still talking about bands, and that as hunters and gatherers in general go, areas like Arnhem Land or the Owens Valley represent an *intermediate* level of population density, one where the social organization was still firmly in the band cluster. In *high* density areas such as the Northwest Coast, family or kin rights to real property began to appear, and the family reasserted itself as a distinct unit, but one whose relationships to the larger group were of a very different sort (See Chapter 14).

5

The Developmental Cycle of the Family in Band Societies

How did people in band societies organize their families to perform the activities in which they cooperated? We can see the reason behind any pattern of organization if we list the activities that tied together certain pairs of family members—first spouses, and second parents and children.

Between spouses, the cooperative connection was essentially life-long. There was, of course, the expectation of sex, at least for most of adult life, and when there were children there were aspects of socialization that had to be shared. All through the productive years of adulthood, there was the division of subsistence labor as well. A woman gained rights to products of the hunt at least partly through her husband's place in the scheme of division of the kill; a man gained rights to products of gathering and processing directly through his wife's own labor. Initially, perhaps, because of sharing in sexual pleasures, upbringing of children, and the fruits of each other's labor, there was the aforementioned strong affective bond that seems to have held spouses together increasingly as they grew older. In short, there is every reason to see the bond between spouses as a basic and a crucial one in the family life of band societies everywhere. They were dependent on each other for a wide variety of necessities.

Between parents and children, on the other hand, the bond was more variable—its content changed greatly in the course of the life cycle. When children were young, they were bound to the parents by the necessity for socialization and also by the division of both procuring and processing labor—the parents procured and processed most of what the children consumed. Typically, in later childhood, both the socialization bond and the division of labor bond were loosened—children learned from others besides their parents, and they procured and processed some of what they

80

consumed themselves. In adolescence and early adulthood, the bonds were typically unimportant. Both generations were capable of procuring and processing their own goods, and socialization was over. Certain forms of division of labor between the generations at this stage, such as bride service (discussed below) can be seen as attempts to secure a pattern of cooperation which would become necessary again when the parents grew old and became dependent on their children again, this time for procuring and processing goods. So the need for parent-child attachment was strongest at the birth of the children, weakened into unimportance when both generations were productive adults, and strengthened again in the parents' old age.

Once again, it is important to emphasize the activities that this pattern of interdependency left out—management and transmissal of property and offices, public representation, and public enabling. In systems in other clusters, which had strongly vertically and horizontally extended family cycles, it was precisely these activities, varying much less with the life cycle than socialization or division of labor, that held extended families together. But in band societies the pattern of interdependence was as described above, and the structure, as well as the structural variation, in the developmental cycle of B-cluster family systems can be explained in terms of that very simple pattern.

The developmental cycle in B-cluster systems, then, was built primarily around the marriage bond, and secondarily around the attachment of married couples, at various times in the life cycle, to couples of adjacent upper or lower generations. The marriage bond itself might be more or less stable in practice—there was some divorce everywhere, in some places reaching substantial proportions—but marriage tended to increase in stability as the couple grew older. Plural marriages, particularly polygyny, occurred practically everywhere; in some areas they fell into a definite pattern. The attachment of the married couple to a senior or junior couple or to the survivor of such a couple could be predominantly patrilocal, matrilocal or optional, and it might shift between these in a regular or irregular pattern through the course of the life cycle.

This basic pattern, of couples or plural couples moving between independence and attachment to senior or junior couples, particularly when one of the couples in question was old and could not provide for itself, repeats itself over and over in B-cluster systems. To represent it, we can develop a specific version of our general family diagram suited to delineating the differences among band cluster systems. We can begin by reviewing the fullest form of the basic diagram, in which the elder and younger generations of a family are both represented, and in which the basic transitions are indicted by successive stages, joined by directional arrows, as in Figure 5-1.

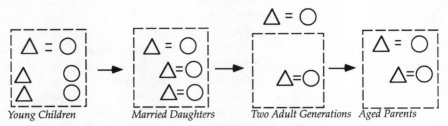

FIGURE 5-1: Basic B-Cluster Developmental Cycle

The first thing we notice is that the boundaries of the family are fuzzy and permeable, as indicated by the dotted line enclosing the basic square. We also see that in the first stage, dependent children and their parents are living together; in the second stage, the children have married and are living with (in this case) the wife's parents; in the third stage, the young couple lives independently; and in the fourth stage, the aged parents once again join the young couple.

Much of this information, however, is redundant to our purposes of comparative analysis. We can assume that the first and third stages are implied, and diagram only the second, showing the residence of the still-dependent young couple upon marriage, and the fourth, showing the provision for the dependent elders (Figure 5-2).

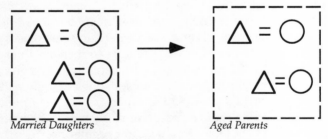

FIGURE 5-2: G/wi Developmental Cycle

The system diagrammed in Figure 5-2 is that of the G/wi of the Central Kalahari Game Reserve, who provide what amounts almost to a type case of band-society family organization. We can begin our account of their developmental cycle with marriage. Though people expressed a preference for cross-cousin marriage, Silberbauer found only about 11% of actual marriages to be between cross-cousins (1981:149-50). Among the G/wi, as among some other Kalahari groups (Marshall 1976:269), marriage took place between a young adult man and a small girl, with the average age at marriage about sixteen for the man and eight for the girl (Silberbauer 1981:149).[1]

The wife at this point was far from economically competent as an adult, and remained under the tutelage of her mother during the first few years of the marriage. The husband moved to reside with her, in a shelter next to that of her parents. At this time, she cooperated with her mother, but they did not share food. Sexual relations between the couple did not begin until the girl's menarche, typically five or six years after marriage, and a period of adolescent sterility after that placed the typical age of the mother at the birth of her first child at around sixteen or seventeen (Silberbauer 1981:149-54). During this early, uxorilocal phase of marriage, divorce might occur if the couple could not get along; separation became more difficult as the couple grew older and assumed responsibility for its own children (Silberbauer 1981:153-4). By the time of the birth of the first child, the couple with its child could subsist entirely on its own, and the ideal then was for them to form an autonomous nuclear family, and go to reside somewhere near the husband's relatives. In fact, they might remain with the wife's people until the birth of the second child, or even permanently—only a minority actually made the move (Silberbauer 1981:154).

The independent nuclear family—whether or not it continued to live near the wife's parents—fended for itself economically as it slowly grew, the husband engaging in cooperative hunting with other adult males, and the wife gathering primarily for the family group. Children had to be spaced at least four, preferably five years apart, in order that the mother might breastfeed each until at least three, and in order that the burden of carrying the children would not be too heavy on the parents. If a couple had three children younger than six or seven, the age at which they were able to walk for themselves on long treks, the burden would be too much for even the mother and father together. Since girls would be married by the time they were nine, and since children over the age of six were cared for primarily by a combination of the family and the play group of peers (Silberbauer 1981:165), the responsibility of parents to their older children became one of feeding them and supervising their socialization, but ceased to be one of constant, close contact. This meant that the typical family would not have more than two fully dependent children at any one time, and the long birth interval meant that most women would raise only three or at most four children. Blurton-Jones has demonstrated, in fact, that for the !Kung, whose ecological situation was not quite as harsh, but similar, a birth interval of about 4 to 5 years not only reduced parents' labor burdens, but also resulted in the maximum number of *surviving* children (Blurton-Jones 1986, 1987).

This isolation phase of the nuclear family continued until one of its daughters married, after which the adult couple was again attached to another couple, this time a junior one, who followed it during the season of band dispersal. Whether the couple again became independent in middle age depended on the age of the couple when the daughter was born—a daughter born to a woman who is 17 would be married when the mother was 25, and would be on her own when the mother was still in her middle thirties. A daughter born to a mother in her thirties would not be independent until the mother was well over fifty, the time of life when people often began to slow down and attach themselves once again to the household of a child, either a son or daughter, cooperating with them and following them into the isolation of the dry season (Silberbauer 1981:159-61).

There was room for considerable variation within this pattern. A married couple might or might not choose to camp with a different group from that of the wife's parents, once a child or two was born. They might, of course, move back and forth between one band and another (Silberbauer 1981:142). Another source of variation was polygyny. For most G/wi men, this was apparently not an attractive option—the sexual abstinence required to sustain the birth interval (and casual affairs on the side were tolerated, if discreet) seems to have been preferable to the burden of supporting two wives at once (Silberbauer 1981:156). Nevertheless, some marriages were polygynous—about 12 percent in Silberbauer's sample—most of these in response to lonely younger sisters who did not want to be separated from their married older sisters, and thus married the same man, or younger widowed or divorced mothers. Co-wives were reported to get along well enough, but an undercurrent of jealousy was always there.

Any kind of formal hierarchy or authority seems to have been absent from the marriage relationship, which was one of extreme identification, of a partial merging of the social personalities of the husband and wife into those of a couple. Information on this aspect of husband-wife relationships is sparse in Silberbauer's monograph (see pp. 161-62), but the neighboring !Kung, whose developmental cycle was otherwise quite similar, the spouse relationship was explicitly characterized as egalitarian (Draper 1975:94).

The developmental cycle of a "traditionally oriented band living in and off the bush in Arnhem Land," studied by Nicholas Peterson, illustrates somewhat different solutions to many of the same kinds of problems faced by the G/wi (Peterson 1970). In this group (to which Peterson steadfastly refuses to give an imposed "tribal name"), the pattern of subsistence was the usual subtropical one, in which the women contributed 60 to 90 percent of the foods (Peterson 1970:12). At the same time, in common with nearly all Australians, these people organized land into clan-held "countries," each of them containing sacred sites important to the men of a particular patriclan. People considered that the clan owned its country, though others were free, with customarily granted permission, to forage on that land. The adaptational pattern here was thus somewhat more complicated than that faced by the G/wi, since the ritual as well as the ecological necessities had to be taken into account. Nevertheless, many of the outcomes were similar, as we shall see.

Here in Arnhem Land, as in the Kalahari, and indeed in all of Australia (Denham, McDaniel, and Atkins 1979:17), there was a great age differential at marriage, with the girl marrying at a very early age and the man not until his late teens or early twenties for the first time. Because authoritative older men retained control over their daughters' marriages, young married men initially had to spend considerable time living with their wives' parents (Figure 5-3). At this stage, local groups might consist of older men and their wives, usually owners of the land upon which they were camped, together with some of their daughters and daughters' husbands, and their unmarried sons. The young women provided vegetable food for themselves and their husbands and children, and also, if they were able, for their mothers, fathers, and unmarried brothers. The young men, by hunting, also provided food for their wives' parents, as well as for their wives and children. So there was a potential uxorilocal extended family at this stage, based on the older generation's necessity or desire to have younger people provide for them. It is noteworthy that the older *men* felt this need in a particularly acute way, because the age differential between them and their children was greater than that between mothers and children (Denham, McDaniel, and Atkins's model posits an average father-child interval of 42 years; 1979:17).

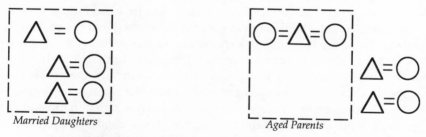

Married Daughters   Aged Parents

FIGURE 5-3: Arnhem Land Developmental Cycle

But this matrilocal extended family did not last out the life cycle. The younger men, living with their wives' parents, saw this arrangement as temporary, because they were anxious to return to their own clans' traditional territories, to play their increasingly important ritual roles and eventually to die there (Peterson 1970:14). So the older men, when they no longer had young daughters and willing sons-in-law, had to resort to other strategies, and this is where polygyny came in. A man in his middle or later years who could take a young second or third wife would not only assure himself of female labor to continue supporting him into his physically declining years, but would also have further potential source of daughters, and thus of sons-in-law. Thus polygyny for older men was a complement to the strategy of co-residence with daughters and their husbands and when a father-in-law either died or married a second, younger wife, a son-in-law was then able to move with his wife and children back to his own clan territory, and begin securing himself economically by taking in sons-in-law and eventually secondary wives of his own.

These people thus supported the aged with the same kind of pattern of temporary attachments of married couples to the wife's parents, wherever these latter might have been, as did the G/wi. The difference is that the polygynous Australian men had an alternative to relying on their children and children's spouses for support in old age, and could thus facilitate the concentration of agnatically related males on their own clans' scared territories. Peterson does not provide any specific information on the nature of authority and dominance in husband-wife relations here, but they seem to have followed the usual Australian pattern of relative male dominance, discussed in more detail below (White 1970:21).

For a final example of the developmental cycle of a B-cluster society, let us move to a very different part of the world and look at the family system of the Netsilik Eskimos of the central Canadian Arctic. Here the problems of adaptation were radically different from those faced by either the G/wi or any Australians. In the first place, in the arctic in general, human adaptation was precarious at best, and all Eskimo groups have tales of starvation and the human response to it prominent in their lore (e.g. Graburn 1969b:50; Balikci 1970:244-45). This reflected itself first and foremost in the age at marriage. A Netsilik woman was not considered marriageable until she had learned the woman's tasks necessary to subsistence, usually at age 14 or older. A man was not considered a competent hunter, and therefore marriageable, until around age twenty. In Eskimo groups the problem of the child bride and the consequent obligatory matrilocal residence was simply absent. Another, even more important difference is that in most of the high arctic, men provided all the subsistence goods. Food was exclusively meat—land mammals, waterfowl, fish, and above all, sea mammals provided the majority of the diet—and almost all hunting was done by men, with females cooperating in only a few of the caribou-hunting and fishing techniques (Balikci 1970). At the same time, women's labor was essential to the survival of the group, for it was they who not only cooked, kept house, and tended children, but most importantly scraped, cured, and sewed the various animal hides used to make the warm clothing necessary for survival in the arctic winters. Among the Netsilik in particular, however, the necessity for women was not of the same sort as that for men. More active males meant more hunters as a proportion of the population, and thus a better chance of everyone being well-fed. A smaller number of females, it seems, could still make all the clothing and do all the housework. This resulted in a strong preference for male children, and almost certainly in a high rate of female infanticide (E. A. Smith and S. A. Smith 1994; Balikci 1970:148-62).

Against this background, let us trace the developmental cycle of a Netsilik family. A couple would typically be married when the woman was fourteen or fifteen, and the man in his early twenties; they might have been betrothed when the girl was still an infant (Balikci 1970:153-54). They probably resided patrilocally: if the husband was the youngest married son, they would share a dwelling (tent in summer, igloo in winter) with his parents (Figure 5-4). Other married brothers ideally occupied nearby dwellings, and in the dispersed summer season of caribou hunting and river fishing, they cooperated economically as a unit, with the eldest female taking charge of the distribution of food (Balikci 1970:119). In the winter, sharing was based on the husband's seal-exchange partnerships. There was thus an economic interdependency between the generations, even when both adult generations were economically productive. There were, however, exceptions to this patrilocal pattern of residence, and for reasons of personal preference or more adequate distribution of labor, some marriages were always uxorilocal, making the local group a mixed one with a virilocal emphasis (Damas 1969:126). Thus the bond between the spouses, even here, remained the primary one.

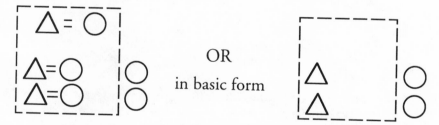

Figure 5-4: Netsilik Developmental Cycle (Note: *Since married sons remain with parents all their lives, there is no need to diagram more than one stage.*)

This is not to imply that the marriage was exclusive or necessarily particularly stable. I have already mentioned both adultery and formalized spouse-exchange as sources of sexual variety, and in addition, with the lopsided adult sex ratio, marriages tended to be unstable. Few men would divorce their wives voluntarily, women being in such short supply, but opportunities for women to run off with a more desirable man were greater, given that such men were always available. Success depended on the relative prowess—physical, diplomatic, and treacherous—of the competing males (Balikci 1970:155-56). In addition, cases of a man murdering another in order to marry the other's wife were also reported. And, remarkably enough, polygyny was reported, though here as elsewhere, only the strongest and most capable of men could afford to support more than one wife (Balikci 1970:156; Graburn 1969:62-3).

In Eskimo marriage generally, the husband tended to be dominant, though not overly so. It was the men who made the decisions on where to camp and where to hunt, and they could coerce, if not actually force, their wives into spouse-exchange arrangements (Balikci 1970:142). Each spouse was reported to beat the other on occasion (Balikci 1970:142; Kjellström 1973:132), but husbands, with their greater strength, must have gotten the better of it most of the time.

In their declining years, Netsilik and other central arctic Eskimos had several strategies available. They might well continue to live with their sons and the sons' wives, and contribute what they could to the domestic economy (Figure5-4). In many cases, old people would adopt children (usually, but not always, their natural grandchildren), to raise as their own, partly to assure a means of support, but also partly to make sure they were doing something useful, and thus not becoming expendable to
the family and band. (Guemple 1979:31). In extreme situations, when the group was threatened with starvation, the old were expected to actively or passively commit suicide, so that they would not slow down the desperate food quest of the others.

Dimensions of Variation in the
Developmental Cycle

These three brief case studies illustrate the common features of the developmental cycle in band societies—the economic and emotional centrality of the marriage relationship, the variability and contingency of the attachment between senior and junior generations of adults, and the resultant lack of stability in lineal family extensions. Other examples could be provided to confirm this general pattern. But at the same time, there was some variability in the family systems of band societies, both in the marriage relationship and in the pattern of attachments between the generations. This section attempts to account for that variability.

Marriage Relationships

Two aspects of the marriage relationship stand out as exhibiting considerable variability—the relative prestige and power of the spouses in a single couple, and the pattern of singular or plural marriages. Let us examine the two in turn.

Gender Equality and Inequality. We find a wide spectrum of relationships between spouses in band societies—from explicitly and ideologically egalitarian, as among most African band groups, to a clear measure of male dominance, as among most Australians and northern hunter-gatherers. The difference seems to hinge on two factors: the contribution of men and women to the subsistence economy, and the existence or lack of a public, ritual sphere of activity dominated by the men.

Central to this comparison, then, is Lee's correlation of female contribution to the subsistence economy with latitude. When we look at the northern groups, particularly the Eskimo, most northerly of all, we find that women's contribution to the division of labor was almost entirely in processing, that they were at best assistants in a few of the many kinds of hunting that brought in the subsistence goods in the first place. Even though women's processing labor was essential to the survival of the group, increase in the number of females did not add incrementally to the potential resource supply of the group, as increase in the number of males did. This may be part of the reason why the Netsilik and certain other Eskimo groups practiced female infanticide, for example, though female infanticide in itself says nothing about the relative power and authority of adult men and women. But more important, men's procuring role explains why the men universally made the decisions about where to camp and when to move— it was they who were responsible for assuring the supply of goods that would keep the people from starvation and freezing. So it is not surprising that, in Eskimo societies, we find men making the important decisions (Balikci 1970:109), husbands beating wives more often than the reverse (Kjellström 1973:132), and in general, boys appreciated more than girls (Kjellström 1973:180-81). Women at best sustained the group's productive resources; men added to them.

When we contrast the position of the sexes in Eskimo division of labor with that among the Mbuti Pygmies or the !Kung and G/wi, we find a very different configuration. In these tropical and sub-tropical societies women, by gathering plant foods and small animals, brought in well over half the subsistence resources. Processing here was not so important altogether, and men and women tended to share in different aspects of this labor. But the women were the primary contributors to the larder (Lee 1968:33). Their work, it has been pointed out many times, was less demanding of strength and endurance, and less hedged about with prohibitions and rewards of prestige for accomplishment, than was that of the men (Marshall 1976:96-7, 130; Turnbull 1965a:167-68). This was perhaps because it involved less chance and less risk. It did, however, involve extensive knowledge, skill and planning, and its results were immediately visible at every mealtime. This placed the women already in a much more equal position to the men. Among the !Kung, at least, this equality probably did not extend to prestige or demeanor in ordinary interactions, but it meant that men had no *authority*, and no basis for authority, over women. As Marshall says, men were dominant and women retiring, but women did not wait on men, and men did not punish women.

When we turn to the Mbuti, we find a much more explicit recognition of the equality and complementarity of the sexes in ideology and ritual, as well as in everyday economic affairs. Not only were men and women both necessary to the success of the hunt—the women acted as beaters—but their ritual role was also as necessary and vital as that of the men. This was expressed in the two major rituals of the Mbuti—the Elima girls' puberty rite and the *molimo* funeral ceremony. In the former, the women were in ascendancy. Girls were secluded in a ceremonial shelter, and boys who wanted to play the game of crashing the gates and gaining admittance had to run the gauntlet of a large number of women ready to chase and beat them with sticks. It was female fertility that was being celebrated here, the life-giving force, and males willingly played a subordinate role. In the *molimo* ceremony, on the other hand, the males tended the sacred fire while the women remained in their huts, fictionally oblivious to what was going on. But on the climactic night of the festival, an old woman danced in the circle of men, scattering the coals of the fire. The men put them back; she scattered them again and again, until she retired. Here the woman was the intruder, overcome by the life-sustaining force of the men (Turnbull 1961:144-65, 184-200).

A similar ritual recognition of the equality of the sexes occurred among the Tiwi of Melville and Bathurst Islands in northern Australia. Here again the female contribution to subsistence was important, even prominent, and the patterns of authority in everyday life were in no way clear. The Tiwi were unique among reported Australian groups, in that they initiated both males and females into adult life in the same ceremony, in the same way, at the same time.

Other examples of egalitarian sex roles among low-latitude band societies with important women's contribution to subsistence occurred among the Shoshoni, where Steward explicitly stated that the sexes were in fact equal in marriage (1938:242), and the Hadza of Tanzania, where marriages were so fragile and based on consensus that neither spouse could leave the group for many weeks and still return to find the other not married to another person (Woodburn 1968:107).

This contrast between woman the gatherer as the equal or nearly equal partner of man the hunter, in low-latitude societies, and woman the seamstress as a definitely junior partner (but hardly a servant) in the northerly climes takes us back to the assertion put forth by Engels a hundred years ago—that in the absence of private property, there cannot be subjugation of the female to the male (1972:118-21). In fact, the case seems not to be so simple. Where women's labor is merely processing labor, where men control access to the means of livelihood, they have the means for the subjugation of the women. It is not because the women's labor is domestic, as opposed to public (Rosaldo 1974:23-5) that women are subordinate in these societies; in fact we have already seen that the domestic-public distinction is of little relevance in the close-knit life of a foraging band. It is that the woman's labor was secondary and derivative. And the reason why their labor was secondary and derivative is that, in the arctic, there was no primary labor or procurement that they could perform and still carry out their essential reproductive role. In a sense, then, Engels was right—where there is no distinction between domestic and public labor, the possibility of egalitarianism, or at least the absence of male authority, exists. But it can only be realized where females make an important primary contribution to subsistence.

When we turn to the majority of the Australian aboriginal groups in light of this formulation, it seems we run into a paradox. Here, as in all sub-tropical or tropical foraging societies, women made the primary contribution to subsistence. And yet, as White states, in Australia generally, the woman was everywhere a junior partner to the man, with the man holding at least formal authority, though it seems to have varied whether he could exercise that authority in practice (White 1970:21; C. Berndt 1970:40-1). Other authors confirm this male authority in specific ethnographic reports. Meggitt, for example, states that a wife almost always got the worst of a quarrel, and that the theoretical obligation of a woman's brothers to intervene when she had a serious complaint against her husband often went ignored in practice, in order to preserve the male dominance in which both the husband and brothers had an interest (1962:88, 92-3). What accounts for this seeming anomaly?

I think, in this case, that we need to return to the domestic/public distinction. Economically, it appears that there was no such distinction, and there is some evidence that in some parts of Australia anyway, the sexes were equal in purely economic terms. Kaberry, for example, reports that in the Kimberly district, it was considered legitimate for either spouse to beat the other for laziness or improvidence (1939:24-5). But where men and women were not equal in Australia was in ritual. Everywhere on the continent, Australian men have developed a complex, sophisticated system of natural philosophy and theology, and explanation of the world and the place of humans in it that depends on male transmission of esoterica, male attachment to important totemic sites, and male conduct of secret and vital rituals, from which the women have usually been excluded. It is perfectly true that women also had their own secret rituals, but men did not consider these as important as the women considered the men's rituals to be. The Australian men, then, developed a public sphere of activity, a system of myth and ritual considered central both to understanding and to perpetuating the place of people in the universe, a system whose full knowledge and participation was restricted to men. The male solidarity expressed in this ritual system seems to be at the root of male dominance in Australian societies. A similar case is presented in Draper's study of the sedentarization of !Kung in the 1960s, when !Kung began living in separate houses, and the men participated in African-style public politics. The relative sexual equality was quickly transformed into male dominance (1975).

In general, then, we can see that male dominance occurred in band societies when males controlled the access to those resources that people considered necessary for society's survival. In the northerly climes, these were economic resources; in Australia, they were of an ideational nature. But the question, of course, still remains as to why the Australians, alone to our knowledge among band societies, have developed such an elaborate, male-oriented belief and ritual system. The question is certainly akin to the questions of why the Australians, who resembled other foragers very closely in their economic activities, have developed such unusually elaborate systems of kinship terminology and marriage sections and subsections. The answer is not obvious—it may be, as Levi-Strauss has suggested (1969:152-53) that they evolved these systems simply out of an intellectual impulse to understand and order the world. This says nothing, of course, about why other foragers did not develop such a ritual system. Once such systems were developed and made central, however, they became the basis of male dominance in those societies.

Singular and Plural Marriage. The second aspect of variation in the structure of the marriage relationship in band societies concerns the incidence of plural marriage. On the surface, there appears to have been little variation here; with a couple of exceptions, all reports mention occasional polygyny, usually comprising three to twenty percent of current marriages. But in fact this statistical similarity conceals two different patterns of polygyny—one based on hunting prowess and social prominence, the other based on age and perhaps also on social prominence.

By far the most common pattern was that based on hunting prowess or other extraordinary ability. For example, among most Eskimo groups, it was the camp leader, the successful hunters, or the shamans who were likely to be polygynous (Balikci 1970:156; Kjellström 1973:115; Damas 1969:125; Graburn 1969:62-3). Only a prominent man could both support more than one wife and keep others from taking one of his wives by force or connivance, especially in those Eskimo societies with an unbalanced sex ratio. The same pattern, though probably based less explicitly on physical intimidation, seems to have prevailed among the sub-arctic groups: Helm states that among the Dogrib, it was probably only a few superior providers who were polygynous in traditional times (1972:74). Polygyny was also mentioned for the Alaskan Tanana and Kutchin (McKennan 1969:109) and for the Mistassini Cree (Rogers 1972:118), but no details are given. Among the Shoshoni, Steward states that a man might have more than one wife if he were an expert hunter, a necessary condition in a group where there was little sharing outside the family for most of the year (1938:240). Among !Kung, about ten percent of males are reported to have been polygynous in the 1950s and '60s (Marshall 1976:263); the percentage was considerably smaller for the G/wi (Silberbauer 1981:155). Finally, polygyny existed but was uncommon among the Mbuti—polygynous men were often, but not always, highly prominent in the band (Turnbull 1965a:183). If we posit that there will be, in most human societies, a certain degree of male competition for mates, then we can see how the most successful, politically and economically, would come out on top in such competition, and this probably accounts for the pattern of polygyny in these widely scattered band societies.

In Australia, however, we find a completely different pattern. Among such widely dispersed groups as the Walbiri (Meggitt 1962:79), the Kimberly peoples (Kaberry 1939:114-15); the groups studied by Peterson in Arnhem Land (1970:14); and even the Tiwi (Hart and Pilling 1960:15-16), polygyny is described as a practice of older men: in fact Rose (1960:91-99) has described the Australian pattern as one of "gerontocratic polygyny." This is clearly something different from the pattern we have seen in other parts of the world—in Australia men were not usually highly polygynous until they were past the time of life when they could hunt effectively.

The key to this pattern seems to be provided by Peterson, who states that the motivation for polygyny in most of Australia was simply support in one's old age. One strategy for an old man was to gather sons-in-law around him to support him when he became dependent, but this was often not feasible for long, because the sons-in-law would eventually want to return to their own people and their own totemic territories. So an old man could take a succession of young wives, who would not only provide for him directly, but by bearing daughters would eventually bring in more sons-in-law (Peterson 1970:146; Meggitt 1962:79). In order to be able to claim rights over young girls, of course, old men had to have certain authority in the society as a whole, but this was often provided by their prominent role in the ritual system. (Perhaps this explains why old men could not marry young girls in other B-cluster societies: they did not have the public, ritual-derived authority that allowed the Australian men to solve their old-age security problems by claiming rights to young girls.) Statistically, the two patterns of polygyny might produce the same percentage of polygynous unions in a synchronic sample, but in terms of the developmental cycle, they stemmed from very different causes and had very different uses for the polygynous men.

Polyandry is also reported to occur in several band societies, including most Eskimos (Kjellström 1973:121-23), Shoshoni, where it appears always to have been of the fraternal variety (Steward 1938:243), and the G/wi, where Silberbauer recorded one, admittedly idiosyncratic case, but one that was accepted generally by the band (1981:155). In no society is polyandry reported to have been particularly common or to have conformed to any rigid or predictable pattern; it seems everywhere to be more of an *ad hoc* solution to particular problems. It is still noteworthy, however, that band society family systems did allow for polyandry so easily; this underlines their essential flexibility and adaptability.

Parent-Child Links

The other dimension of structural variability in B-cluster family systems concerns the pattern of attachment between married couples of two generations. One could attempt to classify band societies in terms of a conventional typology of postmarital residence, into patrilocal, ambilocal or bilocal, and matrilocal, as Ember (1978), for example, has done.[2] But to say the *Ethnographic Atlas* classifies a society as patrilocal, for example, tells us nothing of the developmental cycle dimensions of that residence, whether it is temporary or permanent, whether it refers to actual cooperation in procuring, processing, or socialization, or simply living in the same camp, and how frequently people observe or violate this rule of patrilocality. Instead of taking this approach, I want to look at typical patterns of association between the generations in various band societies, and relate them to the independence or interdependence of the generations at various times in their life cycles.

We begin with the basic developmental cycle shown in Figures 5-1 and 5-2, above, in which a couple first lived with the parents of one of the spouses, then independently, and then with someone who would care for them in old age. An example of a society following this pattern was the Western Shoshoni. Here the couple lived with the parents of the wife, cooperating in the subsistence quest, at least until the birth of their first child. Eventually, they formed with their children an independent nuclear unit, on its own for much of the year, and with no fixed winter place of residence when gathered together with others. Old people might attach themselves to the nuclear families of either sons or daughters, and tried to perform what work they could—old widows often minded children in camp while the parents were out foraging, as shown in Figure 5-5 (Steward 1938:240-43).

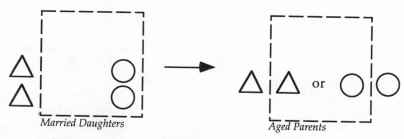

FIGURE 5-5: Shoshoni and Kutchin Developmental Cycle

The Peel River Kutchin of the northern Mackenzie drainage provided another example. When newly married, the couple lived with the wife's parents (Slobodin 1969:58). Afterwards, they became an independent nuclear family, but cooperative hunting put them together with relatives on either side in a hunting group. Old people became dependents of the nuclear families of their children of either sex (Kjellström 1973:58)

The examples could be multiplied, but the pattern repeats itself over and over. In the beginning of marriage was a period often referred to as "bride service." This, I think, is a misleading term, because it implies that it is a husband's payment for the services of his wife, while it seems in most cases to have been a kind of adjustment period in marriage, during which a woman, sometimes sexually mature but not fully competent in the tasks of womanhood, continued to derive help and support from her parents, and when a man was not so much paying for his wife as proving to his wife and her parents that he was a competent hunter and thus a worthy husband.[3] This period lasted a variable amount of time, as indicated in Table 5-1. Once this initial period of residence with the wife's people was over, the independent nuclear family was guided by a wide variety of rules or ideals for residence, but not in any kind of extended household that shared any more activities than it shared with other members of the band as a whole. As indicated in Table 5-1, in many cases the ideal residence in this stage was patrilocal, as among both Kalahari groups and most of the Australians. In practically all of these cases, however, there were reasons why a marriage might remain permanently uxorilocal, though such cases were often in the minority. The independence in this phase is explained by the self-sufficiency of the family in gathering, and in other family activities when the group was dispersed, and by the dependence on a group larger than the family and immediate relatives (i.e., the band), when the group was living together.

Finally, we can see a wide variety of solutions to the problem of care for the dependent aged. Three are noteworthy. First, aged couples might simply attach themselves to the household of a son or daughter. In most of the cases in the table, the preference is left open. Second, many Australian groups practiced what Rose (1960:91-99) called gerontocratic polygyny (see above), where an old man provided for himself and his senior wives by taking plural junior wives. This was only possible where old men were in a powerful enough position to assert their claims over these young girls. Finally, Eskimos especially tended to resort to adoption, taking in their grandchildren as helpers, and thus forming a kind of second-time-around nuclear family, which still, of course, might have to depend on subsistence contributions from others.

Although the majority of societies for which I found detailed enough information displayed this pattern to their developmental cycle, and although it fits well with the subsistence and reproductive requirements of couples as they progress through the life-cycle, it was not the only possible pattern in nomadic bands. Some societies, for example, followed a roughly similar pattern, but dispensed with the initial period of uxorilocal residence. For example, both the Pitjandjara and the Walbiri of the Western Desert had a rule of patrilocal residence upon marriage (the husband was required in fact, to avoid his wife's parents, though he had certain obligations to them), and most, but not all, couples followed this rule. They did not, however, live in extended families with the husband's parents; they simply tended to live in the same camp. In both societies, there were couples who, for one reason or another, did not follow the rule (Tindale 1972:260; Meggitt 1962:57). It is difficult to know in these cases which was cause and which was effect—was avoidance the cause or the result of patrilocal residence—but they were clearly interconnected. The Walbiri, at least, tended to provide for the aged by gerontocratic polygyny (Meggitt 1962:57).

The Mbuti pygmies were another group with a preference for living in the husband's band, though here again there were exceptions. Sometimes a couple would share a hut with the husband's parents when they were first married (Turnbull 1965a:97n). But here the nuclear family was the organizational unit, insofar as there was one—we recall that the family was practically merged with the band for the performance of most activities in this society. This is illustrated graphically by the Mbuti method of providing for the aged—they depended on public welfare, being fed, as honored members of a particular age group, by younger members of the band as a whole (Turnbull 1965a:152).

Only among Eskimo groups do we find a true extended family—a group that had a leader in the senior generation with authority over the younger adult members, and where the economic and other activities of the family were shared, marking the family off from the band economically for at least part of the yearly cycle. We find patrilocal extended families of this sort among both the Netsilik and the Iglulik Eskimo (Damas 1969:118; Balikci 1970:111-13); in both groups, a family without sons might include a daughter and her husband. We can see an ecological rationale for this—in the summer months, the Netsilik band was dispersed, and members of the extended family cooperated closely in fishing and caribou hunting, so it makes sense that they would continue to act in some ways as a unit even when the band was together in the winter camps on the ice. It should be remembered, however, that the neighboring Copper Eskimo found an alternative—meat-sharing partnerships, not based on kinship, operated all year round among this group, and the family system was a nuclear one, with an initial period of uxorilocal residence, as shown in Figure 5-6 (Damas 1972:30).

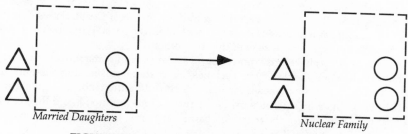

Married Daughters   Nuclear Family

FIGURE 5-6: Copper Eskimo Developmental Cycle

Among the Iglulik, there seems to have been a stronger ecological rationale for the extended family structure—in the summer season, young men went inland to hunt caribou, while the older active adults stayed on the seacoast and hunted walruses from kayaks (Damas 1968:115). So even in the fully productive periods of their lives, there was a division of labor between the two adult generations, and this kept them together in extended families. The extended family structure, of course, provided its own solution to the problems of feeding and clothing the aged, at least outside the times of want, when there was no solution.

We can thus see that, in most band societies, people performed relatively few activities in and for the family, and that even these activities were often shared with the band. The male/female division of labor was everywhere crucial, and for this reason the marital bond was the most important one almost everywhere, though the long-term obligations between spouses were nowhere strong enough to preclude fairly frequent separations and divorces. The bonds that held the generations together were weaker, and so with a few exceptions we find no extended families as corporate groups that remained throughout the adult portion of the life cycle. In most band societies, we find such extended families only when they involved couples that were not fully independent, either because they were just beginning adult life, or because they were too old to support themselves.

Notes

1. Among the Dobe !Kung, marriage occurred somewhat later, at an average age of 16-17 for the woman and 23-30 for the man, but even here the young wife was not considered fully adult at the time of her marriage, and residence was initially uxorilocal (Lee 1979:240-42).

2. Actually, Ember's article is doubly unsatisfactory for our discussion. Not only does she define rules of residence in questionably simplistic, typological terms, she also includes a large number of equestrian hunter-gather societies from the American plains, as well as several societies from the Northwest Coast. She is defining hunter-gatherers as a technological type, not bands as a social type, so many of her societies fall outside the purview of this altogether.

3. Jane Collier's characterization of band societies (and some sedentary hunter-horticulturalists) as "brideservice societies," is perhaps misleading semantically, but in fact her analysis makes clear that she considers the labor and gifts a man contributes to his wife's parents primarily proof of his manhood, and thus reason to enlist their support for the marriage, rather than as some kind of compensation for the gift of the bride (1988:24-26).

PART THREE

The A-Cluster: Family Systems of Sub-Saharan Africa

Prelude: Sebei Elders Discuss Cattle Claims

Sebei elders discuss their claims in the division of cattle occasioned by the death of the herd owner, Kambuya:

MWANGA [quietly]: My friend has now gone into his grave. I am now walking alone on this earth.

SALIMU: I am going to introduce you to our younger brother, and say that you were a great friend of our father's and that he is to treat you as if our own father were still alive.

MWANGA: As I am living far away, I am visiting here.

NDIWA V: Our friend, the son of our mother, I have a different request. I would like you to give me one bull to sell, for I have difficulties. I know it belongs to [Kambuya's estate] and I have been talking to the herdsman, but he says I must go to you, their older brother. I think we can talk about this now.

SALIMU: There is a man who has three cows. He has not paid for them. He is a man from Sipi, and I understand that he is here now.

ANDYEMA: Yes. I understand he has been hiding his cows and trying to avoid paying his debt.

SALIMU: One of these belongs to your mother and, though I ask about it, it is your cow. The second is the same. The third debt came about as follows: he ate a sick cow and offered us a she-goat in return, as the cow was already sick. It is not yours, but belongs to these young children [of Kambuya's young wife]...

SALIMU [addressing Maget]: Do you remember when our father promised you a she-goat?

MAGET: Yes, and he showed me which one it was...

MWANGA: We have been living here a long time, and what I have been hearing is that Salimu is a bad man and that he can't take care of his brothers; but from what I have heard from his own tongue, I think these are mere lies.

SALIMU'S COMPANION: We shall hear from the old men. The thing is that the brothers are afraid of losing their cows—that he will be hiding some. Andyema and Ndiwa never talked to their father as Salimu used to do, and that is why they are afraid..

SALIMU: Next time I will keep quiet and just ask my brothers to tell me which cows in my kraal belong to these brothers. I am not going to hide anything, but they also should say if they have cows belonging to my mother. And I have none of Ndiwa's, just Andyema's. Perhaps I may give Ndiwa some that are *tokapsoy*, because they should be reserved for the young boys...We must decide who will look after these children.

NDIWA V: It is you who will decide that.

SALIMU: When the old man was still alive, I asked him to give me some cows received as bride-price for his sister, but he got annoyed and said "These were for my sister; you have your own sisters to get bride-price from."

NDIWA: I have one cow that the old man said should be given to Andyema, but Andyema should share it with Salimu.

SALIMU: How can a young boy be the head of a shared cow?

SALIMU'S COMPANION: Yes. It is quite impossible for the young boy to be in charge of this cow.

SALIMU: When one of our sisters was married, we were given cows, but Kambuya gave one to his brother. The drought came and killed most of these cattle, and only two bulls were left. One was exchanged for a heifer, and another was given to Andyema when he was young. Turei asked for Andyema's animal and he didn't pay for the *namanya* cow, and we had to take a case against him. Then the heifer was seized by court order and given to me. I brought it to Andyema—it is your cow, brother, keep it as namanya. We exchanged the other bull from this sister for a heifer, and it produced two bulls; the first one died, but the second grew up. Eryeza came to me, saying that the diviner told him that he should kill a brown bull. He took it, but his kraal was raided by the Karamojong, and that bull was taken. Also, the cow was killed by the drought; so I had nothing from this sister. I went to Andyema and asked him to share his cow, but he refused. My father said: "It does not matter—I will give you another." But he did not give it to me; instead, he persuaded Andyema to give me a bull. This was taken by somebody, and I was given a heifer in return; but that heifer died. I was again left without anything. My father said to forget it, that I had to leave this matter alone. But somebody married one of our sisters and gave us only two cows, and those cows died; so I got nothing from that girl. If this young man...were a girl, I would have had a bull from him, but he is a man. His only wrong is that he never does get married. If he had wives, they could give me food and beer.

Walter Goldschmidt, *Kambuya's Cattle* (Berkeley and Los Angeles: University of California Press, 1969), pp. 63–65. Reprinted by permission.

6

The Logic of African Social Organization

In hunting-gathering bands, family organization was part of the process of production and reproduction, and that was all. The goals of family members, male and female, around which family activities were organized, consisted of the reproduction of enough offspring to secure their own livelihood and social continuity, and the production of enough subsistence goods to support themselves and these offspring. As we have seen, this meant that there was no sharp division between the domestic, or subsistence, sphere of activity and the public, or prestige sphere. In fact, the prestige sphere seems to have been subordinated to the domestic, or perhaps absent altogether. It does seem clear that there was, even among members of bands, a kind of innate human drive for prestige, a desire to be respected, to be seen as important, to be looked up to by other people. But in most band societies, this drive was suppressed, because it came into direct conflict with the necessities and possibilities of production and reproduction. The cooperation necessary to secure basic subsistence resources seems to have precluded hierarchy, to have demanded recognition of every person's abilities and contribution, and to have allowed the group to ostracize those who attempted to dominate. In addition, the mobility and fluidity of association and group composition in such situations meant that the loser in any potential status competition could simply move away and leave the potential ruler without a following.

Things were different, however, in most of Africa in pre- and early colonial times. Here in Part Three I focus on a cluster of family systems I call the A-cluster, which includes most of Africa south of the Sahara, excluding both Maghrebi and Ethiopian Highland societies, both of which belong among the C-cluster systems of the European-Mediterranean-Middle-Eastern regions (see Part VI). It also, quite naturally, excludes the few well-known hunting-gathering B-cluster systems of Africa, described in the previous Part. I use the term "Africa" or "A-cluster" because it is less cumbersome than "non-band sub-Saharan Africa outside the Ethiopian Highlands."[1]

In most of Africa south of the Sahara, as in most of the world by the last few centuries, population density and productive technology had both advanced, by invention or diffusion, to the point where agricultural and pastoral subsistence techniques were practiced and associated with much higher population densities than would ever have been possible in most places on a hunting-gathering technological base.[2] Thus both technology and demography are important for understanding the nature of African societies. Agricultural and/or pastoral technology ties groups of people to specific resources much more closely than simple association with hunting or gathering territories, for example. And the higher population densities create interaction between larger groups of people. Both these facts necessitate some sort of large-scale, relatively permanent way of organizing groups of people that are likely to matter to each other. In most of Africa, this meant both territorial organization, usually at more than one level, and kinship organization, usually but not always as some form of unilineal descent. This meant that African families had to operate in the framework of larger territorial and kinship organizations.

But attachment to specific resources, and the larger-scale organization of communities, had another important consequence: it created an outlet, an opportunity for people to engage in competition for prestige and status in groups larger than the family and for ends in addition to the basic goals of production and reproduction. In short, there developed a prestige sphere (Lancaster 1976:553), a public realm, a politico-jural domain (Fortes 1969:63). Whereas in B-cluster family systems both women and men were concerned almost exclusively with production and reproduction (Rosaldo 1974:33), in Africa the men, at least, and in some places also the women, were enabled to participate in the public sphere as well as the domestic. Women's goals for the most part were similar to their goals in B-cluster systems— their role in reproduction, along with the symbolic and political constraints imposed on them because of that role, precluded, at least during their fertile years, much participation in the public, prestige competition.

This participation by men in a separate public sphere is not, of course, unique to Africa, but it had certain characteristics there that justify talking about an African cluster of social, and hence family, systems, despite the wide regional differences within the continent. The means by which African men competed for prestige were strongly influenced by a basic fact of African life, at least in most places before the advent of the colonial era: the goods necessary for subsistence were rarely scarce and thus rarely the object of competition. In particular, almost all African societies recognized a universal right of families or individuals to use land sufficient for their subsistence needs (Colson 1971:194). Where livestock provided the major means of subsistence, (and in many places livestock, though vitally important to the prestige sphere, were not major sources of subsistence materials), there appears not to have been such an explicit recognition of universal rights to stock, but there do seem to have been enough to around, which probably amounts to the same thing in practice. This contrasts explicitly with the often quite unequal distribution of stock in societies with mixed agro-pastoral economies, where livestock were primarily a prestige good. So African men, in competing for status and prestige, did not try to gain control of scarce subsistence resources and make others dependent on them for access to such resources; rather they tried to build up wealth and social capital in the form of prestige resources, usually either livestock or trade goods.

What African men competed for almost everywhere, then, was not land. And in most places it was material wealth only as a means. The end of all this was a following, a group of people loyal to and politically dependent on oneself. Nearly every account of an African society stresses this point, that the ambition of men was to build up a large following of family—wives, sons, political retainers, matrilateral kin, even though the specific ties between leaders and followers varied according to the particular social and economic system. A few examples, taken from widely differing systems in many parts of Africa, will illustrate this point. Among the impoverished, matrilineal Lele of Kasai, for example, "No one could rise far in status without marrying wives and having daughters and granddaughters," as a man's status depended on his control over women (Douglas 1963:65, 113). Among the Yao of Malawi, another matrilineal group but one with much more moveable wealth, "A man's status...depends on the number of persons that he controls" (Mitchell 1951:320). Among the patrilineal Gusii, cattle-keeping agriculturalists of Kenya, "Each household head wanted to have the most populous domestic group possible, with numerous sons as potential fighting force" (Levine 1964:67), and in the patrilineal Shambala kingdom of northern Tanzania, "Within the system prior to contact it was the command over supporters that gave prestige and power to a chief..." (Winans 1964:53). In the Swazi kingdom, "wives and children are regarded as a man's greatest assets" (Kuper 1950:89). In another part of the continent, Bohannan tells us that the patrilineal, agricultural Tiv "correlate a man's wealth and influence with the size of his family and the number of his dependents" (1954:50). And even among the Nuer of the Sudan, so often cited as the epitome of an egalitarian society, Evans-Pritchard states that "It is the ambition of every man...to become a 'bull' and the centre of a cluster of kin" (1951:27). Examples could be multiplied, but the point seems clear: control over human resources was the most important aim of most African men.

This notion receives further support from the observation made by Kopytoff and Miers that African legal systems, more than any others in the world, were concerned with rights over persons: "While all social systems in the world can be analyzed in terms of such rights, Africa stands out...in the legal precision, the multiplicity of detail and variation, and the degree of cultural explicitness in the holding of such rights (1977:11)." The reason, they state, that Africans typically defined these rights with such precision was that "These rights can be manipulated to increase the number of people in one's kin group, to gather dependents and supporters, and to build up wealth and power." (Kopytoff and Miers:9). Africans, in other words, constructed the most detailed parts of their legal systems to deal with the rights that were most important to them: the rights over persons.

But if there was this public sphere in which men competed for prestige and followers, how did they compete? This depended on the nature of production in the particular society. In some parts of Africa, societies can be characterized as poor in prestige goods. Often the labor of the members of such societies was sufficient only to eke out a bare subsistence living, with little or no surplus for trade, tribute, or other activities in the prestige sphere. In such societies, a man could hope to build up a following only by direct means. He could recruit followers through his control over women, to whom he married the potential followers; through his control over ritual means to prosperity, such as rain-making; or through his ability to protect potential followers through military organization. In some such social systems, one can observe an interaction between followers and their labor—labor produced more subsistence goods, which could feed more children or other dependents, which in turn allowed a leader to bring in more laborers. Particularly in poor areas where extensive farming meant ability to mobilize the extreme seasonal peaks in labor demand, control over followers and ability to mobilize their labor went hand in hand. Netting (1968:130-132) has shown this in a contrast between the Cholefein, who practiced extensive cultivation and cited its labor demands as the reason for building large extended families, and the Kofyar, intensive cultivators with nuclear or polygynous-nuclear family households.

In other parts of Africa, however, people were better endowed by nature, and could produce goods that could circulate in a prestige economy, in addition to those needed for subsistence production to support reproduction. In such areas, control over these prestige goods, sometimes termed wealth and nearly always explicitly contrasted with subsistence goods, was closely intertwined with control over potential followers. The best example of this, of course, is the role of cattle in the prestige economies of so many societies of Eastern and Southern Africa. Men could pay cattle for brides, who gave birth to sons and daughters, the daughters in turn bringing in more cattle and allowing access to more brides, etc. In many such societies, the role of bridewealth cattle was almost entirely separate from the subsistence sphere of activity. But cattle were not the only form of wealth—the same effect might be produced by control over long-distance trade goods, or over local products entering into trade. Control over these goods could be converted into control over followers.

In most of these cases, control over followers, though facilitated by wealth, was only tenuously connected to subsistence production. However, this was not always the case. Cattle were not always just wealth, for example—in some societies, especially in the more northerly parts of sub-Saharan Africa, cattle were the primary or even the only means of subsistence. Here the use of cattle to acquire followers had to be tempered by balancing the herd with the human population, so that there was enough labor to take care of the cattle and enough milk to feed the labor force. But even in such situations, there often tended to be a division of interest, with cattle used in an egalitarian manner as providers of food resources, but in a competitive manner as items of wealth (Gulliver 1955:132-133).

Other cases in which the sphere of wealth and the sphere of subsistence production were intertwined occurred in the great savanna kingdoms of West Africa, where the levels of subsistence production and of trade and marketing allowed the formation of occupational groups who did not produce their own subsistence goods. These craft specialists of the towns and the court and local bureaucrats of the state apparatus were both dependent on taxation or market purchase to exchange their own production, of services or craft goods, for food. In such areas, material wealth appears to have become much more of an end in itself than it was even in cattle-wealthy areas of Eastern and Southern Africa, where cattle were still mainly a means to acquire followers, and standards of consumption did not differ drastically from followers to leaders. In these partially urbanized, occupationally differentiated kingdoms of West Africa, it appears that prestige was as much a matter of consumption of wealth as a of acquiring followers, and that the two went hand in hand (Smith 1955:15). But even in these areas, the extraction of surpluses from agriculture, the control of trade and draft production, and the consequent higher standard of living of leaders does not seem to have led to the impoverishment, or the heavy and direct exploitation of followers, for the simple reason that here, as elsewhere in Africa, the means of subsistence production, in this case land, was still not scarce. In other words, while these kingdoms were undergoing the Second Great Transformation, developing some of the characteristics of social complexity, they still belong in the A-cluster, where true social classes based on the economic oppression of the poor did not exist.

In sum, then, all over Africa men competed for prestige, measured primarily in terms of political followings. This competition took place against varying backgrounds of surplus wealth. In addition, it took place in the context of varying systems of territorial and kinship organization, according to which both the domestic and the prestige spheres of activity were organized. If we are going to understand the dynamics of African family systems, then, we have to look at the activities organized in the family in terms not only of subsistence production and reproduction, but in terms of the structure of the larger society in which the family was embedded, both the organizing territorial and kinship principles of that society and its wealth-producing and trading economy, and of course the interaction between the subsistence economy, the wealth economy, and the principles of organization.

Notes

1. In a similar way, "Africa" as used here is also a temporal shorthand. It is intended to refer to the period in the decades before effective changes were made by colonial rule. But the information depends on ethnographies done during the colonial period, which often embody an unconscious myth of the unchanging primitive, along with a more conscious bias toward synchronic analysis, despite all that changed with the imposition of colonial rule. I thus cannot say how successful I have been in describing the true immediate pre-colonial era. The sometimes awkward use of the past tense underscores my anxiety here.

2. Which is cause and which is effect is an interesting subject for argument, but not germane to the subject of this analysis.

7

Family Activities in
Sub-Saharan Africa

The Organization of Procuring

With the development of agriculture and pastoralism as sources of livelihood in Africa, collective subsistence organization of groups larger than the family practically came to an end.[1] In both agricultural and pastoral economies, it is true, there were some infrequent tasks that were performed by large work-parties. But these parties always worked on lands or with stock whose ownership was divided among the families of those who made up the party, and the product was never distributed on a collective basis. Everywhere in Africa, then, people drew subsistence from land or livestock to which their own families had specific rights.

At the same time, as mentioned before, there were few places in precolonial Africa where ownership rights over subsistence resources became a matter of contention or competition. It is mentioned for the Taita of Kenya (Harris and Harris 1965:132), the Sonjo of Tanzania (Gray 1964:241) and a few other groups that buying and selling of land long predated colonial rule, and we can assume that the reason for this was that land rights were in short enough supply that there was some profit to be made by selling them. But even in these few places, this does not seem to have led to landed and landless classes, characteristic of complex societies. In the great majority of African areas, land was a "free good"—if the land a family was farming was insufficient to support an increasing number of family members, the extra members could easily secure rights to cultivate land in some other area. As Malcolm has stated so succinctly for rather sparsely populated region of Tanzania, "Sukumaland is not an island"—there was always land available somewhere (Malcolm 1953:81). But since rights to cultivate land were nearly always available to those who needed them, it also follows that no family would have any reason to claim more land than was needed for the subsistence of its members or, in areas where cash crop production was a source of wealth, at least than the labor of its own members could cultivate. As long as there was a source of free land, there was no source of hired labor, and labor thus became the limiting factor in the amount of land a family could control and cultivate. In areas where surplus products of the land constituted a source of wealth, then, it is easy to see why slaves became a highly desirable commodity (Schneider 1981:80).

Livestock as a means of subsistence is a little more problematical, since livestock was also a kind of wealth, and there was thus always a motivation for those competing for prestige to acquire more stock. But in general, in those few areas where stock were a basis of subsistence, a solution was found that allowed access to stock to everyone. In Somaliland, for example, the stock that produced wealth, primarily camels, were different from the stock that produced subsistence foods, namely sheep and goats (Lewis 1962:5-10). Among the Turkana of Kenya, where the use of cattle for wealth sometimes left certain family units with a scarcity of the subsistence products of the herds, the subsistence products were freely shared—the competition was always over the prestige, or social, rather than the subsistence, or "economic" use of stock (Gulliver 1955:132-33). Among the Hima, the cattle-keeping, ruling "caste" of the Ankole kingdom, there was often a problem of balancing the size of the family with the size of the herd; this may account for the small number of cattle given as bridewealth in comparison to other pastoral peoples (Elom 1973:69). But the Hima were but one segment of the local population, and a person without cattle could possibly have been absorbed into the subordinate, agricultural Iru population. So in effect cattle as a subsistence good, like land, did not give rise to competition between families for their control.

If land (or occasionally stock) as a basis for subsistence was available to all, and if labor was the limiting factor in how much land a family could cultivate or how many stock it could herd, how were families organized for the production of food from this land or stock and the distribution of this food to family members? In other words, what was the nature of the division of labor in subsistence production? In general, there seem to have been two common solutions to this problem—subsistence based on the elementary family centered around a woman, or subsistence based on the patrilocal extended family, centered around a group of related men. Let us examine these two solutions in turn.

Female-Centered Systems

In most of eastern, central, and southern Africa, women were the primary subsistence cultivators, or occasionally men and women shared
equally in the tasks of subsistence (Goody and Buckley 1973:111). But even
where men shared equally in the tasks of cultivation, it was organized
around women. We may take as an example of this type of organization
the Gusii of Kenya, a patrilineal, patrilocal people, holding some cattle but
deriving most of their subsistence from agriculture. Here if a man had a
single wife, he obtained land through allocation from the elders of his
patrilineal group, or through clearing new land (Levine 1964:64). He then
allocated most of this land to his wife, who did the labor of cultivation on
it, and used its proceeds to feed herself, her husband, and her children.
Later in the life cycle, if a man took plural wives (as most did), he allotted
separate fields to each wife, and each wife had the responsibility of feeding herself and her children from these fields, and of contributing food to
her husband (Levine 1964:68). This same pattern was repeated in most of
the societies of East Africa, as for example among the patrilineal, cattle-
keeping Shambala of Tanzania, where husbands did the heaviest work of
ground-breaking, clearing, etc., but left most of the routine agricultural
tasks to their wives (Winans 1964:46). The same was true for the Plateau
Tonga, a group with matrilineal clan organization, and for many other
groups. There were slight variations in the amount of labor contributed by
men in this kind of system—from the patrilineal Tariki of Southwestern
Kenya, (Sangree 1965:44) and the matrilineal Suku of Zaire, where the wife
did all the work on the farm, to groups such as the Gwembe Tonga of Zambia (matrilineal) and the Shona of Zimbabwe (patrilineal) where the contribution, in terms of work, was more nearly equal (Colson 1960:91;
Halleman 1951:362-6). And in many places, cooperative male labor for short
periods was crucial to the success of agricultural endeavors (P.W. Porter
1979). But despite the varying amounts of labor contributed by men, the
organization of agriculture in such systems always had a female focus—
the fields were allocated to a woman, to feed herself and her own children,
and to contribute to the husband's subsistence. In no such system was she
required to share the produce or the labor on her fields with her co-wife.
They might, of course, cooperate, if they got along well. But there was no
obligation to do so. The basic unit of agricultural subsistence organization
was the nuclear family of husband, wife, and children, with the husband
receiving the fruits of labor in more than one such unit when he was polygynous.

There were some variations on this theme. Occasionally junior females were expected to farm together with senior females not just for the initial period of their marriage, but for a considerable segment of the life-cycle. For example, among the patrilineal Taita of Kenya, a son's wife was supposed to farm together with her husband's mother, as long as her husband was co-resident with his parents and had not gone off to seek rights to land elsewhere (Harris and Harris 1964:128,140). And among the matrilineal, matrilocal Bemba, a mother was similarly expected to farm jointly with her married daughters (Richards 1950:228). But these linkages between senior and junior generations seem to be in the distinct minority in East and South African agricultural systems. Usually a wife's obligation to work with her husband's mother ended when the first child was born.

There seems to be no clear explanation of the distribution of this woman-centered complex, though Guyer (1991) states that it probably increased with the spread of American crops beginning in the sixteenth century, and it also seems to coincide with the distribution of the house-property complex, in which men inherited property from their fathers according to their membership in matri-segments, or "houses" of the polygynous family, centered around each of their mothers (Gluckman 1950:197). I will discuss this further below.[2]

Male-Centered Systems

In those parts of Africa where men were the primary subsistence producers (mostly in the agricultural areas of West Africa and in societies where cattle were major sources of subsistence goods), the organization of subsistence production was based not on single women but on groups of men. There were transitional types, such as the Yakö of southeastern Nigeria, where land was allocated to wives but worked by men (Forde 1950:288-9), or the Pastoral Fulani, where again cattle were allocated to various wives, but the men did the labor of herding (Stenning 1958:109). But in the typical system of this male-centered sort, agricultural labor was done by groups of patrilineally related men, and then the was product distributed to the women of the family, who usually cooked for and fed their individual families separately. For example, among the agricultural, patrilineal Tiv of Nigeria, the cultivation group often included full brothers, or a man and his grown, married sons. The food that they produced was then distributed among "consanguineal units" of a woman, any co-wives linked to her house, and the wives of any sons of the wives of that house (Bohannan 1955:24-25). The same was true for the farmers in the Hausa state of Zaria (M.G. Smith 1955:19-20,60) and for the group Goody calls the LoDagaa (1958:61-68). In all these cases, male labor on the land was correlated with male cooperation in the agricultural tasks. There appears to have been no good ecological imperative for such a system, and indeed in some West African systems with male farming, each man held and farmed his own land separately—this was true in much of Yorubaland (Lloyd 1965:552, 556) and for the Gonja (E. Goody 1973:52-3).

There does, however, seem to have been more of an ecological imperative for similar male cooperation in many groups that derived their subsistence from cattle. Among both the Jie and the Turkana, described by Gulliver, the necessity for males of the family to be in different places at the same time, in order to meet the needs of different kinds of stock at various seasons, demanded cooperation among adult males, and in a patrilineal, patrilocal system, the males who cooperated constituted a patrilocal extended family (Gulliver 1955:50-58; 124-8).

It is important in this context to point out, as Guyer (1984) has demonstrated, that there was little *ecological* imperative for specific forms of the division of labor by sex in any of these systems save perhaps those involving long-distance herding. Much more important were the ways in which labor could be mobilized in a particular structure of political relations, once again pointing out the interdependency of the domestic and political spheres of social and economic relations.

In short, in most of Eastern and Southern Africa, procuring was organized around the elementary family, with occasional attached unmarried, divorced, or widowed relatives. In a few cases, extended family structures were mandated by the needs of subsistence production. This was particularly true in pastoral organizations and in some places where extensive cultivation creates heavy seasonal labor demands (Porter 1979; Netting 1968:131). But in most cases, intergenerational ties operated primarily in the sphere of the prestige economy, where fathers retained authority over their sons long after the latter and their wives had become independent for purposes of subsistence production. In West Africa, fathers and sons did cooperate regularly in subsistence agriculture. In some cases, this cooperation was dictated by seasonal labor demands; in other places they cooperated despite the apparent lack of ecological necessity for doing so. Their cooperation in such cases may have been derivative of their connection in the prestige sphere, but since fathers and sons (or, in matrilineal groups, senior and junior matrilineally related males) were connected in the prestige sphere *everywhere* in Africa, this is really no explanation. The best we can say is that such subsistence cooperation between related men, and the consequence that women other than these men's wives and unmarried daughters became dependent upon these men, was historically conditioned in each individual case. But however these various arrangements of the division of labor originated, they had great implications for family structure and family dynamics, topics to be discussed in Chapters 9 and 10.

The Organization of Processing, or Domestic Labor

In most parts of Africa, domestic labor, the work of taking the products of land or stock and transforming them into food, of making clothing and implements, building and repairing houses, and general cleaning and tidying, was rarely problematical, and for that reason seems not to have received much attention from ethnographers. This does not mean that this labor was necessarily light. Minge-Klevana, in a survey of time allocation studies from all over the world, collected six cases from Africa, three of which included "inside" labor time, that is, time devoted to housekeeping and related tasks. In each case, the time was approximately 3-4 hours per day. At the same time, several such studies did not give figures for inside labor at all, showing again the small amount of attention given to the topic (Minge-Klevana 1980:1981). What this seems to indicate is that whereas people, especially women, often gave over considerable time to domestic labor, this labor rarely had much effect on family organization. People did it, but it rarely either required much cooperation or occasioned much conflict.

In Africa, the group in which domestic labor was shared tended to be the elementary family of husband, wife, and children. In most areas, men built and maintained houses, and women prepared food. Other tasks varied greatly as to whether they were assigned to one gender or the other, or whether both genders did them indiscriminately. But whatever the precise division of domestic labor, the woman always seems to have had the greatest burden, because preparation of food was the most time-consuming and regular task, and food in Africa was nearly always prepared by women. And they ordinarily prepared food only for themselves and their husbands and children, in monogamous marriages, or for themselves and their children, contributing a portion of the husband's subsistence, in polygynous marriages. In many societies, a new wife cooked together with her husband's mother, but usually only for a short time, for example until her first child was born. In a few parts of East Africa, women continued their cooperation in cooking, and shared the food among their husbands; this was the case with mother and daughter among the Bemba, (Richards 1950:227); and with husband's mother and sons's wife among the Tiriki (Sangree 1965:54), the Taita (Harris and Harris 1964:128) and the Lovedu (Krige 1964:164-5), where a woman was considered to have right to use her daughters' bridewealth to get a son's wife who could work for her, or to take the wife herself. In all these cases, the senior and junior women were expected to cultivate joint gardens, and the organization of productive labor thus carried over into processing labor.

In cattle-dependent groups with male productive labor, the cooperation between the males appears not to have carried over into domestic cooperation between their wives; among both the Nuer (Evans-Pritchard 1951:127-30) and the Jie (Gulliver 1955:51) women prepared food for themselves and their children separately from other wives of the homestead, even though this food originally came from a common herd. The same was true of the Pastoral Fulani of West Africa (Stenning 1958:97). Similarly, at least some of the agricultural peoples of West Africa with patrilocal joint production groups did not share domestic labor:Goody's account of the LoDagaa differentiates carefully the production groups, consisting often of fathers and married sons or married full brothers, and the consumption groups, consisting of single nuclear units of wife, children, and husband (J. Goody 1958:74-75). Hausa, Tallensi, and Gonja wives of the same compound did share domestic labor, however (Smith 1955:20; Fortes 1949:129; E. Goody 1973:52-4).

The most that can probably be said about the organization of families for domestic labor is that there was rarely much reason for cooperation beyond the conjugal unit, in which labor was divided by gender. There was no greater efficiency, economy of scale, or other obvious reason why women should have cooked and done other domestic tasks jointly. The initial period after marriage, in which a young woman often cooked together with her husband's mother or other senior female, is perhaps best seen as a trial or training period, in which she learned the necessary housekeeping skills under the older woman's supervision. As soon as this was over, as soon as she was responsible for the care and feeding of an infant, she could also be responsible for the care and feeding of a conjugal family unit, and it appears that she usually wanted it that way.

Regulation of Sexuality

In Africa, as everywhere, sex has, as van den Berghe puts it (1979:84), two aspects—procreational and recreational. The procreational aspect was extraordinarily important in African societies, because of the aforementioned relationship between prestige and control of a following, whether through sons who brought in wives and daughters who brought in cattle who could bring in wives for oneself or one's sons, as in many patrilineal systems, or through daughters who brought in sons-in-law, or even sisters' sons who brought in wives and eventually their own sisters' sons, as in various matrilineal systems. To be successful, a man had to procreate. In addition, it was in the interest of women in most of Africa to procreate freely as well. Sons were both an avenue to respect and even, in some cases, a possible entry into the primarily male prestige sphere (H. Schneider 1981:99-101), and a source of emotional support throughout life and security in old age.

But because children of both sexes were so valuable for their labor and for their exchange value, rights over them, a particular kind of rights-in-persons (Kopytoff and Miers 1977:9-11), had to be regulated carefully. There were, in a sense, never quite enough children to go around, and in spite of prolific multiplication, sons and daughters remained scarce and highly desired goods. This meant that procreation, while preferably profuse, could not be random, and rights over sons and daughters had to be assigned according to some system.

This, in turn, is where the procreational and the recreational aspects of sexuality conflicted. If sex for pleasure were given relatively free rein, there needed to be some way of assigning the rights over the offspring, because whatever the motivation for the act that produced them, children were still scarce and desirable goods. Otherwise, sexual activity would have to be restricted to "legitimate" contexts. Sexual regulation in Africa was thus a series of different sorts of attempts to reconcile sexual freedom and rights over offspring.

Given the desirability of children and the necessity to regulate rights over them, it is not surprising that everywhere in Africa, everyone was expected to be married during at least part of the adult phase of the life cycle. Competition for wives, as potential producers of children, usually gave rise to polygynous systems of marriage, a topic discussed more fully below, and this meant delay of marriage for most or all men. But marriage was expected for everyone, and always and everywhere involved certain rights over children on the part of the husband, even if, as in the case of matrilineal systems, these did not extend to membership in his own descent group. And ordinarily marriage was thus expected to involve both sex between the partners and paternal rights of some sort for the husband.

If this were all there were to it, if sex only occurred between married couples, and everyone were married during the whole adult life cycle, then we would not need to discuss the regulation of sexuality at all—we would simply have to know who married whom and why. But of course things were not that simple—sex could occur between unmarried persons or between a married person and someone other than a spouse. It is the regulation of these rights that concerns us here in this section. There are basically two alternatives with regard to assigning the rights to children born out of wedlock or through adultery—one can try to prevent the occurrence, or one can define the rights to a child born from the occurrence in such a way

as not to be disruptive of the system. Different African systems incorporated different solutions to the problem, in regard to both premarital and
extramarital sex.

Prohibition of premarital sex seems to have been rare in African societies. It was instituted among the Muslim Somali, who practiced infibulation
to make it impossible for an unmarried woman to have intercourse (Lewis
1962:35); it may have been related to the dowry system in prestige goods
practiced by these people. Similarly, the aristocratic Hima of Ankole rigidly prohibited sex with unmarried girls, and practiced a similar, dowry-
like system of marital exchanges (Elam 1973:34). And the militaristic Zulu
prohibited sex to the warrior age-grade of men, perhaps originally for reasons of military discipline (Gluckmkan 1950:181). But in general, the attitude toward premarital sex ranged from grudging toleration, as among
the Swazi, where premarital pregnancy lowered the value of a girl's
bridewealth (Kuper 1950:89), to active encouragement, as among the Nuer,
where courting and sex seem to have been the primarily occupations of
both adolescent girls and boys (Evans-Pritchard 1951:49-50). In matrilineal
systems, of course, rights over the children would, to a large extent, go to
the mother's people anyway, and in most patrilineal systems, bridewealth
could still be paid for a girl after she became pregnant, or if this were impossible, the father of her child might make a less-prestigious marriage by
bride-service, as among the Hima (Elam 1973:55-56), Gogo (Rigby 1969:274),
Sukuma (Malcolm 1951:44), and Nyamwezi (Abrahams 1967a:22), among
others. In each of these cases, marrying one's daughter without bridewealth
did not allow one to bring in wives for one's sons, but it did increase one's
following directly by enjoining uxorilocal residence on the couple and giving certain rights in their children to their mother's father's group. Thus
we can see that, in most African situations, a premarital pregnancy might
have been an embarrassment, but it was hardly a disaster, and could be
worked to the advantage of all parties concerned.

Extramarital sex was more complicated. There were two ways to deal
with an adulterous pregnancy: punish the adulterous pair severely to discourage its happening again, or define fatherhood in such a way that the
woman's legal husband (most commonly the person who paid bridewealth
for her) was the father of all her children, regardless of the physical facts of
insemination. Actually, these two courses are not strictly alternatives. In
matter of fact, almost all African legal systems decreed more or less severe
punishments for adultery, if we define adultery as extramarital sex by a
woman without her husband's explicit or tacit permission. Clear-cut examples of this come, for example, from the Nyakyusa, where an adulterer
could legally be speared by the offended husband (Wilson 1950:122) and
the Swazi, where traditional law decreed a severe beating for the woman
and death to her illicit lover (Kuper 1950:89-92), even though, in both cases,

the father was defined as the legal husband, who had paid bridewealth for the woman. And adultery was considered a serious crime even among some matrilineal people, such as the Bemba (Richards 1950:225) and the Mayombe (Richards 1950:216). That adultery was often punished severely despite a legal hedge against losing one's wife's reproductive powers indicates that, however much African men were concerned with sex as procreation, they were also concerned with it as an exclusive emotional relationship, or perhaps as a sign of political power, of control over people. And the reports of sexual jealousy among co-wives, common enough in African ethnography, seem to indicate that many women felt the same way.

But in many cases, punishment for adultery does not seem to have been enough, or else it was deemed ineffective, and social systems defined fatherhood strictly in terms of bridewealth. This can best be illustrated by a famous and extreme case, that of the Nuer of the southern Sudan. Here not only was the person who paid bridewealth for a woman the legal father, but the person did not have to be a potent, live man; indeed it did not have to be a live man or a man at all. In this way, a man could pay cattle out of a deceased brother's herd for a wife for that deceased brother, and beget children for the brother. Even a woman, particularly one with no brothers and a considerable inheritance in cattle, could pay bridewealth and become the legal father of children, who would thus be members of her (and perhaps more importantly, her father's) lineage (Evans-Pritchard 1951:108-112). Although this kind of extreme solution was unusual, it was simply the logical extension of a system, widespread in all parts of Africa, in which bridewealth made the payer the legal father of the children of the woman for whom it was paid. This did not obviate the felt need to discourage extramarital sex on the part of women, but it certainly smoothed out the process of dealing with the apparently inevitable fact of such illicit relationships.

The regulation of sexual activity can thus be seen as an important aspect of African family systems. And in comparison to the extent of such regulation in B-cluster societies, it was much more important in Africa, at least with regard to extramarital sex. One facet of this is easy to explain—in A-cluster systems, it was important to allocate rights over children very carefully, something often of little practical consequence in bands. But on the other hand, this does not explain why most African systems seem to have had more severe punishments for adultery than did bands, even when they had effectively given rights of paternity to husbands regardless of the facts of conception.

With regard to premarital sexuality, the possible social consequences were not much more severe in A-cluster societies than in bands, so we see a roughly similar lack of concern with prohibiting or regulating such activity in most of the family systems of Africa.

The Care and Socialization of Children

As in the case of B-cluster systems, we must divide this according to periods of the child's life. For Africa, the most convenient division seems to be a tripartite one, into the period before weaning, the time between weaning and the onset of training and responsibility for some kind of work, and the period between the onset of light work and the end of childhood at puberty.

Before Weaning

In general, the period of breastfeeding was somewhat shorter here than in band societies: no report gives a breastfeeding period longer than three years, and the norm seems to have been around two to three, as reported for the Tiv (Bohannan 1965:530), Yakö (Forde 1950:290), Swazi (Kuper 1950:94), and Pastoral Fulani (Stenning 1965:391). During the period before weaning, the mother of course took a crucial role in many aspects of the child's care, and she was often the exclusive caretaker for the first few months. After this, however, while the child was still nursing, many African societies assigned a considerable amount of caretaking to someone other than the mother. Among the Tiv, this was an older child of the same sex (Bohannan 1965:529), among the Hausa, an elder sister (Smith 1965:149); among the Tiriki, any related girl seven or eight years older than the child (Sangree 1965:59). In Buganda, mothers were the primary caretakers, but shared their tasks with a wide variety of helpers (Ainsworth 1967:96). In other cases, primary care of such an infant was assumed by a woman past childbearing age: this was true at opposite ends of the continent, among the Pastoral Fulani (Stenning 1958:99) and the Lobedu (Krige 1964:79). Sometimes co-wives helped: a Swazi mother occasionally chose a special friend among her co-wives to help with the children, though co-wives were explicitly prohibited from breastfeeding each other's children (Kuper 1950:96). Tallensi co-wives are reported to have helped each other with childcare freely and often (Fortes 1949:130). In general, men did little childcare at this stage—a Swazi man was not even permitted to hold his child until the age of three months (Kuper 1950:94). On the other hand, Evans-Pritchard reports that Nuer fathers spent a lot of time playing with their infants when the babies' mothers were busy (1951:137).

In general, the pattern at this age seems to have been one in which the mother was still tied to the child by breastfeeding, with provision for care by another person for frequent short periods. This can perhaps be accounted for in many African systems by the long and arduous agricultural labor consigned primarily to women, but it also held true in West African systems where women did not farm, perhaps because in those areas domestic labor tended to be more elaborate and time-consuming.

After Weaning, Before Responsibility

Between weaning and the onset of a child's learning of adult responsibilities, (which usually began at around what Westerners, too, have considered the "age of reason" approximately five to eight years), we find a continuation of some of the same patterns—those systems where a specific caretaker was assigned to infants continued to do so at this age. The mother, of course, was occupied with the next child by now, unless she was recently widowed, divorced, or at the end of her childbearing years, so her part in the child's socialization was, if anything, smaller in this period than previously. And in some places, children this age were sent to grandparents to be reared, even when this meant moving to a different household. Such was the case, for example, among the Kimbu (Shorter 1972:72), and the Fort Jameson Ngoni (Barnes 1951:232).

After the Age of Reason

This trend of dispersal continued and increased once the age of reason was reached. In nearly all African systems, children of this age were started at work of some sort, whether it was simply beginning to learn the tasks associated with one's own gender in adulthood, as among Yakö (Forde 1950:293) and Jie (Gulliver 1965:178), in each case with the appropriate parent, or whether it meant actual responsibility for one's own tasks, particularly in those societies where children of this age were already assigned as nurses to their younger siblings or cousins. In many societies, the independence from the parents' direct supervision took another step at this point, with children sent away for long periods to live with other relatives. Among the Gonja of Ghana, for example, about fifty percent of children in Goody's sample were fostered at this age (E. Goody 1973:182-5), and although this example may be an extreme one, people as far apart as the Tiv (Bohannan 1955:14) and the Plateau Tonga (Colson 1958:224) encouraged children to make long-term visits to other compounds. A special case of this occurred in the Buganda kingdom, where fathers often sent their sons away to relatives, so that the emotional closeness of the parent-child tie would not interfere with the strict upbringing necessary to be successful in

Ganda politics; in special cases, fathers often sent their boys as pages to the court of the Kabaka (King) or of an important local chief, in the hopes that the boys would grow up to assume important positions in the political apparatus (Southwould 1965:106-7).

At this stage also, peer groups became more important—in one case, that of the Plateau Tonga, Colson tells us that the peer group should be considered the most important agent of socialization (Colson 1958:259-60). This, of course, presaged the movement of juveniles, particularly boys, into age-group or age-set activities, first of herding perhaps, and then of raiding in the pre-colonial era, or labor migration in the twentieth century, that were a prelude to the late-marriage enjoined upon nearly all males in a polygynous family system.

The general pattern, then, was one of parents' taking ultimate responsibility for their children's upbringing, but becoming less and less involved with it on a daily basis as the children grew older. And at the stage of adolescence, especially for boys, we find a kind of spatial and physical independence from the parents. The difference, however, between this kind of situation and that found in most band societies, is that in Africa parents continued to control important resources, in land but particularly in wealth and in political and ritual power, that would draw the children back to dependence on them as soon as they were ready for marriage and procreation, made possible only with compliance of their superiors in the kinship system—their parents or, in matrilineal systems, their senior matrilineal relatives. And even in the period of physical independence, the children were often of considerable use to their parents as labor. In fact, one can see clearly here another reason why children were so dearly desired in African societies—not only would they grow up to be or bring in important adult followers or sources of support, they were also quite valuable as helpers while they were still fairly young children, and with parents able to "farm them out" for care in various ways, were little trouble to the parents after they passed infancy.

Management and Transmission of Property and Offices

It is with this family activity that we begin to notice sharp contrasts between the family systems of most of Africa and those of the band societies discussed in Part II. The importance of the family as a unit for the management and transmission of property and offices was much greater in Africa, specifically because there were property rights and rights in persons that had to be transmitted. In the first place, personal status, as mentioned above, was an important goal for nearly all African men, and for many women as well. So there needed to be rules for the passing of this status from one generation to the next. Certain statuses in most African societies, particularly those of high political office, tended to be vested in and transmitted within groups larger than the family, in particular local groups and descent groups. But there were other kinds of personal status, in particular that of family head, which usually carried with them not only prestige, but legal majority and considerable ritual power, that were vested in and transmitted by the family group.

Management and transmission of property were also important. This was not commonly subsistence property, (although it could be in some situations—see below), but rather wealth or property necessary to operate in the public sphere. This kind of property was important not only because it was closely connected with the family head and his position and power in the domestic group, but also because it was often an enabling factor in the family head's participation in the political domain. How many cattle a man inherited, for example, could have a large bearing on the number of followers he was able to build up, and thus on his prestige as well as his suitability for an office vested in his local or kinship group.

In this section, I am not concerned with the particular routes of succession and inheritance—with who passes what to whom; that discussion will be reserved for the section on family structure. What is important here is the demonstration of what kinds of rights and duties African family groups managed and transmitted, and why. I will discuss in turn rights of family headship, rights to property, and rights in women.

Rights to Family Headship and Position in a Kinship Structure

In most African systems, the head of a family group (homestead or compound or sometimes, a minimal lineage segment) not only controlled that group's access to wealth, and thus its ability to contract marriages and otherwise increase itself, but also played important roles in the political and ritual representation of its members in the public sphere (see next section). It is not surprising, then, that in many systems the succession to the position of head was a matter of considerable concern. In Lobedu society, for example, the eldest son of a man's chief wife was designated his successor, and retained jural control over his sons and other dependent members of his compound as long as he lived (Krige 1964:178, 181). Among the Gusii of Kenya, the household headship, the former head's position in the lineage, and the marriage to the widows of the former head were all succeeded to as a package—all these rights did not simply lapse at the decease of their holder, but had to be passed on (LeVine 1964:71-72). Among certain Shona-speaking groups in Zimbabwe, a chosen successor not only assumed his predecessor's position, but his name as well (Halleman 1951:380-81). Examples can be found almost everywhere on the continent—personal succession was of great concern.

Rights to Property

Turning to the inheritance of property, the situation was a bit more complex, because we have to distinguish different sorts of property: land, food, and wealth.

Land. In most of Africa, because land remained a plentiful, "free" good until the early or middle part of the twentieth century, land as a source of subsistence did not usually figure as a matter of disputes in inheritance—access to land could be gotten otherwise than through transmission from one's forbears (see Colson 1971 for a thorough discussion of this). We find, to take an example, that in Sukumaland, while people were very concerned with the inheritance of cattle, they gave little thought to the inheritance of land, because new land could be pioneered (Malcolm 1953:45). Further south, among the Nyakyusa, Gulliver states that "men sought security not in their plots of land, but in their membership in the village community, which assured them of their continuing rights to adequate opportunity for cultivation over the years" (Gulliver 1958:8). This is confirmed in Wilson's account of Nyakyusa inheritance when she says that a man's heir inherited his cattle, and might take his fields if he cared to (Wilson 1950:116). Among the matrilineal Lele, Douglas tells us, rights in cleared land were actually heritable. But in spite of this legal (or perhaps legalistic) provision, these rights remained insignificant, because there was too much free land around to be cleared (Douglas 1963:29). These kinds of statements are typical of discussions of land inheritance in Africa.

There were, however, exceptions, in places where population pressure on land was such that there was a question of accessibility to younger men and women entering adulthood and needing resources for a subsistence base. For example, among the Tonga of the Gwembe valley, we find a considerable difference between the attitude toward bush fields, lying beyond the flood plain of the Zambezi, and river fields, flooded during the rainy season and capable of producing a rich agricultural yield. The rules for inheritance of land applied everywhere, but were only of consequence for the river fields, which were both the scarcest and the most productive sort of land (Colson 1960:79). The Tallensi, in West Africa, made a similar distinction between carefully cultivated and mowed home fields, which were inherited, and the larger, extensive bush farms (Fortes 1949). Among the matrilineal Mayombe of the Lower Congo, Richards attributes the strength of the minimal matrilineage segment, and the attachment of men to this segment, to the shortage and consequent heritability of land: "The strength and importance of the *mvumu* is probably emphasized by the shortage of land, which would tend to make young men anxious to return to their maternal uncles' villages to claim their rights to garden sites" (Richards 1950:220). Among the patrilineal Sonjo of Tanzania, land by the 20th century had long been a scarce commodity, partly because of the defensive perimeter imposed by the presence of hostile Maasai pastoralists, and in this society land buying, selling, and inheritance were of paramount importance long before colonially induced economic change—land could be transferred by sale (goats provided the major form of currency), and the expectations of a son from his father included, prominently, inheritance of agricultural land (Gray 1964:243, 248). What these contrasting examples demonstrate is that African family systems allowed people to organize effectively for the intergenerational transmission of whatever rights were scarce (and thus an object of competition) in a particular society. In most of Africa, these included only rights over persons and rights in wealth, but where rights in land did become scarce, they too were governed by the inheritance system.

Food. A second kind of property that needs to be considered is food. In the long run, of course, this was not important—food crops could generally be stored only for a few seasons, at the longest. But without much of a market in food products in most parts of Africa, and with a season's food stores often the only source of a family's nourishment until the next harvest, it was necessary to have fairly detailed rules about who was entitled to agricultural labor and its product when an important member of a family died in the middle of a particular agricultural season, and the family could not be reorganized equitably for subsistence production until the next season. Thus we find among the Yakö that when a woman died in the growing season, her matrikin were obligated to continue to work in her fields, in order that her family members might be fed (Forde 1950:311). Among the two groups that Goody studied in northern Ghana, the difference between matrilineal inheritance of movable goods among the LoDagaba and patrilineal inheritance among the LoWiili meant differences in the production, consumption, and residential arrangements of domestic groups—father and son, belonging to different matrilineages, would never farm together among the LoDagaba, where the death of one or the other might mean a legitimate, if somewhat immoral, claim to inheritance on the part of the deceased's matrikin (J. Goody 1958:69). Among the Taita, where land sale and inheritance were traditionally important, heirs were specifically enjoined to respect the cultivation rights of widows (Harris and Harris 1964:137).

Wealth. Finally we turn to the inheritance of wealth, an important concern in every society where wealth played a part in building prestige. As the discussions in the Prelude to this part demonstrate, inheritance of wealth (in the Sebei case, cattle) was a frequent topic of both complex rules and bitter disputes. For example, the Tallensi of northern Ghana had an elaborate system of wealth inheritance, distinguishing between wealth that had already been inherited once, which passed to a man's younger brothers and then to his sons, and wealth that had been acquired or created in a man's lifetime, passing first to a man's eldest son and then fraternally to his other sons (Fortes 1949:158). Among the Swazi, another patrilineal people with a rather different, matricentered system of inheritance, Kuper tells us that quarrels and bitterness were extremely common between half-brothers, who were rivals for inheritance, and that the source of most of these quarrels lay in disputes over the inheritance of cattle (Kuper 1950:58). The importance of inheritance of wealth is further illustrated by situations like those of the Ila, where matrilineal clan organization conflicted with patrilineal inheritance of wealth, especially cattle, and where residence was thus patrilocal in spite of the matrilineal basis of kin-group organization (Richards 1950:239). A similar but converse situation existed among the Yakî, where residence was patrilocal, but where inheritance of wealth (in this case not including cattle) was matrilineal, and where people thus retained a lively interest in matrilineal kinship despite the local solidarity of the patrilineal group (Forde 1950:306).

Rights to Women

This is considered separately from rights to headship and to property, because it combined elements of both. While it is a gross oversimplification to state, as Schneider does (1981:99) that women were simply chattels in Africa (he goes on to contradict himself in the next few pages), it is true that rights in women constituted a special and very important kind of the rights-in-persons mentioned before as so crucial to the understanding of African social organization. Men (and occasionally women as well) traded in rights to women—sexual, productive, and reproductive. And because all three of these kinds of rights were vitally important (the last two because they were central to a man's ability to earn a living and build a following, respectively), they were not only allocated very carefully, with a complex system of rules, but also entered into considerations of inheritance and succession. There were several forms of this, perhaps best classified by Gray (1964a:21-22) as including husband succession, where a man stepped into the place of the deceased and his rights to women as an aspect of the deceased's social position, and widow inheritance, where the family headed by the deceased ceased to exist and came under leadership of the successor. Both these forms were widespread, with the husband succession (or levirate) form perhaps more prevalent among the patrilineal cattle-raising peoples, and they both illustrate the importance of rights over women and their transmission between generations.

It should be pointed out, however, that not all African systems included either form of succession to rights in women. Particularly in systems where a wife's incorporation into her husband's group was partial or nonexistent, even young widows were often either free to remarry as they wished, welcome to go live with their brothers and other relatives in their natal homes, or had a choice between these two alternatives. Some variant of this pattern was practiced, for example, among the Lozi (Gluckman 1950:180), the Asante (Fortes 1970:24-25), the Pastoral Fulani (Stenning 1958:98-99) and the Gonja (E. Goody 1973:155). And older, particularly postmenopausal, women, were usually free to remarry or to follow one of their own sons or other relatives and remain as widows.

Representation in Politics and Ritual

A further contrast between most African systems and those of the B-cluster also stems from the existence in Africa of a clearly separate public sphere, or politico-ritual domain of activity. This domain was composed of the relations between members of different family groups, and included activities that we would ordinarily describe as governmental, jural, and ritual. These activities can be considered to have been part of a public, rather than a domestic, domain because, even though all members of the society might be affected by them, not all members were expected or allowed to participate directly. Because certain family members were not allowed to participate in activities that concerned their own welfare, they had to be represented, usually by their family heads. Let us look at some examples of the kinds of activity and the kinds of people who participated or had to be represented.

Political Representation

Representation in government was clearest, perhaps paradoxically, in those societies without formal chiefship or other governmental institutions. In acephalous societies, there was often a council consisting only of household heads, who made decisions on behalf of the entire community. The Tiv, for example, had such a system—a regular council of elders that could only be attended by household heads (Bohannan 1954:6). A similar system prevailed in a very different part of Africa, among the Plateau Tonga , where household heads participated jointly in decisions involving the affairs of an entire neighborhood (Colson 1958:30). And in many places, even if there was no actual council that seated the heads of households, households or compounds were perceived by outsiders as under the direction of their heads, and the heads were expected to represent household members in business with outsiders. This was the case, for example, among the Jie (Gulliver 1955:56) and the Gogo (Rigby 1969:154), both cattle-keeping peoples of East Africa, and among the very different Gonja, West African agriculturalists (E. Goody 1973:40).

Jural Representation

Moving to jural representation, the case is even clearer. Perhaps every legal system on earth has categories of majority and minority, but in Western systems we tend to think of these strictly in terms of age or, if historically minded, in terms of gender. But in Africa traditionally, the scope of jural majority was much narrower. In many places, for example, women were excluded altogether. Thus among the Tallensi (Fortes 1949:99), the Ganda (Richards 1964:257), and the Hausa (Smith 1955:12), as well as many other peoples, women were considered legal minors, under the guardianship of their husbands, and thus technically not allowed to argue their own cases in court. In even greater contrast to European ideas is the legal minority of adult men as long as their fathers or, in some cases, other senior male relatives, were alive. For example, among the Tallensi (Fortes 1949:138), the Lobedu (Krige 1964:178), and the Gusii (LeVine 1964:67), to name a few, a son remained a jural minor as long as his father lived. This of course, along with the father's control over cattle as potential bridewealth, everywhere gave the father considerable authority over his adult sons.

It is noteworthy that in many matrilineal systems women still retained the jural status of minors, but even in those matrilineal systems where marriages were primarily virilocal or neolocal, the legal authority over a married woman resided not with her husband, the head of her residential family, but with her brother, father or other senior male matrilineal relative. This was true for the Suku (Kopytoff 1964:103) and the Plateau Tonga (Colson 1958:281), for example.

Ritual Representation

Ritual representation was also an important activity of family heads in Africa, and an important source of authority over family members. To give some examples, Swazi household heads appealed to the ancestors on behalf of the dependents of their households (Kuper 1950:86). An Arusha man could not have an ancestral shrine while his father was alive, and was thus dependent on his father's offerings (Gulliver 1964:203). The senior members of LoDagaa household groups performed all rituals for their households at their earth-shrines (J. Goody 1958:79-80). And in spite of matriclan organization, a head of a Gwembe Tonga household made offerings for the welfare of himself, his wife, and his children (Colson 1960:106). In other matrilineal groups, this responsibility went not to the household head but, as in the case of jural representation, to the head of the matrilineal group: this was the case among the Yombe (Richards 1950:220). Among the matrilocal Yao, the head of a sorority-group, a man living with his sisters, consulted doctors on behalf of all his sisters and their dependents (Richards 1950:234).

Representation in politics, law, and ritual by the household head was perhaps not quite as simple as illustrated by the normative statements cited above—there were degrees of independence or dependence, especially when members of the senior generation were very old, and the supposedly dependent younger males were already in middle-age, with considerable followings built up by their own efforts. But in general, the point is clear-cut. Families everywhere consisted of ritually and jurally major heads and ritually and jurally minor family members, and the heads represented the minors.

Enabling Participation and Success
in the Public Sphere

The activity of enabling is a third one that sets most African systems apart from those of the B-cluster: there was, after all, a distinct public sphere of competition in Africa, and it was, initially at least, through the buildup of family resources in people and wealth that men (and occasionally women) were enabled to participate effectively in this sphere. Enabling in most of Africa had two aspects. First, it is clear that a man had to be recognized as a family head before he could participate significantly in the public sphere at all—this was explained in the previous section on representation. But second and more importantly, since public success depended on building up a following, a man needed to be not only head of a family but head of a large family before he could start acquiring the extra-domestic influence that would eventually make him a prominent man.

Depending on the nature of the public sphere in a particular society—whether or not there was significant circulation of and competition for material wealth—building up a large family as a stepping-stone to public prominence was done either directly or through the medium of controlling wealth.

Direct Enabling

Where wealth was less plentiful, enabling was primarily accomplished through direct control of followers. In the matrilineal Yao system, for example, a man's status depended on the number of people he controlled, and so he sought to attract daughters' husbands and, if he were particularly successful, to keep his sisters' sons with him (Mitchell 1951:320). A similar strategy obtained among the Bemba, where if a man managed to found a village, attracting a group of followers including his sisters' sons, daughters' husbands, and perhaps even some of his own sons, he achieved a very high status, a prestige reflecting almost entirely on the quality of his own effort and the force of his personality (Richards 1950:228). The Kaguru and related groups of eastern Tanzania also operated in this way (Beidelman 1967:xxi-xiv). The patrilineal Ganda would try to achieve high status by rising to political office, and the king was most likely to favor chiefs who had the most followers (Wrigley 1964:16-24). At the same time, an ordinary man might send his son to the Kabaka's court as a page, hoping that if the boy were successful and rewarded with an important position, the status of the family as a whole would rise (Southwold 1965:106-7).

Enabling Through Wealth

In most cases, attracting of followers was intimately connected with acquiring items of circulating wealth—the one facilitated the other. In some cases, this wealth was obtained through trade. For example, in the Yoruba kingdoms of West Africa, a man could acquire wealth only by trading. If he acquired this wealth, however, he could trade it for prestige by being generous and hospitable, and thus become respected among potential followers, and could eventually invest some of the profits in gifts to the local sovereign, who would grant him office (Lloyd 1965:59-66). Again, in the

Fulani-Hausa kingdom of Zaria, there was great competition for chiefships among those born into the eligible stratum, and the contests seem to have been decided on the basis of who had the most clients (Smith 1955:12). The accumulation of trade goods as an avenue to prestige and office seems to have been more prevalent in West Africa, simply because trade was more highly developed in that area.

Another means for connecting wealth to office was through cattle. In the West African savanna, the nomadic Pastoral Fulani could pursue a strategy similar to that of his sedentary Hausa neighbor: he could make gifts, obtained in trade for his surplus cattle, to his sovereign, the Emir of Bornu, and be rewarded in return with the prestige of an official title (Stenning 1958:108). And all over Eastern and Southern Africa, wherever cattle were kept, they were both an index of status and a means to higher status through the acquisition of dependents. A man paid bridewealth for a wife to marry himself or his son, and thus acquired not only the laboring capacity of the wife (important in a society where women both farmed the land to feed the family and brewed the beer to entertain the guests), but also the reproductive services that would contribute to the further increase of the family.

In many cases, this pattern was intimately connected to formal political power. For example, a Swazi king or chief could contribute some of the cattle from his large herd to the bridewealth paid by one of his subjects. He thus created a further bond between the subject and himself, as well as a debt for part of the bridewealth of any daughter resulting from the union (Kuper 1950:88–89). Among the Ila, a group with matrilineal clan organization but patrilineal inheritance of cattle and patrilocal marriage, a man or even a woman could become so wealthy in cattle that he or she would be chosen as a chief (Richards 1950:238). Among the Taita, the Harrises distinguish two statuses of households. There were ordinary households, where the dependents of a man tended to drift off as he aged, and there were the households of the elders proper, who formed a ruling council of prestigious men (Harris and Harris 1964:146). The difference was that the elders had manipulated their herds to create networks of important social relationships, and had thus become important and respected men (Harris and Harris 1964:131).

In certain patrilineal cattle systems where cattle were unevenly distributed and bridewealth was high, there was a further way in which a following could be created, by accumulating labor in lieu of cattle. In Unyamwezi, for example, there were two kinds of marriages: with bridewealth and without. Marriage with bridewealth transferred the usual bundle of rights over wife and children to the man who paid it. But a man who was unable to come up with bridewealth received only uxorial and not genetricial rights over his wife—the children of such a marriage lived with their mother's people after they were eight or ten years old, and their guardian, for bridewealth purposes, was their mother's brother, who of course was also the beneficiary of their labor (Abrahams 1967a:22). The related Sukumu practiced a similar system (Malcolm 1953:44). And among the Shambala, a chief who wanted to attract followers to his village offered land (a scarce commodity, at least in modern times) to a man who would marry one of his daughters and come to reside in the chief's village (Winans 1964:53). Such a man might either be an ambitious man seeking a closer relationship with the chief, in which case he would pay bridewealth, or he might be a poor man with the inability to pay bridewealth, who would thus come under the control of the chief (Winans, personal communication). In either case, both parties gained, and in either case, the prestige and following of the chief were enhanced.

We can thus see that if man wanted to increase his prestige and social standing, he needed a family to do it—he had to be able to build up rights-in-persons. Sub-saharan Africa was thus the home of widespread accretive family strategies. This is certainly the reason why, as Gray states, "In nearly every account of an African society, we are told that individuals desire as many offspring as possible" (1964:26). It is also, I suggest, the reason why almost all African societies were highly polygynous, by world standards. Women, or the rights over them, were a scarce commodity, one whose reproductive powers were vital to men's competition for success. So naturally men competed for these rights. The offspring produced were valuable in the prestige sphere generally, not, as Marvin Harris and William Divale have suggested (1976), just for military strength, but for status-building generally. This hypothesis can be tested with reference to those few African societies that were not highly polygynous—this matter is discussed in Chapter 10.

Personal Warmth and Affection

Africans, like everyone else, looked to family members for warmth, affection, emotional support. But in contrast to the B-cluster systems, where we observed that such warmth and affection were only loosely correlated with structural relationships in the family, in Africa we find patterns of emotional interaction that were closely tied to patterns of interaction in both the subsistence and prestige spheres of activity. In general, we can say that bonds of affection occurred, or could occur, in relationships where there was little or no possibility of structural conflict; but where there was structural conflict, this would be reflected in the emotional nature of the relationships even in spite of conscious efforts to deny or prevent this.

The only relationship that is reported as being consistently warm and affectionate in African families is that between mother and children. This undoubtedly stemmed in the first instance from the nurturing role of the mother in early childhood, and almost everywhere it remained a strong bond of affection even into adulthood. This seems to have been true regardless of the social system involved: the matrilineal Bemba (Richards 1950:229) and Lele (Douglas 1963:124) showed this affectionate relationship every bit as much as did, for example, the patrilineal Nuer (Evans-Pritchard 1951:138) and Ganda (Fallers 1956:81). Among some patrilineal peoples, the warmth of the mother-child relationship carried over into other relationships in the family. Among the Jie, for example, the mother-son tie is reported to have been the basis of strong and continuing ties between full brothers in adulthood, ties of deep affection that contrasted strikingly with those among half-brothers (Gulliver 1955:51-53). Among the pastoral Somali, mother-son affection combined with husband-wife reserve and mistrust is reported as often leading to father-son conflicts (Lewis 1962:30).

No other relationship was as unambiguous in African societies, as little dependent on family structure, as is that between mother and child. We find a difference already when we look at father-child relationships. Here we find the contrast, predicted by both Malinowski (1955 [1927]:23-26) and Radcliffe-Brown (1924:5-8), though for different reasons, between the relationship in many matrilineal societies, where the father had little authority, and that in patrilineal groups, where the father's authority over the son led to conflict and resentment. For example, among the matrilineal Kongo of Mbanza Manteke, men are reported to have wanted to live with their fathers because there was less conflict and more satisfaction in the relationship (MacGaffey 1977:240). Again, among the matrilineal Suku, who practiced virilocal residence, the father-son tie was reported to be harmonious and warm (Kopytoff 1964:104). This contrasts strongly with the typical pattern among patrilineal peoples such as the Tiriki (Sangree 1965:55), the Gogo (Rigby 1969:97), and the Turkana (Gulliver 1955:133), where rivalry over bridewealth (should the father get himself a second wife or his son a first wife?) is reported to have led to hostility.

The contrast between the fundamental closeness of mother-child relationships in all African systems (perhaps in all social systems anywhere) and the structurally varying relationship between father and child is brought out in the common contrast between full-brother relationships, on the one hand, and half-brother ties on the other. Particularly in patrilineal systems, the full brothers, children of one mother, were often closely cooperative and emotionally close, while the half-brothers, children of different mothers, often quarreled. This is explicitly brought out by Gulliver in his account of the Jie, where he states that this difference was a result of the close ties formed while the brothers were growing up in the household of one mother. Among the Nuer, Evans-Pritchard reports that there was a conscious, but largely unsuccessful effort to ignore this full brother-half brother distinction.

The full brother/half brother contrast was also, of course, connected with the fact that half-brothers grew up, usually in the same compound, as children of co-wives, each attached to his own mother and presumably partaking, at least vicariously, in the quarreling and rivalry that were prevalent between co-wives. In fact, this hostility seems to have existed nearly everywhere: both sexual jealousy and rivalry over material goods seem to have played a part in it. In some languages, such as Nuer (Evans-Pritchard 1951:134-5), the word for jealousy is that same as that for co-wife, but even where the identification did not go that far, the relationship had problems. There were societies, it is true, where cooperation between co-wives was held up as an ideal, and where this cooperation was a reality at least some of the time. Among the Swazi, for example, Kuper reports that, despite underlying suspicion, co-wives were usually friendly. This is also reported to have been the case among the Suku (Kopytoff 1964:105) and the Turkana (Gulliver 1955:130) to name two widely spaced and widely different peoples. But in most societies, it is the rivalry, not the harmony, that is commented on.

This brings us to the relationship between husband and wife. In band societies, as we saw, it was cordial or it was nothing—divorce was the usual solution to a quarrelsome or unhappy marriage. In Africa, though, with the functional dependence of spouses on each other, things were not so simple. Divorce varied greatly in its incidence (see below), and as a matter of fact so did the expectation that husband and wife would be companions to each other. The ideal of companionship was widespread, occurring among peoples so different as the Tallensi (Fortes 1949:87), the Jie (Gulliver 1955:62) and the Plateau Tonga (Colson 1958:132, 140). In other places, however, male companionship was supposed to be with males, and female companionship with females: husband-wife interdependence was economic, in the subsistence or prestige sphere or both, and sexual, but not emotional. This is reported, for example, among the Yakö (Forde 1950:325), the Zulu (Gluckman 1950:179), and the Soga (Fallers 1956:78).

In some places, companionship and emotional closeness, if not found between husband and wife, were still found between brother and sister. This was the case, for example, among the patrilineal Swazi (Kuper 1950:98-99), the bilateral Lozi (Gluckman 1950:79) and the matrilineal Yao (Mitchell 1951:331).

In sum, emotional closeness was an important aspect of the family in African societies, but aside from the mother-child relationship, it was not inherent or universal in the basic structure of any particular kinship or marriage tie, but varied widely with the other kinds of interdependence between the parties to the relationship.

Notes

1. This situation stands in contrast to that found in the O-cluster societies of the Pacific Islands, described in Part IV, Chapters 11-13.

2. Some other societies in which people follow this basic pattern include the Lovedu (Krige 1964:172-4), the Nyakyusa (Wilson 1950:116), the Lozi (Gluckman 1950:193), the Zulu (ibid.), the Kongo of Mbanza Manteke (McGaffey 1977:238), the Nyamwezi (Abrahams 1967a:50; 1967b:52), the Kimbu (Shorter 1972:59), the Sonjo (Gray 1964:237), the Arusha (Gulliver 1964:201); the Gogo (Rigby 1969:28); the Somali (Lewis 1962:5-10); the Ganda (Wrigley 1964:23); and the Soga (Fallers 1957:76-7). This is, of course, nowhere near an exhaustive list.

8

Conceptualizing the Structure
of African Families

Having looked in the previous chapter at the activities organized in and for family groups in African societies, we can now examine the limitations that the organization of these activities placed on family structure.

Family Ties

As in the case of B-cluster systems, we can look at the limitations on family structure in terms of the ties created between people by dependence or interdependence in the various activities. As in band societies, we can look at ties between spouses, and at times between parents and children. In addition, in some African societies, ties between siblings were also important.

Marital Ties

In some ways, ties between spouses were of much the same nature in Africa as in band societies. They depended on each other through the sexual division of labor in procuring and processing of subsistence goods, and sexuality was regulated to the point where spouses primarily depended on each other there, too. In addition, however, spouses in African societies were perhaps more vitally concerned with each other's role in reproduction, since a large number of offspring were so widely desired in Africa.

And of course the labor of spouses was often a vital component in enabling a man to gain respect and advancement in the prestige sphere. All these ties held spouses together. But at the same time, in certain societies the bond between spouses weakened, and this weakening was often associated with the pull of competing ties of a woman with her natal relatives in a patrilocal system or of a man with his natal relatives in any of the several matrilineal arrangements. Thus many African societies had rather high rates of separation and divorce. Nevertheless, during certain phases of the life cycle, the marriage tie was necessary, and even at other times, it continued to hold some force over people.

For reasons explained above, African marriage systems were usually polygynous, so we must look at the structure of polygynous marriages as one of the fundamental building blocks of African family structure almost everywhere. Because of the varying strength of the tie between spouses in various family activities, as well as the pull of competing ties, the durability of marriage and the rate of polygyny were variable in African family systems, and they will be explored in more detail below.

Parent-Child Ties

Here we find a greater difference between B- and A-cluster family systems. We saw that in band societies, parent-child ties were important at first when the children were totally dependent, became less so as the children became capable of subsistence production in their own right, and increased once again in old age, when the elders were dependent on their children for care and support. Only in the few most northerly cases were they interdependent in the full vigor of adulthood, and this interdependence had to do with the particular nature of subsistence pursuits in those few societies. In Africa, certainly the parent-child ties were important in early childhood, though they tended to fade rather quickly when the children became mobile, and became particularly tenuous in adolescence and very young adulthood, especially for boys in societies with age-graded military systems (Gluckman 1950:18). And in old age, Africans, like practically everyone else in the world, had to depend on their children for support.

The interdependence of generations would thus not have varied much from the B-cluster to the A-cluster if subsistence had been the only factor. But the fact that management and transmission of offices and property, representation in the public sphere, and enabling prestige participation were all important activities of the family in Africa meant that the generations were tied much more closely to each other in the A-cluster than among the bands. In some parts of Africa, as mentioned above, there was active subsistence cooperation between senior and junior adult generations. But even where this was unnecessary, the control of the senior generation over wealth, ritual, and jural processes, and the senior generation's need for the junior to provide labor and followers, meant that there was a vital interdependence even in those phases of the life cycle when the generations were perfectly capable of pursuing, and in fact did pursue, their purely subsistence activities wholly independent of each other. In short, there were reasons to have lineally extended families of one sort or another, at least for the performance of some activities, everywhere in Africa.

Family Ties and Family Structure

Similar ties of interdependence in inheritance, representation, and enabling also bound together relatives other than parents and children in African families. Exactly which relatives were so bound—brother and brother, brother and sister, senior and junior matrilineally related males—varied from one system to another. But it was interdependence in such activities, and only occasionally subsistence interdependence, that bound together not only lineally extended, but also laterally extended African families. Finally, it is important to point out, following Goody (1972:4, 5), that the group that was united for the performance of one family activity may not have been the same as the group that was united for the performance of some other activities. In fact, this disparity of groups organized for different activities was particularly characteristic of Africa. These groups, depending on the particular system, were sometimes nested within each other—among the LoDagaba, for example, the consumption group of mother and children was embedded within the production group of one or more males with their wives and children, which was in turn embedded in the residential compound consisting of one or more production groups (J. Goody 1958). Or the differentiation of groups sometimes took the form of overlapping groups, as among the matrilineal Mayombe, where the residential group consisted of husband, wife, and children, living in a village together with the husband's matrilineal relatives, but the group for the division of subsistence labor also included the man's sister, who gave him some of her garden produce, and the woman's brother, to whom she contributed some of her own (Richards 1950). In general, subsistence-oriented family groups tended to be smaller than those concerned with the public sphere, because active participation in the public sphere was limited to jural majors, who tended to be men of the older generation only, or some other restricted group.

Dimensions of Variation

Having seen how interdependency in the performance of various activities held together certain pairs of people in African families, our next task is to outline, very briefly, the way these pairs go together along the relevant dimensions of variation in family structure, both establishing the limits under African conditions and sketching the variation within Africa on each of the dimensions.

Diagrammatic Representation of the Special Features of A-Cluster Families

As in our treatment of B-cluster family structure in Chapter 5, we must modify our general diagram of family process in order to represent clearly the most important aspects of African family process. In particular, we want to be able to indicate the relationship between the group organized for subsistence activities, within the solid circle, and that organized for prestige activities, within the dotted box. In different cases, they may be nested or overlapping, as demonstrated by Figure 8-1.

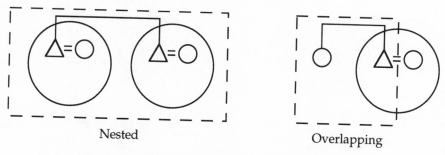

Nested   Overlapping

FIGURE 8-1: Representation of Nested and Overlapping
Subsistence and Prestige Groupings

Another salient aspect of family organization in Africa is generalized polygyny, along with the complex system of transmission of rights and duties that this creates. If we begin with an ordinary kinship diagram of stages in the developmental cycle of a polygynous family, showing its component hearths within the solid circles, as in Figure 8-2, and then impose our basic box-style representation for the prestige group on each stage, as in Figure 8-3, and finally simplify the representation of the polygynous unit, as in Figure 8-4, we can see that the crucial transitions occur between stages

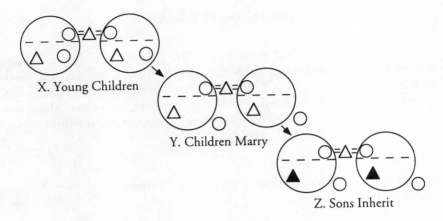

X. Young Children

Y. Children Marry

Z. Sons Inherit

FIGURE 8-2: Stages of a Polygynous Developmental Cycle

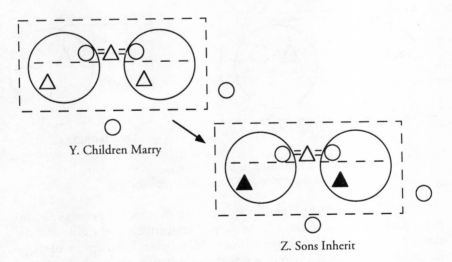

Y. Children Marry

Z. Sons Inherit

FIGURE 8-3: Subsistence and Prestige Groups in a
Polygynous Developmental Cycle

x and y, when the younger generation marries, and between stages y and z, when the rights of various sorts are transmitted to the second generation, either indiscriminately among the children of various wives, for example, as shown in Figure 8-5, or separately according to the specific mother, as shown in Figure 8-6.

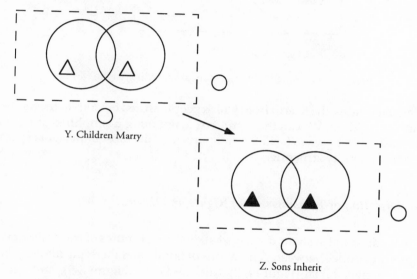

Y. Children Marry

Z. Sons Inherit

FIGURE 8-4: Simplified Representation of Polygynous Developmental Cycle

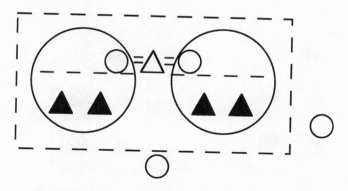

FIGURE 8-5: Inheritance by All Sons Indiscriminately

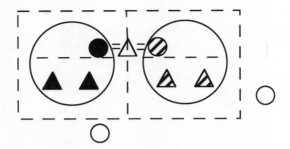

FIGURE 8-6: Patrilineal Inheritance According to the Mother

In all these cases, the hearth from which people are fed belongs to the mother and her children. We can thus omit box x, adopting a simplified structure of two double-boxes to facilitate comparison of the most important aspects of African family structure.

The Direction of Transmission of Rights and Duties

African social systems displayed all five major routes of transmission of rights and duties between generations of family members: patrilineal (Figure 8-7), matrilineal (Figure 8-8), dual-unilineal (Figure 8-9), ambilineal (Figure 8-10), and to a much lesser extent, bilateral (Figure 8-11). There was nothing in the general nature of African social systems that would prevent any of these routes of transmission, but the probable adaptive advantage of unilineal descent groups in organizing larger-scale social relations where there were few limits on demographic expansion (Sahlins 1961) probably contributes to the fact that most African societies had a unilineal form of organization.

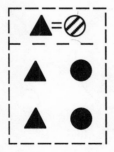

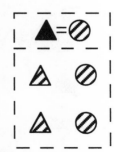

FIGURE 8-7:
Patrilineal Transmission

FIGURE 8-8:
Matrilineal Transmission

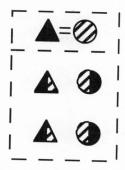

FIGURE 8-9:
Dual-Unilineal Transmission

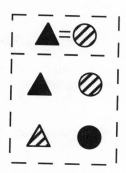

FIGURE 8-10:
Ambilineal Transmission

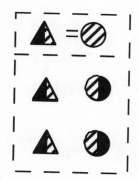

FIGURE 8-11: Bilateral Transmission

But if there were no general constraints on particular routes of transmission, there were certainly constraints operating in certain environments and certain social systems. We have the effects of two kinds of activities to consider here. With regard to subsistence production, there were cases where cooperation between members of a particular gender (usually males) enjoined coresidence of related males. And more importantly, with regard to those functions that connect the family with the public sphere, if there was considerable material wealth circulating in the male-dominated public sphere, then problems arose with matrilineal organization, so that wealthier societies tended to be patrilineal (Schneider 1981: 93). There were, however, ways in which matrilineal systems could be redesigned to get around this point—they will be discussed in Chapter 9. Since the pressures pushing transmission in one direction or another operated differently with regard to different rights or duties being transferred, however, we cannot consider a family system to have been unambiguously, say, matrilineal, unless residence, descent, succession, and inheritance were all matrilineal, and since pressures operated differently in these different areas, we can find family systems where different rights and duties were transmitted thorough different routes.

Restriction or Inclusion of Junior Adults

Here again we must be careful to distinguish family activities dealing with the domestic and with the public sphere. In the domestic sphere, restriction or inclusion was often irrelevant, because adult offspring pursued their subsistence quests separately from their parents. In other cases, though, cooperation was enjoined on one or all offspring of a particular sex. The crucial variables here seem to have to do with availability of land—where population was sparse, people tended to farm separately, but what transmission did exist was inclusive, since there was enough land for all offspring who needed it, as shown in Figure 8-12. A denser population in a particular area, however, might make it easier for only one son or daughter or sister's son to remain near the senior generation, and for the others to go off and pioneer new land elsewhere; this situation is illustrated by Figure 8-13.

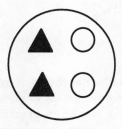   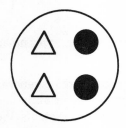

To Sons   To Daughters

FIGURE 8-12: Inclusive Transmission

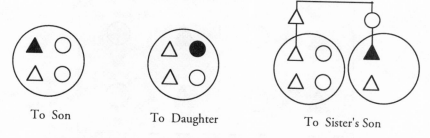

FIGURE 8-13: Restricted Transmission of Subsistence Rights

Turning to the prestige sphere, this dimension became more relevant—wealth and titles, where they existed, were almost always transferred to family members. And there were degrees of inclusion and exclusion. Some titles, for example, passed to a specified son, and one specified son only (Figure 8-14). Others passed laterally along a line of the original holder's full brothers, full and half brothers, or sons, and were thus synchronically exclusive but diachronically inclusive (Figure 8-15). Finally, other rights, particularly those to property, tended to be divided at the holder's death, including everyone of the inheriting gender in the inheritance (Figure 8-16).

FIGURE 8-14: Transmission to the Eldest Son of the First Wife

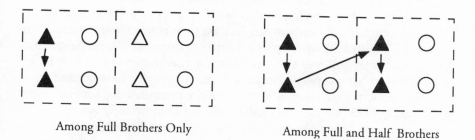

Among Full Brothers Only   Among Full and Half Brothers

FIGURE 8-15: Successive Lateral Transmission

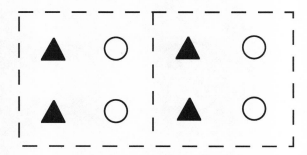

FIGURE 8-16: Partible Inheritance

Participation in Single or Multiple Marriages

People in almost all of Africa were polygynous; as mentioned before, this seems attributable to the scarcity of rights over women as goods and as producers of goods in the prestige sphere. The only exceptions seem to have occurred in societies such as the Sonjo (Gray 1964), where pressure on subsistence resources was so great that the production of offspring had to be balanced with the provision of enough land to support them, and where reproductivity thus seems to have been less than an unambiguous asset. The same seems to have been true for the Hima cattle herders of the Ankole kingdom, who had to balance population against the herds that constituted their subsistence resource, and were consequently not in as fierce competition for rights over women as were most African peoples (Elam 1973:24).

Participation in plural marriages also created another dimension of family organization, concerned in particular with the holding and transmission of property. This is the dimension that contrasts the so-called house-property complex (Gluckman 1950:197; Goody and Buckley 1973:113), in which rights to both use and inheritance of property were divided by "houses", units of full brothers centered on their respective mothers, as in Figure 8-17, with systems of property management and inheritance that did not recognize full-half sibling distinctions, as shown in Figure 8-18. In general, the house-property complex seems to have been associated with the organization of subsistence labor around women-headed units (Goody and Buckley 1973:116-117); this will be discussed more fully below.

Another aspect of single and plural marriages was the temporal aspect— the degree to which marriages were dissoluble, so that men and women might have several spouses consecutively. Much has been written on this topic with regard to Africa (Gluckman 1950: 203-205; Fallers 1957). But in

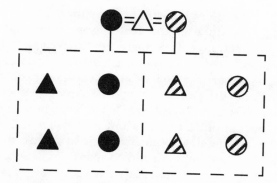

FIGURE 8-17: The House Property Complex

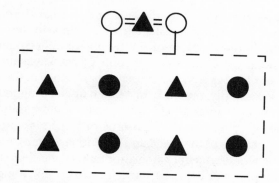

FIGURE 8-18: Property Not Divided by Houses

general it seems to me that the issue is more complex than simply the strength of unilineal descent groups or whether the wife is incorporated into the husband's, or the absolute value of the bridewealth (Schneider 1981: 93). A whole complex of factors operates here, including perhaps most significantly the opportunities presented to a woman to meet her subsistence needs outside of marriage, whether by returning to her natal kin, remarrying, entering into trade, or some other way (Stites n.d.) I will pay attention to variation along this dimension in the case studies that follow.

Time of Transmission

Finally, we have the dimension of the time when rights and duties are transferred from the senior to the junior generation. Once more, we must distinguish rights and duties in the domestic and public spheres. In general in Africa, with a few exceptions that seem to have been related to labor requirements, control over the daily use of subsistence resources was transferred at the time of marriage, that is, at the earliest possible point along this dimension. But in the prestige sphere, the story is diametrically opposite: we have seen already how senior men tended to hold onto their legal, ritual, and wealth-controlling rights as long as they lived. This had important ramifications for the developmental cycle in at least the majority of Eastern, Central and Southern African societies not dependent on cattle for subsistence: there arose in these places two domestic cycles. One was a polygynous nuclear family cycle for the group that cooperated in the subsistence sphere, and the other was the polygynous lineally-and laterally extended family cycle, with many variants, for the group that was interdependent in those activities dealing with the prestige sphere. The interrelationship of these two cycles is shown in Figure 8-19.

All this may seem complex, but the outcome is rather simple. The study of the variation in African domestic cycles is primarily the study of the variations in the domestic cycle of the family's public-sphere activities. These varied along the dimensions of route of transmission, restriction-inclusion, degree of polygyny, and presence or absence of the house-property complex. Secondarily, the study of African developmental cycle variations is the study of the variations in the cycle of the family's domestic-sphere activities varying first of all in time of transmission (most transferred rights at the time of marriage and had done with it) and in the case of those systems where transfer came after marriage (where there was an extended-family phase of the subsistence-group cycle), along the dimensions of route of transmission, inclusion-restriction and presence or absence of house-property complex.

We cannot conclusively explain all this variation. People were constrained in structuring the subsistence-group by the nature of the subsistence economy itself, but these constraints were never enough to determine the form—there seems to be no conclusive reason why extended family farming groups were so much more prevalent in Western than in Eastern Africa, for example. Similarly, the nature and amount of the prestige goods circulating in a society (and these could include office and patronage as well as property) shaped and constrained the structure of the family as organized for participation in the prestige sphere, but they did not determine it—there were alternatives here, too, and the best we can do in many cases is simply to look at the particular historical development in a certain area.

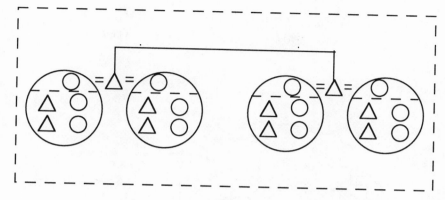

Full Form

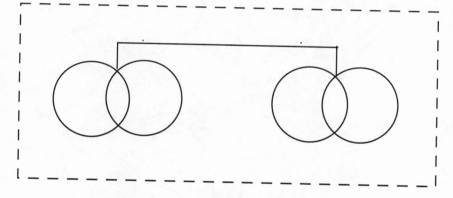

Simplified Form

FIGURE 8-19: Nuclear Subsistence Groups and Extended Prestige Groups

Map 1: Family Systems of Sub-Saharan Africa

9

African Developmental Cycles: Part One

Bearing in mind that there is always, at the time of formation of a social system, "a culture already there", in this chapter I attempt to explain as much as possible of the variation in African family systems. We will look at a number of cases, and show how the systems were affected by the two variables mentioned above—the necessity for subsistence cooperation and the nature and extent of the prestige economy and polity.

We can begin with societies where both these variables were insignificant. The Plateau Tonga of Zambia fit this description well. These shifting cultivators grew various kinds of sorghums and millets, but with a low population density, they had no tradition of land ownership—land was free to anyone who could clear it and work it (Colson 1958:10-11). Husband and wife worked together in the fields, and with their children they managed to provide enough of a labor force that the nuclear family unit could subsist independently, and required little agricultural cooperation with other relatives. So the domestic organization for subsistence purposes was remarkably simple. Residence was totally a matter of personal preference: as Colson says, every fully adult male and every fully adult unmarried female might live wherever he or she chose. Most people tended to live near a relative, but what relative they lived with didn't matter. Thus a survey found that 34.4% of men were living near their matrikin, 39.5% near their patrikin, 9.2% with their wives' kin, 8% with the husband of their own or their wife's kin, and another 8% with no relatives at all, consanguineal or affinal, in their villages (Colson 1958:23).

The reason men could live where they pleased was, as mentioned before, land was a free good, and so never placed any restrictions on residence or movement. At the same time, the sexual division of labor, at least in a few crucial chores, was fairly rigidly defined—a wife was supposed to serve her husband domestically, and indeed a man whose wives were all away from home had to depend on a female relative or neighbor to cook for him (Colson 1958:121, 141). And as the residence survey above indicates, most married couples chose to live with the husband's, rather than the wife's kin.

There was little wealth in this society (see below), and no positions of formal authority. Nevertheless, here as everywhere in Africa, men were concerned to compete for prestige, which could be achieved by having many wives to work for one, and to bear children, eagerly desired by all: "It is the man who is most ambitious who is likely to become a polygynist, for additional wives mean additional labor" (Colson 1958:120). And this competition for wives, here as elsewhere, meant polygyny and a differential age at marriage (J. Goody 1973b:177).[1] Among the Tonga, about 23% of men in a synchronic sample had more than one wife—this means, in effect, that most men who reached middle age could become polygynous (Colson 1958:119).

The developmental cycle of the Tonga subsistence group was thus a very simple one. Women were usually married at about 17 or 18 years of age; men at about 25 (Colson 1958:97-8). At the time of his first marriage, a husband would build for his wife and himself a house in the homestead of an established couple—usually a relative of some sort. Because the bride was so young, still learning the necessary domestic skills, this period of marriage was considered one of domestic tutelage; also the marriage was considered to be a trial one until the bridewealth was fully paid (see below). Marriages were fragile during this initial period, but after the bridewealth was completed, a child or two born, and an independent household set up, they tended to be quite stable—Colson regards the estimated divorce rate of 25-30% as stemming mostly from the instability of the first period of marriage (Colson 1958:175-76).

When the independent household had been set up, perhaps in the same village as the household to which the young couple were formerly attached, it could grow in two ways—by the addition of children, and by the addition of plural wives who, of course, themselves began to add children. Tonga women seem to have regarded polygyny as a real problem. The ideal of companionship in marriage, emphasized in statements by both male and female informants, was difficult, especially for women, to reconcile with the existence of polygyny (Colson 1958:132, 140). And indeed there was very little cooperation between co-wives in any sphere of activity. No woman was required to assist in her co-wife's field or to share anything with her; in fact Colson regards Tonga polygynous marriages simply as "two households sharing a husband" (Colson 1958:119). Such property as existed was also separate—in no case did husband or wife inherit from the other, (Colson 1958:117, 209-10) and this was reflected in the separation of the domestic economies of the co-wives in a polygynous household.

But with or without co-wives, the household grew with the addition of children. While young, these were cared for primarily by their mothers, though fathers helped out when their wives were busy (Colson 1958:141). Children more than a few months old would be put in the care of an older sibling—preferably a girl, but if no girl was available, a boy would do (Colson 1958:264). After the age of six or seven, most children would spend long periods moving about from relative to relative, then coming back home again. Adolescent girls would help their mothers in the fields, thus enabling the family to provide for a growing number of members, but they would be married in their late teens. It would not be too long, however, before a woman got a daughter-in-law or other young woman to help in her fields during the trial phase of her marriage. By the time her daughters were grown and married off, however, a woman would be growing old, and if she were widowed past childbearing age she would ordinarily go to live with one of her children (Colson 1958:134). An older man, of course, could continue living with younger wives, which for most men was probably the pattern until they died. In all, this a simple domestic cycle, consisting of the accretion and final breakup of a polygynous nuclear family.

But what of the prestige sphere, of the group that cooperated in representation, management and transmission, and enabling? Until now, I have deliberately refrained from referring to the fact that the Tonga were organized into dispersed, exogamous matriclans, each in turn divided into "matrilineal groups" (Colson 1958:15-16). This is because the cycle of the domestic family, as organized for subsistence purposes, can be understood without reference to the family members' being members of matrilineages. An absolutely identical cycle could (and did) exist in bilaterally or patrilineally organized communities. But when we turn to the prestige sphere, the matrilineal organization does become relevant. The Tonga had few cattle in the early 20th century—they may previously have had more, but they were eliminated by raiding and disease (Colson 1958:11). What prestige goods were available (and before the mid-20th century these seem to have consisted of hoes, spears, goats, and the like) were used in bridewealth transactions, which transferred rights to sex, a woman's labor, and control over her movements, but no rights over the children (Colson 1958:101). The bridewealth could be paid by any member of the matrilineal group, and was held by a man standing in the relationship of mother's brother to the bride (Colson 1958:18, 48-50). What this meant, of course, was that older, successful male members of matrilineal groups could gain in prestige by taking extra wives for themselves, or by putting their junior male matrikin into their debt by providing the goods necessary for the

younger men to marry. They gained prestige this way, but since the payments were rather small, and since the younger men were in no other way
dependent on their elders, and since a man who did not receive bridewealth
from another had no obligation to that other, the hold of the elders seems
to have been a tenuous one leading neither to localized matrilineal groups
nor to recognized leadership within any sort of corporate matrilineage.The
family, basically a subsistence group with some enabling activity, could
thus exist as an independent subsistence group and still co-exist with the
matrilineal clan organization, because the matrilineal organization was only
minimally necessary to the establishment of a family (and not at all to its
maintenance), and because the matrilineal organization was so weak in its
own right. Thus we find that fathers had considerable authority over their
children, and husbands over their wives (Colson 1958:163-65; 224). We can
represent the domestic (solid circle) and prestige (dotted box) groups in
the Tonga developmental cycle as in Figure 9-1.

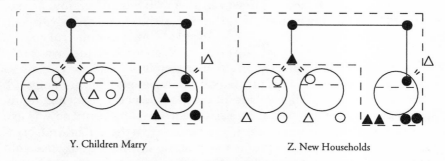

Y. Children Marry   Z. New Households

FIGURE 9-1: The Tonga Developmental Cycle

Among the Suku of Zaire we find a similar situation, with the co-exist-
ence of the parent-child family and the matrilineal kin-group organization, but because the latter was corporate in this society, and had formal,
recognized leadership, the respective roles of family and lineage were more
precisely defined than among the Tonga, and we can already see tension
beginning to arise between them. The Suku all recognized the authority of
a paramount chief called the MeniKongo, who delegated local power to
chiefs and subchiefs, and who stood at the top of a tribute-collection system (Kopytoff 1964:84). Under the sub-chiefs were villages of fifteen to seventy-five people, each "belonging" to a particular corporate matrilineage
headed formally by its eldest member (Kopytoff 1964:84-90). Members of
the lineage might, however, be living in a village belonging to another lineage, because the rule of residence in this society was for sons to live in the
same village as their father, as long as the father was alive (Kopytoff
1964:109).

But if the lineage was not localized, it was still corporate. As mentioned, it had a formally recognized leader, and it also owned medicine and inherited whatever wealth was left by its members (Kopytoff 1964:94). Lineages also dealt in bridewealth—the bridewealth was given by the groom's lineage to his wife's lineage, who immediately turned over 2/3 of the amount to the bride's father, as a payment for rearing her (Kopytoff 1964:96).

In subsistence terms, the initial phase of the developmental cycle of the Suku was much like that of the Tonga—a wife moved to live with her husband, and soon formed an independent farming unit. The husband, in this case, was usually living with his father, rather than, as among the Tonga, with any relative of his choice, but this is explicable by the fact that the Suku, who grew mainly manioc, did not need as much land as the grain-growing Tonga, and thus tended to have much more stable villages (Kopytoff 1964:84). But the subsistence economy was organized in basically the same way—each wife had her own fields (in this case, the men did not help with agriculture), and was completely independent of any co-wives in the domestic sphere (Kopytoff 1964:91-2, 105-6). The real difference in the Suku cycle came when the husband's father died. Because of the matrilineal rules of succession and inheritance, the sons had no further interest in their father's village, and would then usually move to a village owned by their own lineage, where they became the elders of the corporate matrilineal group. They might have had some of their wives with them at this time, but certainly not all— Kopytoff estimated that 50% of middle-aged women were divorced at least once.

In this brief account, we can already see that there was potential conflict between the unity of the family and the existence of a matrilineally organized prestige sphere, controlled by men. The family pulled men one way, toward their fathers' villages and their fathers' relatives, but the political organization, based on matrilineages, pulled them the other way, toward their own lineage villages and their brothers and mothers' brothers. As Kopytoff puts it: "Since the affiliation of each family member in his or her lineage implies very strong economic, social, and supernatural interests outside the family group, the functions left to the family are correspondingly restricted" (Kopytoff 1964:100). But among the Suku, since those activities of the family, namely the subsistence activities, impinged little on the prestige sphere, and since the prestige sphere was primarily the concern of older men, it was still possible to have the family and lineage organized on different bases and co-existing harmoniously enough. In fact, Kopytoff suggests that the delimitation of family members' relationships in contractual terms might actually have contributed to the harmonious relationships between father and son (Kopytoff 1964:100-104). But since this harmonious relationship did not ordinarily involve any power of the father over the son, or any dependence on the father, which a father could use to bind the son to him, the family could still be allowed to co-exist, within certain defined limits, with the corporate matrilineage. Still, in the end, the lineage won out, and old men retired to their lineage villages. Figure 9-2 compares the Tonga and Suku systems.

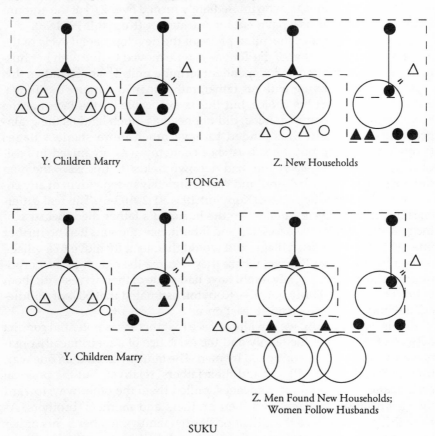

Y. Children Marry   Z. New Households

TONGA

Y. Children Marry

Z. Men Found New Households;
Women Follow Husbands

SUKU

FIGURE 9-2: Tonga and Suku Systems Compared

Among the Tonga and Suku both, the elder men who controlled the resources in the public sphere were willing to allow their matrilineal successors, their sisters' sons and daughters, to remain away from their control at the time of marriage and to live with their husbands' people. One suspects that among the Tonga, this was because they had no firm hold over them anyway, and among the Suku, they knew that the men and the offspring of the women, the male dependents upon whom they would eventually rely to continue the group's prestige and their own following, would eventually be lured back to the lineage's own village when their fathers, and thus their family ties with the older generation, were dead. A Tonga elder, having control over few prestige resources, never built up much of a following anyway, and a Suku elder would get his in time with the return of his sisters' sons. Or to look at it another way, Tonga and Suku matrilineal groups allowed all their members to disperse during young adulthood; the Suku, at least, would get the male members back as elders, and many of the females as divorces.

Among the Yao, however, a matrilineal group of agriculturalists and traders in Malawi, the elders pursued a different strategy, and attempted to keep at least the women of the matrilineal group, as well as its older men, together in one place. As Mitchell remarks, "a man's status in a Yao community depends on the number of persons that he commands, and should he one day wish to set off and form a hamlet of his own...he can do so only though the cooperation of his sorority group" (1951:320). The "sorority group" referred to was the Yao *mbumba*, a group consisting of a man, his sisters, his sisters' children, and his sisters' daughters' children (Mitchell 1951:317). Any man who wanted to be successful, to be head of a hamlet of his own and perhaps gain a chiefly title, had to maintain control over his *mbumba* (Mitchell 1951:317). But to maintain control over his *mbumba*, a man could not let his sisters and their daughters slip out of his control. The obvious solution to all this was to keep the women of the matrilineal group together in a single village, and allow younger men to move in as husbands, and then move back again to their mothers' brothers' villages when they became elders or, better yet, allow them to take their *mbumba*, together with attached husbands, and found a new village altogether. And this, in fact, is exactly what successful Yao men did.

From the standpoint of the subsistence group, things worked out fairly simply. A man who wished to marry a particular woman proposed to the woman's warden, the head of her *mbumba*, and if he accepted, the suitor started to sleep with the woman in her house. There was insignificant bridewealth in this case (Richards 1950:233), but a husband had to remain in his wife's village and work a garden together with his wife as long as he was young and she in her childbearing years (Richards 1950). For young, married couples whose husbands were thus not yet elders, the family was organized for subsistence basically as a nuclear family. But in being so organized, it was subject to conflict between the family principles, which bound children to their fathers, and the lineage principles, which bound them to their mothers and ultimately to the *mbumba* of their mothers' brothers or mothers' mothers' brothers.

This was the origin of what Richards called the matrilineal puzzle, (1950:246), which in matrilocal cases like that of the Yao took the form I refer to as the "husband problem". The in-marrying male was a potential threat to the unity of the sorority group, and his influence thus had to be rigidly circumscribed. This the Yao did—the husband was in no sense considered a member of the community in which he and his wife farmed, and in fact the divorce rate was very high among the Yao (Mitchell 1951:326). Even when a husband did remain married, he was often away visiting his relatives or on trading expeditions (Mitchell 1951:328; Richards 1950:231). The neighboring Cewa, who until the recent introduction of cattle followed a similar system, said that "the husband is a beggar; he has simply followed his wife" (Richards 1950:233-4).

Thus the structure of the prestige sphere, which demanded that the husband's authority and connections be kept at a minimum to ensure the unity of the sorority group, made for a very different domestic cycle of subsistence groups among the Yao. At any one time, a subsistence group might look like a similar group among the Tonga or Suku—a husband, wife, and children existing independently through the agricultural efforts of the parents. But this group was formed at the wife's village, not at the husband's, and was likely not to last very long, because divorce was so common in Yao marriages. In addition, polygyny was difficult as long as a man was in the uxorilocal phase of his marriage.

Eventually, however, if a man lived long enough and was both competent and blessed with sufficient sisters' children, he became the head of his own *mbumba* and moved either to his brothers' village or to his own. At this point, when he became a headman, he could marry virilocally and thus make it easier to become polygynous, which would, of course, give him more powers. So polygyny and prestige, in the form of titles, fed on each other, and a man with daughters might well attract, at least temporarily, sons-in-law to his village along with his sisters' sons, and thus become head of a rather heterogeneous following.

The Yao system represents a further increase in the hold of the matrilineally-organized public sphere over the males of a society, and with it a further weakening of family bonds, indicated not only by the instability of marriages, but by the relatively high authority of women for a central African matrilineal society (Richards 1950:235), and by the contrast between the distant relationship of husband and wife and the close, confiding relationship between brother and sister, even though the latter were not members of the same family group during their primary reproductive years. The richer a society in wealth, that is, in the prestige sphere resources men competed over, the more difficult it was to preserve matrilineal organization. As the Yao case shows, however, it was not impossible, it merely had to be done at the cost of loosening the bonds of the conjugal family (Gough 1961:595). The Yao system, compared to that of the Suku, is illustrated in Figure 9-3.

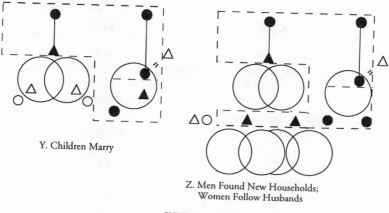

Y. Children Marry

Z. Men Found New Households;
Women Follow Husbands

SUKU

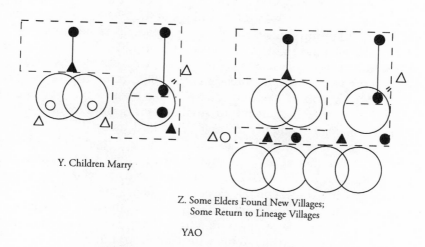

Y. Children Marry

Z. Some Elders Found New Villages;
Some Return to Lineage Villages

YAO

FIGURE 9-3: Suku and Yao Systems Compared

A further step in the interaction between increased wealth and the maintenance of matriliny is represented by the Yombe and Kongo, wealthy matrilineal peoples of the lower Zaire basin. In this area, densely populated even in precolonial times, people engaged in the production and exchange of iron goods, as well as the exchange of copper, ivory, and slaves, for several hundred years (Richards 1950:212). In addition, the Kongo had a highly developed hierarchy of chiefs, culminating in a king, and each permanent village had a formally recognized headman, an office succeeded to within the localized matrilineal group that owned the particular village

(Richards 1950:214). Men thus competed in the prestige sphere not only for control of wealth, but also for access to formal and prestigious office.

A Yombe or Kongo man achieved a prestigious position by being the head of an *mvumu*, a group consisting of himself, his full siblings, and his sisters' children. These *bivumu* controlled access to both land and prestige goods. Since land was scarce in this area, if a man wanted land to farm, he would have to go live with the senior men of his own *mvumu*, who could allocate it to him. In the same way, the valuables that went to pay bridewealth in this society were controlled by the *mvumu* head. So, in a sense, avunculocal residence and high bridewealth reinforced each other here. A man had to go to his mother's brother to get bridewealth valuables, and the return obligation was, of course, to be a political supporter. At the same time, the reason bridewealth was high, something that might at first seem anomalous for a matrilineal society, was that the husband's lineage was claiming the services of the wife and the right to take her away from her own matrilineal relatives and bring her to the husband's lineage village. But the paradox of this system was that even with the high bridewealth payments (3-4 years' earnings in the 1940s), the rights that a husband or his group gained over the wife were really rather minimal. Not only did he have no rights over the children (unlike the Suku case, the bridewealth transactions here went on entirely between the husband's lineage and the wife's, with no intervention by their respective fathers), but even his wife's labor did not go entirely to the family unit—she was expected to give about half the produce of her own gardens to the members of her own *mvumu*, living in their own village (Richards 1950:215).

Superficially, the Yombe-Kongo domestic group, organized for subsistence, looks like that of the other matrilineal peoples we have been discussing—husband, wife or wives, and children lived and labored together—but in fact the matrilineal puzzle asserted itself here, and the husband, as a possible authority over his wife and thus threat to the unit of the brother-sister group, was made to pay a high bridewealth and still did not even have full rights to the fruits of his wife's labor. And the other half of the matrilineal puzzle, what I term the "father problem" was also in evidence. With marriage more stable than, say, in the Yao situation, and with children growing up under their father's immediate guidance, the loyalty of the children might be in question. But again, the Yombe system got around this by making inheritance, land allocation, residence, and bridewealth transactions from the senior to the junior generation all flow exclusively through the matrilineal line. Once again, at the expense of the family, the matrilineal principle managed to hold its own in the face of a large and competitive sphere of both wealth and office. In comparison to the Yao and Suku, the Yombe-Kongo developmental cycle is represented in Figure 9-4.

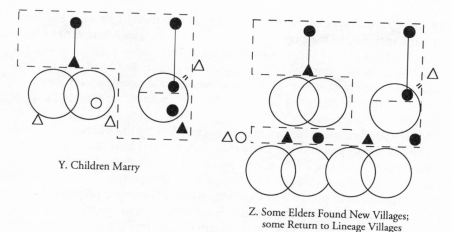

Y. Children Marry

Z. Some Elders Found New Villages;
some Return to Lineage Villages

YAO

Y, Z: Avunculocal Residence; Descent Group also
organizes some subsistence activities

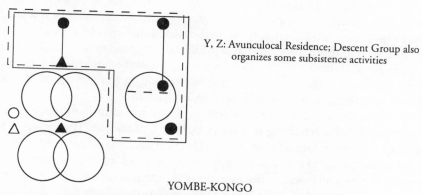

YOMBE-KONGO
FIGURE 9-4: Yao and Yombe-Kongo Systems Compared

An even more highly developed public sphere in conjunction with a matrilineal system was found among the Asante of southern Ghana. Here we find, for Africa at least, a culmination of the sequence of increasing wealth in matrilineal societies that began with the Plateau Tonga. The Asante kingdom, a conquest state, consisted of eight allied chiefdoms with the paramount one at Kumasi providing the Asantahene, or king. The kings and chiefs had lavish courts, maintained by trading native gold and kola nuts for all sorts of luxuries coming from both the trans-Saharan and the coastal trade, by collecting tribute in gold and other commodities from the citizens of Asante itself, and by plunder and capture of slaves in warfare (Fortes 1969:140-41). In addition to the kings and their highly developed courts, there existed also in the towns of Asante considerable communities of occupational specialists of various kinds, and then there were the farm-ers, the majority of the population. The various estates seem to have been at least partially hereditary in matrilineages, but within each matrilineage, whether it owned the Golden Stool itself or merely the headship of a vil-lage ward, there seems to have been considerable competition between members for the offices of head and "queen mother," or female head, of the lineage Fortes (1950:256-7).

This sounds almost like a complex society, but by the definition used in this book it falls just short; if there was clear social differentiation by occu-pations and birth, there was still no real economic exploitation of the lower classes—land was fertile and plentiful, and Asante people, even in the 20th century, could still practice shifting agriculture. There was no private own-ership of land; instead the head of a local matrilineage segment allocated land to the matrilineage members to farm (Fortes 1950:258). What we have is not a complex society, then, but a society with a secure subsistence sphere and a highly differentiated, wealthy, highly competitive public sphere. The important thing about this public sphere for us is that it, like those of the previous groups discussed, was organized matrilineally. Asante as a whole had eight clans, and each of these was divided into maximal localized lin-eages, each of them the owner and principal occupant of an urban ward or of a village (Fortes 1970:9). We thus find the same potential for conflict between the bonds of marriage and fatherhood in the family, on the one hand, and the ties to the public sphere, on the other.

The important group for domestic organization among the Asante was the household, occupying a distinct building of its own (Fortes 1970:10) and cooperating as a subsistence production unit (Basehart 1961:289). At first glance, Asante households appear to have belonged to a diversity of types—some patrilocal, some avunculocal, some neolocal, etc., but Fortes has shown that the composition of households can be explained in terms of the working out, over time, of a series of organizational principles. The first and foremost among these was the close identification of woman and child—as Fortes put it, "A woman and her children constitute the indis-soluble core of Ashanti social organization" (Fortes 1970:19). It follows from this that most Asante, male or female, followed their mothers and lived in their mothers' houses whenever possible, often in preference to living with their spouses. The second principle was that a wife might, especially dur-ing the height of their childbearing years, go to live in a house with a hus-band and his kin, but that men would not go to live in their wives' houses. A third principle was that any senior adult, male or female, could found and head a house and attract dependents to it (Fortes 1970:19). Out of these principles arose a variety of synchronic household structures, as illustrated in Figure 9-5. Some households were headed by women, and contained their sons and daughters, and occasionally their sons' wives, but never their daughters husbands; these might also contain their sisters' children, especially if the sisters themselves were living with the head. Other households were headed by men and might contain, in addition to matrilineal kin, the wives and children of the head and/or of this matrilineal kin (Fortes 1970:25). Fortes notes that, since a woman ordinarily had to choose between living with her husband and living with her mother, households in one town where traditional lineage organization was strongest at the time of his fieldwork tended to rely proportionately more on matrilineal links; in a town where lineage organization had been more severely disrupted by 19th century warfare and 20th century colonialism, marriage ties were more important (Fortes 1970). But the same principles were at work everywhere.

Female
Headed

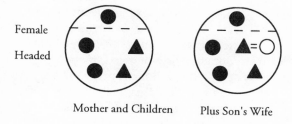

Mother and Children   Plus Son's Wife

Male
Headed

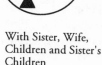

With Sister's Children   With Sister, Wife,   With Wives, Children
                         Children and Sister's   Sister's Children,
                         Children   Sister's Son's Wife

FIGURE 9-5: Examples of Asante Households

These principles, of course, were the familiar ones we have been discussing in the last few cases, and indeed ones verbalized commonly by Asante themselves: there was a conflict between family ties and matrilineal ties, and this provoked tension in the social system. The Asante way of dealing with this conflict was twofold. First, they dichotomized responsibility between, as Malinowski once said referring to quite another part of the world, "mother-right and father-love." An Asante father had no legal rights or responsibilities or authority over his children, but he was expected to take a large part in their upbringing and have a close and warm relationship with them (Fortes 1950:268). Second, the Asante weakened the conjugal bond until it seems to us to hardly befit the name of marriage. The first union for a young pair often began with informal sexual relations, sanctioned, as long as not promiscuous, by the parents of both parties. If it looked like the affair was going to last, it could be made into a marriage by the payment of a couple of bottles of liquor, but it might continue without this legitimation for a long time, as the father accepted paternity of the children. As mentioned above, married couples often spent a large period of their lives wedded but not living together—this was the origin of the famous twilight scene of young girls and boys scurrying about the alleys of the Asante town, their heads laden with food being sent from their own houses to their fathers' houses (Fortes 1970:10). And in Fortes' survey of the more traditional, lineage-oriented town in the 1940s, over half the women over the age of forty were not currently married, far too large a proportion to be accounted for by widowhood alone (Fortes 1970:24). As we would predict from looking at the previous cases, matriliny in such a wealthy society meant the extreme weakening of the marriage tie.

This sequence of matrilineal societies from the poorest in wealth to the richest, as illustrated in Figure 9-6, points out some important things: First, as was stated long ago by Gough, it is true that the more productive a matrilineal society (or, in more precise terms, the more wealth there was for men to compete for in the public sphere), the greater will be the stresses between the matrilineal organization of that public sphere and the ties of fatherhood and marriage in the domestic group (Gough 1961e:595). As we see an increase in the wealth, and thus in the importance of the matrilineal organization, of the public sphere, we also see a process of weakening of paternal and especially conjugal links. At the same time, however, it is not quite true, as Schneider has stated (1981:87) that the main determinant of matrilineal or patrilineal organization in an African society was how much a man could pay for his wife. Certainly this was a factor, because of the strains between matrilineal organization and family organization in a wealthy society. But these strains could be gotten around by various mechanisms of weakening the family. The Yombe husband could pay a lot for his wife, but he did not get very much for it. The Asante husband, who if he was a chief might have many wives and could afford to pay very large amounts for them, nevertheless did not pay much, and got even less. It would be hard to imagine the *emergence* of matriliny in a society already wealthy and remaining wealthy, but matriliny can adapt to wealth, and the two are thus not inversely correlated in any casual or mechanical sense.

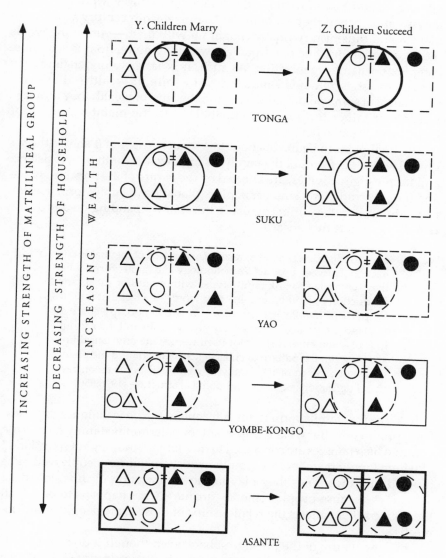

FIGURE 9-6: Comparison of African Matrilineal Systems

This leads us to the second point about this sequence—that it is, or must have been at some time, a historical sequence. Individual societies can certainly gain and lose in wealth—the Tonga, for example, were once probably wealthier than they were in the late nineteenth century when colonialism and thus history finally caught up with them—but on the whole the progression must be one from less wealth to more, from less to more complex forms of organization. As such, it is easier to understand why certain societies remained matrilineal in spite of wealth—they were matrilineal at some point in the past, and the kind of wealth they acquired was, albeit rather tortuously, compatible with the maintenance of the matrilineal organization.

The final point to be made about this sequence is that it shows the degree to which the forms of the family, its organization both for subsistence and for prestige activities, are affected by the nature of the prestige sphere, and thus precludes any kind of simple explanation of family form in terms of productive ecology. In recognizing this, I am expanding on a provocative remark made by Lancaster:

> Evolutionists have failed to recognize this lack of inevitable connection [between productive technology and family form] when they have tried to link family types with modes of subsistence production or land tenure. In other words, the fact that families (or parts of families) account for subsistence, occupy space on the land, and are simultaneously always units in larger groupings of some kind, does not it itself necessitate any causal linkage between the pattern of subsistence behavior and the phenotypic appearance of the family as conceived in terms of traditional definitions of social and political structure [1976:550].

It is true that family form is not determined by the techniques of subsistence production. But what is important for determining family form is the way in which families are connected to the "larger groupings of some kind" of whom family members are simultaneously members. People cannot be divided into their roles they play in the organization of different social activities—because people come in "quanta", what happens to people in the public sphere affects the relationships of those same people in the domestic sphere.

Thus the nature of the prestige sphere, even though it does not determine the way in which people gain their subsistence, does exert a strong effect on the way they organize to gain that subsistence, perhaps a stronger effect than that exerted by the technology of subsistence itself. Here we come back to Guyer's remarks about "naturalism"—more than just technology is needed to explain not only the gender division of labor, as Guyer points out (1984), but the organization of families generally.

Having said all this, however—that matriliny is compatible, although with some difficulty, with wealth, that the fact of their coexistence must be explained by a specific historical sequence in which a matrilineal society got wealthier, and that this in turn has a great influence of family organization—I now want to qualify all of these points. For in the presence of certain types of wealth, particularly cattle as found in Eastern and Southern Africa, matriliny seems almost always to have broken down and transformed itself into something else, and the reason it did so is because of the labor requirements of keeping the cattle, and this in turn had an effect on domestic group organization, particularly but not exclusively in the prestige sphere of functions.

Let us take a couple of examples. My earlier discussion of the plateau Tonga referred to a period in the late nineteenth and early twentieth centuries, when they were poor and the matrilineal organization, weak as it was, went essentially unchallenged. But in the middle decades of this century, they acquired cattle. Having cattle, men turned to the nearest available herdboys to take care of them—their own sons. But this in turn produced a situation where adolescent boys spent a lot of rather boring time and effort herding their fathers' cattle, knowing all the while that they had no interest in them, that they would be inherited, eventually, by their fathers' sisters' children (Colson 1958:234). This, along with the acquisition of other kinds of wealth, led to a demand among some Tonga that they be liberated from the rules of matrilineal inheritance and free to safeguard the economic interests of their households and of their sons (Colson 1958:119), producing a situation like that illustrated in Figure 9-7. At the time of Colson's fieldwork, then, the Tonga were still matrilineal, but system was already showing strains.

FIGURE 9-7: Incomplete Matrilineal-Patrilineal Transistion in Tongaland

Such strains seem to have led considerably further in the case of the Ila peoples of Zambia. Here I cannot demonstrate any historical sequence, but it certainly would not be out of line to posit one. Clan and lineage organization were matrilineal in this system in the recent past, as was, ordinarily, succession to personal status, including office (Richards 1950:236-38). But residence was patrilocal by the early 20th century, as was the inheritance of at least some cattle, a fact that seems understandable when we learn that the patrilocal joint family took responsibility for joint management of its herds. Bridewealth was high, paid in cattle, and in general Richards states that patrilineal inheritance of cattle and patrilocal residence took precedence in the formation of important family groups over the matrilineal descent and personal succession in the society. (Richards 1950:239).

There are many ways in which this might have come about, of course, but at least one possible sequence is one in which a formerly matrilineal society acquired cattle, which were both an item of wealth that in any case put strains on matrilineal organization, and an object of labor that was best handled by cooperation between adult men and their adolescent sons. Cattle thus became patrilineally inherited, and with control over them as bridewealth, the former herdboys maintained their residence in their fathers' villages, even after they had set up independent conjugal families as subsistence units, as seen in Figure 9-8. If this is indeed the case (and I offer no evidence), there remains the question of how long it might have taken before the descent and succession system became patrilineal also. We have, of course, no way of knowing in the absence of direct historical evidence— once a people became fully patrilineal in this way it would be difficult to detect any traces of an earlier matrilineal organization, and the intensive intrusion of the colonial and post-colonial economy into this area obviated any might-have-been.

FIGURE 9-8: Hypothetical Matrilineal-Patrilineal Transistion in Ilaland

I am confident that such shifts in unilineal organization have been common in the past, but I do not think that they constitute any kind of evidence for a prior universal matrilineal stage of organization. Even in the band societies examined in the last chapter, patrilineal descent groups and an eventual ideal of patrilocal residence were found in some places, notably Australia, and patrilineal organization was similarly found in many very poor societies in Africa. Let us continue our tour of African family forms by looking at some of these.

We can begin with the Kimbu, who inhabited the sparsely populated, tsetse-infested, poor-soil forest of part of west-central Tanzania. In this area, it was difficult to scratch out a living by agriculture, though a form of shifting cultivation was practiced. At the same time, honey-collecting was an important subsistence activity, and much hunting was done also (Shorter 1972:46, 55). The Kimbu were organized into patrilineages, each with its recognized head and council of elders (Shorter 1972:69-73); these lineages were divided into chiefly and commoner ranks (Shorter 1972:69-73). The role of the chief was primarily a ritual one—making rain for the precarious agriculture of this area, as well as presenting various offerings on behalf of the entire chiefdom. The chief also had to give permission for people to clear new land within his domain, and for the honey-collecting season to start. He took as his tribute a small portion of the animals killed within his jurisdiction (Shorter 1972:135-6). Succession to chiefship, unlike kin-group organization and inheritance, was matrilineal, though agnates of chiefs formed his important advisory council (Shorter 1972:114, 133).

How were domestic groups organized in such a field of social relations? In terms of subsistence, there was at least an ideal division of labor in which farms belonged to women while the forest and its products—game and honey—were the domain of the men (Shorter 1972:59). In practice, we find here as so many other places that men helped their wives with the heaviest initial tasks of clearing and hoeing before leaving the rest of the agricultural work to the women. New land was acquired by clearing it, with the readily obtained permission of a local chief; rights over particular pieces of land were not important because of the poor quality of the soil and the necessity of moving every few years. The group that benefitted from a woman's labor was apparently the conjugal family—each married man had his own homestead and each wife her own gardens (Shorter 1972:80, 59). It is not clear to what extent the products of men's forest pursuits were shared across homesteads.

In a society with patrilineages, children of course belonged to the lineages of their fathers, and among the Kimbu as elsewhere, it was necessary for the husband to pay something to his bride's people in order to obtain not only sexual rights to her, and rights to her labor, but also the membership of her children in his lineage. But in a poor area like Ukimbu, there was very little wealth available to serve as bridewealth, and so, in spite of the patrilineal rule of descent, marriages were originally uxorilocal in a form of "bride-service". A new husband had to perform services for his wife's parents, and act with extreme respect in their presence, at least for the first few years or until the birth of children of the marriage. A small amount of bridewealth was also paid, but this may have been a recent introduction, and in any case was insignificant in value compared to the bridewealth paid by some of the richer neighbors of the Kimbu, such as the Bungu, Safwa, and Hehe to the south (Shorter 1972:26).

After a few years of marriage, however, a man could move himself and his wife and children (they would likely be moving anyway) to another location where he formed a cluster of homesteads with his own agnates, and where he would eventually be eligible to become one of the local lineage elders (Shorter 1972:73). Some men, however, continued to reside uxorilocally (Shorter 1972:76)

It is instructive, I think, to contrast bride-service in poor African societies such as the Kimbu with the initial period of uxorilocal residence in B-cluster systems. In the band systems uxorilocal residence was a kind of trial period in which the husband proved his worth to the wife's parents, and the wife grew into marriage as she grew into maturity. In African societies, both the husband and wife were older, and proving was not the issue. Uxorilocal residence here was more clearly bride-service, payment of labor in return for rights over a woman. We can see this even more clearly when we consider societies such as Shambala, where bride-service was offered in lieu of bridewealth (Winans, personal communication).

The most striking thing about the Kimbu system (illustrated in Figure 9-9) so far is that with the exception of the compulsory period of uxorilocal residence (which did not, however, result in an extended family for agricultural purposes), the family cycle resembled that of the matrilineal Plateau Tonga as much as it resembled any of the wealthier, more highly developed patrilineal systems that are discussed below.

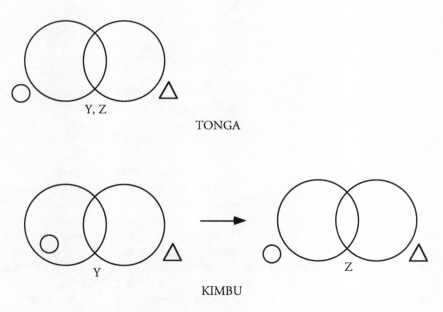

FIGURE 9-9: Tonga and Kimbu Subsistence Group Cycles

The Kimbu subsistence unit of the nuclear family, in later stages of the cycle often expanded to the polygynous family, had considerable freedom of movement after the first couple of years, and the corporate lineages that attracted men to live with their agnates were not so strong or so important that they could form large or very coherent clusters. In terms of ordinary domestic organization, the Kimbu and Plateau Tonga had more in common with each other as poor societies than did the patrilineal Kimbu with, say, the wealthy patrilineal Gusii of Kenya, or the Tonga with the wealthy matrilineal peoples of the lower Zaire basin. The descent system had little influence on the family system at this level of poverty, because the descent system, the organization of the public sphere, had so little to offer in terms of opportunities, and so little that it could use to constrain family behavior, that family heads behaved essentially in family terms.

Where the public sphere did have more influence on families in Ukimbu, however, was among the chiefly lineages. As a kind of paradox, even though descent was patrilineal in this society, the rule of succession to chiefship was matrilineal—the chief's agnates became his councilors, but his sister's son, or failing that, his sister or sister's daughter, succeeded to his own office (Shorter 1972:115). This meant that it was in a chief's interest to keep his sisters, the mothers of his potential successors, close to him, in order to retain control over their offspring. This the chief did by allowing commoner men to marry his sisters, but without paying even the nominal Kimbu bridewealth, and to reside uxorilocally permanently. By this strategy, a chief not only ensured a successor, but also added his son-in-law to his agnates as potential members of his following, and consequently chiefly villages were much larger than ordinary villages (Shorter 1972:115-119). Here we can see that, when the public sphere had something to offer, it did influence the organization of families (Figure 9-10).

We can see the effect of increasing wealth on family organization in patrilineally-organized societies if we look at the northern neighbors of the Kimbu, the Nyamwezi. Nyamwezi country is still classified as *miambo* forest, but the tsetse infestation is more variable here, and it has been possible to keep cattle—at the time of Abrahams' field research in the early 1960s, about 1/3 of the homesteads had some cattle (Abrahams 1967a:9). Cattle were not an important subsistence resource here, however—they were primarily a form of wealth. Subsistence came mainly from agriculture, with a husband-wife unit, sometimes part of a polygynous family when the husband got older, cultivating its own fields allocated, as among the Kimbu, by a local chief. But domestic organization beyond the basic subsistence group differed among the Nyamwezi and the Kimbu. Whereas a Kimbu man might settle with his agnates or not once he had completed the uxorilocal phase of his marriage, and in any case was little dependent on his agnates, a Nyamwezi man, even if he moved away from his father

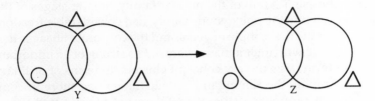

Commoner Subsistence Cycle

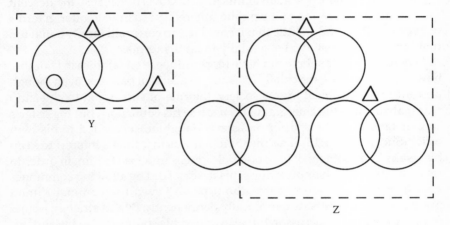

Chiefly Subsistence and Prestige Cycle

FIGURE 9-10: Kimbu Commoner and Chiefly Cycles

during the father's lifetime, was still dependent on the father because of the institution of bridewealth, paid in cattle (Abrahams:52).

But in fact there was a problem here, in that many men, poor as individuals or living in poorer, more tsetse infested parts of Unyamwezi, were not able to come up with the cattle for their sons' marriages. So the Nyamwezi had two kinds of marriages, differing greatly in the rights granted to the husband. Marriage with bridewealth gave the husband both uxorial and genetricial rights—the sons belonged to his patrilineage, and inherited from him. In addition, a man who received bridewealth cattle for his daughters was obligated to use these cattle to pay for the marriage of his son. In non-bridewealth marriage, on the other hand, a man received no genetricial and limited uxorial rights. His children would often go to live with their own, that is, their mother's lineage after the age of eight or so, and the bridewealth of the daughter of a non-bridewealth union was paid to her mother's brother or another of her mother's relatives, not to her father, who had no rights over her because he had not paid bridewealth to marry her mother. In addition, children of a non-bridewealth marriage would not inherit from their father, but would gain limited rights in the inheritance of their mother's brother's goods, as shown in Figure 9-11 (Abrahams 1967:22).

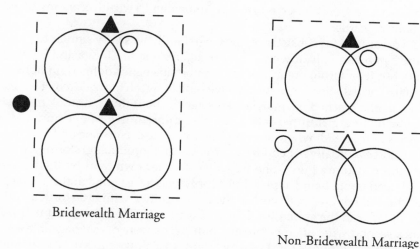

Bridewealth Marriage

Non-Bridewealth Marriage

FIGURE 9-11: Effect of Bridewealth on Prestige Cycle: Nyamwezi

Wealth and its circulation in the public sphere thus affected domestic organization, not in its subsistence aspects (the monogamous or polygynous conjugal family farmed in the same way whether or not bridewealth had been paid for the wife), but in the connection between adult generations that was maintained by the circulation of bridewealth. An adult man's ties were to his father's people or to his mother's people depending on whether not his marriage was made by transfer of wealth. In addition, bridewealth created aspects of the patrilineal house-property complex in this society, in that sons had special rights to the bridewealth cattle of their own full sisters' marriages, while other kinds of goods were inherited form the father regardless of the identity of the mother (Abrahams 1967b:52). It was thus wealth that sustained the patrilineal institutions of this society, including the prestige aspects of family organization. But the patrilineal institutions permeated the society incompletely, because there was not enough wealth to go around.

If we move east form Ukimbu and southeast form Unyamwezi we come to Ugogo, an area where conditions have long favored the herding of cattle. And looking at family organization, we can see the operation of a wealthy, patrilineal family system in its full flower. The Gogo were both farmers and cattle-keepers, and though the possibilities of agriculture in their dry country are described as precarious (Rigby 1969:12), agriculture remained the primary source of subsistence, with cattle products playing a distinctly secondary role (Rigby 1969:26, 46). For our purposes, then, we can describe the Gogo economy as consisting of two essentially independent spheres: a subsistence economy based on growing grains, and a wealth economy based on herding cattle.

As organized for subsistence, the Gogo family was very similar to those of the Kimbu and Nyamwezi (and, for that matter, the Tonga and Suku as well), but its internal organization was perhaps better defined, in light of the patrilineal distinction between wives and between the children of wives. When a man reached the marriageable age of about thirty, he took his first wife, usually a girl in her late teens. She came to live in her husband's father's homestead, where she had her own house. Here she and her husband, and eventually her children, formed a food producing, storing, cooking, and consuming unit. She was allocated her own land by the homestead head (land, being in plentiful supply, was a free good in this region), and she and her husband worked the land together, with little formal division of labor in the agricultural tasks (Rigby 1969:78). When the husband took a second wife, often before any of his sons were of marriageable age, she too received a house and usufruct rights to her own plots of land, where she grew food (again with her husband's assistance), fed herself and her children, and contributed to the domestic support of the husband (Rigby 1969:180). All this time, the man and his wife or wives were living in the same homestead with his father and brothers, at least if his father was alive, but they did not cooperate with the husband's agnates in subsistence activities. When a man's father died, he and his brothers usually dispersed and founded new homesteads of their own, but this made little difference for the subsistence ceremony, where brothers, once adult, did not cooperate anyway. If a woman was widowed young, she might marry an agnate of her husband in widow-inheritance; an older widow usually lived with her son, and was supported, if too old to work, by him and his wives (Rigby 1969:185). As Rigby says, "Agricultural activities and produce are really outside the field of property relations and patrilineal descent" (201), and as such agricultural organization did not differ markedly among the Gogo from that among their poorer, less rigorously patrilineal neighbors.

When we turn from fields to cattle, however, we enter the prestige sphere of the Gogo. Gogo herds were rather large, though not unusually so, by African standards: Rigby estimates an average herd size of 12 per homestead, or a little over one head of cattle per person. Some men were much wealthier, with 100 cattle considered a large herd and a few very rich men owning 800 or 1000. The main use of cattle in this society was as a form of property in social transactions, and it thus stands to reason that "most Gogo men have as their primary aim the accumulation of a large number of live-stock, in general, and cattle in particular" (Rigby 1969:48). A man accumulated cattle by care and breeding, of course, but most importantly by trading, and primarily in bridewealth transactions. Cattle thus meant daughters-in-law, who meant more followers, who meant more opportunities to trade for cattle. Wealth in cattle was thus equated with wealth in dependents, and contrasted with wealth in grain (Rigby 1969:54-5).

How did the competition for cattle and followers (which was really the same thing) affect the family organization? The most important thing to bear in mind is that cattle were controlled by homestead heads. They had certain obligations to fill with the cattle they controlled, but a skillful man could parley a reasonable sized herd into considerable wealth and influence, and could rise to a prominent position as founder of a neighborhood and leader of its council of elders if he had a large number of dependents in his homestead and a considerable number of stock (Rigby 1969:114). So it was in the interests of senior men, homestead heads, to keep control of their cattle, which they did, and it was thus necessary for younger men, who wanted both wives and eventual possibilities of cattle inheritance and political prominence in their own right, to remain in their fathers' homesteads as long as their fathers remained alive. Bridewealth and inheritance were thus the two ways that fathers held their sons to them and gathered up large numbers of dependents. Both bridewealth and inheritance, in turn, influenced the organization of the homestead group, by creating divisions between matricentered houses not just in the subsistence sphere, but in the sphere of control over property. Let us look at each of these control mechanisms in turn.

Bridewealth consisted of fifteen cattle and eleven small stock (Rigby 1969:50). The average herd size of 12 and the existence of herds of a hundred or more underline the difference in the ability of ordinary men and prominent men to acquire wives, daughters-in-law, and thus dependents generally. Bridewealth gave the husband rights to his wife's sexuality and labor, and to the paternity of all of her children (Rigby 1969:244), thus securing not only an increase in the female labor force of the homestead, but the means by which one's own circle of followers, as well as one's own patrilineage, might be increased. A young man was dependent on his father for bridewealth because this was the only way he could gain a wife, but also because it was the only way he could gain rights of paternity over his children. It was possible for a man to marry without bridewealth in Gogo society, but he was then condemned to uxorilocal marriage, dependency on his father-in-law, and his children's belonging to their mother's lineage.

But bridewealth dependency not did not only create father-son solidarity; it also created conflicts, in that a father with a son in his twenties was torn between the possibility of a wife for his son and an additional wife for himself. The moral duty was to get his son a wife, but the strong temptation was to let the lad wait a few years and bring in an additional, younger woman for oneself (Rigby 1969:83). A lot, of course, depended on how much bridewealth a homestead head could bring in for the marriages of his daughters, since girls were married at an earlier age and their bridewealth could thus be used to make marriages for their brothers. There was also a limitation here, set by the fact that cattle were allocated to the house of each wife of a homestead head when she married in. By rights, the cattle allocated to particular house could be used only to acquire a wife for a son of that house, unless the homestead head had the express permission of the wife who was head of that house (Rigby 1969:190). This, of course, could be source of rivalry between houses, but there was nothing a homestead head could do if his wife refused, as she often did, protecting the interests of her own sons, and thus indirectly of herself. The mother's protectiveness of her sons' rights in time enhanced the solidarity of the matrifocal house, as well as exacerbating the rivalry between houses.

Inheritance was the other mechanism by which fathers maintained control over their sons. Men inherited their fathers' cattle when they died, and thus acquired the ability to found their own homesteads and become important elders. They did not necessarily do so immediately upon their father's death—they might remain together under the headship of the eldest brother. But half-brothers almost invariably split not long after their father's death, for they ultimately had rights in different cattle, each set of full brothers inheriting those cattle originally allocated to their own mother's house. If full brothers did stay together until their mother died, they invariably split soon afterward, each becoming head of his own autonomous homestead, though perhaps still living in a neighborhood together with his brothers (Rigby 1969:187-200).

I have discussed the Gogo system at some length, partly because of the rich quality of Rigby's ethnographic writing, but also because their family organization was typical of a large number of cattle-keeping societies in Eastern and Southern Africa. The general form the family in such societies, exemplified by the Gogo case, can be contrasted with the simpler Kimbu and Nyamwezi systems as shown in Figure 9-12. Wherever cattle were found in large numbers, but were not the primary subsistence resource (they might still have been a secondary source of food, hides, etc.), and where land for subsistence purposes is not was not in short supply, we find the same pattern. First, inheritance systems were patrilineal or, if they previously had previously been matrilineal, were strained in a patrilineal direction. This is not only because wealth in general puts strains on a matrilineal system, but also because it takes cooperation among males to

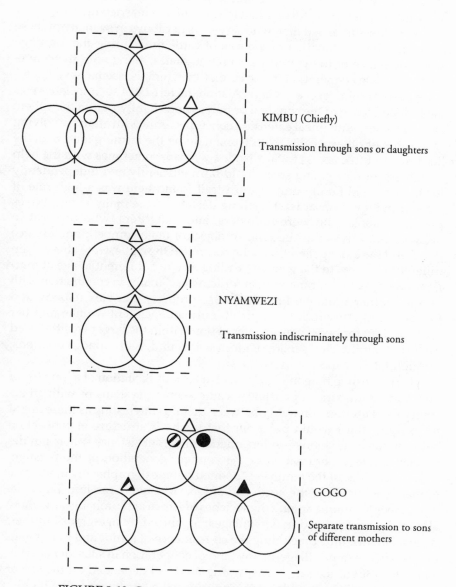

KIMBU (Chiefly)

Transmission through sons or daughters

NYAMWEZI

Transmission indiscriminately through sons

GOGO

Separate transmission to sons
of different mothers

FIGURE 9-12: Comparison of East African Patrilineal Systems

herd cattle. Women with small children were not considered suited to follow cattle to pasture, so this job had to rest with the married men, or, better
still, with the unmarried men who served as herdboys in so many of these
societies. The combination of the role of cattle in ensuring the marriage
and inheritance of the younger generation males, along with the convenience of male cooperation in the care of the animals, seems have led toward patriliny almost everywhere. Also characteristic of such societies was
the independence of the conjugal or polygynous family unit in the sphere
of subsistence, with lineal extension concerned only with affairs involving
with cattle or other wealth. With women doing the farming (and men the
herding) and free access to farmland, a woman, sometimes with the help
daughters and/or young sons, could farm efficiently and independently
for her conjugal family unit. A third trait found here was a high rate of
general polygyny, or at least a strong desire to have many wives. Wives
produced sons, who were followers, and daughters, who brought in
bridewealth. Wives thus became an object of male competition, a scarce
good, and the older generation, who controlled the cattle, were able to gain
differential access to the women, leading also to a differential age at marriage, always older for males than for females. Finally, in conjunction with
all these other traits we find the house-property complex (Goody and
Buckley 1973), in which the agriculturally independent woman and her
own children formed a matri-centered unit within the larger wealth-based
extended family. This general pattern was found, with minor variations,
throughout East and South Africa.

I do not wish to bore the reader with a tedious recitation of a long list of
East and South African patrilineal, cattle-keeping systems or with an account of the minute differences between them, as interesting as these might
be to some. But I would point out that the basic structure of connection
between the generations—independence in the subsistence sphere but dependence and subordination of the younger generation in the prestige-
sphere activities of the family—is pointed out most graphically in the case
of the Nyakyusa near the north end of Lake Malawi in modern Tanzania.
These people, unique among the societies of Africa and probably anywhere
else in the world, lived in age-villages, organized by age-grades of their
male residents, thus precluding the co-residence of senior and junior generations in the same village, or any kind of cooperation in subsistence (Wilson 1963). But at the same time, young men still depended on the senior
generation for bridewealth cattle, and in fact the Nyakyusa had a highly-
developed form of the differentiation between houses, in which a man's
heirs were, in order of preference, a full brother, a brother whose mother
was one's own mother's real or classificatory sister, a half brother linked
by the loan of bridewealth cattle from one house to another, and then a
son, leaving out unlinked half brothers entirely (Wilson 1950:119). Noth-

ing, I think, could be a clearer illustration of the contrast between the polygynous nuclear family cycle in the subsistence sphere and the extended family cycle in the prestige sphere; this contrast is illustrated in Figure 9-14, and lies at the heart of our understanding of many African societies. But it does not work so neatly everywhere; in the next chapters we will consider some cases in which subsistence and wealth goods are not so clearly distinguishable, and in which the developmental cycles of subsistence-holding and wealth-holding groups are thus not quite so separate.

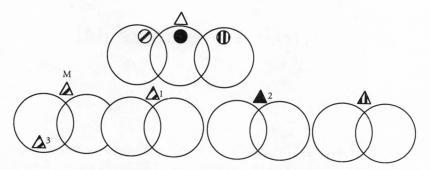

FIGURE 9-13: Nyakyusa Order of Inheritance from M

Notes

1. Goody, however, shows clearly that rates of polygyny cannot be explained by the sexual division of labor alone.

10

African Developmental Cycles: Part Two

If the combination with which we ended Chapter 9—cattle as wealth only, free access to agricultural land, and patriliny—was so widespread and produced such a uniform cluster of developmental cycles, it would stand to reason that if any of these variables were altered, we would find a different form of family organization. And this is in fact true. To show this, we now proceed to examine cases that deviated in one or more of these variables.

First let us look at situations where land was not a free good. In the kingdoms immediately to the north of Lake Victoria, the highly centralized Ganda state and the smaller, but in many ways similar, states of Busoga, the primary resources men were competing for were not cattle—cattle were not suited to the lacustrine environment—but political prominence and eminence at court, achieved through the favor of the hereditary rulers. In these kingdoms, subsistence was as easy, probably, as anywhere in Africa. All that people (and this means almost entirely women) had to do was to plant banana trees and wait for them to grow, and then harvest the fruits. And subsistence was not only easy, it was extraordinarily stable, freeing the Ganda and Soga from the threat of famine that was in the background almost everywhere else on the continent (Wrigley 1964:17).

In the absence of a centralized state, this ease of subsistence probably would have meant relatively free access to land even with the high population density in this area. But in fact chiefs used their territorial rights of granting land in order to create dependence among inhabitants of their districts. This created a rather "Oceanic" pattern (see Part IV), in which regulation of access to subsistence goods was a mechanism of building and maintaining prestige. And the nature of prestige goods—ivory, slaves, patronage or influence at court, and control of access to land, acquired through chiefly favor, trade activity, or inheritance—did not depend on close daily cooperation, as was the case with cattle. In addition, bridewealth was very low (Richards 1964:258), so there was little in either the domestic or the prestige sphere to attach the senior and the junior generation on a day-to-day basis, and Soga sons who reached maturity during their fathers' lifetimes set up their own separate homesteads and began the patrilocal polygynous family cycle anew, as illustrated in Figure 10-1 (Fallers 1956:81; Southwold 1965:101).

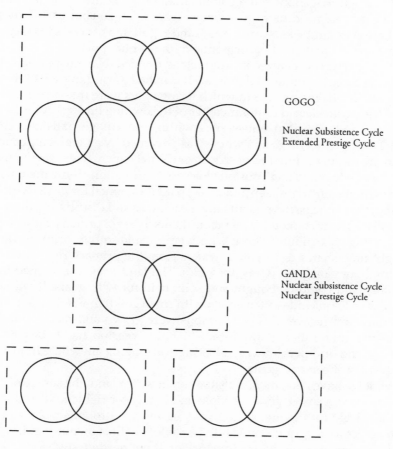

GOGO

Nuclear Subsistence Cycle
Extended Prestige Cycle

GANDA
Nuclear Subsistence Cycle
Nuclear Prestige Cycle

FIGURE 10-1: Subsistence and Prestige Groups

In effect, in these kingdoms, in particular the centralized Buganda Kingdom, the power of the senior generation over the junior was replaced by
the power of the state and its agents over both senior and junior males, so
that the relationship between the nuclear or polygynous nuclear family
and the leadership of the prestige sphere was a direct one, only weakly
mediated by the authority of senior kin. We thus have a polygynous nuclear
family cycle, pure and simple, in these areas.

We can see another kind of effect of scarce land resources on the general,
patrilineal African type if we look at the Sonjo, a predominantly agricultural people of northern Tanzania, who also kept some livestock, but few
cattle. The Sonjo lived in an area surrounded by the pastoral, nomadic, and
generally hostile Maasai, with whom warfare was frequent in the nineteenth century (Gray 1964:235). Agriculture was possible in the Sonjo area
only through irrigation, and a combination of the limited land available,
and the general need to acquire water-rights to make land useful, meant
that here also, land was a scarce good, and regulation of access to land was
an important function of participation in the public sphere.

The Sonjo were organized into patriclans, divided then into patrilineages
of two or three generations depth. Each clan had a ward in each of the six
large Sonjo villages, an area in which its members were free to reside. The
ward leader, an elected senior member of the owning lineage, adjudicated
disputes and allocated house-sites within the village palisade (Gray
1964:233-35). The village as a whole was governed by a hereditary council
of elders, usually composed of sixteen or eighteen men. It was this council,
as a corporate body, that controlled access to irrigation. Some men, those
who owned sufficient sheep and goats, paid the council for primary rights
to land, the council in turn sacrificing the animals and distributing the meat
at a village feast. The council members themselves got primary rights without paying this tribute. Those who were unable to buy primary rights
bought time-shares of irrigation waters from the primary rights owners,
paying honey or grain (Gray 1964:236). The land itself was owned individually, and could be bought and sold, paid for with goats. It was also
possible to lease land—often a man with small children would lease some
land out, and recover it when his sons were grown and ready to marry
wives to farm for them (Gray 1964:240). But wives, too, had to be paid for
in stock, and bridewealth was rather high, averaging anywhere from 60 to
300 head of sheep and goats.

What we have here, then, is a situation in which land, the source of subsistence, was a scarce good—people had to pay for rights to it, and there
was a market for buying, selling, and leasing. Control of stock was thus
both necessary to acquire land and a possible benefit of owning land, which
could be leased out in return for stock or, if not needed, sold. Stock were
wealth, even a medium of exchange, but were of little use without land—

in order to make a marriage for a son, for example, a man needed not only to pay bridewealth for the woman, but also acquire rights to additional land, or, if he had rented or sold land earlier when the son was small, pay goats to get it back again. And in addition, he had to give additional goats to the village council in order to acquire rights to irrigation water, without which land itself was no use. Thus the prestige sphere of wealth transactions impinged directly on the subsistence sphere, and was able to do so because the crucial subsistence resources, land and water, were in short supply.

In this kind of a situation, the family system was again somewhat different from that found among the cattle-peoples. Essentially, Sonjo marriage was monogamous. At any time, an observer might find 10 percent or so of the marriages in a Sonjo village to be polygynous, but these were almost all the result of widow-inheritance, and Gray states that it was very rare for a man to pay bridewealth for more than one wife. The reason, of course, is not that bridewealth was too high in its own right, but that marriage made no sense in the absence of land, and land was in scarce supply, and so it became infeasible for most men to think of acquiring the stock necessary to purchase or redeem the necessary land to allocate to a wife to cultivate, and at the same time to pay the considerable bridewealth. In effect, with land, rather than wives, being the main object of competition and the public good that wealth in stock went to pay for, a braking mechanism was placed on a man's ability to build up a large personal homestead or following. Household membership was thus not allowed to grow too large, being kept in line by the limited availability of land. Differential prestige was still there; in particular those with primary irrigation rights, as well as members of the village council and ward heads, had considerable standing, reinforced by their control of the important resources of stock, water, and land. But it was difficult to translate this into a personal following.

In such a monogamous system, the developmental cycle of course looked different from that of the polygynous systems we have been examining (Figure 10-2). Women did most of the cultivation labor here, with men's work limited to cleaning out and maintaining the irrigation channels (Gray 1964:237). As mentioned above, a marriage required land, and a family's subsistence was gotten as an independent unit, working on that land. Also, the family was likely to remain an autonomous, nuclear family unit, with none of the labor or property divisions typically created by the establishment of separate houses and house-property with the marriage of a second wife. Men throughout their lives remained tied to their fathers in the prestige sphere, however, because they stood to inherit their fathers' stock, land, and irrigation rights (Gray 1964:248). A similar situation prevailed half a continent away among the Kofyar, where land scarcity made inheritance

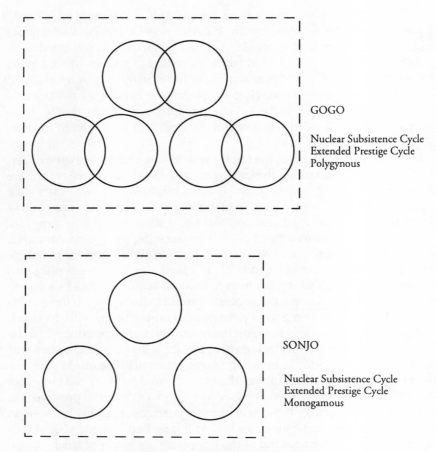

FIGURE 10-2: Gogo and Sonjo Systems Compared

from the senior generation an important way of gaining rights to subsistence resources (Netting 1968:168-172).

A somewhat similar situation of limited access to land occurred among the Lozi of Zambia, but for different reasons. The Lozi lived on mounds in the Zambezi river plain, surrounded not by hostile pastoralists but by seasonal waters. The amount of land available for settlement and agriculture was thus limited by the flood cycle (Gluckman 1950:167). Since rights to land in this area were limited by the number of people who could live on a mound and farm the gardens attached to it, since the mounds themselves were sometimes widely separated form each other by water in the flood season, and since the Lozi were long organized into the centralized Barotsestate, it follows that the important social groups in this society were organized on the basis of the mounds and were thus territorial, or village groups, rather than lineages or any kind of groups based on unilineal kinship principles (Gluckman 1950:177). Each village had a recognized head, who represented all inhabitants of the village in its dealings with the royal court and with the "sector" chiefs subordinate to the king (Gluckman 1951:31, 66). The king and chiefs were not allowed to interfere in the internal affairs of the village-group, but the village head, in turn, was expected to lead his people in paying formal respect to the king, recruiting soldiers for the king's armies, working on public labor projects, and rendering tribute to the court. The king, in turn, was expected to provide protection, grant land to those lacking it, allow people in emergencies to use the products of his own gardens, and give various other kinds of aid in times of need (Gluckman 1951:20). People were thus tied into the national structure by their membership in the territorial, village unit, which was also the group through which they received rights in agricultural land.

In this system, autonomy of the parent-child unit in subsistence production was almost a necessity. With the vagaries of demographic increase and decrease, combined with forced movements of people for military and political reasons (Gluckman 1950:171), there developed a necessity for a conjugal unit to be able to move and take up residence anywhere there was land available. This could not be done at random, but could be done through a variety of kinship connections. Any Lozi had the right to make his or her home in the village of any of his or her parents or grandparents, in effect giving people a wide range of choices within which to adapt to demographic, ecological, or political pressure (Gluckman 1950:171). Wherever a man lived, he had rights of inheritance, but he simultaneously forfeited his rights of inheritance in the villages of his other parents and grandparents. When a man died, his heir was chosen by a council of his bilateral male and female kin from among his sons, brothers, brothers' sons, sisters' sons, sons' sons, or daughters' sons, i.e. from practically any male consanguine of his own or a lower generation (Gluckman 1950:172). The Lozi had, then, rather than the discrete extended family group organized for prestige reasons, as in the patrilineal societies previously described, a bilateral kindred, an overlapping network that could be mobilized for the purposes of transmission of village membership, political office, and property.

Lozi were polygynous, and also kept cattle, but did not use the cattle in bridewealth payments (Gluckman 1950:192). All this made for quite unstable marriage, and for a system in which a woman's primary ties remained with her own kin even though she ordinarily resided virilocally. Since property and succession went to a single heir, not chosen according to any rigid principles, there was no house-property complex in this society—co-wives ordinarily gardened separately, but did not form the focus of houses, as in the classical patrilineal, cattle-paying groups (Gluckman 1950:193). The overall developmental cycle could thus be represented by the accretion and eventual breakup, at the time of marriage of the sons, of the potentially polygynous nuclear family. Its attachments to relatives of other generations were in the nature of a kinship network, not an extended family group.

It is interesting to note that the Sonjo and Lozi reacted to potential land scarcity in different ways. Sonjo developed a patrilineal system, but one in which a balance between people and resources was maintained by a system of land ownership and marriage payments which practically enjoined monogamy and kept the stationary patrilineage from growing too fast at the expense of other local groups. The Lozi system, on the other hand, allowed rapid expansion of the domestic group with polygyny, but facilitated its geographical redistribution in light of available resources (Figure 10-3).

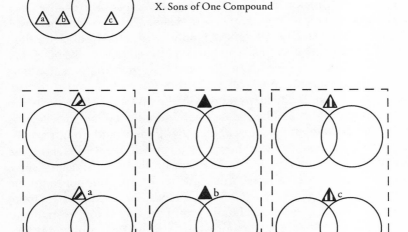

X. Sons of One Compound

Y, Z Settle in Father's or Mother's Villages

FIGURE 10-3: Lozi Developmental Cycle

In neither case did the scarcity of land lead to the impoverishment of some at the expense of others—the products of subsistence work had not yet become involved in the prestige sphere, though prestigious men did power over the allocation of the producer goods. But men prominent in the prestige sphere in both these societies used this control over allocation of producer goods to enhance their prestige directly, not to claim for themselves any portion of the product at the expense of those less fortunate. In this sense, these systems somewhat resemble the systems of Oceanic islands, to be discussed in Part IV.

A third deviation from the model of agriculture as subsistence, cattle as prestige occurred where cattle themselves became the basic subsistence resource. Depending on how many cattle there were, this might have several different kinds of results, in both the subsistence and the prestige aspects of the family developmental cycle. Let us first look at the Turkana of northwestern Kenya, a group whose cattle were plentiful enough to serve both as a reservoir of wealth and as the sole subsistence resource, without the one use much limiting the other. The Turkana lived (and still live) in an area of very low rainfall and high evaporation, where no agriculture is possible, so their stock, including cattle, camels, and goats, were the only source of livelihood (Gulliver 1955:14). But because of the ecology of the Turkana area, to ensure this livelihood required division of labor among a rather large force. Women usually took care of the domestic and watering tasks, while men were in charge of herding and finding pasturage. The latter was a problem. During the brief rainy season, there was pasturage enough for the cattle on the Turkana plains, where the people preferred to live, and there was also browse for the camels and goats. When the dry season came, however, the grass on the plains withered, and the herds had to be divided, with the goats and camels remaining in the plains but the cattle going to the mountains where they could graze on the remaining grass (Gulliver 1955:27-28). Thus any Turkana herd owner had to divide not only the stock but the family's labor, keeping at least one adult male and one adult female in each ecological zone during the dry part of the year. This meant that, although sons desired to be independent from their fathers for subsistence purposes, they could not do so until their own families included enough labor (and this usually meant a son old enough to be a responsible herdboy) so they could be divided between the cattle in the mountains and the browsing stock on the plains (Gulliver 1955:40).

In light of this, the developmental cycle of the Turkana subsistence group had to undergo a patrilocal joint phase of some sort in each generation. Typically, men married late (older unmarried men, in their 20s, usually were put in charge of the secondary cattle homesteads in the mountains, while their fathers remained in the plains), and even after marriage, they remained part of a joint stock-raising and milk-consuming unit until they had sons old enough to take responsibility in the secondary camps, or unless they could persuade an unmarried brother or some other relative to join their subsistence units. A married man with more than one wife usually allocated most of his stock to the houses of the respective wives, and the young men growing up, when they become independent, had as the nuclei of their own herds those cattle originally allocated to their respective mothers' houses (Gulliver 1955:128, 156). When the breakup finally came, when a son took his own stock and his own labor force and became independent from his father for subsistence purposes, he might well take his mother with him, especially if his father had other wives. So eventually, the houses within the polygynous families provided the framework upon which the junior generation divided up into independent families of its own (Gulliver 1955:143). But in whatever phase of the developmental cycle, whether the subsistence unit was the polygynous nuclear family or some variation of the patrilocal extended family, it pooled its resources for subsistence purposes. Cattle belonged to various houses, but their products belonged to the family as a whole as long as it cooperated for subsistence purposes (Gulliver 1955:130).

If the subsistence family cycle among the Turkana included a patrilocal joint phase until the sons developed a large enough labor force to subsist on their own, the wealth-controlling family cycle kept the sons together with their father until his death, in the familiar East African cattle-society manner. Turkana paid very large bridewealth, in the 1950s usually around fifty large stock (cattle and camels) plus a hundred or so goats, and even with the large herds that the Turkana kept, a man, even one who was independent for subsistence purposes, had to rely on his father, if still alive, to contribute most of the bridewealth cattle (Gulliver 1955:22). So the extended family remained together for wealth-controlling purposes until the death of the father. The contrast between the Turkana system, where cattle were both subsistence goods and wealth, and the typical East African mixed system, where cattle were wealth only, is illustrated in Figure 10-4.

Turkana herds were large enough that they could serve as repositories of wealth and sources of food at the same time. In fact, the two uses of cattle seem to have been hardly connected at all in Turkana society. As Gulliver states, there were frequent disputes and arguments about livestock, but these always concerned what he calls the "social" (i.e. the prestige), rather than the "economic" (i.e. subsistence) uses of animals (Gulliver 1955:32). Other pastoral peoples, however, were not so fortunate, and had to curtail the prestige use of cattle in order to insure the economical livelihood of family members. This was the situation among the Wodaabe Pastoral Fulani of Northeast Nigeria, for example—they were exclusively pastoral and kept rather large herds of cattle, but paid no bridewealth.

For the Pastoral Fulani, the problem of subsistence was not, as among the Turkana, simply one of securing enough labor to range widely with the large herds in search of pasture; instead it was one of keeping a rather precarious balance between the labor necessary for the pastoral economy, on the one hand, and the cattle necessary to feed the family, on the other.

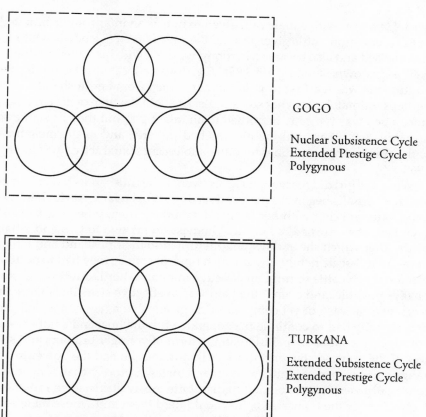

GOGO

Nuclear Subsistence Cycle
Extended Prestige Cycle
Polygynous

TURKANA

Extended Subsistence Cycle
Extended Prestige Cycle
Polygynous

FIGURE 10-4: Gogo and Turkana Systems

No matter what size herd, the minimum labor force consisted of a grown man and a boy, to take care of the herding when the grown man was attending to other business, social or political, and a grown woman and a girl to take care of milking, processing, and other domestic tasks (Stenning 1958:104). The minimum herd necessary to feed this minimal labor unit consisted of one bull and at least 25 head of cattle. If the labor force increased, then the size of the herd had to increase, but in order to build up a really large herd, more labor was required.

In this situation, the payment of large numbers of cattle as bridewealth was obviously precluded—it would, so to speak, have introduced violent fluctuations into the size of herds, throwing them all out of proportion with the laboring units necessary to take care of them and the consuming units dependent on them for subsistence. Instead, a son was prepared for his marriage by a gradual buildup of what would eventually become his herd. He began with a male calf, given to him as an infant, and continued with several more cattle given around the age of seven to ten, when he was circumcised and also became a herdboy, working with his father's cattle as well as his own Stenning 1958:93). A girl was allocated no cattle in her youth—she was fed first from her father's, then from her husband's, and perhaps ultimately from her son's cattle. At about the time of his circumcision, a boy was typically betrothed to an infant girl, but they had little to do with each other until the girl reached puberty, and in the meantime both sexes had opportunities for other adolescent sexual activity (Stenning 1965:392).

When the girl did reach puberty, she went to her husband's father homestead, where she began sleeping and having sexual relations with her husband, and working with her husband's mother. Then, when she became pregnant, she returned to her natal homestead for two to two and a half years, after which she and her child returned to their husband and father to set up full-scale family life, at which time, of course, they had to be allocated enough cattle to form an effective minimum herd. But this was not always possible, and even if the herd was of effective size, the labor force to go with it was not yet complete. This means that a newly married son and his wife had to continue to cooperate with the husband's father—he could supply labor cooperation, in the form of younger brothers and sisters of the married son, or if this was impossible, he had the power to arrange various loans of cattle with other agnates, a process that, for subsistence purposes at least, tended to distribute the available stock rather effectively over the homesteads that could herd them and whose members drank their milk (Stenning 1958:116).

But eventually, the son and his wife became independent. If a man had many sons, he continued to allocate his remaining herds to each one in turn as he reached maturity and had children, until at the end of the cycle an old man had no more sons at home and no more cattle, and became a useless dependent. He and his wife or wives usually lived separately at this time, each sleeping in a makeshift platform on the periphery of a married son's homestead (Stenning 1958:99). In fact, in many cases his wives would have left him even earlier. It was common among the Pastoral Fulani for a man to divorce his wife when she had no children to add to his potential labor forc. When she reached menopause, she was obviously no longer useful for reproductive purposes, and the couple usually separated (Stenning 1958:107). On the other hand, a wife had usually divorced her husband even before this if the ratio of cattle to people in the homestead decreased dramatically, which it could if cattle died in the dry season, if the husband took a second wife (who exercised a claim on the herds and produced offspring who would exercise a further claim), or if the husband used too many cattle to purchase items of real prestige value, such as horses and guns, for himself or to present to a Kanuri chief at Bornu in exchange for a political office or title (Stenning 1958:108).

We thus see again the conflict between the use of cattle for food and the use of cattle for exchange value—the latter, the exclusive province of men, competed directly with the women's concern for their security and that of their children. This need for security precluded the transfer of very large numbers of cattle in bridewealth, as it did among the exclusively pastoral Hima of the Ankole kingdom in Uganda—Hima paid a relatively low bridewealth, many of the cattle were returned with the bride, and they were also concerned with balancing the ratio of cattle with family members so that neither got too large for the other's labor or milk supply (Elam 1973:69).

This does not, however, explain why the Fulani paid no bridewealth at all. Perhaps it was because the most important positions of prestige in this society were acquired not so much by increasing the size of one's household as by solidifying one's household's alliances or by acquiring other prestige goods. The difference between the Turkana, who had large herds and paid high bridewealth, and the Fulani, who had large herds and paid no bridewealth, would thus lie in the fact that the Fulani were part of a wider social order containing some features of complex societies and organized around the Kanuri and Hausa emirates. To achieve real prestige, they had to deal in the prestige goods of this larger social system—guns, houses, and political offices. The Turkana, on the other hand, were part of no social system but their own, and in their system prestige came from building a personal following (Figure 10-5).

In both the preceding cases, the Turkana and the Pastoral Fulani, we saw how the need for male cooperation in subsistence labor—in both these cases, the herding of cattle—created a developmental cycle where patrilineal joint family ties of one sort or another were maintained not only in the prestige sphere, something common to nearly all cattle-keeping societies in Africa, but in the subsistence sphere as well. There were other societies, however, particularly in West Africa, where male participation in labor also held patrilocal extended families together, even though the labor was cultivation of the land.

There is no compelling reason I can see why agricultural labor should be primarily or exclusively the province of women in most East African societies, while it is mainly men's work over most of West Africa (Goody and Buckley 1973:111). Nevertheless, this was the statistical tendency. And where it was the common pattern, across a wide range of wealth and state organization in patrilineal societies in West Africa, it made for patrilocal extended families, cooperating in both the subsistence and the prestige spheres.

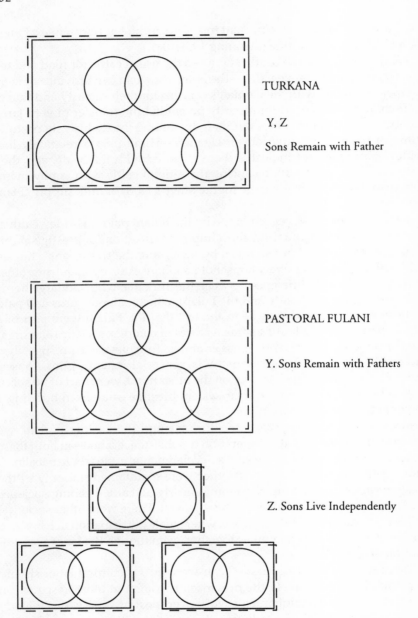

FIGURE 10-5: Turkana and Pastoral Fulani Systems

As a first example of such a family system, let us examine the Tiv of eastern Nigeria, an agricultural people with no cattle in late precolonial times, and only a small amount of trade goods (Bohannan 1965:519-52).

The Tiv had a segmentary lineage system, with a lineage segment about four or five generations deep owning a territory in which all male members of that lineage segment were free to build their compounds and farm any land that was not currently under cultivation in their bush-fallow swidden cycle (Bohannan 1954:8-13). These compounds were occupied by patrilocal joint families made up of polygynous-cycle nuclear families, and cooperated as a whole in their subsistence activities. Men did most of the heavy agricultural work, and women the lighter tasks, in a rather rigid division of labor (Bohannan 1954:21). Among the lands farmed by the members of a compound, each married woman had her own plots, the produce of which went to feed herself and her children, and to contribute food to her husband. But the labor was done cooperatively, under the active supervision of the compound head (Bohannan 1954:22-3). We thus find within the compound a subsistence production group, consisting of all the adult male and female residents of the compound, and a subsistence consumption group, consisting of the nuclear family or the component matrisegment of the polygynous nuclear family. Eventually a compound broke up, usually soon after the death of the senior generation, each son heading an independent compound of his own, which he could locate anywhere in his minimal lineage territory (Bohannan 1954:6). This system is illustrated in Figure 10-6.

What, then, of the prestige sphere? In general, it was very small among the Tiv, and consisted of rights over persons unmediated by control over any form of wealth (there was very little material wealth). Bohannan states that the Tiv "correlated a man's wealth and influence with the size of his family and the number of his dependents" (Bohannan 1954:50), and here as in other patrilineal systems we find that a man accreted dependents by bringing in wives. But with little material wealth that could be paid for wives, they had to be acquired in exchange for other women. This was done by a system in which a small lineage (of shorter span than the territory-owning group) had marriage-ward rights over its member women. One of these could be exchanged in marriage for a woman of another lineage. But since a direct exchange was not always possible, an alternative marriage could be made, in which the eldest daughter of a marriage contracted without giving a woman in exchange then became the marriage-ward of her mother's natal group, thus creating a complex system in which most marriage exchanges, in the early twentieth century, were one or more generations in arrears[1] (Bohannan 1965:526-7).

The important point about this marriage-exchange system, it seems to me, is that it placed the most important transactions in the prestige sphere,

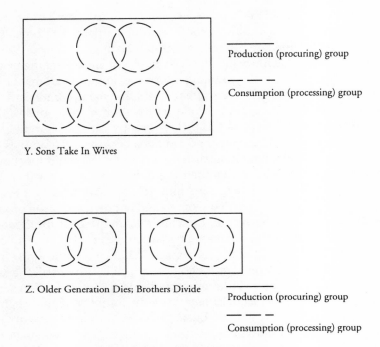

Y. Sons Take In Wives

Production (procuring) group

Consumption (processing) group

Z. Older Generation Dies; Brothers Divide

Production (procuring) group

Consumption (processing) group

FIGURE 10-6: Tiv Subsistence Cycle

those concerning marriage and the recruitment of members to the domestic group and the lineage, outside the control of the leaders of the domestic groups altogether. Domestic groups needed women for labor and reproduction, but they did not get them, as it were, through their own efforts—there was nothing that the domestic group produced, such as cattle, which might enable it to foster its leader's ambitions in the public sphere. Also, with the absence of any significant material wealth, the most important prestige "goods" were rights in persons, acquired only by exchange for rights in other persons. The full complexity of the Tiv system is illustrated in Figure 10-7.

The Tallensi of northern Ghana, still a relatively poor people, but one with some cattle to use in paying bridewealth and for ritual slaughter to enhance one's prestige within one's patrilineage, presented a rather different case of interaction between domestic and prestige spheres, though the domestic organization itself was remarkably similar to that of the Tiv. The Tallensi practiced both fixed and shifting cultivation; although fixed fields were highly valued and carefully tended, competition for land or desire to accumulate it were considered wrong (Fortes 1949:83). Land was worked generally by the homestead group, which followed a patrilocal polygynous-joint family cycle. The senior male of the homestead, while he was

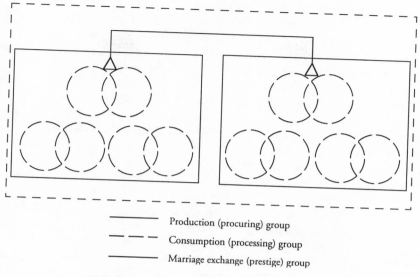

——————— Production (procuring) group

— — — — Consumption (processing) group

——————— Marriage exchange (prestige) group

FIGURE 10-7: Tiv Multilevel Nested Groups

alive, continued to control the products of agriculture, even when he had one or more married sons living in his homestead with him. The household head's granary, looming high in the middle of the compound, symbolized this subsistence-sphere authority in several ways. Only the head himself, or perhaps a trusted senior wife, could enter the granary, which the head or his senior wife did often, in order to get grain for the use of the wives of the homestead. Thus even though they ordinarily cooked separately, wives were dependent on a common source for their staple food (they grew vegetables for sauces and relishes separately in their own gardens near the homestead) (Fortes 1949:128). In addition, a man's eldest son was not allowed even to look into his father's granary while the father was alive: the culmination of the process of generational succession came at the father's funeral, when the son was ritually "shown" his father's granary for the first time (Fortes 1949:208 pl.).

The Tallensi prestige sphere consisted of three interrelated kinds of "goods": followers, stock, and ritual authority. As Fortes points out, children were, for a man "the most ardently desired of all ends" (1949:82). But to achieve this end, a man ordinarily had to have stock, for it took four head of cattle as bridewealth to give a man rights over his children. In such a system, we would expect a relatively high rate of polygyny, and indeed we find one: about 40% of married men were estimated to have more than one wife at any given time (Fortes 1949:126). Polygyny, however, did not mean the creation of house-property, for the rules of inheritance were such that a man's property went first to his eldest son, then to his next son, and so on down the line of brothers, without regard to their maternity. In spite of this, the bond between full brothers was recognized as being qualitatively different from that between half brothers, but this may have stemmed from the residential unity of the maternal segment within the extended household.

Still, possession of stock enabled a man to participate in the public sphere in ways other than through acquiring potential followers by paying bridewealth. Stock were also used in ritual sacrifices performed by the elders of lineages at various levels of the hierarchy of segmentation, and were also used as gifts to the Mamprussi overlords of the Tallensi, who in turn confirmed the givers in office (Fortes 1949:82). The junior generation of males was thus dependent on the elders, who controlled property, not only for wives, but also for ritual protection through ancestral sacrifices and for eventual inheritance of the cattle that would enable them, in their turn, to become fully adult males who had a voice in political affairs and a chance to become important men. It is perhaps noteworthy that although quarrels over inheritance of land were occasionally reported, they were considered wrong, and for two reasons. First, there was considered to be adequate land to go around. Second, land was either the patrimony of the corporate lineage or a grant from a Mamprussi lord, and people ought not to compete for it in the way that they competed for control of followers, wealth, and office.

We should note here that, because of the cooperation of males in agriculture and the household head's control over grain, the domestic group organized for subsistence purposes here often (though not always) coincided with that organized for the prestige sphere. This may have strengthened the overall authority of the household head or even exacerbated the well-known tensions between fathers and sons in this society, but the control exercised by the household head in each sphere was distinct. He could not use the farm labor of his homestead to create cattle, nor could control over prestige goods make much difference in the material standard of living. Here as in most of Africa, subsistence was subsistence and politics was politics—two distinct spheres of operations, here often concentrated in the same group. The difference with an East-African cattle society should thus be clear (Figure 10-8).

As a final example of a society with extended families organized to carry out both the subsistence- and the prestige-sphere activities, we can look at one of the wealthiest and most highly differentiated cities in all of sub-Saharan Africa: the Hausa of the emirate of Zaria. Here as in other emirates of what is now northern Nigeria there was social differentiation of a sort qualitatively different from that found in almost any of our previous examples, with the partial exception of Asante. In Zaria there were different

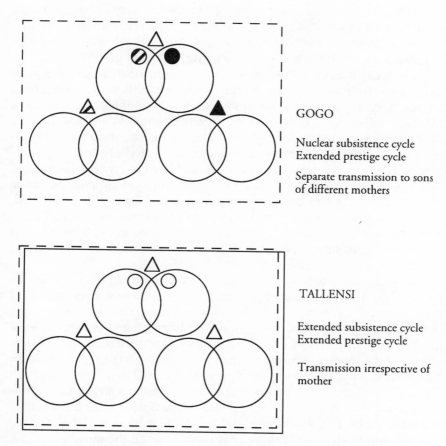

GOGO

Nuclear subsistence cycle
Extended prestige cycle

Separate transmission to sons
of different mothers

TALLENSI

Extended subsistence cycle
Extended prestige cycle

Transmission irrespective of
mother

FIGURE 10-8: Tallensi Compared with an East African Cattle System

occupational orders, living on the whole at different standards of consumption. There were the emir and his officers— both the staff of courtiers and the line organization of chiefs and ward-heads—there were the urban craftspeople, and there were the ordinary farmers. The government and its employees in this society were supported by the tribute collected by chiefs from farmers and, in the 19th century at least, by heads of various craft organizations from the people practicing those crafts (M.G. Smith 1955:6-10). The chiefs, in turn, were supported by being allowed to keep ten percent of the taxes they collected, the majority of which went to the central administration. There were certain lineages whose members were hereditarily eligible to succeed to chiefships, and within these lineages, competition for office was extreme, with wealth a major requisite for being chosen. Wealth in this society was, as elsewhere in Africa, connected with followers—a wealthy man could get clients, and a man with many clients might be appointed to a chiefship, which in turn could bring him more wealth. But wealth here also meant differences in consumption levels—being able to show one's wealth in one's style of living (M.G. Smith 1955:14).

This society thus shows two major differences in the structure of its prestige sphere from what we have seen before. First, there was something approaching a system of social classes. Chiefs, high officials, members of the court did not work for a living, but lived off tribute. While this seems to have stopped short of the kind of exploitation which creates a class of landless laborers (perhaps because there seems not to have been heavy pressure on land), nevertheless some families did live entirely off the fruits of others' labor: there was in a sense a small exploiting class. Second, the goods of the subsistence and prestige spheres were not sharply distinguished, even functionally—consumption at a higher level was an index of prestige, and men in high position could, through a kind of tax-farming, gain subsistence goods in surplus, which might then be marketed and turned into luxury consumer goods (M.G. Smith 1965:128).

The subsistence organization of the Zaria Hausa (or, perhaps more accurately, the agricultural organization, for there were few families, at least in the early 20th century, who did not market some of their crop) resembled closely those we found for the basically undifferentiated Tiv and Tallensi groups. That is, men did all the productive agricultural labor, and they often did it cooperatively, sons remaining with their fathers in common agricultural units for at least some period after their marriages, although they tended to separate from their brothers and fathers and to form separate productive units beginning typically some time in their middle thirties (M.G. Smith 1955:26). Women did the inside work only, and the wives of a patrilocal extended farming unit cooked for all the members of the unit in rotation (M.G. Smith 1955:20).

But this agricultural unit was not just a subsistence unit. Not only could its products be traded in the markets and thus converted to wealth and the possibility of higher status, but with economic differentiation between the various occupational groups in the city, it became important to try to marry within one's own economic level; bridewealth was much higher when marriages violated this norm (M.G. Smith 1955:49). The status of the daughter-in-law's natal family became a matter of concern to the husband's people, and vice-versa. Marriage was no longer simply a way for a man to achieve followers through the reproductive power of the wife, or a way for a woman to ensure her own security with offspring, as in so many African systems. The wife herself became an aspect of the prestige sphere, and in the most prestigious marriages, she was actually secluded in the household, or at least the fiction of seclusion was maintained (M.G. Smith 1955:50-51, 64). And, as we might expect with the wife's parents concerned for her welfare in her husband's family, and that welfare being looked upon as partly con-sisting in standards of consumption, the wife was given a dowry at mar-riage, roughly balancing the value of the bridewealth (M.G. Smith 1955:54). This not only assisted in assuring the daughter a reasonable physical stan-dard of living in her husband's house; it also gave her own family an op-portunity to display its wealth (M.G. Smith 1955:54.). Here, certainly, are the beginnings in sub-Saharan Africa of complex societies with C-cluster kinds of family systems: make the land itself scarce and an object of com-petition, enlarge the "exploiting" class a bit, and you have a typical com-plex society. The intermediate position of the Zaria Hausa between more typical A-cluster systems (here represented by the Tiv) and a patrilineal C-cluster system (here represented by the Greek peasants; see Chapter 19), is shown in Figure 10-9.

Subsistence, Prestige, and African Family Organization

From the preceding "Cook's tour" of some representative African fam-ily systems, we can extract some points that emphasize the unitary nature of most of the family systems to be found on that continent. Most impor-tant is the distinction that has to be drawn between the subsistence activi-ties of the family—productive and processing divisions of labor, as well as child socialization-and the prestige-sphere activities of property manage-ment and transmission, representation, and enabling. Though African domestic groups, as we have seen in Chapter 7, were in fact organized for the performance of all these activities (and sexual and emotional ones as well), what group was organized for one set of activities was usually rela-tively independent of what group was organized for the other set. The developmental cycle of the subsistence group was usually not influenced by much other than the requirements of the particular subsistence technol-ogy. When we look at the other developmental cycle, that of the family prestige activities themselves, particularly with the kind of wealth that or-ganized for the prestige activities, we find that it had little to do with the subsistence strategies, but everything to do with the nature of the wealth that was competed for and exchanged as a means to acquiring prominence in politics and society generally. It is only when we reach something ap-proaching the true complex societies of the Eurasian area that, as Lancaster puts it, the "political economy has become interested ... in the daily round of subsistence" (1976:554), that is, subsistence goods made a difference in the competition for prestige and power. In most of Africa, this did not hap-pen, and even though the same people participated in domestic groups

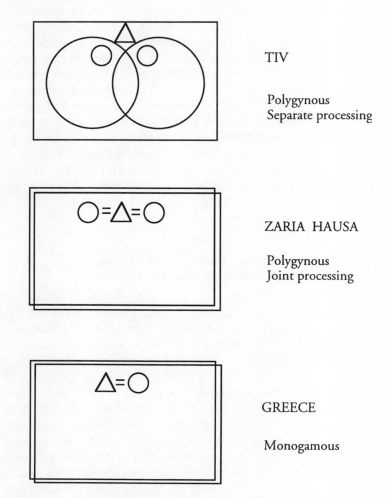

FIGURE 10-9: Hausa as Transitional Between A-Cluster and C-Cluster Systems

organized for the performance of both sets of activities, the groups were not necessarily organized the same way, because the requirements for success in the two spheres were often quite different.

A second point is that the difference between organizing for subsistence and organizing for public competition often, in Africa, coincided with the difference in interests, or goals, between men and women. As the Swazi said in the 1940s, "Polygyny is the nature of men, while the nature of women is satisfied thorough their children" (Kuper 1950:89). This, in a society where wives and children were regarded as a man's greatest assets, meant essentially that men were interested in becoming prominent, while women were interested in maintaining their own security through their offspring. In contrast to B-cluster societies, where both men and women were purely concerned with security, and where striving for prominence was strongly discouraged, here in the A-cluster the striving for security was still there for both sexes, but for the men had become overshadowed by the public or political overlay of striving for status and prominence. But it is important to remember that, in the A-cluster, this public sphere was still but an overlay. Very rarely did it directly influence the organization of domestic groups of subsistence purposes. In terms of the scheme laid out in the introduction to this work, the connection was primarily one-way—it was the enabling connection only, without the allocation connection.

In this regard, it is also important to point out that women often took an active part in public life in certain parts of Africa, but that when they did so, they usually did it by assuming roles ordinarily reserved for the other gender. Gender role boundaries were permeable in many (though certainly not all) African societies, but this does not mean that the roles themselves were not clearly delineated in the first place.

This division of interests between men and women goes a long way, I think, toward explaining what Jack Goody has characterized as an almost universal characteristic of African societies: homogeneous transmission of property, in which, even though property might pass by either a patrilineal or a matrilineal route, it always passed from one man to another, never through daughters (J. Goody 1976:7). The reason this is true is simply that the things inherited, in almost all the societies we have examined, were purely things of prestige sphere, and thus of interest only to men. Women's "nature" in the African definition, could be realized through binding their children to them for physical and emotional support, while property, inheritance, and politics were things of the men.

Finally, I must point out that although the tools developed here for explaining the differences and, in a general evolutionary way, the development of African family systems from the poorest to the richest, in terms of wealth, and simpler "cultural ecology" tools used for explaining differences in subsistence organization, can nevertheless not explain everything. One variable, for example, that defies any kind of definitive explanation, is that of matrilineal and patrilineal organization. Once we assume one or the other of these unilineal systems at some point in history, we can see the pressures exerted in the development of certain kinds of political and economic systems, which tend to make one of these systems evolve in a certain way or even, under some circumstances, change wholly or partially into the other. But we still cannot explain why these systems were there in the first place. This is not, I should emphasize, merely a cop-out. It is a legitimate historical question—unless we refuse to believe that the way society was organized in my parents' time has anything to do with the way

I will conceive of and try to organize society in my own time, such "cultural explanations" are not merely what is left over in the interstices of a materialist explanation; rather they are subjects of legitimate historical inquiry. It just so happens, to my regret, that the historical sources are not there with which to pursue the question. If they were, I have no doubt that we could account for this variation as well.

Notes

1. The British colonial office abolished this system, replacing it with more "conventional," African-style bridewealth, in 1927. This had far-reaching effects on the social system and the economy of the Tiv, but these need not concern us here (Bohannan 1965:527).

PART FOUR

The O-Cluster: Islands of Micronesia and Polynesia

Prelude: An Argument Over Teen Sexuality

Margaret Mead and Derek Freeman present diametrically opposite views of adolescent sexuality in Samoa.

In the strictly clandestine love affair the lover never presents himself at the house of his beloved. His *soa* [ambassador] may go there in a group or upon some trumped-up errand, or he also may avoid the house and find opportunities to speak to the girl while she is fishing or going to and from the plantation: It is his task to sing his friend's praise, counteract the girl's fears and objections, and finally appoint a rendezvous. These affairs are usually of short duration and both boy and girl may be carrying on several at once. One of the recognized causes of a quarrel is the resentment of the first lover against his successor of the same night, "for the boy who came later will mock him." These clandestine lovers make their rendezvous on the outskirts of the village. "Under the palm trees" is the conventionalised designation of this type of intrigue. Very often three or four couples will have a common rendezvous, when either the boys or the girls are relatives who are friends. Should the girl ever grow faint or dizzy, it is the boy's part to climb the nearest palm and fetch down a fresh cocoanut to pour on her face in lieu of eau de cologne. In native theory, barrenness is the punishment of promiscuity, and, vice versa, only persistent monogamy is rewarded by conception. When a pair of clandestine experimenters whose rank is so low that their marriages are not of any great economic importance become genuinely attached to each other and maintain the relationship over several months, marriage often follows. And native sophistication distinguishes between the adept lover whose adventures are many and of short duration and the less skilled man who can find no better proof of his virility than a long affair ending in conception.

Margaret Mead, *Coming of Age in Samoa* (New York: William Morrow, 1928), pp. 91-92. Reprinted by permission.

Samoa, then, is a society predicated on rank, in which female virgins are both highly valued and eagerly sought after. Moreover, although these values are especially characteristic of the higher levels of the rank structure, they also permeate to its lower levels, so that virtually every family cherishes the virginity of its daughters. For example, as Turner noted in 1861, and as Stuebel confirms, although the marriage ceremonies of common people were marked by less display than those of people of high rank, they still involved the testing of the bride's virginity. In other words, while the virginity of the nubile daughters of families of high rank was a matter of quite crucial importance to all concerned, the values of the [sacred virgin] system also traditionally applied to the whole of Samoan society, albeit less stringently to those of lower rank.

It is thus customary in Samoa, as Mead quite failed to report, for the virginity of an adolescent daughter, whatever her rank, to be safeguarded by her brothers, who exercise an active surveillance over her comings and goings, especially at night. Brothers will upbraid, and sometimes beat, a sister should she be found in the company of a boy suspected of having designs on her virginity, while the boy involved is liable to be assaulted with great ferocity.

Derek Freeman, *Margaret Mead and Samoa: The Making and Unmaking of an Anthropological Myth* (Cambridge, Mass.: Harvard University Press, 1983), pp. 236-37. Reprinted by permission.

11

The Nature of Oceanic Societies

Here in Part IV, I consider the family systems of Polynesia and Micronesia, defined as culture areas. Polynesia includes the Pacific Islands from New Zealand in the south to Hawai'i in the north, from Nukuoro and Kapingamarangi in the west to Easter Island in the east, all of which are home to people who speak closely related dialects. Micronesia includes the archipelago societies of the Caroline Islands, Yap in the West to Kosrae in the East, and of the Marshall and Gilbert groups. (The Marianas are linguistically Micronesian, but their social system in modern times has been a product of several centuries of intensive acculturation, and is thus not germane to this study. There is no usable information available about their aboriginal system.)

I include Polynesia and Micronesia together in this chapter because of the similarities in island environment (with the exception of New Zealand, which is practically continental in ecological terms), and in social system. Despite a superficial dissimilarity—in the recent past, most Polynesian descent systems have been patrilineal or patrilineally biased, and most Micronesian systems have been matrilineal, the aspects of the social systems of the two culture areas that are important for understanding family systems are basically the same throughout the two oceanic culture areas, and different in some respects from those of much of Melanesia, which is linguistically closely related as another branch of Austronesian family, but whose social systems lacked strong emphasis on genealogical seniority. I thus speak of the island family systems of Polynesia and Micronesia as O- (for Oceanic) cluster systems.

The Logics of Subsistence and Prestige
Organization on Islands

As in the African case, when we analyze the family systems of the O-cluster we must recognize the importance of understanding both the separateness and the interconnection of the subsistence and prestige spheres of activity. But the nature of the division and the interconnection of the two spheres was quite different from that in Africa. In most African societies, the prestige sphere was the province of men, and except in a few highly stratified societies on the fringe of the A-cluster, it was the province of all men or all men except for slaves. The subsistence sphere was the province of both men and women, but the extent to which women participated in the prestige sphere except as substitutes for men was highly variable: in most places, they participated only minimally, but there were important exceptions. And the more highly developed the prestige sphere was (which in turn is a function of the amount of wealth, or prestige goods available to a particular society), the more separate the two spheres became.

In O-cluster societies, by contrast, the division between subsistence and prestige spheres of activity rested on different grounds. As in most of Africa, women competed in the prestige sphere not as women, but as substitutes for men. But in contrast to the African case, not all men were eligible to compete for prestige. Eligibility instead was limited by two kinds of factors. First there was the limitation of genealogy. In every O-cluster society, birthright played an important part in determining positions of leadership. In fact, genealogy could act in one or the other or a combination of two ways. In societies resembling the ideal type Goldman calls "traditional," genealogy was the primary criterion for leadership roles, high rank, ritual sanctity, and other marks of high status in the prestige sphere (Goldman 1970:20). In such cases, including such diverse environments as New Zealand and Pukapuka in Polynesia (Firth 1959[1929]:106, Beaglehole and Beaglehole 1938:235-36) or Lamotrek in Micronesia (Alkire 1965:28-30), genealogy as a criterion for high position operated *within* a descent group; leaders were genealogically senior members of a group whose genealogically junior members were commoners (Figure 11-1). This type of genealogical seniority was associated with a minimum, for this culture area at least, of status differentiation between chiefs and commoners (Sahlins 1958:104-105). In other cases, corresponding to Goldman's "stratified" ideal type (Goldman 1970:20), genealogy as a criterion for high status operated *between* groups; certain descent groups were set off as aristocratic, with various degrees of power, rank, *tapu*, etc., while even senior members of the non-aristocratic descent groups were excluded from high status positions altogether. Such was the case, for example, in Society Islands (Oliver 1974:751) and Tonga (Clifford 1929:29-31) in Polynesia, and although appearing in less highly developed form in Micronesia generally, appears to have been approached, at least, in such places as Yap (Lingenfelter 1975:136-37) and Palau (Force and Force 1972:9). In both these ways, genealogy acted as a constraint on participation in the prestige sphere. Men without genealogical credentials were precluded from competition for leadership positions, a fact that has important ramifications for the differences between aristocratic and commoner family organization, as shown in Figure 11-2.

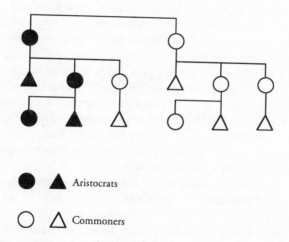

FIGURE 11-1: Aristocrat/Commoner Distinction *Within* Descent Groups

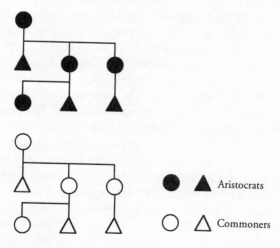

FIGURE 11-2: Aristocrat/Commoner Distinction *Between* Descent Groups

The second factor limiting participation in the prestige sphere was ability or achievement. In most O-cluster societies, men who competed in the prestige sphere needed not only the entitlement of birthright, but also at least some measure of ability, or else their birthright status would be reduced, and they would, in effect, act more like commoners than like chiefs. The extent to which ability made a difference in the right to compete (of course, it always made a difference in how successful a man was in the competition) varied greatly within the O-cluster area. Its importance was highest in that type of society Goldman calls "open" (Goldman 1970:20-21), where ability in warfare and/or economic activity essentially determined who would occupy the effective high statuses in the society, and where any man who was successful in warfare or politics could later on rationalize his position in terms of genealogy and/or *mana*. Examples of this type of society include Mangaia (Hiroa 1934:110) and the Marquesas (Handy 1923:44-45) in Polynesia, and the Marshall archipelago (Spoehr 1949:31) in Micronesia. In the less open societies, whether of Goldman's traditional or stratified type, genealogy remained the prime determinant of high status and thus of eligibility to compete in the prestige sphere, but even there a person in a genealogically impeccable position might be granted the ritual prestige but none of the political or military power of the chiefship, with a genealogically junior but more able man taking over the effective roles of leadership. Such seems to have been the case, for example, among the New Zealand Maori (Firth 1959[1929]:107-08), in Tokelau (MacGregor 1937:51), and on Lamotrek in the Carolines (Alkire 1963). Again, constraints of ability, like those of genealogy, limited participation in prestige activities to a select group of men within the society.

We can thus divide the families of any O-Cluster society into aristocrats and commoners, though in most cases the aristocracy was itself internally ranked according to genealogy, and there was often a fuzzy zone at the border between commoners and lower aristocrats. (There was a further category of slaves in some of the more highly differentiated societies.) Everywhere in the O-cluster aristocrats were entitled to compete in the prestige sphere, while the commoners were excluded. The degree to which aristocrats were separated from commoners varied with the degree to which the prestige sphere of activities was separated from the subsistence sphere, and this, in turn, varied, as in Africa, with the amount of wealth, or prestige goods, available in a particular environment. Exactly what constituted wealth varied from society to society, but I am using the term here as elsewhere to indicate those material goods whose ownership, display, or trade brought prestige to their owner.[1]

In contrast to the situation in Africa, however, the amount of wealth did not determine the extent to which men in general, as participants in the prestige sphere, engaged in activities beyond those necessary to subsist. In the O-cluster, genealogy was always a factor, and the difference between wealthy and poor societies lay in the degree to which aristocratic families, primarily the men of these families, engaged in a game of prestige competition that was closed off to commoners. Even in the poorest societies, those with the smallest amount of circulating wealth or non-subsistence goods, there was always an aristocrat-commoner distinction, because the factor of genealogical differentiation was always present. In the wealthiest and most differentiated societies, aristocrats were separated from commoners by material wealth, leisured lifestyle, ritual sanctity and, importantly for this study, by practicing a very different variant of their society's family system.

Small and Large Island Social Systems

Precisely how did the degree of separation between aristocrats and commoners vary with the nature of the island environment? The distinction usually made is between high, or volcanic islands, and low or coral islands and atolls (Sahlins 1966; Alkire 1978). This is a good approximation but, I think, a bit too geological. There are both small volcanic islands such as Tikopia (Firth 1929) and particularly Anuta (Feinberg 1981), whose small size and high population density makes them economically more like atolls, and systems of atolls, particularly in the Marshalls (Spoehr 1949:74-78), where the availability of resources and the practicality of inter-atoll communication and warfare gave rise to a fairly developed system of social stratification. But in general, the factor of island size, combined with climate, communications, soils, and a host of other factors, made for relative wealth (and thus the possibility of a high degree of stratification) on some islands, and for relative poverty on others. And it was relative wealth or poverty of resources, more than any other factor, that influenced the degree and nature of the aristocrat-commoner distinction.

Small Islands—Gaining
Prestige by Controlling Subsistence

In the environments of poor islands, such as most atolls, the prestige system was constrained not only by the relative lack of wealth, measured in non-subsistence goods and redistributable subsistence surpluses, but also by the necessity, with few resources and a typically high population density, for everyone to play the subsistence game first and foremost. The social system in such places was usually overwhelmingly concerned with a single problem: how to ensure access for everyone to basic productive resources, most importantly agricultural land. For example, Lieber says, "For the people of Kapingamarangi, no other single concern seems to be as omnipresent and as anxiety-provoking as their concern over land" (1974:70). In Tokelau, land is reported to have been the primary form of wealth, and was of consuming interest (MacGregor 1937:53).

This concern was repeated on atoll after atoll, especially when combined with the widely held ideal that no person should ever be deprived of access to the basic means of livelihood (Nason 1970:102). On a small island with a dense population and a typical variation in demographic success of various land-holding groups, this meant that the social system had to operate to ensure redistribution of land access to conform with demographic changes. This could be done in two ways. First, as suggested by Sahlins (1966:50) and confirmed by the Beagleholes' work on Pukapuka, (1938:275-81), the social structure could provide people with membership in a variety of overlapping descent and local groups, through any of which they could gain access to various productive resources. Second, and more importantly, societies could practice what amounted in some cases to almost universal adoption, in order to redistribute people among those groups that held rights to land. Such high rates of adoption were prevalent in almost all small-island societies.

We thus see two constraints on wide aristocrat-commoner status distinctions on small islands. First, there was not much wealth to go around either in the form of subsistence surpluses or of prestige goods, and secondly, everyone had to be assured access, first and foremost, to the subsistence resources which were, after all, the majority of all resources. So typically, on small islands we find a relatively low level of aristocrat-commoner differentiation (Sahlins 1958). But at the same time, even the overwhelming concern with ensuring access to productive resources still allowed for some playing of the prestige game. In most O-cluster societies, high-ranking people controlled titles to various lands, titles that invested them with certain rights such as first fruits, or, in many cases, the right to allocate land on one's own behalf as chief or on behalf of the kin group of which one was leader. In this kind of situation, those who controlled the titles were in a position to be generous, and it was through generosity of all kinds that they could reinforce the ascribed prestige of genealogical rank with the achieved prestige of good leadership. We see this emphasized over and over. For example, in Bikini in the northern Marshalls, authority over land was the greatest desideratum for prestige activity. But at the same time, no one could be deprived of access to the use of land (Kiste 1974:5,54). In

Pukapuka, "The accumulation of wealth has for its end redistribution in the interests of increased prestige" (Beaglehole and Beaglehole 1938:108).

Another important way in which high genealogical position led to the opportunity to be generous and thus gain prestige was through exercising one's rights to first fruits or first fish, and then redistributing the gains among the population. In either case, increased prestige could be gained by those who had genealogical position and used it well; this is the O-cluster version of the allocating connection, in which those who have prestige in the public sphere can reinforce that prestige by allocation of goods to followers. The limitation set by small-island ecology, however, was that prestige was gained only by generosity, and thus could not be used to increase one's own standards of consumption.

Large Islands—Prestige Competition
Unfettered by Subsistence Concerns

At the other end of the scale, on those islands where subsistence seems to have been very little problem at all, there was a wide difference between aristocrats and commoners. Whereas most people living on large islands had it easier economically than most of those living on small ones, simply because of lower population density and more diverse resources, there was still variation among large islands in this regard. Two of the most paradisiacal seem to have been Pohnpei in the Eastern Carolines, and the Society Island group in southeastern Polynesia. Glenn Peterson, writing of Pohnpei, has suggested that what we ordinarily think of as important issues in the subsistence economy, such as land tenure, may have had little relevance on this island: "The productivity of Ponapean farming and localized marriage make issues of land and inheritance somewhat irrelevant for day-to-day existence" (1982:134). In this situation of almost unlimited riches, the subsistence economy had little relationship to the prestige sphere of activity represented by matrilineage politics and chieftainship struggles: "Ponapean matriliny may, in fact, have had little relation to either residence of land tenure" (Peterson 1982:134). The same kind of situation seems to have held true in Tahiti, where there seems to have been enough property to go around without much trouble, and where, for most participants in the subsistence economy, there appears to have been little work necessary to ensure abundance (Oliver 1974:123-25; 254). Pohnpei and Tahiti perhaps represent an extreme, but this kind of situation, where access to subsistence resources was not delimited by poverty of the environment or by small area and large population, seems to have been characteristic of most large islands. (Exceptions, such as Tonga and particularly Yap, resulted in recent times from population growth.) In cases like this, operators in the prestige sphere in a sense got free rein—unconstrained by any necessity to oversee the distribution of access to subsistence resources. Thus aristocrats in such societies were free to play the prestige game to the ultimate—through warfare, tribute and redistribution, ritual and sacrifice, and other activities. It is under favorable material circumstances such as these that we find the elaboration of social inequality so much commented on by early observers of Polynesian and to a lesser extent Micronesian aristocrats.

These differences, between the relative equality of aristocrats and commoners on most small islands, and the great gap that separated their non-subsistence activities on the larger islands, contributed to differences in family organization. In small-island societies, or places where there was little surplus wealth, the important family activities for both aristocrats and commoners were those that dealt with the universal necessities of reproduction and of subsistence production—sex, child-rearing, emotional ties, subsistence organization, and the control and transmission of property, since property was necessary for reproduction and subsistence production. Enabling activity was relatively unimportant, in that it was often impossible or pointless to recruit large amounts of family labor to produce prestige goods, since prestige goods were relatively unimportant in themselves. In the larger island societies, on the other hand, we find a division between aristocratic and commoner family organization. For the commoners, again reproduction and subsistence production were basically the only considerations in planning family strategies. But for the aristocrats, enabling assumed major importance—building a following through control of land, through warfare, or through direction of major rituals was critical to an aristocrat's success in the prestige sphere. An aristocrat thus had an important interest in using his family organization to enable him to achieve these ends. This meant that in many large-island societies, there were aspects of family organization, such as polygyny of aristocrats, domestic slavery, the preservation of "tribal virgins," the careful negotiation of marriage alliances between aristocrats, dowry in land or other goods, and even the curious institution of "non-fraternal polyandry" in the Marquesas islands, all of which helped an aristocrat to use his family to gain prestige in the wider world of politics.

Family activities were thus different in different kinds of O-cluster societies, and in some societies the important activities, and thus the structures they engendered, were very different for aristocrats and for commoners. In Chapters 12 and 13, I examine in detail each set of family activities, along with where they occurred and the way they varied in importance from one O-cluster society to another.

Notes

1. Weiner (1985) has pointed out that in Polynesia wealth could acquire its prestige-giving value not only through exchange but through retention and display; this point is developed further with regard to Northwest Coast societies in Part V.

12

Making a Living and
Making a Name on an Island

Procuring: Farming Like Africans,
Fishing Like Bands

Subsistence production in Polynesian and Micronesian societies was predominantly two things: farming and fishing. On many of the smaller islands, fish and other marine animals may have constituted the bulk of the diet, or at least a large proportion (Hatanaka 1971:254; Kirch and Yen 1982:351); even on large islands, where not all families had direct access to fishing grounds, fish still served as the primary source of protein, and were part of the daily diet for most people (Handy and Pukui 1958:6; Oliver 1974:253). And every family, everywhere, with the exception of a few high-ranking chiefs in the most stratified societies, engaged in agriculture, primarily producing food for its own consumption. Understanding family organization for subsistence production, then, means analyzing separately organization for farming and for fishing.

Farming: A Household Enterprise

Although a variety of crops are grown on Pacific islands, they can be roughly divided into two types: tree crops and root crops. Tree crops, including coconut, breadfruit, and pandanus, require little labor to cultivate, so that the main concern of families who depended partly upon such crops was not the organization of labor (except processing labor, to be covered in the next section), but rather the organization of rights to the fruit of various trees and orchards. It was in the cultivation of root crops (most importantly true taro, or Colocasia, and giant taro, or Cyrtosperma) that the organization of family labor became important. Both these crops are grown in pits, or swamps, and require labor for digging and maintaining the pits, and for planting, weeding, and harvesting.

Some cooperation might have been necessary for digging and maintaining taro beds, but usually agriculture of this labor-intensive kind, as well as the much less laborious cultivation of tree crops, can be conducted by the members of a single family or by a small group of kin. Variation in the composition of the group that farms cooperatively and eats the products of its labor seems, in fact, to have depended more on the larger social organization in which the family was embedded than on the ecological or labor requirements of the land. With similar crops in most parts of the Pacific, we nevertheless find a wide variation in both the sexual division of labor and the nature of the group that shared farm produce.

In most O-cluster societies, it was a household, passing through a developmental cycle with nuclear and various extended forms, that was the effective farming unit. This was true whether the women did most of the farm work, as seems to have been the case in Western Carolines, from Palau (Force and Force 1972:14-15) to Woleai (Alkire 1978:55, 58), Lamotrek (Alkire 1965:84, 96) and Ifaluk (Burrows and Spiro 1957:51-52), or whether men were primarily responsible, as in Polynesian islands ranging in size from the atolls of Niutao in the Tuvalu group (Noricks 1983:573-5) or the Tokelau group (MacGregor 1937:42) through medium-sized islands such as Uvea and Futuna (Burrows 1938a:67-68, 94; 1938b:65-66, 140), to the large and highly stratified society of Tahiti (Oliver 1974:229, 249). Households also produced for their own consumption in those societies where men and women shared more or less equally in the agricultural labor, both where there was no clear cut division of labor between them, as Firth reports for Tikopia (1963:61, 92-29), or, more commonly, where men and women each had definite tasks to perform, as on the Eastern Caroline atoll of Etal (Nason 1970:95; 1981:157), and in many islands in Polynesia, from the atoll of Pukapuka (Beaglehole and Beaglehole 1938:90) or the tiny volcanic island of Anuta (Feinberg 1981:22-23, 76-78) to medium-sized islands such as Rapa (Hanson 1970:65, 72) or Rarotonga (Crocombe 1964:23) or Ta'u in Samoa (Mead 1969:24, 67) to the large land mass cultivated by the New Zealand Maori (Firth 1959:111, Heuer 1969:458). In all these cases, one or more members of the household, which was usually a residential group with a common cookhouse and one or more dwelling houses depending on the number of nuclear families composing it, produced agricultural goods that were then consumed by the household as a unit. A variant of this kind of arrangement also occurred on Yap, with the difference that in Yapese society, the nuclear family, occasionally together with attached relatives, was the household, and joint families never formed (Lingenfelter 1975:21, 26).

There were also two other kinds of arrangements in which the household was not the exclusive unit for the procurement and consumption of agricultural goods. The first occurred in those areas where sibling solidarity, an important phenomenon in most Polynesian and Micronesian societies (Ortner 1981:369-370), overrode the household unit even in subsistence production and distribution. This kind of arrangement occurred in some of the atolls in the Marshall group (Pollock 1974:123-24; Rynkiewich 1976:95, 108-9), where men produced agricultural goods for their own households but also for their sisters', on the Carolinian atoll of Namonuito, where women did most of the production (Thomas 1980:175), not only for their own households, but also for other members of their fathers' matriclans, and on the Polynesian outlier of Kapingamarangi (Lieber 1974:82), where the set of brothers and sisters performed agricultural labor jointly under the direction of the eldest brother and eldest sister, and then divided the produce among the siblings' respective households. The second kind of arrangement occurred only on a few high islands, such as those of the Truk archipelago, where male members of the matrilineal group worked cooperatively, even though they lived matrilocally (Caughey 1977:68-69; Goodenough 1951:31), and in Hawaii, where extended kin groups, or *ohana*, contained households living in different ecological zones, with the agricultural households who lived inland expected to trade farm products for fish with their coastal relatives (Handy and Pukui 1972:2-5, 44). This last arrangement conformed to Sahlins' characterization of ramage-type systems, where a descent group was built up of households living in different environments, who engaged in exchange of subsistence products (Sahlins 1957:48).[1]

With the exception of this last case, in which ecological conditions seem to have compelled related households to exchange farm produce almost every day (less frequent ceremonial exchange, of course, existed everywhere), the other cases in which households exchanged produce regularly seem not to have derived directly from any ecological imperative. Instead, cooperation in such cases came from the extension of kin solidarity, particularly among siblings, into the agricultural aspect of subsistence, even though, from a practical standpoint, agriculture could have been easily and satisfactorily handled on a household level.

Fishing: Cooperation and Risk-Spreading

Fishing was an altogether different matter. Individuals could do some fishing, such as gathering shellfish on a reef, spearfishing, or even the remarkable Anutan technique of swimming out beyond a reef and fishing with a hook and line (Feinberg 1981:31). But by far the majority of fishing expeditions involved canoes, either in the placid waters of a lagoon or in the more dangerous open ocean, and canoe fishing involved cooperation, usually between members of different households. In this regard, fishing resembles hunting, as practiced in the B-cluster societies described in Part II. Fishing also resembles hunting in that it is a chance activity—sometimes the catch is large, sometimes meager. For both these reasons— the necessity of cooperation and the variability of the catch—fishing was less often a purely household activity, though household fishing is reported for Arno (Rynckiewich 1976:108-9) and Majuro (Spoehr 1949:139) in the Marshalls, for Palau (Force and Force 1972:14), and for the Polynesians of Niutao in Tuvalu (Noricks 1983:573-75), Tahiti (Oliver 1974:229, 310), Rarotonga (Crocombe 1974:23, 32) and Manu'a (Mead 1928:17, 1969:24).

Far more common, however, was some sort of venture in which several men or women cooperated in fishing, and the produce was divided among a number of households. In Raroia in the Tuamotus, for example, members of fishing expeditions were expected to distribute their shares of the catch to unspecified "relatives" (Danielsson 1955:52). On Kapingamarangi, a man's share of the fish catch went first to the households of his sibset and then, if there were still fish left over, to other relatives (Lieber 1968:45, 113, 123-240). And in Tonga, a man was required to give fish to his sister as well as to his wife (Rogers 1977:162).

In other places, there were other, even more inclusive arrangements for distribution of the fish catch. In Yap (Lingenfelter 1975:26), Bikini (Kiste 1974:250), Ifaluk (Burrows and Spiro 1957:147), Anuta (Feinberg 1981:22-23, 81) and Rapa (Hanson 1970:82-83), men fished cooperatively in canoes, and then distributed shares of the catch to the households of all crewmembers. In much of the Caroline group, men fished cooperatively and then distributed the catch to a large group, such as the matrilineal relatives living on the islet in Etal (Nason 1970:130), the group of matrilineally related men that shared a canoe-house in Lamotrek (Alkire 1965:84), or even the whole islet in Woleai (Alkire 1978:47). In Pukapuka, all the young men or all the old men of one of the three villages would fish cooperatively, and distribute the catch to the whole village (Beaglehole and Beaglehole 1938:54); and in Tikopia, the whole fleet of a particular village would go out to sea together, and distribute the catch among all their households (Firth 1968:54). In Truk, where women's fishing on the reef was an important source of food, the catch would be shared among all members of the women's matrilineages (Caughey 1977:16, 68-69, 121; Goodenough 1951:75).

The less exclusively domestic nature of the fishing economy is not difficult to understand, in terms of the technical requirements of fishing and the unreliability of the catch, but it had important ramifications for household solidarity. In this respect, the fishing economy of the O-cluster societies resembled the hunting economy of the B-cluster; it compelled people to organize subsistence activities in a group larger than the family. This means that the importance of the family for subsistence in these societies fell somewhere between the B-cluster, where hunting was cooperative and gathering, while in some sense domestic, involved morally obligatory sharing, and the A-cluster, where the subsistence economy, in contrast to the prestige economy, was entirely domestic in most cases. Here in the O-cluster, farming was domestic but fishing was cooperative, as shown in Figure 12-1.

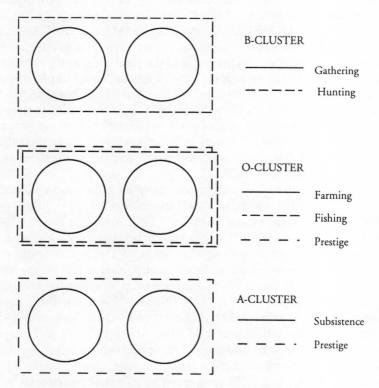

FIGURE 12-1: Nested Groups in B-, O-, and A-Clusters

This is one of the reasons, I think, why "domestic groups" are in some senses harder to define in the O-cluster than in Africa. The household group was not always the unit of subsistence production, and sometimes, even where it was, this was not considered to be a particularly important fact. At Arno, in the Marshalls, for example, Rynkiewich reports that "The household is not an important ideational group among the Arno Marshallese, but it is an important action group" (1976:108). On the other hand, the household was hardly obscure in many parts of this region. At Anuta, for example, the household was the basic unit of island social structure in practically every respect, even though its members engaged regularly in cooperative fishing expeditions (Feinberg, 1981).

Processing

Cooking, storing food, making clothing and mats, building houses, and building canoes were the important processing activities in this region. In most areas, fresh food was available throughout most of the year (though some storage was necessary in dry seasons in places such as the Marquesas), and the requirements of protection from elements were not particularly important, except perhaps in New Zealand, which was the only O-cluster society to fall outside the tropical zone. The organization of processing activities is fairly simple to describe. Canoe-building was usually the province of experts, and thus was not something that members of most households did anyway. Men built houses almost everywhere, and they did so cooperatively, but they did not, of course, do it very often. Cooking, cleaning, and making mats and clothing were the important everyday processing activities, and everywhere in the O-cluster, these were primarily organized in the residential household. The only differences seem to have been in the sexual division of labor. Where cleaning and tidying seem always to have been women's work, cooking varied. In some parts of Western Polynesia, cooking seems to have been a male activity, as in Uvea (Burrows 1938a:65, 93), Futuna (Burrows 1938b:67, 97), and Manu'a (Mead 1928:28, 30; 1969:62, 67), or an activity performed jointly by men and women, as in Anuta (Feinberg 1981:92) and Tikopia (Firth 1963:95, 118). In other areas, women tended to cook, though I must admit that much of the literature is remarkably unclear on this rather basic aspect of the sexual division of labor.

The only exceptions to the pattern of cooking in a nuclear or extended family cookhouse seem to have come in two complex, highly stratified societies: Yap in Micronesia and Hawai'i in Polynesia. In Yap, considerations of tabu and pollution prevented men and women from sharing food, so that in each nuclear family, the men and the women had separate cookhouses: they drew from a common food supply, but cooked and ate separately (Lingenfelter 1975:23). Similar conditions seem to have obtained in Ka'u, on the island of Hawaii, where the men and the women, amounting throughout most of the domestic cycle to an extended household, cooked separately because the men, in general, were *kapu* (sacred) in contrast to the women, who were profane, or noa (Handy and Pukui 1972:7-12, 44). What is striking about these cases is that they constitute the only exceptions to the household as the basic processing group, thus underlining the general rule for the area that there was no good reason, arising from the nature of the work itself, to spread domestic labor among groups larger than the residential group, or to divide the residential group for such purposes into some kind of sub-units. Cooking, cleaning, and so forth were basically unproblematical, and it was only in a few cases, where ideological or ritual reasons concerned with the hierarchical structure of the society as a whole impinged on the organization of the domestic group, that this group's function of subsistence processing was organized in a different way.

Regulating Sexuality: Differences of Rank

Oceanic societies, particularly those of Polynesia (the "South Seas") enjoy a popular reputation as paradises of free love. In many ways, that reputation, if not entirely accurate, has a basis in fact, particularly in the fact of free sexual license for unmarried adolescents and young adults. But in the O-cluster, as elsewhere, sexuality was only as free as it could be and not threaten a system that both allocated rights and privileges over persons in a certain way, and also took account of the jealous or possessive side of human sexual emotions.

The best way, I think, to account for the pattern of sexual regulation in Polynesia and Micronesia is to look at the consequences of unregulated sex. These were, here as elsewhere, of two kinds: jealousy and pregnancy. Pregnancy was structurally more important, because it created persons who had to be affiliated to certain kin groups and, in the more stratified societies, to social strata as well. But the situation here was different from what we found in Africa, where it was the ambition of every man to control the sexuality of either wives or sisters, in order to increase his own following. In the O-cluster, by contrast, sexual activity was more strictly regulated in families that had greater status differentials to maintain.

Commoners and Small Islanders:
More or Less Free Love

In O-cluster societies, most non-aristocratic men were not concerned with building up followings. Men of low or small islands had to be concerned, instead, with distributing people among landholding and resource-using groups in such a way that basic subsistence goods would be available to all. This could be taken care of by adoption and other measures, as discussed below, but it meant that it was usually no particular advantage for a man to have a maximum number of children—the more he had, the more he had to adopt out. Advantages might come, however, from the alliances created by adoption.

For a woman, whatever children she had were hers anyway, unless, again, there were too many, and some were adopted away. For this reason, in such societies there was not the kind of competition for women that in Africa was associated with bridewealth, a high age-differential at marriage, and general polygyny. Rather there was typically monogamy. Men and women married at approximately the same age, and there was neither an asymmetrical, bridewealth-type exchange of goods at marriage or, on some islands at least, even a formal marriage ceremony.[2]

The same was typically true for commoners in the more complex, stratified societies of many of the large islands. Commoners had little if any chance to play the prestige game. Commoners everywhere in the O-cluster could compete for prestige as warriors or craft specialists, but these were individual achievements different from the building of followings that was so important to chiefs. Thus, they apparently rarely either competed for wives, as laborers and child-producers, or attempted to maximize their reproductive rates, as African men always attempted to do.

What all this adds up to, for large-island commoners and most of the people of small islands (sometimes excluding chiefs), is very little reason to regulate the sexuality of unmarried family members, and only somewhat more stringent regulations against extramarital sex. In the case of premarital sexual activity, Polynesian and Micronesian commoners, like members of many B-cluster societies, had the relative economic and political luxury of being able to indulge their sexual appetites when these were the strongest—in the adolescent and early adult years—subject to the restrictions imposed by the incest taboo, which could rule out a lot of partners due to classificatory nature of kinship systems. In nearly all the societies reported, adolescence was a time of busying oneself with affairs. We find this pattern in both the Marshalls and the Carolines in Micronesia and throughout the less stratified societies of Polynesia. Examples are too nu-

merous to list in their entirety, but we might mention such diverse societies
as Pukarua in the Tuamotus, where "sexual adventure was the privilege of
the adolescent" (Hatanaka 1971:260); Mangareva, where adolescent sexuality was characterized as "as free of inhibitions...as in other regions" (Buck
1938:128); commoners in Tahiti, where both young women and men were
freely sexual from early adolescence (Oliver 1974:354); Futuna, where there
was complete sexual license for unmarried men and women (Burrows
1937:54-5); Ifaluk, where premarital sex was explicitly allowed by custom,
though lovers were expected to be discreet (Burrows and Spiro 1957:123);
and Majuro, where adolescents, expected to have active sexual lives, were
normally "busy with their amours in the evenings" (Spoehr 1949:138, 195).

In some societies, adolescent sex even enjoyed a degree of institutionalization; in the Marquesas, for example, all "youths and maidens" were expected to participate in the activities of the *ka'ioi*, a kind of adolescent social club (Handy 1923:39-40), and the Western Caroline high islands of Yap
and Palau, where the young men not only had their own private affairs,
but were also served, sexually and otherwise, by young women appointed
as official hostesses to the young men's clubhouses (Force and Force
1972:22-24, 29; Lingenfelter 1975:44). Even the double standard shows up
here only in a weakened form. Few authors mention that adolescent men
had more legitimate sexual freedom than young women; and even in such
cases the distinction seems to have been a mild one. In Eastern Truk, for
example, Caughey mentions that if a young woman gained a reputation
for promiscuity, it might affect her marriage chances (1977:113), and in the
Polynesian atoll of Tongareva, Buck tells us, a young woman had to be
more discreet about her affairs than was necessary for a man (1932a:34).

As in the other societies we have examined so far, Oceanic commoners
and inhabitants of small islands treated extramarital sex much more harshly
than they did premarital sex.[3] In general, it is very difficult to determine
how much of the disapproval of extramarital sex was part of the pre-contact culture, and how much was introduced by the missionaries. But evidence from small, not heavily missionized societies in recent decades suggests that extramarital sex was never totally free or completely condoned.
In some places, authors report only mild disapproval. On Ifaluk, for example, most married people were expected to have lovers, although people
were said to have felt ashamed if their spouses' affairs were found out
(Burrows and Spiro 1957:304). Futunans (Burrows 1936:66) and Pukapukans
(Beaglehole and Beaglehole 1938:285-91) also apparently took a rather tolerant attitude toward extramarital adventures. But in most places, at least
in modern times, adultery was considered a more or less serious, if not
really heinous, offense. In some cases, such as Palau (Force and Force
1972:24), Etal (Nason 1970:91), and Tonga (Gifford 1929:189), this was apparently true whether the offender was husband or wife; in others, for

example Lamotrek (Alkire 1965:57); Tikopia (Firth 1963:118-19), and among the New Zealand Maori (Heuer 1969:460; Firth 1959:120), women were more severely punished. In some cases, adultery might have been cause for divorce, confiscation of property, or beatings, but in no case was it a cause for killing or other serious and lasting punishment, unless it involved chiefs, a topic to which we now turn.

Aristocrats: Protecting the Value of the Virgin

The aristocracy, in particular the aristocracy of the large and stratified societies, played by different rules. It was important for a chief in an "open" or "stratified" society, to use Goldman's terms, to build up a following by any means possible; though his rank might never be taken away from him, his power certainly could be, and there was sometimes the possibility of moving up in rank, if one had enough followers. Various kinds of accretions to one's household, through polygyny and through the high reproductive success that polygyny can give a man, were some of the ways to build up a following. And aristocrats in any society, even the least stratified ones, were interested in building up political, military, and economic alliances with chiefs from neighboring descent groups, districts, or islands. In this kind of situation, the sexuality and reproductive powers of a potential spouse for a high-ranking man became valuable commodities. Men playing the power game could not afford to allow these commodities to be expended in pursuit of the woman's own personal sexual inclinations: they were needed for followings and alliances.

For the aristocrats of the more stratified societies, then, female sexuality was often highly guarded until marriage. This was true, for example, in the now-famous "princess" or "sacred virgin" of Samoa, a young woman of high-rank in her descent group, who was kept virgin and secluded until marriage, which was usually homogamous by rank and always arranged for political advantage of the descent group of which she was a member (Mead 1978:98). The same kind of strict restrictions on the sexuality of high-ranking young women obtained among the New Zealand Maori (Heuer 1969:453, 460), in the Ka'u district of Hawai'i, where girls of chiefly families were betrothed even before birth (Handy and Pukui 1972:53, 109, 105, 161), and in Tahiti, where such restrictions were combined with apparently strict endogamy for each of the three social strata of *ari'i*, *ra'atira*, and *manafune* (Oliver 1974:358, 354, 611, 751). In Tonga, this restriction was apparently, perhaps in imitation of chiefly practice, extended to commoner females as well, the only case in Polynesia where we find female premarital sexuality reported as disapproved for all females in pre-missionary times (Gifford 1929:21).

It is interesting to note that, in parts of Polynesia, this seclusion and virginity of high-ranking females was practiced even in rather small, unstratified societies. This appears to have been the case in both Manihiki-Rakahanga, where higher-ranking women were secluded (Buck 1932b:41), and Pukapuka (Hecht 1977:196), where each patrilineage had its "Sacred Maid" who was kept virgin for life. In the latter case, however, we can already see the transformation of the sacred virgin institution into purely symbolic terms in an unstratified society. If she was kept virgin for life, she could hardly be used, either by her father and brothers to make marriage alliances, or by her high-ranking husband to produce progeny.

Probably the most unusual form of utilization of control of sexuality in the service of prestige was the practice of marriage between closely related couples (sometimes even brother and sister) in the highest-ranking chiefly families of Hawai'i (Handy and Pukui 1972:109). In this case, the families involved were already secure enough in their high-ranking position that they did not need to worry about alliances with others; indeed, it seems to be the case that the politically powerful chiefs, who had to have at least some contact with commoners in order to rule, ranked somewhere in the middle of the chiefly ladder of ritual sanctity. So the most *kapu* of all needed to preserve and, if possible even intensify, their sacrosanct status and that of their offspring, something that they could do by the heightening purity of a marriage with a close relative, but of course, a close relative whose sexuality had been highly guarded before the marriage.

The contrast between the commoner and the aristocratic patterns with regard to premarital sex lies in some sense behind the controversy between Derek Freeman and the supporters of the deceased Margaret Mead over the nature of Samoan adolescence, as illustrated by the quotations in the Prelude to this Part. In fact, they do not disagree particularly startlingly on the facts of the case. Mead does not (contrary to the stereotype put forth by those who have not read her work) describe Samoa as a paradise of free love, and Freeman does not neglect status differences in the strictness of sexual mores. Mead describes the cult of the sacred virgin in great detail, as well as the furtive and clandestine nature of adolescent sexual relations. Freeman also admits that the cult of virginity was most prevalent among the elite. Where they disagree is in the signficance of the findings. Mead contended that stress in adolescence in 20th-century America was the result of inculcation of guilt about sex by Puritan morality, and that such guilt did not exist in Samoa (1928:242-248), showing that there was nothing innate in human biology that caused adolescent stress and rebellion. Freeman, on the other hand, contends that the very real conflicts over adolescent sexuality in Samoa (which Mead does not deny) lead to a situation in which unconflicted adolescent sexuality is rarer, and sexual violence more common than Mead admitted (1983:226-253), demonstrating that cultural differences in sexuality cannot escape the bounds of biology. From my perspective, I can do no better than quote Theodore Schwartz's comment, "Can the same society both stress virginity and encourage permarital sexual experimentation?" It seems to me that the answer must be affirmative [1983:925].

We must realize here that societies do not stress things, only people do, and that people in different social positions (male and female, aristocrat and commoner, married and unmarried) have different interests in their own and others' sexuality, differences that are easily explained in terms of their differential participation in prestige competition. When we observe that a similar pattern is found in other O-cluster systems, it seems clear that the supposed contradictions in the two portrayals of the Samoan system were nothing of the sort; both empirical observation and logic tell us that the system must have worked this way.

When we turn to extramarital sexuality on the part of the aristocracy, we again find a situation that differed from that of the commoners. On the one hand, adultery with the wife of a high chief was often punished, as in Pohnpei (Riesenberg 1968:73-75), but in many of these societies, members of the higher aristocracy were allowed free sexual relations with those of lower classes. In less stratified societies, such as the atoll of Kapingamarangi, (Lieber 1968:113-4), or the "open" society of Mangaia (Buck 1934:154), this allowed only male chiefs to have sexual relations with women of inferior standing, but in some of the more stratified societies, such as Pohnpei (Riesenberg 1968:73-75) or Tahiti (Oliver 1974:764), either a man or woman of sufficiently high rank could take lovers from among his or her social inferiors, apparently with impunity. In the case of Tahiti, we are told that the children of a union between a high-ranking woman and an inferior man would be killed at birth (Oliver 1974:764), but in the Marquesas, where wives of high chiefs took secondary husbands from commoners or the destitute, these latter were valuable not only as potential sires of offspring, but also as laborers in the household.

In summary, then, we can say that the regulation of sexuality in O-cluster societies depended on its connection to prestige activities. For those ineligible to compete in the prestige sphere, sexuality was virtually unregulated beyond the confines of the incest taboo before marriage, and although regulated in the interests of marital harmony afterwards, not regulated too strictly. On the other hand, for aristocrats engaged in prestige competition, sexuality was regulated in a variety of ways designed to allow them to manipulate women's sexual and reproductive powers to men's (and sometimes women's) political, economic, and ritual advantage.

Care and Socialization of Children

As in the African case, it makes sense when examining the O-cluster societies to divide child rearing into three periods: the period of infancy, when the unweaned child needed both constant care and access to the mother, or occasionally a wet-nurse; the period from weaning to the beginning of education in adult knowledge and skills, typically somewhere from seven to ten years of age, during which the child needed supervision, but less constant and less expert; and the period after the child began to learn adult skills, when the child was still dependent, but did not need supervision, but instead needed to begin accompanying and imitating adults going about their business, and to take instruction in lore and other knowledge from elders. The requirements for child rearing in these three periods were quite different, and we thus have to consider each period separately.

Before we do so, however, we should point out that a child in an O-cluster family system was rarely being raised to take up an adult role that involved exclusive or even primary allegiance to, or reliance on, other family members. A typical adult would, as mentioned above, cooperate with members of other families in subsistence tasks, particularly fishing; gain access to productive resources from various relatives through inheritance or adoption; and maintain some of his or her closest adult relationships with siblings of the same or opposite sex, many of whom were likely to be resident in different households and dependent for their livelihoods on different resources. There was no single group, *The Family*, that performed all the family activities in these societies, and so a child as a potential contributor to more than one kind of group was worth investing in for various kinds of relatives, and a child as a potential user of more than one group's resources was the responsibility of various kinds of relatives. So sharing of childcare beyond the nuclear family, and commonly beyond the residential household, made sense in terms of what the child was being socialized for.

Keeping this in mind, let us look at the changing needs of the child in the three stages of socialization, along with the kinds of groups that organized to meet these needs.

Infancy

It was unusual for a child in early infancy to be separated from the mother for a very long period, though wet nursing does seem to have been a fairly common practice, being reported for Arno in the Marshalls (Rynkiewich 1976:103), for Tokelau (MacGregor 1937:38), and Manu'a (Mead 1928:21), among other societies, and mentioned as prohibited only in the Beagleholes' account of Pukapuka (1938:272). Dependency on the mother was typically extended into the third or fourth year by continued breastfeeding, and the average age at weaning was anywhere from two years, as in Namonuito (Thomas 1980:175), or Tokelau (MacGregor 1937:38), to the "three or four years" reported by Burrows and Spiro on Ifaluk (1957:253). Even children already promised for adoption usually remained in their natal household until weaned or even longer as in Lamotrek (Alkire 1965:60) and the Polynesian outlier atoll of Nukuoro (Carroll 1970:124).

During the later part of this infant-dependent period, however, mothers seem to have often left much of the care of their infants to other caretakers. As in Africa, a wide variety of relatives are reported to have taken large parts of the responsibility for older infants. These might, for example, be household members, such as older sisters reported for Manu'a (Mead 1928:22) or Tahiti (Oliver 1974:697, 742), or elder siblings of either sex, as was the case in Majuro (Spoehr 1949:212), Kapingamarangi (Lieber 1968:46-7), and Futuna (Burrows 1936:59), or the father, as reported for Anuta (Feinberg 1981:85) and nearby Tikopia (Firth 1963:127). In some of these and other cases, caretakers might be relatives who were not household members, such as classificatory mothers in Namonuito (Thomas 1980:175), Pukapuka (Hecht 1977:194), and Anuta (Feinberg 1981:83)—all societies with quite different family structures—or the father's sister reported for Tokelau (Huntsman and Hooper 1975:424). The point is that relatives of various kinds, not limited in general by sex, age, household membership, or kin affiliation, found it in their interest in various O-cluster societies to help with infant care.

Early Childhood

When we move to the next period, between weaning and the commencement of serious learning of adult skills, we find an even lighter emphasis on the residential household as a unit of socialization. Once again, caretakers ranged from elder siblings to grandmothers to fathers, but the caretakers had less to do, and the natal mother might remain tied to her children by bonds of affection only. This was particularly true in the very frequent cases where children had been adopted out. Once children had been adopted, they were either expected to take up residence with their adoptive families (in any case, almost always relatives of their natal families) as in Pukapuka (Beaglehole and Beaglehole 2938:251), or the very different society of Ka'u, Hawai'i (Handy and Pukui 1972:71) or they gained the option of residence with one family or the other, depending on the terms of the adoption, as in Tonga, where we read that adoption varied "from a complete transfer to a mere formality" (Gifford 1929:26), or according to whim, as in Ifaluk (Burrows and Spiro 1957:268) or Pukarua (Hatanaka 1972:26), where children apparently could move around whenever they got tired of or angry at one or the other set of parents.

The Later Childhood Learning Period

Moving to middle and later childhood, when children actually began to learn agriculture, fishing, household chores, cooking, clothing manufacture, and the other kinds of skills necessary to become economically functional adults, along with the lore necessary for social adulthood, and when children's labor could begin to make a contribution, a still different pattern of socialization (or perhaps, more accurately, education) developed. The parent of the same sex almost always had some responsibility for his or her own or adopted children's education, but it was rare that the parent's responsibility was considered exclusive—I have found this reported only in Yap (Lingenfelter 1975:21, 42). It is noteworthy that in this society the economic discreteness of the individual household surpassed that found in other Oceanic societies; it lends support then, as a negative instance, to the rule that people were not socializing their children simply to be members of a family corporation.

Far more common was the arrangement where the parents cooperated with other relatives in the socialization of their children; these relatives might be specified, as in the case of Anuta, where the father's parents, who were household members, and the mother's brothers, who were not, both helped in socialization (Feinberg 1981:87), or they might remain unspecified, as in Truk (Caughey 1977:126; Goodenough 1951:52, 124), or in Tahiti (Oliver 1972:700-01). On some islands, the parents' role was not even primary once the children grew to this stage. This was particularly the case in Etal (Nason 1981:163), in Ka'u, on the island of Hawai'i (Handy and Pukui 1972:90), on the atoll pair of Manihiki-Rakahanga (Buck 1932b:39), and among the New Zealand Maori (Heuer 1969:460); in all of these systems the primary role in the education and training of children for adulthood was taken by the grandparents, who not only had more to tell but had more time to tell it, being not so actively involved in the daily subsistence activities as the children's parents.

In general, then, children were socialized by relatives, but certainly not exclusively by those relatives who belonged to their own residential households. The family as organized for the socialization of Polynesian and

Micronesian children was more like a child-centered kin network than like a discrete, corporate group.

Management and Transmission of Property and Titles

Rights to Land, the Most Important Property

By far the most important kind of property in most O-cluster societies was land. This, perhaps more than anything else, distinguishes Oceanic from African-type social systems. The reason for this emphasis on land is simple—unlike most Africans, most Polynesians and Micronesians lived at fairly high population densities, on islands surrounded by oceans dotted with other, equally densely populated islands. There were, in fact, a number of Polynesian and Micronesian societies in which land ownership and inheritance were not major concerns, but these were precisely those societies where there was surplus land and low population density and where access to subsistence resources was not restricted by availability of lands. For example, Mead says of Manu'a that land had never been used up by the 1920s, and ambitious people could always clear more (1969:65). Similarly, on Pohnpei, one of the largest and most productive islands in Micronesia, "The productivity of Ponapean farming....made issues of land inheritance somewhat irrelevant for day-to-day existence" (Petersen 1982:134). On Easter Island, in the Marquesas, and in Tahiti, land was plentiful enough that there was always enough available to all, with some uncultivated expanse left over (Mietraux 1940:142; Handy 1923:57-8; Oliver 1974:766-67).

These societies were, however, the exception—the few islands where size and productivity freed their inhabitants from worries about access to agricultural subsistence. On the remainder of the high islands in the area, and on all the low islands, access to land was a central concern. For example, in the large and stratified society of Yap, "The People of Yap, from time immemorial, have defined authority and power in terms of their land" (Lingenfelter 1975:1). In the stratified, multi-atoll society of the Marshall Islands, "Social statuses entailing authority over land were the supreme prizes in the competitive arena of Marshallese life" (Kiste 1974:5). In Polynesia, "For the people of Kapingamarangi Atoll, no other single concern seems to be as omnipresent and as anxiety-provoking as their concern over land" (Lieber 1974:70). On the larger island of Rarotonga, the chiefly titles, the most important indicators of prestige in the society, were always associated with land (Crocombe 1964:38), and so on. In Hawai'i and Tonga, the necessity of supporting large chiefly establishments meant pressure on land and agricultural intensification, even though the basic population/ land ratio was not notably high (Kirch 1984:161-168).

How, then, were land rights held and transmitted in these societies? There were several patterns, but the most important one was found over a wide range of societies in both Polynesia and Micronesia. This was the pattern in which titles to land were vested in some extended kin group, and the individuals belonging to this kin group had rights of access to the group's land. Since these kin groups were never wholly endogamous (in fact, in many cases they were exogamous), residential households consisted of members of more than one such kin group. Each member of a household, then, would be able to claim rights in the lands held by his or her kin group or groups (in some cases, people could claim rights, for example, in both mother's and fathers's group's lands). The land on which the household subsisted was thus a combination of several plots, often in varying eco-logical zones, each forming part of the estate of one of the extended kin groups to which one or more of its members belonged. In this system, rights to the use of land and rights to transmit the use of land within or between generations were held in the extended kin group, which was rarely local-ized. Rights to the produce of the land, while theoretically extending to all members of the landholding kin group, were exercised from day to day on a household basis.

This system worked basically the same way in spite of considerable varia-tion in both kin-group recruitment and household residence. It was found, for example, in the matrilineal, ambilocal Marshalls (Rynkiewich 1976:97-99, 108, 112; Pollock 1974:l04), as well as in several societies in the prima-rily matrilocal, matrilineal central Carolines, such as the Woleai group (Alkire 1974:50-55) and Namonuito (Thomas 1980:174-75). It worked es-sentially the same way in many Polynesian societies, where decent-group recruitment was primarily patrilineal and residence patrilocal, such as Uvea (Burrows 1947:68), Futuna, (Burrows 1936:80-82), the New Zealand Maori (Heuer 1969:469-70), and Rapa, at the opposite end of Polynesia (Hanson 1970:20). The same kind of systems, in fact, also operated in societies where the landholding corporation was a kind of cognatic "stock" of descendants of an ancestor through both lines, as in Tokelau (Huntsman and Hooper 1976:259), and in Pukarua in the Eastern Tuamotus (Hatanaka 1971:314). This system allowed productive processes to be organized at the house-hold level, while keeping ultimate control over the allocation of resources in the hands of the descent-group leadership, whether chief, council, or a combination of the two.

A slight variation on this system occurred in areas where most land was owned by descent-based corporations, but land could also be owned individually. In such systems, a household's productive lands would consist of some that its members obtained use of by their descent-group membership, and others which its members held outright, and could then pass on to their heirs by individual inheritance. This type of system obtained in Truk (Caughey 1977:54, 65-68; Goodenough 1951:31-42) and on the nearby atoll of Etal (Nason 1970:76) as well as on some Polynesian atolls from Kapingamarangi (Lieber 1974:81-82) to Rangiroa in the Tuamotus (Ottino 1970:111, 117n).

Another system assigned rights in land directly to individuals, thus making a household's subsistence land out of the wholly owned plots of its members. This seems not to have been a very widespread system; I have found it described only for the Gilberts (Geddes 1977:380-1; Lundsgaarde and Silverman 1972:101-2; Goodenough 1955:73) and for Nukuoro (Carroll 1970:134-37).

All these systems essentially worked the same way. The problem at hand was to ensure that a household, the group that usually shared in the agricultural division of labor, had rights to enough land and enough different kinds of land to be able to provide subsistence for its members. By allowing the household access to land from various sources, through the individual rights or kin-group memberships of its various members, the system accomplished just that. Both household membership and activation of land rights tended to be flexible, and together they managed to assure the family's subsistence. At the same time, insofar as rights in kin-group held land were under control of group leadership, it enhanced the prestige of the leaders and their control over their followers when the leaders, as nominal owners or custodians, had the right to grant or withhold land from group members.

There was, however, another way to organize land ownership—simply on the basis of the household[4] itself. Particularly in a few Western Polynesian societies, such as Tikopia (Firth 1963:316), Anuta (Feinberg 1979:37; 1981:76), and the Tuvalu or Ellice group (Brady 1974:139-40; Noricks 1983:573-4), but also on the Eastern Carolinian atoll of Pingelap (Damas 1979:181) the patrilocal joint family was the effective landholding, land using, and land inheriting group. This system had fewer sources of flexibility than the systems described above, but as long as transfers—of land or of people, through adoption and alternate residence—were available, as was the case in all these societies, people could still manipulate the system to distribute people and resources in a satisfactory way.

Other Material Resources

Compared to land, other material resources were considerably less important for the family systems of O-cluster societies. Trees could be individually owned in some places; in others, they went with the land they
grew on; in either case, it was the owners' households who usually shared
in the produce. Resources necessary for fishing, such as canoes and fish
weirs, were sometimes collectively owned, as by the canoe house group of
related patrilocal extended families in Anuta (Feinberg 1981:81), or by the
matrilineage, as in Truk (Caughey 1977:69.) The inheritance of durable
wealth was more important in some places than in others. In some areas,
relevant kinds of wealth consisted primarily of food surpluses collected as
tribute, but on other islands, inherited valuables could be an important
aspect of prestige or high status. Weiner has shown (1985) how cloaks and
nephrite ornaments represented valuable prestige items for the Maori, and
that the passage of these between generations at birth, marriage, and death
was an important aspect of the maintenance of status and prestige in families. The same seems to have been true of Palauan shell "money" (Force
and Force 1972:8) and of Yapese shell and stone "money" (Lingenfelter
1975:64), as well as Samoan fine mats preserved and handed down over
several generations in Tonga (Debra Connelly, personal communication).

Titles and Offices

The other kind of rights and duties that were managed and transmitted,
and had an important place in O-cluster social systems, were the many
offices and titles that characterized both the kinship and the political system. We will understand the transmission of such offices and titles better
by considering the next two kinds of family activities: representation and
enabling.

Representation: The Councils of Governing

Another characteristic that O-cluster societies shared with those of Africa was the existence of separate domestic and public, or politico-jural,
spheres of activity, the latter being the arena in which some people, primarily men, competed for social prestige. And in both clusters, this meant
that certain family or kin groups were composed of both active partici-

pants in the prestige competition and other people whose sphere of activity was confined primarily to the family group itself. This, in turn, meant that the family operated in both clusters in ways that were shaped by the family's embeddedness in the larger social system, and did so in two ways. First, participants in the public sphere represented the other members of their families in the activities of that sphere. Second, the mobilization of family efforts enabled some of their members to participate effectively in public activities. We will consider representation first.

As in Africa, family heads represented the other members of their families both in public ritual and in governing councils. The emphasis, however, in most of the literature is on representation in government, so I will concentrate my discussion there. Almost all O-cluster systems seem in precontact times to have had some sort of political council system at some level of the society. Chiefs, it appears, were very rarely autocratic, but usually sought the advice of their council members before making important decisions. For example, in Pukapuka, Hecht considers real economic and political power to have resided in the hands of the council of elders, rather than in those of the *aliki* (1977:197). In the much more highly stratified society of Mangareva, most chiefs still sought the advice of a council of tribal elders (Buck 1938:157). In Rapa in aboriginal times, a chief not only needed to consult his council of elders, but could be deposed by them under certain circumstances (Hanson 1970:22). Geddes has even characterized the southern Gilberts as "democratic," noting that effective power in these islands was exercised by the council of lineage heads which convened in the village meeting house (Geddes 1977:371).

If the council was a widespread institution in the Pacific, what exactly were the groups that were represented to it? They seem to have been of two kinds: extended kin groups, either unilineal or ambilineal, whose core was a group of siblings, and household groups, whose core was one or more married couples. The first type seems to have prevailed in the southern Gilberts (Geddes 1977:371, 375, 380; Goodenough 1957:73-74); and in most of the atolls in the central Carolines, where councils seem to have consisted of lineage heads, either all with chiefly titles, as in Etal (Nason 1981:156), or some with chiefly rank and others commoners, but holding council seats by virtue of their headship of their kin groups, as on Lamotrek (Alkire 1965:30-35). This type of kin-group representation seems to have been present in Polynesia as well, as in Mangaia (Buck 1934:110), in Tokelau (MacGregor 1937:43), and in Tikopia (Firth 1963:314). Whether this should be termed "family" representation is a debatable point. On the one hand, the groups represented fall outside many usual definitions of families, because they included no married couples, unless the groups were endogamous, something rather rare at such a low level of segmentation. On the other hand, such groups, with cores of siblings, fit the more general definition adopted here, of families as groups of relatives living together. For example, in Romonum, Truk, the lineages represented in the meeting house ranged in size from three to thirty-four people (Goodenough 1951:70-71); in nearby Etal, a council of eleven chiefs represented a total of 300 people. We can thus at least say that this sort of representation of small descent groups is an activity of small, quasi-familial groups.

The other sort of representative system took the household or group of households as the unit to be represented: here representation was unambiguously a family activity. The best-known system of this sort was probably the *fono* system of Manu'a: each household, which was organized on ambilocal principles of residence, with patrilocal choices prevailing, was headed by someone with a title, which entitled the head to a seat on the fono, or council (Mead 1969:12, 16). In a very different area, in Yap, the household head was charged with representing the household in all external and political matters (Lingenfelter 1975:42). In the Tuamotuan atoll of Raroia, important decisions were made by a council of all household heads (Danielsson 1955:44).

With regard to many other islands, we are told only that a council of elders or a tribal council or a council of adult males was important, but without structure being specified. In general, the variety of political representation systems reflects a tension or perhaps a balance characteristic of this area between brother-sister ties and husband-wife ties as the important organizing principle of these societies. Both kinds of representation were also important in the ritual sphere: in Tahiti, and Ka'u, Hawai'i, household heads made ritual offerings on behalf of household members (Oliver 1974:624; Handy and Pukui 1972:5-9), while in Tikopia, the ritual representatives were the senior elders of patrilineage segments (Firth 1963:314).

Enabling

The second way in which the family system was conditioned by its embeddedness in a larger society was through family resources enabling family members to compete in the larger sphere of prestige activities. The degree to which this was an important family activity varied widely, however. For commoners in stratified societies, it appears to have been unimportant, since commoners had very little chance of mobility in such situations. For example, Handy and Pukui say of Hawai'i, the most stratified society in the whole cluster, that "The commoner has no greater ambition than success in fishing and farming." Similarly, in Tahiti the three strata in the status system were clearly separated, to the point that stratum endogamy prevailed, and a commoner had little chance to play the game of status mobility (Oliver 1974:751).

For different reasons, enabling was relatively unimportant in many of the small, resource-poor societies. This was partly the case because there were few resources that an ambitious man could accumulate and redistribute, and partly because such societies seem to have been organized primarily along Goldman's "traditional" lines, with the authority vested in the genealogically determined chief only somewhat susceptible to modification. For example, Alkire presents a case from Lamotrek, where the paramount chief of the whole atoll was a disabled young woman. Because of her gender and disability, her authority was attenuated, but by no means eclipsed (Alkire 1965:68). And those who did assume some of her authority in her place were still entitled to do so by their fairly close genealogical connection with her. Similarly, on Tikopia, although it was easier for a chief to meet his ritual obligations if he had control of the sources of wealth, this had not affected the actual ranking or the ritual prestige of the four chiefs of that island in recent generations (Firth 1963:313-315).

We should not, however, belittle the importance of enabling as an activity for important families, even in small societies. Nowhere was chiefly or other power conferred by genealogy alone; one had everywhere to earn at least part of one's inheritance. Both in the rigidly stratified societies such as Hawai'i and Tahiti, and in the relatively poor, genealogically based societies such as Tikopia; in most of the Polynesian atolls from Tokelau to the Tuamotus, and in the low-island societies of the Carolines, those born into high status could either enhance or dilute that status by judicious control and manipulation of resources such as land, goods, and food. In the real "open" societies, such as Mangaia, the Marquesas, Rarotonga, and others, nearly everyone could manipulate these resources to attempt to gain prestige.

The ultimate end of the manipulation of human and other resources in an Oceanic society was a following: increased prestige in the eyes of as many people as possible. In most Oceanic societies, one gained a following by being generous with goods or land, or by mobilizing followers for successful warfare.

Generosity with Goods

Generosity with goods is illustrated by Eastern Truk, where, according to Caughey, "To accumulate food and give it away to those less fortunate gives one prestige and humiliates the other." In this case, generosity was an important part of a good reputation (Caughey 1977:57-8). In the same way, in Futuna prestige was said to depend on generosity (Burrows 1936:58). In Manu'a, accumulation and exchange of wealth was the only way to validate status and status transactions. In Mangareva, while control over land and goods was an important requisite for high status, the highest ranking chiefs of the archipelago could still be deposed if they kept too much tribute for their own families and refused to redistribute enough (Buck 1938:165). In all these cases, an important man could gain followers not by owning and consuming goods, as in C-cluster societies, but by redistributing them. As Firth says of the Maori, "The fixed wealth of a man of rank was not immensely in excess of that of an ordinary tribesman; the difference lay in the larger quantities which kept continually passing through his hands" (1959:134).

Allocation of Land Rights

Redistribution of wealth was not the only way that resources could be turned into prestige. In those societies where there was land shortage, control over and distribution of land had the same effect. This was true at the same time that there seems to have been a general cultural norm throughout the O-cluster that no family could be denied the land necessary for at least a subsistence income. The seeming paradox is resolved when we remember that those who held onto land, who were interested in using it to gain prestige, had no better use for the surplus portion than to grant some sort of rights to the land to people at a lower level, who would thus become or remain their followers. For example, in Yap, where land was the key to political power (Lingenfelter 1975:1), a wealthy man could give away land to poor relatives and thus gain in influence and power (Lingenfelter 1975:89). Similarly, Nason says of Etal that "The ability to accumulate more property than one had received through inheritance, or to obligate others to one, makes a person an influential adult in the community" (1981:162). In Mangareva, land grants from chiefs could make commoners wealthy, but doing so increased the prestige of the chief (Buck 1938:145). In Kapingamarangi, the prestige of the traditional chiefs was based on their landholdings and thus on their ability to grant land to others (Lieber 1968:170). This kind of ability to gain prestige by controlling land and allowing others to use it stood at the base of what Sahlins (1958:7) has termed the pattern of "overlapping stewardship" in so many Oceanic societies. Each level of land rights (except the lowest, or usufruct level) brought prestige directly to its holder, and also brought prestige indirectly though providing certain taxes, gifts, or first fruits offerings that the holder could use in redistribution of goods.

Success in Warfare

The third way to gain or build a following was through military success. This was particularly true in those societies Goldman terms "open", where most of the important status positions were open to those who could effectively compete for them. This could operate in several ways. First, a conqueror would have extra land to distribute to past or potential followers. In the Marshalls, for example, a paramount chief claimed one level of title to all the land in his domain, so that in a sense all the lineages who held the actual usufruct rights held that land of the paramount (Milne and Steward 1967:15). Similar arrangements prevailed in Mangaia, where the victor in a civil war became the "Temporal Lord" of the island, redistributing land to his loyal warriors and incorporating the defeated into his tribe in a lower status (Buck 1934:105, 110, 123), and Rapa, where fugitives from defeat were often taken into the victor's tribes (Hanson 1970:21).

Another way that a conqueror could build or enlarge a following was by making the vanquished into direct dependents, taking them into his household as servants or slaves. This was done in the Marshalls (Spoehr 1949:115) and among the New Zealand Maori (Firth 1959:109-110). A third way that victory enlarged a following was by making it easier for the victor to form marriage alliances with other powerful men, thus gaining both wives, who contributed the household labor that often allowed distribution, and allies, who would increase the likelihood of further victories and more power. Marriage alliances as an important strategy for powerful men are reported from such diverse places as Pohnpei (Petersen 1982:137), New Zealand (Heuer 1969:453), The Marquesas (Handy 1923:45) and the atoll of Tongareva (Buck 1932a:35).

The Enabling Process

Given that generosity and military success were ways of recruiting followers, how did men maneuver within the family systems of O-cluster societies to enable either displays of generosity or military success? Probably in two different ways. First, certain aspects of the family systems of the aristocracy in particular were designed to begin building an important man's following by building its inner core: the man's own household. Chiefly polygyny, reported almost everywhere, certainly contributed to this, as did the above-mentioned practice of taking in defeated refugees and fugitives as households servants. The polyandrous system of the Marquesas (Otterbein 1963) certainly facilitated this process also. Second, extra household members meant extra labor, either in producing valuable goods to be given away, as in Pohnpei (Petersen 1982:136-37) and in Manu'a (Mead 1969:24), or, more commonly, in preparing for ceremonies at which the household head displayed his generosity.

This is why we find various structural features of the most prominent households in all O-cluster societies, features like polygyny, marriage alliances, and domestic servitude, that were ordinarily not present among commoners. For those who could participate in prestige competition, accretions to the family and alliances with other prominent families were important instruments in that competition.

Emotional and Affective Ties

As in Africa, emotional warmth and closeness were not only important aspects of family ties, but aspects that were not randomly distributed across kin categories. Instead, emotions were patterned according to the specific relationships of the people involved. Unlike the African case, however, the pattern of emotional ties in the Polynesian and Micronesian family systems was remarkably uniform across the whole area, from stratified to poor societies, from high islands to low, from matrilineal to patrilineal systems, from Micronesia to Polynesia.

As was the case elsewhere, mother-child ties were intense, strong, lasting, and usually mixed affection with respect. This was the case in such diverse societies as Tahiti (Oliver 1974:725), Anuta (Feinberg 1981:84), and Tonga (Gifford 1929:18). It seems to be a universal pattern that the strong affective bond established between mother and child in infancy continues into adulthood, and the Oceanic societies were certainly no exception. With regard to father-child ties, we find a less warm, more respectful and obedient relationship. This was the case, for example, in Eastern Truk (Caughey 1977:74-5); in Yap (Lingenfelter 1975:43), Tongareva (Buck 1932a:51), and Kapingamarangi (Lieber 1968:74-75). The expected structural contrast between matrilineal and patrilineal systems does not appear here, perhaps because the descent-group principle was always mitigated by other considerations of residence and by the often optional or contingent nature of property and other rights within a descent group. The father, in a sense, did not start out either all-powerful or irrelevant to the child's authority relationships; depending on the child's later choices, he might play a more or less important structural role in the descent group. He always played the same, relatively authoritative role in the household.

The grandparent/grandchild relationship, on the other hand, is everywhere reported to have been one of the loosest, freest relationships in the family system, usually with much indulgence on the part of the grandparents, much affection and joking in both directions. We find this pattern in places as widespread as Rapa (Hanson 1970:104) and Rangiroa (Ottino 1970:103) in Eastern Polynesia; Kapingamarangi in the far west of Polynesia (Lieber 1968:75-76), and the Marshall group in Micronesia (Kiste and Rynkiewich 1976:85; Spoehr 1949:197). This free and easy relationship, as mentioned above, sometimes contained an important component of instruction and learning.

Turning from cross-generation to same-generation relationships, we find a similar consistency in their patterning. Siblings of the same sex were usually solidary and free with each other, though they might be rivals as well (sometimes there is a distinction, in polygynous marriages, between full- and half-siblings, with the latter reflecting the jealousy of their respective mothers—see Oliver 1974:727). Siblings of the opposite sex, on the other hand, usually stood in a complex relationship to one another. In one respect, their relationship was usually considered to be one of the firmest, longest-lasting, and most important ties in the social system, and they were expected to aid and support each other. At the same time, the relationship was usually a formal, restrained one, in which sexual joking was never allowed, and more extreme forms of avoidance were sometimes the practice, as in Yap (Lingenfelter 1975:45), Tokelau (Huntsman and Hooper 1975:425:6, 1976:251), and Manu'a (Mead 1928:44). Even where avoidance was not the rule, as in Pukapuka and Tikopia, a certain amount of respect between brother and sister was expected (Hecht 1977:195; Firth 1963:179).

The other cross-sex, same generation relationship, that between husband and wife, was usually freer and sometimes considered not particularly solidary in ideology. This was the case, for example, in Majuro in the Marshalls (Spoehr 1949:198), in Anuta (Feinberg 1981:90), and at Pukarua in the Tuamotus (Hatanaka 1971:261), where the relationship is described as quite impulsive and not as important as ties between consanguineal kin. The difference between the formal brother-sister tie and the loose husband-wife tie can be explained, I think, by the fact that, while the complementarity of the two kinds of ties was central to O-cluster family structure, the husband-wife tie, because it was based on day-to-day cooperation in subsistence and often other tasks, took care of itself and needed no particular cultural requirement. The brother-sister tie, on the other hand, was necessary for the solidarity of descent groups, but after adolescence the brother and sister rarely cooperated on a day-to-day basis, since they lived in different households. So the cultural emphasis on this tie was necessary, and the relationship was defined in formal terms, with the result that, while the tie was clearly emotionally strong, it was not one of easy comfort or give-and-take, as was the case with the marital bond. Also, the marital bond was dissoluble, and substitutable, while the brother-sister tie was permanent and irreplaceable.

We can see, then, that all eight kinds of family activities were present in O-cluster societies, with the important qualifier that enabling was important only in certain circumstances.

Notes

1. I do not find such an arrangement for systematic exchange of products among households on other high islands, however, as Sahlins predicted. What seems to have happened instead is that landholding corporations to which individuals belonged had ecologically diverse landholdings, so that each household had access to a variety of different kinds of resources. Finney (1966) has shown that households on Tahiti had easy access to a variety of agricultural zones.

2. Western Polynesian islands, such as Tokelau (MacGregor 1937:41) or Anuta (Feinberg 1981:122-23) did have a formal but reciprocal exchange of goods at marriage.

3. This was not true all over the world; the opposite seems to have been the case on the Northwest Coast—see Part V.

4. "Household" is used here not in the sense of a co-resident group but of one that "eats together," i.e. the processing group.

13

Oceanic Family Structure

How did organizing to live on islands in a system of hereditary rank and prestige competition shape the ways in which families were organized in Micronesia and Polynesia? We can begin, as we did for Africa, by looking at the kinds of ties that bound certain people in carrying out the activities described in Chapters 11 and 12. Having done this, we can then proceed to describe the way these ties aggregated people into family groups.

Family Ties

Parents and Children

The most important ties in O-cluster societies were those between parent and child, between husband and wife, and between siblings. Parent-child ties persisted throughout the life-cycle, but as in other areas, their intensity varied with time. Children were, of course, dependent on their parents for nurturance and subsistence from the start. Their dependence and loyalty, however, were sometimes split or transferred by the very common practice of adoption. Depending on the society, and often on the individual case, adoption could mean different things for different adoptees. It might mean recognition of a formal tie between the two sets of parents, and continued dependence on the natal parents for all subsistence and nurturance, or split loyalties and responsibilities, a situation where the child often exercised considerable option in deciding whom he or she would

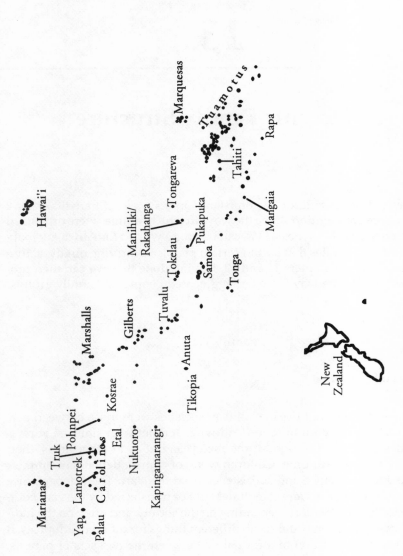

Map 2: Micronesian and Polynesian Islands

live and eat with at a particular time, or even complete transfer of economic responsibilities (though not necessarily of affection) from the natal to the adoptive parents. Whether a child was adopted or not, he or she gradually moved away from the parents through childhood, and in adolescence might well spend most of his or her time in a separate clubhouse for boys or, more rarely, for girls. But adolescent clubhouses were not households—their members did not form a subsistence community—so that even the most independent of adolescents still cooperated and shared in the benefits of their parents' subsistence activities.

In adulthood, married couples usually lived with one set of parents or the other, so that they continued to cooperate with their parents in everyday subsistence activities. But even in situations where parents and children, for some reason, did not share in subsistence activities, they still retained important ties for three reasons. First, people were always dependent on membership in descent groups and descent lines for access to land and other resources, and the resources held by these descent lines were controlled by their senior members. Second, there was the aforementioned role of grandparents in the socialization of their grandchildren, something that gave delight to grandparents and grandchildren, and convenience to the intermediate generation. Finally, in old age people were everywhere dependent for care on their children. All this meant that intergenerational ties, however organized in a particular case, were an important part of Oceanic family organization throughout the life-cycle of the individual.

Husbands and Wives

These ties varied in importance throughout the O-cluster. On the one hand, there was no society in Polynesia or Micronesia where husband and wife were not an interdependent pair for purposes of procuring and processing subsistence goods. On the other hand, their other kinds of interdependence were weaker. Only in a few cases, such as Anuta (Feinberg 1981:76) did they share community property, and although it was often possible, for example, for a husband to work land belonging to his wife's descent group as long as they were married, he had no permanent rights in such land. Husband and wife of course had common interests in children, but both the possibility of adoption and the fact that the children's own property interests were not dependent on their parents' rights as a couple meant that these were not a particularly cohesive force either. What all this meant was that there was rarely even any kind of formal marriage ceremony for commoners in these societies, and that divorce was easy and fairly frequent. Close emotional bonds did, however, hold many couples together for a lifetime.

All this was different, however, in the case of the aristocracy, whose marriages were intimately bound up not only with subsistence, but with access to titles, with preserving stratum endogamy and the ritual sanctity that accompanied it, and with the creation of political and military alliances with other elite families. For this reason, we find the widespread cult of virginity for the daughters of important families, along with arranged marriages accompanied by lavish gift exchanges. For aristocrats or others actively involved in prestige competition, marriage was the stuff of enabling and of politics, and as such was both more important and probably more durable than among commoners.

Brothers and Sisters

Sibling ties were important in all O-cluster societies, and varied less than any other kind of ties in their importance through the life cycle. In most societies, of course, the full group of brothers and sisters that grew up together was split in adolescence by the beginning of single-sex adolescent activity groups, and by their exclusion, because of the incest taboo, from the sexuality that was the usual form of contact between adolescent boys and girls. And when the siblings married, rules or choices of residence inevitably divided some of them in terms of residence. But siblings remained, all over Oceania, members of descent groups that held land and titles, and as such, they continued to have an interest in each other's doings. And this common interest remained throughout the whole life-cycle, even though adult brothers and sisters were usually required to practice considerable reserve with one another.

Dimensions of Variation

Directions of Transmission of Rights and Duties

In most Micronesian societies, descent groups were organized on a matrilineal principle, and much transmission of individual rights also proceeded through the matrilineal route. Conversely, in Polynesia descent group organization and transmission of rights were primarily patrilineal.

But in neither case did the resultant descent groups or mechanisms of transmission look much like those we found in unilineal societies of Africa. This, I think, was true for two reasons. First, in all O-cluster societies, choice and secondary rights of membership and inheritance were important. Choice could be exercised at several points in the life-cycle, but the most important of these were childhood adoption and marriage. If, for any of a variety of reasons, a child was adopted from one descent group or descent line to another, this affected the rights the child would succeed to or inherit, which in turn affected the child's eventual choice of residence at marriage. Residence at marriage might sometimes, as in Rapa (Hanson 1970:20-21), actually determine which member of the couple would be the primary conduit for their children's inheritance; but even if it did not, it certainly was closely tied up with the practical matter of which descent group's resources would be the couple's principal source of subsistence. And finally, even when a person gained principal access to rights and duties through one parent, secondary or conditional access through the other parent was rarely ruled out. All this meant that the actual composition of family groups was not rigidly structured by rules of descent, but was conditional upon many other factors as well, factors that ultimately led back to the old island problem of ensuring equable distribution of scarce subsistence resources.

Inclusion or Restriction of the Junior Generation

The second reason why Oceanic descent groups did not look like their African counterparts is the Oceanic emphasis on genealogical seniority. Always in matters of titles and offices, and sometimes in matters of land and property as well, eldest children, particularly eldest sons, had a special position. This meant that within a descent group at any level, from a small lineage segment to one of the six "canoes" of the Maori, there were senior and junior lines, and the senior lines, at least in those groups with some claim to aristocratic status, had an advantage in prestige competition and thus would take into account prestige considerations when making marriage, residence, and other choices. It was thus not only the rule of descent but the rule of seniority that was a factor in organizing the cross-generational ties in family groups. While all children had to be provided with subsistence resources, the senior ones ordinarily were connected to their parents for purposes of succession much more strongly than were their genealogically junior siblings and cousins. In a sense then, the subsistence group was inclusive, while the political or prestige group was restrictive, and most often restricted on grounds of genealogical seniority.

Single and Plural Marriages

Here the situation was quite simple. In society after society, from the least to the most complex, we find that commoners were monogamous (with the easy possibility of divorce and remarriage) while aristocrats were polygynous, for two reasons. First, more wives meant more alliances with other important families. Second, more wives meant more labor power and more ability to make the ceremonial exchanges and redistribution incumbent on an important chief. At the same time, of course, chiefly status and the goods and deference due from one's commoner retainers made it easier for a chief's household to gainfully employ more wives. The polyandrous marriage system of the Marquesas can, in a sense, be seen as further increasing an important man's household's labor power by bringing in male "wives"; I discuss this system in more detail below.

Time of Transmission

The time of transmission of property rights from one generation to the next was not ordinarily an important concern in O-cluster societies, though in a few places, such as Etal (Nason 1981; 1970:108), a parent who wanted to be supported in old age ensured this support partly by a maintaining a balance between transferring property rights to children and withholding them from them. But in general, the time of transfer of personal statuses was much more salient. Since personal statuses, such as chiefships, family headships, and titles of various sorts, were part of what enabled a man in particular either to simply control material resources, as in the case of a family head, or to participate effectively in political activity, there is a sense in which men of the older generation never wanted to give up these statuses, and sons might well have been impatient for their fathers to leave the scene. On the other hand, there was not much variability here either—chiefs held on to their titles, and thus their formal prerogatives at least, until they died. In general, then, the pattern was for members of the younger generation to gain access to subsistence property at the time of marriage, either through their own parents, their spouses' parents, or some other relative, but to have to wait until the death of the senior generation to come into the most important titles.

We thus find a general type of family developmental cycle in O-cluster societies, in which a family was not so much, as in Africa or in the complex societies, (see Part VI) an organic unit that grew and transformed itself as the generations passed through it, but rather a set of temporary agglomerations of people who were dependent on each other in a variety of ways, either as individuals or as members of larger kin groups. The family cycle was a kind of process of aggregation and splitting of individuals as they pursued their own goals throughout the life cycle. All the enumerated family activities were present, and this made the family a more important unit than in the B-cluster. But the family boundaries were rendered vague by the importance of the adult sibling bond and by the flexibility of residence and adoption. So even more than in the A-cluster, societies of the O-cluster contained family groups with nested and overlapping boundaries.

Variation in O-Cluster Families: A [Captain] Cook's Tour

To illustrate the variations in the Oceanic families, then, we again need to tailor our basic diagram of the developmental cycle to highlight those particular characteristics most important in the O-cluster. Here we need not worry much about plural marriages; chiefs had them, but ordinarily rights and duties were not allocated according to anything corresponding to the African "house." We can thus discard the double box of Chapters 9 and 10. We continue, however, drawing different kinds of boundaries, according to the system being illustrated. In the case of the atoll and small island systems, for example, the relevant groups are the food producing and consuming groups, enclosed within the solid line, and the resource-owning groups, enclosed by the dashed line (Figure 13-1). As in the A-cluster, we need show only one transition (when the rights and duties are passed to the next generation), so we can abbreviate the sequence down to the post-transition phase in the cycle, as usual implying the first diagram in the sequence (Figure 13-2).

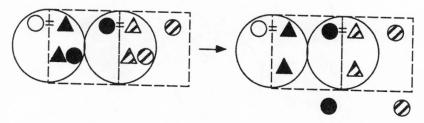

X. Children in natal families

Y. Sons take wives (implied)
Daughters marry out

FIGURE 13-1: Two Phases of an O-Cluster Developmental Cycle

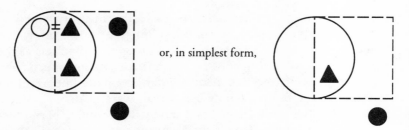

FIGURE 13-2: Simplified Representation of an O-Cluster Developmental Cycle

In the larger systems, where family members are important in enabling the ambitions of family leaders, we retain the solid line for the food procuring and processing group, but add a dotted (not dashed) line for the extended household that cooperates in enabling its leader (Figure 13-3).

At the same time, however, the nature and prevalence of adoption are important variables in O-cluster families, so we need to indicate adoption, which can be done, if necessary, by leaving a little breach in the rectangle surrounding the subsistence group, in order to let infants and children in or out (Figure 13-4).

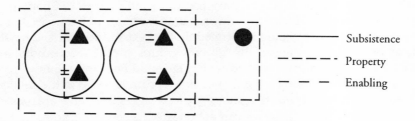

FIGURE 13-3: Overlapping and Nested Groups

FIGURE 13-4: A Subsistence Group with Children Adopted In or Out

Small Island Systems—Adjustive Strategies

I will begin with family systems in which the main concerns were those addressed by the typical adjustive family strategy—insuring a workable balance between resources, primarily land and labor, and human subsistence needs. Sahlins (1957) predicted that this would be true of low island societies, where people would adjust the balance between resources and human needs by maintaining memberships in a large number of overlapping groups. Each of these groups would be organized according to a different principle, and each would be an avenue through which individuals could gain access to property rights. There were, in fact, many other ways of accomplishing the same ends, but in all systems the ability to adjust group membership and to exercise options of property use were important. Within these constraints, however, there were a large number of ways that the developmental cycle of a family group could work itself out.

I will begin with systems in which the adjustment of the needs/resources balance was accomplished by making access to group resources contingent on use, by allowing choices and frequent changes of marital residence, and by a high rate of adoption. One such system prevailed among the commoners of nearly all the atolls of the Marshall group, with only very slight variation from one atoll to another. (The Marshall group was ruled by a number of warring paramount chiefs, each of whom held sway over several atolls at once. But beyond the hints that the high chiefs were often very polygynous [Kiste 1974:49], that their marriages were endogamous and arranged [Kiste 1974; Spoehr 1949:74], and that their households sometimes contained domestic servants recruited from war refugees [Spoehr 1949:115; Kiste 1974:20-21], we have no record of how the family system of the chiefly class actually worked.)

The family system of the Marshallese commoners, however, is much better described. It was based on the principle of the matrilineage as the effective landowning group (though the paramount chief had certain rights of overlordship), with households displaying very fluid residence and adoption patterns. Land in the Marshalls was divided into strips, called *wato*, that ran from the ocean to the lagoon side of an atoll, and thus were likely to contain land suitable for more than one kind of agriculture, as well as for housing (Milne and Steward 1967:2; Pollock 1974:105). Each of these *wato* effectively belonged to a matrilineage, or *bwij*, and all members of the matrilineage were eligible to claim rights of residence or use to that lineage's land. The *bwij* landholdings were administered by the lineage head, or *alab*, typically the eldest male of the landholding group (Rynkiewich 1976:112). In effect, this seems to mean that any member of a *bwij* could live on or work any land belonging to his or her lineage that was not already being worked by somebody else. In addition, the *alab* could, with the consent of the lineage members, allocate lifetime usufruct rights to land to the children of the lineage's male members, giving people the option of access to their fathers' lineage lands as well as their own (Kiste 1974:56; Rynkiewich 1976:112). Husbands and wives, as long as they remained married, also were free to use each other's lands (Pollock 1974:104).

Under such conditions, a viable household was one in which one or more members, through their matrilineage membership or their connections to their father's lineage, provided the household with land that they could use for housing and for agriculture. In addition, a household needed at least one able-bodied adult male to take part in fishing expeditions, someone to do agriculture, and an adult female to cook and make mats (Rynkiewich 1976:108-109). Beyond this, the number of people consuming a household's production had, of course, to be adjusted to the productive capacity of that household as determined by its land and labor supply.

All these needs could be met in a very flexible way, and the flexibility of the Marshallese developmental cycle reflects this. We can begin the description of the cycle at the point where a married couple, previously part of a joint household of some kind, broke off and formed a household of its own, perhaps with some of its children. The marriage itself was not the result of a formal betrothal or ceremony, but rather the culmination of a process in which, "after a period of initial experimentation, individuals gradually settled into fairly stable unions with compatible partners" (Kiste 1974:49). The couple's residence was located on the land of either the husband's or the wife's matrilineage, and consisted of a dwelling house and a cookhouse. When the original couple's children grew up and married, they might either stay or leave to live with relatives of the other spouse—there was no particular preference for virilocal or uxorilocal residence, and indeed couples might move back and forth between several households with which they had ties (Pollock 1974:109; Spoehr 1949:113-114; Kiste 1974:70). When there was more than one nuclear family unit in the household, each had its separate dwelling house, but they all shared a common cookhouse. When children were born to the second generation, they too might stay, leave, or alternate residences after marriage. Eventually the original couple died, and it is possible that classificatory siblings might live together in a household for awhile, but eventually it broke up, and the cycle began again (Spoehr 1949:113-15).[1]

We can thus discern the outline of an ambilateral joint-family domestic cycle as in Figure 13-5, but we must not imagine that all or even a majority of households followed this outline very closely. Couples and their children usually remained together as long as the husband and wife remained

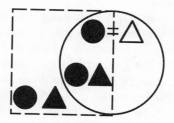

FIGURE 13-5: Basic Marshallese Cycle

married and the children were still minors, but the nuclear family unit often moved between various households to which it was related and on whose land the family members had rights by virtue of lineage memberships, as demonstrated in Figure 13-6. They did this in order to live closer to resources they wanted to use, or in order to be with different people. In addition, adoption was very common, as it was throughout the O-cluster area. Adoption might or might not, depending on the individual circumstance, involve a transfer of residence or a shift in the primary parental responsibility for the adopted child (Rynkiewich 1976:101; Spoehr 1949:210-211); it also varied whether an adopted child gained land rights in his or her adopted lineage (Spoehr 1949:211; Kiste 1974:51). Thus adoption might or might not mean a change in household membership. Finally, divorce was very common throughout the Marshalls (Pollock 1974:104; Spoehr 1949:158). This, too, could disrupt the pattern of the developmental cycle.

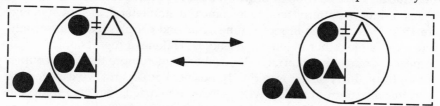

FIGURE 13-6: Marshallese Nuclear Family Moving
Between Resource-Owning Groups

We thus find in the Marshall archipelago a system in which descent-group membership was fairly rigid, and descent groups owned land. But the resources were adjusted to human needs by an extremely flexible system of residence and by allowing people rights in many different pieces of land. When we look at family composition, it should not be surprising that we do not come up with any clear pattern. Household size in the Marshalls typically varied from 3 or 4 to 30 or more people, with averages reported in the mid-20th century as 15 on Bikini (Kiste 1974:69), 7 to 9 on Arno (Rynkiewich 1976:108), 8 on Majuro (Spoehr 1949:103-04), and 15 on Namu

(Pollock 1974:123). Only through examining the processes and principles by which people aggregate into family groups can we see that the pattern of family organization in the Marshalls was other than random.

In the Tuamotus, another group of Atolls thousands of miles from the Marshalls and belonging to the Polynesian linguistic and cultural area, we find a quite similar developmental cycle, but based on entirely different principles of association. Before the inhabitants of the archipelago were gathered into nucleated settlements in historic times, the primary unit of social organization above the level of the family was an ambilineal descent group, called *'ati* on Rangiroa (Ottino 1970:88-89). Recruitment to the *'ati* could be through either the father or the mother; in pre-contact times apparently *'ati* membership depended on the parents' residence. These descent groups were divided, for purposes of landholding, into branches called *feti'i*; each *feti'i* consisted of the descendants of a common pair of grandparents (Ottino 1970:89; Hatanaka 1971:314). Primary members of the *feti'i* were those who lived and worked on the *feti'i* land; although all members of the sibling set held theoretically equal rights to the use of the group's land, only those who resided there ordinarily passed such rights down to the next generation.

On the surface, this seems like a more restrictive system for family organization than that found in the Marshalls. But in practice, the family cycle worked out in a similar way. There was no particular preference for residence on the land of the husband's or the wife's group at marriage (Hatanaka 1972:20-24), so in practice, both in precontact times and in the 1960s, residence patterns tended to come out ambilateral, as shown in Figure 13-7. Here, at least in recent times, married couples had a lesser tendency to live together in joint households; Hatanaka reports only 8 of 37 domestic groups on Pukarua in 1962-63 contained more than one couple. But eight of thirty-seven is certainly not negligible, and we can deduce from this a pattern in which, when a couple married, they had to decide whether to affiliate with the husband's or the wife's *feti'i*, choosing each of

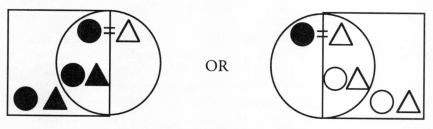

OR

FIGURE 13-7: Ambilateral Transmission and Ambilocal Residence
in the Tuamotus

these approximately half the time. The outlines of an ambilateral joint family system are once again visible, but again the household census would not reveal this in any clear way.

The vagaries of developmental cycle changes were compounded in Pukarua, as in the Marshalls, by mechanisms that served to ensure universal access to material resources. The difference seems to be that in the Tuamotus, a couple had to make a more-or-less permanent residence choice at the time of marriage, a choice that affected their primary descent group affiliation and their children's descent group membership, whereas in the Marshalls descent group recruitment was matrilineal in any case, unaffected by the choice of residence which was, in fact, not stable even after marriage. But if the Tuamotuans had to make a choice at marriage, they could still readjust descent group membership or household organization by the practice of frequent adoption—as Ottino comments, the purpose of adoption was to "work out a reallocation of children which would be more in accord with specific social needs" (1967:476). In both these archipelagos, then, we find family systems that solved the problems of adjusting the balance of people and resources by allowing choices and options in activating rights granted through descent, choices that were exercised by differential decisions in marriage, divorce, residence, adoption, and land utilization. Despite the very different descent ideologies of the two archipelagos, the family systems worked out in very similar ways; each displayed an ambilateral joint-family cycle with much opportunity for splitting, re-aggregating, and transfer of membership.

Most of the atolls in the Marshalls and the Tuamotus are quite large, with land areas typically two or more square kilometers and lagoons up to several tens of kilometers long. In such situations, the resources held by a descent group were apt to be spread over great distances, so that residential flexibility was necessary if people were to balance themselves and their resources over the years or over the generations. In some of the very small atolls of the Carolines, on the other hand, the same balance of people and resources could be achieved even with definite preferences for marital residence, at least as long as some deviations were allowed. Such was the case, for example on Lamotrek, a small atoll with less than one square kilometer of land area (Alkire 1965:22-23). The population of Lamotrek, together with those of its sister atoll Elato and the nearby raised coral island of Satawal, was organized into nine exogamous, ranked matriclans, the three highest ranking of which held chiefly titles that were normally assumed by the genealogically eldest males of the clans (Alkire 1965:30). Each clan was segmented into sub-clans, which were the units of land ownership; the sub-clans, in turn, were segmented into matrilineages (Alkire 1965:43-45). Each lineage had a homestead, which was divided into a home plot, where its residential core of women lived with their husbands, and other plots that were mostly agricultural but might be residential as well. In 1962 and 1963, when Alkire conducted his field research on the atoll, there were 201 residents and 26 homesteads, giving an average of slightly less than eight people per household (Alkire 1965:26-27).

In this system, land rights were granted by sub-clan membership; they could cross lineage lines in inheritance, but the group that controlled the land was the lineage (or occasionally lineage segment) that lived on it and whose women members cultivated it. Marriages here were usually arranged between the partners' respective lineages. Residence was thus preferentially uxorilocal; Alkire found 68% of the people resided uxorilocally, (as shown in Figure 13-8), another 12% virilocally, and 17% lived with the adoptive relatives of one sort or another. With predominantly uxorilocal residence of this sort, the brothers of the sibling group controlling the estate would be dispersed around the inhabited islet, but this would not be any serious handicap, because the male part in subsistence labor was in fishing, which was done communally—the women of the owning lineage, who lived on the land themselves, did the agricultural labor (Alkire 1965:83-84).

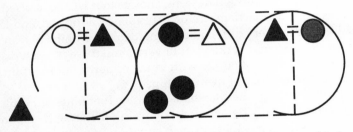

FIGURE 13-8: Uxorilocal Residence and Property-Group Dispersal in Lamotrek

The outline of the Lamotrek developmental cycle was thus that of an uxorilocal joint family, but this outline does not take into account the vagaries of demography. If a lineage got too large, its constituent descent lines could split to form new lineages, each with its own estate and homestead. At the same time, if a lineage diminished in size, its male members might, with their relatives' approval, give land to their own children; in this way the descent line, the group of real siblings within the lineage, gained an estate of its own and was thus aided in the process of breaking off and becoming a lineage in its own right (Alkire 1965:50-52). This mechanism was one way that descent groups could maintain their existence, recruit members unilineally, enforce a residence rule in the great majority of cases, and still manage to readjust the balance between people and resources.

Once again, here as elsewhere, adoption aided in the process. In Lamotrek, an adopted child assumed almost all the rights and duties of a natal child, while retaining the ultimate option to reaffiliate with the natal lineage. Although over half the inhabitants of Lamotrek and Satawal had been adopted at the time of Alkire's visit in 1962-63, in fact only some of these had actually transferred residence and primary affiliation to the adoptive lineage. Adoption thus appears, among other things, as a way of hedging bets. A lineage adopted its child to another (usually within the same clan), and thus not only managed to reinforce distant kin ties, but also more importantly established for that child the option of using resources belonging to, and contributing labor to the subsistence activities of, either the natal or the adopted lineage. The three mechanisms of patrilateral land-transfer, frequent adoption with optional activation of rights in the adopted lineage, and arranged marriage thus served to allocate resources to consumers very efficiently, even though descent group membership was always matrilineally transmitted and residence was overwhelmingly uxorilocal (Alkire 1965:54).

There were many other ways in which atoll societies managed to adjust descent-group membership, residence, and access to resources to ensure an equable, if not necessarily equal, distribution. For example, on Tongareva, succession to titles and inheritance of land rights were normally patrilineal, and residence thus usually patrilocal (Buck 1932a:39-41). But at the same time, flexibility was possible. People could dispose of some of their landholdings by testament (Buck 1932a:41). If a husband was likely to come into fewer land rights than his wife, the couple might live uxorilocally, and their sons, according to the situation, might remain as members of their mother's group, or might be adopted back to their father's family. Households were often large, amounting to as many as fifteen people with a single food supply and single cookhouse, and the largest ones usually took the form of the patrilocal joint family. But again the rules provided for flexibility.

In the Tokelau group, still another pattern prevailed. Here the people were organized according to membership in cognatic stocks, each consisting of the descendants of a common ancestral couple several generations back. Rights to land were held by these various stocks: the children of the daughters of the founding couple, the *tama fafine*, lived on the land (following a preferential rule of uxorilocal residence), worked it cooperatively, and distributed its fruits. The children of the males, on the other hand, the *tama tane*, had rights to decide on the use and reallocation of the property (Huntsman and Hooper 1976:260). Here there was a rather uniform rule of residence, but the relationship of people to resources was made extremely flexible by the fact that a person could claim membership in as many stocks as he or she could trace genealogically back to their founders. The redistribution of land relative to people was accomplished here by Sahlins's suggested mechanism of allowing people rights in resources through membership in many different groups, rights that could be activated or ignored according to individual needs.

The same kind of mechanism also operated in Pukapuka. The social organization of this rather large atoll (5 square kilometers) in central Polynesia was extremely complex, people belonging both to segmentary matrilineages and to segmentary patrilineages. Land was held by matrilineages, by patrilineages, and by the village as a whole, in the case of certain valuable taro beds in the middle of the islands (Beaglehole and Beaglehole 1938:32-45). In addition, if a man dug and maintained new taro pits, these became his personal property, to be inherited patrilineally. In the case of lineage-held land, people ordinarily gained shares in lands held by both their patrilineages and matrilineages.

Marital residence in Pukapuka was usually patrilocal, though if a wife had access to a better quality or greater variety of land rights than her husband, the couple might go to live with her people. In either case, the couple would be affiliated with the *village* where they resided (Beaglehole and Beaglehole 1938:221). This meant that a single married couple had access to the landholdings of at least five groups: the husband's patrilineage, the husband's matrilineage, the wife's patrilineage, the wife's matrilineage, and the village where the two of them resided. The unit of consumption was ordinarily not the nuclear family however, but rather, at least at some phases of the developmental cycle, a patrilocal, matrilocal, or occasionally ambilocal extended family. This family would occupy a group of dwellings, usually one for each couple and its younger children, plus a common cookhouse. So the cooking and consumption group had access to the produce of lands of the patrilineages and matrilineages of all the married-in members, as well as those of the set of siblings who formed the core of the extended household. In addition, produce of the village reserve lands, those not divided into plots for individual families, was divided *per capita* among all the households in the village, and fish caught by communal expeditions of old men or of young men were also distributed in this way (Beaglehole and Beaglehole 1938:38, 54).

We thus have a picture of a system which made maximum use of the principle of membership in overlapping groups as a means of assuring individual access to productive resources. In addition, as in the other systems we have examined, adoption was widespread in Pukapuka, with the adoptive child sometimes gaining complete rights in the adoptive parents' household and lineages, including rights to land inheritance, and at other times receiving only the rights to be fed as a member of the adoptive household, not to gain land access as a member of the adoptive parents' lineages (Beaglehole and Beaglehole 1938:251-52). And marriage, despite its being solemnized, in a rather Western Polynesia manner, by the exchange of mats on both sides, was still fairly flexible. Divorce was easy, and widows and widowers could practice the levirate and sororate as well (Beaglehole and Beaglehole 1938:292-95). Adoption and marriage options thus added to the mechanisms for ensuring the distribution of labor and resources.

The atoll systems from the Marshalls, the Tuamotus, the Lamotrek group, Tongareva, the Tokelaus, and Pukapuka are all compared in the Figure 13-9. All these distributive mechanisms served to ensure adequate subsistence for the entire population of the atoll—the Beagleholes stated that no one ever suffered from lack of food or shelter (1938:108). At the same time, it did not mean that the society was not competitive—in fact there was considerable competition for access to land rights and for production of wealth in the form of food surpluses and mats. As the Beagleholes stated, "The accumulation of wealth has for its end redistribution in the interests of increased prestige" (1938:34-35). And although the economic position of chiefs was in no sense very superior to that of commoners—not enough even to make polygyny profitable (Beaglehole and Beaglehole 1938:292)—still, chiefly lineages took their ritually elevated position seriously, embodying it in the person of the *mayakitanga* or "sacred maid," a woman of that lineage who remained virgin for life (Hecht 1977:196). That she was not married for political advantage, as was her counterpart in the more stratified society of Samoa, indicates once again that prestige in this society did not stem from control over the quest for security in subsistence, and indeed, except for a few chiefly patrilineage branches, prestige was independent of the family system.

We can see a common theme in all the atoll family systems we have examined so far. In none of the systems (except for the high-ranking Marshallese chiefs, of whose family system we know very little) did family members serve to enable the political competition of their family heads. In every case, the project of the family was to assure that the resources necessary to the family's continued existence—land, labor, and childcare—were distributed in such a way that no one was deprived of the basic necessities. In every case, this assurance came from having a series of choices for each individual—whom to marry, where to live, whether to adopt children in or out, which land rights to exercise and which to forego—all of which gave individuals, married couples, and/or sibling sets room to maneuver within the system. As a result, in none of these systems was the land-using group entirely congruent with the land-holding group, or indeed with any of the several landholding groups.

There was, however, another way to ensure distribution of resources on a small island, as illustrated by the case of Anuta, which is not an atoll but is atoll-sized and shares many of the same constraints in adjusting population and resources. On Anuta, the *patongia*, ideally a patrilocal joint family, was both the unit of land ownership and the unit of subsistence production and consumption, as well as being the nearly exclusive sphere of

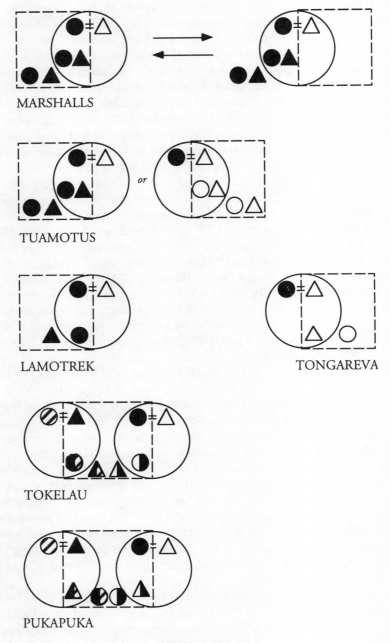

FIGURE 13-9: Atoll Systems Compared

child-rearing and an area of demonstrably closer emotional ties than those with non-members (Feinberg 1979:327; 1981:83-87, 76). A woman, upon marriage, joined her husband's *patongia*, so there were no divided loyalties or resource-access options within the extended family group. Members of the *patongia* were expected to eat together (though they did not always do so), and to live in the *patongia's* house and on its land. This system looks fundamentally different from those described above (Figure 13-10); the subsistence and the landowning groups are fully congruent.

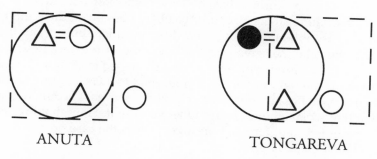

ANUTA   TONGAREVA

FIGURE 13-10: Anuta System Compared with Tongareva,
Another Patrilineal System

How, then, could resources be distributed equably when the social system contained only one kind of group at the family level, and when group membership was so inflexible? Even in this case, there were some mechanisms for readjustment of people to resources when necessary. For example, even though all land belonged to one or another *patongia* and ideally stayed in that estate across the transfer of generations, in fact wives sometimes brought shares of their natal *patongia's* land along with them at marriage, thus matching the transfer of labor power and consumers with the transfer of land resources (Feinberg 1981:80). We also find that, while a *patongia* would ordinarily not transfer title to its lands to another family, it would often allow a related family to use some of its surplus plots, and since every *patongia* on the island was related in a known way to every other one, this meant that a family could grant usufruct rights to anyone who needed them (Feinberg 1981:76; Feinberg 1979:328). Also, though every tree and every taro plant on the island stood on somebody's land, in fact rights to the produce of land did not always go to the owner of the land, but in the case of crops that required work to cultivate, to the cultivator, and in the case of crops, such as coconuts, that required no work, to anyone who wanted to take them (Feinberg 1981:78). In effect, this means that a *patongia* that was short of land had two kinds of recourse: it could borrow some land from a related (that is, Anutan) family, and it could take coconuts and other tree crops from anywhere. And here as elsewhere, fish, an important part of the diet, belonged to the households of the fishermen or, in the case of fishing expeditions in a canoe, to those households who shared in the ownership of the canoe. Every household, of course, had rights in one canoe or another (Feinberg 1981:81-82). What at first looks like a rather rigid and unworkable system of fixed household shares of resources thus turns out, on closer examination, to have been a system in which *ownership* of the resources was fixed, but use of the products was not.

The question then arises, what good was ownership if it did not involve the right to exclude others from use? Feinberg does not address this question in his description of Anutan social organization, but I think the answer is rather like that given for the operation of territorial ownership among Australian hunter-gatherer bands, discussed in Chapter 5. Ownership gives me the right to say this is mine, and to increase your indebtedness to me when I grant you the right to use this, even if I could not, without violating social ethnics, refuse to let you use it. Household resources thus contributed to differential prestige, as was the case on neighboring Tikopia (Firth 1963:314-315).

Larger Islands and the Accretive Strategies of the Elite

All the systems described so far existed on small islands, and as such shared the important characteristic of limited access to subsistence resources, so that the primary goal of families was to adjust the balance between resources and people. The next group of family systems to be examined, however, existed on those larger islands where population pressure did not render subsistence resources particularly scarce. In such environments, social systems developed in which there was considerable political power to be exercised over areas much larger than found in the atoll societies, so that there was considerable competition for prestige resources in larger political and economic arenas. Men who wanted to build, maintain, or enhance their social standing in such societies did so not by genealogically-based control over the allocation of scarce resources, but by control over followers and over territory, the latter often exercised by military means. In such systems household members contributed in various ways to the household heads' competition for social power and prestige—enabling became important in determining the nature of family organization. Subsistence activities of the family were still important here, of course, but family organization for subsistence was concerned more with providing an adequate and suitably divided supply of labor than it was with ensuring access to material resources. So enabling came into its own—the ability to build up a large, strong, and well-connected family was crucial to a man's success in political competition, and ambitious men pursued accretive family strategies. Let us look at some of these systems, in particular at the ways in which certain characteristics of family organization contributed to family heads' political success.

We can start with the Maori of New Zealand. Although their society was, in Goldman's classification, a "traditional" one, that is, one in which high status rested primarily on genealogy, it becomes clear when examining descriptions of the Maori that in fact genealogical position was not enough—if a chief wanted to be respected in his position and powerful in politics he had to build a loyal following. Chiefly position was indeed determined by genealogy in the first instance—a chief was the genealogically senior male in the highest ranking descent line of the *hapu*, or localized, patrilineally-biased ambilineal descent group (Firth 1959:103). Commoners in this society had a family system mostly innocent of the need to enable political participation. Commoners married within the *hapu*, did so without ceremony, and ordinarily resided patrilocally in *whanau*, or household groups, that appear to have gone through a patrilocal joint family cycle (Heuer 1969:454; Firth 1959:105, 111). Their family organization thus appears to have been primarily concerned with ensuring family subsistence and continuity.

Chiefs, however, had additional concerns. They were concerned with building their political power and prestige, and did so primarily in two ways: by leading their *hapu* (often congruent with village communities) in warfare, and by being generous to their followers in distributions of wealth. To do either of these effectively, a chief needed to build a household that was both large and well-connected, and much of the difference between chiefly and commoner family organization stemmed from the devices used by chiefs to increase the size and better the connections of their households.

A larger household meant both more effective military organization and, more importantly, more labor to produce the goods that a chief could give away to show his generosity. So chiefs increased their household size in several ways. First, there was polygyny. Only chiefs were commonly polygynous, and one way of estimating a chief's wealth was in terms of the number of wives (Heuer 1969:455-56; Firth 1959:129). This was because, as Firth indicates, "the social importance of polygyny lay in the fact that it buttressed the position and authority of the chief, both directly, by giving him land and prestige (the land came as a "marriage portion" of a woman marrying a chief), and indirectly, by providing him with an amount of economic resources which could be distributed to secure the services and allegiance of his people" (1959:130). Wives made woven and plaited goods, often given away in ceremonial exchanges, and also prepared all the food, which was also an important vessel for generosity (Heuer 1969:458). Second, a chief could increase the size of his household by bringing in war captives as household servants or slaves, further adding to the labor capacity (Firth 1959:109-110).

But a successful chief needed not only a big household, but also alliances with other chiefs. This means that it was to the advantage of a chief not only to make plural marriages, but to make good marriages, and in both directions—his daughters ought to marry well, and his wives ought to be of good family. For this reason, marriage could not be left to the emotions of the young, as among Maori commoners, but had to be arranged. And unlike commoners, chiefs ordinarily married outside the *hapu* or even the tribe (Heuer 1969:453). For a system of arranged marriages to work, of course, the sexuality of young women had to be controlled, and indeed we find that daughters of chiefs, unlike other young women, were allowed no sexual freedom. And when they were married, they not only took a portion in land with them (Firth 1959:130), they also married with a formal ceremony, something absent from the marriage of the common people (Heuer 1969:454).

All in all, then, the need of chiefs to make their households large and well-connected made for a considerably more complex household organization than prevailed among the commoners. The polygynous household of a chief brought about the co-wife relationship, one that was said to be frequently, if not always, fraught with rivalry (Firth 1959:131; Heuer 1969:456-57), and which sometimes entailed the setting up of separate cookhouses within the chief's family. One wife was the head wife, and her children took precedence in succeeding to chiefly titles (Heuer 1969:456).The Maori chiefly family system is illustrated in Figure 13-11.

FIGURE 13-11: Maori Chief's Prestige Cycle Showing Succession
to Sons of Senior Wife

If a Maori chief gained his title by genealogy but created and maintained his prestige and power by being militarily strong and economically generous, on the island of Mangaia in the Cook group, genealogy played a much smaller role, though the effects of chiefly activity on the family system of important men were similar to those found in New Zealand. Mangaia, with a probable pre-contact population of two to three thousand (Buck 1934:6), was divided into several tribes, each a unit of warfare and a local unit occupying a group of mainly contiguous lands, crossing the several ecological zones that made up the island from reef to mountaintop (Buck 1934:105-107). There was in each tribe a man with the impeccable chiefly title of *ariki*, but by late precontact times his powers seem to have dwindled until they were primarily ritual. Instead, it was the war leader of each tribe, a non-hereditary position, that possessed the most political and economic power, and after each round of the civil wars that rocked the island in those times, the war leader of the victorious tribe became Temporal Lord of Mangaia, rewarding his loyal subordinates with land grants and with the rule of various districts on the island (Buck 1934:110, 123-124). In this kind of a system, it was not only the genealogically eldest who could engage in competition for power and prestige, it was in essence anybody. Some presumably never gave it a thought, and devoted themselves and their families solely to survival and reproduction. Others, however, competed actively through participation in war and the enjoyment of its spoils. Since these latter were not in any titular sense 'chiefs,' I will refer to them as 'the elite' and contrast them not with 'commoners' but with 'common people'.

The developmental cycle of the common people's families appears to have followed a familiar Polynesian form. Patrilocal residence was usual, but matrilocal was possible. Marriage occurred without ceremony, after a period of free adolescent sexuality. Monogamy was the rule; adoption was easy (Buck 1934:91-96).

Among the elite, however, the same kind of considerations as occurred among the Maori influenced their family cycle in very different directions from what we saw of the common people. An elite man's power and influence depended largely on the number of people who give him allegiance, and this in turn depended both on the size and composition of the household and on its ability to contract advantageous marriages (Buck 1934:90, 110). We thus find that elite men were not only polygynous (Buck 1934:92-93), but also accumulated large households by bringing in a variety of miscellaneous relatives, as well as members of subjugated tribes who sought the great man's protection and were rewarded with the status of menial servants, who of course increased the household's labor power.

And as in New Zealand, members of the elite were concerned not only with accumulating followers in their own, sometimes very large households, but also with obtaining the allegiance of outsiders. This probably happened simply as a virtue of having a large household that would be militarily strong, but it was also facilitated by making good marriages. Whereas marriage among the common people was established merely by cohabitation, among the elite it was arranged by the parents, with status the first consideration (Buck 1934.:90-91). Once again, as in New Zealand, competition for status meant that the family members of a prominent or ambitious man were caught up in enabling; the difference was that on Mangaia, determining who could compete for status had much less to do with genealogy that it did among the Maori. The two systems are compared in Figure 13-12.

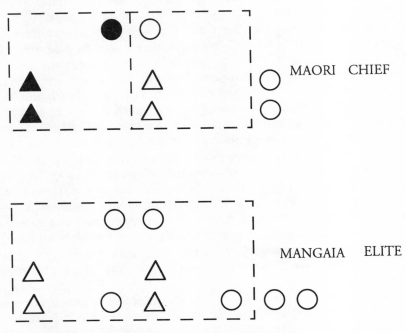

FIGURE 13-12: Accretive Strategies of Maori and Mangaia Elites

Lest it be thought that the kind of accretive family strategy pursued by important men was purely an Eastern Polynesian phenomenon, we might note that a very similar system was in effect on the Micronesian high island of Pohnpei. We do not know as many details of the social organization of Pohnpei in pre-contact times as we know for New Zealand or the Cook islands, but what we do know suggests that, in spite of a culture area difference and the usual Micronesian preference for matrilineal descent group organization and official succession, the family system of the Pohnpeians showed the same difference between chiefs and commoners that was found among the Maori and the Mangaians, and that the family system of the Pohnpeian chiefs itself worked in a very similar way to the chiefly systems in the two Polynesian societies.

Consider first the following contrasts. Among commoners, residence was optional, with perhaps a matrilocal preference (Petersen 1982:133; Riesenberg 1968:72), but chiefs commonly violated this preference, bringing their wives to live with them (Riesenberg 1968:72). While commoners were monogamous, lower-ranking chiefs commonly had two wives, but the highest-ranking chiefs were known to have married as many as ten or twelve women. While commoners usually married within the local group, chiefs endeavored to take wives from other chiefly lines, for purposes of political alliance (Petersen 1982:134; Riesenberg 1968:73).

From these sources, we gain little picture of what the Pohnpeian developmental cycle actually looked like, but we can explain the ways in which chiefly polygyny and exogamy served to increase their status and prestige. Pohnpeian chiefs gained prestige by warfare and by putting on large ceremonial feasts. Women not only produced taro, the most important food crop, but they also made the wealth goods—belts, baskets, mats, blankets, ornaments—that were given away by chiefs at feasts that celebrated their marriages, taking of titles, or other important events. The more women in the household, the more goods it could produce, and the more prestige the household head could gain by giving the goods away. Despite the difference in social systems, Pohnpeian chiefs seem to have manipulated family resources to serve political needs in much the same way as their Eastern Polynesian counterparts. We can thus present the family systems of those societies in which prominent men followed accretive strategies in the Figure 13-13, showing the matrilineal and patrilineal variants side-by-side, with the commoners' families on the top and the elite on the bottom.

This kind of family accretion, in which a powerful or ambitious man, as head of household, tries to increase his power and influence by accumulating labor resources within his family, can go a long way, I think, toward explaining and putting into context what has been considered one of the most bizarre of the world's family systems—the famous "non-fraternal polyandrous" system of the Marquesas. On these rugged islands, cursed with a dry and unpredictable climate necessitating reliance on stored foods, and with no fringing reefs, meaning all fishing had to be done in the deep sea, tribes isolated in the deep valleys of the larger islands constantly fought with one another, forming and breaking alliances, conquering and being scattered by conquest (Handy 1923:6-9, 24-27, 35-37).

High status in the Marquesas, as on Mangaia, seems to have had little to do with genealogy. Each territorial tribe had its "chief", but significantly even the word for chief, *haka-iki*, meant "made chief"—chiefship was won in politics and warfare, not conferred by birth (Handy 1923:44-45). The power of a chief depended on his ability to control territory—the land of his tribe's valley was his in overlordship, and he allotted it to the families of the tribe in return for their service in war and in economic pursuits (Handy 1923:57).

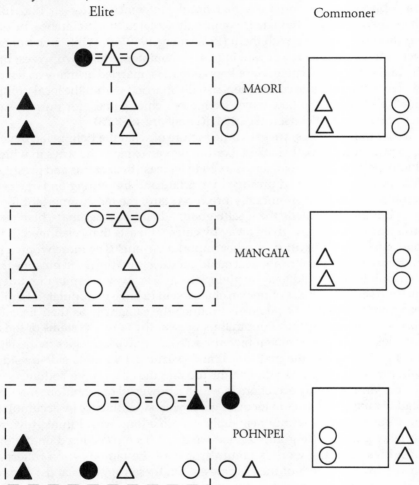

FIGURE 13-13: Accretive Elite and Adjustive Commoner Households

πIn this kind of an "open" social system, it was theoretically possible for just about anyone to engage in prestige competition, but of course in reality there were only a few chiefs, and even with the fluid social system, in the absence of major catastrophes or unforeseen shifts in fortune, a chief's children, particularly his first born, had a decided advantage in achieving the *haka-iki status*. This means that most people were neither wealthy nor influential, and that their goals in building families were to ensure access to sufficient land (which could be gotten by inheritance, by allotment from a chief, or by reclaiming unused ground). We have no concrete information on the developmental cycle of ordinary families in the Marquesas, but we can infer from what little information is available that marriage was sometimes with close relatives, in order not to disperse the inheritance of property (Handy 1923:100) that it was almost certainly monogamous, and that adoption was a common practice, the motive of the adopter usually being to increase the family's labor power, necessary in the arduous tasks of fishing and food preservation (Handy 1923:81).

Of the families of influential men, including chiefs, we know a lot more, because their family system fascinated early explorers and later ethnologists alike, and because it was superficially unlike any other found in a known human society. A member of the Marquesan elite, like his counterpart on Mangaia, in New Zealand, or on Pohnpei, pursued an accretive family strategy. Handy tells us that "a chief arrives at this position through social prestige and power resultant upon being the head of a large and wealthy family, allied with other powerful families by means of affiancing, marriage, adoption, and by making namesakes" (Handy 1923:45). In order to build up the family to the greatest possible extent, elite Marquesans employed many of the same strategies we have seen in the previous examples. For example, a chief could take multiple wives (Handy 1923:46; Otterbein 1963:157-58), could adopt and/or foster large numbers of children, could take in all manner of relatives as household members, and could gain servants from poor members of his own tribe or from among the defeated (Handy 1923:46).

But the accretive family strategy of the Marquesans did not stop there. One other way to gain important additional male labor power for a chief's family was to allow lower-class men to marry as secondary husbands of the chief's wife or wives. This might happen in any of several ways. For example, a man of modest means might marry uxorilocally to gain access to land inherited from his wife's family. Later on, a wealthy man (perhaps a chief) took both of them into his household, marrying the wife himself and bringing her original husband along in a now secondary, subordinate role, but still in a sexual relationship with the wife. Or a high-status man and one of lesser status might form a sort of partnership, and marry the same woman at the same time. In this kind of a situation, the higher-status of the two husbands would become the household head. Alternatively, a middle-aged or older man of high status might want to marry a young woman from a poorer family, an arrangement attractive to her and her family because of the potential access to resources from the wealthy husband. The young woman, however, might insist on bringing her lover or lovers with her into the marriage (here as elsewhere in Polynesia, premari-

lovers with her into the marriage (here as elsewhere in Polynesia, premarital sexuality was free at least for lower-status people), an arrangement that would also provide labor for the household and thus be advantageous to the family head. There was a fourth arrangement, less formal and, in Otterbein's view, not deserving of the title "marriage", where young men simply attached themselves for sexual purposes to the household of wealthy man with attractive wives (Otterbein 1963:156-58).

In a synchronic sense, all these arrangements simply look like a system in which a woman had plural husbands, as indicated in Figure 13-14.

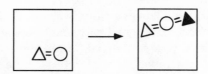

A. A low-status couple marries a prominent man

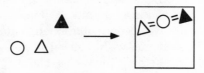

B. A high- and a low-status man marry the same woman at the same time

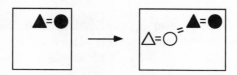

C. A high-status man takes a secondary wife along with her husband or lover

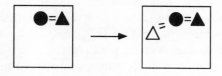

D. A young man marries a wealthy man's wife as a secondary husband

FIGURE 13-14: Processes of Formation of Marquesan Polyandrous Households

But the important thing to understand is that the polyandrous arrangement was not woman-centered. Its result was, indeed, more than one husband for a woman, but the structure centered around the household head. In every kind of polyandrous arrangement, the household head, the senior male or primary husband, seems to have been the authority figure in the family. Junior husbands were almost always of lower status than the household head, and since the head's wife was raised to the status of her husband, it appears that she ordinarily had authority in domestic matters over secondary husbands, and in fact over secondary wives as well (Otterbein 1963:157-58).

Seen in this way, some of the mystery of Marquesan polyandry evaporates. It was, on the whole, simply part of an accretive family strategy followed by wealthy and powerful men in an open social system. The practice of polyandry may have been encouraged by a somewhat imbalanced sex ratio brought on by female infanticide (Otterbein 1963:157). This would be plausible in a country where warfare and male labor were the most important assets, and where periodic droughts may have made it disadvantageous to try to raise babies born at certain lean seasons. It also had consequences for sexual practices of married women, who seem to have gained access to a greater variety of partners than was the case in many other O-cluster family systems. But it is not a bizarre system at all; it fit in very closely with the accretive family systems so common in a certain type of island society. Figure 13-15 puts the Marquesan system into its Oceanic context.

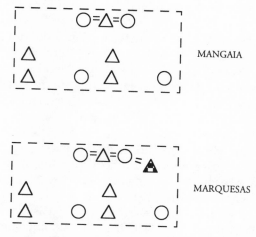

FIGURE 13-15: The Close Relationship Between Marquesan Polyandry and Other Accretive Systems

Family systems of the accretive type (including those of Samoa and Mangareva in addition to the systems discussed in detail), were thus characteristic of high-status groups in societies where gaining or maintaining high status depended on building a following through generosity and making alliances.

The Highly Stratified Societies — Enter the Exclusive Strategy

When we come to systems in which hereditary rank divided the society into definite strata, with mobility between the strata difficult and high status thus no longer achievable, we find not only accretion but exclusivity coming into play in shaping the family system. In many such systems, accretion was still a characteristic of the families of the elite, but it was accretion for a different reason. A large and wealthy household was the result of high status, not a factor contributing to that high status. In such family systems, concern with differential rank worked both ways—on the one hand, it encouraged accretion, because people could gain benefits from being retainers of a high chief, or subordinate members of his household, but it also in this case made for a certain exclusiveness—the high rank of the prestigious household members should not be diluted by indiscriminate contact with those of lower rank even if they were useful as retainers and servants. We thus find in such societies a concern with the preservation of rank, with the exclusion of people of lower rank from certain positions in the family.

The societies displaying the exclusive tendency did not all do so to the same degree. In Tonga, for example, both the accretive and the exclusive tendencies were clearly visible. The society was divided into three distinct strata—*eiki*, *matapule*, and commoners; within the *eiki* stratum were various ranks, genealogically determined, culminating in the lineage of the Tui Tonga, the highest ranking chief. Chiefs had certain prerogatives—they could commandeer labor for monumental construction, for example, and exercised territorial rights to the lands in their domains, rights that included first fruits and choice fish grown or caught by their subjects (Gifford 1929:73, 102-108). Commoner family organization seems to have been unremarkable—residence was ordinarily patrilocal, unions were monogamous, and the nuclear family seems to have existed, in many cases at least, as a fairly autonomous unit (Gifford 1929:15-17, 31). But among chiefs, things were different. Chiefs practiced now-familiar strategies to augment their households—they were commonly polygynous, and often took kin of inferior rank as household servants. When a chief married, his wife would often bring several of her relatives to form part of the chief's family (Gifford 1929:15-17, 31).

So far, the Tongan family system looks just like one of the accretive systems just described, but there was in fact an exclusive tendency at work as well. The high-ranking chiefs, at least, did not just practice polygyny, at least not polygyny of the indiscriminate type. Rather the Tui Tonga and other chiefs of very high rank accumulated large harems, but harems with internal differentiation. The Tui Tonga tried to marry the daughter of another high-ranking chief as his "great chief wife," and he might take other high-ranking wives as well (Gifford 1929:61). Other chiefs, including the *hau* or secular paramount, arranged marriages designed to preserve their higher rank and sanctity: Marriages between the *hau* and the Tamaha, the sister's daughter of the Tui Tonga, or between the *hau* and chiefly women of Samoa both served this purpose (Kirch 1984:226). But the Tui Tonga did not stop there—he also took subordinate wives, who were sometimes younger, and thus-lower-ranking, relatives of his important wives. We thus see in the Tongan system (Figure 13-16) at least the beginning of the distinctions of rank that became so important in the more highly exclusive systems of Tahiti, to be described below.

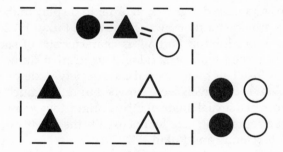

FIGURE 13-16: Higher Ranking Wives Produce Heirs

We know little about the family system of aboriginal Hawai'i. The only detailed description seems to be that of Handy and Pukui (1972), but even that was collected in the mid-twentieth century at a time when the living system had changed considerably. The memories of even the oldest and best-informed people in the area only reached back to a time two generations after the true native stratification system, and the effects it must have had on the family patterns of the different strata, had been transformed by colonial contact and the recasting of hierarchy in more European-like terms. Nevertheless, there are tantalizing glimpses available in the literature, and these glimpses at least hint that the Hawai'ian system was, like the Tongan, composed of both accretive and exclusive features.

The distinction between commoner and chiefly *(ali'i)* family systems seems reasonably clear, at least in its basic outline. Commoners married monogamously and uxorilocally, and nearly always married within their own social stratum (Handy and Pukui 1972:44, 105, 161). There was no particular period of betrothal, no formal marriage ceremony, no attempt to arrange marriages, and there was the possibility of divorce for whichever partner decided to just pick up and leave (Handy and Pukui 1972:105-110). Among the elite, however, we find features typical of an accretive family system. *Ali'i* were commonly polygynous (Handy and Pukui 1972:58), and household retainers, usually relatives of junior lines of chiefly lineages, were common in chiefs' households (Handy and Pukui 1972:199).

But at the same time, among the Hawai'ian elite, we find other tendencies of a more exclusive nature, a tendency toward concern with rank overriding concern for building up a large household. For example, we find more concern here than elsewhere with marrying someone of the right social standing. The firstborn of distinguished families were often betrothed before birth to partners of similar social distinction (Handy and Pukui 1972:105). When families of means married their sons and daughters, they not only held lavish feasts, using tribute from their subjects to display their generosity, they also endeavored to provide dowry in land and goods to both their sons and their daughters, in order to display to the community their ability to provide for their own (Handy and Pukui 1972:106). Dowry, as we will see more fully in Part VI, is characteristic of societies where families are concerned with preserving their relative status, and is most prevalent in C-cluster, or preindustrial class-society, systems. Finally, marriages with lower social levels were frowned upon, so much so that if offspring were born of a sexual union of mixed origin, they were usually killed at birth, or else adopted out, in order not to sully the sanctity of their higher-ranking parents (Handy and Pukui 1972:79).

Homogamy, of course, is not in itself exclusivity in a family system; we have seen a degree of homogamy in all the accretive systems as well. But homogamy in this case seems to have been directed toward the goals of exclusivity. And there were other features of the Hawai'ian system that suggest even more of an exclusive emphasis. In the first place, there was a great concern with differential rank or sanctity within the household itself. Only in Hawai'i and Yap (see below) do we find evidence of an attempt to exclude women, whose sanctity was always lower, from eating with men, even of the same household (Handy and Pukui 1972:12). And finally, of course, an aspect unique to the Hawai'ian system demonstrates its exclusive character most fully for the highest ranking families. This was the custom of marriage with close relatives. In the accretive systems, the higher the status, the more distant marriage is likely to be, since people are concerned with making alliances. But among the most elite families of Hawai'i, in fact the opposite held true. High-ranking chiefs were more *kapu* or sacred, than other people, and a marriage at a distance could only dilute that sacredness. For the very highest ranking chiefs, those who were too sacred to even engage in political activity and had to go about only by night, in order to avoid contact with the profanity of even the temporal rulers, marriage with the full sister was the desired rule, and a child of a brother-sister marriage, from whose ancestry all diluting influence had been excluded, was the highest ranking and most *kapu* of all.

Thus while the Tongan and Hawai'ian systems both showed accretive and exclusive tendencies, the Hawai'ian stood somewhat closer to the exclusive pole of the continuum, particularly in the family practices of the highest-ranking people in the islands. When we move to Tahiti, we find a system in which the exclusive tendency was apparently paramount for all members of the highest social stratum.

In the Society Islands, of which Tahiti is the largest and best-known, there were in pre-contact times three social strata—*ari'i*, *ra'atira*, and *manahune*, most clearly distinguished by their homogamy (Oliver 1974:751). *Ari'i*, in addition to being temporal and military rulers, also had rights of overlordship to most land, rights that granted them tribute from tenants, little of which they commonly redistributed (Oliver 1974:1128). *Ra'atira* were apparently not the junior relatives of *ari'i*, but rather members of lineages ranking lower than those of the chiefs, but not subject to the overlordship of the *ari'i* (Oliver 1974:769-70). Commoners were those with no ritual rank, and whose lands were most encumbered by rights of overlordship of *ali'i* and/or *ra'atira*. There is little information about the family system of the commoners, except that marriage was typically casual, after a period of free license in adolescence, and residence was typically virilocal, with the possibility of uxorilocality in circumstances that favored it (Oliver 1974:801).

If the Tahitian commoner system resembled that found on other, similar large islands, there are hints that the family process of the *ra'atira*, or perhaps others in the middle ranks of Tahitian society (such as prominent ritual and craft specialists or warriors) showed the accretive tendencies of the elites of some of the "open" societies. We find, for example, that the *ra'atira*, in contrast to the *ari'i* (see below) were usually polygynous, and because it was people of this middle stratum who controlled much of the land and wealth of the society, their poorer and lower ranking relatives often attached themselves to the households of the *ra'atira*, giving them great numbers of retainers (Ellis 1829, vol. II:344-345, quoted in Oliver 1974:771).

What, then, of the *ari'i*? Their family system, in fact, seems to have been more exclusive then accretive. A high-ranking chief had only one wife, a wife who was betrothed early and whose marriage was certainly arranged with considerations of rank in mind (Oliver 1974:732, 751). The marriage was concerned not only with alliance between high-ranking lines, but also with the legitimation (and limitation) of the children who would succeed to important titles and positions (Oliver 1974:805). This, of course, necessitated an elaborate wedding ceremony (Oliver 1974:805). But people of chiefly rank in Tahiti did not wish, nor were they required, to restrict their sexual relations to others of similar rank, nor were they expected to do much of the productive or domestic labor for their families. Both these needs were taken care of by lower-ranked people.

Whereas ra'atira were polygynous, ari'i were strictly monogamous in terms of high-ranking, legitimate marriages designed to produce successors and heirs. But both males and females of the highest stratum were permitted sexual relations with lower-ranking people, sexual relations neither officially sanctioned nor productive of legitimate heirs. Male ari'i had concubines in addition to their wives, and the concubines' children were excluded from succession (Oliver 1974:464-65). Ari'i women's sex lives increased in freedom as they got older. Women of title-holding families were generally prohibited from premarital sex, in anticipation of an advantageous marriage to a man of similarly high rank. During the early part of the marriage, their sexual relations were restricted to their husbands, until they had given birth to a legitimate successor. Once this successor was born, however, high-ranking women had the same sexual freedom as their husbands, taking numerous lovers from all classes of the population, particularly from the chiefly household's military retainers. Children of these unions, however, were usually killed at birth (Oliver 1974:611, 827-28, 764).

The households of ari'i also apparently contained many servants and followers, but these were completely separate from their masters in terms of their lack of titles, their subordinate status, and their requirement to perform most of the household labor (Oliver 1974:785).

The highest ranking families of Tahiti, then, practiced a family system that resembled that of the highest status families of Hawai'i: it served the preservation and enhancement of their high status not by building followings, which were built by other means, but by serving to set those of high-rank apart from those underneath them. In Tahiti, more than in any other society, we thus see family systems functioning separately on three levels of society. For the commoners, the family system served primarily to establish a division of labor, assure access to resources (which was not difficult), and to provide child-rearing and emotional interdependence. Among the ra'atira, the family system served the additional purpose of enabling— building a following that would help to raise the family head's status and thus allow him to further increase his following. Among the highest rank, where status and following were already secure, the family system served to emphasize the separation between the ari'i and their followers. We can sum up the family systems of the elite of Tonga, Hawai'i, and Tahiti in Figure 13-17.

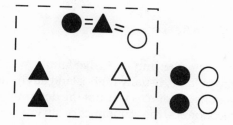

Tonga: Higher-Ranking Wives Produce Heirs

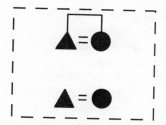

Hawai'i: Marriage With Close Relatives Preserves Rank

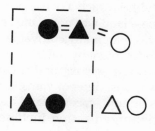

Tahiti: Offspring of Lower-Ranking Spouses Excluded from Prestige Group

FIGURE 13-17: Elite Polynesian Exclusive Strategies

Yap and the Return to Subsistence Concerns

All the accretive, accretive-exclusive, and exclusive family systems we have discussed so far occurred in large, usually high-island environments, where population pressure against resources was not the determining factor in social organization. If economics, the economics of survival, was the most salient consideration for the adjustive family systems of the small islands, it was politics, the politics of competition, prestige, warfare, and status, that dominated the concerns, and thus also the family-building strategies, of the elite of the larger islands, while the commoners were left to exist, ordinarily without any privation, as the subjects and soldiers of the elite. There is, however, another possibility, that of a large, high island on which population pressure was extreme, and existed together with a large-scale political system in which important people competed for power and prestige. There was, in fact, in the O-cluster at least one system of this kind, on the islands of Yap in the western Carolines.

Yap was by far the most densely populated high island in the Pacific, with an estimated pre-contact population of 50,000 people in an area of 38.6 square miles, giving it a population density three times that of the Society Islands, a density approached elsewhere only on small atolls with adjustive mechanisms primary in their family and social systems. Yet Yap was a competitive polity, with marked social strata and endemic territorial warfare. How, in such a situation, did the family system work, both to insure access to resources and to boost the position of competitive participants in the elite political system?

The Yapese polity, as might be expected from such a dense population, was organized around access to land. Yapese land was not of the best quality, and much of the mountain interior was marginally cultivable, but the Yapese made up for their poor natural endowment by the intensive cultivation of high-yield root crops, particularly *Cyrtosperma*, or giant taro, and secondarily true taro, or *Colocasia*, and various kinds of yams. They also cultivated tree crops, including banana, chestnut, coconut, and breadfruit (Lingenfelter 1975:11-12). Yapese social organization included both patrilineal and matrilineal descent groups. Local organization consisted of a hierarchy of patrilineal, patrilocal units, beginning with the nuclear family, which was the basic household unit performing the functions of subsistence procuring and processing, as well as childcare and education (Lingenfelter:21-23). Nuclear families were nested into what Lingenfelter calls "patriclans", but what are probably less confusingly referred to as patrilocal joint families. Each of these was composed of several nuclear families, whose heads were related as brothers or patrilateral parallel cousins. These were the units of land-ownership at the basic level, and generally lived together on a common house-site, with each nuclear family having its own sleeping and cooking houses. The men of the joint family cooperated in fishing, and the patrilineally inherited titles were transferred within this group. Next up the line was the patrilineage, which held titles to several joint family estates, and acted as a political and ceremonial unit in wider affairs, with its head, or *matam*, representing the entire lineage, including several constituent joint families, in politics and ritual (Lingenfelter 1975:53-55). The nested nature of Yapese patrilineal groups is diagrammed in Figure 13-18.

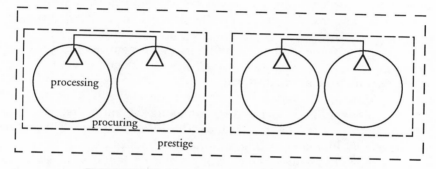

FIGURE 13-18: Nested Patrilineal Groups on Yap

At the same time, however, every Yapese also belonged to matrilineal descent groups. These could not, of course, be localized if the patrilineal groups were, but they were still important for their members in several ways. The lower level of matrilineal group, called "subsib" by Lingenfelter, occasionally held rights to a landed estate, but its primary activities were ritual and life-crisis support of its members. In addition, subsibs were strictly exogamous, marriage within one being considered tantamount to incest within the nuclear family (Lingenfelter 1975:33-34). Above the subsib was the sib, a named, totemic matriclan, but its functions had been displaced in Yapese society by the ascendancy of the patrilineal clans and the territorial organization built on the localized clan basis (Labby 1976:114).

What made a man powerful in the Yapese system? Rank and control of titled estates seem to have been the most important factors, and they went together. In many places, since men ranked above women and had access to the titles of the important estates, they ate more desirable food. At the same time, men were ranked into eating categories, based on a combination of seniority in years and importance of the title of their estates (Lingenfelter 1975:93-97). The holders of the highest-ranking estates composed the village subsection, village section, and village chiefs, and the village chiefs were organized according to a shifting network of ranks and alliances into a "national" system (Lingenfelter 1975:ch. 6-7).

In this kind of a political system room for maneuver through accretive devices was extremely limited. High-ranking titled estates were, in fact, often poor ones, because it was through generosity and reciprocity that a successful chief bound his people to him, and this often meant giving land away in return for allegiance (Lingenfelter 1975:119). For this reason, polygyny was rare, even for chiefs, being practiced only in the form of the levirate (Lingenfelter 1975:43). Marriage had to be within one's rank, and it, together with adoption, provided means of making alliances with other important families. The family system thus showed mild exclusive tendencies, but these were not confined to the elite families, since social intercourse in Yap seems to have been restricted by notions of rank on every account.

We have thus come full circle. While family organization on Yap reflected the structure of rank and inequality on the islands, making the system similar to those of the stratified societies of Polynesia, the constraints of landholding provided little room for family heads to build up large and powerful households through accretion, making the family system similar to the adjustive ones of the small islands. The difference here is that powerful men could, by manipulating the process of adjustment and granting usufruct rights to lower-ranking or impoverished families (Lingenfelter 1975.:143), increase or maintain a higher, more exalted status in the large-scale system of Yap than was ever possible on any atoll or tiny high island. The relationships between the four broad sub-clusters of family systems are illustrated in Figure 13-19.

Comments

We can see common cultural themes running through the family systems of all the O-cluster societies, themes that may well be aboriginal to Malayo-Polynesian ideas of social organization. There was rarely a rigidly unilineal ideology; even where clans existed, their importance was balanced by the presence of complementary ties in the other direction. Genealogical rank was everywhere important, often a determining factor in establishing social status. Monogamy was the rule and the basis upon which marriage relationships were predicated; where polygyny occurred it was as a function of high status, and was considered a mark of distinction. And everywhere the brother-sister tie was strong, mitigating the importance of the conjugal bond.

Within the cluster, however, we find considerable variation in the way the family systems worked. This variation was not so much dependent on descent-group organization; whether patriliny or matriliny was the rule,

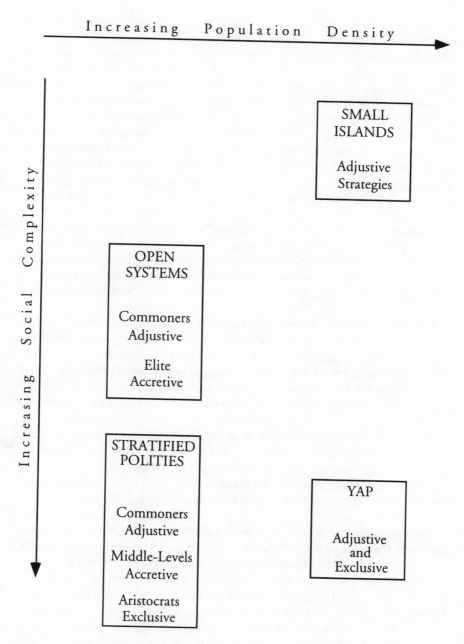

FIGURE 13-19: Relationships Among O-Cluster Systems

family cycles in otherwise similar types of social systems tended to look similar. Rather, I would submit, the pattern of variation in family organization is directly related to the prestige structures of the society, and these, in turn, arose out of the environmental conditions in which a society existed. Where resources were scarce and needed to be carefully balanced against the needs of the population, adjustive systems predominated, characterized by flexibility of access to property rights, almost universal monogamy, and very high rates of adoption. Where economic resources were not the main point of contention, systems of large-scale politics and status competition tended to arise, and these gave birth to family systems that allowed members of the elite, whether determined primarily by genealogy or by achievement, to build up family human and material resources in pursuit of their political ends, while leaving the commoners of the society with little to worry about but fishing, farming, sex, raising children, and caring for the aged. Finally, where political systems evolved distinct and unequal social strata, members of the highest strata were concerned with building their families in such a way as to reinforce their separation from their inferiors, while still ensuring themselves access to food, sex, and power in abundance.

The fundamental differences between the O-cluster and the B-cluster are twofold. First, oceanic people had to worry in rather precise and long-term ways about adjusting the people-resources balance. Band members, on the other hand, could adjust this balance ad hoc. This difference stemmed directly from the fixed nature of agricultural land, as opposed to the shifting nature of foraging foods. That this difference was not complete, that family groups in O-cluster societies still shared a bit of the flexibility and ambiguity of band-type families, may be due to the similarity of fishing, also an important subsistence activity in Oceania, with the foraging activities that bands practice. Second, at least on the larger islands, O-cluster societies did develop distinct spheres of political activity, so that men competing in these spheres often shaped their family organizations to aid them in this competition.

The fundamental difference between O-cluster and African societies is also dual. First, the Malayo-Polynesian emphasis on genealogical seniority as a criterion for status meant that status competition in Oceania was more restricted than it was in Africa. Second, the relations between people and resources were fundamentally different in the small islands of Oceania and the broad expanses of Africa. In those Oceanic societies where population/resource balance was a lesser concern, the genealogically entitled elite at least began to pursue accretive family strategies, such as polygyny and the taking in of lower-class or poor relatives, that look remarkably similar to African ones. By the same token, in those few parts of Africa where there was a severe population-resource problem, as among the Sonjo or the Hima, monogamous, adjustive family system began to take on distinctly "Oceanic" characteristics. The place of the O-cluster in the entire constellation of family systems described so far is suggested by Figure 13-20.

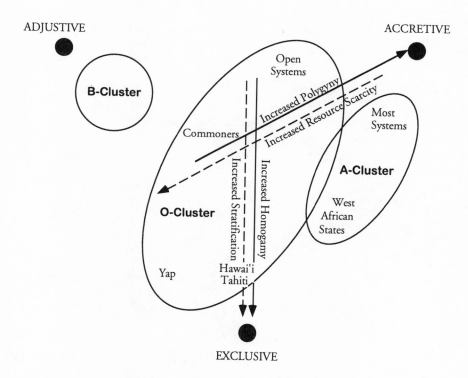

FIGURE 13-20: Place of O-Cluster in the Constellation of Family Systems

Notes

1. Spoehr's analysis of the developmental cycle is one of the earliest I know of, roughly contemporary with, and presumably not cognizant of, Fortes's work with the Asante material (1949). Both, interestingly enough, arose out of situations were household censuses would have yielded no discernable patterns of "family composition".

PART FIVE

The N-Cluster: Societies of the Northwest Coast of North America

Prelude: Growing Up in a Kwakiutl House

Charlie Nowell describes life in an old-style house at Fort Rupert in the 1870s.

When I was a child, I was living in a community house with people living on the four corners of the house. They have their fires in the four corners. I and my parents were living on the back right-hand corner as you come in the door. My oldest brother was living in the other back corner with his wife, and he had no children then. My other brother, the one next to the eldest, was living with us. He wasn't married yet. On the other place was a man called Poodlas. He was the husband of my aunt, my mother's sister. Her children were there, too; she had three boys and one girl. They were all older than I was.

...The best part of the house is in back. It is always the head man of the house that spends the most for the building of the house. It is the head man that gives the potlatch. The others is helping in the work and pays for the work that is done, and the lumber that goes into his part of the house where he is going to live. Each person is responsible for his corner of the house, and, if it needs repairing, it is up to him who lives there. If the center of the house needs repairing, they all help. We all lived in separate bedrooms. These bedrooms are private, and I never heard of anybody going into another one's bedroom, that lived in the same house, by mistake. Even in the old days, the bedrooms had doors that shut. If anybody wants my brother, and he is in his bedroom, they come into the house and call him from outside his bedroom. The door to the house is public to everybody. This is the one in the front of the house, and anybody can come in without knocking or hollering out. Sometimes there is a small door leading to the back ground, but this is only used by the members of the household.

One in our house always gets up early and starts the fire and wake us up in the morning. Poodlas usually got up first and asked us to have breakfast at his place. He didn't have to; he just liked to get up early. He would get up and boil dried salmon, which was our main food, and serve it to us all with some *olachen* grease. After that, there will be something which we call "after-food."

287

...Sometimes we would have clover root as our after-food...In the olden days, the women had their own clover patches marked with sticks on the four corners, and, if one woman gets in another's patch, they fight over it.

Sometimes they used to pick up sticks and hit each other with them, and their menfolks used to come sometimes, too, and butt in...Clover patches are women's property, and it comes down to her daughter. If they have no daughter, the boy get it, and then when he gets a wife the wife uses it. It is only this way with patches of roots. They berries don't belong to anybody.

...In summertime, we have everything: fresh salmon, halibut, flounder, cod, hair seals, clams, cockles, horse clams, fruits, and potatoes, but we don't eat all the different kinds of roots in the summertime. We eat all the different kinds of ducks, but we don't eat sea gulls, cormorants, and loons. They are too tough and too hard to pluck. I guess we would if we didn't have anything else to eat, but we always did. We eat eagles in the wintertime, when they get fat eating fish. We don't eat frogs, nor do we eat snakes... When I was very young, I used to sleep sometimes beside my father. When I lie in bed beside him, he talked to me about our ancestors. He told me about my grandfather and his father and his father, and what they did, and about how our ancestors knew about the flood...

My father also tells me about the potlatches which has come down from our ancestors, how our great-grandfathers used to give potlatches, and so on down to his time. He told me to be careful not to quit the potlatch, but to look after my blankets when I grew up, and not to spend my earnings foolishly, but to keep them and loan them out so that I could collect them whenever I want to give a potlatch. "In giving potlatches," he says, "is the only good name you'll have when you grow up, but if you are careless and spend your money foolishly, then you'll be no more good. You'll be one of the common people without any rank."

Clellan S. Ford, *Smoke from Their Fires: The Life of a Kwakiutl Chief* (New Haven: Yale University Press, 1941) pp. 48-56. Reprinted by permission.

ALASKA

Tlingit

BRITISH

Matrilineal

Area

Tsimshian

COLUMBIA

Heiltsuk

Haida

Haisla

Bella Coola

Owikeno

Kwakwak'awakw

Wakashan

Westcoast

Area

Halkomelem

Straits
Salish

Klallam

Puget
Salish

Twana

Quinault

Salish

WASHINGTON

Puyallup-Nisqually

Area

Chinook

Tillamook

Alsea

OREGON

Southern

Area

Karok

Yurok

Hupa

CALIFORNIA

Map 3: Northwest Coast Societies

14

The Logic of Social Organization on the Northwest Coast

Rank Societies on Foraging Base

The Northwest Coast of North America, extending from Cape Mendocino in California to Yakutat Bay in Southeastern Alaska, presents us with yet a third cluster of family systems within the supercluster of rank societies. The N-cluster shows both similarities to and differences from the family systems of the A- and O-clusters. In particular, Northwest Coast family systems in the 18th century resembled those of Africa in that they existed in a natural setting of abundance of resources (Suttles 1968), making for a loose and artificial allocation connection between prestige and subsistence spheres. In this, Northwest Coast societies contrast to the land-scarce systems of much of the O-cluster. On the other hand, Northwest societies shared with Oceanic groups an emphasis on hereditary rank, often based on genealogical seniority, effectively limiting prestige competition to certain aristocratic lines. In this, they contrast to Africa. Finally, Northwest Coast societies differed from those of both Africa and Oceania in their emphasis on wealth as a predominant factor in social status. In all three clusters, wealth and status were closely intertwined, but the emphasis was different in each place. Whereas for the Africans and Oceanians, wealth was a means to a following; for the Northwest Indians, wealth was itself an integral part of high status, sometimes more important than a political following itself. We can represent the salient features of the three clusters of societies in a simple chart (Table 14-1):

TABLE 14-1: Features of A-, O-, and N-Cluster Social Systems

Cluster	Subsistence Resource Availability	Genealogical Restriction of Competition	Primary Factor in High Status
A	Abundant	Absent	Following
O	Scarce	Present	Following
N	Abundant	Present	Wealth

This particular variant of a rank society cluster of systems was built on the basis of a technology that included almost no cultivated crops (though tobacco was grown in northwest California) and dogs as the only domesticated animals. This foraging subsistence base can mislead the observer, who is in some instances liable to see Northwest Coast societies as part of a "hunting-gathering type," or to wonder how the N-cluster societies could be so different from other foragers. But this is a fundamentally misleading tack to take: the extremely rich natural resources of the Northwest Coast area, particularly the abundant and generally reliable runs of anadromous fish (salmon and steelhead trout, herring and eulachon) provided the material equivalent of agricultural or pastoral resources, and permitted the development of a society whose scale and complexity were in every way comparable to those of shifting agriculturalists, agro-pastoralists, or intensive gardeners in other parts of the world. In some purely subsistence areas of life, particularly in the organization of food gathering (berries, roots, mollusks, etc.) and of sea-mammal hunting, we can see on the Northwest Coast traces reminiscent of the organization of B-cluster societies. But the organization of fishing, the single most important subsistence activity of most of the Northwest Coast groups, differed in its organization both from B-cluster hunting and fishing and from O-cluster fishing: the difference was between river and ocean fishing, and will be dealt with below. The point is simply that the Northwest Coast societies belong firmly in the "rank-society supercluster;" despite the foraging technology, the closest comparisons are with Africa and Oceania, not with bands.

The Prestige Sphere

Northwest Coast societies are renowned in anthropology because of their elaborate systems of status rivalry and competition. Though the account in Benedict's *Patterns of Culture* (1934) is both exaggerated and based on post-contact elaborations of the aboriginal system, even the accounts of more responsible observers bear titles such as Rosman and Rubel's *Feasting with Mine Enemy* (1972), Drucker and Heizer's *To Make my Name Good* (1967) and *Codere's Fighting with Property* (1950) each pointing to a different aspect of the system of prestige competition in this area, each emphasizing a different factor but agreeing on the overall importance of status and status rivalry. What was the logic of this system?

Simply stated, people possessed high status in Northwest Coast societies when they possessed certain things: abundance of subsistence goods, access to subsistence areas, durable material wealth items, privileges, spirit power and good manners. These six kinds of status goods varied in relative importance from one part of the coast to another, and the methods by which they were converted to high status also varied: in some places, one merely possessed them, while in other areas one had to give at least some of them away. But everywhere on the Coast there was an inseparable relationship between the status itself and the goods that accompanied it. It was not just that having the goods gave one the status; it was also that having the status gave one access to the goods. This was true for all six kinds of status goods, but each in fact operated somewhat differently with respect to status, and it seems worthwhile to consider each in turn.

Subsistence Surpluses

A surplus of subsistence goods was not connected directly to status: no man would be famous for being owner of lots of fish or eulachon grease, for example. But possession of such a surplus could be converted to high status in two ways. First, at least among some Salish groups (Suttles 1960:301), food could sometimes be exchanged directly for wealth or for trade items that could be converted into wealth. A concrete example of this is provided by Bierwert (n.d.) who shows that South Vancouver Island *si'em* (important people), by virtue of their large fishing parties, could accumulate fish surpluses that could then be traded across the straits for wool and other imports. The Nooksack, themselves an upriver group and therefore relatively poor, still had a system of exchanging food with affines for wealth goods (Amoss 1978:26-27).

The second way that control of surplus food could lead to wealth was much more general on the Northwest Coast: in all the areas where feasting and potlatching were necessary to validate claims to high status, giving a feast or potlatch demanded, along with wealth items to give away, a large amount of food to feed the guests, who often stayed for several days, and to give them to take home with them when they left. And it was, of course, precisely those in high-status positions who could draw on the food resources of their relatives to accumulate enough to make a large distribution. This relationship is documented for such diverse Northern and Central Coast groups as the Tlingit, whose chief's duty it was always to be able to extend hospitality (Oberg 1973:120; Olson 1967:12); the Heiltsuk or Bella Bella (Olson 1955:326), the Bella Coola (McIlwaith 1948:189), and Coast Salish peoples such as the Twana (Elmendorf 1960:311), all of whom stored food all year in order to be able to make large distributions, and the upriver Upper Skagit, among whom high status depended partly on relatives' willingness to supply food to be given away at feasts and potlatches (Collins 1974:128). Among the Westcoast peoples of Vancouver Island, perhaps the most rigidly hierarchical of Northwest Coast groups, chiefs were owed tribute of a sort by their followers: both successful deer and bear hunters and extraordinarily successful fishermen were expected to contribute large amounts of their catch to the chief, who in turn distributed the fish or meat at a feast or potlatch (Drucker 1951:251-4).

Ownership of Subsistence Areas

In the preceding examples, it is control of a food surplus, whether gotten by one's own efforts or by contributions from dependents, that leads indirectly to high status. But there were other kinds of situations on the Northwest Coast where it was not so much control of the food itself as ownership of the subsistence areas that conferred or confirmed high social status. Such uneven ownership was far from being a universal phenomenon: particularly among groups without highly elaborated status systems, such as the Quinault (Olson 1936:94), Tillamook (Sauter and Johnson 1974:28), and Twana (Elmendorf 1960:262-68), most subsistence resources were publicly owned, and such prestige as chiefs had was derived from other sources. But in other areas, subsistence resources were differentially owned, either by kin- or house groups, as among Haisla and other northerly peoples (Olson 1940:180), by chiefs as stewards for the kin-groups of which they were the heads, as among the Westcoast people (Drucker 1951:57-8), or by individuals, as among Salish groups such as the Katzie (Suttles 1955, Bierwert n.d.:21-23), Straits (Suttles 1951:56) and Klallam

(Gunther 1927:201). In no case did this mean that owners could refuse access to the needy, or even to others who simply wanted to use their areas for reasons of convenience. As a Sto:lo told Duff, "I have never heard of an Indian stopping anyone from getting food." (Duff 1952:207). But in all cases, the owners exacted a price in the form of recognizing the superior status of those who give (Bierwert n.d.:21-3). This kind of trade of prestige for food in fact allowed the simultaneous expression of the principle of social hierarchy and of the deep-seated idea that no one should be denied the basic necessities of life, a principle common to all rank societies (Fried 1967:109).

Wealth

Material wealth items, durable things whose primary use was in status competition itself, were the third sort of goods connected with high status on the Northwest Coast, and the single type of good whose possession and manipulation was a universal characteristic of N-cluster societies, from Yurok to Yakutat. Northwest Coast societies, particularly those of the northern and Wakashan sections, are justly famous for the artistic quality of many of their wealth objects, from totem poles to goat-wool blankets to seal clubs to enormous canoes.[1] And in general we may surmise that it was not just the aesthetic pleasure in creating such objects (which in itself must have been considerable) but also the knowledge of the social importance of the thing created that led to the expenditure of so much time, energy, and creativity even on such everyday things as cooking utensils and hunting weapons.

Material wealth items were important in two ways: as things that one kept and displayed as a marker of one's high status, and as things one gave away at potlatches. Things one kept and displayed were common to the whole coast, including the most southerly portions, where potlatches or other large-scale distributions were unknown. At the southern limit of the Coast, in the Yurok, Karok, and Hupa areas, for example, status depended on the accumulation of wealth, gotten through marriage exchanges and blood money, and displayed in the form of dentalium shells, deerskins, obsidian blades, and other objects at dances and other important social rituals (Kroeber 1925:2; Goldschmidt and Driver 1940:105-6, 118). Among the Lower Chinook, where the potlatch existed but in "much attenuated" form (Ray 1938:94), nevertheless the mere possession of wealth brought power (Ray 1938:78). But even among the groups where the potlatch was prominent, high status involved possession of certain goods that were not given away. These included memorial poles and house-post carvings among many northern groups, for example, as well as masks, costumes, and other ritual regalia almost everywhere. In many cases, these "ungivable" wealth items were closely connected with the inheritance of privileges, a class of goods discussed below.

The other way that material goods were connected with status is more famous but in fact existed in a smaller area—this is the giving of goods away at potlatches, ceremonies in which an important man or couple (Murdock 1936:9) gave away wealth in order to validate a claim to status, a claim usually involving a privilege or name or high-ranking title that itself could not be given, but remained in the giver's family. So much has been written about the potlatch that it seems superfluous to give a full account here: suffice it to say that the ceremony varied widely in its emphasis, frequency, and lavishness in different parts of the Northwest Coast, but that the common feature was that the giver enhanced or validated his own status and/or that of other family members by giving the ceremony. In some cases, as in Nootka, the status itself was entirely inherited, but nevertheless had to be validated (Drucker 1951:234-5) in others, how well and how frequently one potlatched was the primary determinant of status, thus allowing for a certain amount of mobility, at least among those whose status was reasonably high-born in the first place. This seems to have been the case, for example, among most of the Coast Salish groups; particularly the Puyallup-Nisqually (Marion Smith 1940:48), the Upper Skagit (Collins 1974:125) and Sto:lo (Bierwert n.d.:19) emphasized achievement along with or even instead of birth as the main criterion for status, and the ability to give potlatches was the most important form of achievement.

Privileges

The fourth sort of goods that were closely connected to high status in N-cluster societies consisted of what are usually called privileges; these were probably most important north of the Strait of Juan de Fuca (Suttles 1951:500-502). A privilege, in this terminology, is the right to use some sort of object or performance, and in the societies where access to privileges was important, they formed the most visible and important means of validating social status. For example, Drucker gives a summary account of the types of privileges owned by a Westcoast chief at Kyuquot on the northwestern coast of Vancouver Island: he had numerous personal names, along with four war-chief names, including one meaning "they don't like him." He had special names that only he could bestow upon male slaves and female slaves. Certain names for pet dogs or seagulls were his alone to use. There were three posts in his house carved with designs that only he could use, and he also had the privilege of erecting two kinds of poles outside his house, as well as of using certain names for his visiting canoe. Perhaps the most striking and characteristic of this chief's privileges were his entitlement to certain ritual displays performed at potlatches, shamans' dances, and other ceremonies; these included "*tu-ta*, a figure of the thunderbird that arose from the floor and flew across the house while the chief sang his songs, ...*qamin*, a small carving representing a bird (a dancer pretended to give birth to the figure, which then ran back and forth across the floor); *huhuqw*, a monster with the body of a bear and birdlike head with a huge beak, that sat on the floor and snatched at little birds that flew about..." and many others. This chief also owned the right to cut infants' umbilical cords, the ornaments used in a young woman's hair at her puberty ceremony, and of course the all-important second-ranking seat at local potlatches and feasts (Drucker 1951:258-62).

Although the Westcoast and their close linguistic and cultural relatives the Southern Kwakiutl elaborated the complex of inherited privileges more highly than elsewhere, nowhere on the coast was it entirely absent. Northern and Central groups that had highly developed privilege complexes included the Tlingit, who counted as privileges anything that was decorated with a clan design, as well as face-painting motifs, for example (Olson 1967:37); the Owikeno of Rivers Inlet, among whom titles and privileges are asserted to have been more important than material wealth, and who counted as privileges dances and a ornamental poles, among other objects (Olson 1954:232); and the Makah and their Salish-speaking neighbors, the Straits and Halkomelem, all of whom counted as privileges names, dances, songs, costumes, and other ceremonial displays (Colson 1953:192; Bierwert n.d.:55; Suttles 1951:55). Farther south, the privilege complex was attenuated, being confined primarily to the use of personal names, but we find the use of names and their validation at potlatches as a common feature of prestige competition among such groups as the Twana (Elmendorf 1960:328), the Puget Sound Salish (Haeberlin and Gunther 1930:52) and the lower Chinook (Ray 1938:66).

Wherever privileges were found, whether in highly elaborated or simpler form, they demonstrate clearly the type of connection between status and goods on the Northwest Coast. Privileges ordinarily had to be inherited (I say ordinarily, because it is clear that powerful people sometimes invented them anew and then had them passed on to their descendants); in other words, one had to have high status to have privileges. On the other hand, the ownership of privileges had to be validated at potlatches or other ceremonial occasions, at which the privileges themselves were displayed and talked about, and material goods and food were given away. One had to earn one's inheritance, but one could only earn it if one had a right to inherit it in the first place.

Spirit Power

A fifth kind of prestige good was spirit power. It is safe to say that everywhere on the Coast, contact with a guardian spirit, usually achieved through a conscious quest, was important for acquiring at least one important status in the society: that of shaman. But it was among the peoples of what is now western washington and southwestern British Columbia in particular that spirit power had its greatest importance as something that was necessary for wealth and high status. Among the Makah and Quileute, non-Salish speaking peoples of the Olympic Peninsula, for example, boys all went on spirit quests in their mid-teens to gain competence in all sorts of activities, including those that would bring wealth (Colson 1953:4; Powell and Jensen 1976:25). Straits, Klallam, and Twana all had a tradition of particular kinds of spirits that would bring various powers, including the ability to acquire wealth and good fortune, markers of high status (Suttles 1951:53; Gunther 1927:289-95; Elmendorf 1960:335). Among the Lower Chinook at the mouth of the Columbia, spirits were said not to bring power or high position in themselves, but rather to assist people in acquiring the wealth that was requisite for high status (Ray 1938:78). This probably sums up the entire complex well: spirit power was not something that was displayed in the proud manner of northern crests or given away as were material goods in potlatches (though spirit-dancing ceremonies, held in the winter by Salish groups, allowed for the demonstration of the power of one's familiar spirit; see Amoss 1978). Rather spirit power was something that many groups considered necessary for the kind of competence that it took to gain wealth. Therefore, the wealthy and prominent not only needed spirit power, but obviously possessed it: if they had not, they would not be wealthy or prominent.

Good Manners

Closely connected with spirit power as a requisite for high status, but existing also in many places where the spirit-power complex was not so important, was the idea of advice or good manners, the notion that those of high position knew more about good behavior and behaved in a more cultivated manner than their poorer or lower-ranking neighbors. For example, the Tlingit of Yakutat felt that a good chief had self-restraint and a mild-temper; to be boastful or arrogant was unchiefly (DeLaguna 1972:467). At the other end of the Coast, the Yurok assumed that a rich person would have good manners (Kroeber 1925:39). Neither of these peoples had a very prominent spirit power complex, except for shamans. But among many Salish groups, similar notions about the connection between high status and good behavior were tied in closely with ideas relating to spirit power. For example, the *siab*, or important person, among the Upper Skagit was expected to have good manners and dignity in addition to wealth (Collins 1974:123). Similarly, an important person in Nooksack was supposed to have, besides wealth, such characteristics as dignity, open-handedness, restraint, and knowledge (Amoss 1978:10). The Twana assumption was that an important factor in social success was diligence: the poor were thought of as lazy and lackadaisical (Elmendorf 1960:331-33). In all these places, it is difficult to prove that the high status people actually behaved more correctly than the poor; it is even harder to accept the idea that the poor did not even know how one was supposed to behave. What seems to have been happening, instead, is that upper-status people maintained the myth of good behavior as a justification for something everyone knew: that they were both wealthier and born of higher-status parents (Suttles 1960). And this, in turn, connects back to the idea of spirit power: it was only through discipline and self-restraint that one acquired the purity to be able to make contact with a spirit.

Geographical Variation in the
Organization of the Prestige Sphere

All along the coast, control over some or all of these six kinds of goods—food surpluses, subsistence territories, wealth goods (including slaves), privileges, spirit power, and proper behavior—was the basis of a highly organized, rivalrous competition for prestige and high status. But the relative importance of these various kinds of goods, and the way people were organized for access to and competition over them, varied from one part of the Northwest Coast to another. This variation, in fact, can be seen as occurring along two dimensions: a North-South dimension, which has no obvious ecological or technological base, but rather consists of four variations on the general Northwest Coast theme of close connectedness of wealth and high status; and seaward-inland dimension, in which the upriver people in any river system tended to have a simpler, less elaborate version of the local logic of social relations, based on their materially poorer environment. I will consider these two dimensions of variation in turn.

The North-South Dimension:
Four Logics of Status Competition

The Southern Area: Owning and Displaying Wealth. The southernmost and simplest sub-system of the Northwest Coast cultures extended from the Northwest California cultures of Yurok, Karok, Hupa, Wiyot, and Toilowa as far as the Tillamook on the northern coast of Oregon; the Lower Chinook at the mouth of the Columbia River were transitional between this sub-area and the next. The primary distinguishing feature of this area was a negative one: these people did not potlatch; thus the connection between wealth and status was involved entirely with the acquisition, possession, and display of wealth items, and not at all with giving them away (Drucker 1939:61). Wealth items, which in this area included a variety of goods such as deerskins and obsidian blades in Northwestern California (Goldschmidt and Driver 1940:105; Kroeber 1925:26-28), as well as dentalium-shell "money" apparently almost everywhere, were acquired by marriage exchanges, trade, collection of fines (among the California groups), and other routes, as well as, of course, by manufacture or other kinds of effort. And in all these groups, wealth was the primary determinant of social status, far more important in native thinking than birth or genealogical position (Goldschmidt and Driver 1940:106; Kroeber 1925:3; Ray 1938:48; Drucker 1939b:92). In northwestern California, there was an elaborate complex of dances, exemplified by the White Deerskin dance of the Hupa, at which important persons demonstrated their status by displaying their wealth items publicly: men danced at gatherings of several village communities, and dancers representing each community tried to outdo each other by displaying—holding up for public view during the dance—the obsidian blades, deerskins, and bright red woodpecker-scalp bands (Kroeber 1925:53-55).

This region seems in a way peripheral to the Northwest Coast, because it does not display any of the characteristic prestige goods whose control was so crucial to high status in more northerly regions, except the one central kind of goods—wealth objects. Spirit power and spirit quests were also present; aside from shamans, who were almost uniformly female and thus unlikely to become important wealthy personages (Kroeber 1925:4), spirit power was seen as an avenue toward gaining and holding family wealth (Keeling 1992:69). Surpluses of food were rarely given away: even in the marginal Chinook area, where the potlatch did exist in attenuated form, attendance was restricted to a few high-status people; this must have meant that feeding the guests was not much of a problem (Ray 1938:50). And among groups farther south, potlatches did not exist. Similarly, control over subsistence areas was not apparently important; Yurok did own fishing places, but everyone seems to have had a place; this would mean little prestige would be gained by lending (Kroeber 1925:33, 37). Among the Tillamook on the Oregon coast, subsistence areas were public (Sauter and Johnson 1974:28-30). Advice is mentioned only rarely, but inherited privileges were a concomitant of aristocratic status at least among the Yurok (Pilling 1989:423-24). Still, it was primarily wealth, usually pursued by individual initiative, sometimes with a substantial "head start" for those of high birth, that was a significant prestige good in this area. Nevertheless, that the pursuit of wealth was the primary preoccupation of people active in the public sphere in these societies is enough to classify them as a subtype, if a rather inelaborate one, of the cultures of the Northwest Coast.

The Salish Area: Spirit Power and Hereditary Achievement. The second subsystem begins at the mouth of the Columbia River and extends Northward to the southern tip of Vancouver Island and adjacent areas on the British Columbia mainland. This area was populated mainly by Salish-speaking peoples, including the Puget Sound Salish in the middle of the area, and their close relatives the Nooksack in the river valley of the same name. Also in the core of this group are the Klallam of the south coast of the Strait of Juan de Fuca and the Twana of Hood Canal, as well as three coastal groups: the non-Salish speaking Makah and Quileute and the Salish-speaking Quinault. The Chehalis to the south of Puget Sound probably also belong here. The Chinook at the Columbia River mouth were marginal between this pattern and the more southerly one; the Straits and Halkomelem Salish to the north still belong in this group but display some influence from the more northerly Wakashan pattern.

In this second area, the logic of social status lies in a mutual interdependency of four factors: spirit power, wealth, position, and advice. Spirit power enabled one to gain wealth, wealth allowed for the validation of high social position, high social position brought one the advice, or good manners, appropriate to one's rank, and this advice gave one the moral purity and determination to quest successfully for spirit power. The guardian spirit complex reached its greatest importance in this section of the coast; Suttles asserts that spirit power played a key role here comparable to that played by inherited privileges farther north (Suttles 1951:500-502). As mentioned above, spirit power in this region was considered to be the means by which one acquired the wherewithal to accomplish anything of value in the society, including artistic skill, bravery in warfare, healing prowess, or, most importantly, the wealth that brought high position. But spirit power could not be displayed or boasted of directly; even in the winter spirit dances, the actual nature of the power being displayed was hidden behind conventional forms of costumes, songs, and dances (Amoss 1978:50, 161). The greatest proof that one indeed "had something" came in the results; a great warrior was assumed to have a warrior power; a successful hunter, a hunter power; and a wealthy individual, a wealth power. Spirit power was at one level a powerful subjective experience for the possessor; but this experience was kept largely secret and only hinted at publicly (Amoss 1978:49). At another level, spirit power was a rationalization for one's manifest skill or high position. Once one had an important power, particularly a wealth power, then one could gain high status and validate one's claims to such status by giving away masses of food and wealth objects at a potlatch.

Such a system, in which anyone with a particular kind of acquired spirit power could theoretically rise to the most respected position in the society, would seem to be a wide-open one, one in which achievement was more important for status than ascription. But in fact, inheritance played a large part in the determination of high status in this region. The wealth necessary to validate claims to high status was not in itself inherited; most of it was procured in trade or manufactured by family members (Suttles 1968:66-67; Bierwert n.d.:71; Suttles 1951:492). But the ability to engage in trade or to make the affinal connections that could result in a large network of supporters depended on heredity, either through inherited ownership of a subsistence area producing surplus to be traded, or through a genealogically validated high position that would allow one to marry distantly and well (Bierwert n.d.:5; Suttles 1951:492; Gunther 1927:241). And so, within the large stratum of "good people" who had neither stigmatized nor outright slave status to prevent them from engaging in prestige competition, there were in fact a smaller number of families who seemed to have a consistent advantage, and to gain high status positions in successive generations (Suttles 1958).

But a system like this runs up against a problem of self-justification. If everyone knows that certain families are better, or in the modern idiom "high-class," but at the same time the wealth with which they validate their status has to be earned or created anew in each generation, how is the high-class status passed on? The answer is through the myth of advice or good manners. High status people had it; low status people did not, and those who had it passed it on to their children through a rigorous process of education and training. And it was only those who knew how to act properly who gained the spirit power (not to speak of the human respect) that would enable them to have high status. We thus come full-circle, and can see the logic of a system of "hereditary achievement." Statuses themselves were not fixed; they were not even named, except by the general Salish term *siab* or *siem*, meaning simply respected or high-status person. Individuals, not kin groups, held these statuses; there were no named kin groups. And yet support of kin was vital if status was to be achieved or maintained.

The Wakashan Area: The Elaboration of Ranking. The social system in the next area to the north, the area of the Wakashan-speaking Westcoast and Kwakwaka'wakw peoples, was also one of "hereditary achievement," but with more emphasis on the heredity, a paradoxically equal amount of emphasis on the achievement, and a much more rigid structure in which people operated. This area extended from the northern and central Nootkans (Drucker 1951) of the west coast of Vancouver Island through the famous Southern Kwakiutl and their neighbor tribes, on the northern tip of that island and adjacent areas of the mainland, to more northerly Kwakwaka'wakw-speaking[2] peoples such as the Owikeno and Bella Bella, or Heiltsuk.[3] The Salish-speaking Bella Coola, though located in the northern part of this region, had a mixture of "classical Salish" and Central features. Finally, the Kwakwaka'wakw-speaking Haisla, bordering on Tsimshian territory, were transitional between this area and the northern, or matrilineal, group.

This area, as mentioned above, continued the tradition of the area immediately to the south, where hereditary achievement culminated in the validation of status through the distribution of wealth at the potlatch. But the social framework in which the game of status competition was played out was a much more highly structured one in this area than in Washington or southernmost British Columbia. Here spirit power and advice, so important to the south, declined in prominence to be replaced by inherited privileges and elaborate systems of reciprocally-ranked titles. The privileges were legion, as described previously, involving songs, dances, tricks, carvings, names, ornaments, stories, and many other kinds of things. Some were invented anew by their holders, but most were passed down through a complex and somewhat fluid system of bilateral inheritance. These privileges were held either individually or by a local-kin groups (called *numaym* or *namima* in Kwakwaka'wakw; the Nootkans do not seem to have used this name). These groups were preferentially patrilineal, but one could claim membership in one's mother's group under certain circumstances, or even gain rights from the groups of both parents (Drucker 1951:2; 9-20; Drucker and Heizer 1967:10-12; Boas 1920:360; Ford 1941:14). The local groups were clustered into named tribes (the name Kwakiutl properly refers to one of these tribes), and the tribes in turn sometimes into confederacies (Ford 1941:16; Drucker 1951:219-20). Within the confederacy, if such existed, tribes were ranked; within the tribe, local kin-groups were ranked. Within each local kin group, in turn, there was a series of graded, named statuses, each with its accompanying privileges. The privilege most directly and obviously connected to the status system was that of a particular seat at a potlatch or other ceremony; by means of these seats all named statuses in a tribe or confederacy of tribes were ranked with respect to each other.

This was the grid upon which the Nootkan- and Kwakwaka'wakw-speaking peoples acted out their competition for prestige. The titles that constituted the grid were normally passed on to a direct, lineal heir, preferably the eldest son of the previous holder (Ford 1941:36; Drucker 1951:267). But the route of transmission was not fixed or unalterable, which is where the achievement part of hereditary achievement enters the picture. A Westcoast or Kwakwaka'wakw chief, like the *siem* of his southern neighbors, had to validate his position by demonstrating his worthiness to hold it, and this meant, in fact, accumulating and redistributing wealth. The name, as Drucker and Heizer put it (1967) had to be made good; the chief had to show himself the rightful holder of the headship of a local group and of a place in a ranked series of statuses, and he could only do this by means of displays appropriate to the position. Even though the Westcoast and Kwakwaka'wakw chiefs probably were separated from the commoners of their communities by a wider gulf than existed elsewhere on the Northwest Coast (Drucker 1951:243-4), this gulf was in fact neither clearly demarcated—lower aristocratic statuses graded imperceptibly into commoners—nor constant, since the statuses had to be reclaimed in each generation. Here the principle of individual ranking precluded the operation of the principle of group stratification.

The Matrilineal Area: Stratification by Household. The northernmost part of the coast exhibited a still different social configuration, one in which the Central-type grid of reciprocally ranked statuses was replaced as the field of social action by a series of matrilineages organized into moieties or phratries. This group consisted of the Haida on the Queen Charlotte Islands, the Tsimshian of the Nass and Skeena River Valleys, and the Tlingit of the Alaskan coast northward to Yakutat Bay. The northernmost Kwakwaka'wakw-speaking group, the Haisla, exhibited some features transitional between this group and the group immediately to the south.

In this northernmost region, the first basic division of society was into exogamous, named matrimoieties or martiphratries: the Tlingit had two, called Raven and Eagle or Raven and Wolf; the Haida, also two, called Eagle and Raven, and the Tsimshian four, called, on the coast at least, Eagle, Raven, Killer-whale (or "Blackfish") and Wolf (Garfield 1939:231). These moieties were in turn divided into a number of matriclans each, most of the clans having representatives at more than one location (Murdock 1936:6; Garfield 1939:182). These were further divided into lineages, each lineage consisting of all the members of a clan located at a particular village, and itself consisting of several avunculocal joint households (Olson 1967:5; Swanton 1905:68; Garfield 1939:182).[4]

The high-status positions in these societies were those of the chiefs of the household and lineage. The local lineages in a particular village were ranked with respect to each other, and as the chief of the highest-ranking household within a lineage was reckoned the chief of the lineage, so was the chief of the highest ranking lineage in a village reckoned the village chief (Murdock 1939:16; Olson 1967:47; Garfield 1939:182). Where clans extended over more than one village, they were not uniformly ranked, and of course there was no ranking of phratries or moieties. Hence the important positions were household, lineage, and village chiefs.

This sounds like a rather rigid status system, but in fact it was more flexible than that of the Wakashan groups. Here the reciprocal rankings of households and lineages were not fixed, but rather varied with accomplishments, primarily the potlatching, of the heads or head couples (in the Haida case) of the various groups (Olson 1967:47; Stearns 1984:197; Garfield 1939:178-80). It thus required, as in the Wakashan and Salish groups, achievement to claim one's heredity. But the units that were reciprocally ranked in the Northern Coast societies were not individual statuses or seats, but rather households and lineages. There was thus less internal ranking within a household—eligible males tended to succeed to household chiefships as they became senior in age and generation—and more concern with the standing of a household or lineage as a whole, whose status might go up or down according to the wealth and accomplishments of its members. At the same time, while the Northern groups lacked the characteristic Wakashan grid of ranked statuses, they did practice a kind of status homogamy, in which members of high-ranking lineages and households tended to marry each other, creating homogeneous strata linked by marriage, something that approached the systems of marriage classes found in the most stratified societies of the O-cluster.

We thus find a uniform theme in the overall organization of Northwest Coast societies: they were all organized around the pursuit of wealth and concomitant high status on the part of ambitious individuals. The relative abundance of subsistence resources all along the coast meant that the amount of time and effort devoted to the pursuit of wealth and status by high-ranking individuals and their supporters did not impinge on the basic right to subsistence, which was guaranteed to all. But within this theme we have found four significant kinds of variations: in the southernmost group, status accrued to individuals, and was conferred by the possession of wealth items. In the next group north, the Coast Salish and their neighbors, wealth items had to be given away as well as possessed. One who did so was recognized as a high-status person, one with spirit power and advice. In the Wakashan group, redistribution of wealth continued to play a role, but here status conferred wealth more than wealth status, and the status was one in a rigid hierarchy of individual rankings. Finally, in the northern group, redistribution of wealth was still the key to high status, but redistribution of wealth was organized by, and high status conferred on, the avunculocal joint household or localized exogamous matrilineage rather than on the ranked individual.

The Seaward-Inland Dimension:
Richer and Poorer Versions of Four Social Logics

The variation just described between the four variations on the theme of status and wealth competition seems to have had little if any ecological base. Despite a suggestion by Suttles (1958) that the difference between the rudimentarily stratified system of the Coast Salish and the elaborately ranked system of the Kwakwaka'wakw had to do with the fact that the Salish territory was both richer and more varied in its natural resources than that of the more northerly Kwakwaka'wakw, in fact this does not explain, for example, why the Salish shared with the Northern groups the rudiments of a stratified system (though a different sort of rudiments) while the intermediate Wakashans elaborated on the principle of ranking. Similarly, why the Northern groups were organized around the all-important matrilineal principle, while the whole rest of the coast was bilateral or weakly patrilineal, cannot be derived from environmental factors any more than can the difference between largely matrilineal Micronesia and largely patrilineal Polynesia within the O-cluster pattern.

But there were differences among Northwest Coast societies than can be attributed to ecological or environmental factors, and these are the differences between more and less elaborated versions of the four logics of status competition. *Within* each type of society, its own patterns tend to be more elaborated, its own versions of status competition more active and more intense, in the wealthier (usually seaward) portions of the territory, and weaker and less elaborated in the poorer, (usually inland) regions. We can illustrate this with an example from three of the four basic logical types of Northwest Coast societies.

The Southern Area: Yurok and Chimariko. We begin with a brief example from the southernmost region of the Coast, comparing the "core" culture of the Yurok with the much less highly developed system of the Chimariko. The Yurok occupied the lower reaches of the Klamath river, from its confluence with the Trinity to the ocean; this was one of the richest parts of the North California coast. Here they developed the most elaborate version of the first, or southern variant of Northwest Coast culture, including a highly complex system of wealth transfers through trade, marriage payments, and fines, all of them reckoned in dentalium shell "money" or its equivalent. In addition, the Yurok, along with their near-upstream neighbors the Karok and the Hupa, developed the wealth-display dance ceremonial to its most complete form (Kroeber 1925:4-5; 22-25; Goldschmidt and Driver 1940:103-106). Their economy was wealthy enough that they could acquire and hold slaves as indicators of prestige; people were enslaved in the first place because of debt, but were also bought and sold (Kroeber 1925:32). The picture here is one of considerable wealth, a high velocity of circulation, and the development of significant social differentiation based on wealth.

As Kroeber points out (1925:6-7), the elaborate features of Northwestern Californian culture drop off gradually as one proceeds upstream into the interior; even the Yurok's closest neighbors, the Hupa and Karok, had slightly less elaborate material culture and slightly less apparent wealth circulating in the economy, as indicated by the lower frequency of dance ceremonials. If we follow this progression from relative wealth to poverty a bit further inland, to the Chimariko on the north fork of the Trinity River above Hupa territory, we can see the attenuation of the status system, due primarily to the relative poverty of the upriver environment. The Chimariko were still concerned with wealth and its acquisition, but they had very little wealth to work with. They had no redwood trees with which to make the great Yurok-style trading canoes, and anyway their little river was too narrow and shallow for canoes. They used dentalium shells as a kind of money, but the shells were very hard for them to get; and they never managed to produce or acquire enough wealth items to be able to purchase slaves or indeed to force someone into deep enough debt to become enslaved. They had no individual ownership of fishing rights or other subsistence territories. With this paucity of wealth, it is not surprising that they did not hold the great wealth-display ceremonials of the Yurok, Karok, and Hupa (Kroeber 1925:111).

The difference between the Yurok and the Chimariko is one of elaboration in the status system, based on the differential availability of wealth; daily subsistence is not at issue here. The Chimariko, like their wealthier downriver neighbors, disdained the diet of earthworms and grasshoppers characteristic of peoples farther inland than themselves, and the lack of ownership of fishing places seems to indicate that there were plenty of fish to go around. Chimariko houses were less elaborate than those of the Yurok, but constructed on the same principles. Still, the social systems were noticeably different, and that difference lies in the availability to the Yurok, but not to the Chimariko, of the kinds of prestige goods characteristic of the entire Northwest Coast. We have no direct information on advice, and we know that spirit power, confined in this region almost entirely to female shamans, is not at issue here. But we find that the other kinds of prestige goods were simply more abundant in Yurok territory—they had a *surplus* of subsistence goods that could be traded; they had individual ownership of fishing places, and most importantly they had wealth—obsidian blades, woodpecker scalps, deerskins, dentalium shells, and slaves. This is what allowed them to elaborate the southernmost version of Northwest Coast status systems.

The Salish Area. There is a similar scale of elaboration within the Coast Salish group, with the rather crude distinction usually made between the more developed prestige systems of the saltwater peoples and the less developed systems upriver. This distinction is illustrated well by the comparison made by Bierwert among three Halkomelem-speaking groups. The Sto:lo, who lived on the upper reaches of the Frazer River, had a fairly undeveloped system of status differentiation. People agreed that some were *siem*, or respected people, and others were not, and those who could accumulate preserved resources and trade them for exotic goods had access to "what 'rank' there was in Sto:lo society" (Bierwert n.d.:19-20). But Bierwert characterizes the Sto:lo as being more "egalitarian" in their subsistence access than their downriver neighbors, and as having fewer social distinctions in general than the Katzie of the Pitt Lake region or the Musqueam, Nanaimo, and Saanich, who inhabited the two sides of the Strait of Georgia. These latter peoples, particularly the Katzie, had much more restricted access to subsistence goods, with social relations characterized by "obligations of status," and by more restricted access to siem for *distribution* of resources (Bierwert n.d.:30). Similarly the Upper Skagit, an inland group speaking Puget Sound Salish, characterized themselves as having fewer slaves and a general lack of social distinctions, as compared with their salt water neighbors: one Upper Skagit summed it up to Collins by saying "Everyone was the same up here" (Collins 1974:129).

Amoss (1993) has shown in a stimulating analysis how the generally reported greater status differences in saltwater societies may have been directly related to subsistence, with the coming of the wool dog to the Salish area. Before the introduction of the wool dog (in the late seventeenth or early eighteenth century?) there was a rough equality of trade between the saltwater and upriver peoples. The saltwater peoples had more food, but they had to trade much of the surplus upriver in return for mountain-goat wool, which was only available in the mountains and was essential for weaving blankets that were the most important wealth item given away at potlatches. This made for a rough equivalence, with trade and marriage in both directions. But, according to this still-unproven scenario, when the wool dog was introduced to the lowland villages, its hair could be used to supplement or even supplant mountain-goat wool, which relieved the saltwater people of having to trade their food surpluses upstream, and instead allowed them to use the extra food to feed the dogs. This made the saltwater people richer, and meant that marriages tended to be in a downriver direction, and also that the saltwater people could purchase more slaves. With more slaves and/or more wives to weave the blankets, their wealth was further augmented. But of course, according to the general Northwest Coast pattern, the wealth was concentrated in the hands of a few successful operators, or *siab*, so that not only the number of slaves, but the degree of differentiation among free people, was increased.

The Wakashan Area. We can also find relationships between resources and relative wealth or poverty in at least one Wakashan area, that of the Southern Kwakwaka'wakw. In this area, there were twenty-five local groups or tribes (at the time of the first descriptions by outsiders in the middle and late 19th century), each of them headed by a recognized chief and all of them ranked with respect to each other (Ford 1941:15-16; Boas 1940:359). Internally, the ambilateral descent groups within each tribe were also ranked, each with its own chief and its own, again internally ranked, houses (Boas 1940:359). The various local groups all had access to some coastal areas and some important fish runs, so there was no question here of upriver and saltwater groups. But Donald and Mitchell have shown that the relative ranking of the local groups was strongly correlated with the availability of important subsistence resources, specifically salmon runs, in the groups' territories. These groups with larger and more reliable salmon runs tended to be ranked higher, presumably because they had more of a surplus that could be converted in some manner to wealth, or else could form the basis for entertaining larger audiences at potlatches and other ceremonies (Donald and Mitchell 1975). There is no direct proof here that the higher-ranking groups necessarily had more elaborate ranking systems than those farther down in the order, but there does seem to be a clear relationship between resource abundance and the ability to achieve high status.

We can thus see that Northwest Coast societies present a large number of variations on a common theme. Everywhere people were conscious of wealth and status, and those who could (usually men) strove to gain this wealth and status by operating in a network of social relations that was constructed on principles of status differentiation by a combination of birth and achievement. But the specific principles of differentiation varied from one part of the Coast to another, as did the nature of the goods that conferred or enabled the conferral of high status. And from richer to poorer groups, the opportunities to gain status, as well as the gaps between the high- and low-ranking, diminished. The family systems of the Northwest Coast reflect organization to perform all eight basic kinds of family activities. In general, the subsistence needs of all groups were very similar, but the prestige systems varied so greatly that the family organization differed from one group to another, and from high- to low-status families within a group, according to the dictates of the prestige system. Enabling family members to preserve and enhance status was the activity that largely determined how families were organized to carry out the other activities as well. The ownership and transmission of property, for example, was an arena in which to maneuver for status. Likewise, children were socialized with a view to making them better able to compete. Sex was closely or loosely regulated according to the implications of unregulated sex for the status chances of the participants' families, and so forth. It follows that variation in family organization on the Northwest Coast follows very closely the variation in the organization of systems of prestige competition. Each pattern of prestige competition has a corresponding pattern of family organization and domestic developmental cycle, and in contrast to the African case, on the Northwest Coast these patterns are reflected in the organization of the family for each of its activities. In Chapter 15, we will look at the ways in which the Coast societies were similar in their organization of each activity, and in Chapter 16 we will be examine the differences among the family systems themselves.

Notes

1. I do not mean to imply a personal judgment that northern art was superior to that from other sections of the Coast; I merely observe that it is more famous in the Western artworld.

2. The terminology used here reflects the attempt in recent years to develop inclusive names for ethnic groups. The old terms, Nootka and Kwakiutl, were adopted from particular local groups to refer to all speakers of the respective languages, but members of other local groups within the same linguistic collectivities successfully argued that more inclusive terms could be found. Thus the larger collectivity of what are still called Nootkan speakers refer to themselves as a political unit by the term Westcoast, and the peoples formerly collectively known as Kwakiutl now use the name Kwakwaka'wakw. I retain Kwakiutl in some cases for the particular local group of this name on northern Vancouver Island. I am indebted to Pamela Creasy, a Kwakiutl in the local sense, for straightening out this usage for me.

3. The Nitinat, Nootka speakers of the southwestern coast of Vancouver Island, seem to have left us no information; I have been unable to determine whether their system was more like their northern neighbors or like that of the Makah, Nootka speakers of the Cape Flattery region who shared most of the social characteristics of the Coast Salish.

4. The terminology used for matrilineal segments of northern coast societies differs from one author to the next. As far as I can determine, the various authors' usages correspond as follows:

Garfield(1939)	DeLaguna (1972)	Olson (1967)	Oberg (1973)	Swanton (1905)
Tsimshian	*Tlingit*	*Tlingit*	*Tlingit*	*Haida*
Clan	Moiety	<u>Moiety</u>	Phratry	
House	Sib	(group of clans with a name)	Clan	
Lineage	<u>Lineage</u>	Clan		Family
Dwelling	House	<u>Household</u>		Household
Family	Family	Family		

The underlined terms are the ones I have selected, in accordance with what seems to be the closest possible concurrence with recent anthropological usage.

15

Family Activities in Northwest Coast Societies: Similarities and Generalities

A very general key to understanding the activities performed in and by various kinds of family groups in N-cluster societies is provided by a remark made by Suttles, especially concerning the Straits Salish, but in fact applicable to all groups south of the northern matrilineal area: He remarks that the "family" (by which he means the nuclear family, sometimes augmented by attached close relatives, what I call below the "small-family") could feed and clothe itself, and was thus the basic unit in production of subsistence resources. But it was the larger household, consisting of several small-families, that made possible the demonstration of status or, in other words, that was organized for the purpose of prestige competition. In fact, as is demonstrated below, variation in Coast family systems can be seen in terms of variation in which activities were performed by the small-family and which by the household.

Procuring: Technological and Social Determination

Two kinds of principles operated to determine the social organization of procuring on the Northwest Coast. Environmental and technical principles governed the organization of the groups that cooperated in the tasks of procuring, while social principles governed the organization of rights to the products. These two kinds of principles seem to have operated relatively independently of one another, with the result that the same kinds of rights of consumption sometimes existed over products whose procurement needed to be organized according to different principles of organization.

Rights of access were of two kinds: those based on ownership of resource areas and those based on participation in procuring activities. We can refer to these more simply as ownership rights and participation rights. Ownership rights, here as in the A- and especially O- clusters, were often multi-layered, with rights of stewardship or overlordship belonging to chiefs or other people important in the supra-household political organization. Ownership rights varied considerably from one society to another, and within societies often from one resource to another. The simplest situation was one like that of the Tillamook, where very few subsistence areas were owned: some fishing places were owned by villages, who gave free permission to others to use them, while hunting and gathering areas seem to have been free to all, unencumbered by rights of ownership (Sauter and Johnson 1974:28-30). A considerably more complicated situation prevailed, for example among the Straits Salish. Here fishing locations, clam beds, and root beds were the most important subsistence resources—some locations of each kind were owned, while others were free to public access. Reef-netting locations, for example, were individually owned, usually by household heads (Suttles 1951:162). Clam beds were generally in the public domain, but some of them were owned, as were some camas beds, by individual women (Suttles 1951:60, 68). Hunting nets were individually owned, making the owner of a net the head and organizer of a hunting expedition (Suttles 1951:88). An even more highly developed system of ownership prevailed among the Westcoast people, where chieftainship included, as one of its prerogatives, overlordship of all subsistence resources within the territory of the group subject to the chief. These might include, for example, fishing locations on rivers, inlets, bays, etc.; hunting rights in mountain areas, as well as rights to waterfowl taken anywhere within the domain; roots and berry patches; and salvage rights to the beached carcasses of whales and, later on, ships washed up in the chief's territory (Drucker 1951:250-255). But if the chief of the confederacy claimed overlordship rights to all these resources, lower-level notables claimed more immediate rights to some of them: tribute from berry harvests, for example, appears to have been given to several different levels of chiefs, as were portions of whale carcasses (Drucker 1951:250-255).

In general, ownership rights seem to have been of two kinds. First, there was the right to grant permission (rarely if ever the right to refuse it) to others wanting to use one's owned subsistence territories. The reward for ownership in this sense was the ability to play host, to be the owner. We find this kind of pattern described for peoples from the Haisla (Olson 1940:180) to the Halkomelem (Bierwert n.d.:26) and Upper Skagit (Collins 1974:80-81). Second, there was sometimes the right to tribute in the form of a portion of first catch, first fruits, etc., which the owner was often then obligated to redistribute in a communal feast. Tribute obligations, with correspondent feasting, seem to have been confined to strongly hierarchical peoples like the Westcoast (Drucker 1951:251), through economic rights deriving from ownership are also reported for the Yurok, where a fishing-location owner used "leases" as a method of gaining wealth (Kroeber 1925:33-34).

Rights of ownership were thus a way of distinguishing owners of resources from other potential users, with benefits to the owners in enhanced prestige or enhanced ability to acquire prestige. They were not a way of excluding anyone from access to subsistence goods. This is an example of the general trend referred to above, namely that the organization of families for subsistence activities tended to be regulated, at least partially, by the organization for the pursuit of prestige. And indeed, differences in the groups that held ownership rights tended to be associated with differences in the groups that competed in the prestige system of a particular society. Among the individualistic Yurok, who had no extended kin groups of any sort, all resource ownership was individual; even when several men had ownership rights to the same fishing site, they did so as individual shareholders, and used the site in rotation (Kroeber 1925:33-35). Among the Tillamook and Upper Skagit, widely separated Salish groups with weakly developed prestige hierarchies, resource owning groups were villages or extended kin groups, a pattern that was consonant with the relatively egalitarian nature of, respectively, Oregonian groups and upriver peoples in the Washington-B.C. Salish region (Amoss 1993). Among the strongly hierarchical Westcoast, the resource owners were individual chiefs at various levels, and among the matrilineal Tlingit, the ownership groups were variously the matriclans, the localized lineages, or the avunculocal house groups, depending on the resources (Olson 1967:24; DeLaguna 1972:383).

The second sort of rights of access were the participation rights. These were rights to consumption of subsistence resources arising out of participation in the subsistence activity itself or out of being part of a family group of which the participant was a member. There were two ways in which these consumption groups were organized. In the northern or matrilineal section of the Coast, each household had a central fireplace, and all members of the household who brought in subsistence goods shared them communally with the entire household (Olson 1967:11; Murdock 1936:16; Stearns 1984:193; Garfield 1939:277, 326). In the case of the Tsimshian, this household communalism was so strong that it carried over even to summer fishing sites, where the entire winter household camped together (Garfield 1939:277, 326). On the entire rest of the coast, the effective unit for sharing subsistence resources was a sub-household unit usually referred to in the literature by the imprecise term "family," but consisting in most cases of a nuclear family as the core, often with attached senior relatives, unmarried siblings of the spouses, and so on. (I will use the arbitrary term "small-family" to describe this group.) This family group typically had its own fireplace within the large house, and cooked and ate its own food, though with much sharing among families within the household. We find this pattern from the Alsea (Drucker 1939:85) to Chinook (Ray 1938:125), to the Puyallup-Nisqually (Smith 1951:272) and Halkomelem peoples in general (Bierwert n.d.:3). The Wakashan peoples practiced a slight variation on this pattern, in that sharing among families seems to have been a bit more obligatory, though they still cooked separately and kept separate supplies; they also had a communal fireplace, in addition to the individual family fireplaces, for feasts or entertaining visitors (Jewitt 1975:27; Kenyon 1980:94; Ford 1941:6). In Charlie Nowell's story, the prelude to this Part, we see that everyday behavior in this regard was flexible—a man who got up early, for example, often fed the whole household at breakfast.

These kinds of patterns of access rights, being so uniform outside the matrilineal area (and uniform within that area as well) contrast to the actual organization of the subsistence activities, which are determined much more by environmental and technical aspects of the activities themselves. In general, there was a fairly standard social division of labor, with men fishing, hunting for land and sea animals, and procuring construction materials. Women generally gathered plant foods (mostly berries and roots) as well as marine invertebrates. Both sexes gathered firewood. Their sexual division of labor established the "small-family" as the minimum group that shared participation rights to subsistence resources.

Along with this sexual division of labor, the specific nature of subsistence tasks shaped the groups that performed them. For example, many kinds of salmon fishing, practiced up and down the coast, required cooperation of several men at weirs or in boats of various kinds, while other methods, such as dip-netting, were individual processes. The Twana and the Westcoast, for instance, practiced both these kinds of salmon fishing; in each case the small-family of the fisherman was the ultimate recipient of the fish (Elmendorf 1960:72, 106-7; Drucker 1951:41). Among the Straits Salish, the primary method of salmon fishing was reef-netting; the owner of the net would collect a crew and supervise the work, then divide the catch among the crew members, each of whom would take his portion home to his small-family (Suttles 1951:179-80; 272). In most of the coast, women went gathering in groups, probably as much for companionship as for efficiency, and each brought back the take to her own small-family (see, for example Olson 1954:229 on the Owikeno; Drucker 1951:39 on the Westcoast; Smith 1940:4 on the Puyallup-Nisqually). In a sense, then, the organization of procurement activities was largely independent of the organization of rights to products; this is reminiscent of the situation in B-cluster societies, and reflects probably the only major sense in which the foraging technology of the Northwest Coast groups is reflected in their social organization.

Again, however, we find exception to this generalization in the northern matrilineal groups. Here the household was not only the possessor of many ownership rights and nearly all participation rights, but also the effective unit for the organization of subsistence activities. Among the Tlingit, for example, men fished and hunted in household groups (Olson 1967:11; DeLaguna 1972:310), while the women of a household similarly went together to gather (Olson 1967:24), as they did among the Haida (Blackman 1982:34). This is but one example of a pattern we will see in examining the organization of many of the activities of the family: in the matrilineal area, it was the extended household that was the primary solidary unit.

Processing

The labor of processing was extremely important to the subsistence economy of the Northwest Coast, and ethnographies of the area often describe in detail the multiple processes involved. Most of these were performed by women, and the most notable were cleaning and preserving fish, necessary to take full advantage of the seasonal abundance of salmon and other species. In addition, women's processing labor included drying other kinds of foods, such as roots, berries, and shellfish, making barkcloth, and sewing clothing, and general cleanup and maintenance of the household space. Both sexes engaged in the manufacture of various tools and utensils. Men were primarily responsible for house construction and the making and maintenance of weapons of hunting and war. So much is clear; the sexual division of labor is reasonably uniform throughout the area. But what is not often talked about in the accounts is the group to which processing applied—did someone skilled in making, say, spoons, make them for his own small-family, for the household, for anyone who paid? We know that specialists in the manufacture of wealth goods were paid, but what about smaller subsistence articles? Perhaps this side of life was too domestic to attract the attention of the ethnographers. What I can deduce is as follows:

Cooking on most occasions was divided by fireplaces, which means that in the matrilineal area, it was accomplished communally by the women of the household (DeLaguna 1972:308-310), and elsewhere by a woman or women for the small-family (see Ford 1941:11 for the Southern Kwakwaka'wakw; Drucker 1951:114 for the Westcoast; Smith 1940:139 for the Puyallup-Nisqually). Preserving fish and other goods, perhaps the most arduous and time-consuming of a woman's tasks, seems to have been performed on the same basis: Suttles illustrates this for the Straits Salish, showing us how all the members of a reef-net crew received individual shares of the crew's catch; then each fisherman's wife cleaned and dried the fish for her own family (Suttles 1951:180). The same pattern seems to be true for making clothes; at least Drucker describes this for the Westcoast people (1951:114).

Some processing tasks required larger-scale cooperation; these were primarily the work of housebuilding and, in those areas where whaling occurred, the butchering of the whale carcass. With regard to housebuilding, among the Tsimshian male members of all the households of a local matrilineage would join together to build a new structure for one of them (Garfield 1939:275-76); among the Twana, who had no unilineal descent groups, it was the village men who put up a dwelling for any household in the village.

Regulation of Sexuality

Premarital sex in Northwest Coast societies was regulated by the ambition of families to make a good marriage; extramarital sex was regulated by jealousy and possessiveness. Premarital sex was therefore regulated more strictly; its consequences were potentially more serious for the social structure and involved many people, whereas the consequences of extramarital sex involved primarily the triangle only.

If a woman became pregnant before marriage, or in some cases if she was known to have had sexual relations before marriage, this decreased her chances of making a marriage alliance that was profitable to those members of her family who would try to use marital connections to enhance their status. Hence premarital sex was regulated tightly or loosely according to how important such considerations of matchmaking were to the woman's family. I can find nothing about premarital sexuality or its prohibition among the northern matrilineal groups. This may be just a coincidental oversight of the eight or ten ethnographers whose work I have consulted, but I would suggest it is no accident. The matrilineal groups married close; all of them had a preference for cousin marriage (usually matrilateral or double cross-cousin marriage), and at least in the cases of the Tlingit and Haida (Olson 1967:20; Blackman 1982:30, 60-61), it seems to have been very prevalent; the actual frequency among the Tsimshian has been disputed by Vaughan (1984:63). In addition, in a matrilineal system any child who has a mother has a moiety and clan affiliation automatically.

It thus follows that an early pregnancy could be taken care of very neatly and without fuss by arranging a marriage with a male cousin, very probably one from the same household. Thus premarital virginity would not be of much concern.

But as soon as we move south out of the matrilineal region, the picture changes. These peoples reckoned descent either bilaterally with a patrilineal bias or according to no fixed system; in either case both the father's and the mother's identity are important to the place of the child, and a woman who has had a child by another man (unless he can be persuaded to marry her quietly and discreetly) is of lesser value to a potential husband's family as an affine. And even if an adolescent father can be persuaded to marry his girlfriend, this deprives her parents of any choice or maneuvering room in arranging a marriage. They may get a son-in-law, but they probably will not get the one they want. So people with ambitions watched their daughters carefully, as is documented from just about every group on the coast south of the Tsimshian and Haida. We find, for example, that parents always tried to chaperon their postpubertal daughters carefully among the Owikeno (Olson 1954:225), the Southern Kwakwaka'wakw (Ford 1941:34), the Upper Skagit (Collins 1974:228), the Klallam (Gunther 1927:240), the Nooksack, who specifically justified this practice in terms of leaving marriage options open (Amoss 1978:13), and the Quinault (Olson 1936:106-107). And the fact that daughters were chaperoned explicitly to prevent their pregnancy, not to preserve their virginity, is demonstrated by the observation that the Southern Kwakwaka'wakw and their linguistic relatives the Owikeno freely allowed sexual play among young children, who had no possibility of getting pregnant, then began to chaperon their daughters at puberty (Olson 1954:225; Ford 1941:34).

For other groups, we have even stronger evidence that regulation of adolescent female sexuality was concerned with the possibilities of matchmaking: we find that the higher-status families, those with the greatest positive and negative changes in prestige competition, were the ones who chaperoned their daughters most carefully. For example, the Bella Coola chief's daughter was watched very carefully, but other adolescent females less so (McIlwraith 1948:372). Among the Twana, unmarried males were supposed to gain some sexual experience; this could be gained either with a married woman or with an unmarried woman of a low-status family (Elmendorf 1960:433). Among the Puyallup-Nisqually, a Salish group with a relatively small degree of inherited status distinction, it was the "ambitious" families that were said to guard their daughters carefully (Smith 1940:168-69). The chief's daughter among the Westcoast people was kept in a state of semi-seclusion until her marriage (Drucker 1951:143-45; 286-87). And finally, among the Yurok, every family guarded its postpubertal daughters, but the wealthy (who in this society were identical with the high-status) guarded them more carefully (Kroeber 1935:49).

With extramarital sex, the consequences were less systematic and more personal. Adultery could result in divorce in some areas, fines or revenge in others, but it might be ignored altogether if kept discreet. There seem to have been three patterns of regulations and sanctions regarding extramarital sexuality. Among the northern matrilineal groups, it depended on who the partners were. The levirate, which in this region meant moving a younger matrilineal male relative into a deceased husband's position, meant that sex between a husband's brother and brother's wife was considered acceptable and proper, as was intercourse between a mother's brother's wife and a husband's sister's son: in either case the relationship was a prelude to a marriage that would probably happen after the death of the older man (Garfield 1939:234; DeLaguna 1972:484-85; Olson 1967:23). Otherwise, a wife's affairs might lead to divorce (Krause 1956 [1878]:154), to killing the paramour (Krause 1956 [1878]:154-55), or to fines paid to the husband (Olson 1967:23).

The second pattern occurred among the Kwakwaka'wakw and Westcoast groups, and was one of relative tolerance of any reasonably discreet extramarital sexual activity. Among the Southern Kwakwaka'wakw, "Marriage did not demand fidelity of either the husband or his wife" (Ford 1941:38-39); in Westcoast communities, discreet affairs were implicitly approved, people were admonished by their chiefs not to be too jealous, and fighting over adultery was strongly disapproved (Drucker 1951:287, 305, 309). This pattern, more than anything, tends to emphasize the tendency of N-cluster societies in general to see affinal alliances as the most important part of marriage. If something like the sexual infidelity of one of the spouses is allowed to disrupt marriage and affinal relations, serious disruptions in the system will result, especially since in these groups important privileges and other property rights were often transferred as part of marriage payments. So better to urge people to stay calm and be tolerant.

The third pattern seems fairly uniform, with minor variations, from the Coast Salish area on southward. In all these societies, extramarital sex was recognized as being a potentially serious offense, one that could lead to divorce, heavy fines, or physical revenge. For example, in the Straits Salish area, an offended husband might beat or abandon his wife; and offended wife might abandon her husband (Suttles 1951:471). Among the Puyallup-Nisqually, a husband could theoretically kill or beat his wife's lover, or abandon the wife. The wife, if offended, could leave her husband. But here as elsewhere, the decision to do something about a spouse's affair seems to have been a personal one; again discretion was the key (Smith 1940:169), because even an unexpected pregnancy would not have serious structural consequences if the mother were already married.

Care and Training of Children

Socialization of children in N-cluster societies had three kinds of purposes: the care and watching of children considered too young to begin to learn systematically (up to about four or five years), the training of older children in subsistence tasks, and the education of children for participation in the prestige competitions of the society. The first of these, here as everywhere, began as the almost exclusive responsibility of the mother, though even with infants, other caretakers sometimes took a turn: casual wet-nursing is reported for the Puyallup-Nisqually (M.W. Smith 1940:150) as well as the Southern Kwakwaka'wakw (Ford 1941:32), and grandparents or other relatives often cared for infants among such peoples as the Tlingit (DeLaguna 1972:309, 506), the Upper Skagit (Collins 1974:96-7), and the Straits Salish (Suttles 1951:437). Older sisters (I suspect they may have sometimes been classificatory sisters) also took care of infants in some places (Ford 1941:32; Collins 1974:224).

Children almost everywhere on the Coast seem to have nursed for two to three years or perhaps slightly longer; such intervals are reported for the Tlingit (Krause 1956 [1878]:152), the Haisla (Lopatin 1945:48), the Bella Coola (McIlwraith 1948:363), the Quinault (Olson 1936:100), and the Lower Chinook (Ray 1938:71). It appears not to have been long between the end of nursing and the start of a child's formal education, reported to have begun as early as four or five years of age (Ford 1941:33-34; Collins 1974:222; Olson 1936:102).

A child's formal education had two parts—training in the subsistence arts and training in the things necessary to achieve and maintain status. The former is less discussed in the literature, but seems to have consisted mainly of imitation, and in most cases imitation of the parents, along with other relatives, whom the child accompanied on the subsistence quest. The Bella Coola child, for example, was supposed to learn the subsistence tasks by accompanying the same-sex parent on the subsistence quest (McIlwraith 1948:143), as was the Westcoast child (Drucker 1951:273), and the child of the Southern Kwakwaka'wakw (Ford 1941:8). This evidence tends to agree with Suttles' dictum, cited earlier, that it was primarily the "small-family," the group of parents, children, and attached relatives, that was responsible for subsistence procuring and processing. Even among the matrilineal Tlingit, the father began the education of his sons; it was taken over by the mother's brother when the boys moved to their uncle's house (if indeed they did actually move) at eight to ten years old (Krause 1956 [1878]:106; DeLaguna 1972:419).

To learn the subsistence arts was of course important, but it is something that most people were expected to be good at. On the other hand, certain other things had to be learned if one was going to distinguish oneself from one's peers and compete successfully for high status. Everywhere, one had to learn good manners and proper behavior, or "advice." Among the Northern and Central groups, one had to learn the history and traditions, and especially the ancestry of the inherited privileges, of one's household or ancestral line. And in the Coast Salish and southern areas, one had to achieve the purity and discipline necessary to make contact with a spirit helper. Clearly it was not enough to bring up one's children to be skilled in the arts of everyday living; in many ways the most important goal of education was to teach them how to be high-status or important people.

Ordinarily, this training was not carried out exclusively by the child's parents. It is reported that parents played a primary role in the teaching of their children among the Bella Coola (McIlwraith 1948:368-69), the Southern Kwakwaka'wakw (Ford 1941:34-35), and the Upper Skagit (Collins 1974:225), but even in these cases the parents' role was not exclusive. In most Coast groups, the parents' role was not even primary. In Westcoast households, both parents and grandparents participated in the instruction of children in behavior, morals, traditions, and methods of carrying out rituals (Drucker 1951:131-33, 323). For Quinault children, advice in the form of lectures came nightly, again from either a parent or a grandparent (Colson 1936:102). And in most Coast societies, it was specifically the elders, often referred to as grandparents, who did most of the training. Since most households would consist of three generations, with all members of the second and third generations descendants of the members of the first, what this probably means in effect is that the elders of a household took responsibility for training the children of that household. For example, among the Straits Salish a grandparent or other related elder took the responsibility of taking the children for cold morning baths, as well as for lecturing them in manners, hospitality, and generosity, all aspects of the "advice that was thought a mark of high status in that society" (Suttles 1951:393). Among the neighboring Nooksack, an older relative was supposed to teach the children to discipline themselves and to overcome fear, so that they might be successful in the spirit quest (Amoss 1978:13). The Chinook elders prepared their grandchildren for spirit questing also (Ray 1938:78-79), and the Tillamook grandparents were thought of as their grandchildren's main teachers.

Among the Sto:lo, this instruction and discipline of young people was explicitly connected to the household: the eldest male of the household was responsible for training the boys, as the eldest female was for the girls (Duff 1952:210). And among the Tlingit, the household socialized its children, but the labor was divided: the house chief was responsible for giving the lectures and instructions, while a boy's own mother's brother had the duty of directly supervising the individual boy's training, including the cold morning baths that were designed as toughening exercises (Krause 1956 [1878]:152; DeLaguna 1972:512; Oberg 1973:25).

This emphasis on the elders, particularly the elders of the household, and on the moral and spiritual training that they could provide, points out two important features of N-cluster societies. First, as organization for status competition was at a level above that of the small-family, so was the training for such competition rarely carried out within the small-family group. Second, members of the societies appeared to be more concerned with the political economy of status and prestige than with the domestic economy of subsistence. But it was the larger-scale domestic group—the household—that inculcated in the children the values of the political economy. Once again, the organization and functioning of the domestic group were shaped by the role that its members played in the wider, political sphere.

Management and Transmission of
Property and Offices

Northwest Coast social systems, like those of Sub-Saharan Africa, were built on two seemingly contradictory principles concerning access to valued things. Subsistence goods were not to be denied to anyone—"anything to eat is for everybody." At the same time, however, Northwest Coast societies operated on a principle of ranking, which meant unequal status among members of society, status that was bolstered, at least, by unequal access to valued goods. But if goods were abundant and the society recognized an explicit right of everyone to be fed and clothed, it had to have some other mechanism to allow unequal access to goods to form and support ranking. This unequal access was of two kinds: unequally direct access to subsistence goods, and quantitatively unequal access to prestige goods. By the first I mean that while everyone had a right to food and other basic material necessities, some people were considered to own these things directly, while others got them from the owners. And prestige goods had no guarantee of universal access.

Family groups on the Coast were responsible for preserving both these kinds of unequal access and for allowing those with lesser rights to gain some access through the mediation of higher-ranking family members. Common membership in family groups thus served the interests of the high-ranking, in that it organized subordinates as followers through allowing the high-ranking to control goods. But once the ranking system was established, family groups were necessary to maintain it, to allow those without strong rights of access to gain indirect access through common family membership with the great ones. Through the pervasive ideology of chiefly generosity, this system made a structure of domination look like a structure of benevolence, with chiefs allowing others to gain access to needed goods and to bask in the reflective glory of their patrons' accomplishments. But as long as the maxim of universal subsistence and the ideology of chiefly generosity held, the structure of domination remained a benign one—everyone belonged to a family group and nobody was deprived of a livelihood, except slaves. Except slaves—there is a temptation to see slaves as outside the social system, because they are often described as objects of wealth that could be given away or destroyed at potlatches (Drucker 1949:111), rather than as social persons. But this is, or course, a fundamentally erroneous notion—slaves were people like anybody else, and we must not succumb to the temptation to regard slaves as either solely property or solely persons. They were both. What distinguished them most from free members of the society is that they were not members of family groups, if they were newly captured or bought, and thus enjoyed even the most rudimentary rights only at the sufferance of their masters. Even slaves who had been in a community for awhile and who had married and had children of their own were members of families with no rights, with no possibility of providing access to any kinds of goods. The very insignificance of such families, the fact that their members remained powerless as the orphaned or widowed slaves of recent capture, points up the importance of the families of non-slaves as groups for the management and transmission of property and other goods.

Families did not always own or regulate access to subsistence resources, because not all subsistence resources were owned. In some groups, in fact, most subsistence resources were free of access. Among the Twana, for example, hunting territories and the shore resources of the Hood Canal were available to anybody; no economic resources were owned by local groups or kin groups of any kind. Stations on the fishing weirs across streams were owned by individual men, but all seem to have had access to a station (Elmendorf 1960:268-69). This simply meant that access to subsistence resources was not a factor in determining social status in this group. The same thing seems to have been true for the Klallam (Gunther 1927:202), and for the Quinault, whose hunting territories were free of access, and whose salmon weirs belonged to the local community as a whole, with platforms on their weirs belonging to the small-family groups (Olson 1936:94). Similar situations seem to have prevailed among the Sto:lo, who had communal hunting grounds and individually owned dip-net stations (Bierwert n.d.:11-14), and the Tillamook, among whom fishing rights were owned by villages or by individuals, and hunting rights were free to all (Sauter and Johnson 1974:28-30).

All of the foregoing groups belong to the Coast Salish area, and are among the least "hierarchical" of the Salish societies. For other Salish groups, however, control of subsistence resources was one key to prestige, and it was certain high-ranking household heads who held that key. If we proceed just down the Frazer River from the Sto:lo, for example, we come to another Halkomelem-speaking group, the Katzie. Here, though sockeye and eulachon runs were free of access, the most important fishing resources, the sturgeon nets and the fall-season dog salmon stations, were owned by individuals and households respectively (Bierwert n.d.:24; Suttles 1955:22). Those who owned the prized sites or nets were of course generous with their catch, but they kept enough surplus for themselves to be able to trade up and down river for wealth items, which would enable them to stage the potlatches that would accord them status of *siem*, or honored ones. Similarly, among the Straits Salish groups, fishing locations, root beds, clam beds, hunting nets were all owned by individuals, but these individuals were almost always the heads of prominent households, meaning that access to these goods was through household membership, and that the members of certain fortunate households could inherit them (Suttles 1951:52-56, 68, 218).

Among the Yurok and Hupa, access to subsistence goods was also unequally direct, but for different reasons. Rather than being the property of households of important household heads (which is sort of a trusteeship for the household) all subsistence goods and locations among these Northwestern California peoples were individually owned, and each had its precise value, and could be inherited, usually by sons but occasionally by daughters or close patrilateral kin (Kroeber 1925:20, 33, 39). Since the control of wealth, all of it measured against a universal standard, was the only basis for status in these societies, we can see that control of subsistence resources, even if the fruits had to be shared, was a potential source of the differential wealth of families, especially important since inheritance was a very common way of acquiring wealth (Kroeber 1925:39).

Among the Westcoast and Southern Kwakwaka'wakw, we find a third pattern, in which individual small-families acquired rights to subsistence resources not by being members of particular households (households held no property rights except to the houses themselves) but by their heads' membership in extended kin and/or territorial groups. The Westcoast chief was the nominal owner of village sites, inland and coastal waters, salmon streams, and beached whale carcasses. He granted usufruct, essentially, to all followers, sometimes through the intermediary of lesser-ranking chiefs in his own kin group or other kin groups that shared the locality (Drucker 1951:247-251). In this society, the most generous chief, the one who accorded subsistence rights and reflective glory (see below) most lavishly, was the most successful chief, the chief with the greatest following to enable him to accumulate more wealth and further raise his status (Drucker 1951:273). Similarly, among the Southern Kwakwaka'wakw, the famous *numaym* or *namima*, a patri-slanted ambilateral kin group, was the basic unit through which small-families derived their access to economic rights. As among the Westcoast, the chiefs of the kin group were the owners, or more properly the stewards, of its economic resources (Drucker and Heizer 1967:11-12).

Finally, there is the pattern of subsistence resource ownership by unilineal kin groups. We find this with patrilineages among the Makah, where the lineage was the owner, and its most important household head the steward, of fishing grounds, berry patches, and strips of coastline (Colson 1953:4, 193). And, as expected, a similar pattern occurs among the matrilineal groups to the north, including the incompletely matrilineal Haisla and the fully matrilineal Tsimshian, Haida, and Tlingit. In all these groups, whatever subsistence resources were not free of access (and there seem to have been some of these in Tlingit and Haida territory) were owned by localized matrilineages. In some cases, these localized lineages consisted of one household only; where lineages had multiple households in a village, the effective ownership may have been by the house chiefs or the lineage chiefs, depending on the specific nature of the resources (DeLaguna 1972:383, 361, 407; Olson 1967:12, 24; Olson 1940:180:Halpin 1984:17-18; Swan 1905:71; Stearns 1984:193). These lineages and households were enduring corporations, and all but slaves were in a sense full members of these corporations; status as household or lineage members and access to subsistence resources was thus passed down through the generations.

There is thus considerable variation both in the degree to which inequality of direct access to resource areas was a support of social status differences and in the manner in which family membership organized that support. For non-subsistence goods, the situation is somewhat simpler. Everywhere on the coast, both tangible wealth and intangible privileges were differentially held, and everywhere they were transmitted down the generations. The patterns in which they were held and transmitted, however, varied. Beginning from the North this time, we find these wealth items and privileges among the matrilineal groups being held by and transmitted in the matrilineage (Olson 1967:1; Halpin 1984:17-18; Olson 1940:170). Among the Southern Kwakwaka'wakw and Westcoast, the privileges and wealth were attached to a position that itself was a title or seat held by the ranking member of an ambilateral kin group; the goods passed to the next generation within that kin group or to a child's spouse as a marriage gift (Drucker and Heizer 1967:11-12; Boas 1940:360-65; Drucker 1951:257, 265-67; Kenyon 1980:106). From the Coast Salish area south, these material and immaterial prestige goods (and the immaterial ones become less important as we go southward) were owned by individuals, and passed down to relatives in various and usually not very regular patterns.

In each of these patterns, family groups played a role in managing and organizing the transmission of property between generations. In all areas, someone who was a member of the household of someone who held rights and privileges of a high-ranking sort could both benefit from the secondary distribution of potlatch goods and bask in the reflective glory of the successes of the household head. In the northern and central patterns, membership in an important household also conferred more direct benefits. In the northern groups, the rights and privileges really belonged more to the kin group, and stewardship of its resources came to many if not most males by virtue of seniority in the group (Olson 1967). In the Southern Kwakwaka'wakw and Westcoast groups, the rights and privileges belonged to the head, but if he wanted to keep his position he was generous to his followers, not just with material goods but with names, minor privileges, initiations into societies, the use of certain ornaments, and so forth (Drucker 1951:273). In the Coast Salish groups, the benefits of household membership seem less tangible, but even here such attenuated privileges as names were usually transmitted to direct descendants, who tended to be household members at some point in their lives (Suttles 1951:404; Elmendorf 1960:328; Haeberlin and Gunther 1930:46).

Political and Ritual Representation

Everywhere on the Northwest coast, the position of household head was a recognized one, with the head having either power over the household members or at least increased prestige. But it is difficult to find information on how and in what contexts household heads represented the interests of other household members in public contexts. I suspect that the phenomenon was more frequent and important than the relatively few references to it in the sources suggest. What those references describe are two kinds of representation of households by their heads: representation in political councils and representation at potlatches and other ceremonies.

Household-based councils seem to have been a feature primarily of the northern matrilineal groups. For example, at Yakutat each clan had a series of chiefs, each of whom was head of a household. One of these was the most important, or head chief, recognized as chief of the local population of that clan, while other household heads acted as a sort of clan council (DeLaguna 1972:462). In the Tsimshian area, by contrast, the council seems to have covered a whole tribe, or local settlement group, with heads of various households, regardless of clan affiliation, forming a local or tribal council. Outside the Northern groups, we find descriptions of similar council representation among the Makah, where the head of the household exercised the privileges owned by the household and controlled their use, and where, in Colson's description, the individual acted more as a member of a household than as a citizen of a village (Colson 1953:19).

The other form of representation recorded in the literature concerns attendance at various kinds of ceremonies. This seems to have been particularly common in the Coast Salish area. For example, among the Straits peoples the household head often represented his household at a feast, taking food home to other members who did not attend (Suttles 1951:307-08). Among the Halkomelem speakers, immediately to the north, sometimes more than one member of a household attended a potlatch, but the household head acted as a speaker on behalf of all household members.

Finally, we find a sort of representation among the Tlingit (and the other northern groups as well), in which the ranked unit in the community was the household as a whole, not the individual as in the Westcoast and Southern Kwakwaka'wakw societies. In the northern groups, then, the rank of the household head and the rank of the household were in a sense synonymous; all household members shared in their leader's rank, and most of the male members, at least, could expect to hold that rank personally when they, in their genealogical turn, succeeded to the household headship. Meanwhile, if the household were to give a potlatch, the household head would officiate on behalf of the household as a whole (Olson 1967:48).

Enabling

It is probably no exaggeration to say that, on the Northwest Coast, it was the activity of enabling that held the household together. Whereas the small-family seems to have been able to meet its subsistence needs either by itself or by means of ad hoc cooperation with other small-families, the prestige of important men was dependent on displaying and giving away wealth, and it was through mobilization of the household members that a man could accumulate enough wealth to be able to potlatch. Everywhere but in the northern matrilineal area, important men were concerned with attracting relatives to their households in order to use these relatives' labor to augment their wealth, and ordinary people were attracted to the households of wealthy men as places where they could, in return for labor and support, gain access to some of the privileges or other benefits the prominent household heads could provide. Even among the northern groups, where the households were the subsistence units, they were just as importantly organized to support their leaders in prestige competition.

If the measure of high status on the Northwest Coast was the ability to display and/or distribute wealth and privileges, the process of enabling was the process through which a prominent household could accumulate such resources for distribution or display. And there were two basic routes toward such accumulation. Privileges could be inherited, or wealth created, within the household, transmitted from the previous generation or created by the labor of the members. Or wealth could be accumulated by calling in debts (or creating new debts) from affines or other relatives. Enabling thus consisted of processes through which household heads gained access either to the labor of household members or to alliances, usually through marriage, with other households that could be called on to contribute goods. These two kinds of enabling, through household labor and through creating alliances, are illustrated in descriptions of the Tlingit:

> All men of the household were expected to aid in the house chief's endeavors to maintain or raise his social standing, and thereby enhance the prestige of the house and, by extension, that of the clan [Olson 1967:48].

the Westcoast:

> It was commonly recognized that the individual chief's ability to "keep up his name"...depended on the people living in his house, [Drucker 1951:273].

and the Sto:lo:

> Potlatching was a circulation system in which the house groups and nuclear families could maximize the amount of currency they circulated by careful and fortuitous credit manipulation. [Bierwert n.d.:53].

Let us consider these two kinds of enabling in more detail. The most obvious ways in which households enabled their members' prestige activities was by manufacturing wealth objects or preserving and preparing food surpluses to be given to guests at feasts, potlatches, or other ceremonies. And in aboriginal times the bulk of this labor seems to have been done primarily by women. Native blankets, one of the most important of wealth items, were usually manufactured by women out of goat hair, dog hair, feathers, or other animal products; it often took several months to manufacture a fine blanket. (See Krause 1956:1878-79 for Tlingit; Drucker and Heizer 1967:14 for Southern Kwakwaka'wakw; Suttles 1951: 492 for Straits Salish). In addition, food surpluses were important, and these were usually produced by women's processing labor. Men's work was also important in creating wealth—they made carved goods among the Haida (Murdock 1936:3), for example, but women's labor seems to have been most important, as Suttles observes for the Straits peoples:

> The products of men's industries—canoes, house posts, planks, tools were more important as capital than as wealth. But the products of female crafts—mats, baskets, blankets, skin clothing—while they were useful, were more purely wealth. A surplus of goods classed as wealth was probably more often produced by women than by men (1951:492).

The great importance of women's labor in enabling has several interesting implications. First, it seems to be connected to the general importance of women in prestige activities on the Northwest Coast, not as substitutes for men, as in African and Oceanic areas, but in their own right as women. Whereas men were usually the publicly recognized leaders, the chiefs and potlatch-givers (although Murdock has described the Haida potlatch as being given by a couple [1936:9]) women seem everywhere to have played an important role behind the scenes. This is well expressed in the modern Sto:lo metaphor of men as the nose and women as the backbone: it is the nose of the fish that stands out in front and leads, but it is the backbone that provides the propulsion: women were equally involved in creating prestige for the household with men (Bierwert 1986:339-44). And this seems to fit well with the idea of status homogamy among high-status people; the wife as well as her husband was from a respected heritage. This contrasts strongly with African cases in which men and women shared power: in Africa those who shared power were brother and sister, not husband and wife.

A second implication of the importance of female labor for creating wealth concerns the distribution of polygyny on the Northwest coast. N-cluster polygyny was much more like that found in Oceania than like the African version: on the Coast only high-status men had more than one wife. And the motivation for polygyny, at least in some cases, was to have more women in the household, and thus more labor to create wealth items to give away (Collins 1974:79).

A third implication concerns social change in the nineteenth century. During this time, immediately prior to the period of "competitive potlatching" analyzed by Benedict, there was an enormous inflation of the currencies of the Northwest Coast status system. In particular, Hudson's Bay Company blankets began to fill the area and could be gotten very cheaply. Instead of a few native blankets, each a product of months of skilled labor, there were literally heaps of cheap woolen blankets; quantity seems to have partially replaced quality as a criterion of goods given away. It is quite possible that, with this inflation and the consequent displacement of the products of women's labor, the position of women in the prestige system became less important.

The other kind of enabling was through creating alliances with households who could be called upon to supply goods to an ambitious or high-ranking person; this was ordinarily done by creating marriages. And marriages brought the possibility of wealth into the household in two ways. First, of course, they created affines, pure and simple; and transactions with affines were ways of acquiring wealth directly, as when Straits and other Salish groups took surplus food to affines and expected wealth items in return (Suttles 1951:313), or indirectly, lending and borrowing and then calling in all debts when a big ceremony was due. And of course the higher-ranking and more prestigious the affines, the more they would likely be able to supply. This goes a long way toward accounting for the insistence on status homogamy among groups as widely separated as the Bella Coola (McIlwraith 1948:376), the Makah (Colson 1953:203), the Twana (Elmendorf 1960:362), the Westcoast (Drucker 1951:244), and others.

But marriage alliances did not just create potential wealth; in many societies they created wealth directly through dowry and buy-back marriage. Dowry, the passage of prestige goods from the wife's own family to the family she was marrying into, was widely practiced on the coast, from as far south as the Yurok (Kroeber 1925:29) to the Westcoast and the Bella Coola, where important privileges often descended to women, and were brought to the virilocal marriage as part of the marriage contract (Kenyon 1980:107; McIlwraith 1948:376). The buy-back marriage was an institution of the Northern Kwakwaka'wakw, reported for both the Owikeno and the Bella Bella groups. In these societies, a chief would often arrange a marriage between himself and a small girl, as young as five years old, and pay a brideprice for her. Then her own people would arrange to "buy her back" for two or more times the value of the original brideprice. The gain accruing to the chief went to pay for potlatches; her family gained the advantage of having an important chief as an affine (Olson 1954:223; 1955:334).

Both these kinds of enabling depended, of course, on leaders' being able to attract lower-ranking small-families to be members of their households. This was no problem in the matrilineal area, where small-families were not very discrete units and the entire household shared the prestige and rank of its temporary leader, but it was more of a question in other areas, where small-families were relatively independent for subsistence. This problem seems to have been solved in two ways: chiefs could promise the allocation of subsistence areas they controlled, as in the Westcoast case, or they could perform services for their dependents, such as giving them minor names, helping with ceremonies, and distributing freely among their own household members food and wealth items they had been given by other chiefs at potlatches. But it is clear that, as much as leadership meant the ability to distribute and display wealth, this ability was itself dependent on building a following. As in Africa and Oceania, wealth and following were closely intertwined, but on the Northwest Coast, a following enabled wealth, rather than the other way around.

Emotional Ties

Northwest Coast ethnography is frustratingly sparse on the topic of emotional relationships within families; only June McCormick Collins' *Valley of the Spirits*, dealing with the Upper Skagit, and two works dealing with the Tlingit, Frederica de Laguna's *Under Mount Saint Elias* and Kalervo Oberg's *The Spatial Economy of the Tlingit Indians* provide anything like systematic or coherent accounts of these relationships in traditional N-cluster societies. My remarks must then be brief and tentative.

First, it is clear that, as in other rank-society clusters, emotional relationships on the Northwest Coast were structured according to family ties; expectations for some kinds of relationships were much different from expectations for others, as would be expected in this kind of society. We can see this clearly if we divide relationships into five categories: alternate generations, adjacent generations, same-generation affines, siblings, and spouses.

The relationships between spouses are probably best characterized by solidarity without merging—each spouse clearly retained his or her ties to the natal family after marriage (Collins 1974:106-7; Ray 1938:128). Whether this kind of solidarity meant a rough equality of power and respect, as suggested by Blackman for the Haida (1980:31-32), Ray for the Lower Chinook (1938:118), and Bierwert for the Sto:lo (1986:ch.4), or whether it meant a pattern of male dominance and female subordination, as suggested by Olson for the Owikeno (1954:285), Swan for the Makah (1870:11), or DeLaguna for the Tlingit (1972:483), may have more to do with the prejudices and assumptions of the ethnographers than with the quality of the relationships themselves. Either way, perhaps the best way to characterize husband-wife relationships on the Coast is as solidary and identifying, but maintaining a considerable amount of individual independence.

There is no clear picture of sibling ties in the literature. For example, Garfield says of the Tsimshian that the relationship between brothers was characterized by rivalry and jealousy (1939:328), while DeLaguna says of the Tlingit, whose family system was very similar, that brothers identified closely with each others' interests and cooperated closely. Sisters are reported to have been close and cooperative (Collins 1974:91; DeLaguna

1972:484-85), but most sources do not mention sisters at all. The only discussions of brother-sister ties I have come across concerned the matrilineal peoples of the north coast, who practiced a mild form of avoidance, but at the same time had important economic obligations to each other (DeLaguna 1972:483; Oberg 1973:26; Olson 1940:185).

The picture for same-generation affines is similarly confusing: Collins says that among the Upper Skagit, both wife's brother-sister's husband relationships and husband's sister-brother's wife relationships were characterized by joking—here as elsewhere perhaps a cover for possible jealousy and rivalry (1974:109). For the Tlingit, DeLaguna reports no special emotional relationship between male affines of the same generation (1972:494-5), while Oberg tells us that these men were often close confidants.

From all this, it is impossible to tell where the trust and where the tensions would have fallen among relatives of the same generation. When we move to adjacent generations, the picture is little better; there is much material in the literature about how parents socialized their children, but very little about how they got along. Collins does say that the relationships with the same-sex parent remained close into adulthood, and there is nothing in the literature that would cause me to question the generality of this statement. For the Tlingit, the information is fuller; we learn that children were emotionally close to both their parents, and that, as in matrilineal systems around the globe, the relationship to the father was an affectionate one, while that to the mother's brother was more distant and authoritarian (DeLaguna 1972:478-9; Oberg 1973:24-25). In addition, the wicked stepparent motif, prominent in the lore of the Salish peoples (Collins 1974:93; Suttles 1951:290), was absent from Tlingit culture, because the step-parent in that society was invariably the father's brother or mother's sister, owing to strict practice of the levirate (DeLaguna 1978:478).

One place where the emotional quality of family relationships is clear in the Northwest Coast literature, however, is in the discussion of grandparents and grandchildren. Despite the leadership role of the grandparental generation, despite their explicit duty to train the grandchildren for the spirit quest or for knowledge of lore and privilege, the relationship between grandparents and grandchildren is always reported to have been close, warm, and affectionate. Among the non-matrilineal peoples, this relationship was perhaps most often that between true grandparents and true grandchildren (Collins 1974:93-94; Ford 1941:39); in the northern area the important elders might be either the grandparents or the senior generation of the avunculocal household; the bonds might be even stronger when, with bilateral cross-cousin marriage, the father's father and the mother's mother's brother were the same man (DeLaguna 1972:476). It is apparently no exaggeration to characterize the Tlingit as having a much

stronger emotional bond between alternate than between adjacent generations DeLaguna 1972:476), and if this was general throughout the coast
(which I think it probably was), it may explain the sparsity of references to
parent-child emotional ties in the literature. In any case, the emphasis on
love between grandparents and grandchildren points out the importance
of the extended household, along with the subsistence-oriented small-family, in Northwest Coast family structure, the topic of Chapter 16.

16

Family Structure on the
Northwest Coast

The most important principle for understanding the developmental cycle of N-cluster families is the principle of two distinct, but related, levels of family organization. The lower level was what I have called the "small-family," the group, usually centered around a single married couple and their children, often with attached relatives. This small-family was embedded in a larger level I refer to as the household, which inhabited a single permanent dwelling and consisted of a group of related small-families. There is variation from one area to another in the nature of the activities organized at each of the two levels, but nowhere is one level ever independent of the other.

To represent this structural variation, I employ yet another version of the general family diagram used elsewhere in this book. As in the African and Oceanic cases, the diagram shows a specific phase in the family developmental cycle with three generations of adults alive at one time, when the middle generation has married and given birth to children. Earlier and later phases, indicated here, are implied in the diagrams of specific systems. The most important feature of the N-cluster diagram system is the relative strength of the small-family, indicated by the family circle, and of the household, indicated by the rectangular outlines of the typical Northwest Coast longhouse, as in Figure 16-1.

To examine the variation in the activities organized at the two levels and in the relationship between them, we shall take a tour up the coast. We shall find a general progression from south to north of decreasing importance of the small-family and increasing importance of the household. We

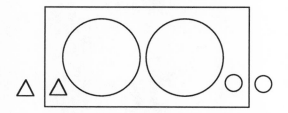

Figure 16-1: A Hypothetical N-Cluster System

begin with the southern area, where the household is undeveloped. We then proceed northward, to examine a few variations on the most common kind of system, in which both levels are important and inter-connected, and then finish by examining the northern areas, where the small-family is of minor importance and the household is the group in and for which almost all family activities are organized.

The Southern Area: The
Relative Independence of the Small-Family

The Yurok and their neighbors, as mentioned before, can be seen as marginal to the Northwest Coast culture area in several ways, probably most importantly because they gained status primarily by the display of wealth and not by its distribution. But they are marginal in terms of their family organization as well, for they did not have the large joint household characteristic of the rest of the coast. The Yurok and their close neighbors, the Karok and Hupa, had two kinds of house buildings—dwelling houses and sweat-houses.[1] Each dwelling was occupied by a single small-family (sometimes including more than one adult male); each sweathouse, on the average, was occupied by the adult males of three or so dwelling houses (Kroeber 1925:81-82). Access to resources was individually owned, and it appears that the dwelling-house group, or small-family, consumed fish and plant foods brought to the family by those family members who had rights of access to the subsistence territories. The small-family was, then, self-sufficient in food and other subsistence resources, though there seems to have been considerable sharing as when, for instance, a man caught a large amount of fish and was expected to give liberally of the catch to all comers (Kroeber 1925:34).

If access to subsistence goods was individually owned in these societies, so was the wealth that was so important in Yurok and neighboring cultures. A man was prominent in Yurok society if he possessed and could display deerskins, woodpecker-scalp bands, obsidian blades, and most importantly dentalium shells, the standard of value in terms of which all other goods were priced. A man could acquire wealth in several ways: by trade up the coast, by inheritance (most wealth was passed on to the sons, though some went to daughters as dowry or to other patrilateral kin) by receiving bridewealth for one's daughters, or by receiving blood money for the death of a close relative (Goldschmidt and Driver 1940:106). The manipulation of bridewealth payments must have required considerable skill as well as demographic good fortune, for a daughter's bridewealth had to go to pay for a wife for a son, making both the sex ratio of children and the timing of loans and payments crucial to family success (Kroeber 1925:29-30), as well as precluding any easy or spectacular short-term changes in status (Kroeber 1925:40).

Brides brought with suitable brideprices normally married virilocally, and married sons and their wives usually shared a house with the husband's parents for at least some time after their marriage, as indicated by the average number of persons in a dwelling house, reported by Kroeber as 7.5 for the whole Yurok area, too large to be accounted for by even the most fertile nuclear-family households. In addition, a man whose father and father's brothers could not afford the full brideprice might marry uxorilocally, coming to live with the bride's father for a few years; whether in the same house or a neighboring one is not clear from the sources (Kroeber 1925:29). In the event of divorce, all marriage payments had to be returned, meaning that people were usually unwilling to see their daughters divorced unless there was evidence of abuse or maltreatment (Kroeber 1925:30). Finally, on the death of a spouse, the sororate and levirate were considered obligatory; in either case the groom's people made a small payment to the bride's people (Kroeber 1925:30-31).

It is not clear from the sources to what extent the labor of family members contributed to the wealth- and prestige-seeking activities of the family head, but at least the other kind of enabling, the kind that comes from marriages that are advantageous for contacts and dowry, definitely operated in the Yurok family. By manipulating full-bridewelath marriages with status equals and "half" or uxorilocal marriages with status inferiors, a prominent man could substantially reinforce or raise his own and his family's status.

In the context of the two levels of Northwest Coast family organization, the Yurok-Karok-Hupa small-family organization seems to be that of a generally virilocal, joint family cycle, dividing when the father dies or perhaps beforehand, which combines most of the family functions into one. The subsistence activities were organized on a house (small-family) basis, and what enabling went on pertained to essentially the same house group, though enabling by labor of family members seems to have been much less important than it was further north on the Coast. There was, however, another level of organization—that of the sweat-house. There was, as mentioned, approximately one sweat-house for each three family houses. This sweat-house was the property of one man, presumably a man of prominence in the local group, and was used not only as a men's clubhouse but as a sleeping-house for the adult males of several dwelling-houses, ordinarily a total of six or seven men among the Yurok, and all the men of a village, however many that may have been, among the Hupa (Kroeber 1925:82; Goldschmidt and Driver 1940:104). The men who used a sweathouse were almost always relatives, consanguineal or affinal, of the sweathouse owner. Some of the sweathouse-sharing groups were known as "great houses," or "aristocrats," and maintained high reputations along with their members' ownership of wealth and a few inherited privileges (Pilling 1989). The sweathouse, then, apparently without much of an organizing function in either the subsistence or prestige sphere, still appears to be an incipient form of the larger family group which, farther up the coast, develops into the joint household organized everywhere for prestige functions and in the most northerly areas for subsistence functions as well. If we represent the small-family level by the family circle and the larger level by the rectangular household, we can represent the Yurok-Karok-Hupa situation like this: all family activities are preformed by the basic base-group; the larger level, represented by the sweat-house, although associated with status and status homogamy, is not yet a corporate group (Figure 16-2).

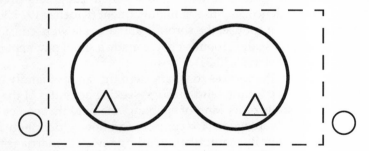

FIGURE 16-2: Yurok System

The Alsea of the central Oregon coast had a family system with some of the same features as the Yurok and other Northwestern California groups, but which already began to display the two-level configuration characteristic of most of the coast. Like the Yurok, the Alsea had no unilineal descent groups, but unlike the California groups, they did have village headmen, from one to three in each community (Olson 1939:92). As among the Yurok, Alsea marriages were usually virilocal by brideprice, but with an uxorilocal alternative (Olson 1939:93). Wealth here appears to have been individually owned, as it was farther south, and to have been connected to status by display rather than by distribution. Ways of gaining wealth were by trade, brideprice, and dowry, which among the Alsea appears to have been an expected transaction in all marriages (Olson 1939:93-94). In all these characteristics, the Alsea family seems to have resembled that of the California groups quite closely; virilocal small-families with some uxorilocal couples, organized in all probability for most of the subsistence and prestige functions.

But there is a difference—the sweathouse is absent in the Alsea area, and the household, consisting of several small-families, begins to appear. The winter dwelling of the Alsea was a large, rectangular pit-house, containing from one to four families, each with its own fireplace in its own section of the house. It is not clear from the sparse accounts given Olson by three aged informants in the 1930s whether the household group, when it contained more than one family, was organized to perform any kind of functions other than just living in the same building, or whether household mates had some kind of greater obligation to each other than did kin who did not reside together, or even if families living in the same household were necessarily related. But at least the residential pattern here seems to be that of the great majority of the Northwest Coast, from this area north to the Kwakwaka'wakw-speaking groups. We can represent the Alsea family as in Figure 16-3: here the larger household becomes a firm residential structure.

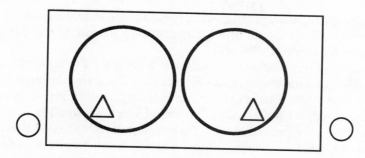

FIGURE 16-3: Alsea System

As we continue to move northward along the Coast, we see more and more of the two-level pattern emerging. Among the Tillamook, just north of the Alsea, houses are routinely reported to have had three families, each with its own fireplace (Sauter and Johnson 1974:107). With the next group to the north, the Lower Chinook, we enter the realm where potlatching and the distribution of wealth were at least as important as the display and ownership of wealth, and where virilocal small-family cycles were embedded in the larger cycle of a multi-family household, where each family had its partitioned off room and its own fireplace, but all were related to each other and to the household head, who was the most prestigious of the family heads in the household (Ray 1938:125-128). It is not clear from Ray's accounts exactly what the constituent small-families in a household shared with each other, that is, how important the household was as an organization for the performance of the prestige functions.

The Salish Area

One step farther north, however, takes us into the Coast Salish area proper, where we find a typical pattern of two-level organization operating almost everywhere. One account from this area that focuses particularly clearly on small-family and household organization, and on the relationships between them, is Marion Smith's *The Puyallup Nisqually* (1940). These were Salish-speaking people living along the southern shores of Puget Sound. They had a definite system of social rank, but little inheritance of status, making achievement the primary criterion for respect and authority: "Individuals who held places of respect and authority in the community were those who fitted most perfectly into a preconceived idea of what the requirements for the positions were" (Smith 1940:48). This preconceived idea, in turn, was of a person who was wealthy, and who displayed his wealth by giving it away: "High-class persons consistently gave away more than others, the first man of a group naturally assuming the role of the most generous (Smith 1940:147)."

There were three kinds of social units among the Puyallup-Nisqually: small-families, households, and villages. The village was the largest political unit, and might consist of from one to three households (Smith 1940:4). The household, in turn, usually consisted of four to six small-families, who lived in the house permanently in the winter season, and used it as a kind of home base during spring, summer, and fall. Subsistence resources were owned by villages, if ownership is the right word; members of a village community could use the resources within the river drainage that the village controlled, and might use resources of other friendly villages by permission (Smith 1940:24).

Here the small-family was unambiguously the subsistence unit. Each small-family provisioned itself with the food resources hunted and gathered by its members—men did the hunting and most of the fishing, while women did the gathering (Smith 1940:4, 135-39). Other resources came to the family groups similarly—men worked bone, horn, and stone, while women did sewing, spinning, weaving, and mat-making (Smith 1940:139). In addition, processing labor was likewise the province of the small-family; the food foraged by its members was brought to the family's fire in its own section of the house, where it was cooked for the family under the supervision of the senior woman (Smith 1940:193). During the seasons when the people were not living continuously in the main house, each small-family went its separate way to fish, gather, hunt, and preserve food for the coming winter, food that it would cook and eat at its own fireplace (Smith 1940:35).

The developmental cycle of the Puyallup-Nisqually small-family was a fairly simple one. Let us begin with a married couple with several children, and no attached relatives. The children of both sexes would be married in their late teens or early twenties, and take up residence in small-families separate from those of either partner's parents. They might continue to live in the same household as the parents of one or the other partner, or might move into a separate household in the same village (marriage within the household was forbidden) (Smith 1940:34, 42, 166-68). As a couple's children married off, however, there developed more of a tendency for the younger ones to marry and remain within the small-family of one or the other partner, thereby causing a "shift in nucleus" (Smith 1940:33) from the older couple, now grandparents, to the younger. Widows and widowers both ideally practiced the levirate or sororate, but in the end old people remained as a dependent generation above that of the effective heads of the subsistence-oriented small-family. In effect, then, the small-family in this society was following a stem-family cycle, with one of the younger children remaining part of the family on marriage, and forming its new nucleus in the succeeding generation.

If small-families were thus independent in their organization for subsistence functions, they combined into households to face the outside world and to organize for prestige activities. Each household consisted of from four to six small-families, usually but not always related to each other (Smith 1940:34). It was this household that tried to present itself to the outside world as "socially and economically enviable" (Smith 1940:34). The household group would ordinarily not contain more than one famous craft specialist, one well-known warrior, or one wealthy and prominent man, a man who was competing for wider prestige by accumulating and then redistributing wealth at potlatches. The house group was exogamous, and tried to arrange for its members the most advantageous weddings possible, which meant marriages with people of as high status and as distant provenance as possible (Smith 1940:166). These marriages were accompanied by exchanges of goods in both directions, which ended with the birth of the couple's first child. Because arrangements for marriage were so important for creating the alliances that would help in enabling a man's prominence, premarital sex for women was guarded against; it was easier for young men to gain experience with older married women than with younger women (Smith 1940:198). Similarly, socialization was at least partly an affair of the household. It was common enough for children to actually reside with small-families other than their parents', and in addition the job of socialization was divided between parents, who often punished children, and grandparents, often the elders of the household, who encouraged and taught the children with a kind of emotional support that they could not have used with their own sons and daughters (Smith 1940:188).

The developmental cycle of the household is more difficult to deduce from the report than is that of the small-family; this may be partly because it did not follow any regular pattern. But since small-families were free to move between households, the process seems to have been one of household heads, ambitious men who could hope to potlatch to display their status, accreting families to their own households as their fame and fortune grew. What is not clear is what happened when a household head died. Most probably a new head emerged, either from among the heirs to the former head's names and heritable wealth (slaves, canoes, horses, houses) or from among the heads of families within the household—often this was the same person. That man would then be able to pursue the same sort of strategy, using the labor and the marriage alliances of his household members to accumulate enough goods to give a potlatch, and to be recognized in his own right as an important and wealthy man. We can represent the developmental cycle of the small-family, as well as its firm embeddedness in the household, in Figure 16-4.

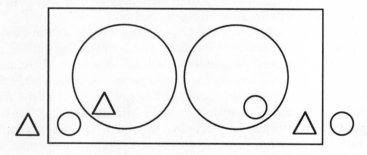

FIGURE 16-4: Puyallup-Nisqually System

This pattern of two-level small-family and household organization seems to have been uniform throughout the Coast Salish area: it was found, with minor variations, among the Quinault (Olson 1936), the Puget Sound Salish (Haeberlin and Gunther 1930), the Nooksack (Amoss 1974), the Twana (Elmendorf 1960), and the Klallam (Gunther 1927). Its most important features were the emphasis on achieved, rather than ascribed status, meaning little inheritance of wealth and/or privileges, and a consequent requirement for ambitious men to build up large and hard-working households to support their quest for the wealth that would bring them high status. The accretive strategies of these wealthy and ambitious men pursued produced, almost everywhere, a series of similar family phenomena: polygyny for high-status men only, a direct correlation between status and marriage distance, more elaborate ceremonies and exchanges at the marriages of the prominent, a preference, but not a hard-and-fast requirement, for virilocal marriage, and a pattern of household organization in which the most prominent households usually contained more small-families, and often lived in larger buildings, than the households of less important men. In some cases, in fact, there seem to have been households of "no-account" or "low class" people, who commonly followed the pattern of one small-family in a simple dwelling, and had no joint households at all (Suttles 1958). This would be expected logically from the fact that these people, because of slave origin or some other bad reputation and lack of "advice," were precluded from the status competition engaged in by all "good people," (*siab* or *siem*). Since the extended household organized only for prestige functions, there was no reason for the no-account people to form extended households.

When we move one step farther north again, into the area of the Straits- and then the Halkomelem-speaking Salish, we find the basic pattern of achieved status still intact, but with an increasing admixture of a few inherited privileges and perhaps a larger number of inherited rights to subsistence goods that could be parlayed into surpluses, which could in turn be converted to wealth to be distributed at potlatches (Suttles 1951:55, 62; Bierwert n.d.:71-72; Duff 1952:171-72). The basic two-level pattern found in the core Coast Salish area remains in this, its northern fringe, but with the slight difference that there seems to have been more of an emphasis on inherited property and privileges in determining which were the prominent households and who were their heads.

The Straits and Halkomelem peoples were thus a transition, in family organization as in some other ways, between the relatively achievement-oriented societies of the Puget Sound region and the inheritance-oriented societies of the Westcoast and Kwakwaka'wakw area. One important feature that appears in these transitional groups, because of the existence of certain privileges in this area, is that dowry, or pre-mortem inheritance (Goody 1973) becomes an important part of the transactions in wealth that went on in the marriages of at least the prominent people in the society. Among wealthy Straits families, for example, a woman marrying virilocally might bring to her new home either a name or a dance rattle, both of them important privileges (Suttles 1951:289). Similarly, among the Halkomelem groups, the important Sxwayhwxe dance, performed at marriages and other special occasions (Bierwert 1986:474-500) might often be transmitted through a daughter at the time of her marriage, passing on to her descendants and thus in effect crossing over from one house group to another (Bierwert n.d.:63-64). Figure 16-5 shows the differences between the Puget Sound peoples and the Straits and Halkomelem, who add the factor of dowry.

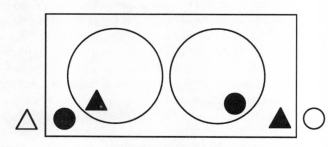

Puyallup-Nisqually

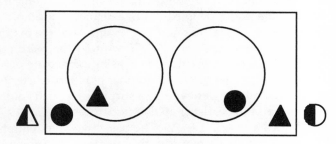

Straits and Halkomelem

FIGURE 16-5: Salish Transmission Systems

The Wakashan Area

When we move one step further north, into the realm of the Wakashan-speaking Westcoast and Southern Kwakwaka'wakw peoples, we of course enter the area of paramount importance of inherited privileges, and this had its effect on family organization, particularly as household heads used marriages and other family connections to increase their followings and their access to wealth, both inherited and created. At the same time, there seems to have been in this area a further diminution of the importance of the small-family, and organization of more and more activities at the level of the household. Let us look at the most fully described case, the Westcoast peoples of Nootka Sound, as an example of how the family activities were allocated in these groups and how this influenced the developmental cycle both at the level of the small-family and at the level of the household.

We can see the relative weakness of the small-family in this area if we look at its activities. There were, for sure, some subsistence goods that were procured and processed by members of the small-family for other members of the small-family. For example, women gathered marine invertebrates, either in large parties with other women or in pairs with their husbands; in either case, most of what the woman or the couple brought back was consumed by her or their small-family at its own fireplace, one of many owned by the small-families within a household (Drucker 1951:39; Jewitt 1975:27). Similarly, men both collected roe and hunted waterfowl and small seals individually and in pairs, and each gave his catch to his wife to be prepared for the small-family to consume (Drucker 1951:42-45). But other subsistence goods were collected and owned by larger groups. For example, berry patches were usually owned by households, and the chiefs of those households sent the women of the household together to collect berries at the beginning of the season; only after the chief had collected and redistributed the first one or two pickings were the patches opened up for exploitation by individual women on behalf of their small-families (Drucker 1951:57). And whaling, the most famous food-producing activity of the Westcoast, was a large-group activity. Only fairly high-ranking chiefs had the privilege of sponsoring whaling expeditions; the crew of the expedition consisted of from one to three boats, each manned by eight men, with the chief as the harpooner and various of his retainers as paddlers and helpers (Drucker 1951:50-55). The whale, if caught, was divided according to the positions with respect to whaling crew, with the harpooner, the paddlers of his canoe, the heads of other canoes, the crews of other canoes, and all the other retainers of the chief all eventually getting portions of the meat and blubber (Drucker 1951:50-55). The processing, at least at the initial stage, was also done collectively, and only after the shares were distributed did the management of whale products revert to the small-family group.

Whales, of course, are hardly family-size catches, and in addition, evidence seems to demonstrate that they were seldom caught: when John Jewitt was a slave of the chief Maquinna, the chief and his crews caught but three whales in a season of effort (Jewitt 1975:63). But there are other indications that even domestic processing labor was often not confined to the small-family level. At least among the closely related Southern Kwakwaka'wakw, even though each family had its own fireplace and its own provisions (Ford 1941:5, 11), there was in fact much informal sharing of food among the families within the household. In the story quoted in the Prelude to this

Part, for example, Charlie Nowell recalls that in the household where he grew up, there were four families, but that they almost always ate breakfast together at a particular family's fire, because the head of that family was a light sleeper who liked to get up early and fix breakfast for the whole household (Ford 1941:50).

We also find here, as in many of the central Coast Salish groups, an emphasis on socialization by a wider group than the small-family. In the first place, there seems to have been considerable flexibility of residence, even for fairly young children: Jewitt reports that children often moved around to live with people who were not their parents. And when socialization did begin, the emphasis seems to have been on two kinds of things: learning of advice and learning of traditions, privileges, and rituals owned by one's household or local kin group. And quite naturally, much of this instruction was carried out by the leaders of the larger group, the custodians of such knowledge, elders who may or may not have been members of the child's own small-family (Drucker 1951:131-35).

Seeing such a lack of emphasis on the small-family even in the performance of such functions as elsewhere belong to it, we should not be surprised that, when we move on to the activities connected to the prestige sphere of competition, the small-family fades into insignificance as we find important men maneuvering on much larger scales. As mentioned before, the Westcoast seem to have had the most rigid hierarchy of individual statuses of any groups on the Northwest Coast, but even there an important man had to make his name good in order to retain the respect that his birthright potentially entitled him to. This meant, of course, that it was in the interests of chiefs to build up followings of relatives and other commoners, and they used their various kinds of ownership rights to do so.

First, chiefs were, in this area, the ultimate owners of most subsistence resources as well as of house-sites. This meant that every small-family that did not itself currently hold a chiefly position (or even one that held a minor chiefly position, subject to a more important "overlord") had to attach itself to the retinue of a chief in one way or another in order to just gain access to salmon streams, clam beds, berry patches, or whale carcasses, among other things. And the chiefs, in emphasizing their overlordship of subsistence resources, exacted a symbolic price from their retainers: a tribute in first fruits of berry patches, for example, or in the first day's catch at fishing sites, or in portions of seals caught in a chief's inlets or offshore waters (Drucker 1951:250-255). This in itself would weaken the notion that the fruits of the subsistence quest belonged to the family that procured them.

Ownership of house-sites worked in a similar fashion. Everybody needed a place to live, but it was impossible to just build a house on an empty plot of land: in addition to the danger of a single unprotected family in time of enemy raids, this would also be an insult to the ownership rights of the chiefs who claimed the house-sites. In fact, everybody became a member of the household of a chief of some sort or another, from a minor luminary who was simply the chief of a house to the most important first-ranking chief of an entire tribal confederation. Since these chiefs wanted more re-tainers for the prestige a large household would bring, for the possibility of more affinal alliances by having more married couples in the house-hold, and for the labor of household members, especially women, there was competition between chiefs for household followers, resulting in both a fluidity of residence, with small-families frequently moving to the house-hold of a "better" chief, and larger households (and larger houses) for more important chiefs (Drucker 1951:273, 278-79; Jewitt 1975:25, 76). Slaves, of course, also entered into this equation: they provided both prestige and labor for a chief's enterprises, and the higher-ranking chiefs had more slaves and slave families living in the households (Jewitt 1975:38-39). It is also perhaps significant here that the Westcoast and Kwakwaka'wakw appar-ently had no class of no-account people such as was found among Salish peoples farther south: any retainers were valuable to a chief, and chiefs both owned all housing sites and claimed a right to all retainers.

The amount of control that chiefs had over people's lives thus broad-ened people's everyday attention and activities from the level of the small-family to the level of the household. And this, in turn, meant that the de-velopmental cycles of the household and of the small-family were inter-twined. The small-family, in its own right, did not look very different in its developmental cycle from the small-families of groups farther south: it depended on a system of mainly-virilocal marriage and mainly-patrilineal inheritance. Young married couples always joined the small-family of one partner or the other, usually the husband, meaning that small-families of-ten grew to the stem or even joint form before breaking up on the death of senior members (Drucker 1951:281-282). Whatever rights and property the head of a small-family held were usually passed on formally to his heirs (usually sons, but sometimes daughters) at potlatches given during their youth; the marriage of an heir involved further transfer of rights, includ-ing the all-important transfer (usually of movable rights, such as wealth and privileges) from one family to its affines through dowry. The higher-ranking the family, of course, the larger the number of rights transferred, and the more interest the chief of the family's household would have in the arrangements for the marriage. When the marriage was in his own family, the wealth and alliances that might accrue were all the greater, so impor-tant chiefs were often highly polygynous. The chief, in turn, might bestow certain privileges upon the new couple; at minimum he and his retainers would perform some of their display privileges connected with marriage ceremonies (Drucker 1951:267, 287-91). In this way, the timing and personnel of the small-family's developmental cycle would be the concern of and to a certain extent under the control of that family's house or local chief.

The developmental cycle of the household was, here as farther south, more varied than that of the small-family; it involved the successor to a chiefship attempting to retain the householders loyal to his predecessor and, if possible, to add to the families within this household. Within the household, families were strictly ranked by the places their fires occupied in the house itself: the back right-hand corner facing the door was the chief's own family's place, and the back left-hand corner belonged to the small-family of the second most important man. The two front corners, on the wall that contained the door, were the third-ranking places; they were followed in importance by the middles of the two long sides and, in exceptionally large houses, by the places between the centers and the ends of the two long sides (Drucker 1951:71).[2] A successful chief was one who could not only recruit various relatives' small-families to his household and keep them there, but could also manipulate the affinal alliances of his household members, including his own small-family, to his greatest advantage. His reward for such successful manipulation, of course, was access to more goods and privileges through dowries and through members' labor, enabling him to give more frequent and lavish potlatches and other ceremonies, increasing his prestige, and thus in turn enabling him to conclude more and better affinal alliances, thereby starting the cycle all over again. The intertwining of the developmental cycle of the small-family with that of the household, together with the diminishing importance of the small-family, is illustrated in Figure 16-6.

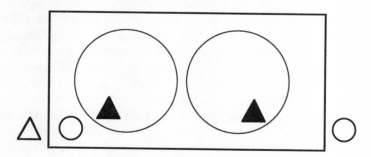

FIGURE 16-6: Westcoast System

There are two paradoxes in this system. One is that, with the strict hereditary succession to rigidly ranked social positions, the real prestige and power of a chief were so intimately connected with the welfare and satisfaction of his retainers, his junior relatives. Because the chief controlled so much, his junior relatives were unusually dependent on him; but because the expectation of a chief was to have retainers, and commoners had the option of changing chiefs (they were rarely related to just one), he was just as dependent on his retainers. Thus the interdependence of chief and retainer contributed to the importance of the household and higher levels and the relative unimportance of the small-family, even in performing basic subsistence functions. The second paradox is that, even though the household level was crucial in performing enabling activities for chiefs, and in organizing many subsistence and socialization activities, the household itself was a very shifting group, far from rigid in its composition. It was the very importance of this level, and the consequent competition among chiefs for retainers, that allowed the household to be so flexible and shifting in its composition.

Moving north from the Kwakiutl proper and their neighbors, we find between them and the matrilineal groups a series of Kwakwaka'wakw-speaking peoples who possessed social institutions reminiscent in certain ways both of the rank-centered structure of the Southern Kwakwaka'wakw and of the matri-clan structure of the northern groups, but without much elaboration of either kind of institution. We also find the Salish-speaking Bella Coola. Though we know less than we might like about the Kwakwaka'wakw-speaking groups, we find that the Bella Coola provide an instructive case for understanding the relationship between powerful chieftainship (of the Westcoast-Southern Kwakwaka'wakw type) and the weakening of the small-family. Bella Coola social organization seems to show influence from both the Salish language family, to which the Bella Coola belong, and the central Coast complex of inherited privileges, in which they are geographically located. The "Salishness" of their organization comes out in the lack of formal statuses of chieftainship or rigid hierarchies of rank. McIlwraith reports, for example, that the Bella Bella or Heiltsuk, Kwakwaka'wakw speakers immediately to the north, are a bit puzzled by the fluidity of the Bella Coola status system: "We laugh at you Bella Coolas, because each of you is always trying to be chief. Our system is much better; we all help our chiefs" (McIlwraith 1948:137). Names, privileges, and subsistence areas among the Bella Coola all belonged to a group McIlwraith has called the "ancestral family", a kind of ambilateral descent group (McIlwraith 1948:126). This ancestral family was loosely structured, generally centered in a particular village but without fixed leadership or even clear criteria of membership; people could in fact gain access to privileges or subsistence rights from the ancestral families of both parents, and rights owned in the ancestral families could often be passed on to daughters as well as to sons (McIlwraith 1948:126-30).

In this fluid system, both small-family and household members depended to a large extent on the ability of the leaders of the groups to attract followers. At the small-family level, residence was usually virilocal, but a powerful man could draw his daughter's husband to live with him, if not as part of the same small-family, at least in the same household (McIlwraith 1948:195). Similarly, powerful men could enlarge their small-families by adopting more distant relatives, usually from within the ancestral family; the natural parents would adopt their children out to a prominent relative because of the promise that he would bestow prestigious names or other privileges upon them. The developmental cycle of the small-family was thus a very fluid one; its boundaries were shifting and its principles of recruitment flexible. As McIlwraith says, there were "No well-defined degrees of relationship in which responsibility rests," but at the same time "everyone knows...how many persons share the family life of the individual" (McIlwraith 1948:148). And from the rather sparse information that McIlwraith gives us on this topic, we can infer that, for subsistence procurement, the small-family was usually the effective unit (McIlwraith 1948:147, 367).

The difference between this system and that of the Westcoast seems to lie in the relative powerlessness of the Bella Coola chief, as well as in the flexibility of the status system. Here important men gained access to wealth and privileges, and could manipulate them to attract people to their small-families as well as to their households—the households of important men might have as many as ten small-families living in them, as opposed to two or three families in the houses of less important men (McIlwraith 1948:142). The Bella Coola system, and its relation to its Salish relatives and Wakashan neighbors, is illustrated in Figure 16-7.

We do not know as much about the Northern Kwakwaka'wakw groups; we can perhaps assume that they had a more rigid hierarchy of ranks than the Bella Coola, but it is also clear that important titles did not go automatically to genealogical heirs unless they had the wherewithal to pay for them; this was true of the Owikeno, or Rivers Inlet people (Olson 1954:220), as well as Bella Bella (Olson 1955:329). In addition, subsistence areas were sometimes owned by clans of chiefs among the Haisla (Olson 1940:180), or by unspecified groups among the Owikeno (Olson 1954:229), but these seem not to have involved any tribute obligations, or to have given chiefs power to control the subsistence activities or movements of their subjects (Olson 1940:180). In this way, the Northern Kwakwaka'wakw groups look more like the Bella Coola than like their linguistic relatives to the south, but unfortunately we have no information on the functional importance of the small-family in any of these groups; a vain search of the literature did not even tell me whether a Haisla house had one fireplace or many.

More interesting for the study of the Northern Kwakwaka'wakw was their possession of some but not all of the matrilineal features of the North Coast groups. The Owikeno, the most southerly of this constellation, had very few matrilineal features; the Heiltsuk more, and the Haisla, bordering on Tsimshian territory, displayed the most influence. The Haisla, in spite of their exogamous matriclans, still had a basically patrilocal marriage system. This combination produced a kind of marriage exchange peculiar to the Northern Kwakwaka'wakw groups, and known as the buy-back system. A Haisla marriage, or at least one in which the families had any pretention or ambition toward high status, began as did marriages among Salish and Central Coast peoples, with gifts from the groom's family to the

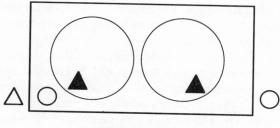

WESTCOAST

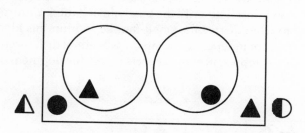

STRAITS AND HALKOMELEM

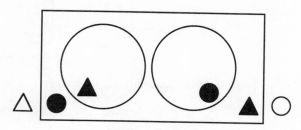

BELLA COOLA

FIGURE 16-7: Salish and Wakashan Systems

bride's. A year after this came the actual wedding, which involved exchanges of gifts in both directions and was followed by a year or so of uxorilocal residence by the new couple. At the end of this uxorilocal period, the bride's family gave a large amount of goods (it had to be at least twice the original bridewealth) to the groom's family, to "buy her back" into their own clan, at which time the couple took up residence with the *husband's* people, and ordinarily remained in the husband's house unless the husband came into an important title upon the death of his mother's brother, at which time he and his family would take up residence in the mother's brother's house, assuming headship of that house, and the titles that went with it, belonging to his own clan. If, as was preferred, his bride was his mother's brother's daughter, they would of course be taking up uxorilocal residence once more (Olson 1940:178, 186-87; Lopatin 1945:23). Attempting to reconstruct a pattern of household composition from this description, we find the typical household of a prominent man consisting of his own wife or wives (if he was very prominent, he would tend to be polygynous), his unmarried sons and daughters, his married sons and their wives and children, and perhaps a married daughter with her temporarily uxorilocal husband. Matriclan relatives, if they were in his house at all, would consist of his own brothers; his sisters' sons would not take up residence in the clan household until the head himself died. Unfortunately, we do not know to what degree the small-families within this kind of household were discrete or independent units, so we cannot draw accurate circles, but we can at least represent some aspects of the developmental cycle (Figure 16-8).

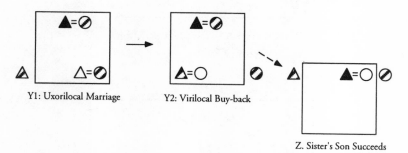

Y1: Uxorilocal Marriage   Y2: Virilocal Buy-back

Z. Sister's Son Succeeds

FIGURE 16-8: Haisla Buy-back Marriage

The Northern, Matrilineal Area:
The Absorption of the Small-Family

Turning now to the matrilineal peoples themselves, the Tsimshian, Haida, and Tlingit, we find a system that organized the same kinds of concern with status and prestige according to a very different structural logic, one that gave the organization of family activities and the family developmental cycle among these peoples a quite different character from that found on the rest of the coast, but a character that is in some ways reminiscent of the matrilineally-organized family systems of certain wealthy peoples in the A-cluster. Let us look more closely at the family organization of the Northern Coast; we will use as our primary example the Tlingit system, since that is best described, but will make frequent references to Tsimshian and Haida materials as well, since their family systems were virtually identical to that of the Tlingit.

Simply stated, the household of the North Coast matrilineal peoples, a group often described as avunculocal but probably in fact usually uxorilocal at the same time, was the locus of practically every family activity, making the small-family an almost superfluous unit, one with few if any defined activities. This breakdown of the boundaries of the small-family can be seen as the result of three factors: ranked matriclans and lineages, cross-cousin marriage, and avunculocality.

The first factor, ranked matriclans and lineages, has already been touched on above. In this area, one clan, and within one clan one lineage, was recognized in each village to be the most prestigious in the area; clans and lineages vied with each other, under directions of their senior males, in the same kinds of prestige competition engaged in by important individuals in other parts of the Northwest Coast. And here as elsewhere, this meant status homogamy (Olson 1967:19; Garfield 1939:232). Since it was the lineages, rather than the individual positions or seats, that were reciprocally ranked in these societies, the combination of ranking and status homogamy tended to give rise to definite endogamous strata, referred to in the literature as classes or castes (Garfield 1939:177), though even these, some authors point out, were subject to changes in rank with the rise and fall of the fortunes of various lineages and households (Olson 1967:47; Murdock 1936:18).

If one belonged to a more or less definite social stratum, and had to marry within it, one also had to marry into the opposite moiety. This was the origin of the second structural factor: cross-cousin marriage. In a strictly observed moiety system, of course, all members of one generation in the opposite moiety are cross-cousins, and if cross-cousin marriage is the rule, all of them are thus potential spouses. Similarly, all in one's own moiety are siblings and forbidden as marriage partners. Tlingit, Tsimshian, and Haida did not carry the logic to this extreme, and in fact distinguished cousins of various degrees of known relationship from members of the opposite moiety to whom no relationship could be traced. But it is noteworthy that, in some abstract sense, one did have to marry a cross-cousin, in that one could not marry a Kwakwaka'wakw or a Westcoast, because these people had no clan affiliation and thus did not fit into the social universe of the northern groups. But the preferred marriage for these groups was with an actual cross cousin of first or second degree, preferably a matrilateral (from the male perspective) or a double cross-cousin. Florence Davidson's Haida genealogy (Blackman 1982:60-61) in fact shows a large percentage of actual matrilateral or bilateral cross-cousin marriages; on the other hand, Vaughan found very few close cousin marriages in a survey of Tsimshian unions (1984:63).

The third structural factor in this system was avunculocal residence. Unlike the practice of incompletely matrilineal Haisla, the Tlingit and their neighbors brought residence into concert with matriliny by having a couple live in the household of the husband's mother's brother. The prescribed pattern was for a boy to live with his parents until he was from eight to eleven years old, and then move to his mother's brother's household, where he would eventually bring his bride and settle into the hierarchy of matrilineally related males who would succeed in time to positions of leadership in the household and have responsibility for furthering the prestige of the household in the lineage and village (Garfield 1939:278; Murdock 1936:15; Olson 1967:5).

Taken together, these three factors tended to produce endogamous household clusters. For example, consider the case in which there were two chiefly lineages in a community, belonging to opposite moieties. They would, quite naturally, tend to marry each other, and a system of bilateral cross-cousin marriage would evolve, the women of one clan marrying the men of the other. Each boy would be raised by his father and mother, living in his father's clan's house. At puberty or before, he would move to his own clan's (his mother's brother's) house, where he would marry a woman of the other clan, that is to say a daughter of his mother's brother, a woman who in fact grew up in the house to which the boy moved when he was an adolescent. In other words, nobody moved at marriage. The boy, since puberty, had been living in his mother's brother's house, and the girl, since birth, had been living in her father's house, which was of course the same house, since the boy's mother's brother was the girl's father. The household would thus consist of three kinds of people: males of the owning clan, aged nine or ten and above; their wives and daughters, all of the opposite clan, of all ages; and boys of the opposite clan, who will remain in the house only until puberty. The residential core of the house was, in a sense, not the owning clan at all, but the females of the opposite clan, who spent their whole lives there. (Figure 16-9).

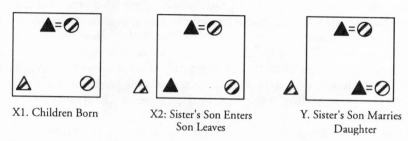

X1. Children Born   X2: Sister's Son Enters   Y. Sister's Son Marries
                           Son Leaves   Daughter

FIGURE 16-9: Idealized Northern Two-Moiety Household Developmental Cycle

And within each of these three categories of residents in our ideal household, various members of the category were in a sense interchangeable with each other, through the institutions of levirate-sororate, nearly automatic succession to chiefship, and free sexuality between people of opposite moieties. As mentioned above, extramarital sex was not considered an infraction if committed with a member of the opposite sex who was married to one's own clan-mate; what this meant in our ideal household was that acceptable partners other than the spouse would be any adult of the opposite sex in the household. And when one spouse died, it would be expected that the survivor would marry a clan-mate of the deceased; once again, in our ideal household, that could be any adult of the opposite sex. Finally, brothers were in a sense interchangeable, since it was the house and not the leader who was ranked and who was the holder of important wealth (including slaves) and privileges (Stearns 1984:193; Garfield 1939:276; Halpin 1984:17; Olson 1967:5, 12).

It is not entirely clear the extent to which actual North Coast households conformed to the ideal; certainly many marriages involved a man marrying a woman from a household other than that to which he moved upon puberty. But even in such cases, the categories of persons within the household were the same, and it was considered ideal if all the wives of a household came from the same clan (Olson 1967:5).

The inevitable corollary of these rather unusual structural properties in the Tlingit and neighboring family systems was a lack of differentiation between the family units that made up a household. This lack of differentiation is borne out first by the statements of observers. Oberg says of the Tlingit, for example, that "economically and politically the family is of little importance" (1973:23), a sentiment echoed by Olson, who remarks that "Household and clan are far more important than family" (Olson 1967:48).

But the unimportance of the small-family is further borne out when we examine the family activities and their performance. With respect to the prestige activities, of course, there is no question; here as elsewhere on the Coast, those who competed for prestige, who controlled wealth and privileges, who built followings and used these followings to enable their own advancement, were heads of households. But the importance of the household level here reached to all the subsistence activities as well. To begin with, socialization was carried on primarily at the household level; the elders of the household were said to be responsible for the socialization of their children, sisters' children, and children's children (DeLaguna 1972:465).

But we have found socialization centered at the household level even in the Coast Salish area; here in Tlingit country sexuality seems to have been regulated more at the household than at the nuclear family level, as evidenced by the freedom of sexual activity with other members of the household (who would be of the right moiety), as well as the expectation of the levirate and of chiefly polygyny, both of which conformed to the two-side configuration, which was re-figured in the structure of the avunculocal household.

And, most importantly, procuring and processing were organized by and for the household. Subsistence resources were sometimes owned by whole clans, sometimes by households (Olson 1967:12); subsistence activities were organized by the house head and the participants were members of the household—men in the case of hunting, fishing, and wood-gathering; women in the case of berry-picking (Olson 1967:11-12; DeLaguna 1972:408). This was true even in the case of summer camps away from the main house-site; these places were also owned by households (Olson 1967:12). Among the Tsimshian as well, the entire house-group moved together to the summer fishing grounds (Garfield 1939:277). And in all these groups, it was the household head who directed the economic activities of everyone in the household, and the results of the subsistence quest were distributed to the household as a whole (Stearns 1984:193; DeLaguna 1972:310; Olson 1967:11).

In fact, in the northern corner of the Northwest Coast, not only procuring but also processing labor was organized at the household, not the small-family level. One characteristic that distinguished the house itself among the matrilineal groups from those of the Westcoast, Kwakwaka'wakw, and Salish, was that the Tlingit, or Tsimshian, household had only one fireplace, used in rotation or cooperatively, as the occasion required, by the various women of the household (DeLaguna 1972:301, 308; Krause 1956 [1878]:107; Garfield 1939:275-76). It is thus clear from the details as well as the generalizations that, as Olson says, the household was the effective unit in the daily life as well as in the prestige structures of the northern peoples (Olson 1967:24). This contrasts dramatically with the case of the Coast Salish mentioned earlier, where units above the small-family level were concerned primarily with the prestige sphere, and the small-family was self-sufficient on an everyday basis. We can illustrate the relative importance of small-family and household on the northern Coast in Figure 16-10.

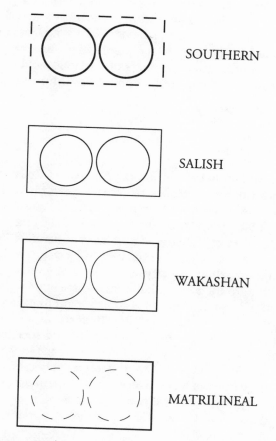

SOUTHERN

SALISH

WAKASHAN

MATRILINEAL

FIGURE 16-10: Relative Importance of Small-Family and Household in N-Cluster Systems

It would be difficult to account for this "household communism" (Olson 1967:11) among the northern peoples by any dramatic differences between this area and those to the south in climate, ecology, or technology. It is clear that it was the matrilineal organization of the larger society that contributed to the de-emphasis on conjugal relations (the basis of the small-family) here as in other parts of the world. It is not so much that the loyalties of the respective spouses were drawn away from the domestic bonds by stronger pulls of matriliny, as we saw to be the case in Ashanti or the other African societies, for example, but that there was another level of domestic relationships here, that of the avunculocal-uxorilocal household, that subsumed both marital and lineage bonds, and thus obviated any structural tension between one and the other. The combination of avunculocal residence and matrilateral or bilateral cross-cousin marriage (the latter partly a requirement of status homogamy) allowed the unity and solidarity of the marital pair, so common on the Northwest Coast, to persist in the face of strong matrilineal organization, to the point where, among the Haida at least, husband and wife, as co-members of the household, were the unit that organized and gave the important potlatches (Murdock 1936:9).

Implications

The variation in family systems on the Northwest Coast illustrates an important paradox of rank societies, one that is clearer here than in either of the other two clusters we have examined in detail. The subsistence organization of these family systems varied quite widely, and in a way that seems little influenced by the subsistence tasks at hand. Abundance was the key word on the coast, and abundance of subsistence resources meant that people could turn their primary strategizing attention (if not the majority of their time) to the accumulation and display or redistribution of goods in pursuit of prestige. And it was this pursuit that shaped the organization not only of the prestige activities themselves, but of the groups that combined to carry out the basic subsistence and socialization activities. Individual subsistence pursuits, of course, sometimes needed to be organized in a particular manner, but this organization cross-cut that of family groups in a variety of ways. People on the Northwest Coast needed to eat, and they worked long and hard for their food. But they did not allow their work to get in the way of their more important business, the pursuit of wealth and prestige.

Thus we see that in all three clusters belonging to the broad category of rank societies, there was a distinction between a subsistence and a prestige sphere of activity, and this distinction tended to correlate roughly with the differences between domestic and public arenas of action. And in all three cases, the connection between subsistence and prestige activities was primarily in a single direction: the domestic group's control over material and labor resources enabled its members to participate more effectively in prestige competition. In no case was the participation in prestige competition a primary determining factor in shaping the nature of the family's subsistence functioning. Subsistence goods were incompletely convertible into prestige, and the universal right to subsistence was recognized. The C- (or complex society) cluster, to which we now turn, worked differently.

Notes

1. Neither of these was very impressive looking when compared with the magnificent, often carved and painted "longhouses" of the rest of the Northwest Coast. They were built out of planks, as were their more northerly counterparts, but were smaller and without ornamentation.

2. In the Westcoast houses there were no partitions between the living spaces of the constituent small-families, a further indication that the small-family was less of a discrete functional unit here than among the Coast Salish groups.

PART SIX

The C-Cluster:
Premodern, Complex Societies

Prelude: Dowry Negotiations in Lahore, 1925

The author's father (Daddyji), pays a visit to his future wife's father (Babuji) to negotiate the terms of his marriage to the author's mother:

Soon the house was filled with the whirr and clatter of sewing machines as several tailors busied themselves with the clothes for the dowry. Bulaki Ram, before his death, had accumulated and put by much of Mamaji's dowry: a collection of gold jewelry, seven silk-cràpe saris with heavy intricate old embroidery, six heavy silk suits (with matching veils) embroidered with heavy gold thread, four silk sleeping suits, twelve tablecloths, a silver tea set, twelve big silver glasses, brass dinnerware, two chairs, a bed, twelve sheets, twelve pillow cases. Her dowry clothes were all sewn with silk thread, and there wasn't so much as a cotton tape in her pajama trousers. But to make her dowry complete she needed a few more petticoats and blouses, tea cozies and kitchen towels.

Mamaji heard the putt-putt of a motorcycle, then footsteps, and the sound of the unbolting of the doors downstairs. She knew that it was he, and that he had come to see Babuji. She stationed herself behind a curtain, listening, her face hot with worry that someone would guess the secret joy she was feeling and make fun of her...

After a silence, Babuji asked, "What kind of watch would you like in the dowry?"

"I already have a watch, thank you," she heard him say.

She felt weak and frightened. He has everything, she thought. There is nothing we can give him. He will withdraw like the other one. (In later years, he would often reânact the scene for her—how he had held up his wrist and proudly shown Babuji his big wristwatch—and each time she would feel weak and frightened all over again.)

"She will have plenty of changes of clothes," Babuji said. "For winter, for summer, and for monsoon—day wear and evening wear. There are, of course, the usual ornaments of twenty-two carat gold. In addition, I plan to give you two thousand rupees. I would like to give you more but I have four daughters."

"Babuji, like you, we are Arya Samajists" [Members of a Hindu reform society] came the reply. "We don't believe in dowries."

"How would you like the two thousand rupees—in cash? What do you need?" [Later, Daddyji (Mehta's father) learned that Babuji had been afraid that yet another son-in-law would slip through his hands and had therefore been determined to impress him with the lavishness of the dowry.]

"I don't really need anything."

"What about a motorcar?" Babuji asked.

"I already have a motorcycle."

"That's dangerous," Babuji said. "A married man should not ride one of those things."

"One day, I hope to have a motorcar," Daddyji said.

"A motorcar would look impressive in the dowry, and it would be a good talking point for the neighbors," Babuji said. "Many prominent Lahoris are giving motorcars in dowries these days."

Overcome with fear that she might be discovered, Mamaji ran up to the chaubara.

Ved Mehta, *Mamaji* (New York: Oxford University Press, 1979), pp. 128-130. Reprinted by permission of The Wylie Agency, Inc.

17

Introduction to the Family in C-Cluster Societies

Social Class and the Family

The societies of this group, which I call the C- (for complex) cluster, differed fundamentally from those of the A-, O-, and N-clusters. The C-cluster consists of the family systems of what we would call pre-modern (see Chapter 21) or pre-industrial, complex societies, societies that had undergone the Second Great Transformation, and thus developed systems of social classes (groups with differential access to the means of production) and state organizations. These systems occupied most of Europe, Northern Africa, and Asia, as well as the colonized parts of North and South America, before the Industrial Revolution, or as I prefer to call it here, the Third Great Transformation. Insofar as there are still many parts of the world in which the modernizing changes of the Third Great Transformation are incomplete, there are today still many people (often referred to as peasants) in Asia and Latin America who are practicing C-cluster family systems, although the majority of the world's urban-dwellers are now firmly engaged in the different logics of the M-cluster (Part VII). Nevertheless, since I am writing this book from an M-cluster perspective, I will use the past tense to describe C-cluster systems; most of the descriptions upon which I rely refer to the early and middle decades of the twentieth century, though a substantial minority describe systems as they existed centuries ago.

In the C-cluster, there was still a division between subsistence and prestige pursuits, between domestic and public arenas, but their connection had become a double one: not only did family organization enable prestige competition in the larger arena, but success or failure in this prestige competition was an important factor in determining the nature of family activity and organization, including organization for subsistence activities. The same resources that were important for daily subsistence were important for achieving success in prestige competition. This meant, as Lancaster has stated it, the "the political economy has become interested in the daily round of subsistence" (1976:554). The causes and consequences of this "interest" are both important to our understanding of C-cluster family systems.

The origins of the two-way subsistence-prestige connection are points of considerable contention, which need not concern us here: basically they lie in the process of the origins of private property and the state. But however private property and the state originally arose, they have important implications for the study of family systems. First, the existence of the institution of private property in productive goods meant, in effect, that access to these goods would be differentially distributed among the population. Because the same goods were useful for ensuring subsistence and for competing for prestige, competitors in the prestige sphere had in a sense snatched away the legal security of subsistence that was there in rank societies, presenting families in the C-cluster with the possibility of losing their rights to subsistence in the face of someone else's rights to become rich and powerful. This also meant, in effect, that productive goods in such systems tended to become scarce, in the sense that there was never enough to go around. This scarcity had little to do with any kind of absolute balance of population against resources, because in a system where social status depends on acquiring and keeping as many productive goods as possible, people who are competing for status will always want more—more of the same goods that are necessary for every family's subsistence.

Families in C-cluster societies, then, were dependent for their livelihood and for their public status on the extent to which they could gain and maintain control over productive goods, or property. This, in turn, had three important effects on family organization. First, it meant that family strategies in this cluster were primarily of an adjustive nature—the problem in building a family was always to adjust the balance of consumers and resources to the family's advantage. This might, in some cases, mean adjusting the balance by creating as much labor as possible, but this was the case only in particular kinds of circumstances, and did not lead to a totally accretive strategy such as we saw practiced in Africa and in the "open" societies of the O-cluster.

Second, exclusive rights to productive property, and a state organization whose primary function was to guarantee those rights, led to differential rights among different groups in the society, that is, to social classes. When social classes differed in the nature of their rights of access to property, the families that belonged to the various classes might well differ in the family strategies and types of family organization available to them. We should, in other words, be able to find differences within any C-cluster society with regard to the way families were organized in different classes, whose member families enjoyed different kinds of property rights. This, as will be noted in more detail later, has important ramifications for the study of family organization in general: comparisons within societies, between social classes that share very closely related cultural traditions but differ widely in their access to resources, enable us to examine more confidently the effect of purely economic variables on family organization.

Third, the existence of a state organization that guaranteed families' rights to property meant that there was a further variable that needs to be taken into account when studying variation in family organization: the variable of law. In complex, state societies (including both C- and M-cluster societies), rights to productive resources, as well as obligations of family members to larger collectivities, are often determined by the state, an organization serving the interests of particular classes in their domination of other classes. Families in these systems thus had to adjust themselves, not only to the economic realities of their property system, but to the legal realities of the state that had authority over them. And here, in contrast to the political institutions of the previous clusters, the state, as a representative of the dominant class, often had an interest, not in ensuring access to subsistence resources with a reasonable amount of equity, but rather in protecting the rights of successful competitors for resources to hold on to those resources.

It should be noted here that the presence of private property and state organizations imposed a unity on the nature of C-cluster family organization worldwide, a unity that we found missing when we were forced to acknowledge the division of rank societies into geographic clusters, of which the A-, O-, and N-clusters were examples. As with the pure subsistence requirements of the simplest societies (the B-cluster), in the C-cluster families had to adjust to a system in which land, labor, and capital goods were all, to an extent, convertible not only into each other, but also into both a family's subsistence and its chances in prestige competition. Because of this forced unity, we can group together systems from Japan and England, from China and the Balkans, from Java and Spain, and expect them to be explicable in the same kinds of terms. It is in the pre-industrial, but complex, stratified, state societies of the "great civilizations" of Asia, Northern Africa, and Europe, that we find a particular kind of family system, a system which, in the end, can be explained, both in its commonalities and in its geographic particulars, by the necessity of families to adjust their membership and operation to their particular rights to property in the basic factors of production: land, labor, and capital.

C-Cluster Family Activities

This unity of C-cluster family organization manifested itself both in the way the families carried out the eight types of family activities, and in the structures they built and maintained in order to organize those activities. In C-cluster societies, all eight kinds of family activities outlined in this book were concentrated in the family itself, and usually in a single household group. When Engels wrote of *The Origin of the Family, Private Property, and the State*, he assumed that the family was invented in order to serve the system of social classes that private property and the state brought about and maintained. As we have seen in the earlier chapters of this book, he was wrong: societies without private property or the state still had family systems. But Engels was not totally off the mark: it is in those societies with private property and the state, in particular those of the C-cluster where private property was the basis of most families' livelihood, that we find the family in its most important and structurally discrete form. Let us examine the effect of the private-property/state system on the eight kinds of family activities.

Procurement of Subsistence Goods

When we speak of private property in C-cluster societies, we rarely mean property belonging to single individuals. Rather we mean property, the rights to income from and disposal of which belonged to a defined family (usually literally household) group. The work or other activity that turned property into subsistence was nearly always performed by family members, and only family members were ordinarily considered to have rights to the income from such property. Transactions between families were carried out strictly on the basis of balanced reciprocity (Sahlins 1972:194-95), whether the balance was conceived of as exchange of labor for labor, as was the case, for example, in the Tokugawa period Japanese village (Beardsley, Hall, and Ward 1959:259-60), whether it was in the form of labor for money, when family members would work for others on a hired basis, as between father and son in the Spanish village of Valdemara (Freeman 1970:67-77), or whether it was conceived of in terms of an exchange of land rights for produce, as in English feudal labor services (Homans 1941:340), Chinese land rents (Yang 1959:40) or Central Italian *mezzadria* sharecropping (Silverman 1968:6). The family produced for itself, either consuming or selling what it produced, and either producing or buying what it consumed.

Processing of Goods for Subsistence and Other Needs

In C-cluster societies, since subsistence goods all derived ultimately from a family's access to property or its equivalent, the sale of labor, it seems natural that family members would process what they or other family members brought in. And this was indeed the case; even such processing as was often done communally, as for example the house-building party or the hiring of domestic servants such as cooks, was arranged strictly on a basis of balanced reciprocity. It is certainly not surprising that this should have been so, given the fact that processing was usually a domestic activity even in the non-class societies of the A-, O-, N-, and even the B-cluster.

One aspect of subsistence activity that took on a particular cast in the C-cluster was the sexual division of labor between the procuring and the processing tasks. Whereas in the other clusters we found a wide variation from society to society in the extent to which, for example, women and men did farm work, we find in most C-cluster systems that most processing labor was thought to be women's work, while most procuring labor, including farming, herding, trading, and the majority of wage-earning, was thought to be the proper province of men (J. Goody 1976:33; Boserup 1970:25-27). Engels (1972:137) thought that this division of labor was something intrinsic to the species, but did not become the basis of male power and dominance until the advent of private property and the state. But we know now that this sexual division of labor did not become the general pattern at all until the advent of private property and the state organization.

We are not sure exactly why this should be so. Goody (1976:33), suggests that this sexual division of labor was a consequence of the almost universal use of the plow in agriculture in complex societies. Plowing with animals, this argument goes, is heavy work, requiring considerable upper-body strength, and thus was best performed by larger, stronger males. This may well be the case, but it is probably not enough of an explanation; after all, in many East African systems the heaviest work of ground-breaking with large hoes was done by men, while the rest of the work of the agricultural season still fell to the women.

Another, perhaps more plausible explanation is that, in C-cluster systems, subsistence work was not just subsistence work—it served also to advance family members' interests in wider-scale prestige competitions. And here, as in the A-, C-, and N-clusters, it was ordinarily the males who competed in these prestige-producing activities. When subsistence became a potential factor in a family's social standing, men would want to gain the credit for the more visible or public part of subsistence activities, and this was the procuring, done outside the home, in contrast to the less visible processing, done inside. Thus while various kinds of labor in the home may have made indispensible contributions to the prestige of a family though enabling male family members' participation in public activities, the women's contribution seems to have been pushed into the background. This was as true where women's enabling production was of prestige goods only, as in Pohnpei or among the Coast Salish, as it was in most complex societies, where their activity, being by nature inconspicuous (Cronin 1977:76-80) remained in the domestic setting and was confined primarily to processing.

Regulation of Sexuality

The confinement of sexuality to marriage, that is to say to a legally defined relationship within the family, was also at its strongest in the C-cluster. Over and over in these systems, we find the greatest strictures on premarital sexuality, especially for women, along with the direct penalties for extramarital sexual relations, again particularly for women. Statistical evidence, such as that presented by Goody (1976:34-36), shows that restrictions on premarital sex were closely correlated with diverging devolution of property, a variable closely identified with what we are calling C-cluster societies. In addition, ethnographic descriptions confirm that this was a major concern in these groups. For example, the ideal for all classes in traditional China was not only an arranged marriage, but one in which the bride and groom had never set eyes on each other before the wedding. Much is written, as well, about the "honor and shame" complex of Mediterranean societies, in which a family's shame is closely connected with the sexual fidelity of its sisters and wives (Campbell 1966; Brandes 1980). And in classical Indian theory, the highest-status marriage was conceived of as the "gift of the virgin."

Many more examples could be cited for this strict sexual morality, but it is more important to suggest reasons for this concern. They have, I think, more than anything else, to do with the class nature of such societies. This class nature meant, as we have said before, that families were dependent on property for both their subsistence income and their social status, and this, in turn, meant that as the generations replaced their predecessors in the family, they were going to be dependent on the inheritance of property in order to maintain that status. This was as true for the daughters, in nearly all such systems, as it was for the sons, and indeed in almost all C-cluster societies daughters received significant portions of goods either upon their marriages or upon the retirement or death of their parents. But gaining one's own inheritance was not enough to maintain one's status in the next generation; one also had to marry well, or at least as well as one could.

And parents and grandparents, anxious to see their children marry well, were concerned with controlling whom they might marry. This, of course, meant that they had to restrict their children's choices of spouses, and in order to do so, it was best to be safe, not to let the young ones decide on the basis of personal likes, as they might well have done if they had been allowed to have sexual relations. So homogamy and the general concern with making a good marriage—one that would allow access to a spouse's inheritance—meant restricting premarital sexuality.

There was, of course, more to it than just that. Any sex outside marriage created the possibility of an unwanted pregnancy and an illegitimate child, something that was of little concern in the B-cluster and at most an easily overcome inconvenience in the A- and O-clusters, but was a disaster in a complex society, where the child thus conceived gained valuable access to property. So an unwanted child born out of wedlock was likely to force a marriage, which might be a bad one, and a child born to a married woman as a result of a known extramarital dalliance was likely to precipitate a conflict over not only the child's own rights, but very likely those of its natural father as well. Consequently, C-cluster systems were the strictest of all about sexual conduct.

Socialization of Children

Children in complex, premodern societies were raised not only by family members but for the family's sake. Quite expectedly, since children were needed to contribute labor power to a family, as well as security for its members in their old age, and since children were also going to be dependent, at least in their formative years and in many cases for considerably longer, on the property they gained from their natal family, it was only family members who had a real interest in socializing them.

But in complex societies, it is not just that family members carried out the great majority of childrearing tasks. The purpose of childrearing in these societies was not simply to raise children who knew the skills to be adult members of their societies. More importantly, the task of childrearing was to train the children to be loyal to family and to family values.[1] This is perhaps most graphically illustrated by cases in which agencies other than the family, namely various kinds of school systems organized and managed by government, lineage, or other organizations, nevertheless inculcated children first and foremost with the values of loyalty and devotion to the family and its causes. The schoolbook of the traditional Japanese temple school, for example, had as its very first line the sentiment that "The debt you owe to your parents is deeper than the oceans and higher than the mountains" (Hibbett and Itasaka 1967; II, 31). In the traditional Chinese school, the students early on learned not only the *Classic of Filial Piety* but also the Twenty Four Stories of Filial Devotion, in each one of which a child or children perform extreme, even grotesque feats of self-sacrifice on behalf of their parents. In southern Italian villages, children quickly learned that trust and devotion were proper inside the family; wariness and suspicion outside (Silverman 1968:15; Cronin 1977:72). And so on. The concentration of the means toward livelihood and status in the control of the discrete family group meant that children in C-cluster families were socialized both by and for this group.

Management and Transmission of Property

As mentioned above, one of the most important distinguishing characteristics of C-cluster societies was the development of private property in productive goods whose value was convertible from subsistence to prestige needs and vice versa. This distinguishes these societies from those of the A-, O-, and N-clusters, where rights in subsistence were still guaranteed to all members of a local or descent group. In C-cluster social systems one's livelihood depended on one's family's property rights, at least in the majority of cases. These property rights might consist of anything from various kinds of customary overlordship, giving the owning family the right to collect rents or taxes; through the kind of arrangements we usually refer to as freeholding, where the family had rights of income and disposal to its property, though sometimes subject to taxes or other encumbrances; to customary rights to work and retain some of the income from property, but subject to heavy encumbrances and without the right to dispose of the property except in certain closely regulated ways. These latter kinds of rights were those of tenants, sharecroppers, or serfs, and of course belonged to the lower classes in the society. But still they were property rights, and securing and maintaining them was vital to the family's subsistence. In many if not all premodern, complex societies, there were also classes of people who had no rights to productive property of any kind, and had to depend for their livelihood on the sale of labor. For these people, family organization was usually somewhat different from that of the classes who held property rights, and in fact examination of these differences within various complex societies is a central topic of a later part of this chapter. But the labor-selling classes always formed a minority in pre-modern situations; this in fact is one way to distinguish premodern from modern societies, in which property-holding families are in a minority, and the majority of families gain their livelihood from the sale of their members' labor.

Concomitant with the prevailing tendency in premodern, complex societies for families to derive their subsistence and livelihood from property, was the ideational tendency to group family, house, and productive property into a single unit. For example, the Basque villagers of Murélaga in northern Spain conceived of family and property as a unit, including people, house, land, and a particular standing place in the village church (Douglass 1969:87). In Japanese, *ie* means house, home, family, all rolled into one (Nakane 1967:2). In China, which unlike either the Basque country or Japan had a joint-family developmental cycle, the idea of *jia* encompasses a house, an estate, and a group of people (M. Cohen 1970). The same is true of the taravad of the Nayars and other property-owning castes in Kerala: *taravad* means house-site, house, property, and the people who inhabit the house and work the property, in the case of the Central Nayars, a matrilineage segment (Gough 1961a:323, Moore 1985). Once again, examples are too numerous to list.

But the importance of property for C-cluster families did not stop at this management or at its identification with the family group and its house; since each generation had to gain property rights from the last, systems of inheritance were of paramount concern to all C-cluster family systems. Exactly who got what from whom, and at what point in the life cycle, was a matter of endless concern to the people whose livelihood depended on it. In fact, here as nowhere else in our survey of family systems, considerations of inheritance were themselves paramount in shaping the developmental cycle of the family group. The crucial time for the developmental cycle of the Irish family, for example, was when the father, at his son's marriage, "gave over the farm" to his heir (Arensberg and Kimball 1940:123). Once the son had the farm, his was the position of authority in the family. In the Chinese joint family system, the crucial time was the time of division of property among equally inheriting brothers; a father who was no longer the head of a joint family was an aged dependent who was no longer the head of anything. In the Swiss alpine village of Kippel, marriage had to be delayed until property transfer was feasible, and this gave rise to a pattern of late marriage that was very wide-spread in European nuclear and stem-family systems (J. Friedel 1974:27).

Thus we see that, in a sense, the C-cluster family was, first and foremost, a group for the holding, management, and transmission of property rights. More than anything else, the C-cluster family's connection to property determined its other aspects: much of the subsistence organization and division of labor, sexual restrictiveness, family-centered socialization, political representation, enabling of prestige activity, and even the pattern of emotional closeness and cleavage in the family was determined, or at least strongly influenced, by the basic nature of the family as a property-holding unit.

Representation in Larger Social Groups

The premodern state was not, in contrast to its modern counterpart, structured as an organization of citizens, each of whom has direct rights and responsibilities with respect to the state itself. Rather the premodern state was built up of pre-existing, component units, the smallest and most basic of which was usually the household or legal family unit. It was ordinarily only the head of the family unit who had direct contact with the state and its agencies, through payment of taxes, negotiating with state representatives, attending and speaking at assemblies, and in other ways.[2] Representation thus became an extremely important activity of the family group, and the position of family head entailed not only authority over other members of the family, but also participation in larger-scale social groups as the family's political or ritual representative.

This representation could take several forms. One of the most important of these was representation for the purposes of exacting from a family those things that it, according to the state's laws, owed to the state. Taxation in premodern states was typically based either on property, something owned by the family, or on some sort of household population characteristic, such as number of adult males, total number of persons, or some other formula. Corvée labor and military conscription were also organized on a household basis. In Qing Dynasty China, for example, the household head was responsible not only for paying land and head taxes, but also for the good conduct of family members (van der Sprenkel 1962:47). The Serbian household head, similarly, was responsible not only for the tax, sometimes figured on a population basis, and sometimes directly on a household basis, but also, in certain areas, for supplying recruits for defense of the military frontier.

Another kind of representation was legal rather than political—in many complex societies only people who held certain statuses in a family were considered competent to appear in court. Thus in medieval England, the household head was responsible in court for the behavior of all members of his family (Homans 1941:209). This same kind of legal representation by the family head, and consequent legal minority of other family members, was a feature of court systems in East Asia as well.

A final kind of representation was ritual. In many different C-cluster family systems, the descent and inheritance that formed the continuity of the family group across generations were celebrated and reinforced in the practice of ancestor worship or veneration. When people made offerings to the ancestors, they did so not on their own individual behalf, but on behalf of the entire family group that kept the ancestral shrines. This was true whether, as among the Central Kerala Nayar, it was only the formal household head who could perform certain offerings (Gough 1961d:343), or whether, as in China and Japan, other members of the household group could perform the rites, at least on certain occasions (Freedman 1958:85; Smith 1975:118-119).

This enhanced emphasis on representation was closely connected to the power of the state apparatus in C-cluster societies. The family here was not only organized to provide for the subsistence and enable the prestige competition of its members; it also became a convenient unit through which the state organization could control the society's members and enforce its rights to use some of their resources for its own ends. In the C-cluster, the state reinforced the unity and importance of the family by making it an instrument through which it carried out its own policies.

Enabling Members' Participation in Prestige Activities

Enabling was universally important in C-cluster systems. Without family members' activities that produced, directly or indirectly, access to property and the fruits thereof, a member of a complex society could not hope to maintain or improve his social status or that of his family. The Chinese father who sat his sons down after dinner to exhort them to work harder for the benefit of the unbroken chain of ancestors and descendants that is their family (Yang 1945:129-30), the Catalonian younger brother who left the family home to make his way as a laborer, merchant, or professional, and thus to add to the fortunes of the family that raised him (Hanson 1977:86); the Irish parents who carefully negotiated their children's marriage as to strike the ideal balance between the bride's fortune and the groom's farm (Arensberg and Kimball 1940:114-122), all these and many others were using the labor, property, or other resources of the family in order to enhance their own status and their family's.

At the same time, however, families in complex societies in a sense had more restricted opportunities to use their labor and property to enhance their status than did their counterparts in the A- cluster and some of the more open systems of the O- and N-clusters. This restriction stemmed from the aforementioned two-way connection between the subsistence and prestige spheres of activity in C-cluster societies. The amount of resources a family could muster to enhance or maintain its status was often restricted by its own position in the larger social system. More labor or more followers in East Africa or an open system in Polynesia, for example, could be converted to more wealth and thus higher status, because there was access to the necessary material resources if the labor was there. In complex societies, however, access to material resources was often more problematical.

Increased labor in the family may have been useful in certain situations, particularly if there were opportunities for migration and/or diversification of the family's economic activities. In other kinds of situations, however, there were simply no extra resources to support the laborers, and in this kind of a situation the best family strategy was to restrict membership, as the Japanese did during the Edo period by practicing a high rate of infanticide (Hanley 1985:217-18), or as many people in the stem-family systems of Japan and Western Europe did by restricting marriage to those who could be allocated an adequate share of scarce property resources.

What this meant in general is that family members in C-cluster systems always had to consider the consequences of the allocation of property and labor for their social status, but that in many cases the lack of resources or the rigidity of social class divisions, often reinforced by law, meant that there was a very small amount of room to maneuver in. Where social mobility within or between classes was great, the enabling possibilities for a family were great, and more labor or more property could be converted into higher status directly. Where mobility was restricted, however, by law or by lack of resources, enabling simply meant holding the line—using family resources to maintain the status that a family already possessed.

Emotional Ties and Solidarity

In keeping with the generally more rigid patterns of family membership and authority in class societies, family emotional ties became both more sharply distinguished from emotional ties outside the family and more regularly patterned within the family. Each C-cluster family system, depending on its pattern of the developmental cycle and on its structure of authority within the family, developed its own pattern of emotional interactions, but all adhered to some basic patterns.

The first general pattern was the sharp line between ties to family members and to people outside the family. This line was at its sharpest in places like Sicily, where the proverb said that *"Il veru parenti sunnu chiddi dintra la casa"* (Cronin 1977:72) and where the extreme family exclusivity led Banfield to coin the term "amoral familism" (Banfield 1958). But this kind of exclusivity was not confined to the "amorally familistic" societies of the northern shore of the Mediterranean. It also occurred in Japan, for example, where ties between adult siblings were inconsequential, because they belonged to different households, or ie (Nakane 1967:7), and in China, where ties between brothers remained strong only as long as the brothers remained together in an undivided household (M. Cohen 1976:204-205).

The second general pattern is that the constellation of positive and negative emotional relationships in C-cluster families tended to be fixed and stereotypical within any particular system. In general, of the three kinds of elementary family ties found in human societies, those between brother and sister were much less important in the C-cluster societies than in the systems we have looked at previously; this happened because the house-hold, as a residential and budgeting unit, had such overwhelming impor-tance here that ties between members of different households, as adult brother and sister were almost everywhere, began to fade as soon as both siblings were married. On the other hand, both husband-wife ties and par-ent-child ties were important in all these societies, the relative importance depending on the particular family system. For example, in the aforemen-tioned nuclear family systems of southern Italy and Sicily, parent-child ties typically remained emotionally strong only until marriage of the children. But in stem-family Ireland or Japan, (Arensberg and Kimball 1940:54-60; Nakane 1967:19-26) or in joint-family China and many parts of India (M. Wolf 1972:217; Roland 1988), cross-generational ties retained a high emo-tional content throughout life. The various ways in which husband-wife ties came into conflict with parent-child, and particularly mother-son ties, varied with particular family systems.

The Concentration of Activities and the Discreteness of the Family Group

Because all eight kinds of activities were concentrated in the family, and because the importance of so many these activities derived from the family's place in society as a unit with access to property rights, in C-cluster sys-tems the group that cooperated for the performance of one activity was usually the same group that cooperated for the performance of another. There was very little of the nested or overlapping groups so important in Africa, the Pacific, or the Northwest Coast. The people with rights in a particular piece of property also lived together, produced and consumed and traded their subsistence goods together, and had a single representa-tive to the state or the ancestors, as well as a common interest in promoting the prestige activities of one or more of their members. There was typically a family group in the C-cluster, and it is usually perfectly clear who its members were and were not. The family had become more closely con-nected to the larger society, because both enabling and allocation tied them together, but it had also become more sharply distinguished from the rest of society, because it was a discrete group for the performance of most of the activities necessary to the livelihood and fortunes of its members.

Having emphasized the unity and discreteness of the family group in C-cluster systems, however, I must now back off a little and recall that this unity and discreteness were not absolute, but simply much greater than in other clusters. Even in the C-cluster, there were sometimes differences between the groups that cooperated for some activities and those that cooperated for others. In order to understand the developmental cycle of C-cluster family systems in fact, we must consider the developmental process of two different kinds of groups: those who resided together and cooperated in everyday subsistence activities, and those who held ultimate rights to a family estate, or a bundle of family property rights. These groups were, in fact, usually conceptually the same in C-cluster societies, so much so that there was rarely, for example, a separate word for the two kinds of family groups. And in a large percentage of the cases for a large proportion of the time, there was in fact no difference between the two kinds of groups. But in many systems the two kinds of groups developed at different rates—people, for example, left their natal residence before they settled their individual rights to shares of the family estate, or a joint family broke up into separate households before it broke up into separate property-holding units. In almost every case I know of, the residential group and the property group were organized according to the same principles, but in many cases the timing of their development was dissimilar. Thus when we consider the developmental cycle of C-cluster families, we will occasionally have to examine the cycle of the household separately from the cycle of the property-owning group.

Dimensions of Variation in C-Cluster Family Structure

The discrete, multi-activity family units of the C-cluster are, then, relatively unambiguous and easy to find, and they also represent a rather small range of variation on the structural dimensions set out in Chapter 2. For this reason, and also because a single family system, or structure, may have varied considerably from class to class or occupational group to occupational group within a society, the C-cluster societies are an ideal ground for the study of the minutiae of structural variation in the developmental cycles of both the household and the property group. This variation, as we see it in C-cluster family systems, can be studied systematically if we organize the particulars of C-cluster structural variation according to the general dimensions of family variation explained in Chapter 2, along with some other dimensions particular to the C-cluster.

The Direction of Connections Between the Elder and Younger Generations

This manifested itself in C-cluster systems in two ways: On the level of the residential group, it was the variation from residence with the husband's people at marriage to residence with the wife's people at marriage. In those systems where the transmission of rights to family headship came at marriage, this dimension was precluded. On the level of the property-managing group, this dimension was always important in C-cluster systems and manifested itself as variation from a patrilineal emphasis through bilaterality to a matrilineal emphasis in inheritance. It is doubtful whether, in any complex society, inheritance was entirely patrilineal or matrilineal; these arrangements would conflict with the phenomenon of diverging devolution (Goody 1976) which was, in some form or another, universal in this group of societies.

Inclusion or Restriction of Junior Adults

This dimension was manifested in C-cluster systems on the residential level by the variation from stem to joint family systems (again, where the couple established its own household at marriage, this variable was irrelevant). In the stem family systems, the household endured across generations, while in the joint systems, it ceased to exist in each generation when the siblings who formerly shared it established their own independent households.

On the property level, this dimension was represented by the variation from single heirship, in all its myriad forms, to equally partible inheritance.

Individual Participation in Marital Pairs

Marriages in C-cluster systems were generally monogamous. Where higher class males had more than one mate, the mates after the first one tended to have a secondary, distinctly inferior status (Goody 1976:51-52). Monogamy in these societies seems to have gone together with the necessity to maintain a family's status through the generations by making a suitable match; this precluded matching one's daughter as a secondary wife under most circumstances. The result of this was that the dimension from monogamy to polygyny was not a relevant one for comparisons made within the C-cluster.

There were polyandrous unions in several societies of the C-cluster, primarily in Tibet and parts of South Asia. These unions, as explained below, did not create separate descent lines based on half-siblingship, as did the polygynous unions such as those we examined in the A-cluster. The variable of individual participation in marital pairs thus distinguishes the C-cluster from other clusters, but was not important for explaining or describing variation among the societies of the cluster itself.

Time of Transfer of Statuses from the Senior to the Junior Generation

This is a crucial variable among C-cluster systems. It encompasses, on the residential level, the difference between nuclear systems, on the one hand, in which residential group headship went to the junior generation at the time of its marriage, and on the other hand both stem and joint systems, in which headship passed to the junior generations only on retirement or death of the senior.

On the level of the property group, this dimension consisted in the difference between dowry systems, in which some members of the junior generation, usually but not always females, received property at the time of their marriage, and non-dowry systems, in which inheritance came only at the retirement or death of the parents.

Other Dimensions of Variation

There are two other dimensions of variation that are important to understanding the nature of C-cluster systems. These, however, differ from the previously mentioned dimensions in that they are not manifestations of structural principles of people combining and splitting in unified households, but are rather dimensions of deviation from the multi-activity, property-centered family that is the ideal type of the C-cluster.

The first of these concerns deviation from the property-centered ideal. The deviation is represented by bridewealth, or horizontal exchange of goods at marriage, a phenomenon characteristic of accretive systems of the A-cluster in particular, while the C-cluster norm is represented by dowry, or vertical transmission of goods at marriage, characteristic of C-cluster systems where property had to be adjusted to consumption needs. One would like to think of these as pure types, but in fact they are not, and on the fringes of the C-cluster we can see systems whose marriage exchanges looked more like bridewealth than like dowry.

The other dimension of variation concerns deviation from the multi-activity, discrete group as the norm of the C-cluster: the deviation is represented by what I call split maintenance, a system in which a member or members of a household received some of their income from the proceeds of property to which they held rights, not as members of that household, but as members of a kin group some of whose members resided in other households. This, in fact, always manifested itself as a division of different activities between a husband-wife centered household and a brother-sister centered property group; it was characteristic primarily of matrilineally-oriented societies when it (rarely) occurred in the C-cluster. The norm, in which all activities were organized in and for the same group, and a household's property maintained its members, I call household maintenance.

Notes

1. The advocacy of "family values" by cultural conservatives in the United States in the 1990s is, more than anything else, an attempt to return to C-cluster morality and security. See Chapter 23.

2. The most notable exception here seems to be military service, which as often as not was performed not by household heads but by younger, more dispensable, and more commandable males.

18

A Tour of C-Cluster
Family Systems: Part One

Having set in Chapter 17 the parameters within which C-cluster family systems vary, our next task is to examine the variation within those parameters. This we will do in two stages. First, in Chapters 18 and 19, we will take a tour of C-cluster family systems, preceding where possible by small steps from one system to another, both showing the range of variation and examining several systems in detail. Having done this, we will return to the dimensions of variation set out above, and attempt to explain what kinds of factors dispose family systems to move toward one or another value on the various dimensions of variation.

In order to illustrate the variations among family systems of the C-cluster, we can once again reduce our basic diagram to a single square, since neither overlapping and nested groups nor polygyny play a large part in the developmental cycle here. We can, at the same time, add certain symbols that express the details variation in such important areas as inheritance of property rights is indicated by partially or wholly filling in the triangle and/or circle symbols. For example, if all children inherit equally and bilaterally, both circles and both triangles will be filled in; if daughters inherit half as much as sons (as in Islamic law), this can be indicated by filling in the triangles solid and the circles half way. Finally, if there is only one heir, his or hers will be the only symbol filled in, though others receiving movable property portions will be indicated by placing a dot in the middle of the symbol. These conventions are shown in Figure 18-1.

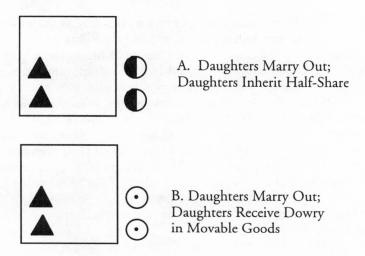

A. Daughters Marry Out;
Daughters Inherit Half-Share

B. Daughters Marry Out;
Daughters Receive Dowry
in Movable Goods

FIGURE 18-1: Samples of Inheritance Systems

If necessary, we can introduce an even greater degree of precision with regard to inheritance by indicating the time at which the inheritance of property takes place: we place a cross (indicating death) to indicate inheritance upon the death of a parent; an "r" to indicate inheritance upon the retirement of a parent, and an = sign (the conventional symbol for marriage in kinship diagrams) to indicate a dowry, or portion given upon marriage, as shown in Figure 18-2.

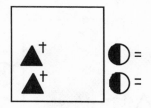

FIGURE 18-2: Timing of Inheritance

Now for the tour. For the sake of presentation, I will begin in Japan, specifically in the Japan of the Old Civil Code, promulgated in Meiji times and in force until after World War II. This code made into the legal norm what had been the predominant, though by no means exclusive, pattern of development and devolution in the Japanese family (Nakane 1967:8). According to custom all over Japan, property was vested not in individuals, couples, or descent lines but in the *ie* (household) as a corporate group. The *ie* property was held in a kind of trusteeship by the household head, who could acquire, sell, and manage property but only as a representative of the household corporation, not as individual owner of the property. According to the predominant system, membership in the *ie* was determined by succession, and there could be but a single successor in each generation. Children of members were members until they reached majority, at which time they either succeeded, became a successor in another house, married a successor in another house, or established a new *ie*. Wives of successors became members upon marrying in, and in some areas unmarried siblings could remain in the *ie* throughout their lifetimes if they remained celibate (Nakane 1967:6). The developmental cycle of the Japanese *ie* was thus that of a "stem family" which could be extended lineally to three or, rarely, four generations (Smith 1978:53; Dore 1978:138) but could not be extended laterally by the addition of married siblings of the head or the successor.

The identity of the successor varied somewhat. He *was* always a real or fictitious son (Nakane 1967:4) but whether he was a real or a fictitious one and which one he was depended partly on local custom and partly on the exigencies of the particular case. In those cases in which primogeniture was the preferred form (as it was in the early 20th century) the *ie* thus was a group which was headed, in turn, by a succession of fathers and eldest sons and contained their wives and unmarried children together with retired heads and their wives whenever these were alive and had not migrated elsewhere. We can diagram the primogenitural *ie*, the ideal system of most of pre-War Japan, in terms of its developmental cycle as shown in Figure 18-3.

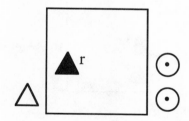

FIGURE 18-3: Japanese Primogenitural System

As in all other systems, however, some Japanese had to cope with the exigencies of a situation in which there was no suitable successor according to the primary rule of primogeniture. Not only the economics of supporting the dependent members but also the ideology of ancestor worship dictated that the ie not be allowed to die out except in cases of fragmentation by major disaster. In some instances the eldest son was either thought incompetent to succeed or had a better deal elsewhere, and in these cases a younger son might become the successor. If there was no natural son one could be adopted (Nakane 1967:5) or, more commonly, brought in as a *muko-yoshi*, or adopted son-in-law. This institution, found everywhere in Japan (Smith 1977:56; Dore 1978:162-4; Beardsley, Hall and Ward 1959:238), involved bringing in a husband for a natural or adopted daughter of the household, conferring upon him the household surname, and grooming him to be eventual successor. By such means succession was almost always secured.

There was in this system a close tie between succession and marriage; only a successor or a daughter who married a *muko* successor was allowed to marry and remain in the *ie*. Succession, however, did not happen immediately upon marriage. For one thing, when the formal retirement of the household head completed the succession the statuses of father and son were reversed; father was respected as an elder but was under the economic and legal sway of his son (Nakane 1967:17). So typically succession was delayed, even in peasant households, until after the father turned 60 (Beardsley, Hall, and Ward 1959:220-221).

The Japanese developmental cycle was thus a stem-family cycle with a true single-successor pattern. The Japanese ideal was also as close as one finds to a system of single-heir inheritance. Though it was not true always and everywhere, by the pre-war period there was a growing tendency for all the productive property of the *ie* to be transmitted along with the succession (Beardsley, Hall, and Ward 1965:241). Daughters marrying out were taken care of by a system referred to by Goody as "indirect dowry." The groom's family paid a sum known as the *yuino* to the bride's parents, and this plus considerably more was used to prepare the bride for the wedding and to purchase the household items which she would bring with her to her new home (Smith 1978:193; Nakane 1967:153; Beardsley, Hall, and Ward 1959:324-5). Younger sons, however, were usually given only education (Nakane 1967:7) unless they were to form independent branch households, which tended to occur regularly only in those areas where extra land was available and opportunities for taking up alternative occupations were limited (Beardsley, Hall, and Ward 1959:239-40; Nakane 1967:119). In an ordinary succession they were not provided with property but were expected to make their living as *muko-yoshi* or by taking up urban occupations or, occasionally, to remain celibate for awhile in their natal *ie* (Nakane 1967:6).

We find other quite similar single-successor, single-heir primogenitural systems scattered around the world. A well-known example comes from Medieval England (Homans 1941). This system differed slightly from the Japanese primogenitural system in that a daughter could inherit in lieu of sons (something rendered unnecessary in Japan by the institution of *muko-yoshi*) and in that the widow of a deceased head of household inherited lifetime usufruct (free bench) to all or part of the estate (Homans 1941:180-

2). Also, the connection between marriage and succession appears to have been much closer in Medieval England than in Japan; the father made over the estate to his son at the time of marriage. (If he was a serf, he did so by surrendering it to his lord, who then reassigned it to his son and heir [Homans 1941:109].) Also, sons not inheriting received small portions, or settlements, from their fathers' goods and chattels, but not from his land, in the same way that daughters received dowries, not including land, upon their marriages (Homans 1941:140-2). If we place the inheritance system of the primogenitural English villagers diagrammatically alongside that of the 20th century Japanese, we find only a slight difference from the single-heir pole, as shown in Figure 18-4, which shows how the single-successor developmental cycle of the two places appears the same in its structurally significant details.

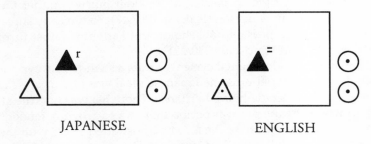

JAPANESE   ENGLISH

FIGURE 18-4: Primogenitural Systems of Japan and England

Primogeniture, while common enough, is certainly not the only kind of single-successor or single-heir system. There are at least eight other logical possibilities. Instead of passing to the eldest son, succession can pass to the youngest son, to a son chosen by the father or the parents, to the eldest child irrespective of sex, to the youngest child irrespective of sex, to any child chosen by the parents, to the eldest daughter, to the youngest daughter, or to a daughter chosen by the parents. We find ultimogeniture, or succession by the youngest son, occurring locally both in Medieval England, where it was known as Borough English (Homans 1941:126-7), and in Tokugawa Japan (Nakane 1967:9). Inheritance by a chosen son is described by Arensberg and Kimball in their study of rural West Ireland in the early 20th century (1968). There the successor and heir was a son chosen by the father, but in this case a substantial portion of the estate was also given as a cash dowry upon the marriage of a daughter. This portion was usually negotiated to be approximately equal in value to the farm the groom was inheriting. As in the English case, the transfer of authority over property coincided with the marriage, encouraging fathers to put off the marriages of their successor-sons as long as possible. Including in our diagram now a representative group of systems in which there is a single male successor, we arrive at the arrangement shown in Figure 18-5. Stem-family systems descending through single male successors can also be found, with minor variations on this same theme, in Slovenia (Winner 1971), parts of France (Goubert 1977) and Germany (Berkner 1976) among other places. No attempt is made here to give a complete listing.

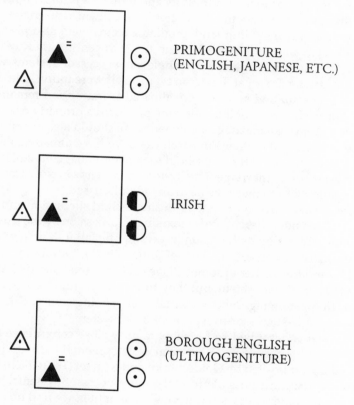

PRIMOGENITURE
(ENGLISH, JAPANESE, ETC.)

IRISH

BOROUGH ENGLISH
(ULTIMOGENITURE)

FIGURE 18-5: Patrilineal, Single-Successor Systems

Single-successor systems that approach the single-heir pole and pass headship not through sons but through children irrespective of sex, or through daughters, appear to be much rarer than those passing through sons. (Indeed, Goldschmidt and Kunkel, 1971, do not recognize either of these types as occurring in their typology of peasant family and inheritance systems.) There were, however, clear-cut cases of inheritance through a chosen child irrespective of sex: the Basques of the villages of Echalar and Murélaga as described by William Douglass (1969, 1975) provide the most detailed example. In these communities the entire household estate,

including land, house, and space in the village church, was considered indivisible and was inherited by a child chosen by the parents according to a
variety of factors. There was a slight statistical preference for sons over
daughters in Murélaga (79 of 117 marriages) but little if any preference in
Echalar (41 of 71 marriages were virilocal, with the grooms inheriting
[Douglass 1975:43-45]). The sons and/or daughters who did not inherit,
whether they stayed in the community and took up a trade, migrated elsewhere, or married into another household, were given at marriage a dowry
in cash but never including land. Similar systems were also practiced in
the south of France and in Wallonia in the 16th century (LeRoy Ladurie
1976:61-63). The similarities to the single-son-successor systems we have
been considering are great. First, the estate itself were indivisible. Second,
only the successor and spouse were allowed to marry and remain on the
estate. Third, children not inheriting the productive property or the house
were paid off in cash marriage settlements. We should also note that in the
Basque case, as in the other European cases we have already considered,
the new head couple of the household took over management of the lands
and the estate upon marriage. This system thus stands in close transformational relationship to those we have already discussed.

There are also two other systems of single-child succession and inheritance which do not differentiate by sex: single succession by the eldest child
and single succession by the youngest child. The latter system was found
among agricultural tenants in parts of Brittany in the 19th century (Segalen
1977:229) and the former in some villages of Japan (Nakane 1967:9). I have
few details on either system, but they fit into a diagram we can compose
(Figure 18-6), showing developmental cycle of single-successor-son systems and single-successor-irrespective-of-sex systems.

The systems described so far show a fairly close congruence between
residence and inheritance, or between developmental cycle and devolution, of the kind posited by Goldschmidt and Kunkel (1971:1062). If we are
to move to the third possible row of single-successor systems, however,
those in which the succession is through a daughter, we find no empirical
cases with single inheritance of all the productive goods. In order to place
any systems in this row we need to move to systems in which succession is
single but inheritance, though showing a single-tendency, is slightly partible, even in terms of immovable goods. We find such a system among the
fisherfolk and certain farmers of Galicia in Northwestern Spain. Here, as
reported by Lison-Tolosana, the successor was a chosen daughter, and
marital residence was correspondingly uxorilocal. This chosen daughter,
among farmers, often got the house and whatever fields existed, pushing
the system toward a single-heiress type, but in other cases she got the house
and a field, with the other fields divided equally among her and her brothers and sisters (Lison-Tolosana 1976:306). Among fisherfolk, in some areas

and a field, with the other fields divided equally among her and her brothers and sisters (Lison-Tolosana 1976:306). Among fisherfolk, in some areas

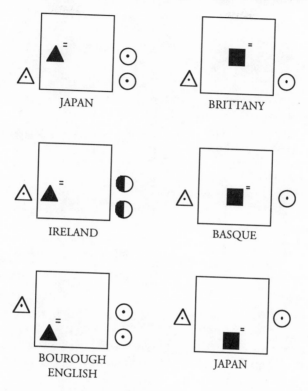

FIGURE 18-6: Single-Successor Systems Through Sons and Through Either Sex

fishing boats went to the successor-daughter, in others, to sons. But the daughter always succeeded and got the house, and always with some other inheritance (Lison-Tolosana 1971:242-272). Here it was the woman, the successor, who made all the decisions about the household economy. With the proviso that single-succession in this case was not necessarily associated with single inheritance (though it appears to have been associated with single inheritance of the majority of the productive property) we can fit this Galician fishing system into an expanded system of systems as shown in Figure 18-7. In the third row, we find no empirical cases of the systems which would belong on the left (single-succession and inheritance through the eldest daughter) or on the right (single-succession and inheritance through the youngest daughter). In sum, then, we find empirical cases of seven of the nine logical possibilities for single-successor and single-heir systems.

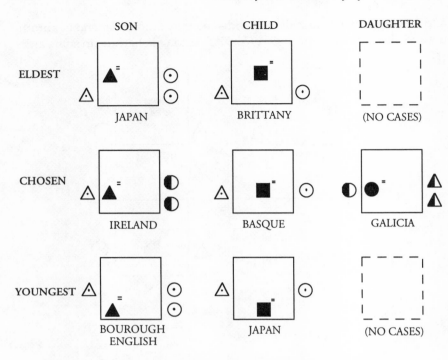

FIGURE 18-7: Summary of Single-Successor Systems

If we were to follow a strict typological approach such as that advanced by Goldschmidt and Kunkel (1971) we would now move on to the systems of partible inheritance and either joint or nuclear family developmental cycles. But there is no clear break, as we shall see, between single-successor and joint systems, between single-heir and partible systems. We can learn more about the variation by considering some of the intermediate types; progressing logically from the stem, single-successor types to the joint, partible types. The first step was already taken when we mentioned that in some of the Galician families, succession was single but inheritance was partible. We find parallel intermediate systems in the two upper rows of our diagram as well. In the other regions of Galicia, for example, we see in the mountain villages a system where an eldest son, if he was interested, succeeded to the family headship and married virilocally, becoming legal owner of the land upon his marriage and granting to his parents a right of lifetime usufruct. But he did not inherit everything, not even all the productive property. He got the lion's share, to be sure, usually two-thirds of the parents' estate, but the remaining third was distributed among all his remaining brothers and sisters (Lison-Tolosana 1976:305-6). A very similar system was practiced in central Italy before the introduction of the

Napoleonic Code (Silverman 1975:81-2). In other parts of the plains of Galicia there was still a designated successor, in this case a *chosen* son, who continued to live in the family house and manage the largest part of the estate, but here he got only one-third of the estate plus an equal share, with his brothers and sisters, of the remainder. The relationship between these systems and the ones to which they are closely related is illustrated in Figure 18-8.

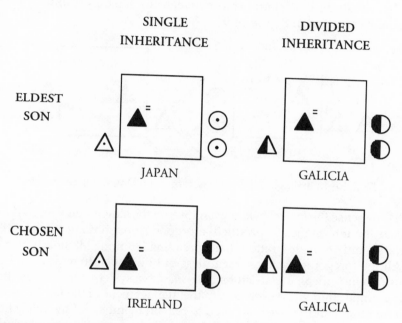

SINGLE INHERITANCE

DIVIDED INHERITANCE

ELDEST SON

JAPAN

GALICIA

CHOSEN SON

IRELAND

GALICIA

FIGURE 18-8: Single-Successor Systems with Single and Divided Inheritance

Another instance of single succession but divided inheritance is the *Bunke* (branch household) system practiced in some parts of Japan. *Bunke* occured occasionally almost everywhere in the country but seem to have always been more common in the less-developed northeastern (Tohoku) region (Nakane 1967:49, 121). Since an *ie* as a *corporation* was indivisible, it always had to have a single successor, but since the trustee, the household head, was allowed considerable liberty in managing the *ie* property, it was possible to set up a non-successor son by dividing the *estate*. This allowed a son other than the successor to marry and live from the proceeds of the estate, though usually from a smaller portion of it than that retained by the original *ie*. This established a new *ie* called a *bunke*, which began with the non-successor who received productive property. He, in his turn, might transmit the property of his new *ie* intact or might establish a *bunke* for one of his non-successor sons, if he had any. Where the creation of *bunke* was practiced regularly we may speak of it as a system, and note that it shares characteristics of the systems discussed immediately previously: there is a single successor but more than one heir. Where the *bunke* system differs from the Galician ones is that in the Japanese variant only a son would ordinarily be set up in a *bunke*, and setting up one child in such a branch household did not require the parents to similarly set up any of the others. We can illustrate the relationship between the Japanese *bunke* and the Galician systems as in Figure 18-9.

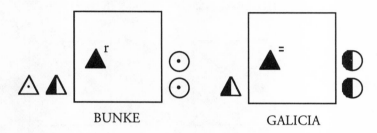

BUNKE   GALICIA

FIGURE 18-9: Single-Successor Systems with Divided Inheritance

In one sense the *bunke* system was closer to the single-heir pole in that it spread the inheritance of productive property only among two siblings, and then only to males, rather than spreading it among all the siblings.

All the foregoing systems, regardless of how much they deviate from the single-*heir* ideal, are strictly single-*successor* systems, insofar as there was a single child who succeeded to the management of the family estate, and no other children were allowed to remain members of the household corporation after they married. But there were other systems in which this sharply drawn line of household membership was somewhat blurred, while the inheritance of the estate, at least its productive resources, remained intact. Proceeding logically along a continuum, then, from single-successor to ever more inclusive systems, we will eventually arrive at the pole of laterally fully extendable families.

We begin in yet another region of Spain—this time Catalonia, in the 19th century. At least among landowners, and among grape-growing families who held secure heritable tenant rights to their vineyards, the family headship and the management of the estate passed to the eldest son, or *hereu*; failing sons, these rights passed to the eldest daughter, or *pubilla*, who took in an uxorilocal husband (Hansen 1977:84-6). The *hereu* was a single successor in the sense of managing the undivided estate (see below) and living in the original home, the *casa pairal*, but his younger brothers were not entirely excluded from the family corporation. In fact, the second son, known as the *caballer*, was expected to add to the family estate by pursuing a profession, operating a business, or practicing a trade, depending on the social class of the family. The head of the family (his father or elder brother) was expected to use the resources of the family estate to stake him to the necessary education and capital, and the *caballer*, in turn, was expected to add to the estate through his efforts. He might, if he were successful, eventually establish a family corporation of his own upon division of the inheritance, but if he were unsuccessful the *hereu* was required to take him back (Hansen 1977:84-6). Three fourths of the estate was inherited outright by the *hereu* but the remaining quarter, the *llegitim*, was divided among all the siblings of the *hereu* upon the father's death. Here is a system, then, in which not only single inheritance but also single succession was somewhat blurred by the inclusion of the *caballer* and his earnings in the family corporation and its estate, at least temporarily. Figure 18-10 indicates the relationship of this system to those previously discussed.

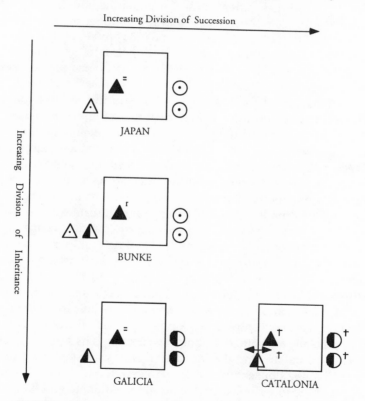

FIGURE 18-10: Systems Deviating from the Single-Succession
and Inheritance Pole

One step further down the road toward extendable families and partible inheritance we find the system practiced by the enserfed Lettish peasants of the Baltic provinces of the Russian empire at the end of the 18th century. These peasants cultivated holdings of a conventional size which, though they could be divided, were actually divided rather infrequently (Plakans 1975:12-13). These holdings required three to five adult males to work them and it became the task of the *Wirt* (the relevant census documents are written in German), or family head, to ensure that the requisite labor was available on his farmstead. He could do this by accretion of either relatives or non-relatives, and where relatives were available they lived with him as part of a single household. This meant that in the soul revision (census) of 1797, about one-third of the households on the estate of Daudzewos were laterally extended, including married brothers of the head and their families. But, unlike the situation in a truly partible system, the younger brothers of the head could not remain on the holding indefinitely, and when they and their older brothers divided the household, the holding remained intact. Both the sisters and the younger brothers got some movable portion, the sisters at marriage and the younger brothers at household division, but the younger brothers and their families were excluded from the inheritance of the holding which, as mentioned before, was normally indivisible. It is probable (Plakans 1975:34) that the younger brothers thus cast off joined the lower economic stratum of *Einwohner*, who worked contractually on the farmsteads of non-relatives as part of their "hosts'" productive group but with a separate budget and no rights to any of the inheritance. In this system, while the estate remained indivisible, the boundaries of the household were broken down even more than in the Catalonian case; at least one married brother of the successor ordinarily remained as a member of the successor's household even after his own marriage. But eventually he too had to leave and the estate remained undivided. The inheritance system here was nearly identical to the Galician and Catalonian cases with non-successors getting cash portions only, but the developmental cycle was rather different. We can diagram its relationship to the ones previously discussed as in Figure 18-11.

We began with systems which had both a single successor, excluding married siblings from the household, and a single heir to all the productive property. We have shown two kinds of deviation from this pattern: Cases like the Galician (both its mountain virilocal and its seacoast uxorilocal forms), Central Italian, and the Japanese *bunke* systems which preserved the integrity of the household and the succession but allowed some division of part of the inheritance; and cases like Catalonian and Baltic which preserved the integrity of the productive property part of the inheritance, but allowed household membership, and thus rights to the income from property, at least temporarily, to married siblings of the household head.

Increasing Family Extension

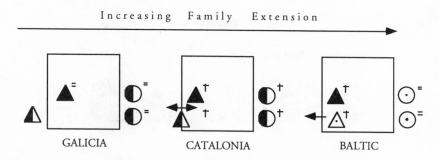

FIGURE 18-11: Family Extension by Inclusion of Siblings of a Successor

One step further from the single-successor, single heir norm is the Yi dynasty Korean system which, while preserving the ultimate integrity of the household succession (and thus being not quite a partible system), allowed *both* temporary rights of residence and maintenance and eventual shares of the productive property inheritance to the married siblings (in this case, ordinarily brothers only) of the successor. Among the propertied classes of late Yi Korea (1700-1910), and persisting in customary law to the present day, every household had to have a successor both to become the legal head and to carry on the rites of worship for the household ancestors. This household successor had to be a real or adopted son; apparently the institutions of adopted sons-in-law and filiacentric marriage,[1] so common in the patrilineally-biased, virilocal systems of many complex societies (Goody 1990), were rare in Korea as they were in North China (Sorensen 1981:259-60; 1988:154-65; Gamble 1954:29). But succession to the headship by one son did not preclude the others from residing in the household, contributing their labor, and earning maintenance from the family estate. Indeed they were expected to do so, and most families with more than one son thus went through a joint phase in their developmental cycles. Eventually, however, like the younger brothers in the Baltic households, they split off—this might happen before or at the death of their father. When they did split they established new households of their own (known as "little houses") and got some property to go with them. The successor kept two-thirds of the property if there were only two brothers; if there were more than two the successor kept half and the others divided the property equally among them (Sorensen 1981:157-58; 259-60). This system approached even more closely to the partible, joint-cycle ideal but had not reached it yet, because of the inequality of inheritance and the importance of succession to the household headship and ancestral rites. Figure 18-12 shows its relationship to the other systems we have been considering.

All the systems we have considered so far are predicated on some kind of close connection between monogamous marriage on the one hand and

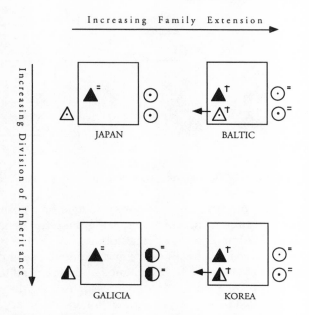

FIGURE 18-12: Family Extension and Division of Inheritance

succession and inheritance on the other. In the single-successor systems only the successor/heir can be married and remain part of the household. The Galician and *bunke* systems follow the same rule, though they allow some division of the property. The Catalonian and Baltic systems, in order to keep the inheritance intact, admit married siblings temporarily but then exclude them from the household eventually. The Korean system preserves the succession by eventually expelling the married siblings, but it must divide the property to do so. And when we get to the Korean system we are poised on the edge of true partibility. But before we step over (for it is only a small step by now) we must examine another route to the edge. This is a route through systems which keep the household intact by allowing only one marital unit in each generation but allowing more than one brother to remain in the household nevertheless. We can see this route clearly if we go back to the single-successor systems and recall that in most of these there was often a place for unmarried siblings of the successor in the household: they had rights of maintenance through no rights to inheritance or management. The first step away from the single-successor pole in this direction is taken by examining the system practiced by the noble Venetian Donà family over a long period from the Renaissance to the 19th century (James Davis 1975). This family was faced with the problem of keeping its estate intact (it originally had mercantile wealth but came more and more to depend on landholdings) in the face of a Venetian law of equal inheritance among brothers. Sisters could be taken care of by dowries in movable goods—though these did place a strain on the estate, they did not require its division—but any brother who grew to majority was entitled to a separate and equal share. The Donö circumvented this problem neatly by allowing only one son in each generation to marry and produce offspring. The unmarried brothers received their shares of the patrimony upon the death of the father, but since they had no legitimate issue (there was a flourishing prostitutes' quarter which provided sexual services for these unmarried men) their shares of the inheritance reverted to their patrilateral nephews, the sons of their married brothers, when the childless uncles died. While they were alive they had rights to reside under one roof and did so when they were in town. The palace of the Donà family, with quarters for both married and unmarried members, was built by the family's most famous member, Leonardo Donà of Venice, in the early 17th century, who himself never married (James Davis 1975:4-6). This system illustrates another strategy for accomplishing the exclusive goal of accommodating non-successors within a household without dividing it but at the cost of not allowing the non-successor to marry. Its relationship to single-successor systems is illustrated in Figure 18-13. In the single-successor system, the unmarried brother can remain, but has no inheritance rights. In the Venetian system, he can remain with inheritance rights, but these revert to the successor line upon his death.

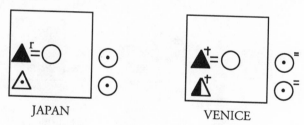

JAPAN   VENICE

FIGURE 18-13: Accommodating an Unmarried Sibling of the Successor

The Venetian system allows property rights to all brothers but allows only one of them to form a marital unit. The next step down this particular path to partibility is found in the polyandrous system of Tibet, which allowed all the brothers to form a marital unit but required them to share the marriage among them. In Tibet among both the nobility (Epstein, personal communication) and the tax-paying serfs, who held hereditary rights to farm certain parcels of land (Goldstein 1971:66), only one marriage was allowed in the household in each generation. But unlike the previous cases, where this excluded any more than one successor from either marriage or

permanent membership in the household corporation, the Tibetans provided for both marriage and household membership by the practice of
polyandry: two (or very occasionally more) brothers took a single wife between them. This allowed for sexuality in the family for both of them, it
allowed them to reside in the house and contribute their labor to the estate,
and it gave them all descendants. What it did not do was differentiate between them; both of them were husbands of the wife and fathers of the
children. Since it was ordinarily difficult for more than two brothers to
share a wife, such extra sons were ordinarily either married uxorilocally
into families which had only daughters, or else entered the monkhood
(Goldstein 1971:68). A family with only one daughter could take in an
uxorilocal son-in-law; if it had two daughters left over after one had become a nun it could take in a single son-in-law for both of them in a polygynous uxorilocal family. Finally, if a man's wife died while he was still
young he would prevent the step-sibling problem by taking another wife
in common with his son or sons. The practices are diverse and seem bizarre; the principle, however, is clear. The family and its estate could not be
divided; population could not be allowed to increase until it strained the
available resources, which ordinarily are not great; nevertheless all sons
had to be provided for. Figure 18-14 shows the relation of the Tibetan system to the single-successor and Venetian systems.

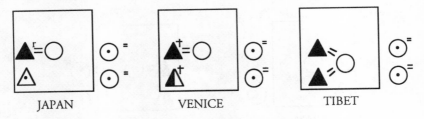

JAPAN   VENICE   TIBET

FIGURE 18-14: Polyandry as a Way of Maintaining Undivided Inheritance

The Tibetan system and certain closely related systems among the Ti-
betan-speaking populations of the Himalayas (Goldstein 1976) necessarily
involved a large surplus of unmarried women: some women had a single
husband and some had two, but rarely did a man have two wives. In both
the Himalayas (Goldstein 1976:228) and Tibet proper (Epstein, personal
communication)[2] there were thus large numbers of maiden aunts living at
home, along with some female servants in wealthy households and of course
nuns in nunneries. But there were other systems in the Himalayas that
preserved the integrity of the household estate, accommodated all the brothers in a family, and at the same time achieved a high rate of marriage among
the women. These are the "polygynandrous" or "group-marriage" systems

of the Pahari of Janusar Bawar as described by Berreman (1975). In this case, polygyny and polyandry were, in fact, practiced by the same families. The developmental cycle began when a group of brothers took a wife, usually around the time of the eldest brother's maturity. As the brothers matured they all became husbands of this wife, and they might also take another wife or wives, so that in effect there was for at least part of the developmental cycle a group-marriage situation (Goldstein 1976:132-35). No particular woman was considered the wife of a particular brother, and the children were considered equally the children of all their "fathers." Berreman demonstrates (Goldstein 1976) how the family at any particular time in the cycle could appear monogamous, polyandrous, polygynous, or polygynandrous, where in fact all these forms were stages and variations of a single developmental cycle (Figure 18-15).

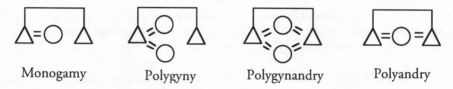

Monogamy   Polygyny   Polygynandry   Polyandry

FIGURE 18-15: Stages in a Hypothetical Janusari Developmental Cycle

This system, however, did allow for division of household and property—in fact, if a particular husband and wife in a polyandrous or polygynandrous family wanted exclusive sexual rights to each other they had to divide the household and the patrimony and set up a separate household. This did not happen automatically in each generation, however, so that in many families a single household was preserved by merging the social personalities of the brothers into a single "successor" who was allowed, unlike the Tibetan brother-group, to have more than one wife. The relationship between this system and those previously discussed is shown in Figure 18-16.

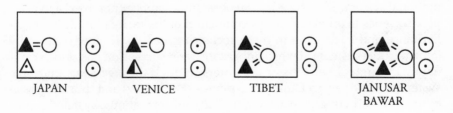

JAPAN   VENICE   TIBET   JANUSAR
                                   BAWAR

FIGURE 18-16: Celibacy, Polyandry, and Polygynandry
to Maintain Undivided Inheritance

In Garhwal, another part of the Pahari area, we come even closer to a fully partible system. Here married brothers lived together after their marriages, as in the Janusar Bawar system, but each married his own separate wife (Berreman 1963:150, 171-72). The children of each couple were its own, and when the brothers or their sons decided to divide their household and property, they divided it equally and formed separate households. This sounds like the fully partible systems of India and China (see below) but actually represents an intermediate step, because brothers in this system shared sexual rights with each others' wives as long as the couples remained part of a single household. This system thus preserved the sexual side of the true polyandry of their Janusar Bawar neighbors while dividing the other rights and duties of household and estate.

We have thus traced two series of logical steps away from single-successor systems: one, through Galician and some northern Japanese systems in one of its sub-routes and through Catalonian and Baltic systems in its other subroutes, leads to the Korean system. The other, through Venetian and Tibetan forms, leads to the Janusari and then to the almost totally partible Garhwal system. The Korean and the Pahari systems both differ but slightly from the fully partible inheritance, joint family systems of China, India, the Balkans, and the Middle East. When we put both these routes with the sub-routes of one in a single diagram we get Figure 18-17.[3]

Before going on to describe the fully partible systems a couple of comments are in order concerning what has been described so far. First, the transformational routes shown are those from single patrilineal inheritance and succession with virilocal residence through various intermediate forms to fully partible, joint patrilineal forms with virilocal residence. There do exist, though rarely, single-heir systems with transmission through daughters and uxorilocal residence (see the Galician fishing system, above) as well as partible, joint matrilineal systems with uxorilocal residence (see below, the Mappillas and the Tamil Moors). There is thus a logical possibility of finding intermediate systems parallel to the intermediate patrilineal systems we have described already and of constructing a parallel transformational system. That these logical possibilities appear not to exist in complex societies is probably simply a function of the rarity of matrilineal inheritance and succession in these societies generally. I know of no fully joint, partible systems in which inheritance and succession pass indiscriminately through either sons or daughters (though the *diga-binna* marriage system of Kandyan Sri Lanka comes close—see below) and thus the possibility of constructing such an "ambilineal transformational system" beginning with the Basque single-successor type is also empirically precluded.

Second, it is interesting to examine the degrees to which the cases described so far conform to Goody's model of "diverging devolution," in

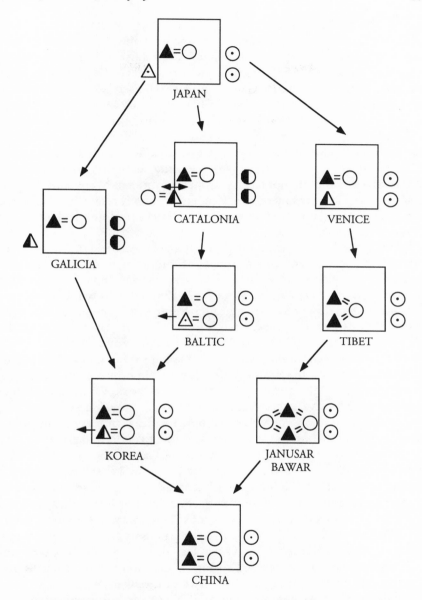

FIGURE 18-17: How to Get from Japan to China Through Logical Progression

which "Women were usually residual heiresses to their brothers in addition to which they received a dowry if they married away" (Goody 1976:21).
Taking the first point, women as residual heiresses, we find this generally
to be true. Leaving aside those cases (the Galician fisherfolk and the Basques)

where women had a prior or equal right to inherit, we find women as residual heiresses in Japan (Nakane 1967:5, etc.), Medieval England (Homans
1941:139), and early 20th century Ireland (Arensberg and Kimball 1968:109-
10) among the single-heir systems for which we have information, as well
as in the slightly less "single" Catalonian case (Hensen 1977:84) and among
the Polyandrous Tibetans (Goldstein 1971:69). Only according to Korean
law (Sorensen, personal communication) was it the case that adoption of
an agnate was the required way of insuring an heir for a sonless family, so
that uxorilocal marriage could only be resorted to if their was no agnate
available. Even here, though, it is noteworthy that the agnate had to be
adopted as a son and did not receive property by means of any lateral transmission as a residual collateral heir. Keeping the family estate together seems
to be associated with transmitting it to a direct lineal descendant, as we
would have predicted.

What about the other aspect of diverging devolution—the payment of a
dowry to daughters who are marrying out? Again, in every case for which
we have information, this appears to have been done. In Japan (Beardsley,
Hall, and Ward 1959:324-5; Nakane 1967:153) and in Korea this was partially an indirect dowry traveling through the groom's parents to the couple;
in the other cases there was a straightforward dowry (Homans 1941:140-
42); Arensberg and Kimball 1940:140-42; Berkner 1976:78; Hansen 1977:98;
Epstein, personal communication). But it is important to note at the same
time that in none of these cases (with the possible exception of Calenberg,
for which Berkner gives no clear indication) was the dowry in land or other
productive property: it was always in the form of movable goods; usually
clothing, jewelry, household furnishings, bedding, money, or, most frequently, a combination of most or all of these. Even in Ireland, where the
value of the fortune was supposed to match the value of the farm (Arensberg
and Kimball 1968:110) the fortune was paid in cash. What this indicates to
me is simply that even in the face of the necessity to give a dowry for reasons of prestige or simply of propriety (see below) systems that attempted
to keep the family estate intact could not split the estate by giving some of
its productive property away to a daughter who was going to marry out.
(Korea, where the family estate was, in fact, divided among brothers, was
a strongly agnatically organized society, a situation which typically precludes women from inheriting productive property anyway).

Finally, we should reiterate that in all these cases for which we have
information, excepting the Korean which is almost a fully partible system,
there is a close connection between inheritance and marriage. In the European cases in particular not only was marriage at home a necessary and
sufficient condition for inheritance, but inheritance occurred at the time of
marriage—the heir took over the farm and the parents, legally at least, became dependents of their married child and his or her spouse (Hansen

1977:85-6; Homans 1941:154-57; Arensberg and Kimball 1968:118-21). Even in Japan, where the parents retained their superior position in the household after the marriage of the heir, they did not retain it into extreme old age but were expected to retire sometime in their seventh decade (Nakane 1967:17). In generalized terms, we can thus say that we have a "single-transmission complex," including single succession to an enduring household, single inheritance of productive property, exclusion of married siblings of the successor from the family corporation and its house, daughters as either alternative heiresses or occasionally the heiresses of choice, dowry in movable wealth only, and early transmission of the rights and duties of headship from the senior generation to the junior. All aspects of this complex except the restriction of the dowry to movable wealth tend to be weakened as we move from the strictly single-succession systems to the fully partible systems, the topic of Chapter 19.

Notes

1. Sorensen (1988:164-65) says that uxorilocal marriage was sometimes resorted to when a household was sonless; this brought in extra labor for the household. But these unions were not filiacentric; the children all took their father's name, and were not allowed to succeed to household headship. Why Korea did not adopt the common, filiacentric alternative remains something of a mystery.

2. I am indebted to Lawrence Epstein for providing me with much valuable information and clarification concerning the Tibetan family.

3. It is perhaps noteworthy, though not crucial to the argument, that two possible series of systems ranging from single to partible are also geographically arranged series: Japan-Korea-China and Tibet-Himalayas-India.

19

A Tour of C-Cluster Family Systems: Part Two

We began Chapter 18 with a description of the variation within that group of systems that approach closely to the ideal of the "single-transmission complex" and moved through a progressive weakening of that complex until we reached systems verging on full partibility. In this chapter we begin with the fully partible, joint systems, describing the variation within that group. I will begin with the Chinese system. The most important characteristics of this system were the patrilocal joint family and equal division of household and property. In sharp contrast to, say, the Japanese system, but not too different from the Korean, all brothers in a Chinese family, or *jia*, were expected to marry and to stay in the family when they did so, bringing their wives to live virilocally. When they lived together as members of a joint family there was one person, the family head, who controlled the budget and the labor of the family members and who represented the family in its dealings with other families and with the community at large. This head was normally the eldest male, more often the father than the elder brother of other married adult males who might have resided in the household.

Exactly how long the family remained in its joint phase depended on a combination of demographic, psychological, and economic factors, but more than one married brother meant eventual division. This division might occur as early as the marriage of the second youngest brother (who would have a viable domestic unit after division, as would the youngest brother if his mother were alive to cook for him) or as late as several years after the death of the father. The key factor in determining such division seems to have been the balance between the economic advantages of keeping the joint household and economy (Cohen 1968; 1976:ch. 5) and the psychological tensions created between the nuclear family units (Cohen 1976:202) or "uterine families" (M. Wolf 1972:164-65) created by the marriage of the respective brothers. If the family coresided, its consumption was always unified and its production usually so, though it was possible, for example, for several brothers to hold wage-earning jobs and turn over their earnings to their father for redistribution. It was also possible for members of a family to live in different places and still retain rights in a joint family corporation. They might budget separately for their own daily needs or those of their nuclear families but send remittances back to their parents in the original home, or simply retain potential rights in the division of the estate (M. Cohen 1970:31). But as long as no formal division had taken place there still existed a joint corporation, even if its members were dispersed.

When division did take place, it was two processes, usually but not always occurring at the same time (Ahern 1973:196-7). First the household itself, the consumption unit, divided, with each new household building its own separate brick cooking stove and budgeting separately. This might happen either before or at the same time as the division of the property. If division of the household came first, brothers would work the property together and each take equal shares of the product rather than relying on a redistributor to attend to their daily needs. The division of the property itself depended on the category of property. For property which had already been inherited, usually by far the most important category, the cardinal principle was equal division *per stirpes*. In some areas the eldest son received a slightly larger share in recognition of the extra expenses of his primary role in ancestor worship (Fei 1939:66); alternatively, a small share was sometimes given to the eldest grandson (M. Wolf 1970:196). This in fact came under the control of his father (that is, the eldest son), though the eldest grandson's brothers had no rights in his property once they had divided from him. But both these deviations from the ideal of equality were minor; even where they were practiced they seem not to have been carried out in every case, and they were not practiced everywhere. For the second category of property, that which had been acquired by the family since the last inheritance, a different principle applied: sons got shares corresponding to the degree of their own contribution to the acquisition (Sung 1981). The third category of property was women's property. While men could not hold property except as members of a family corporation, women had "private" property which they were entitled to manage and spend at their own discretion. This property came from their dowries, paid in movable goods and wealth, and in some cases from other gifts given to them at the time of their weddings (Cohen 1969; 1976:ch. 6). This almost never included land, but since land was a tradeable commodity, women were sometimes able to buy land with the capital they had accumulated by manipulation of their original dowry and wedding gifts. This property was merged into the estate of the women's conjugal family when it divided from the conjugal families of the husband's brothers and became an independent *jia* in its own right.

If the joint family had managed to last until after the death of both parents this single process of property division was the end of it; the cycle began again in the next generation. If one or both parents were alive at the time of division, however, there were problems of residence and support of the older people. Several solutions were common. In one, a share of the property could be set aside for the parents as *lao-ben* (capital for old age). They could either attach themselves and their *lao-ben* to the *jia* of one of their sons, or they could live with each son in rotation, using the proceeds of their *lao-ben* to pay for their support. If, as was probably most common, the separated *jia* of brothers continued to live in separate quarters but in the same building or group of buildings, the aged parents might simply have their own quarters but eat with the family of each of their sons in turn; no separate parental share of property was necessary in such a case. When the parents died the *lao-ben* would be used to pay the funeral expenses; if any was left over it would be divided equally between the sons.

We thus have a developmental cycle which moved from the joint family to a series of nuclear families or a stem family and one or more nuclear families each of which could, in turn, develop into a joint family in its own generation before it eventually divided (A. Wolf 1985). A characteristic of this joint-family cycle that made it different from the systems described previously is that there was no continuity of the household or the estate. There was continuity of descent, expressed by the patrilineal transmission of surnames and by the rites of ancestor worship, but the joint family itself, together with the resources it had accumulated, ceased to exist upon family division. It might, in some areas, eventually develop into a patrilineage or lineage segment (Freedman 1958:47; Baker 1969:100) but this was a fundamentally different kind of group, because it did not share a common budget and was itself composed of property-holding *jia*. Partibility meant just that: the family and its estate were eventually divided; only their former component parts continued.

Another noteworthy characteristic of the joint-family cycle was that not every family passed through a joint phase in every generation, and thus there was not always a division. Not every family in a single-successor system passes through a stem phase in every generation either, but this makes little difference with respect to the logic of development and devolution. But in the joint system if there is only one son the developmental cycle looks exactly like that of a single-successor system. If there was no son two alternatives were available in China: a son could be adopted, preferably but not always from an agnate, or a man of a different surname could be married to a natural or adopted daughter. In either case the principle of lineal transmission remained intact. In fact, even not marrying was no bar to inheritance or to succession. An unmarried man could adopt a son; a woman with no brothers could bear children out of wedlock who would be the rightful successors to their grandparents and heirs to their property. In sum, a different basic principle appears to be at work here: not the continuity of the household and estate but the continuity of the descent line was the most important consideration. We indicate the relationship between the Korean and the Chinese systems in Figure 19-1.

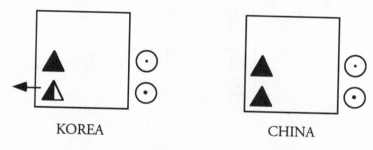

KOREA   CHINA

FIGURE 19-1: Korean and Chinese Systems

There are several other family development and inheritance systems which closely resemble the Chinese in its important particulars of virilocal residence, a possible joint phase in the developmental cycle, equal division of property *per stirpes*, a dowry consisting of solely of movable wealth for women with brothers, and daughters as residual heiresses in lieu of real or adopted sons. This is essentially the same system that was practiced in Serbia since medieval times (Hammel 1972; Halpern 1972; Halpern and Halpern 1972), in Bulgaria (Sanders 1949), in Russia (Czap 1978; Benet 1970:100-6), and of course in most of India (Tambiah 1972). All these systems exhibited congruence between the system of patrilocal residence for all sons and the system of equal patrilineal inheritance of productive property,[1] with the daughters getting no share. But not all systems displayed such congruence; it is possible to have patrilocal joint families and still have bilateral inheritance of productive property. Let us look at a few Greek examples to see how this works.

Everywhere in Greece kinship is reckoned bilaterally, and the law of inheritance in recent times has prescribed equal shares to sons and daughters. But this masks great differences in practice, and tells us nothing of residence and domestic cycle, which have not always been congruent with the local inheritance practices. Let us take as a start the Sarakatsani shepherds of the Zagori mountains in the period after World War II, as described by J. K. Campbell (1964). The developmental cycle of the Sarakatsani was almost identical to that of the Chinese: marriages were virilocal; brothers formed extended families that resided, cooked, and managed their labor together; and sometime after the marriage of the youngest daughter the brothers divided households and property, in this case flocks (J.K. Campbell 1964:44). In the early 20th century a bride's dowry consisted only of wealth, but after 1945 it gradually came to include a sizeable number of sheep, so that the value of a dowry was typically half that of a son's share when he and his brothers divided the flocks. Figure 19-2 shows the Sarakatsani system in relationship to the Chinese.

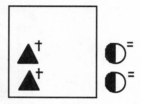

FIGURE 19-2: Patrilocal Extended Family Systems

If we move to another part of Greece, the agricultural village of Vasilika on the Boetian plains at around the same time (Friedl 1962) we find a system with an even greater degree of incongruity between the inheritance practices and the developmental cycle. Here, at least until migration to cities made theirs essentially a stem system, the peasants lived in patrilocal, extended families with a cycle of growth and division essentially no different from that of the Sarakatsani. But in this village sons and daughters in effect inherited equally. Daughters brought their shares with them at marriage, while sons ordinarily had to wait to gain full control until the division of the household, but their shares ended up equal. That there was an incongruity here was fully recognized by the villagers themselves: in village-exogamous marriages the bride's dowry land was inconveniently far away for the husband and wife to till, and they thus tried to arrange to trade with someone from the wife's village who was in a similar predicament, or else sell some land and buy another piece (Friedl 1962:59). This system is related to those of the Sarakatsani and Chinese as shown in Figure 19-3. Proceeding from left to right, we retain the patrilocal joint family but move from patrilineal to equal bilateral inheritance of productive property. The same progression appears to have been followed by at least some people on the Great Hungarian Plain: patrilocal joint families and strict patrilineal inheritance in the 19th century were replaced in the early 20th by a system in which some families still passed through a patrilocal joint

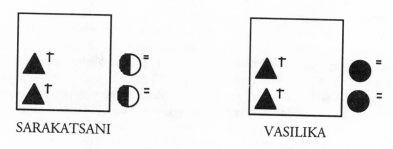

FIGURE 19-3: Greek Patrilocal Joint Family Systems

stage, but daughters regularly claimed and received equal inheritance rights Fel and Hofer 1969:256, 403-6).

A logical progression of types from a congruent one of patrilocal joint family and patrilineal inheritance to a less congruent one of patrilocal joint family and equal inheritance between sons and daughters should lead us, as its next step, back toward congruence with bilateral inheritance and an ambilocal joint family. Empirically, however, we find no such system with fully joint families—joint in residence, consumption, and production. So we shall take another tack, first going back to the congruent patrilocal joint/ patrilineal system, this time in India, and proceeding to show its relation-ship with various matrilineally organized forms.

Whereas in complex societies with patrilineal inheritance, patrilocal resi-dence was the only common arrangement, in systems with matrilineal in-heritance two types of residence are possible. These are the matrilocal, which is, in terms of recruitment to the household, the exact counterpart of the patrilocal, and the avunculocal, which shares with the patrilocal the pas-sage of property and other rights between unilineally related males of ad-jacent generations. We find inheritance and developmental cycles in south India and Sri Lanka which followed both these patterns.

The example of a matrilocal grouping which appears to fit best into the system we have been describing is that of the Tamil Moor merchants of the east coast of Sri Lanka. These Muslims nearly all lived matrilocally in an extended household with the wife's parents for at least the first few years of the marriage (Yalman 1967:297-99). There was among this group an inti-mate connection between marriage, inheritance, and property management, so we have to treat the three subjects together. Most property in this group was passed on to the next generation at the time of marriage. There were two transactions of importance: a couple gave a cash payment to their in-marrying son-in-law, and at the same time gave their daughter a dowry in land, which the parents, however, often continued to manage and which would gradually pass into the management of the son-in-law (Yalman 1967:291-94). This was in fact a sort of matrilineal inheritance, or at least the transmissal of property, which was in fact a conjugal estate, through the daughters as the primary heiresses. If there remained some property after all the daughters had married out, it was divided, usually more or less equally, among daughters and sons. This is an interesting case, because a system which would be bilateral inheritance with matrilocal residence, and thus the counterpart of the Vasilika system, was transformed by the institution of large dowries into one of matrilocal residence and primarily matrilineal inheritance, somewhere between the counterpart of the Chinese and the Sarakatsani systems. The Tamil Moors thus represent, potentially at least, the matrilocal reflection of the whole range of patrilocal joint families discussed in the previous pages. We can diagram their relationships, real and potential, as in Figure 19-4.

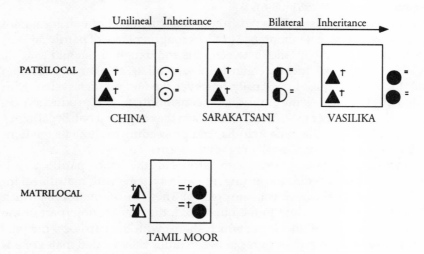

FIGURE 19-4: Patrilocal and Matrilocal Residence with
Unilineal and Bilateral Inheritance

The other likely possibility in conjunction with matrilineal inheritance is avunculocal residence which, like patrilocal residence, is a species of virilocal residence or residence at the husband's place. If matrilocal residence is the mirror image of patrilocal residence, avunculocal residence is its matrilineal equivalent, in that it keeps the male holder and the male heir, as adults at least, in the same household. An avunculocal system which fits into the series of systems we are discussing here is that of the Tiyyar of Central Kerala, as described by Gough (1961a). These people were agricultural sub-tenants of the dominant Nayar groups, and like the Nayars, matrilineal. But unlike the Nayars they had a system closely related to those we have been discussing. Residence in the 18th century was avunculocal, and boys moved at puberty or marriage to the households of their mothers' brothers, where they formed part of an avunculocal extended family which was both a work group and a consumption group, at least in some cases (Gough 1961a:407). There was, in addition to the collective tenancy rights to land, held by the matrilineally related males of a household and used to feed their wives and children as well, also a small dowry transferred at marriage and consisting, like the dowry we have seen in so many other systems, of household goods and jewelry. It is not clear from Gough's account whether such avunculocal extended families as did exist were partible in each generation in a parallel to the Chinese and Tamil Muslim systems. In other ways, however, the Tiyyar system is parallel to the other two, as indicated in Figure 19-5.

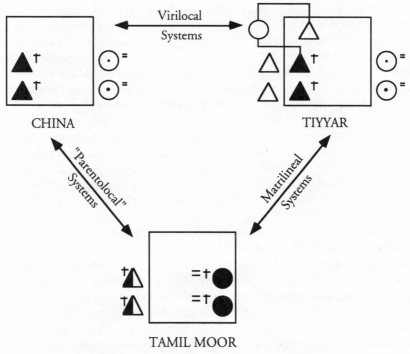

FIGURE 19-5: Three Kinds of Joint Systems

All the systems we have discussed so far, whether they be partible-joint, impartible/single-successor, or somewhere in between, have been characterized by a complex of two important characteristics: the inheritance of the in-marrying spouse was wholly or primarily transferred at marriage in the form of a dowry, either in land or in movable goods, and the maintenance of all members of a household, both those who were born or adopted there and those who have married in, came entirely from resources belonging to that household or to the persons themselves as personal property. In other words, inheritance rarely crossed household lines from a natal to a marital household of one who had already transferred residence; maintenance almost never crossed those household lines. There is another group of systems, however, in which this was not the case; these were characterized by the absence of dowry and by the actual or residual obligation of maintenance of a married-out child by his or her natal group. These occurred in both patrilineal and matrilineal variants, but probably for somewhat different reasons; since our tour vehicle is sitting over on the matrilineal side right now we shall begin with these groups.

A matrilocal system of this sort (which I shall call a "split maintenance system," as opposed to a "household maintenance system"—see Chapter 17) was that of the Mappillas, Muslim landlords and merchants of North Kerala, as described by Gough (1961b). In this group, residence upon marriage was matrilocal, and the living group often consisted of a matrilocal joint family. But since property was held by groups of matrilineally related people, men were not living with their own property-holding groups. In consequence of this, when a man of a wealthy family became the eldest in his matrilineal property-holding group he often went, with or without his wife, back to his natal family, where he presided over the estate on which resided his sisters' daughters and their husbands and children. And as a matter of fact, among the wealthier classes as well, even men who were living matrilocally with their wives' groups were still given a large percentage of the maintenance costs of themselves and sometimes their wives and children by the heads of their own matrilineal groups (Gough 1961b:424).

The Mappillas thus had matrilocal joint families, as did the Sri Lanka Tamil Moors, but the Mappilla joint families did not maintain all their members, leaving much of this function to the matrilineal groups of the inmarrying men. Between the aristocratic and middle-class Mappillas, however, there was a difference here; the middle-class male was much more likely to support himself and his wife and children through business efforts of his own. This is particularly significant when we realize that these businesses were often started or helped along by dowry payments which the man received from the wife's matrilineal group. Among the wealthier classes, whose matrilineal groups maintained their absent members, real dowry payments were confined to women's jewelry (Gough 1961b:429-430). Thus we see that even within the Mappilla group dowry was associated with household maintenance, and a much diminished dowry with split maintenance. The relationship of the household maintenance system of the Sri Lanka Tamil Moors and the split maintenance system of the Mappillas, both matrilocal, is shown in Figure 19-6.

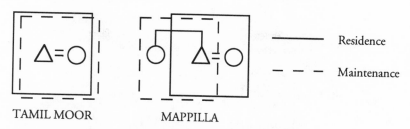

TAMIL MOOR   MAPPILLA

——— Residence

– – – Maintenance

FIGURE 19-6: Matrilocal Household- and Split-Maintenance Systems

The difference between the Tamil Moors and the Mappillas is paralleled by that between the Tiyyars of North Kerala and their landlords and caste superiors, the Nayars (Gough 1961c). The Nayars in this area, at least some of them, lived in avunculocal extended families, each under the authority of the senior male, or karanavan, and including with him junior matrilineally related males such as his younger brothers, his sisters' sons, and sometimes his sisters' daughters' sons, together with their wives and children. But the wives' connection with their husbands' avunculocal families was less encompassing than that of the Tiyyars. A man was supposed to provide some of the support for his wife and children, but another part of their support was sent by the women's own *taravads* (matrilineal property groups), to which their children, of course, also belonged (Gough 1961c:398). At the same time the marriage of a Nayar woman in this area involved no dowry but simply her husband's presenting her with a loin-cloth at the time of marriage (Gough 1961c:398; 1961a:411). And finally, a Nayar woman, unlike her Tiyyar counterpart, usually did not remain resident in or economically dependent upon her husband's group after his death, but returned to her natal family to live with her matrilineal relatives. Thus in two senses there was no conjugal estate created: a woman was not wholly dependent on her husband's family for maintenance, and marriage transactions did not involve a direct or an indirect dowry. The Northern Nayar woman, like the matrilocally marrying Mappilla man, resided in her spouse's family's house, but was only a marginal member of that family; she was only a temporary resident, and even while she did live there, part of her support came from her own relatives. Figure 19-7 shows the relationship between the Tamil Moor, Mappilla, Tiyyar, and Nayar systems.

Our progression so far should make the famous system of the Central Kerala Nayars (Gough 1961d), with their "duolocal residence," considerably less mysterious.[2] The loosening of the bond to the conjugal household and the corresponding strengthening of the bond to the natal household, even for the spouse who marries out, reached its logical culmination here, where the bond with the natal household was so strong that there

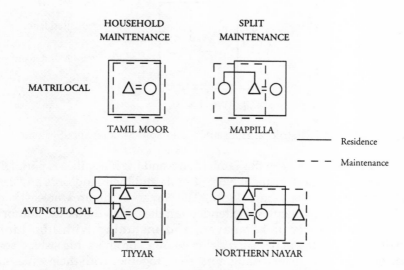

FIGURE 19-7: Matrilineal Household- and Split-Maintenance Systems

was no conjugal household; both spouses continued to reside in their re-spective natal families, with the husband visiting the wife for sex and companionship but having no rights of maintenance whatsoever in her household. And with such a residential arrangement it comes as no surprise that the Central Kerala Nayars paid no dowry, and that both women and men customarily had several sexual partners (Gough 1961d:358-9). The duolocal system of the Central Kerala Nayars was thus merely a logical extension of the principles operating for both the avunculocal Northern Nayars and the matrilocal Mappillas. Figure 19-8 shows the relationship.

With the Central Nayar we have reached a congruent system again: rights in property and rights of maintenance passed along the same lines as house-hold residence: both men and women acquired all these rights exclusively from their mothers. We should also note that in terms of its cycle of growth and division the Central Nayar household followed the same kind of principles we saw in operation earlier with the patrilocal extended households of the Chinese and others, only here the unit which divides from its parallel units is a sister and her descendants or the descendants of one sister. Since the Nayar did not allow such division until anyone who would have rights in all of the units created by the division (a brother, mother, mother's sister, or mother's brother) was dead, Nayar households were apparently quite large (Gough 1961d:344; Fuller 1976:52-6). But they followed the same basic principles of *per stirpes* division which we have seen as characteristic of partible systems.

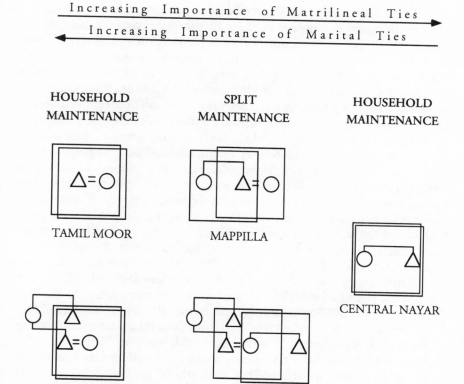

FIGURE 19-8: The Central Nayar in Context

We should also point out that, as in the African cases treated in chapter 8, the ideal of the Nayar *taravad* organized entirely along lines of affiliation to the mother's household, where property-based matrifilial ties totally outweighed the more bilaterally-balanced ties of affection, was most characteristic of the most aristocratic families, i.e. those in which the estate of the *taravad* (in land or political titles or both), was the largest and had the most hold on the household members. In poorer *taravads*, with little or no property or political estate, the distinction between the rules of inheritance from the mother's brother and from the father was irrelevant, since there was nothing to inherit (Moore 1985:536-37). It was in the presence of important property that the matrilineal principle was elaborated to a point near its logical conclusion, here as with the Asante, described in Chapter 9.

Our discussion of split-maintenance systems has so far concentrated on some matrilineal groups in South Asia, but I suggest that it can help us to understand an otherwise somewhat puzzling deviation on the patrilineal side: the family systems of the Arabs. Now according to Islamic Law, a kind of diverging devolution ought to be practiced: sons should each get two shares of their father's inheritance, with daughters getting one share. And in fact something approaching this arrangement seems to have taken place in a few cases, notably among wealthy merchant families in Basra in the early 20th century where a bride's dowry, though consisting entirely of movable wealth, appears to have been not only valuable but a subject of considerable negotiations prior to the marriage (Van Ess 1961: 35). And some Christian Arab villagers in Lebanon also gave shares of their inheritance to daughters (Peters 1976:70-1). But for the most part the range among Arab family and inheritance systems described in the literature goes from a large bride-price, an indirect dowry worth much less than the bride-price, and no female inheritance of property at the father's death, as among certain peasants in Iraq (Fernea 1965:44), in parts of Palestine (Cohen 1965) and among the Iraqi marsh dwellers (Salim 1962:60), to a much more common pattern of bride-price only, no appreciable dowry, and no *post mortem* female inheritance of property either. This pattern obtained, with minor variations, among the Bedouin of the Negev (Marx 1967:114, 185) and of Cyrenaica (Peters 1965:128-31); in farming communities in Galilee (Rosenfeld 1963:248-50), on the Turkish-Syrian Border (Aswad 1967:142-3), and in Tunisia (Cuisinier 1976:138-42); and in a mixed pastoral-farming community in the Western Desert of Egypt (Mohsen 1967:225).

There was thus at least a tendency away from both dowry and observance of the Islamic inheritance law in nearly all the communities in the recent past on which I have material, and in some of them we find something approaching the kind of bridewealth system which ought, according to Goody, not be found in complex societies (1972:23). Nearly all these communities had family systems that included a joint phase in their developmental cycles, and every one of them practiced partible inheritance, at least among sons. So it would seem legitimate to look for parallels to some of the matrilineal joint family systems of South Asia which we have just been describing. And as a matter of fact we find them in the notion of split maintenance. It is true that in most of the Arab communities studied, a woman's husband was supposed to maintain her. But at the same time, almost everywhere Arabs were aware of the provisions of Islamic Law, which give the daughter a half share of the inheritance. They got around this provision, however, by stating that a woman, upon her marriage, had to renounce her legal share of the inheritance in return for a guarantee of protection from her brothers, and of maintenance from them in case of divorce (Aswad 1967:143; Cuisinier 1976:142; Mohsen 1967:232). This was, on the level of family ideology, parallel to split maintenance. It is also notable that in many Arab communities agnates and not daughters, or sometimes agnates in addition to daughters, were residual heirs (Marx 1967:185). Thus the relationship of the Arab system to the Chinese/Indian system resembles the relationship of the Mappilla system to the Tamil Moor system and the relationship of the Northern Nayar system to the Northern Tiyyar system, as illustrated in Figure 19-9.

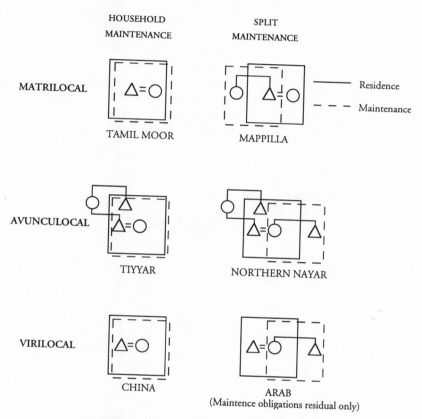

FIGURE 19-9: Patrilineal and Matrilineal Versions
of Household- and Split-Maintenance

I should mention briefly here, though I will treat the subject in more detail in the next section, that the Arabs and the South Indian Groups arrived at the split-maintenance systems through rather different routes, which had to do with the differences between matriliny and patriliny in situations where males had effective control over property. But the systems are parallel in several of their aspects.

This concludes our discussion of family systems with fully partible inheritance, and where the family passed through a phase in its cycle where it was joint in residence, production, and budgeting or consumption. As a matter of fact, we see already in the split maintenance systems—matrilocal, avunculocal, and patrilocal—some movement away from the fully joint form, at least in procuring, processing, and management and transmission of property. Now it is time to move away from joint/partible systems in another direction. As we moved from stem-family systems with single successors to joint-family systems with partible succession and inheritance, we now begin a progression which will lead us to systems of full partibility of inheritance but with a nuclear family cycle.

We begin with systems in which all children of a particular sex reside and consume jointly with their parents, as in a joint system, but serially rather than at the same time, leading to an end result of several nuclear families plus a stem family including the parents. Perhaps the simplest, or at least one of the most congruent and thus easy to understand, systems of this type is that of the Thai-Lao of northeast Thailand (Keyes 1975, 1976). We can, rather arbitrarily, begin the description of the domestic cycle of the Thai-Lao with a nuclear family living in its own house and farming land inherited through the wife. As the children of the couple grew up, the sons would ordinarily move out to live in their wives' families, and the daughters brought in husbands in matrilocal residence. When the first daughter married, she and her husband resided with her parents, participated in their production activities, and shared a common budget with them. When the next daughter married, however, the first daughter moved out of the parental house and established a separate household, usually within the same walled compound. This household was residentially separate and ate separately, but remained economically dependent on the parents' household, sharing in their productive labor and receiving rice from the parents' granary, not directly from the fields (Keyes 1975:282-3). If there was a third daughter, the second would move out and found a semi-independent nuclear family upon *her* marriage, and so on down the line. The last daughter to marry, however, did not move out at all; she continued to live with her parents as long as they were alive, and inherited the parental household when they died. When the latter surviving parent did die, full title to the land was parceled out equally among the married daughters, and the family of each became a fully independent household with separate production, consumption, and residence (Keyes 1975:282-3). If a family had no daughter, one son, usually the youngest, stayed in the parental household; he brought his wife in and inherited the house and land (Keyes 1975:284). It is important to recognize here that the connection between marriage and inheritance, strong in the stem-systems and progressively weakened as we proceeded toward the fully partible joint systems, is reasserting itself here: only *married* daughters inherited land. The connection is still not as strong as it will get, however: the land was given to them not at marriage but at their parents' death. This is a difficult system to diagram but we might illustrate it as in Figure 19-10, showing that the brothers are excluded upon marriage, but that the elder sisters remain for awhile after marriage but never in co-residence with their younger *married* sisters, and thus never forming a joint household.

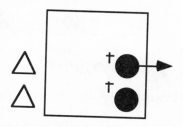

FIGURE 19-10: Northeastern Thai-Lao System

An essentially similar system was practiced by the Thai of the Central Plain of Thailand in the 19th century, as described by Piker (1975:304-6). The in-marrying son brought with him what Piker describes as a "bride-price," apparently in movable goods, which might constitute a substantial portion of the inheritance. If we move to the system practiced in the north of Thailand in the 1970's (Potter 1977) we find that men received full shares of the inheritance, along with their sisters, at the time of their parents' death. We thus have a progression from partible matrilineal inheritance through a system in which men got movable goods in what was essentially a male dower, to one in which males received an equal share of the land inheritance along with females. The developmental cycle of the three cases was, however, almost exactly the same. Their relationship is illustrated in Figure 19-11. In each case, the dotted enclosure indicates continued membership in a production group, even after separate households have been established.

A comparable system with virilocal residence was found in southern Vietnam before the American war (Hickey 1964:91). Here each brother and his wife lived virilocally for a time after marriage, but everyone but the youngest eventually moved out and set up a household either in a common compound with the parents or nearby. The youngest brother, like the youngest sister in the Thai cases, remained with the parents and was expected to provide for them in their old age. There was a difference other than that of residence rules between this system and those of the Thai, however; the Thai formed a two-level domestic group with the larger, property-holding group remaining essentially joint until the death of the parents but the smaller, budgeting and co-residential groups forming anew

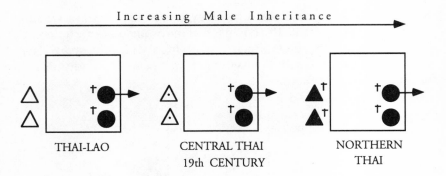

FIGURE 19-11: Inheritance Variation in Matrilocal Thai Systems

with the marriage of each daughter. In the Vietnamese system, when the older sons moved out upon their younger brothers' marriages they no longer worked the property jointly, though the parents continued to hold the ultimate rights over it, which they disposed of by testament, sometimes giving portions to both sons and daughters and sometimes, if there was not enough land to go around, giving portions to sons only. The relationship between the Thai and Vietnamese systems is shown in Figure 19-12.

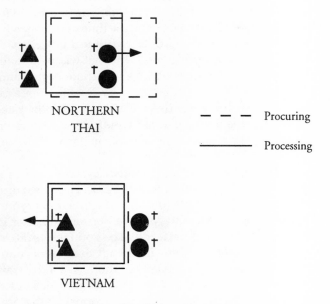

FIGURE 19-12: Northern Thai and Vietnamese Systems

The previous two systems, the uxorilocal Thai and the virilocal Viet-namese, both included a period of co-residence for the newly married couple and the appropriate spouse's parents before establishing nuclear house-holds for the older siblings and a stem household for the youngest, in the Thai case as part of a joint production group and in the Vietnamese as independent producers. We can now move a step further away from joint systems by examining a system in which fully independent consumption groups were set up immediately upon the marriage of each spouse but remained part of a joint productive group with the parents and some of the siblings of one of the spouses. This was the *diga-binna* system of the Kandyan Sinhalese, as described by Yalman (1967:100). In this system procuring was almost always carried on jointly, but processing and consumption were separate, and consumption groups were invariably nuclear families. In terms of the linearity of inheritance and the direction of marital residence, this system lies intermediate between those of the Thai and Vietnamese: where the couple lived and which spouse's productive group they joined in a particular case depended on ad hoc considerations of the availability of property and sometimes irrigation rights (Leach 1961:138). Among the wealthier classes, couples almost always married *diga* (virilocally), arrang-ing *binna* (uxorilocal) unions only when there was no son. Among small property holders, however, *binna* was less rare, as it could be resorted to when the wife's family needed labor and had eventual land inheritance to offer in return. Among the poor, the distinction had no meaning, as there was no property to be worked (Yalman 1967:126).

The effect of all this was that joint productive groups could take many forms, including sometimes brothers, sometimes brothers and sisters, and occasionally only sisters and their spouses. Inheritance in this system ef-fectively turned out bilateral, though the quantities might not actually be equal. A wealthy girl who married *diga* lost her *post mortem* inheritance rights but gained property *inter vivos* by a large dowry (Yalman 1967:132). A son who married *binna* did not get a dower but retained his ultimate rights to inheritance. And of course sons who married *diga* and daughters who married *binna* received full shares. Figure 19-13 shows this system in relationship to the Thai and Vietnamese systems.

From here it is but a short step to basically nuclear-family systems, in which all children set up independent households upon marriage. There is, however, a great deal of variation within the broad range of nuclear family systems, variation which arranges itself around two dimensions: what kinds of property go to sons and to daughters and at what point in the developmental cycle the property changes hands. Closest to the sys-tems we have been examining are those in which, although nuclear fami-lies with separate residence and budgeting are established upon marriage, property does not devolve until the death of the parents. Such a system

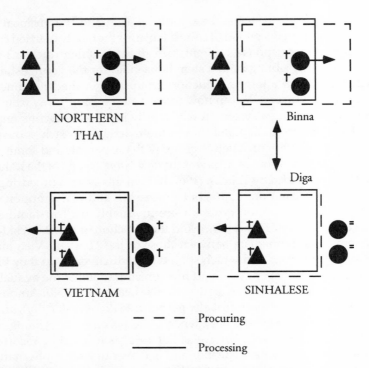

NORTHERN
THAI

Binna

Diga

VIETNAM

SINHALESE

– – –   Procuring

———   Processing

FIGURE 19-13: Logical Transformations of the Kandyan Sinhalese System

with equal inheritance for sons and daughters appears to have been common in recent times in Castile. For example, in the village of Valdemara, a small mountain community, marriage set up new nuclear families but without their own productive property. The bride brought to the marriage a trousseau only, and while a married man's father was alive he had his own share of his father's property to farm, but it was not his—he had to pay rent to his father for the privilege of farming it. When a man died his widow had lifetime rights of ownership to half his property, and his children, male and female, each got an equal share of the remainder, supporting their mother out of the land, which remained her property. When she died her half of her husband's property was shared out equally among her children (Freeman 1970:67-77; see also Brandes 1975:107-21).

A similar system obtained on the island of Nisios in Greece, but with the difference that only sons inherited major shares of productive property. Here, when marriage established a nuclear family the bride brought with her a house, furniture, and clothing, and perhaps a few "grain terraces or olive trees," perhaps not (Kenna 1975:349-50). But her dowry property, even if it did include an orchard, was never enough to support herself and her husband. So the husband needed to find work. He could work on the lands of his own father, but if he did he received wages like any other laborer; or he might choose to take a job on someone else's farm or outside the community. Only when his father died did he inherit a share of the land.

We thus have a progression of systems in which the transfer of rights to productive property did not happen until the death of the senior generation. This was true perforce in nearly all joint-family systems (though occasionally dowries could establish independent funds beside the main funds of the household) and it was true in systems of the Thai type where nuclear residential consumption units were formed upon each marriage but the production remained joint and the property was under control of the senior generation. In the Spanish and Greek systems just described we have moved a step farther away: both residence/consumption and production became, in effect, separate upon marriage, but ownership of the property still remained with the parents until their deaths. We can diagram the relationship between the four types of systems as in Figure 19-14.

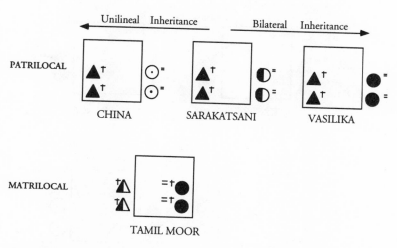

FIGURE 19-14: Patrilineal Progression from Joint to Nuclear Systems

Another step in this direction leads us to the type of system practiced in early modern times in most of the northwest of France (Le Roy Ladurie 1976:53-5). In provinces other than Normandy all children were given shares of the land to work at the time of their marriage. They were thus, unlike their Castilian counterparts, independent of their parents and did not need to establish sharecropping or wage-labor arrangements. But the independence of their estate was only temporary—at the time of the parents' death all children who had been given marriage portions had to restore their property to a common pool, together with whatever property the parents had retained for themselves, to be divided again, this time with absolutely equal shares going to each child. In Normandy the system was somewhat different: daughters were given but a "pittance" (Le Roy Ladurie 1976:53) at the time of their marriage and sons were given rather larger portions. When the father died the sons all had to restore their portions and divide them equally among their brothers. We thus find that this kind of system, with temporary marriage settlements and a final inheritance at the death of the parents, resembled the previous system of no inheritance until the parents died in that it had both a patrilineal and a bilateral inheritance variant. We show the Castilian, Nisios, Western France, and Norman systems in their interrelations in Figure 19-15.

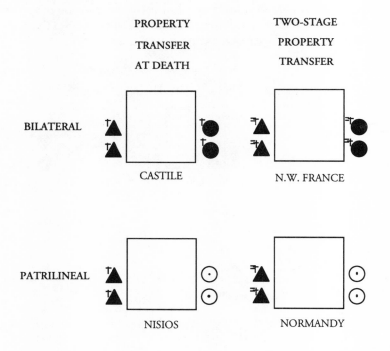

FIGURE 19-15: One- and Two-Stage Property Transfer in Nuclear Systems

From these systems, in which final transfer of all property had to wait until the death of the parents, we move to systems in which some property was transferred at the time of marriage, while other property did not pass to the junior generation until the parents died. These, like the last two types examined, had several variants. We begin with a bilateral one, found in the town of Milocca in Western Sicily in the 1920's (Gower Chapman 1971). In this town, inheritance of land was strictly bilateral and equal, but the shares of sons and daughters came at different times. Daughters received a large dowry at marriage, including land among the landed classes, and this dowry was looked at as an advance against the eventual portion they would receive at their parents' death. Sons, on the other hand, received only movable goods at the time of their marriages and had to wait until their parents' death to receive their land inheritance. Where the Milocca system was one of strictly equal inheritance, it is easy to see how the giving of portions of productive property at the time of marriage, if looked upon as final settlements rather than just temporary stakes, could lead to a skewing of this kind of system in either the patrilineal or the matrilineal direction. We can find patrilineal skewing among the Ilocano rice farmers described by Lewis (1971). Here males were the ones who received the large portions in the form of a *sebong* or "male land dowry." Since making a good match for one's son depended on being able to be generous with the *sebong*, and since it was often in the interests of parents to endow one of their children with a larger estate than the others, what often happened in fact was that a system that was in theory one of equal bilateral inheritance approached in practice either primogeniture or ultimogeniture, and that in any case males ended up inheriting more land than did females (Lewis 1971:89-93).

By contrast, Greece again provides us with an example of such a system skewed in the other direction. Casselberry and Valavanes (1976) report that in the village they call Piyi, on the Dodecanese island they call Nisi, the productive goods of a family, which consist primarily of vegetable gardens, were given, along with houses, as dowries to the family's daughters when they married. If there was any land left over, the authors state, it might be given to the sons of the family, but the clear implication is that, in fact, the large dowries often took up all or most of the property and that the portions inherited by the sons upon their parents' death were insignificant in comparison to the dowries of their wives and sisters. Thus the system, in theory like all Greek systems a bilateral one, became in practice something approaching matrilineal inheritance. It is noteworthy in this respect that even though couples set up independent nuclear families upon their marriages, they often lived in or near the houses of the brides.

There is still one other type of system which belongs to this general group, in which part of the inheritance is transferred at marriage and part at death. But unlike the Milocchese, Ilocano, and Piyi systems this system, found in the Greek Cypriot village of Alona (Peristiany 1963), finds both spouses receiving part of their inheritance, including a house and some land, upon their marriage and the rest of their shares, divided equally among all their siblings, upon the death of their parents. Figure 19-16 illustrates four variants within this general group, which itself stands intermediate between those systems where all property is transferred at death and those where all property is transferred at marriage.

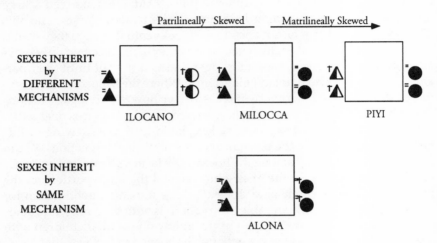

FIGURE 19-16: Variation in Two-Stage Inheritance in Nuclear Systems

Before passing to the systems where all property is transferred at marriage, we should mention one more intermediate type, as found in most of Java in the mid-20th century (Geertz 1961). The Javanese have two formal inheritance codes, the Islamic, which prescribes one share for a daughter and two for a son, and the "true Javanese," which enjoins equal division between sons and daughters (Geertz 1961:46-7). But as a matter of fact neither was followed strictly, nor was there any particular prescribed time for the transmissal of property. Rather parents, throughout their lifetime, gave various portions of his property to various children—as they matured, when were married or divorced—in short, when the father thought they needed some property he gave them some. At the parents' death, to be sure, there was a formal division of the property, but again this did not actually follow any rigid rules; the needs of each individual heir, along with other considerations, actually dictated what the final settlement would be (Geertz 1961:52).

Within the broad group of nuclear-family systems we have been moving from those in which there was little connection between property rights and marriage to those in which the tie between property rights and marriage was very close: in any of the systems where dowry or dower (male dowry) was given, acquisition of property and marriage are in a sense inseparable. In many of these systems such as that of Milocca (Gower Chapman 1971:102) this meant that parents who wanted to hold on to their resources as long as possible often delayed the marriage of their daughters as long as possible. This association between marriage and inheritance became even closer in the Swiss Alpine village of Kippel (J. Friedl 1974). Here inheritance was equal and bilateral but was not given in the form of dowry, but rather as a share in the estate upon the retirement or death of the parents. In consequence, people waited to marry until "one or both came into inheritance" (J. Friedl 1974:27) making for an average age of marriage of 29 for women and 32 for men in the early 20th century (J. Friedl 1974). The close relationship between marriage and property, and consequent late marriage, meant in this case that a large portion of people never married, as many as 30% in the early 20th century (J. Friedl 1974:28). And interestingly enough these three factors together—marriage only when property can be transferred, late marriage, and a high proportion never marrying—are the same cluster that we found earlier in so many European stem family systems. In fact, all we need to do is take the small step from a large portion never marrying to a rule restricting marriage on the holding specifically to one heir and we have come full-circle; this is the connection (though not empirically represented by intermediate steps) between the nuclear cycles we have been talking about and the stem-type systems with which we began our tour of C-cluster systems.

Before summarizing this grand tour, one or two comments are in order about the nuclear family systems themselves. First, it is clearly not true in every case that the relationship between nuclear family cycle and partible bilateral inheritance, proposed by Goldschmidt and Kunkel (1971:1063), necessarily held. Nuclear family organization, in a sizable minority of cases, worked together with patrilineal inheritance and in one case with something approaching matrilineal inheritance. Second, in examining nuclear family systems we get the clearest idea of the association between dowry and a conjugal fund, as described by Goody (1972:17). Either dowry created a conjugal fund, or there was no conjugal fund and the newly married couple had to fend for itself through wage labor, sharecropping, or some similar arrangement. Finally, it is evident why I put the Thai system where I did. While it appears intermediate between nuclear and stem systems, as well as between nuclear and joint systems, it fits in most effectively in the latter position because it forms part of the bridge between systems in which marriage and property have no connection and those in which their connection becomes closer.

Leaving out the matrilineal-bilateral-patrilineal dimension for now, we can summarize the relationships among C-cluster family systems in greatly simplified form in Figure 19-17. Our tour has thus taken us all the way around the world of premodern, complex societies and C-cluster family systems; the final chapter in this Part attempts to explain some of the variation described here.

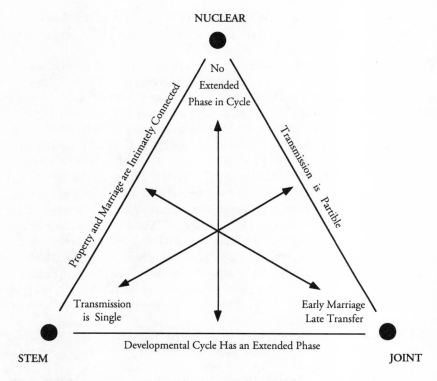

FIGURE 19-17: Dimensions of Variation Among Nuclear, Stem, and Joint Cycles

Notes

1. In Russia, land was often not heritable, being redistributed by the village council, or *mir,* but other property could be inherited, and the rules for inheritance closely resemble those practiced in Serbia, China, and India. See Benet 1970:7-11, 100-6.

2. The Western Naze people, in Ninglang and Yanyuan Counties in southwest China, have continued to this day to practice a system virtually identical to that of the Nayars before the British conquest, though they were forced to marry and live virilocally during the Great Proletarian Cultural Revolution. For detailed accounts of Western Naze family organization, see Shih 1993 and Weng 1993.

20

Explaining Variation in
C-Cluster Systems

Having examined the range of variation among C-cluster family systems in some detail, we now proceed to the next portion of our task: explaining this variation in terms of the dimensions of variability set out in Chapter 2 and related specifically to C-cluster systems in Chapter 17.

I have, of course, done this for other clusters in previous chapters. but in those cases I faced a rather intractable problem: the societies composing a single cluster vary widely in their cultural tradition. This is particularly true of the B-cluster, but also a major factor in the A- and N-clusters, and not a negligible one even in the culturally rather "uniform" societies of Eastern Oceania. In none of these cases could I say with confidence that the differences in family structure from one community to another were clearly attributable to the differences in their natural and social environments. There was always the possibility that people with different historical or cultural traditions had come up with different alternatives for solving the same environmentally-posed set of problems. It was only in the rare cases where I could compare, for example, the aristocracy with the commoners on Tahiti, or the royal clan of the Bemba with its subjects, that I could be confident that I was seeing the effect of environmental or social context variation pure and simple.

In the C-cluster, happily (and also in the M-cluster; see Part VII) things are different. We have numerous cases where communities, or even social strata within a community, differ both in the environments to which their families need to adapt and in the structures of the developmental cycle of these families. When we find two groups of people who share a very similar cultural tradition and nevertheless differ in their family organization, we can say with confidence that the difference is due to factors other than a differing ideology of how families ought to be organized. We can use this sort of intra-societal comparison to make assertions about what affects family organization, and we can make these assertions with some confidence, because we can better control the factor of cultural or historical contingency.

We must not, however, assume that differences in natural and social environment can account for all observed differences in C-cluster family systems. Environmental differences can be shown to be important in controlled comparison precisely because it is controlled comparison—controlling for the cultural and historical factors that may, in some cases, play an equally important part with the environmental ones in shaping family organization. In examining C-cluster family systems, when we move away from situations in which we can control for cultural differences, toward situations in which cultural differences are apparent, we find that these cultural differences may in fact play a large part in shaping the actual family organization, even when the communities that differ culturally are quite similar in their environmental situation. This is illustrated in the Wolf and Cole's study of German and Italians in a single valley in South Tirol (1974), for example, as well as in Geertz' discussion of the differences between Orthodox Muslims and others in Java (1961:46-9), and in Rogers and Solomon's paper (1983) in which they show that many aspects of family organization and of intrafamilial relationships differ, in two pairs of farming communities in France and Illinois, both according to different ideologies of inheritance and in the degree to which the various communities conform to their ideologies. Once we move beyond intra-societal comparisons to comparisons between societies or between culturally very different ethnic groups within a society, we must take both adaptation and ideology into account if we are going to explain differences in family organization.

Having stated this caveat, my purpose in the remainder of this chapter is to push controlled comparisons and the effect of natural and social environment as far as I can. To do this, I will examine intra-societal differences in family organization with respect to each of the specific C-cluster dimensions of variation set out in Chapter 17. In each case, I will consider my argument to carry the most weight if I can make parallel intra-societal comparisons in two or more different societies. For example, if I can show that French farmers differ from French fishers in the same way that Thai farmers differ from Thai fishers, I consider that I have controlled as well as possible for cultural differences, because even in two sets of culturally very different communities, the same environmental factors are operating in the same way. I will discuss each of several dimensions of variation in turn, in each case attempting to show the action of the same kinds of factors in more than one society.

Direction of Transmission

Inheritance

Let us begin with the first dimension, that of the direction of transfer of rights and duties from the senior generation to the junior. It will be most convenient to discuss the inheritance aspect of this dimension first. There are two kinds of situations in complex societies in which inheritance systems can be pushed toward the matrilineal pole. First, there are those rare systems in Kerala and Sri Lanka which were explicitly matrilineal. The societies had matrilineal descent groups, and the family structure and inheritance reflected this ideology of descent. To determine under what circumstances such groups might have arisen is essentially a problem in inter-societal comparison and thus very difficult to answer in terms of the kinds of variables I have been examining. There is some possibility that matrilineal systems had more chance of emerging in circumstances where men were absent from home in warfare or trading a good deal of the time, and as a matter of fact these groups (except the Tiyyars) do fit that model. But there have been many other groups where men have been absent in warfare or trading for long periods of time, and it is only in Kerala and Sri Lanka, and in a very small group in Southwest China, the Western Naze (Shih 1993; Weng 1994) that we find any explicitly matrilineal groups in complex societies. My best guess, and it is only a guess, is that these were areas where matrilineal descent groups occurred before the emergence of male-controlled private property, and that by certain kinds of adjustments parallel to those we saw in African societies where matriliny coexisted with increasing wealth, particularly by the weakening of the conjugal bond, such groups kept their matrilineal systems through the process of emergence of complex, stratified society. In other places, perhaps, the contradiction between matrilineal inheritance and male-controlled private property was resolved by a shift to bilateral or patrilineal inheritance. But in the absence of social history this must remain a conjecture.

Far more interesting for this kind of analysis are those situations, also quite rare, where a society with a bilateral inheritance ideology is pushed toward the matrilineal end of the continuum by environmental or economic constraints. Three obvious cases of this are reported from Greece and one from Galicia. Let us first look at the Greek cases. I already mentioned the system on the island of "Piyi" described by Casselberry and Valavanes (1976) where residence was often matrilocal with respect to household, usually "matrilocal" with respect to village in a neolocal household, and where most of the heritable property (house and productive vegetable gardens) was given as "dowry" at the time of the daughter's marriage. On another island, Kalymnos of the Sponge Fishermen, dowry seems to have exhausted most of the family's resources (Bernard 1976:296), though the author gives no precise information as to what percentage of the inheritance it formed, and anyway these were maritime people who did not depend on land for livelihood. In both these communities there was much seasonal migration of men, either as laborers or as sponge divers, and it may be that matrilocality and the transmission of such property as gardens and houses, along with the marriage pattern, made sense for communities in which the women formed the core of the stable population, while men were away much of the time. Another Greek community is perhaps more conclusive in this regard: in the recently depopulated Maniot (southern Peloponnesian) community of Aspidea (Allen 1976) there was a recent shift from equal inheritance to a matrilineal bias, and from virilocal to uxorilocal residence, with the declining importance of agriculture and the rise in male migrant labor.

The other case of a shift toward matrilineal inheritance is that of the Galician fisherfolk and some farmers (Lisón-Tolosana 1976:197). Here we see a pattern similar to that in Greece; whereas Galician farmers displayed a patrilineal bias in their inheritance, the fisherfolk on the coast made the daughter the successor and passed the inheritance through her. Again, the relatively mobile existence of fishermen and the relatively stable residential community of fishwives may well account for this shift toward the matrilineal. Even in those areas of Galicia where farming combined with a shift in the direction of matrilineal inheritance, out-migration of males for labor purposes was very common (Lisón-Tolosana 1971:272).

Finally we should mention Thailand. There is evidence (Keyes 1975:53; Piker 1975:308-9; Tambiah 1970:12) that inheritance was once almost exclusively matrilineal in all parts of Thailand. Since the 19th century in Central Thailand, however, and in the middle of the 20th in the North and Northeast, there has been a shift toward bilateral inheritance while maintaining matrilocal residence (Keyes 1977:141; Tambiah 1970:12). This seems puzzling until we realize that, before the shift, it was usually possible in most places for a man who did not come into enough land through his wife's inheritance to obtain more by pioneering. When all the available land had come under cultivation, however, and population began to pressure the land, it was more important to men to assure themselves supplies of land not dependent on their marriages, so they began to claim equal shares with their sisters. There is also at least indirect evidence of a similar shift in northern Thailand: Keyes (1977:141) states that the traditional pattern there was matrilineal inheritance, while Potter (1978:53) states that the men in her family case study all received shares of their own parents' inheritance.

Having spoken about intra-societal variation between matrilineal and bilateral, or between matrilineal and patrilineal inheritance, I now turn to those societies which show variation between the two more common forms, patrilineal and bilateral inheritance. Much of the difference here is explicable in terms of economically-based stratification and participation in a money economy, which tend to push systems toward significant dowry, and also tend to push them from patrilineal toward bilateral inheritance. This is particularly true in systems where there are no organized patrilineal extended kinship groups, though it can also happen where such groups are present. Let us take some examples.

In both southern and central Italy, there seems to have been effectively patrilineal inheritance of productive goods in the 19th century. By the early 20th century, however, there seems to have been a general shift to bilateral inheritance, this shift coinciding with the monetization and commercialization of the Italian agricultural economy (John Davis 1973:87-90). The same process also took place in Hungary, though perhaps somewhat later. But by the period immediately preceding collectivization of land in the 1960s, what had been a patrilineal system had become a bilateral one, despite the continued preference for patrilocal residence (Fél and Hofer 1969:256). The Sarakatsani shepherds of western Greece moved at least part way along the dimension from patrilineal to bilateral inheritance in the middle of the 20th century: dowries, previously including only household goods, began to include a large number of sheep at that time.

Examples could be added, but the trend is clear: entrance into a modern economy means social status based on wealth, or at the very least, considerations of wealth as important in a family's standing and its future. And as such, all members of the family must be provided for. But another explanation also presents itself, and needs to be dealt with before we can proceed. In many parts of Europe in the 19th century, legal codes were enacted prescribing bilateral inheritance. Napoleon's reforms certainly played some part here, but it should also be noted that in some places, such as Italy, the Napoleonic reforms were rescinded after his defeat, and partible inheritance did not become universal until later in the century (John Davis 1976:88-9; Silverman 1975:81). Where the introduction of laws of bilateral inheritance might be seen as an attempt to modernize, or to raise the status of daughters or wives, it thus seems clear that such measures, in and of themselves, are not enough.

The Nationalist government of China also introduced such laws in the 1920s (Fei 1939:79-82) and even if that government's inability to enforce those laws while it ruled portions of the Chinese mainland may be explained simply by the fact that it was unable to enforce many laws of any kind during that time, it is striking that the people of rural Taiwan, even in the 1980s, went to great lengths to circumvent the law of bilateral inheritance: before a woman could marry, she had to sign a statement legally relinquishing her rights to her natal family's land. When we consider that even in the People's Republic, what property a family does own (and this cannot include land, which is still collectively owned, though it is now usually privately worked) passes to sons under a similar arrangement, we must conclude that simple passage of a law of bilateral inheritance is insufficient to actually establish that system in local custom. It must be, after all, the kind of economic forces which we have seen as crucial in accounting for others kinds of variation in family organization. But at the same time, economic factors, in and of themselves, appear to be no more sufficient than changing the law. After all, rural Taiwan is now part of a commercial capitalist economy. Perhaps what is happening there is that the increased value of dowries, even if they do not include land or capital goods, in effect bring the Taiwanese inheritance system closer to the bilateral pole than was formerly the case. If this is true, we might well cite the patrilineal kinship ideology as a reason why inheritance has not become more equal than it has. The issue is not resolved, but we can probably say with confidence that a money economy and legal action have both tended to push formerly patrilineal inheritance systems in a bilateral direction, but that patrilineal kinship ideologies have tended to retard that movement.

Residence

Within that group of systems where marital residence is something else than neolocal, that is, where married couples go to live with one set of parents or the other, which set do they go to live with? The relationship to the former dimension is obvious: in general, matrilocal residence implies matrilineal inheritance, and as a matter of fact, avunculocal residence can only exist with matrilineal inheritance or, at that very least, with matrilineal descent. But there are problems, and there is no exact correspondence in complex societies between inheritance and residence patterns. We find matrilocal, patrilocal, and ambilocal systems in concert with various degrees of unilateral and bilateral inheritance and, as a matter of fact, even neolocal residence is known to occur with either patrilineal or bilateral inheritance. So we need to treat this aspect of the dimension separately

We can begin parallel to our last section, discussing factors pushing a system toward matrilocal residence. The clearest examples here come from Galicia and Greece, the very places where we found *de facto* matrilineally biased inheritance in the absence of an ideology of matrilineal descent. All the Greek cases (Casselberry and Valavanes 1976; Bernard 1976; Allen 1976) involved males absent from the community for a long period of time, either as migrant laborers or as fishermen. Similarly, the matrilocal Galicians were the fishing people as well. We thus have an explicit contrast in two parts of Europe between predominantly virilocal or neolocal farmers and predominantly matrilocal fishing people, a contrast probably best explained by the fact that, with males absent for long periods of time, it makes more sense for the females to form the core of the domestic group. Since a domestic core of mother-in-law and daughter-in-law, where it exists, inevitably generates friction, and since the house, inhabited by the women, is not intimately tied to the sources of income, brought in mostly (though not entirely) by men, it makes sense to form a female core of mothers and daughters, and this is just what is done. Important to remember here, too, is that the Greeks and Galicians are both bilateral in their basic kinship institutions; Chinese fishers never, as far as we know (Wang 1971; Ward 1966; Diamond 1969) lived matrilocally.

Aside from these few cases, however, stem family systems have been overwhelmingly patrilocal, at least by preference (the occasional uxorilocal marriage in a family with no sons does not concern us here). In Britain, southern France, Slovenia, Ireland, most of Galicia, Catalonia, and Japan residence was patrilocal, and this went along with patrilineal inheritance of agricultural land, which in all these societies was worked primarily by males. These cases all stand in contrast to those mentioned in the previous paragraph: where there is an intimate connection between the land and the house, and the males work the land, they will furnish the continuity in the household as well.

Ambilocal stem systems, the third possible type, are unfortunately quite rare, and I have examined no cases in which ambilocality clearly contrasts with patrilocality or matrilocality in the same society. In Douglass' study of two Basque villages, he notes that a preference for male primogeniture and virilocal residence in Murçlaġa was correlated with nucleated farm settlements and cooperation between males laboring on farms; in nearby Echalar, a statistically more evenly ambilocal residence pattern, with the resident child inheriting, was correlated with dispersed farmsteads and the lack of settlements as corporate groups (1975:50-70); this is certainly an effect of economic conditions on the household, but in the absence of comparable cases, I cannot posit any general principles at work here.

Turning to joint family systems, again there is surprisingly little basis for comparison. True ambilocal joint families, sharing in production and consumption, appear not to have existed;[1] the only species of joint families are patrilocal, matrilocal and, among a few 18th century Tiyyars, avunculocal. And matrilocal joint families are found in only a few places, all of them in conjunction with matrilineal inheritance. All other joint families are patrilocal, found in conjunction with both patrilineal and bilateral inheritance patterns and occasionally, as in the Baltic estates, even in conjunction with impartible patrilineal inheritance. It thus appears that joint family systems will be patrilocal except in the case of matrilineal inheritance, and that patrilocal joint families are thus better explained in opposition to nuclear families than in contrast to joint families of some other type.

Inclusion or Restriction of Juniors

This dimension divides into two aspects—a residential one ranging from single-succession to breakup of the corporation, and an inheritance one ranging from impartible to partible inheritance. In order to understand these dimensions we have to consider the advantages or disadvantages to a family in pursuing one or the other of these strategies. If a family keeps itself and its estate intact, transmitting them to a single successor and heir, it has preserved the integrity of a functioning social and economic unit— the family and its resources. This strategy has the disadvantage, at the same time, of providing for some offspring better than for others. The opposite strategy, fragmenting the household and parting the inheritance, has the disadvantage of destroying the working unit but the advantage of providing for all children equally. We should expect, then, that situations in which the goal of keeping the holding intact is more important should push a system toward the impartible/single-succession pole, while situations in which the goal of taking care of all children is more important should push a system toward the partible/fragmentation pole.Such is in fact the case in many societies. We can begin, for example, in Lower Saxony in the 17th century. Here in the neighboring districts of Calenberg and Göttingen we find two quite different family systems. In Calenberg inheritance was impartible, and the family usually passed through a stem phase in each generation—65% of the families in the 1689 tax lists for this area were in fact of the stem form (Berkner 1976:87). By contrast, in neighboring Göttingen, where inheritance was partible, 90% of the families in the same year were of the nuclear type, with only 6% stem families (Berkner 1976:87). It might appear that this is a situation in which different districts simply have different customs, but in fact it is more interesting than that. We find that in Calenberg almost all the land was held in *Meierrecht*, a kind of tenancy which prevented partition. In Göttingen, on the other hand, most of the land was held in one or another form of free tenure and could be divided legally. And where the peasants were free to divide their land they did so, thus providing for all their children and producing what was in fact a purely nuclear-family cycle (Berkner 1976:95).

This case is relatively straightforward—German peasants in these areas divided their land when they could, but kept it intact and passed it to a single heir when that was what the terms of their tenancy contracts required. More interesting perhaps are cases in which the inheritance ideology clearly specifies partition or remaining intact but the actual practice reveals a wide range, depending entirely on the economic circumstances. We can illustrate this clearly by comparing the cases of China and Japan. In China, as mentioned earlier, the customary law everywhere was equal inheritance among sons. In the early 20th century in the area of Taiwan where I conducted field research, however, this kind of equal inheritance often did not come about in fact. Poorer families with many sons were always on the lookout for ways to provide for some of them without splitting up the small amounts of property (sometimes tea gardens, sometimes just houses and movable property) that they had. As a result, poor families often passed their meager property to one son only. Another would marry into a family with an inheriting daughter, or might be apprenticed to a merchant or artisan family in a nearby town. Sons who left the family in such ways usually did so without any claim on the family's property, thus producing the effect, in practice, of transmissal to a single heir even though all the sons, if they did remain, had equal rights to the inheritance. A similar situation can be observed in mid-century Greece (Friedl 1962:48) where educational expenses could legally be deducted from the son's share, so that he received in fact only a nominal portion of the estate. And in postwar rural Korea, with its incompletely partible system, we find remote mountain villages where all but one son routinely migrated out and never formed joint families with their brothers. In the village studied by Sorensen (1988:204) there had not been a single joint family for over ten years.

If we look at premodern Japan, by contrast, we can see exactly the inverse situation. It will be recalled that even though the household was indivisible, it was possible to divide the patrimony and form a branch household (*bunke*) attached to the share which had been divided off. In some villages, *bunke* were created in practically every case in which a household had more than one son; they tended to form networks of hierarchical relationships between households, known as *dozoku*. These *dozoku* were not found everywhere, however; according to Nakane (1967:119-1230) they existed only in villages with particular economic conditions, namely enough available resources to support the branch households. In villages dependent on such non-agricultural pursuits as fishing and forestry, *dozuku*, and hence *bunke*, were also seldom formed, because economic opportunities were more flexible in occupations not tied to particular plots of land. In short, where surplus children had to be taken care of locally or not at all, and where sufficient resources were available, inheritance was regularly parted. But where there were no resources available, or where other occupations were open, inheritance remained impartible. The same seems to have been the case in some parts of Medieval England, where taking assarts (newly reclaimed land) sometimes allowed a non-successor son to inherit a place in the village.

A final example of economic conditions producing a local difference between partition of inheritance and keeping it intact, and in this case also producing a similar difference between a stem family cycle and, in this instance a nuclear family cycle, comes from the South Italian town of Matera (Tentori 1976). The population of this town was divided into two discrete classes, the *signori*, or landholders, and the peasantry, most of them tenants working for a *signor*. The *signori* practiced, into the postwar period, what in effect was a stem-family, impartible inheritance system, in which formerly only one son was allowed to marry (Tentori 1976:275), thus keeping the family estate intact. In more recent times younger sons still found difficulty marrying, though most of them entered the professions. The peasants and shepherds, on the other hand, had no propertied estate to worry about splitting up or not, and expected all children to marry and to set up independent nuclear families upon their marriages.

All these cases, then, are variations on a single pattern in which certain kinds of economic or legal forces made it advisable or necessary to keep holdings intact, thus pushing inheritance systems toward the impartible pole, while other kinds of forces made such a consideration much less important and allowed people to provide for all their children by some sort of partible inheritance. In this light, I think Goldschmidt and Kunkel were correct, at a rather simple level, to hypothesize that impartible inheritance is correlated with feudal-type systems in which landholdings are legally impartible at the will of the lord, thus allowing the lord to maintain stable relations with a number of vassals or retainers (1971:1065). Such was indeed the case in Medieval England, where the lord's permission had to be secured in order to part an estate held in villeinage (Homans 1941:200-1), in the case of Calenberg described above, and in that of the Baltic serf families, where the will of the lord to keep the holdings intact meant that even what was once a joint family eventually had to break up and have its entire estate inherited by one of the brothers. But this is only one kind of situation which would push a system toward impartibility. After all, neither the *signori* of Matera nor the poor Chinese tea-growers were acting in response to anything but economic good sense when they maneuvered around their societies' partible inheritance ideologies to keep their holdings intact. That they had to resort to special maneuvers (keeping younger sons celibate in Matera; sending sons off to be apprenticed in Taiwan) shows the strength of the partible inheritance ideology itself.

Time of Transfer

Residence

We can pass over our third dimension, that of participation in single or multiple marriages, because multiple marriages are rare in the C-cluster., Instead we move on to our fourth dimension: the time of transfer of rights and duties from the senior to the junior generation. This, in its residential aspect, which I will consider first, manifests itself as variation from neolocal residence, in which a couple establishes a new household upon marriage, to forms in which married couples live with members of the senior generation until the elders' death.

This residential aspect of the dimension has several possible manifestations, but some of these are not important empirically. In general, impartible inheritance is found with stem-family cycles, and stem-family cycles preclude, logically and by definition, any system of neolocal residence. The stem family, with impartible inheritance, is predicated on the continuity of the family unit, and thus the inheriting child necessarily takes up residence with his or her parents and remains with them throughout their lives. Even where the parents may move into separate quarters such as the "West Room" of the early 20th century West Irish peasants (Arensberg and Kimball 1968:129) or the "Inkyo house" found in some parts of Japan (Nakane 1967:11-13) they remain part of the same procuring and processing unit. Where we find meaningful variation along this dimension, then, is within that group of family systems which are ultimately divisible—at one extreme through the formation of joint families which eventually divide, through to the other extreme of formation of nuclear families upon marriage. Another way to look at this variation is to examine the percentage of time in each generation that a typical family in a particular system spends in a joint state, ranging from 100% in cases where families remain joint until children of the jointly residing siblings are married to 0% in cases where nuclear families are formed upon marriage. (In fact, of course, in no system will we ever find 100% joint families in a census, because there will be some families which produce fewer than two children of the sex that customarily resides with the parents.)

Variation along this dimension is reasonably easy to understand in terms similar to those used to explain variation from single-successor to divisible systems; there are certain economic imperatives that keep a family together. These imperatives can be either those of labor, or capital, or both, depending on the particular situation. Let us consider some examples which will illustrate this point, beginning with a contrast drawn by Silverman (1968,

1975) between central and southern Italy, both of which have operated under the Italian law of equal inheritance since 1861 (Silverman 1975:82). In central Italy, Silverman explains, most land was held under a relatively stable system of sharecropping known as *mezzadria*, in which families took out long-term leases on agricultural estates, paying their *padrone* one half of the crop. In a situation of this sort, the more labor available in the family the larger and more efficient a *mezzadria* it could manage. The ideal, then, was for all the sons of a family to bring their brides into their natal household and form a joint family; if this was not feasible, or if there was only one son, still a stem family could be formed. That this imperative worked in response to the particular economic situation of the family is evident upon examination of the percentages of families of particular occupations in the town of Montecastello who were living in stem or joint families in 1960. *Mezzadri*, who needed to pool family labor to greatest advantage, had 52.6% stem or joint families and merchants, to whom it would be advantageous to pool capital, had 65%. By contrast, only 12% of the professionals and 18% of the artisans and laborers were living in joint or stem family households, reflecting a much lesser tendency to form such households (Silverman 1975:179-85).

The situation in the Italian South was considerably different. Here, Silverman reports, land came to farmers not in integrated, fairly large units, but in independent, small parcels from several different landlords (Silverman 1968:12-14). Here another kind of economic imperative was at work: the imperative to maintain flexibility in the relationship of labor to land. For this reason, the nuclear family, formed upon marriage, was almost universally the rule in most parts of southern Italy and Sicily (Silverman 1968:12-14; John Davis 1973:33; Gower Chapman 1971:77-9; Cronin 1970:45; Banfield 1958).

Variation along the same dimension occurred in China, and can be explained by resort to similar factors. We find in many studies of the Chinese family that large extended families tended to be more typical of the elite classes or at least of the wealthier peasants in communities where no members of the elite resided (M. Cohen 1970:36; Gamble 1954:84; Fei 1939:28-29; Wolf and Huang 1980:67) and it is not necessary to look far to find the reasons why. They are perhaps best illustrated in Cohen's study of tobacco farmers and non-tobacco farmers in a Hakka-speaking village in Southern Taiwan in the 1960s (1968; 1976). In this village, people who grew tobacco under government license lived side by side with those who had no such license; because people lost their license if they did not cultivate, and because new licenses were difficult to obtain, these groups remained relatively stable for many years. And when we look at the distribution of family types among the two kinds of farm families we find that the percentage of joint families among the tobacco growers was 46%, while among the non-tobacco growers only 16% of the families were of the joint form.

Since nearly all families went through at least a brief joint phase in their developmental cycle if they had the requisite personnel, what we see here is a contrast between those who remained in a joint phase for longer, delaying the transfer of property rights until quite late in the life cycle, and those who transferred the rights early, shortening the joint phase of the family. And when we look at the labor requirements of tobacco we understand why—it required very heavy labor, much of which could be done by either males or females, during short but intense peak seasons. Families who stayed together in the joint form could use all but one able bodied adult (a woman who did the housework) in the tobacco harvest and processing, while those who split were forced to allot one woman's labor per family to housework and had to make up their agricultural deficit with hired labor, thus cutting into their profits. So tobacco-growing families stayed together. For families that grew only rice, however, the labor imperatives were not so pressing, and they could divide their families earlier without experiencing severe economic loss (Cohen 1968:167). It is interesting to note also that among the non-tobacco growing families those who did go through a fairly long joint phase in their cycles were those who had mercantile interest in addition to their farms, whose family economy is diversified. These families found it advantageous to stay together, not only in the allotment of labor but in the pooling of capital for possible expansion and to absorb losses. When we think that most elite families in traditional China had diversified economic interests, usually including commerce of some sort (Lippitt 1978:286-87) we understand why investigators found a larger percentage of joint families among the Chinese elite: not because they were wealthy *per se*, but because they had diversified economies, they tended to stay together.

Other examples from Chinese society make this point even more clear. Ward (1966), for example, cites data from her study of a fishing village in Hong Kong to show that purse-seine fishermen who operated with larger boats and larger crews had more complex families (a joint phase in the cycle) than did the long-line fishermen whose nuclear family cycle was a response to the needs for small crews on small boats. Wang (1971) reports a study of another fishing community in which the desirability for flexibility in forming crews led to a family cycle in which each son formed an independent nuclear family: there were never any joint families in this community because the cycle simply did not pass through a joint phase.

These are merely detailed examples of a pattern which seems to have held worldwide until the decline of property in the later phases of the C- to M- transition: where there was partible inheritance and variation from early to late transfer of property rights, the wealthier classes, who were usually those with more diversified holdings or perhaps the only ones with any holdings at all, tended to hold their joint families together longer. Brief examples which might be cited come from Vilyatpur in the Punjab (Kessinger 1974:200) where laborers with no property had by far the highest percentage of simple families in a census; from Serbia, where large holdings and efficient agriculture are reported to have increased the size to which patrilocal joint families expanded (Halpern 1972:405; Hammel 1972:370-1) and even from the famous matrilineal groups of Kerala. Here, for example among the matrilineal Mappillas, the wealthier classes, who relied on landholdings, persisted in forming joint families to a much greater degree than did the middle and lower classes who entered the modern economy in small business or as wage laborers (Gough 1961b:423). Even among the lowly Tiyyars it was those who could obtain long-term land leases from their Nayar overlords who actually formed avunculocal extended families (Gough 1961a:407).

Property and Inheritance

We turn now to consider the time of transmission of *property* rights; which usually means the giving or not giving of dowry.[2] Goody has maintained that the giving of dowry (for this is much more common than the dowering of the groom) is one of the most common characteristics of diverging devolution, in which male property is transmitted through both sexes (1976:8). But, as mentioned in Chapter 19, when we actually look at a wide range of variation among family forms in complex societies, we find great discrepancies in the amount of property that actually accompanies an outmarrying daughter or son upon marriage. There seems to have been no complex society in which a bride or groom left the natal household to form a conjugal household without at least some clothing, furniture, or cooking pots, but there is a wide variation between those systems in which dowry was merely given in movables and those in which it actually included productive property such as land or business capital. There is no sharp distinction here, particularly in societies where land and other goods are easily convertible into one another in terms of cash value to those of greater value. And as a matter of fact there does seem to be a relatively clear pattern: dowry is a significant portion of family resources in those cases where families are concerned to establish their relative prestige in the community, and is not given, or is much smaller, where such considerations are not important. The role of the dowry in securing a prestigious match for a family's daughter is well illustrated in Ved Mehta's account of his mother's marriage negotiations, presented in the Prelude to Part VI. Liking what she sees from her furtive perch behind the curtain, she is confronted head on with the need to balance material goods and family status in order for the marriage to go forward.

The primary purpose of dowry thus seems to be the making of a match—both marrying one's daughter to a suitable station and impressing the community with the ability of one's family to provide for its own. I remember being laughed at as a stupid foreigner during my field research when I did not yet understand this point. A young woman in the village where I lived was to be married the next day to a man from the local town, and the groom's brothers had come, as is the local custom, to pick up the dowry. They had, however, not come in proper style. For one thing, they had ridden in the truck on which the goods were to be transported, rather than hiring a separate taxicab to precede the dowry itself. And the truck they had brought was a rather ragged, smallish one; it was not clear whether it would hold all the furniture, clothing, motorcycle, television, refrigerator, sewing machine, stereo set, gas range, small appliances, grandfather clocks and other goods which the bride's brothers had assembled at so much expense. When I suggested they could make two trips, well...

We can hypothesize from this and from other instances of dowry-giving that dowry will be more likely to occur, and will be bigger and more important, when the intermarrying parties are part of a system of social inequality in which relative wealth plays a part and where there might be some question as to their relative status. (This is true whether the alternative to a large dowry is a small dowry with no horizontal exchange of marriage gifts or whether it is a horizontal exchange of the bridewealth type; dowry as an alternative to bridewealth is discussed as part of the next dimension below.) We can illustrate this with reference to intra-societal variation in several societies; let us begin with some northern Mediterranean societies, examining the circumstances which give rise to large dowries (often in land) or small dowries consisting of a trousseau, perhaps furniture or a house, but no productive property.

We can begin with the simplest case, that of the late Franco era in the regions of Spain subject to the inheritance laws of Castile. Here four ethnographic case studies will illustrate our point quite nicely. In the mountain community of Valdemara, studied by Freeman (1970), there was little economic distinction among the households of the community, and in fact the *común de vecinos* itself exercised certain economic rights in common, such as the grazing of all *vecinos'* stock on fallow fields and the communal ownership of a threshing machine purchased in 1965. Here there was no distribution of productive property at the time of marriage—all inheritance came at the death of the parents. The daughter received linen and furniture as a marriage portion, and might bring clothes to the nuclear family which she and her husband established. The son was given usufruct to some plots of land, but had to pay rent to his father, who retained ownership (Freeman

1970:73). Similar customs obtained in the relatively egalitarian community of Becedes in the Sierra de Bejar, described by Brandes. Here the bridegroom's family gave some jewelry to the bride, and the bride and groom both contributed to the establishment of the conjugal household, usually at the time of marriage (Brandes 1975:165). But the parents retained the land until they died: even if a father could no longer work his land he retained ownership and sharecropped it with his children's families (Brandes 1975:120-1).

A third case of the absence of significant dowry is even more interesting—it concerns the pueblo of "Alcalá de la Sierra," described by Pitt-Rivers. Here, although there were considerable variations in wealth among village families (Pitt-Rivers 1961:34-46), there was at the same time "a strong reluctance to accord superior status to [members of the pueblo] who are economically superior" (Pitt-Rivers 1961:65). And in this community, dowry, though not unknown, was rare; in fact it was quite unusual for a husband or wife to have any productive property from parents while the parents were still alive (Pitt Rivers 1961:99). It was not the fact of economic distinctions, but the recognition that such distinctions conferred social status, that gave rise to the dowry system.

The confirmation of this relationship, at least in Spain, comes from the community of Belmonte de los Caballeros, in Aragón. Here concentration of landownership in a few hands led to a stratified system of owners and sharecropping tenants, with apparently no countervailing tendency toward ignoring these economic distinctions. And here dowry was crucially important for making a good marriage. A son had to receive his rights to a plot of land outright in order to be married, and even though a daughter was only *required* to bring furnishings and linen to the marriage, her family often included a plot of land in her portion as well, "so as not to be outdone" (Lisón-Tolosana 1966:158). It is also important here to realize that marriage portions were a direct expression of social status. If one partner to the marriage, for example, had higher education, that could in a sense become part of the marriage portion, substituting for the property which would otherwise be given (Lisón-Tolosana 1966:161).

It is important to realize that, in all these Spanish communities, inheritance was, by law and custom, equal and bilateral. It is not a question of transmission of property through females—that happened in all these places—but of the timing of the transmission and of the assertion and validation of a family's status in the community by the display of wealth that it could give with its daughter or son in marriage.

If we turn from Spain to Greece we find that the relationship between dowry and economic stratification was less clear: those communities where dowry is reported to have constituted the *majority* of the inheritance were island villages with uxorilocal residence (Bernard 1976; Allen 1976;

Casselberry and Valavanes 1976:215). In other island communities where residence was virilocal or neolocal, dowry tended to be small and to consist of movables; these communities also appear to have been relatively egalitarian, as does the remote mountain village of Ambeli studied by du Boulay (1974:20; see also Dubisch 1976:318, 321; Kenna 1976:349; Peristiany 1968). Only in Friedl's Vasilika (1962) does there appear to have been a significant dowry associated with an outmarrying daughter, and in this community negotiation for dowry appears to have been a part of the families' jockeying for wealth and social position (1962:54). We thus do not receive strong confirmation for the relationship between dowry and economically-based stratification, but what data do exist seem to support the hypothesis.

For a final brief example, we can turn to Italy, where every single community or social group which I found documented practiced dowry in land or, where there was no land, movable dowry as a significant portion of a family's resources, explicitly connected in every case with establishing the relative position of the families in an economically stratified community. Italy thus offers a partial confirmation of this relationship, though a full confirmation would have to await data on what kinds of Italian families did not give significant dowry (Cronin 1970:45; Gower Chapman 1971:97; Tentori 1976:277; John Davis 1977:301; Silverman 1975:82; James Davis 1975:106). It is interesting to note that, according to John Davis, land and house dowries, common in the mid-20th century in the community of Pisticci in the Potenza, were a result of entrance of the village into a money economy: only movable marriage portions were given in the early 19th century (1977:88-89).

Horizontal and Vertical Marriage Payments

We turn now to our next dimension, and take up dowry again, this time not as an alternative to inheritance exclusively *mortis causa*, but as an alternative to the horizontal transfer of marriage gifts, that is to say bridewealth. In the cases to follow, we will see a typical pattern in which there was always a gift from the groom's family to the bride's family before the wedding. The crucial dimension of variation, however, is embodied in whether this gift then became part of a circulating fund, used by the bride's parents to find themselves a daughter-in-law, in which case the transfer of property became bridewealth, or whether the gift to the bride's parents was then passed on to the bridal couple, in which case it became the indirect part of a dowry (Goody 1972:20). It is important to realize, too, that this is no more a dichotomy than any other dimension: it is possible for *part* of the betrothal gift to be retained or circulated by the bride's parents while the other part is passed on to the couple as dowry.[3] It should also be noted that societies where there is a variation extending from near the bridewealth to near the dowry end of the dimension are almost always those with an ideology of patrilineal descent. Perhaps because of this, they display less *tendency* than do the purely bilateral societies to include land as part of a dowry, though there are certainly cases in such societies where land is included. So when we talk about a continuum from nearly pure bridewealth to large dowry in such societies, the dowry, though lavish, usually consists entirely of movable goods. As mentioned before, however, the distinction between land and movables becomes less important the more a money economy allows the conversion of one kind of value into the other.

Looking, then, at such societies, we can see a clear association between large dowries and a system of economically-based social stratification, and can often see this association as part of a historical process. Aside from long term trends, such as that documented by Hughes from bridewealth among the ancient Germanic tribes to *Morgengabe*, or a gift from the groom's family to the bride, in medieval times, to dowry as we know it in the commercial and aristocratic houses of the late middle ages (Hughes 1978), we also find short-term historical trends which exhibit both a transition from bridewealth to dowry and, in one special case, the reverse process.

First, there seem to be a number of societies in which dowry was originally an urban phenomenon, but spread to the countryside with the direct entrance of a peasant class into a system of social stratification based on wealth and including some degree of mobility. In Japan, for example, peasants seem to have paid very little if any dowry during the Tokugawa and early Meiji periods—peasants were part of a legally defined class which, as long as it remained in the rural areas, had little possibility of economic mobility. But with the rise of industrial capitalism in Japan, the custom of dowry, which had been developed in the cities (Nakane 1967:153n), spread to the rural areas until, in some communities at least, the *yuino*, or betrothal gift, which had once been something like a bridewealth (Nakane 1967:153n 153), had become but a minor indirect part of the dowry: Smith (1978:193) gives a ratio of *yuino* to dowry of about 1:5 in 1975.

In the Balkans, we find a similar process going on. In very early times (14th century) we find the only evidence of dowry to be in cases where women with no brothers nevertheless married virilocally: this is not really diverging inheritance from the standpoint of their own individual families (Hammel 1980:249). In more modern times dowry in land reached the villages of Serbia. Whereas whatever goods were given with the bride in 1870 consisted chiefly of money and movables, by the middle of the 20th century some land was given as part of a marriage portion (Halpern and Halpern 1972:18). Halpern (1967:192) attributes the growth of dowry in real property to "Western influence," but it seems more reasonable here to attribute it to the growth of a money economy, in which households' relative prestige came to be at least partly determined by how much wealth they controlled and could pass on to their daughters.

Further cases continue to strengthen this point. I mentioned previously the rather striking fact that apparently almost nowhere among Arab peasants or pastoralists is the Islamic law, which prescribes single shares for daughters and double shares for sons, actually followed. The closest we can find to a large dowry for a bride comes from an urban setting (Van Ess 1961:27) and it may be noteworthy in this regard also that Islamic law itself was developed in a merchant society, not among the pastoralist tribes (Rahman 1979:12).

Similar relationships between dowry and economic stratification are found in Turkey, another country with patrilineal descent. According to Stirling's account of the villages Sakaltutan and Elbasi, a bride did bring a trousseau to her marriage (it would be difficult to conceive of patrilocal marriage in a complex society without this), but that the value of the trousseau was outweighed by the "bridewealth" given to her family by the family of the groom. In the nearby town of Kayseri, however, there was a gift in gold from the groom's parents to the bride herself (a vertical marriage transaction) whose value outweighed that of the "brideprice" (Stirling 1965:186). When we turn to the town of Tutunelli in southwestern Turkey, we find that the bride brought a house to the marriage and that the groom's family furnished that house as well as giving the bride substantial gifts. Some inheritance of productive property went to sons and daughters at their marriages, while the rest waited until the death of the parents (Benedict 1976:234-6). I would suggest that this town-country difference on the scale from bridewealth to dowry is another example of the association between dowry and economic stratification as a basis for prestige. Stirling tells us that in the villages there remained into the postwar period certain forms of communal pasturage and that land, while privately owned, was not sold (Stirling 1965:47-9). This would seem much less likely, at the very least, to be a field for economically based stratification than would the heterogenous commercial environment of the towns.

Finally, let us examine the evidence from Tambiah's detailed article on dowry and women's property rights in South Asia (1972). He tells us that both the classical legal sources and modern custom recognize marriages with dowry and marriages by brideprice, but that in the classical legal sources, castes ranking below Brahmins were not allowed to marry with dowry (1972:69) while even in modern custom, though economic considerations may dictate the choice of one form of marriage or another, it is only in giving the dowry with the bride that a family can contract a totally prestigious marriage.

So far, I have given both diachronic examples of a change from bridewealth to dowry and synchronic comparisons which I consider to be parallel—two communities with conditions parallel to those existing at two different times in the diachronic examples. One final case ought to clinch my point—a case in which a system based on indirect dowry moved back to bridewealth with the elimination of economically-based social stratification, and then saw dowry revive once again when stratification once more came to be based on wealth. This comes from the Chinese People's Republic—specifically the southern Province of Guangdong before and after the era of collective agriculture from the middle 1950s to the late 1970s. Whereas in the 1940s and 50s in this area a betrothal gift to the bride's family usually covered only a part of the expenses of providing the bride with a suitable dowry, by the late 1960s and 1970s, with agriculture collectivized and social prestige based more on political than on wealth considerations, the dowry shrunk to a small trousseau while the betrothal gift became a true bridewealth, used by the bride's family to find a bride for its own son, and increased even in proportion to peasant income, which itself went up considerably in that period (Parish and Whyte 1978:181-8). When stratification based on wealth disappeared, so with it the dowry system.

In the 1980s, however, agriculture was decollectivized and both family farming (though without actual ownership of the land) and private entrepreneurial activity became common. With this change, those areas in which dowry had been a significant expense before collectivization revived the custom at even higher levels (Siu 1993). We thus see that the payment of dowry fluctuated almost in lock-step with state-imposed changes in economic organization and thus in the system of social status.

Thus we have demonstrated that both when dowry is contrasted to no dowry and inheritance at death (an aspect of the time of transfer dimension) and when dowry is contrasted to bridewealth (the vertical-horizontal marriage transaction dimension) dowry is associated with a family's desire to compete in a system of social stratification based at least partially upon wealth. But local economic stratification based on family wealth is contrasted with something quite different in each case. In the case of contrast between dowry and inheritance at death, both kinds of systems occur where families depend on their own property estates for their members' livelihood. The difference is, that in those cases where dowry is not given, the social status of the family relative to others in the local community is not dependent on the family's being able to display its relative wealth. Both these kinds of family systems belong firmly within the C-cluster, where families are dependent on their own estates for their living.

In the case of the contrast between dowry and bridewealth, however, the situation is more problematical. It appears that bridewealth (as opposed to indirect dowry) occurs in those communities on the periphery of complex societies, such as Arab nomads, in which extended kin groups, such as patrilineages, still retain significant rights, at least to the allocation of property, where the family estate has not come entirely into its own as the basis of livelihood. Such communities are, of course, fully part of the C-cluster, but they share only partially that characteristic of complex societies which makes most families dependent on propertied estates.

Household and Split Maintenance

This brings us to the other dimension that distinguishes family systems central to the C-cluster from some of the systems on its periphery: the dimension from household to split maintenance. It is apparent that this dimension runs conceptually parallel to that between transfer of rights at marriage and at death, but empirically the parallel is lost. Where split maintenance in complex societies is always associated with the absence of dowry, in fact most cases of the absence of dowry do not involve split maintenance, except in the perhaps trivial sense that an out-marrying spouse maintains claims on property he or she will eventually inherit. But this is not split *maintenance*. In the previous section of this essay, we discussed two cases of split maintenance: among some of the matrilineal groups of Kerala where an out-marrying spouse is actively provided with some of his or her livelihood by his or her own matrilineal group, and among most of the Arab nomads where a woman gives up her right to a share in the inheritance in return for the protection and potential maintenance, in case of divorce, from her brother. Thus one case concerns a matrilineal and the other a patrilineal system. And as fits the difference between patrilineal and matrilineal systems generally, there seem to be two different causes behind the appearance of split maintenance in these two cases.

First let us look at the Arab case. It is evident, as mentioned above, that this type of potential split maintenance was commonest among the Bedouin populations where private ownership of livestock, the main productive good, was not fully developed, and where patrilineages retained significant collective rights over property. Such retention of lineage rights must perforce weaken any possibility of stratification based on individual wealth, especially between members of one's own lineage. This is also consistent with the fact that in at least some cases a man's residual heirs were not his daughters but his collateral agnates (E. Marx 1967:185). What all this means is that the exclusive lineal transmission of property, the basic component of diverging devolution (Goody 1976:7), was not developed among these Arab groups. The lineage estate was more important than the conjugal estate, and the lineage rather than the family provided the residual heirs; it is thus quite natural that a woman's own patrilineage should have had some obligation to protect and maintain her, even after she was married. The C-cluster norm of the discrete, property-holding family was not fully developed here; like the family systems with true bridewealth, those with split maintenance were peripheral to the C-cluster.

The case of the matrilineal groups of Kerala, however, is almost the opposite. They are central to the cluster, but they were matrilineal. It is not that private property rights were still subordinate to lineage rights here, or that economically-based stratification was undeveloped, but rather that the development of private, or more accurately, family property rights controlled by males, along with economically based stratification, came into contradiction with (presumably pre-existing) matrilineal inheritance, and that to resolve the contradiction one or the other had to give way. This may have happened at other times in other places with matrilineal organization giving way; I have no evidence. But here the opposite happened and the conjugal estate, along with its major features such as dowry and household maintenance, was not allowed to develop fully.

The contradiction can be seen most clearly in the case of the matrilocal Mappillas. With matrilocal residence the heirs to property were not co-resident with the holders of that property, their mothers' brothers. If the heirs were to become fully incorporated into the families of their wives they would have been lost to their own matrilineal groups. In order for their own matrilineal groups to hang on to them, they had to continue the economic connection through support while they were matrilocally resident, eventual return upon assuming family headship, and of course the promise of inheritance. In the case of the avunculocal northern Nayar, the danger was not that a man would become too closely associated with his wife and father-in-law, but rather that he would become too closely associated with his children. In order for a matrilineal group to hang on to its youngest male members, who were living with their fathers rather than with their mothers' brothers, it also had to provide them with part of their support, which it did by continuing to support their mothers, even though their mothers were living, at least temporarily, in their husbands' groups. With the central Nayar, of course, the property-holding group was again congruent with the residential and budgeting group and the problem of household maintenance vs. split maintenance was again rendered irrelevant: naturally the matrilineage segment-cum-household maintained all its own members.

Conclusion

From the survey of C-cluster family systems in Chapters 18 and 19, and from the initial attempts in this chapter to demonstrate the factors that push C-cluster systems in one direction or another along the different dimensions of variation, several general points emerge, all of them stemming from what I have all along maintained to be the single most important characteristic of family systems in pre-industrial, complex societies: the fact that the majority of families depended for their subsistence livelihood on rights to private family property. This basic characteristic leads to some more concrete generalizations about the nature of the family in C-cluster societies.

First, family strategies in this cluster were a mix of adjustment and exclusion, with essentially no accretion. In every case where there was property, this made subsistence goods scarce, and so any family had to adjust its membership to the resources available, and these resources were primarily its property or property to which it had rights of access. In the C-cluster societies there was never an advantage to trying to expand one's family to the largest size possible: even in those peasant societies where high fertility was valued, eventually the family came up against the necessity of having to provide in some way or other for all its members, and this it could do by restricting transfer of rights to some members of the junior generation, or by dividing rights equally while trying to expand. But in no case was the expansion limited only by fertility; in every case the family was competing for resources with other families, and thus had to adjust its membership and its resources.

But C-cluster family systems were not simply adjustive, as were those of the B-cluster and of some of the smaller, less productive islands of the O-cluster. Since C-cluster family systems existed by definition in stratified societies, parents were concerned to marry their sons and daughters to wives and husbands of the appropriate stratum, that is a stratum very near or above one's own in the social hierarchy. This meant the strict regulation of sexuality, or where sexual relations were allowed (usually for males) with partners that ranked well below one's own family in the hierarchy, such relations had little chance of being legitimized as marriage or of having its children legitimized. As we saw with the most highly developed societies in the O-cluster, an exclusive family strategy is a way of validating and protecting one's social rank. The difference is that in the O-cluster, only a few of the highest ranking families had this concern, where in the C-cluster, class homogamy through the society is an indication that families at nearly all levels were concerned to preserve and defend their rank against those ranking lower. Thus in the C-cluster, adjustive and exclusive concerns belonged to the *same families*, rather than being divided up by stratum, which was the case in the highly ranked societies of Oceania.

The second generalization is that the requirements of adjustment and exclusion, which are first and foremost strategies for organizing management and transmission of property, gave rise in different groups within a society to different forms of the developmental cycle of the family group and different forms of the practice of property inheritance. Over and over, we have seen, for example, how wealth-based stratification within one community and the lack of such wealth-based stratification in another can explain the presence and absence of dowry in the two cases, or how the possibility of bringing new resources under cultivation, as opposed to the closing off of that possibility, led to more or less inclusive systems with regard to members of the junior generation. These and other kinds of trends held true in many different societies, societies whose basic ideologies of family organization varied greatly from one another. At the same time, it has been equally clear that the kinds of class variables, or, more broadly stated, the kinds of differences in strategic possibilities from one group to another, cannot explain all the variation between one society and another. Pre-existing cultural ideas about how families ought to function are always important, even when the actual functioning of families represents an adaptation of these ideologies to the concrete conditions of life that individual families or groups of families face.

The third generalization that we can draw is that some of the greatest differences within any C-cluster society were those between the propertied and the propertyless classes, as described above, for example, in reference to Tentori's work on the *signori* and the poor of Matera, or Gough's distinction between the developmental cycles of aristocratic, middle-class, and propertyless Mappillas. In practically any C-cluster society, the strictures placed on sexuality, marriage, and even emotional relationships by the relationship to property were noticeably loosened in the social groups within that society who held no property, and had to depend on the sale of labor for their livelihood. This simply constitutes a further demonstration that property holding, property management, and the possibilities of property inheritance are the most salient characteristics determining the form of the family developmental cycle in pre-modern, complex societies.

Notes

1. This is in marked contrast to the O-cluster, where such families were com-

mon. The difference may be attributable to the more flexible rules of inheritance of land access in the Oceanic societies.

2. Such transfer is not limited to transfer through *females*, which is implied in the term dowry, but can also include transfer through males. Spiro (1977:192) uses the term *dower* for such a transfer through males, and although there is probably same historical reason for not using that term (see John Davis 1977:184; Hughes 1978) it seems that most convenient one and I will use it here. For a fuller account of the variation in dowry in C-cluster societies, see Harrell and Dickey 1985.

3. This point has also been recognized by Silverman (1975:240n).

PART SEVEN

The M-Cluster:
Families in Modern Society

Prelude: The Debate About the Family

Barbara Dafoe Whitehead and Stephanie Coontz are two of the many U.S. writers engaging in the debate on the family.

> According to a growing body of social-scientific evidence, children in families disrupted by divorce and out-of-wedlock birth do worse than children in intact families on several measures of well-being. Children in single-parent families are six times as likely to be poor. They are also likely to stay poor longer. Twenty-two percent of children in one-parent families will experience poverty during childhood for seven years or more, as compared with only two percent of children in two-parent families. A 1988 survey by the National Center for Health Statistics found that children in single-parent families are two to three times as likely to have emotional and behavioral problems. They are also more likely to drop out of high school, to get pregnant as teenagers, to abuse drugs, and to be in trouble with the law. Compared with children in intact families, children from disrupted families are at a much higher risk for physical or sexual abuse...
>
> Despite this growing body of evidence, it is nearly impossible to discuss changes in family structure without provoking angry protest. Many people see the discussion as no more than an attack on struggling single mothers and their children: Why blame single mothers when they are doing the very best they can? After all, the decision to end a marriage or a relationship is wrenching, and few parents are indifferent to the painful burden this decision imposes on their children. Many take the perilous step toward single parenthood as a last resort, after their best efforts to hold a marriage together have failed. Consequently, it can seen particularly cruel and unfeeling to remind parents of the hardships their children might suffer as a result of family breakup. Other people believe that the dramatic changes in family structure, though regrettable, are impossible to reverse. Family breakup is an inevitable feature of American life, and anyone who thinks otherwise is indulging in nostalgia or trying to turn back the clock. Since these new family forms are here to stay, the reasoning goes, we must accord respect to single parents, not criticize them...
>
> [This is] a debate over deeply held and often conflicting values.

How do we begin to reconcile our long-standing belief in equality and diversity with an impressive body of evidence that suggests that not all family structures produce equal outcomes for children? How can we square traditional notions of public support for dependent women and children with a belief in women's right to pursue autonomy and independence in childbearing and child-rearing? How do we uphold the freedom of adults to pursue individual happiness in their private relationships and at the same time respond to the needs of children for stability, security, and permanence in their family lives? What do we do when the interests of adults and children conflict? These are the difficult issues at stake in the debate over family structure.

Barbara Dafoe Whitehead, "Dan Quayle Was Right," *Atlantic Monthly,* April 1993, pp. 47-48. Reprinted by permission.

I am not going to recite a litany of ways in which modern families have "abandoned traditional commitments," failed their children, or "lost their moral compass." Nor, however, will I offer soothing words about achieving "self-actualization," making divorce a "growth experience," or celebrating the "new family pluralism."

Most Americans welcome the expanded tolerance for alternative family forms and reproductive arrangements, although they are perplexed by the difficult boundary disputes that accompany new family definitions. Courts have been asked to decide what happens to fertilized ova if the partners split up and to rule whether sperm donors or surrogate mothers have higher rights. It is surely wrong to consider a woman who agrees to become a surrogate mother nothing more than a "carrier" for the fetus, but isn't the woman who made plans to receive that baby for nine months also an expectant mother? What about child-custody disputes between lesbian or gay partners? Do paternal grandparents have any right to visit their grandchildren if their daughter-in-law has custody and forbids the relationship to continue? How does a divorced woman relate to the "wife-in-law" she gains when her husband remarries, a woman who may actually take more care of her children on visitation weekends than her ex-husband does?

Contrary to the doomsday scenario, there have been undeniable gains associated with the democratization of family relations, the expansion of women's options outside the family and men's responsibilities within it, the erosion of ethnocentric and moralistic norms about what a proper family must be and do, and the new tolerance for unconventional family relations. But these gains have been accompanied by unanticipated and difficult new inequalities. While divorce has been a vital option for many, family dissolution often impoverishes women and children and, at least in our current social context, puts some youth "at risk." Even though many families as well as individual women benefit from women's new work opportunities, child care by profit-making companies, state agencies, and unregulated homeworkers all have major drawbacks. There seems to be an erosion of commitment to social obligations in general, and to children in particular, within America. There are no easy answers to such problems.

But then again, there never were...

Stephanie Coontz, *The Way We Never Were, American Families and the Nostalgia Trap.* (New York: Basic Books, 1992), pp. 1-4. Reprinted by permission.

21

Modernity and the Embattled Family

Modernity as a Social Type

The most recent great transformation, based on the growth of industry and science, has created a new form of society in the nineteenth and twentieth centuries, and with it a new form of family organization. I choose to call these both by the superficially fuzzy adjective "modern," and to designate the cluster of family systems treated in this chapter as the M- (for modern) cluster.

This form of society is emerging at different rates in different parts of the world; in Europe, much of the former USSR, North America, and Japan, its development away from its predecessor, C-cluster systems is almost complete; in China, Southeast Asia, India, and most of Latin America and the Middle East, the modern social forms occur primarily in the cities, though of course the cities themselves in turn affect the countryside, which is thus no longer purely C-cluster, while not fully modern either. But the modern social formation has come to dominate much of the globe, and we can thus study it as a new phase of history, which brings with new rules and new forms for family organization.

The term "modern" seems to be in a certain disrepute among social scientists; it has connotations that lead to laziness in ethnographic description and to disrespect for, or even disinterest in, cultural or culturally particular phenomena. In popular thinking, "modern" is equated with "Western;" "modernization" with "Westernization" or even "Americanization." Modernization theorists have told us that economic development, liberation from poverty and misery, is possible if only we build certain kinds of economic and political structures or instill certain motivations in previously unmodern people's consciousness. Not only does this theory of economic development seem naive after the oil shocks, famines, epidemics, environmental disasters, and debt crises of the 1970s and 80s, but even those countries that have developed economically have still shown limits to how "Western" or Western-like they might become.

"Modern" also has value implications, differing according to the user's politics or philosophy of history. For those who believe in progress, modern is better than pre-modern: it means longer life, distancing of worries about many diseases, liberation from heavy physical labor, and access to technology not only of cornucopious material production, but of unimagined (and itself liberating) communication and transfer of information. To be modern is to expand one's horizons, multiply one's choices, set free one's energy and potential. For others, modernity is bad. The "World We Have Lost" is deeply to be mourned: we have lost community, attachment, assurance that our life means something or is worth something. In their place we have alienation, suspicion, loss of faith, and meaninglessness. To be modern is to long for the communal past of history or perhaps only of imagination.

Neither of these value judgments is going to help us much in understanding family systems in the industrial areas of the world. Why, then, when I analyze the family systems of the industrialized areas, do I not simply speak of the family in industrial societies, and forget about that troublesome term, "modern?" Especially when I maintain that the development of an industrial social formation brings with it similar changes in family activities, leading to similar alterations in family forms, everywhere in the world? It is tempting to do so and be done with it, except for an important paradox of culture. One of the things that has happened in the modern societies is that people have come to analyze and even criticize their own societies incessantly, something that people in C-cluster societies did not do. Song Dynasty China may have had instructions for household management or for women's behavior; India the Laws of Manu, the Bible its commandments about filiality and adultery, and Christianity its elaborations on these commandments. In this sense, people in C-cluster societies analyzed their family systems. They also criticized current practice for not living up to culturally-assumed ideals. But they rarely criticized the basic ideals themselves. It is only in modern societies that the mainstream of social thought has questioned, rather than simply advocated, the fundamental nature of the social system. Whatever changes have gone on in family forms and activities in modern societies, they have been interpreted, praised, lamented, analyzed, puzzled over and, most importantly, subjected to recommendations and admonitions. As the Prelude to this Part shows so clearly, the family systems of M-cluster societies are not just groups that share activities and go through developmental cycles; they are ideology, counter-ideology, discussion and debate.[1]

This discussion and debate has created a paradox, one that makes culture, in many ways, more important to modern societies than to those of the C-cluster. We find a general congruence between ideology and social system, between mental structure and behavioral organization, in the C-societies, though sometimes mitigated by the inability of exploited classes and other groups to realize the cultural ideal. But in the M-cluster, the ideologues are free to criticize, to debate, to advocate something different. The result is that the criticism of the family is part of the family system. The behavior need not coincide with the ideology; this gives the formulators of the ideal a kind of free rein to shape the organization in ways contrary to, or at least different from, those that might be prescribed by adaptational concerns. Whereas among the A-, O-, and N- clusters, we saw actors organizing the same basic activities in different ways, in the M-cluster we see people arguing both for and against the idea that the family should in fact organize certain activities at all. Thus we have, in nineteenth and twentieth century North America, for example, both utopian socialists who advocated the family's abolition and cultural conservatives who advocated the restoration of what they saw as its former functional unity. We even have an ongoing debate about how to define the family in the first place, illustrated graphically by the fact that when Jimmy Carter tried to convene a White House conference on the family, the project failed because prospective participants could not agree on who should participate (Van Horn 1988:152). The choices that industrial social formations have offered to modern people thus provide a bulwark against that very uniformity that was predicted by "modernization" or "convergence" theorists (see Goode 1963). Within certain limits, we can invent our own family ideologies. This is because the activities that must be organized by the family have, in fact, diminished with the creation of industrial society.

In terms of family organization, this creates a paradox. M-cluster family systems have much in common with B-cluster systems and with C-cluster systems, and have almost nothing in common with the systems of the A-, O-, and N- clusters, or with the systems of rank societies generally. The similarity to B-cluster systems derives from the fact that, with industrialization, there is not as much that the family has to do anymore, and in some ways this resembles the situation in foraging bands. The connection to the C-cluster is historical: both the institutions and the ideologies of modern societies are partially left over from the C-cluster, our immediate past when the family-based organization of activities was most unified and when ideology and practice closely coincided, at least for those classes that formulated the ideology. And this left-over ideology, the historical relic that gives people comfort in the face of the ocean of modern possibilities and threats, in turn gives rise to counter-ideologies; hence the debate over the family, a debate that is so much a part of the family system, is born (Wells 1982:158-168), mainstream, establishment publications such as *Newsweek* (1990) devote whole special issues to the future of the American family, and "family values" becomes a political slogan familiar to every informed citizen.

In the last instance, then, it does come down to the transformation of the productive forces; as they are transformed they decrease the necessity to organize things in the family, giving rise to the choices and debate that are the essence of the M-cluster's distinctiveness. This Part, then, begins with a brief description of the important aspects of the modern transformation of productive forces. In Chapter 22, I proceed to an activity-by-activity enumeration of the diminishing importance of the modern family. In Chapter 23, I then consider how this lessening importance has worked itself into the redefinition and reduction of the structural links that make up the family. From there it is any easy step to viewing the combination of this redefinition and the demographic changes that have been part of the transformation of productive forces—this combination is the development of radically new developmental cycles.

This development, however, is at the same time restrained in various ways by various societies' left-over C-cluster ideals and pushed in unpredictable directions by radical ideologies. So I then proceed to examine the critiques of the family in Chapter 24, both the radical critique which, in Utopian communes from Oneida to Galilee and in certain branches of feminist and lesbian-feminist theory and practice, tries to abolish the family altogether and organize life's activities differently, and the alternative critique, theorized and practiced in particular by many lesbians and some gay males, which tries to re-create the structure and activities of the family but with different personnel. Looming against these, though not considered in detail, is the conservative critique, articulated by primarily fundamentalist Christian "pro-family" groups, which proposes that an idealized version of the C-cluster family be "restored" as an antidote to the moral decay of modern life. All of these critiques are examples in the domestic domain of the luxury and desperation of modern-day diversity, a diversity that constitutes the unity of M-cluster family systems.

Modern Economy and Society as Background for the Family

The most important aspect of the transformation from pre-modern to modern society is the development of the industrial capitalist mode of production, whose salient feature is in turn the movement of manufacture from the home or small workshop to the factory. In studying the development of M-cluster family systems, I have become convinced that industry is the key factor in explaining all the most important modern social changes. Pre-industrial capitalism (if that term be allowed) retained most of the important features of the agrarian societies out of which it emerged; the really important transformations did not come until the development of industry.[2]

The development of industry has worked in concert with the development of scientific and technical knowledge to produce a number of social changes that have radically altered the context in which the family is organized. Here I trace briefly the major changes in social organization that the development of science and industry have brought about.

The first major effect of industry is the creation of unprecedented economies of scale in manufacturing. Before the harnessing of steam power, only perhaps in monumental construction or in waterworks (Wittfogel 1957) was it necessary or advantageous to have more than a few tens of workers in one place at one time; premodern cities were primarily trade and administrative centers and only secondarily centers of manufacture, the latter more because of the advantages of concentrating trade than because of the advantages of concentrating labor for manufacturing itself (Sjoberg 1960:197). And most production, including manufacturing, went on in rural communities and small towns (Mumford 1961:456). But with the development of mechanized industry, large concentrations of industrial producers came to confer an advantage on the owners of large-scale capital.

This brings us to the second major effect of industry, the concentration of capital in a few hands.[3] Commercial capital was probably similarly concentrated previously, but commercial capital never dominated production in the way that industrial capital was later able to do. And non-capital owners, in many cases dependent on wages paid by capital owners, were increasingly induced or forced to concentrate in the neighborhood of the capital plant itself.

But capital in an industrial system is not only concentrated; it is also fluid, bringing with it the necessity of hiring and firing workers at a great rate.[4] Even in those systems such as Japan, where large employers often provide lifetime employment, the vagaries of the market are served by flexible employment in smaller firms (Kondo 1990:49-51).

The tendency toward labor mobility is compounded by the development of the technology of motion in all M-systems. With industry and its accompanying technology comes the ability to move, not only large amounts of goods, but also large numbers of people rapidly over long distances. Whereas people until the early 1800s could only move as fast as they or a horse could walk (or run over short distances), now a day or two is sufficient time to go from just about anywhere to just about anywhere else.

Taken all together these four factors—economies of scale in manufacturing, concentration of capital in private or state hands, fluidity of capital and of the labor market, and development of the technology of motion—lead to the rapid growth of cities as a percentage of population in all the industrial countries. Urbanization, in turn, particularly when it is characterized by constant mobility, contributes to one of *the* most salient and talked-about features of modernity—the dislocation from the community and its consensual norms. Writers on the topic of modernity, in fact, often see this as the crucial feature of present-day existence and the source of the malaise at the heart of modern society. Marshall Berman, for example, sees the great virtue of the bourgeoisie as the capacity for "creative chaos" and "innovative self-destruction" (1982:98-99); this is possible because industry and urbanization have wrenched people out of the "little world" of the promodern village (1982:59-60). Leszek Kolakowski sees modernity as a state in which "Concepts of home, the family house, the links from generation to generation...seem to be on the way to extinction" (1985:150). The dislocation from the community that formerly presented people with proper and unquestionable life plans has left people in a state where they can choose for themselves, a state of unprecedented freedom or unprecedented anomie, or perhaps both at the same time.

These and other major effects of both industry and its partner, science, have led to different, related aspects of the modern condition. For example, the development of the advanced technology of motion leads not only to the concentration of people in great cities, but also to their propensity to move around a lot. In 1960 in the United States about 1.5% of people over 18 years old had lived their whole lives in a single house; about one in five American families was estimated to move each year at that time (Burgess, Locke, and Thomes 1963:366-67). Not only the anonymity of the urban high-rise, but the short duration of neighborly relations and the frequent removal from kin relations contribute to the feeling of dislocation so eloquently described by the above authors.

Another result of the growth of industry, and an extremely important one, is a growth in productivity of all kinds of labor, including mechanized farming, and thus the ability to both produce unprecedented surpluses and devote an ever-dwindling proportion of the working population to agricultural labor or even, in the so called "post-industrial" countries, to the manufacturing processes that started it all.[5] This has a pair of effects central to the modern experience. First, it means that a large amount of people's time can be spent in other than production of material goods. The development of universal education, taking older children and young adults out of the work force and putting them into ever-longer courses of study, is one phenomenon facilitated by this increased productive efficiency. The second effect is the growth of materially non-productive occupations: the professions and the now-predominant (at least in North America, where it accounts for over half the employment [United Nations 1988:77-83]) service sector of the economy. And when two things converge—the material forces of production increasingly concentrated in a few hands, and the society being able to support more and more of its members as students or as dealers in professional and other services—this means that a smaller and smaller percentage of the population depends on property as the source of its livelihood. Though figures are hard to come by, we may take the example of Japan, where this transition is probably slower than in most places, but where only 25% of households had property-based (farming or self-employed) incomes in 1980, a reduction from 43% in 1955 (Fuse 1984:2-3). By 1993, the figure had fallen much further, to 12% (Statistics Bureau 1995:56). We saw in Part VI how the dependence on property in C-cluster societies concentrated so many activities in a single household group. In Modern society, these strings have been loosened again. It is not that everyone in premodern, complex societies was dependent on property for livelihood; only most people were. (Those who were not owners in the full sense were often still holders of various kinds of heritable tenancy or usufruct rights.) That small percentage that lived from wages in fact had family systems much more like the M-cluster norm, as will be recalled from certain Sri Lankan and South Italian cases in Chapter 19. Conversely, not everyone in M-cluster societies is a wage earner. Only most people are. Those who are very wealthy and live on investments, the declining numbers of family farmers, and the group of small- and medium-business owners are the exceptions in M-cluster societies, as are wage-earners in C-cluster societies. And the modern property owners' families in fact show important traces of C-cluster elements. And in societies such as China and much of what was known in the 70s and 80s as "The Third World," where rural people are still primarily family-based producers, C-cluster norms still predominate, though weakened by the incursion of modern ideas through media and education. But the norm in fully modern societies is for people to be wage-earners, and this is the second great characteristic (along with the dislocation of community) of modern society that we must understand if we wish to comprehend that kind of society's family system.

Other aspects of industry and science lead to still other salient features of modern societies. Science brings with it a major transformation in the statistics of human demography. Mortality rates have plunged in the industrial countries, to the point where infant mortality is between one-half and two percent for most of the industrial world, and where in modern North America, Europe, and Japan over 95% of the people live to age 45. This has meant that fewer children need be born in order to have a certain number of children survive. And there also seems to be less reason to want children in the first place; both the increase in the efficiency of production and the presence of occupational mobility, which requires education to realize, have led to a sharp decline in the value of child labor. This, along with greater rates of survivorship, has meant less overall motivation to bear children.

Science, along with the universalization of education, has also led to a rapid growth in the amount of knowledge possessed by modern societies, and also to a wider social sphere of the knowledgeable. All sorts of ideas are now accessible to all sorts of people. This, along with the aforementioned dislocation from the local community, means an unprecedented ability to question the culture and society in which one was socialized, once again the great freedom and terror of modern existence.

One particularly relevant aspect of this great freedom to criticize is freedom to criticize family rules and expectations of several kinds, a freedom mentioned in the first section of this chapter. Different aspects of this freedom to formulate and criticize family rules have different roots in addition to the common ones of dislocation and wider dissemination of knowledge. Freedom to criticize parent-child links also stems from the reduced dependence on property for livelihood, and freedom to question gender roles has several additional causes. Lack of dependence on property, male controlled in the law of most C-cluster societies, is certainly one factor, as pointed out by Engels long ago (1884). Others are the reduced incentives to bear children, the ability of the newly-grown service sector to do some socialization of the children that are born, and the declines in domestic production for subsistence (Kyrk 1953:247-251; Fuse 1984:2-3) and in domestic processing labor. In addition, safe and reliable methods of contraception have made it possible for women to postpone or even forego childbearing without resorting to celibacy.

This ability to question and to devise new rules, emerging out of dislocation as it does, has given rise to its opposite, a search for assurance, in all walks of modern life. Berman points out that, in spite of the great virtues of the bourgeoisie in creative chaos and innovative self-destruction, the members of that class seek to be the party of order, to deny their own creative nature (1982:99). And Kolakowski sees a desperate search for order amidst uncertainty:

> The search for new forms of religiosity, the success of various charismatic sects, the exploration of the wisdom and legends of the eternally mysterious Orient, various techniques of collective psychotherapy—all these are symptoms of the same bizarre disease, which is intimately linked with the vague feeling of having lost the ability of so-called direct communication [1985:159].

As with culture in general, so with the family in particular—we long for some sort of security, seeking it in a return to the old forms or the creation of something novel and better, or we celebrate the creative chaos and indulge our instincts or our rationalizations of what is best for our self-development. For from the dissolution of the old socially-anchored self there has developed the new individualistic self, whose goal is to realize its own potential and abilities, the self that believes in what Bellah and his associates (1985) call expressive individualism, consciously formulated or simply accepted as really real (Geertz 1965:35-40) by the enculturated. When this self turns its thoughts to the family, it envisions a family predicated on the abilities of individuals to find maximum "self-fulfillment" or "self-realization" (what in previous times might have been called "happiness") in interpersonal relationships. This "companionship family" (Burgess, Locke, and Thomes 1963:3) is possible because the family is no longer burdened by the demands of the community-centered, property-based C-cluster society. But before we turn to what this family has become, we must first examine how and why it lost so many of its activities, and with these the centrality that it held in C-cluster societies.

Notes

1. In this and many other regards, I fail to see much of a relevant difference between "modern" and "post-modern." What writers have defined as post-modern (Lyotard 1984) seems to me to be nothing but a full realization of the direction of modernity. Writers who distinguish "high modern" from "post-modern" (see Harvey 1989:39-65), do so on the basis of high modernism as a series of universal schemes of society-building (such as fascism, communism, and Fordism), while post-modernism consists of a plurality of possibilities and the recognition that the world cannot be wholly designed. Insofar as this historical progression has taken place, it has simply consisted of the final abandonment of the totalizing ideologies characteristic of pre-modern forms, of the final realization of the debatable nature of reality that is the hallmark of the modern era. In this sense, socialism in particular, along with fascism, can be seen as a modern form that retains more of the premodern, of the C-cluster certainty of the proper way, than do the "late capitalist" (which may turn out to be early capitalist) forms prevalent in Western Europe and North America in the last decade of the twentieth century.

2. Strange as it would have seemed when I began this book in 1979, socialism requires nothing but a footnote here. The state socialism practiced in the USSR and its East European satellites, as well as in China between 1956 and the 1980s, did not differ greatly from capitalist modern societies in those characteristics that are most important for the evolution of the family, namely urbanism, widely available con-

traception, and the replacement of property by salary as the primary means of income.

3. This was at least as true of socialist systems, where the few hands are those of the state, as it is in the capitalist systems where the means of production are in the grip of private interests. This distinction, however, is fading, since socialist economic systems are now being replaced by more plural systems in Eastern Europe, Russia, and some other former Soviet republics, and even in China, where the Communist Party still holds sway, the percentage of state-owned industrial output had dropped to 57% by 1988, and has certainly dropped even farther since then (Naughton 1992:22).

4. In socialist industrial systems this tendency was usually constrained by state policy guaranteeing employment at the cost of labor productivity; this was an important difference between socialist and capitalist variants of industrial society. But even in socialist China, the state owners of capital moved in the 1980s to reduce the guarantee of employment and to develop a labor market everywhere but in the state-owned industries of the large cities (D. Davis 1990), and by the end of 1991, state-owned industry accounted for just over half of industrial output.

5. In the United States, employment in manufacturing declined from 24% of the total labor force in 1980 to about 22% in 1985; in the United Kingdom, the decline was more precipitous, from 33% in 1975 to 26% in 1985. Switzerland, Sweden, Canada, and France experienced similar declines (United Nations 1988:77-83)

22

What Families Do and Don't Do Anymore in Modern Societies

From the B-cluster through the various tribal clusters to the C-cluster, we saw the gradual buildup of activities organized in the family: more activties came into existence, and those that already existed became more and more concentrated in the family group. This process culminated in the C-cluster household, the private-property holding family, a group that concentrated all eight of the basic family activities in itself, and thus became the fundamental economic, sexual, legal, political, educational, ritual, and even emotional building block of larger social units. With the drastic changes in productive forces that happened with the industrial and scientific revolutions, however, all this has rapidly fallen apart; people do fewer things as families now than they have since band days. Let us examine, each activity one by one and show how the role of the family in each has been weakened by the shift to industrial society.

Procuring: From Property to Salary

There are two senses in which procuring historically has been an activity performed in and for the family. In the first sense, the family itself is a work group, laboring together to produce income for all its members. We see this kind of procuring at work, for example, when there is a family farm on which various family members perform various tasks, or in a family shop where family members perform tasks of supply, accounting, waiting on customers, maintenance, etc. In the second sense, the family is a procuring group in that all members of the family share the goods brought in through the labor of one or more members. If a Japanese husband brings home a salary, for example, and he, his wife, and their children all gain their material goods with that salary, or if an African woman works fields while her husband hunts, as among the Kimbu, then the family is acting as a procuring group in the second sense, in that it is sharing the fruits of the labor of one or more members, even though it is not a working group.

We have, of course, seen numerous examples of both these types of procuring groups as we have traced the history of the family in pre-modern times. The first type, which involves the family as a work group, with very little inter-family cooperation in productive labor, is probably most characteristic of C-cluster family systems, where property is also concentrated in the family, and family members tend to work on or with their own property. Chayanov's description of late 19th and early 20th-century Russian peasant households, for example, is based on the premise that all major economic decisions, including the allocation of inputs of all kinds to various tasks, are made on the basis of certain calculations about the needs of the family, and all land, labor, and capital are controlled by the family corporation and used for its benefit (Chayanov 1966 [1925]:90-92).[1] And most accounts of recent changes in the American family begin from a baseline of an integrated family economy, which Hazel Kyrk characterizes as "making goods (1953:247-250)," and Burgess, Locke, and Thomes refer to as the "Institutional Family (1963)."

When we move into modern society, however, with the sweeping changes described above, we see a great decline in the number of families that persist as work groups. In industrial societies all over the world, the percentage of people engaged in any kind of agriculture is a fraction of its former level; currently about 10% in Japan, 8% in France, 7% in Australia, 6% in Canada, 5% in West Germany, 3% in the United States and Belgium, and 2.5% in the United Kingdom (United Nations 1988:77-83). These figures for all agriculturalists are, of course, larger than the percentage of family farmers. In addition, the percentages of people engaged in other family businesses never grows very large, even with the commercialization typical of modern society. In Japan, for example, by 1980 64% of families depended entirely on wages earned by family members in non-family enterprises (Fuse 1984:2-3; Musselwhite 1987:36); the percentage had increased to 72% by 1993 (Statistical Bureau 1995:56), and the totals were even higher in most of the rest of the industrialized world, both capitalist and socialist. Indeed in the socialist societies, there existed but a minuscule number of families that constituted work groups. In today's China, though family farmers once again form the bulk of the population (placing most of the country's families squarely back in the C-cluster after a partial transformation to M-characteristics under collective agriculture), urban business-owning families only accounted for 4% of the urban population in 1987 (Gold 1990:166).

The decline of families as work groups has contributed to the decline in the interdependencies of generations, and also to the decline in incentives for fertility. Children no longer are very beholden to their parents, because the parents do not control a potential source of the children's livelihood, and parents no longer see children either as old-age security or as a source of labor for a family enterprise. This decline has also contributed to the demise or weakening of former systems of family extension. In Japan, for example, where the stem family prevailed in pre-industrial and early-industrial times, recent history has shown a trend toward older people living alone, with 18% of older couples living apart from their children in 1980 (Fuse 1984:9-10). When agriculture was collectivized in China in the 1950s, patrilocal joint households became virtually unknown (Parish and Whyte 1977:134), only to reappear after family agriculture was restored (Zhao 1985).

There are, however, countertrends to the general decline of the family as a procuring group. In some societies, the beginning stages of industrialization come about not entirely at the hands of large industrialists, but as a complex process that involves links between large- and small-scale capital, with small entrepreneurs providing both commercial services and labor-intensive manufacturing. In such societies, of which Taiwan is the prototype example, pooling of incomes and labor is an advantageous strategy for those families engaged in entrepreneurship, making them not only significantly larger than the families of wage workers, but also larger than the peasant families from which they emerged (see Cohen 1968, 1976; Harrell 1982). This illustrates the danger of generalizing too much about family forms in complex societies, whether of the C- or M-cluster. In any of these societies, families of different social classes control different kinds of resources, and this affects whether or not the families are work groups.

The general decline in families as work groups is thus well-defined for industrial societies, but in fact the second way in which the family in other societies has served as a procuring group—with all family members living from the income of some family members—also declines in importance with industrialization. This trend is a result of the almost complete monetization of the industrial economy. A person with money can purchase any kind of goods or services; no longer is a division of labor within the family necessary for a person to gain different kinds of goods, as was the case, for example, when women gathered while men hunted, as in most band societies; or women farmed while men hunted, as in many extensive agricultural societies of Africa, or women traded while men farmed, as in certain West African societies; or even if men plowed the fields while women tended the barnyard animals, a common pattern in 19th century America. In industrial societies, anyone's labor is convertible into any kind of good or service through the medium of money, and division of labor within the family in procuring is no longer necessary.[2] At the same time, many modern states have instituted old-age pensions or social security systems; this and the possibility of private savings for old age have weakened intergenerational interdependencies, since the aged are no longer dependent on their adult offspring for procuring. This has had profound effects on family composition and family developmental cycle, as discussed below.

Processing: The Re-invention of Interdependency

In premodern societies of all types, the interdependency between the procurers and processors has often been at the base of family economic organization. The clearest case of this is of course the Inuit (see Chapter 2), where the men do nearly all the procuring—hunting and fishing—and the women do nearly all the processing—butchering, cooking, scraping, and sewing—and both kinds of work are absolutely necessary to the continuance of life in the harsh Arctic. Since such interdependency is at the heart of the bourgeois ideal of the 19th and early 20th centuries, Engels built an entire theory of the family on this relationship, assuming that men always got the goods and women always processed them. This meant that his model of primitive society had to be one in which procuring and processing were equally valued; it did not occur to him that women might have done much of the procuring (1985 [1884]:78-80). But in fact it seems rare that these two kinds of labor are given equal prestige. Inuit males are in fact more dominant than are males in other foraging societies where women contribute some portion of the procuring labor. The prestige of the "breadwinner" is proverbial in 20th century America. And much of the impetus for the feminist movement and for equal-opportunity laws passed in North America and Western Europe in recent years has come from women's desire for equality in careers, that is, equal opportunity to participate in procuring labor. In fact, processing labor itself has become synonymous with drudgery: from the "Fuck Housework" posters of the 1970s to polls about how much cooking, cleaning, and shopping husbands actually do, to attempts to set monetary values on housework, processing is seen as low-prestige, forced, not-very-creative labor.

It follows from all this that if the "modern" family is really going to live up to its name, to participate in that loosening of bonds, that widening of possibilities, that questioning of definitions that itself defines the modern condition, the assumption of basic interdependency between the procuring male and the processing female is going to have to be questioned; if the former basic interdependency does not completely disappear, it at least has to become one option among many. And certain aspects of modern technology have made such a thing possible. There is simply a lot less necessary processing labor in the world of washing machines, permanent press, frozen dinners, takeout, diaper services, and greatly reduced standards of cleanliness than there was in the C-cluster world of starched collars and elaborate dinners made from fresh ingredients, not to mention the less fastidious but even more labor-intensive self-sufficient farm family of the same era.

Where children are present, of course, processing as a family activity is much less optional. Adults must process for children as they must procure for them. But modern changes also lead to lower fertility and a higher rate of optional childlessness. One need enter a family relationship involving processing only if one wants to; one can lead a singles life if one prefers; this is another of the options of modernity that reduce the inevitability of certain kinds of family interdependence.

At the same time, however, there seems to be a kind of cultural resistance to elimination or substantial reduction in processing labor. This resistance seems to have two sources. First, there is the pursuit of standard of living, which is built into the prestige structure of modern societies. Standard of living means not only "labor-saving devices," such as washing machines and microwave ovens, it also means spacious and gracious, living in a larger house and a better-appointed one, one that is going to need more care. This pursuit of standard of living is probably necessary to the successful workings of the modern economy; since "basic" needs have long been met for most members of the society, the focus of productive growth is on the creation and meeting of culturally-determined needs, which provide both further incentives to procuring work and more processing work to maintain the symbols of prestige and success.

The second source of the resistance to reduction in processing labor is the ideology of bourgeois wife-and-motherhood. In order to provide a pleasant environment for husbands and children, wives and mothers as far afield as Taiwan and the United States have at various times been expected to spend large amounts of time in processing work. The mother in Japan, for example, though precluded from having a big house, is still supposed to make the little apartment as cozy an environment as possible for the youngster's serious study in pursuit of examination success (Vogel 1963); recent student desks in Japan include an electric "mother-call button." The cult of domesticity of the 1950s and 1960s in the United States, where the floor gleams and the dirt all comes out of the collar, created and glorified processing work, while hewing to the assumption that procuring work was prior and thus more important. And even in the mid-1980s, with 68 percent of U.S. married women working outside the home, women spent about nineteen hours more per week on housework than did men (Hochschild 1989:2-3; 272), and even among two-job, professionally successful couples, there was usually the assumption that the wife was primarily resposible for processing labor and for the organization of the household (Hochschild 1989:22-32).

Both the pursuit of the standard of living and the cult of wife-and-motherhood can be seen as aspects of the modern economy, which needs both growth (provided by the perpetual and limitless increase in perceived needs) and an adjustable labor supply (which can spend all its time processing when there is a contraction in the number of jobs available in the public sector). But there is a cultural element also. If, as modern technology in fact allows, processing becomes reduced to a simple matter of an hour or so a day for each person, there is no interdependency—employed persons can simply keep house for themselves. This happens, of course, as is demonstrated by the ever-increasing number of one-person households in the industrial countries (see Chapter 22). But it runs up against deep-seated ideological feelings that the family ought to be some sort of solidary unit, either for the benefit of the children, or just because that's the way things should be. And the solidary unit is only necessary if a division of labor is maintained. So kinds of processing that could be dispensed with are instead celebrated, in order to buttress the otherwise fragile functional interdependencies that bind families.

Sexuality: "The Breakdown of Traditional Values"

The press tells us practically unceasingly (though perhaps less so than ten years ago) that there has been a "sexual revolution" in 20th century society. This has had several aspects. First, there has been a dramatic increase in the incidence of premarital sex. In the United States, this increase occurred between the cohort born before 1890 and the cohorts born after 1910 (Burgess, Locke, and Thomes 1963:355-56). In Australia, it seems not to have happened until after World War II (Game and Poole 1983:97-98); the same seems true of the former German Democratic Republic (Edwards 1985:160). There the transformation in attitudes is nearly complete—a poll taken in the early 1980s, 98% voiced no disapproval of premarital sexuality—but still about 50% of the population in fact reports having only one partner, pre- and post- maritally. In the Netherlands in 1985, 72% approved of premarital sex, not necessarily restricted to one partner (van de Kaa 1987:8). In some areas, however, the attitudes and behavior are still strongly skewed by gender, with much greater approval and easier access to premarital sex for boys than for girls. This appears to have been the case, for example, during the postwar era in northern Italy (Pearlin 1974:145) as well as in Japan (Vogel 1963:222).

The second aspect of the "sexual revolution" is the eroticization of marriage, which in modern societies is thought to be primarily a bond of affection, with a strong sexual component, and not a bond of practical interdependency, as is the case in the C-cluster and, for that matter, in all the rank-society clusters as well. This trend was commented on as early as the 1950s in England, where Elizabeth Bott showed that for the most "modern" families of the upper-middle classes, families that were no longer part of the close kin- and neighborhood networks still characteristic of working-class London, sex was a much more important factor in marriage than it was for the families still embodied in what were in effect left-over C-cluster networks. Bott remarks that "One almost got the feeling that these husbands and wives felt a moral obligation to enjoy sexual relations (1957:83)." Similarly, in postwar Australia, the "level of erotic activity in marriage has soared (Game and Poole 1983:97-98)." Florian Znaniecki, writing of the United States in the 1930s and 1940s, has referred to this general phenomenon as the "merging of erotic and conjugal structures (1941:60)," which had been separate in Europe and its descendants from Ancient Greece to the 19th Century, i.e., in what we would call C-cluster family organization. Bellah and his colleagues see this as an aspect of the general trend in American society toward what they call "expressive individualism." For the expressive individualist, a good marriage is one that is good for the self, one that involves "egalitarian love between therapeutically self-actualized persons (1985:90-100)."

Interestingly, these two aspects of the "sexual revolution," the permitting of premarital sex and the eroticization of marriage, have not led to a third that might be expected: general tolerance of extramarital sex. Where extramarital sex is tolerated, it seems to be in places such as Japan (Fuse 1984:7) and Italy (Pearlin 1974:145) where there is a strong double standard or, looking at it another way, where the erotic expectations of marriage are much less than in the societies described above. In the societies with eroticized marriage, the approved solution to an intolerable marital sexual relationship is ending the marriage, since the marriage exists for self-fulfillment of sexual and other needs. Since other kinds of interdependencies have weakened, there are few barriers to divorce, and since an unfulfilling marriage is an impediment to self-development, it is considered a normal, salutary thing to end it. This is reflected in rising divorce rates in many countries; in the 1980s, it was predicted that 50% of marriages would end in divorce in the United States (van Horn 1988:152); 45.4% in Sweden; 45.1% in Denmark, 40.4% in England and Wales, and 32.4% in Hungary (van de Kaa 1987:16).

An actual third aspect of the "sexual revolution" does exist, however: it is the increasing public visibility of and tolerance for "alternative sexual lifestyles," that is, something besides the combination a little pre-marital experimentation and then settling down in marriage which is still probably the ideal in most modern societies. These alternatives can be of any sort, but the most common seem to be the heterosexual "singles life" and various kinds of homosexual patterns, including both the equivalent singles pattern and more stable homosexual relationships approximating marriage. These latter relationships increasingly include the possibility of raising children, especially among Lesbian couples, a further indication both of the increasing (though by no means universal) tolerance of these alternatives and of the irrelevance of sexual division of labor for procuring and processing in the modern family.

All this adds up to much less control over sexuality, much less restriction to family contexts, than has been the norm in any C-cluster society, and less than in many of the societies of the rank-society clusters. When we look for causes of sexual tolerance in modernity, we come up with four; three, not surprisingly, have to do with the connection between sex and children. First there is the declining importance of the consequences of unwanted pregnancy. Pregnancy no longer forces marriage, as rising illegitimacy rates testify. In the United States in 1955, 4.8% of births occurred to unmarried women; in 1975, the proportion was 14.3% (Wells 1982:235). In an extreme case, a survey of Black underclass births in Seattle in the late 1970s revealed that 51% of first births were to women outside any stable sexual relationship; in the same population, boys were expected to father children without being married (LaFargue 1981:137-143). In some European countries, first births out-of wedlock have become the norm: births outside marriage accounted for over 40% of all births in Denmark and Sweden in the early 1980s, and in both these countries the mean age at first marriage was about a year later (26.4 in Denmark and 27.3 in Sweden) than the mean age at birth of first child (van de Kaa 1987:11-12,15). And if a pregnancy does cause personal hardship, abortion is now more or less freely available in most industrial countries.

If pregnancy no longer forces marriage, however, it still strongly suggests it, and this leads us to the second reason for decreased family control over sexuality: decreased family interest in whom one marries. In all the property-based systems of the C-cluster, making a good match was an integral part of most people's strategies for maintaining or improving their families' economic and social positions. But with the shift from property to salary as the primary basis of livelihood comes a decline in the family as the locus of management and transmission of property, and that along with various kinds of state support for the elderly brings about a decreased intergenerational interdependency in modern families generally. The parents thus have less interest in whom the children marry, and they also have less leverage over the choice of spouse, because the property they control no longer forms the basis of the children's livelihood. Again, an unwanted pregnancy is much less of a threat: it can either be aborted or, if the choice is to have the child, this can either be done out of wedlock or the pregnant woman can marry the father—it is of little consequence to the woman's parents who the grandchild's father is. All this leaves the field clear for romantic love to "unseat material considerations (Shorter 1975:5)" as the primary consideration in choosing a mate.

The third and perhaps most important reason for the loosening of sexual strictures is of course the development of readily available, reliable methods of contraception. This contributes both to the tolerance of premarital sex and to the eroticization of marriage, as well as to the increased acceptance of the sexually active single as a stage in the life-cycle or even as a life-long pattern (Sternlieb and Hughes 1986:24). Increased sexual activity in any of these contexts no longer brings with it the problems of childbearing and childrearing.

None of these three changes, important as they are for explaining increased tolerance of and emphasis on heterosexual activity before and during marriage, is sufficient to explain both the increased participation and increased public acceptance of homosexuality and lifelong "singlehood." To explain these, we must look to the decreasing value of children in modern society altogether. Children no longer provide much to their parents in the way of financial support, labor interdependency, or old-age security. It is no longer even important for a woman to be a mother to be fully accepted in her adult female social role. In the Netherlands in 1986, for example, 86% of survey respondents approved of voluntary childlessness; this figure contrasts to 22% approval as recently as 1965. And it is predicted that about 25% of the Americans born between 1945 and 1960 (the baby-boomers) will remain childless (van Horn 1988:159). So sexual styles that preclude children are no longer a threat to the perpetuation of the social order, as long as they remain minority sexual styles, which until the present at least they still do. If, as has begun to happen in some European countries, as well as Japan, in the last two decades, birth rates drop and remain well below replacement levels, this may change (Edwards 1985:3; Lutz 1994:7; Statistics Bureau 1995:62). But for the present, the sexual revolution seems here to stay. Concern over sexually transmitted diseases may diminish the number of partners for the average person, but it is unlikely to slow the basic trend. The really strong restrictions on sexuality, stemming from property, inheritance, and intergenerational division of labor, have disappeared with the full flowering of the modern industrial society.

Socialization: From Control to Actualization, Mainly by Mothers

Like family procuring, processing, and control of sexuality, socializing children is less important in most adults' lives in modern societies than it was in earlier times. But like these other activities, socialization as a family activity has not simply declined with modernity; it has changed in a series of ways, all of which reflect the general nature of modern social change.

In the first place, even in the face of its own decline, the socialization of children is celebrated as the most important activity of the family in much modern moral rhetoric. For example, in the old German Democratic Republic, legal codes decreed that socialization was the most important duty of the family (Edwards 1985:14). Recent newspaper and magazine articles in the United States also emphasize that the current "problems" with the family center to a large part on the raising of children: a recent special issue of Newsweek on the 21st century family devotes five of eight major articles to issues of bringing up children, what's wrong with how we do it, and how we might change it in the future (1990).

This concern with and nervous celebration of family-based socialization is, however, not really a reassertion of the strength of families as socializing units, but rather a reaction to a realization that changes in the social division of labor that are part of modernity in fact do two things to lessen the importance of familial socialization. First, they make children an optional part of life, and second, they provide opportunities to socialize children through means other than the family. Let us look at these two factors in turn.

The most striking aspect of the changing position of children in M-cluster families is that they are no longer necessary; in fact from many perspectives they are no longer desirable. Whereas in all the previous clusters from bands to complex societies, children contributed to the life projects of their parents by helping with procuring, processing, enabling, representation (mostly of mothers) and emotional solidarity, in modern society most of these are stripped away. As seen above, children rarely help in any kind of household division of labor in modern societies; in fact they are to an extraordinary degree passive recipients of parental labor clear into their late teens and early twenties. This also means that their labor does not enable their parents' success in the public sphere; in fact in modern societies enabling generally works the other way around, with the parents laboring toward providing the children with an education that will further their own station in life. Representation barely exists in modern life; when it does parents represent minor children; adults do not represent other adults.

Thus it is only the emotional value of children that remains; recent articles by American social philosophers have explicitly argued that the relationship between parents and children should be based on the respective rights of the individual parents and children, rather than on any special bond or obligation between them (English 1979:351; Blustein 1979:118-120).

Even the emotional value of children is conditional, however. This is largely because, in the atmosphere in which the purpose of life is the search for and fulfillment of the self (Bellah et al. 1985:101), relationships to other people are simply a means to this actualization, rather than ends in themselves. Thus for some people, children may be a means to self-fulfillment; for others, the lifelong conjugal-erotic relationship and or a public-sphere commitment to a career may be more important. And unlike the situation in A-cluster societies, for example, where a man's career is a failure unless he has sons and sons-in-law as followers, in M-cluster societies children and career, or children and marriage, are often seen as conflicting rather than complementary.

Another factor in lessening the emotional value of children is precisely the increase in the emotional value of marriage, something present to some degree in such diverse modern societies as England (Bott 1957:83), the former German Democratic Republic (Edwards 1985:164) and Japan (Lebra 1984:24). For women in many C-cluster family systems, the husband was not a source of emotional support; this had to be gained from the children. Now, however, this is not true; marriage is expected to have an affective as well as an erotic component, while bonds with children are not only optional but temporary.

With children no longer valuable in spheres other than the emotional, and even their emotional value somewhat lessened, and with contraceptives readily available, it is no surprise that fertility has dropped in many modern societies: people want and have fewer children than before. This trend seems to have reached its extremes in the societies of central Europe in the 1970s, when several countries actually had negative rates of natural increase; in the GDR this was nevertheless accompanied by continued relatively early marriage (Edwards 1985:3), indicating that spouse and career were beginning to compete with children as desirables. As early as the 1950s, 2/3 of the Italians surveyed wanted no more than two or three children (Gini and Corranti 1954:350-351); now their total fertility rate, along with that of the rest of Western Europe, averages only 1.5. In the USSR in the 50s and 60s, about 1/4 of marriages were childless, while nearly half of those couples who did have children had only one, and abortions exceeded live births in many urban areas (Liegele 1970:36-38).

All this demonstrates that in many modern societies, one can go through life as a socially normal person without having children. This by itself lessens the importance of child socialization for the family, but that importance is further weakened by the fact that much of the socialization that does go on is now done by groups other than the family. Nurseries, kindergartens, and schools now take a good portion of the average child's day in most modern countries; although the age at which such intensive care outside the home varies from a few months in many of the former socialist societies (Liegele 1970:13; Edwards 1985:22-28) to school age for many families in Japan, the fact remains that such extrafamilial socializers are available everywhere, and that there is continual demand for more in almost all modern societies, a demand that reflects the decline of the sexual division of labor and the inclusion of women in the societal ideal of fulfillment through career advancement.

At the same time, we should not exaggerate the decline of family members' roles in socializing those children that do get born in modern societies. This is particularly true in those forms of the modern family that retain a significant sexual division of labor; in all these cases, the mother remains the primary caretaker and a woman's role in her young adult years is defined principally in terms of her job as a socializer of children. This is true in the working-class families in England studied by Bott (1957:54, 72-80) and by Young and Willmott (1973:92), and also in the lower-class Black families in the United States where, however, the primary caretaker may or may not be the biological mother (LaFargue 1981:43-4). But this pattern is most salient in Japan, where virtually all home socialization is done by mothers, and it is assumed that a woman is going to follow a rigidly structured life-course, with marriage between the ages of 22 and 25, one or two children born a few years after this, and devotion to the children's welfare and education until they are grown and ready to assume employment on their own (DeVos and Wagatsuma 1972:78; Vogel 1963:184-5; Brinton 1986:18-19).

In sum, we can say that socialization remains important as a family activity in modern society, more so than procuring, processing, or regulation of sexuality. Children, after all, are still necessary to the continuity of society, even if some people would rather not be the ones to rear them. Unlike the activities previously discussed, whose diminution was a result of spontaneously occurring forces of the modernization process itself, substantially reducing the role of parents and other family members in the socialization of children is something that requires conscious and radical social engineering, something which, as I discuss in Chapter 24, has been tried, but not very often and even less often with enduring results.

The diminishing importance of children to the family has also led to a change in the content of child socialization. Now instead of socializing the child to be a loyal and productive member of the group—socializing the child for the parents' or the family's benefit—the emphasis is on socializing the child to provide maximal opportunities for the child's own success in a social role. Independence has become the goal of American child-training, for example: Newsweek's special issue on the 21st century family laments the failure of America's adolescents to mature, as evidenced by a growing number still living with their parents in their 20s (1990:54-60). Even in Japan, where independence is not highly valued even in adults, it is the molding of children, particularly boys, for career success through school examinations that is the highest duty of every good mother (Rohlen 1983). Since they are no longer of particular value to the parents, the children must be socialized to meet the current social ideal for the individual.

Management and Transmission: The Triumph of Achievement

The single aspect of the modernization process that has the greatest potential effect on the importance of the family is the steady decrease in the percentage of people whose income depends on the returns from property. As mentioned above, this is a universal characteristic of modernizing societies, but not of all families in modernizing societies. In essence, moving from the C-cluster to the M-cluster means tipping the balance between property-dependent and wage-dependent families, with the latter overwhelmingly predominant in the M-cluster.

It is almost a truism to point out that the family activity most affected by the transition from property- to wage- based income is the management and transmissal of property. In North American and European societies, family property is important only for a few specific segments of the population. For the wealthy, fortunes are such that they are sufficient to provide income for family members, and promises of inheritance are important enough that they continue to exist as a means of social control; thus both the management of property as a means of procuring and the transmissal of property through inheritance continue to be important for the wealthiest families. Among business owners and family farmers, by contrast, management of property is still important, since it is a source of livelihood not only for those active in its management, but for dependents and sometimes wage-earners as well, but transmissal of property—the inheritance of the family farm or business, is rarely enough of a lure to be an effective way for parents to exercise control over their adult children. For these people, the ideology of family unity on the farm or in the business is important (Tauxe 1989), but the reality in most cases is that most of the children, sometimes all of them, pursue other lines of work.

When we come to the other kind of transmissal, that of offices, we find it is basically irrelevant in M-cluster societies. There are a few royal families in Europe (even one in Japan), and a somewhat larger number of noble ones whose titles confer prestige and may still be as important as their diminishing benefices. But nearly all political offices and positions in large corporations are filled by means other than familial succession. Even Japan abolished the legal requirement of family succession, along with the legal status of family head, in its 1947 constitution.

Another legal factor that has been associated with the reduced importance of family as a property-owning group is that it has become increasingly possible in M-cluster societies for persons to own property as individuals rather than as members of families. Although in the United States, for example, laws vary from state to state as to whether spouses' property is presumed to be held in common, it is rarely the case that family heads are trustees of property held by the family group. And in purely ideological terms, most people in North America think of "mine" rather than of "ours."

The decline in the importance of management and transmission has had extreme consequences for relationships between the generations, as pointed out in Chapter 23. No longer do parents have any power over their adult children; it is even argued that adult children, by rights, owe their parents nothing in return for the years of socialization and care (English 1979).

Nevertheless, even though management and transmission are much less important for the majority in M-cluster societies, they are not gone altogether. In Japan, for example, even though there is no legal requirement for a family head to be succeeded, into the 1970s most families operated as if there were, and found a successor to the headship (R.J. Smith 1978:55). And in all these countries the decline in the importance of productive property among the middle and lower classes has been offset to a slight degree by the increase in consumer property. For dependent children in the middle classes of Europe and North America, the family is the source of television, stereo, and a car to drive on weekends, as well as a warm and roomy house. And it is common in the United States for parents to help their children with the down payment when they buy a house for themselves. But when American RVs can proudly sport bumper stickers proclaiming "We're spending our children's inheritance," we realize that even in the ideal M-cluster family, property and inheritance count for a lot less than they used to.

Representation: The Rise of Citizenship

In C-cluster societies, where the family typically stands as an intermediary between the individual and the state, and often between the individual and the church, family members (usually family heads or head couples) represent other family members in three spheres: political, legal-economic, and religious.

The transition from C- to M-cluster societies, from agrarian empires to industrial states, has also been characterized by political scientists as the transition from folk to mass society, from a C-cluster social order in which the state deals with the individual through a series of intermediary groups, of which the family is the smallest, to an M-cluster social order in which the state deals directly with the individual (Kornhauser 1959). When the state deals directly with the individual, representation of some members of the family by others no longer operates.

In general, M-cluster societies have indeed abolished the family as a political intermediary between the state and the individual. In place of family membership, modern governments have substituted citizenship, a system in which the political rights and obligations of adults accrue to them directly as individuals. So, for example, all the Western industrial countries instituted universal adult suffrage in the early part of the 20th century (except Switzerland, where women's franchise is still incomplete in some cantons), and Japan, under allied pressure, did the same after its defeat in World War II. No longer does the household head have either a vote or the opportunity to hold office to the exclusion of other household members.

At the same time, however, as some societies have instituted universal adult suffrage, representation still operates surreptitiously in the political sphere. In the Taiwanese village where I lived in the early 1970s, representatives of candidates for local office would come around a few days before elections and ask the household head how many votes (that is, how many voters) the household had. If the head agreed to vote for the candidate, his[3] representatives gave the household head a certain amount of money per vote, assuming that the head would deliver the votes of the rest of the household. This demonstrates that the legal systems characteristic of M-societies, when applied in a situation where the household was still organized according to C-principles, were subverted to the C-pattern, and representation still operated.

In the legal-economic sphere, the decline of representation is less complete than in the political. This is true for two reasons. First, all modern governments establish an age of majority below which people are not full citizens—they cannot enter into contracts, own real property except as it is managed for them by trustees, or in most cases bring suit or be held responsible in ordinary courts of law. So parents are still considered responsible for their minor dependents, and as such can be said to represent them. The situation here, however, seems to be changing somewhat, at least in the United States, where it has gradually become possible for children to bring suit and to hold property in certain situations (Katz, et al. 1979:328-333).

Second, many M-societies' property laws still deny equal ownership rights to married women, or have until recent decades, or even where rights are equal, establish a community of property rights upon marriage, so that a married couple has a joint estate, and in certain circumstances spouses can represent each other. The strength of this belief is underlined by the recent publicity for a series of "palimony" settlements, in which a man who has lived in a non-marital relationship with a woman is nevertheless held to have had with her a community of property (Cunningham , et al. 1993:69-77; Freeman 1995:151; Rollier 1977:54-55; Picker 1977:322-323).

What seems not to happen, even in the legal-economic sphere, is that a formally designated household head represents all the other members of the family in a property transaction or in a legal suit. In fact, the formal position of household head no longer exists in fully modernized societies: in Japan, probably the last M-society to have such a position, it was abolished in the new civil code of 1947, even if the informal power of the head remains strong in some situations. That China still has such a formal, legal position today is a reflection of its as yet incomplete transformation.

Although these changes are not complete, they have strong implications for the declining importance of the family in modern societies. No longer is someone who is not part of any family group at a disadvantage with regard to the state, since the state grants all adult individuals the same legal and political status. At the same time, this lack of family representation among adults serves to underscore the importance of representation of children. Even children who have no parents must have legal guardians to represent them to the state; in this way the statuses of adult and child are more clearly distinguished than in the C-cluster societies, where there are a series of family-based statuses ranging from household head to minor children.

Representation is not, however, only political and legal-economic; it is also religious, and in societies from both the rank-society supercluster and the C-cluster, the ability of senior members of family groups (households or kin groups) to represent their juniors in ancestral worship or other religious activity was an important source of the seniors' prestige and power. In the West, the relationship of the individual to God was always important in the Christian tradition; it became more so in the Protestant Reformation, where the priestly authority was de-emphasized in some sects and abolished in others. Now, in most Christian churches, religion is an individual matter for adults, and even children have much more opportunity to deal with God than with Caesar.

There are, however, exceptions. In Japan, for example, worship of the family ancestors (Smith 1975) still involves the senior members' representing the family as a whole. And even in the Christian tradition, there is at least one increasingly important church, the Church of Jesus Christ of Latter-Day Saints, in which the priestly power of the senior male to represent his wife and children is seen as a foundation of the family which, in turn, is a bulwark of God's kingdom on earth (Wallace 1987). The LDS vision of the family, however, is a self-consciously retrograde one, in which a strict division of physical and spiritual labor is seen as a defense against the fragmenting influences of modernity; it belongs to the conservative critique which is an integral and reactionary part of modernity. For the majority, representation in religions, as in political, and legal-economic matters, exists only when adults represent children or when husband and wife are assumed to have a commonality of interest.

Enabling: For the Children's Sake

The activity of enabling, something we saw as supremely important among the upwardly mobile in the tribal clusters and the C-cluster, becomes much less important in M-cluster societies. Social status is no longer dependent, in every instance, on the labor or other contribution of family members. If the African chief needed wives and sons, and the Polynesian chief followers and marriage alliances, the noble or bourgeois in the premodern complex society still required family connections and household labor to improve or maintain his position. But with the advent of modernity, one of the most important changes has been the direct participation of the individual in games of social status, games he or she can play without the backing of family members. The two young college graduates who start an electronics company in their basement, the autodidactic philosopher who wins literary fame and fortune while working on the docks, the teenage Asian sailor who jumps ship, joins the U.S. army, and becomes a prominent economist, all are U.S. Pacific coast exemplars of those whose dramatic rise in social status had nothing to do with family labor or family connections, as are the greengrocer's daughter who became Prime Minister of Britain and the shipyard electrician who became President of Poland. It is possible in modern societies for a single individual to succeed.

But the diminishing importance of enabling does not mean that this process has entirely disappeared. There are still several ways in which belonging to a family enables one to preserve or enhance social status; the difference is that these are for the most part no longer necessary; the same results can be achieved without the aid of family members' labor or connections. But in M-cluster societies, even the optional work of enabling takes on a different emphasis than it did in the tribal and C-cluster societies.

Whereas in the earlier stages, it was almost always the family head whose career was being promoted by the efforts of subordinate members of the family, in the M-societies the hierarchy is less inevitable: there are situations in which family heads benefit by their family members' help, but there are probably more situations in which it is the junior members that benefit from the concrete aid and sacrifice of their elders. Let us first look at the former situation, less common but more linked to previous societies, and then at the more exclusively modern phenomenon of child-enabling.

Family heads in many M-cluster societies still benefit greatly in their careers by the labor of other family members. The fact that males have very little responsibility for processing or socialization in such modern societies as Australia (Game and Poole 1983:89), East Germany (Edwards, 1985:37), Italy (Pearlin 1974:146), Japan (Brinton 1986:), the United States (Hochschild 1989) and the USSR (Liegele 1970:45-6; Gray 1990) means that in a situation where gender roles in the public sphere are legally equalized and men and women are thus playing the same prestige games—even Japan passed an equal employment opportunity law in 1988—men have a head start; they have wives to take care of all their domestic requirements, whereas women who are competing in the same work arenas find it necessary either to do all the housework and childrearing in addition to the career work, or else forego marriage and children entirely, something that was probably the norm for career women in the United States several decades ago, and is still a prominent pattern in Japan. In a sense, then, the second shift is more than anything else an enabling shift, one that enables the guy who is free from it to pursue his career plans unencumbered. But unlike his counterpart in, say, the Northwest Coast or late imperial China, he can play the career game with no wife, no children, and no household responsibilities either.

Another type of enabling that works to the benefit of (usually male) family heads in modern societies concerns political support. Candidates for high office, especially in the United States, not only require immense amounts of enabling labor from their families, but also display their family lives as credentials for holding office. It is perhaps impossible still for anyone without at least a spouse and preferably children to be elected U.S. president, probably because the "family values" left over from the C-cluster but considered vital to correcting America's problems are an important plank in all U.S. political platforms.

These examples notwithstanding, enabling of the family head's career, something that characterized all tribal and agrarian societies, is less prominent in modern societies than the enabling of the children—the work and sacrifices made by parents not in order to raise their own social status, but rather to enable their children to get an effective start in life. Whereas this was accomplished in the property-based systems of the C-cluster by giving dowry—a payment that not only provided resources but confirmed the status of the family the bride was coming from—in the wage-based systems of the M-cluster property of this sort is usually not the most important factor in giving a son or a daughter a start. Instead, education is, and it is in the education—usually the formal education—of the younger generation that we see the greatest efforts toward enabling in modern societies. Let us look at some examples.

Prime among the societies whose families put extreme effort into enabling children's social climbing is Japan. In middle-class families in that country today, one of the most important roles of the housewife and mother is to facilitate and help in the children's education, and specifically for enabling reasons: it was the mother's help and support for her children's education, rather than the parents' inheritance or instruction in a trade, which would ensure the children's future (Tsurumi 1970:45). This central importance of education, enabled by the mother, becomes a central concern for the Japanese household as a whole. People are supposed to keep quiet while the child (particularly the male child) is studying, particularly during the all-important exam-preparation period during the first part of the senior year in high school (Ishida 1971:51-2). It is even reported that fathers who know best for their sons will leave the boys to their books and mothers, so as not to disturb the study process (Fuse 1984, part 2:8). With the withdrawal of the father from the family and the loose marriage bond that results, it is probably no exaggeration that ensuring children's school success is the most important perceived task of the Japanese married woman; in fact women's own education is considered valuable in large part because they will be able to help their sons with their examinations (Brinton 1986).

While the Japanese case is an extreme one, it is common in modern societies that the elder generation contributes labor and material resources to enable the social status of the young. For example, mothers in the Soviet Union, though they could hardly afford to be so dedicated to their children's education as their Japanese counterparts, nevertheless considered education as the children's main chance for social mobility, and devoted considerable time and effort toward facilitating that education (Liegele 1970:151). The same was true of middle-class families in postwar England, and a survey of Blacks and Whites of several social classes in the United States in the 1980s revealed that children's success, as measured in education, was an important goal for all of them, though the motivations and sacrifices were stronger among black and white middle classes, who saw a realistic chance for upward mobility, than they were among the poor (Willie 1985:72, 155, 189-90).

Help in education, of course, is not the only way in which parents enable their children's social success in M-cluster societies. They also call on connections to start them in their careers, a fact underscored by the observation that most of the managing directors of British corporations in the 1970s obtained their posts through family connections (Young and Willmott 1973:243). This, like the work parents put into their children's education, is the reverse of the situation found, for example, where the Maori chief is careful to marry his children to the families who will provide the best affinal alliances. There, children's connections serve the household head; here, the household head's connections serve the children.

This sort of enabling of the young, so predominant in M-cluster societies, differs in one very important way from the kind of enabling we saw as so prevalent earlier, in which subordinates work on behalf of the household head. In the latter form, those who do the enabling labor expect to benefit from it, however indirectly: the rising status of the household head raises the status of the family as a whole, and short of revolution in the family system, raising the family's status is one of the best outcomes subordinate members can hope for. But in the modern child-enabling form, there is little direct benefit for the parents who do the enabling labor or provide the crucial connections—in many cases the only thing the parents gain from it is vicarious pride in the children's achievement. This, however, seems to be enough for many people in many modern societies.

But not for everyone. As mentioned above, the lessening economic and social-security value of children has led to continual drops in fertility throughout the transition from C- to M-systems (Wells 1982:92; Mitchell 1976:104-121). The fact that having children entails a felt obligation to give them a start in the world (as it does everywhere), but that, having put so much effort and so many resources into the children's education and socialization, one can expect nothing but pride in return, certainly contributes to declining fertility. Many people in M-cluster societies are not willing to have children and then not work hard on their behalf; as an alternative they have no children at all.

Emotional Support: The One Thing Remaining?

It seems the press these days is full of statements that the family, once a functional group, is now an emotional group; these statements echo in weakened form the pronouncements of American family sociologists beginning in the 1920s and 1930s. But this is of course a mistaken dichotomy; in the M-cluster as elsewhere emotional support and attachment are a primary "function" of the family, a "function" as much in the Malinowskian sense of fulfillment of a need as in the structural-functional sense. And the family sociologists of that era in fact recognized that emotional bonds were what, if anything, was likely to hold the family together in the face of the decline of everything else. When I read through the first several years of the journal Living, which started in 1939 (and then changed its name to Marriage and Family Living and finally, in the 1970s, to Journal of Marriage and the Family) I found a consistent emphasis on the idea that the perceived "crisis in the family" was due to the rising divorce rate, and that the rising divorce rate was in turn due to the decline in the family's importance in every sphere other than the emotional.

This kind of analysis carried over into postwar works on the family: the third edition of Burgess, Locke, and Thomes's textbook was entitled The Family: from Institution to Companionship, with companionship defined as behavior arising from mutual affection (1963:3). Edwin Shorter, in 1975, followed a similar line of analysis, seeing sentiment as the main factor in the emerging modern form of the family, with sentiment itself concentrated in three areas: in the erotic/romantic relationship between husband and wife, which was inherently unstable, in the maternal attachment to the infant, which had become much stronger as total fertility had declined, and in the emotional boundary between the family and the rest of the world, a boundary that replaced a former economic one (Shorter 1975:5).

But it is not just academic writing that assumes the primacy of emotional ties in American family life: even a casual survey of women's magazines reveals a strong concentration on achieving sexual satisfaction, and depending on the particular magazine, sexual satisfaction is often seen as the foundation of a stable family life. It is also a commonplace in modern America that without a strong erotic/romantic relationship between husband and wife, the entire family unit is in danger, because the couple must, for the sake of the individual development of the people involved in it, divorce when erotic/conjugal life is no longer what it used to be.

In addition to the emphasis on the emotional bond of spouses as sex partners and leisure companions, there is also a popular emphasis on the importance of maternal-child bonding and of parental love as the basis for strong and responsible character of children, a character that will, paradoxically, allow them to grow to adults that are not dependent on others but are strong and self-fulfilled as individuals (Bellah et al. 1985:56). And in the achievement of this ideal individual, the family plays a crucial role as "... a place of love and happiness where you can count on other family members" (Bellah et al., 1985:87).

Lest we think that the reduction of the whole family to a purely emotional group is merely an outgrowth of a peculiarly American "expressive individualism," however, we should hasten to point out that this process seems nearly universal in societies undergoing the modern transformation. For example, students of the English family see the primary developments in the period since the second world war as leading to almost precisely the same configuration found in the American case. In the prewar neighborhoods of London, for example, husband and wife had separate social spheres, but were held together by a division of labor based in procuring and processing alone, for the working class, but also in community of property for the propertied classes. Since the War, however, the move has been into a single social sphere, particularly in those cases in which the stability of the old working-class neighborhood has been replaced by the occupational and spatial mobility of the truly modern society (Young and Willmott 1957:28; Bott 1957:90). We see the move of the husband away from the pub, and the wife away from the local women's network, both gravitating toward the family circle in which they, as couple, are the key link; here "A partnership in leisure has replaced a partnership in work (Young and Willmott 1973:98)."

A similar redefinition of important social relationships, concentrating on emotional bonds, has gone on in Australia, where the nuclear family has assumed "a centrality in the emotional lives of the mass of the population as the arena of mutual fulfillment (Game and Poole 1983:81)," and where modern analysts, like their U.S counterparts, see the emergence of an incompletely realizable ideal of domestic/erotic companionship as the main factor in Australia's rapidly rising divorce rate (Game and Poole 1983:89). Even in northern Italy, Pearlin has characterized the nature of marriage as changing from a relationship between spouses, most of whose lives are lived in separate spheres, to one of "companionate marriage," especially in the generations who have come of age after World War II. At the same time, postwar northern Italians also considered the emotional content of parent-child ties to be extremely important, and consciously used affectionate relations with their children to make the children dependent (Pearlin 1974:43); this was a strategy more characteristic of the middle-class, where other kinds of interdependency were weaker, than of the working class (Pearlin 1974:125). Recent statistics showing that that northern Italy now has one of the world's lowest birth rates (van de Kaa 1987:19) are commensurate with the growth of the idea that the quality of the parent-child relationship is so important.

This brings us to the Japanese case, where husband-wife emotional dependence is less emphasized, where many marriages are still semi-arranged and the husband in the urban middle-class family spends most of his time either at work or socializing with workmates. In this kind of situation, the primary emotional ties are created between mother and child, a pair who see each other frequently in the father's absence, and also tend to sleep together and share other kinds of physical contact (Ishida 1970:51-52). With the increasing differentiation of the procuring and processing roles of the husband and wife (in C-cluster Japan, they did the same kind of work on the farm or in the shop; now the husband is a *sarariiman* ['salary-man'] or worker, while the wife is mostly a mother and 'homemaker'), the mother-child emotional ties have gotten even closer than they were in traditional families, where some analysts still saw them as the basis of all relationships in the society (Doi 1973:72-75; Okonogi 1978-9).

But even Japan does not stand totally contrary to the modern trend; even in the presence of the kind of division of labor that is decreasing in importance in other C-cluster societies, the husband-wife dependance and the emotional unity of the family are still concepts that are discussed and that are embodied in the controversial "ideology" of *mai-homu shugi* or my-home-ism; it is at least thought that emotional ties should form the core of family life, even if few people actually experience a life in which this kind of emotional ties are central.

This all adds up to a cluster of family systems in which, given the lessening importance of all the first seven activities, the eighth comes into its own not only as a force that intrudes, willy-nilly, into the carefully planned lives of property-based families, as in the C-cluster, but that becomes the reason for forming family bonds in the first place. And since the family bond that has the greatest emotional content in these societies—the bond between spouses—is also the one which is central to the family structure, we have a kind of life cycle and configuration of family process that much resembles that found all the way back in the B-cluster. It is to this pattern of processual configuration that we turn in Chapter 23.

Notes

1. One of the reasons Marshall Sahlins's "Domestic Mode of Production" analysis (Sahlins 1972:41-148) didn't work, and in fact was contradicted by Sahlins himself in the second part of his own article, is that he seems not to have understood that Chayanov was talking about what we would call C-cluster family systems. Sahlins tried to impose this idea of family autarky on tribal systems, where in fact we all know there is much less boundedness to the family group, in terms of procuring and other functions. He then went on in the second part of his article to show that the DMP never existed in a pure form. Of course not; it was a mixture of a C-cluster domestic organization with a tribal lack of stratification, something we know from our previous analysis does not and probably cannot exist.

2. It would seem logically that the same argument would apply to division of labor between procuring and processing. This has happened, but not everywhere and almost nowhere completely; see below under processing.

3. There were sometimes female candidates for local legislative offices, since the constitution specified there were to be a certain percentage of women representatives. But there were never more female candidates than were sufficient to fill the quotas, so they were elected automatically without anyone needing to vote for them.

23

Modern Family Process

The whole series of changes in family activities that has come about as part of the transition to modern society has thus radically altered the configuration and the strength of structural bonds. The activities whose importance has declined most seriously in the C to M transition—enabling, representation, and especially the management and control of property (with nearly everyone now a wage-earner)—are precisely those activities that held senior and junior generations together after the younger generation attained adulthood in C-cluster and to an extent in tribal systems as well. The result, as will be documented below, is not only a decline in residentially extended families (which, after all, were not a feature of certain C-cluster systems, such as those of western and central Europe), but more importantly a perceived loosening of all kinds of connections between parents and their adult children. At the same time, the diminishing importance of the division of labor in the activities of procuring and processing (as these became more easily available to individuals in conjunction with the service economy), along with the loosening of the family's power to regulate the sexuality of its members and the increase in the perceived importance of emotional attachments, has meant not so much a loosening as a transformation of the ties between husband and wife, moving from functional interdependence to idealized emotional attachment.

Changes in the Basic Dyads
Making Up the Family

The change in the activities organized in the family leads to a pattern of family process similar to that found in many B-cluster systems: pair-bonding is potentially life-long, but parent-child attachments vary greatly with the life cycle. At the same time, differences in the content of pair bonding make the M-cluster configuration somewhat different in certain ways from its B-cluster counterpart.

In B-cluster families, pair bonding was shaped by the requisites of procuring, processing, sex, and emotional attachment. In modern systems, pair bonds often involve interdependence in the division of procuring and processing labor, as in the USSR, where women were ordinarily responsible for all household chores (Liegele 1970:40), or in Japan, where Walter Edwards (1987:68) has characterized the modern pattern as "harmonious but hierarchical." But this kind of interdependency is easily circumvented. Women or men can procure for themselves through wage earning, and the majority of women in almost all M-cluster societies are in fact employed: this percentage reached 88% in the German Democratic Republic in 1984 (G. E. Edwards 1985:10), 54% in the US in 1986 (Briggs 1987:178), and slightly over 50% and growing even in Japan, where women consistently stay out of the workforce only when they have small children (Fuse 1984, II:3; Statistics Bureau 1995:82-83). (That it is almost everywhere more difficult for women to earn the same level of wages as their male counterparts is something of an *incentive* to continue marriage or other pairing, but it is not an *imperative* to do so.) Similarly, the availability of almost all of what members of most modern societies consider life's material necessities in already-processed forms such as fast foods, frozen entrées,[1] and permanent-press clothing, as well as the increased availability of processing services for hire—everything from dog-walking to Christmas decorating—means that men and women alike can process or pay for processing when necessary. The fact that people currently in pair bonds generally give the major processing role to the women, and thus recreate an interdependency that is not there by functional necessity, testifies to the effectiveness of gender ideology and perhaps even male physical strength in enforcing certain roles on women, but it is probably not a significant factor in encouraging people to *form* pair bonds; even single young men *can* live on their own, as 28 percent of males between 25 and 34 were doing in the US in 1980, and 39% percent of males from 20-24 were doing in Denmark, 26% in the Federal Republic of Germany, and 15% in the Netherlands and France in 1985 (van de Kaa 1987:33).

The importance of pairing in modern systems is similar to that in B-cluster systems in that it involves a "pairadox": pair-bonding is lifelong, in the sense that it never becomes irrelevant as it often did to the Ashanti or traditional Chinese widow, for example; even people in their seventies and eighties marry for companionship in the US and other countries. But at the same time, pair-bonding is fragile, because of the lack of interdependency in most life activities and the volatility of the emotional ties that form its basis: in almost every industrial country, divorce rates have risen in the twentieth century. In the United States, for example, divorces accounted for 3.5% of marriage terminations from 1860-1864, 24.6% in 1920-24, and over 40% since 1970 (Wells 1982:167-68); similar rates obtained in England, Denmark, and Sweden (van de Kaa 1987:16), and in the German Democratic Republic and the USSR (United Nations 1988:470-472.)

Parent-child bonds, on the other hand, are even weaker and more contingent on the phases of the life-cycle in modern systems than they were in the B-cluster. Since socialization of children remains primarily a family activity in nearly all M-cluster systems, parent-child bonds are strong in early childhood. In fact, the decrease in the number of children, the greatly increased chances of survival from birth to adulthood (98.8% of Japanese lived to age forty in the late 20th century, along with 98.2% of Canadians and 97.1% of Americans [United Nations 1988:378-403]) and the reversal of the enabling process, which now primarily consists of parents' enabling their children's success in wider spheres, have led to an ideological and in many cases behavioral *increase* in the importance of parent-child bonds in the early stages of childhood or even longer. This is true in northern Italy, where middle-class parents consciously use affection as a strategy with which to ensure their children's loyalty, a strategy much less apparent among more "traditional" working-class families. In Japan, many mothers in the postwar era felt that their attachment to their children should be so all-consuming as to preclude much other activity (Tsurumi 1970:279), and most people make a distinction between the outside world (*soto*), where propriety and self-restraint are the norm, and the inside world of the home (*uchi*), where it is good and natural to affirm affinity by *amae*, or displays of emotional self-indulgence in a context of dependency (Peak 1989:97; Doi 1973)

At various stages of adolescence, however (earlier perhaps in North America and Europe than in Japan) parent-child bonding loosens. There is widespread feeling, for example, in the contemporary U.S., that children should be independent of their parents in all respects except perhaps a residue of emotional ties by the time they reach the age of about twenty. And the separation is reinforced by generational differences in cultural preferences and, at least at times of rapid change, in ethical and moral values as well. In the modern situation, cultural differences operate as a kind of symbolic marker of generational separation, in the same way as "elite" and "mass" cultural preferences reinforce and to an extent create class divisions between the bourgeoisie and the lower middle classes (Bourdieu 1984). If each generation has its own rock music and its own films, this is not because of any intrinsic preference for one style of electric guitar over another, but rather reflects the necessity for the children to establish their own defining cultural traits in a world where practical interdependence no longer exists, but parents still attempt to hold on to their adolescent children's affection. Once interdependency is loosened in this way, it remains tenuous throughout the years when both generations are adult, as it does in so many band societies.

When the elder generation becomes unable to perform labor, in B-cluster systems this creates a second period of intergenerational dependency. In most M-systems, however, it is expected that old-age pensions, social security, and personal savings will replace labor as a procuring source for the old, so that dependency on the younger generation does not really develop until the older is incapable of processing for itself, at which point various kinds of residential, cooking, and other arrangements may be made. In some cases, however, even processing needs are taken care of not by adult offspring but by institutions such as retirement manors and, in cases of real disability, nursing homes. For example, in the Netherlands in 1985, there were about 8 places in old-age homes and nursing homes for every hundred people over 65; in the United States, the proportion of over-65 people actually living in institutions is usually given at about 5%, rising to more than 20% of those over 85; in Poland, where the M-transition was much slower; only about 1.4 percent of the over-65 population lived outside a family household (Gerritsen et. al. 1990; Eustis, Greenberg, and Patten 1984:29; Synak 1989). This secondary period of dependency is thus more contingent in M- than in B-systems, or indeed than anywhere else.

If family solidarity in any society is composed of a series of intertwined bonds among individuals, it becomes clear that in the M-cluster, with the extreme loosening of parent-child bonds in the middle phase of the life-cycle, as well as the increased emotional importance of the husband-wife tie, along with the simultaneously decreasing importance of procuring and processing, and the increasing fragility of that same tie, the family developmental cycle will be one that de-emphasizes intergenerational ties and tries to build itself around the emotional attachment of husband and wife, parents and small children. This kind of structure, I submit, is and must be inherently unstable; those caught in it will either lament its instability and try to keep it coherent, or they will declare themselves free from any rules or conventions whatsoever, and go on to invent alternative forms.

The forms that result from this process of weakening and reinvention are discussed in the section after next. But before proceeding to this description, I must give some attention to another aspect of the modern condition that effects family process: the demographic shifts that attend the appearance of science and industry in the modern world.

Demographic Change

Probably for the first time in human history, the transformation from C-to M-cluster societies has included a fundamental demographic revolution. While the transitions from the nomadic existence of the B-cluster to the settled agricultural life of the tribal societies represented in this book by the A-, O-, and N- cluster examples may have entailed somewhat raised fertility, due to shorter child-spacing, and perhaps slightly lowered mortality (though this would depend on particular environments), the demographic regime of the tribal and C-cluster societies must have differed more in degree than in kind—fertility and mortality remained at several times their modern levels for thousands of years. But then, suddenly between 1750 and the present, everything has changed radically; both mortality and fertility have been cut to a fraction of their former rates. So we must consider explicitly the demographic characteristics of the M-cluster societies if we are going to understand modern family systems.

Demographic changes in the C- to M- transition and beyond stem from two primary sets of causes. First, science has reduced mortality to the point where almost everyone lives to be old, and people no longer need to bear two children to produce one potential adult, as was the case until the last two hundred years almost everywhere. Second, the declines and changes in interdependencies, as outlined above, have reduced the desirability of children, making them optional instead of necessary in most modern cultures. These two sets of causes have resulted in lower mortality at all ages, in lowered fertility by all measures, and in less frequent and later marriage.

In pre-modern society, much if not most mortality occurred in the childhood years, which is another way of saying that most people never became adults. Now, as mentioned above, over 95% of infants born in Western Europe, North America, and Japan can expect to reach age 40. Almost none die as infants, as indicated by the infant-mortality rates for 1985 and 1986 shown in Table 23-1. At the same time, life expectancies in all these countries are between 70 and 75 years for males, and over 75 for females.

The net cultural effect of this drastically reduced mortality is that people can plan their lives and their families' futures with the expectation that everyone born will grow to be at least middle-aged if not old, an expectation that has ramifications not only for fertility and marriage behavior, but for issues concerned with aging and the relationships between adult generations.

Along with mortality changes come transformations in fertility. Of course, the classic demographic transition, shown in Figure 23-1, posits a historical sequence beginning with high mortality and high fertility, continuing with a period in which mortality is reduced, but fertility remains high because of cultural values and ingrained habits, followed again by a period in which people have learned that they no longer need to have a lot of children to have a few survive, and fertility declines to a level approxi-

Table 23-1: Infant Mortality in Selected Countries, 1985-86

Country	Infant Mortality per 1000 live births
Australia	10.0
Denmark	7.9
Finland	6.3
France	7.9
Federal R. of Germany	8.9
Italy	10.9
Japan	5.5
Netherlands	8.1
Singapore	9.1
United States	10.3
United Kingdom	9.4

Source: United Nations, *Demographic Yearbook*, 1988, pp. 304-308

mately the same as that of mortality, as shown in Figure 23-1. During the interim period of the demographic transition, there is a population boom, as high excess of births over deaths is expressed as rapid rates of natural increase; after the fertility decline, population growth should subside to manageable levels (Wrigley 1969:184-202).

The fertility decline has been going on in the modernizing and modern societies since at least 1800, when the first national records were kept. Crude birth rates from European countries shown in Table 23-2 illustrate this. Except for the slight recovery after the disruptions of World War II, every country has a consistent downward trend in birth rates during these years.

Total fertility rates (the number of children a woman can expect to have if she lives out her childbearing years) provide an even more vivid indicator of declining fertility, though they are not available for as long a time series in most places. In late colonial North America, total fertility rates are estimated at about 7.4; 35.9% of families had nine or more children during the late 18th century, meaning that about half the population grew up in families of nine or more siblings; by contrast only ten percent of couples had three or fewer children, and only 2.6% of children grew up in such

Table 23-2: Crude Birth Rates in Selected European Countries, 1780-1960

Year	Finland	France and Wales	England	Italy	Russia
1780	41.2				
1800	37.6	32.9			
1820	36.6	31.7			
1840	34.7	27.9	32.0		
1860	36.4	26.2	34.3	38.0[a]	49.7[b]
1880	36.5	24.6	34.2	33.9	49.7
1900	32.6	21.3	29.6	33.0	49.3
1920	27.0	21.4	28.1	32.2	30.9
1940	18.3	13.6	14.1	23.5	31.2
1960	18.5	17.9	17.1	18.1	24.9

[a]1862
[b]1861

Source: Adapted from B.R. Mitchell, *European Historical Statistics, 1750-1970* (New York: Columbia University Press, 1976) pp. 104-121.

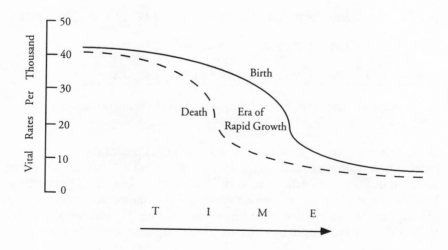

Figure 23-1: Demographic Transition Curve

small families (Wells 1982:50-51). Similar family sizes prevailed in England, with total marital fertility ranging from 6.5 through 7.0 throughout the sixteenth to eighteenth centuries (Wrigley and Schofield 1981:254)

By the 19th century, however, U.S. fertility had experienced considerable decline. Women married at the end of the 18th century (who had their families in the early 1800s) produced an average of 6.4 children; those married 1800-1849 had 4.9 children; and those born 1870-1879 had a total fertility rate of 2.8, representing a crude birth rate of around 25 per thousand in 1920. By the late 19th century, only .5% families had ten children or more, while over fifty percent had two or fewer (Wells 1982:92).The decline continued in the 20th century. Measured by a slightly different statistic, the U.S. general fertility rate per 1000 women of childbearing age declined from 130 in 1900 to just under 90 in 1940. There was an upswing between 1946 and 1960 (the famous "baby boom"), when the rate rose to about 120, but since then it has dipped to levels below those of the Great Depression; it is currently about 60, corresponding to a crude birth rate of around 13 or 14 per thousand (van Horn 1988:2). In Europe, there has been a parallel decline; there was no substantial baby boom in the 40s and 50s, and since 1950, the total fertility rates of most European countries have declined drastically, as shown in Table 23-3.

Table 23-3: Total Fertility Rates in Selected European Countires, 1950-1985

Year	Den	Swed	UK	Fran	WGerm	Neth	Italy	Port	EGerm	Czech
1950	2.58	2.30	2.22	2.93	2.10	3.09	2.49	3.04	2.30	3.04
1965	2.61	2.42	2.83	2.84	2.50	3.04	2.55	3.07	2.48	2.37
1985	1.45	1.73	1.80	1.82	1.29	1.50	1.42	1.87	1.74	2.07

Source: Adapted from van de Kaa, "Europe's Second Demographic Revoultion," *Population Bulletin* 42:1, 1987, p. 19.

At present, fertility in western Europe in general is at the replacement level or below; the regional average total fertility in 1994 was 1.5 births per woman. But the implications of such fertility declines extend beyond the level of the expansion or contraction of the population as a whole; they also mean that sibling sets continue to get smaller. We can see this if we look at the percentages of live births by birth order in selected countries in 1985, as shown in Table 23-4.

Table 23-4: Percentage of Live Births by Birth Order, Europe 1985

Birth Order	1	2	3	4	5	6+
Canada	44	35	14	4	1	1
United States	42	33	15	6	2	2
Japan	42	39	16	2	*	*
Denmark	47	36	13	3	1	*
Finland	40	35	16	5	2	2
German Dem Rep	48	37	11	2	1	1
France	42	35	15	4	2	2
England and Wales	40	36	15	5	2	1

*Less than one percent.
Source: United Nations, *Demographic Yearbook,* 1988, pp. 669-742.

In all of these countries, a quarter or fewer of live births are third-and higher-order children. By contrast, the pattern in countries that have not yet laid the demographic foundations of modernity is quite different, as illustrated by two of the countries for which data are available. Here, as shown in Table 23-5, over half the births are third- and higher-order, and fifth and higher order births compose almost a quarter, as against a twenty-fifth or less in the M-cluster societies.

Table 23-5: Percentage of Live Births by Birth Order, Philippines and Egypt, 1985

Birth Order	1	2	3	4	5	6+
Philippines	28	20	15	11	7	16
Egypt	19	21	19	15	10	14

Source: United Nations, *Demographic Yearbook,* 1988, pp. 660, 701.

Another way to look at the shrinking size of sibling sets implied by lowered fertility is to look at the percentages of women of various parities among women aged 40-44, the youngest cohort that can be expected to have basically completed its childbearing (Table 23-6). In all these countries, two is the modal number of children born to mothers of this cohort; in Canada, Australia, and the United States, almost as many women have had three children as have had two, while in East Germany, the second most popular number is one. In each case, around one woman in ten or twelve is childless, while only a quarter or slightly more of all women (and only an eighth in East Germany) have borne four or more.

Table 23-6: Percentages of Women by Parity, Ages 40-44, M-Cluster Countries

	Number of live births						
	0	1	2	3	4	5	6+
Canada 1981	7	10	29	25	15	7	3
United States 1980	11	10	24	23	15	8	9
German DemRep 1981	9	27	34	17	7	3	2
Australia 1981	8	14	27	26	15	6	5

Source: United Nations, Demographic Yearbook, 1986, pp. 1040-1073.

Once again, a contrast with the data in Table 23-7 may be instructive. In Kenya and Rwanda, where A-cluster accretive strategies still survive, the modal number of children borne is nine, while women with four or fewer children constitute well under a quarter of the cohort. Nepal, showing more C-cluster than rank society influences, is somewhat less radically different from our M-cluster examples, partly because the rate of childlessness is so high, but the modal parity is four, and a third of the cohort has borne five or more children, still presenting us with a picture where large sibling sets are the norm, and only a few people grow up with one sibling or none.

Table 23-7: Percentages of Women by Parity, Ages 40–44, Incompletely M-Cluster Countries

	Number of live births						
	0	1	2	3	4	5	6+
Rwanda 1978	2	2	2	3	5	7	79
Kenya 1979	4	3	4	4	5	7	67
Nepal 1981	21	6	9	11	13	12	21

Source: United Nations, Demographic Yearbook, 1986, pp. 1040-1073.

Reasons for the drastic fertility drop in modern times are really of two kinds, and emerge in historical sequence. During the early stages of the modernization process, children continue to be seen as an asset, and women in most societies continue to assume that being a good wife and mother is their highest calling. As Van Horn observes for the United States, "Society's tenacious belief that women should remain the custodians of the home diminished not at all in the first four decades of the twentieth century" (1988:47). At this stage, in which functional differentiation of male and female roles increases as men take outside jobs and women become custodians of the home (Young and Willmott 1973:73-84), fertility falls primarily *because* mortality falls. People still perceive five or so children as the ideal family size, but they can achieve this by giving birth to four or five children, instead of bearing nine or ten in the hopes that four or five will survive.

The latter period, which van de Kaa (1987) calls the "second demographic transition," marks the full flowering of the societal and cultural complex that I have described above as modernity. In this period, the majority of people discard previous assumptions about the value of children and about gender roles. The assumption of functionally differential roles for men and women is discarded, with the resulting belief that women and men are qualified for almost all the same work, and for all the same social positions. This provides two disincentives to childbearing: first, having children may get in the way of the goal of self-fulfillment (van de Kaa 1987:6); among the upper-middle classes especially it is no longer assumed that home and family are the only proper context for a woman's energies (Van Horn 1988:187-193). Secondly, when women do enter the work-force with the goal of *either* self-fulfillment or simply making ends meet, it is still assumed that they will be primarily responsible for socialization (Hochschild 1989); the ever-debated question of "balancing a career and a family" comes up, and in the competition between these two the family, if not losing out entirely, is delayed or shrunk or both. In short, the fertility decline of modern times has two components: the first is an adjustment to lower mortality, and the second is an adjustment to changing gender roles and to the increased "opportunity costs" of bearing children (van de Kaa 1987:6).

This fertility decline is also accompanied in its later stages by other demographic changes, including declining overall rates of marriage and rising marriage ages. For example, as shown in Table 23-8, the total marriage rate in Europe, which was around 1000 in 1965, had slipped to six or seven hundred by the mid-eighties (van de Kaa 1987:14).[2]

In the United States in the same period, the percentage never married in the age-group 30-34 rose from 11.9% of men and 6.9% of women in 1960 to 20.8% of men and 13.5% of women in 1985. Some of those, of course, would

Table 23-8:Total First Marriage Rate, Selected European Countries, 1965-85

	DN	SF	S	UK*	AU	F	ND	GR	IT	E
1965	1026	959	986	1038	923	1013	1124	1218	998	1008
1985	527	610	479	666	637	530	627	942	731	684

*England and Wales only.
Source: Adapted from Dirk J. van de Kaa, "Europe's Demographic Transition," *Population Bulletin* 42:1, March, 1987, p. 14.

later marry, but this reflects a significant portion of people who would never marry at all (Sternlieb and Hughes 1986:16).

These figures also reflect the delay of marriage in the United States in the last three decades, a trend that reverses the tendency toward earlier marriage of the baby-boom years (Wells 1982:231-232). Similarly, mean ages at first marriage in northern and western Europe have risen from around 22.5-23.5 in the late sixties to between 23.6 (United Kingdom) and 27.3 (Sweden) in the mid-1980s (van de Kaa 1987:15).

Along with the higher divorce rates mentioned earlier, the changes in marriage rates and mean ages at first marriage seem to reflect a profound attitude change: no longer, in Western Europe and North America, is marriage assumed to be something that just about every adult should be involved in. There are many factors here. One is the increased acceptability and safety of premarital sex. A second is the wider acceptance of alternatives to marriage, such as permanent singlehood, cohabitation, single-parenthood, and various kinds of temporary and permanent homosexual unions (Sternlieb and Hughes 1986:24). A third is the tendency of people born after 1945 to "prolong their youth until age thirty and either postpone assuming traditional adult roles or reject them completely (Van Horn 1986:156-57)" in the name of career or other kinds of self-fulfillment. This whole complex of attitudes is reflected dramatically in a longitudinal study of Dutch attitudes reported by van de Kaa: in 1965, 60% agreed that married people were generally happier than single people. In 1983, only 18% agreed with the same statement (1987:8).

New Variations on the Developmental Cycle

This complex of demographic changes—later and less universal marriage, later and drastically lower fertility, and dramatically decreased mortality at all ages—acts in concert with the loosening and redefinition of bonds between family members to produce new variations on the domestic developmental cycle, characteristic of the M-cluster. Before we describe this new cycle in detail, it is important to stress two cautions: first, the contested nature of modern social institutions means that nowhere is there a single developmental cycle; rather there is a series of choices throughout the individual life cycle that combine to produce a series of related developmental patterns in any society, varying by class, ethnic group, religious affiliation, and simply individual preference. Second, there are economic and other constraints that lead to class differences in the developmental cycle in all industrialized countries, but particularly in the United States, where class differences in income, education, and lifestyle are much greater than those in Europe or Japan. The particular patterns that have become known as the "Black underclass family," discussed below, are the most dramatic instance of the importance of class variation. Third, there seem to be cultural differences among countries as well; in particular Japan has not followed the same road to modernity as have the peoples of Europe and North America, and the family system of modern Japan is an important exception to the overall pattern seen in Western societies. There may also be cultural differences at work in the distinctions between White and Black family patterns in the United States, though these seem less important than class differences. In spite of these variations, however, there are general patterns, and we turn to these before we consider variations and exceptions.

The course of the developmental cycle in M-cluster family systems is by and large determined by the demographic changes and the changes in family activities associated with the C- to M-transition. By the time the M-pattern is fully realized, interpersonal dependencies can be seen as falling into the following pattern:

Each individual has three kinds of potential dependencies: vertical links upward, to parent or parents; vertical links downward, to children; and horizontal links, to spouse or other partner. The life cycle of the individual is a composite of these links as they change in importance over time. Vertical links upward are important for the first fifteen to twenty years of the individual's life, because of interdependency in processing, procuring, representation, and socialization. They may become important again when the individual's parents become aged, because of processing and procuring needs, and occasionally the need for representation, as when the aged are judged legally or practically incompetent. Vertical links downward are important for that proportion of the population that chooses to bear children; the pattern is the same as with the upward links, in that there is a relatively fixed period of seventeen to twenty-five years when one takes care of one's children, and a sometimes a variable period in which one's children take care of one's aging self.

Horizontal links are the most variable in this M-pattern, for reasons detailed above; though processing and procuring interdependencies are possible, they are not necessary; sexual and emotional links are generally thought more important, but even these are not necessarily sought in the context of permanent pairing. So the typical individual life course has become a series of pairings and unpairings—some officially marriages, others merely cohabitations; these pairings are influenced by the current status of vertical links, particularly the early phase of downward links to one's children, in that people with children are more likely to seek pairing relationships or remain in them than are people with no dependent children at the time. But the rising number of single-parent families recorded in all M-cluster systems testifies that the presence of a downward vertical link does not necessarily require a horizontal link at the same time.

The pattern of actual household forms across time or in a cross-sectional survey is thus the result of the timing of the decisions of individuals to form or break vertical and horizontal links, by bearing children, leaving home, moving in with, moving apart from, marrying, separating, and divorcing. Within the specific demographic parameters now current in Western Europe and North America, we can put forth a tentative model of what the developmental cycle of M-cluster family systems now looks like. We will first describe a kind of ideal-type model, which pertains nowhere in particular, along with particular species of that type as they exist in various countries. Then we will discuss two outlier models that require significant revision of the principles set out to explain the ideal type.

The Ideal Type: Western Europe and the North American "Mainstream"

In this model, since the formation and dissolution of horizontal links is irregular and dependent on individual perceptions of emotional ties, any consistency we find in such family systems will take the shape of a series of stages in the formation and dissolution of vertical ties. In such a model, there are five possible stages in the individual life-cycle, and the individual's family configuration derives from a conjunction of that individual's stage and the stages of others with which the individual is tied. We can illustrate the outline of this cycle schematically in Figure 23-2.

For the M-cluster developmental cycle, we have eliminated the box indicating the solidary unit; in the M-cluster cycle it is ephemeral at best, and the important links are between individuals, as illustrated by the vertical and horizontal lines.

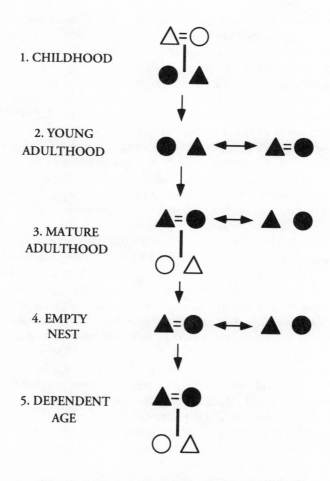

Figure 23-2: Stages in an M-Cluster Developmental Cycle

The individual stages of this cycle are as described here:

Stage 1: Childhood. This stage lasts from birth to leaving home. In contrast to the C-cluster pattern, where leaving home was usually tied to marriage, and the A-cluster pattern, where leaving home was tied to marriage for women and to the assumption of a warrior occupational role for men, who would remain unmarried throughout this stage, the M-cluster pattern defines leaving home as an autonomous event, tied to a perceived maturation and ability to live independently, and often to the assumption of full-time employment or higher education, but not necessarily to singlehood or marriage. Typically the phase of childhood lasts between sixteen and 24 years. In a study of six Western European countries, Kiernan found that at least 88% of sixteen and seventeen-year-olds of both sexes were living with at least one parent in all six countries, while less than half the men, and outside Ireland a fifth or less of the women, were still living with parents at ages 22-24, as shown in Table 23-9.

During this first, or childhood stage, the ideal is everywhere that a child will grow up in a home with two parents. In many places, this ideal is also the statistical norm: in West Germany 83 percent (van de Kaa 1987:35) or 90 percent (Schwartz 1988:77) of children under 18 were living with both parents in the early 1980s, a percentage thought to be comparable to those found in other West European countries. Even in Sweden, where over 40% of children are born to unmarried women, 74 percent of children were living with two parents in 1982 (Schwartz 1988:77). Among Whites in the US, over 80% of families with children were two-parent families (Rawlings 1984:7).

That most children grow up in a household with two parents, however, should not be allowed to obscure the fact that divorce, separation, re-cohabitation, and separation from cohabitation enter into the lives of many children even in the mainstream areas. In Germany, for example, even if well over eighty percent of children were living with two parents in any cross-sectional sample, a quarter lived in a one-parent household at some time during their childhood, a statistic that reflects the presence of divorce and remarriage (Schwartz 1988:77). Similarly, in the United States, with a divorce rate about twice that of West Germany, we can expect a much greater movement into- and out of one- and two- parent arrangements; this accounts for the popular attention paid to "step-families" as one of the important challenges for the American family in the nineties (Newsweek 1989).

For most children in all these societies, the one-parent configuration, while common, is usually temporary (van de Kaa 1987:35).

Combined with the low total fertility rates detailed above, this pattern of divorce and remarriage contributes to a childhood stage in which children live in two-generation families most of the time (by the 1980s, three-generation households were only 2.5 percent of Canadian and 5% of German households [Schwartz 1977:73-74]), and in which they may or may not oscillate between families with one and two adults. Another variation within this basic pattern, but one for which I have found no numerical data, is the joint custody after divorce arrangement, in which children alternate monthly, weekly, or more often between the households of two parents, either of which may itself contain the parent alone or the parent and a new partner. Insofar as children pass through one-parent arrangements during their overall childhood stage, they are overwhelmingly more likely to live with their mother than with their father. In 1983, for example, the following percentages in Table 23-10 obtained.Only about one child in fifty is living with just the father in these three M-cluster societies.

Table 23-9: Percentage of Children Living with Parent or Parents at Various Ages, 1982

		16-17	18-19	20-21	22-24
UNITED KINGDOM					
	Males	100	93	70	43
	Females	88	68	35	16
IRELAND					
	Males	100	92	83	43
	Females	98	93	85	42
NETHERLANDS					
	Males	98	96	82	38
	Females	98	88	48	12
FRANCE					
	Males	94	81	70	38
	Females	97	82	45	14
WEST GERMANY					
	Males	98	84	80	29
	Females	92	68	48	20
DENMARK					
	Males	89	71	33	20
	Females	100	47	20	2

Source: Kathleen Kiernan, " Leaving Home: Living Arrangements of Young People in Six West-European Countries," *European Journal of Population*, 1986 (2), p. 179.

Table 23-10: Percentages of Children Living with One Parent Only, 1983

	Mother Only	*Father Only*
United States Whites	15.1	2.3
Sweden	24	2
West Germany	8	2

Source: Adapted from Karl Schwarz , "Household Trends in Europe after World War II," in Nico Keiolman, Anton Kuijsten, and Ad voss, eds, *Modelling Household Formation and Dissolution*, (Oxford: Clarendon Press, 1988) p.77; Steve Rawlings, *Household and Family Characteristics*, March 1983. *Current Population Reports: Population Characteristics, Series 20, No. 388.*[a] (Washington, D.C.: U.S. Bureau of the Census 1984), p. 7.

It is also rare for children to be living with no parents at all. Among White Americans in 1982, only 2% of children were living with neither parent; for black Americans the figure is 8%, of which almost all are living with another relative, often a grandmother (Matley and Johnson 1983:16)

Stage 2: Young Adulthood or Pre-parenthood. The transition from C- to M-cluster social forms has meant for many people the development of an entirely new phase in the life cycle: the young adult time between leaving home and becoming a parent. In certain phases of Western European history, this phase existed for some proportion of the population in the form of domestic service, where unmarried young adults became functionally interdependent with households of unrelated people (Laslett 1972:56-57). But now this stage is something different—a period in which young adults are functionally independent or virtually independent of anyone in an older generation, living "on their own."

The length of this stage without important vertical ties varies greatly; so does the presence or absence of horizontal ties over the course of the stage. In the United States and Western Europe both, most people have left the parental home by the age of 21 or 22 (see above), and the average age at the birth of the first child is somewhere from 23 to 27 (van de Kaa 1987:15; HHS 1989:15-16). In the United States, class differences in fertility behavior have re-emerged in the cohorts born since 1945, so that, particularly among the wealthier and more educated segments of the population, "This cohort tended to prolong their youth until age thirty and either postponed assuming traditional adult roles or rejected them completely (van Horn 1988:157)."

Whether this stage of young adulthood lasts a few months or more than a decade, it involves both variety and fluidity of living arrangements. In Great Britain, for example, over half the males and over three-quarters of the females aged 20-24 and living away from their parents were already married (Kiernan 1986:181-182); while in West Germany and Denmark, the same group of people tended to either cohabit with a person of the opposite sex or live alone. Other countries showed still other, divergent patterns, shown in Table 23-11. It appears from these figures that the most common pattern in Great Britain and Ireland is to go directly from parents' home to marriage, or if not directly, at a very short interval. This is less common in the Netherlands and France, which have higher rates of cohabitation and living alone, a pattern seen even more intensely in West Germany and especially Denmark. I know of no exactly comparable figures for the United States, but it is noteworthy that 23 percent of all households in the US in 1983 consisted of single persons, and that about seven or eight percent of all households consisted of never-married persons, most of them presumably in their twenties (Rawlings 1984:198). About two percent of households consisted of cohabiting couples, of which a majority

Table 23-11: Living Arrangements of 20-24 Year Olds, 1982

	With parents	Married	Cohabiting	Alone	Sharing
UNITED KINGDOM					
Male	58	28	3	4	8
Females	23	59	6	6	7
IRELAND					
Males	62	21	0	4	13
Females	57	29	1	3	10
NETHERLANDS					
Males	58	17	10	11	4
Females	28	48	7	8	9
FRANCE					
Males	52	18	14	13	4
Females	27	43	12	17	2
WEST GERMANY					
Males	43	11	19	21	5
Females	31	2	14	23	4
DENMARK					
Males	26	11	24	29	10
Females	11	12	42	31	4

Source: Adapted from Kathleen Kiernan, "Leaving Home: Living Arrangements of Young People in Six West-European Countries," *European Journal of Population*, 1986(2), pp. 179-182.

were under forty (Sternlieb and Hughes 1986:17-18). The pattern thus appears to be something like that found in France or Germany, with marriage, cohabitation, and living alone all common choices for people in their twenties.

Given that marriage has always been an option for this age-group, we need to explain the rise of cohabitation and living alone as alternatives. Clearly living alone has been made viable by the simplification of procuring and processing labor (anyone can microwave a meal, order a pizza, drop off the clothes at the laundry or throw them into the coin laundromat), as well as the possibility of earning a living wage from a wide variety of employments available to people in this age bracket. The shift in sexual morality has undoubtedly also played a part here; permanent or even long-term commitment is no longer a prerequisite for sexual relations (Mintz and Kellogg 1988:205-210). In addition, reliable contraception has, as mentioned above, fundamentally altered the relationship between sex and responsibility.

Cohabitation reflects, I think, a deeper and more fundamental value-shift, one that has less to do with the availability of fast food and other services and more to do with broad trends of secularization (marriage need no longer give God's approval to sexual relations), and the shift from fulfillment of duty to individual self-realization that seems to characterize personal goals in general in the M-cluster societies. That there still appears to be considerable opposition to the practice, particularly among the generations born before World War II, whereas there is no opposition to living alone, indicates that cohabitation stems from a value-shift that is not yet complete, at least in United States society.

At the same time, cohabitation as a process is much less distinct than cohabitation as a social and ethical issue. As reported by Schmid (1988:20), most cohabiting relationships begin simply as sexual relationships between people living in some other arrangement, and gradually move from spending occasional nights together to moving in and giving up one or the other apartment or room. It is also clear that cohabitation is considered a temporary stage by most people living this way. Wells (1982:231) reports that about 40% of cohabiting unions in the US will end up as marriage, and in most Western countries, the decision to bear children usually means a decision to convert from cohabitation to marriage. The only exceptions are Denmark and Sweden, where most first children are born to cohabiting couples, but even there the percentage of all coresident couples who are married moves from 31% in the 20-24 age group to 82% of those between 30 and 34 (van de Kaa 1988:18). In other words, where C-cluster morals disapproved of sex outside marriage altogether, in the United States and most of Western Europe, sex outside marriage is fine, but not childbearing; whereas in Sweden and Denmark, even childbearing is not enough to risk making the marital commitment. In the end, however, even Swedes and Danes mostly get married. Young adulthood is thus a transitional stage for most people in most M-cluster societies. There is, however, a growing proportion who have decided to forego childbearing entirely, and thus to blur the distinction between the young adult phase and the next phase—parenthood. In the early 1980s, for example, about 11% of U.S. women aged 40-44 had borne no children, and were thus likely to remain childless; the corresponding figures were 9% for Canada and 7% for Australia (United Nations 1988:1040-1126). Van Horn (1988:159) predicts that of the total baby-boom cohort in the US (born 1945-1960) as many as 25% will remain childless. Even marriage does not necessarily mean childbearing: in 1992, 15.3% of the *married* women in the U.S. had borne no children (Bachu 1993:xx). In a 1986 survey done in the Netherlands, 86% of those polled stated that voluntary childlessness was acceptable, up from 22% in 1960. As children have lost economic value and gained in opportunity costs, they are increasingly seen as one avenue to self-fulfillment among others, so that not everyone needs them. For the childless, there is no clear division between young adulthood and maturity.

Stage Three: Mature Adulthood. For those who do make the clear transition to mature adulthood as marked by childbearing, there is in the Western European countries and particularly the United States a wide range of variation in the age at which the first children are born. Mean ages for all Western M-cluster societies are in the middle-twenties, but they mask a wide range, which in the United States at least is heavily influenced by class. Among people with only high-school education or less, first childbirth typically occurs in the early twenties or even earlier (the teenage pregnancy pattern of the underclass will be discussed below), while it is common for professional women, if they become mothers at all, to wait until after thirty[3] or even forty to enter into childbearing. Since those who wait until later tend to have fewer children (van Horn 1988:162), this means that the total fertility of the higher socioeconomic groups is less than that of those further down the scale.

As Europe had no baby-boom, it appears to have less class differential in timing of childbearing; none of my sources mentions this as an important factor in the developmental cycle. But in all Western M-cluster systems, childbearing is both later and sparser than it was before or during the C- to M-transition.

The transition to parenthood in M-cluster systems is also almost completely independent of the transition to partnerhood. Most people have lived with a sexual partner (or had multiple partners without living with them) for several years, even up to two decades, before childbearing. This contributes not only to the expressed fear of losing one's freedom and independence with the advent of a child, but also to the expressed idea that having children is some kind of awesome responsibility that ought not to be entered into lightly—the contrast with the pre-modern idea that children are a natural part of everyone's life course could hardly be more striking. During the period of adulthood with children, the normative pattern is to remain in a couple relationship, and almost everywhere this is still normatively a martial relationship, though this is showing signs of change in two directions. First, more and more unmarried women are bearing children. In the U.S. in 1992, 11.6 percent of women 15-44, and 36.5% of women 30-39, had borne at least one child out of wedlock (Bachu 1993:xix). In many cases, however, unmarried women who bear children marry soon after children are born. Second, it is no longer the case that a couple with children can automatically expect to stay together while these children grow up. Instead couples repeat in their own generation the pattern described above for the childhood stage, in which uncouplings and recouplings are a feature of about 40% or so of the couples who enter this phase. Divorce, even for people with young children, is no longer so stigmatized, and this leads to a situation in which about 20% of families with children are single-parent families in the United States (Rawlings 1984:7), and from ten to twenty percent in various European countries (Schmid 1988:19). Recouplings, of course, mean that "step-families," once primarily caused by the early death of one parent and consequent remarriage for purposes of achieving a processing and procuring division of labor, are now almost exclusively the result of divorce and remarriage, both undertaken for emotional reasons.

The period of adulthood with children is perhaps the phase of the life-cycle thought most typical or normative in M-society, but it in fact lasts a shorter time than was common in earlier societies with higher total fertility rates. The low total fertility rates of North America and Europe (see above, p. 31) mean that less than ten percent of births are fourth- and higher-order, and that the majority of those who do have children have only one or two. This, in turn, means that even with the use of contraception in child-spacing, the interval between first and last childbirth is rarely more than eight to ten years, and is quite commonly zero (if only one child is born) to three or four years (if two children are deliberately spaced). Given that most children tend to move out of the parental home by age 22 or so, this means the total length of the period of adulthood with children varies from about 18 years to no more than 32, and that most people are emerging into the "empty nest" phase of the life-cycle between ages forty and sixty.

Stage Four: Empty Nest. The empty-nest, the couple or single-parent whose children have grown up and left home, is a phenomenon almost exclusively of M-cluster developmental cycles. In many C-systems, of course, including those stem-family systems of England, Japan, much of France and Germany, as well as the joint-family systems of Eastern Europe and most of Asia, the possibility rarely came up, because at least one child was expected to remain in the parents' home even after marriage. But even in systems where the nuclear family was the norm (see above, Chapter 19), as in Colonial North America, the nest seldom emptied for a married couple. An average of 7-10 children born over a period of twenty to twenty-five years, a consequent forty to forty-five year duration of the adulthood with children stage, combined with much higher mortality rates at all ages, meant that most couples experienced the death of one spouse before the last child left home (Wells 1982:54-55). Widows living alone were more common than couples whose children were all grown, but even they outlived the departure of their youngest child by only an average of four or five years, though of course some lived much longer. Widows with young children were likely to remarry.

In the "mainstream" M-cluster system, things are more complex. A sizable portion of people have no children, and those who do vary in the onset of childbearing from the late teens to the mid-forties. For men who marry a second time, sometimes to wives two or three decades their junior, children can be born at 60 or older, putting survival to the child's maturity much in doubt.[4] On the other hand, couples who have only one or two children while in their early twenties can have their nests emptied out by age 45, looking forward to 30 years or more before the first spouse dies. At the same time, the empty-nest phase, like the earlier ones, is susceptible to divorce and remarriage, to the same kind of pattern of pairing and unpairing.

Stage 5: Old Age Dependency. Statistics about graying populations abound in today's news media. The 20% or more people who are over 65 in most Western European countries today (Keyfitz and Flieger 1990), and the even greater percentage expected by the year 2030 (Bulatao et al. 1990) are caused both by increasing life expectancies—around eighty for females and seventy-five for males in all the M-cluster societies—and more importantly by the lowering of fertility that straightens the sides of the population pyramid until they are almost vertical to age sixty or so. The great majority of old people, however, will continue to live with a partner or alone for most of this phase of the life-cycle. Schwartz, for example, estimates that German women aged 60 had a life-expectancy of 20.8 years, of which they could expect to spend 10.0 years living alone; for men, less likely to outlive their spouses, the corresponding figures were 16.5 and 2.2. At 75, women could expect to live 5.9 of their remaining 9.7 years alone; men 1.7 of their remaining 7.6 years (Schwartz 1988:81-82). Similarly, in the United States in 1980, widows over 65 were the largest category of single-person households (Bureau of the Census 1981:4).

If most old people live alone, they are not necessarily completely independent; there seems to be a preference almost everywhere for elders who are losing physical and mental competence to continue to live separately from their offspring, but to have some regular contact with them, perhaps increasing as the parents need help with more aspects of daily life. A 1986 survey found, for example, that in Denmark and the United States, only about 3% of respondents thought that living together with aged parents was a good idea, but less than one-half of one percent preferred to have no regular contact with them (Martin 1989:16). These preferred arrangements are also reflected in the fact that in Canada, three- and four-generation families, most of which would include a dependent elder at some time during their duration, declined from 4% to 2.5% of all households between 1971 and 1981, and that in Germany, while 5% of adults grew up in a household that included their grandparents, by 1982 there were only 500,000 three- or four-generation households in the country, almost all of them in rural areas (Schwarz 1988:74-75).

Institutionalization may, of course, be the last phase in the life-cycle of the elderly, but statistics show that institutionalized elderly form only about 8% percent of the population over 65 in the Netherlands, for example (Gerritsen et. al. 1990), and in the United States, 14% of the men and 23% of the women over 85, but only 4.2% of the men and 6.8% of the women between 75 and 84, and only a little over 1% of the men and women between 65 and 74 (O'Brien 1987:8, 12).

Household Frequencies

The synchronic manifestation of the developmental cycle is, of course, the percentage distribution of household types. Although such a synchronic view can be misleading—different processes can lead to the same outcome— it may still be useful to present a tabulation of the household types in certain countries that display the processes outlined above.

We can begin with figures for 1983 in the United States shown in Table 23-12.

Table 23-12: Percentages of Household Types, United States 1983

	Perecent of Households in such Households	Percent of Persons
Family Households	73.1	88.2
Married Couples	59.5	77.8
With Children under 18	29.0	45.1
Male Head, Single	2.4	2.5
Female Head, Single	11.3	12.9
With Children under 18	6.8	8.1
Non-family Households	26.8	11.8
Alone	22.9	8.4
Male	8.9	3.3
Female	14.1	5.1

Source: Steve Rawlings, Household and Family Characteristics, March 1983. Current Population Reports: Population Characteristics, Series 20, No. 388. (Washington, D.C.: U.S. bureau of the Census., 1984) pp. 2-3.

In light of the previous discussion of trends in demographic rates and loosening of horizontal and vertical ties, it is striking that the figures appear so conservative. Over three-quarters of the population is living in households with married couples at the head, indicating that marriage is still the expected state for most of the population. Even though the increasing emotional requirements of spousehood make it harder to maintain a marriage, people seem to be re-coupling at a great rate—about half of divorced mothers are reported to remarry within two years of their divorce (Mintz and Kellogg 1988:228). Of families with children under eighteen, again over three-quarters are headed by married couples, and the great majority of the rest are headed by women. Singles, either in the young adult phase, between childless marriages, or widowed, account for over a fifth of the households, but less than ten percent of the population. While 28.2 percent of males between the ages of 25 and 34 were living alone, only 13.7 percent lived alone between 35 and 44. The corresponding figures for females were 11.2 and 4.8 percent (Bureau of the Census 1980:4). In other words, singlehood, as outlined above, is a stage.

When we consider that almost all the singles are in phases of the life cycle before, between, or after coupling relationships, we again see the similarity between M- and B-cluster systems: pairing (including cohabiting pairs, which account for about two percent) seems to be the normative state of adults in this society, even though people rapidly change pairs. If we consider that families with children under 18 account for the vast bulk of families with two generations (since children tend to move out by 21 or 22), then only 35% of the households consist of two or more generations, though slightly over half the population is living in two (or more) generation households. Another way to think of this is that almost everyone spends an average of 20 years in the childhood phase, and those who have children (between 80 and 90 percent) spend another 20 years or so in households with their children, then about half of an eighty-year life span is spent in a two-generation household, which is reflected in the figure of about half the people at any one time living in those households.

The interpretation of these U.S. figures is supported by parallel European trends; witness the following tabulation for West Germany in 1981, shown in Table 23-13. The overall trends here are similar to those in the comparable U.S. households, but there are differences. The United States sample includes a much larger number of both males and females living with no partners, with or without children, which probably reflects the divorce rate in the U.S., which is about twice what it is in Germany. More Germans than Americans live in households with children under 18 (66 percent as opposed to 55), which may reflect again the lower divorce rate and the consequent propensity for children to be living in houses with more members. More Germans live singly than Americans, but a smaller percentage of the singles are divorced in Germany (about 11%) as opposed to about 26.4% of the males and 17% of the females living without relatives in the U.S. (Schwarz 1983:575; Rawlings 1983:198).

Table 23-13: Percentages of Household Types, Germany, 1981

	Percent of Households	Percent of Persons in such Households
Family Households	66.2	83.8
Married Couples	62.2	78.5
With Children under 18	40.0	61.5
Male Head, Single	.6	.8
Female Head, Single	3.4	4.5
With Children under 18	3.1	4.2
Non-family Households	33.8	14.2
Alone	30.8	12.5
Male	9.5	3.9
Female	21.3	8.6

Source: Adapted from Karl Schwarz, "Household Trends in Europe after World War II," in Nico Keilman, Anton Kuijsten, and Af Vossen, eds., *Modelling Household Formation and Dissolution* (Oxford: Clarendon Press, 1983), p. 575.

From these two examples, we can see that a particular pattern of the developmental cycle has emerged. Families with children still take up a major portion of most people's life cycle, and form a small majority of the total households in the population. The addition of significant life-cycle stages of young adulthood and empty-nesthood, however, means that one-generation households, including singles, widows, and empty-nest couples, come to occupy a considerable proportion of the population. In addition, the redefinition of marriage away from processing, procuring, and property interdependencies, and toward serving as a means of self-fulfillment, has created a pattern of coupling and uncoupling that further increases the variety in the households seen in any synchronic sample.

This rather schematic sketch, I think, serves to delineate the most common pattern of the developmental cycle in M-cluster families. But it is by no means the only pattern. Three important exceptions need also be described. First, in the United States, and not in Western European countries or Japan, there is an alternative pattern that has grown up in the so-called "underclass" of inner-city, undereducated, primarily unemployed people, most of them African-Americans. As Willie (1985) has pointed out, this is not "the Black family;" middle-class and working-class African-Americans have family patterns almost identical to those of Euro-Americans. But a significant underclass family pattern has emerged, and it reflects the particular nature of class differences in contemporary U.S. society.

Second, Japan conforms not at all to the pattern seen in Europe and in the "mainstream" United States. The stem-family cycle still predominates in Japan, as does the procuring-processing division of labor; the stage of single young-adulthood is an exception rather than an expectation.

Finally, in all these societies (perhaps less so in Japan) the debate on the proper nature of the family, the arguments that by my definition make such families modern, have given rise to a small number of people who participate in family critiques, including both the alternative family forms, such as gay and lesbian families, and the radically critical practices such as Utopian communes. There are not enough people experimenting with these forms to show up at all in the gross statistics presented above, but they deserve attention because they, more than anyone, are calling into question, and thus into direct view, the very nature of family functions. I treat the underclass and Japanese variants in the remainder of this chapter, then proceed in Chapter 24 to treat the alternative forms in the context of the discourse and arguments about alternatives to the family.

The American Black Underclass Predicament: Its Family Dimension

Among poor black people in the United States, particularly in the inner-city ghettoes that have become increasingly homogeneous in their poverty (Lemann 1986), there exists a pattern of dyadic relationships, demographic rates, and developmental cycle that is radically different from that found in other communities in the United States and Europe. I will refer to this pattern as the Black American underclass family, or underclass family for short, with the understanding that this pattern is not universal in the Black underclass (Glasgow 1980), and that it exists to a smaller extent among poor people of other ethnic groups as well. In other words this, like the more common pattern outlined in the above sections and the "Japanese alternative" described below, is an ideal type; there is a continuous scale of variation from the ideal type underclass family to the ideal type of the general M-cluster family pattern.

The Black underclass, the locus of this ideal type family pattern, can be characterized as poor, mostly isolated in depopulated inner-city ghettoes, largely unemployed and partially unemployable, and undereducated. Glasgow perhaps sums up its essence best when he says that "The underclass is distinguished from the lower class principally by its lack of mobility (1980:8)." In this situation, access to resources—money, housing, childcare, education, information—is unpredictable, and it is most difficult for people to form stable marital bonds and parent-child links that will assure the independence and support of all the members of a couple-headed household (Martin and Martin 1978:5-16). In response to this uncertainty, members of the Black underclass have developed a more flexible and adaptable pattern of family relationships.

The most important contrast between the Black underclass family pattern and the general M-cluster pattern is the relative flexibility of dyadic ties in the Black underclass pattern. In place of the pattern of solid parent-child ties that remain strong through childhood but then dissolve rather quickly in adolescence and early childhood, the Black underclass pattern consists of ties that are still strong but somewhat negotiable in childhood, but that remain available throughout adult life. And in place of the general M-pattern of pairing as the normative and most common state throughout adulthood, the Black underclass shows an ideal of pairing, but one that is often put aside for other considerations. Thus both vertical and horizontal ties are less fixed by the life cycle and more adaptable to specific exigencies.

These flexible ties attach individuals into two kinds of social networks: female-centered, extended family networks and male-centered, street-corner, tavern, and other outside networks (Scott and Black 1989; Martin and Martin 1978; LaFargue 1981). The family networks, with which we are most concerned here, each center around a head (LaFargue 1981) or "dominant family figure" (Martin and Martin 1978), which may be either a married couple of the older generation or, more commonly, a senior woman, who may be married, divorced, or never-married. This recognized family head usually lives at a headquarters house that becomes the physical center of the family network. The members of the network may live primarily in this headquarters house, but more commonly, especially in big cities, are dispersed in a series of houses and apartments. These residential units, or households, are only partly independent; members depend on the family head and on other members of the extended family network for various family functions. Family network members who gain access to resources are expected to share with other members. The satellite residential units, which Martin and Martin (1978) call "sub-extended families" are not independent nuclear family units because they are not self-sufficient; instead they are residentially separate parts of the larger extended family network. Even with the existence of these residentially separate units, however, extended *households* accounted for 30% of family households in the total U.S. Black population (Farley and Allen 1987:177-78).

The flexibility and adaptability of dyadic ties, and the extended family networks that are made up of these ties, results in an individual life-cycle and a family developmental cycle that are considerably different from those in the general M-cluster pattern shown in Figure 23-2.

A slight majority of children are born to unmarried women: in 1983, 58% of Black children and 86% of those born to women under 20 years of age (Edelman 1987:3); presumably this includes a higher percentage of those in the underclass. Depending on the circumstances of the woman who bears the children, she may take the primary role in socializing them herself, or she may give this over to her mother, grandmother, older sister, or another relative; thus the question "Who gave you birth?" is different from "Who is your mother," the latter referring to the primary caretaker. At the same time, there is a distinction made for a woman who is not the biological mother of a child, as to whether she is "raising" the child, meaning she has primary responsibility, or just "keeping" the child for the biological mother temporarily. The younger the biological mother, the more likely the social mother will be someone else (LaFargue 1981:41-43, 137-39). Biological fathers of children may or may not play an active role in procuring and socialization; some of them marry the mothers while others contribute money or other kinds of support; they may or may not live with the mothers (Scott and Black 1989:20; LaFargue 1981:139).

A child will thus grow up in a family that includes the primary caretaker (who may or may not change over the years) and a shifting collection of other relatives. Sometime in the teens, the child will become sexually active; boys will father children, of whom they will be proud, and to whose support they may or may not contribute, and girls will become pregnant. In most cases, they will not marry the father of their child, but will repeat their mother's pattern of raising the child themselves or giving it to another female relative to raise.

People entering their twenties may enter into marriage or an equivalent long-term pair relationship involving coresidence and sharing of procuring, processing, and socialization. They are, however, less likely to do so than people outside the Black underclass. In 1983, 11.9% of Black males were married by age 24, and 44.3% by age 29 (Edelman 1987:10). 32% of the total number of Black female household heads were never-married in 1982; this contrasts with only 11% unmarried White female household heads, most of whom were divorced (Matley and Johnson 1983:15).

The remainder of the life-cycle consists for most people of moving into and out of a series of pair-relationships, with less compulsion to remarry after divorce than in the general M-cluster pattern: among Black adults, there were 220 divorced people per 1000 currently married people in 1982; this contrasts with 107 per thousand among the White population (Matley and Johnson 1982:16). For males and females both, a stable pair relationship confers social respect as well as providing sex and division of labor benefits (LaFargue 1981:147).

One common pattern of pair relationships results from the low sex ratio in most ghetto communities: Scott estimates that in some urban ghetto areas, the sex ratio may be as low as 85 males per 100 females (1986:173-74). This is the pattern of polygyny, in which a man either has continuous and semi-stable relationships with two or more women, each part of an extended family network but living as a sub-extended family with her children, or a married man forms a subordinate relationship with an unmarried woman, and shares some resources with her household as well as with that of his wife (Scott 1986:173-174). Within a general situation of fragile conjugal ties, this polygynous pattern is simply one more variation.

This pattern of extended family networks, flexible and adaptable conjugal and parent-child ties, and residential dispersion of the extended family group, seems to be an adaptive response to an environment in which availability of resources is unpredictable: establish a series of links, any of which can be activated when it seems necessary or advantageous. When looked at through the ordinary statistical categories of the U.S. Census or other standard sociological measures, however, it seems to present a pattern of dispersed, female-headed, sub-nuclear family households, without access to the earning power of an attached husband and father. By 1993, 62.9% of black households consisted of single-parent families (Rawlings 1994:xv). There has thus arisen a considerable debate over whether this might be a pathological or an adaptive family system. (For an early but still pertinent review of this debate, see Martin and Martin 1978:103-114). I think the fairest evaluation is that the system is an adaptive one for dealing with the situation of scarce resources found in the underclass environment, but at the same time, given its ethic of sharing within the network, as well as ostracism of those who exit the extended family network and form independent nuclear families, it is not conducive to helping members escape the underclass predicament. As Martin and Martin point out, some economically successful married couples who originated in the extended family leave and form nuclear families outside the ghetto, at which point they retain only minimal contact with the extended family network. In other words, the family serves well to organize the activities of processing, procuring, sex, socialization, and emotional support, but it lacks the ability to support the enabling activities that allow members to be successful in outside social arenas. When people see themselves as lacking the possibility of economic success and social mobility, the system protects and takes care of them, but when they see their way to possible economic success, they try to escape from this system.

This interpretation is strengthened by the fact that the kinds of statistics that translate this Black Underclass family pattern into conventional household categories are heavily dependent on income, which is a rough measure of closeness to or distance from the underclass environment. Consider the figures in from the 1980 census, shown in Table 23-14.

Table 23-14:Household Headship by Household Income Level, Black and White, U.S., 1980

	<$5000	$10,000-14,999	$20,000-24,999	>$50,000
BLACK				
Couple	13.5	41.0	62.0	71.8
Male Head	2.1	5.0	5.3	3.9
Female Head	35.6	29.3	17.3	10.9
Non-Family	48.8	24.7	15.4	7.4
WHITE				
Couple	8.6	54.5	75.7	86.1
Male Head	1.2	2.1	2.8	2.5
Female Head	12.4	11.7	5.8	2.4
Non-Family	67.8	31.7	15.7	9.0

Source: Adapted from Reynolds Farley and Walter Allen, *The Color Line and the Quality of Life in America* (New York: Russell Sage Foundation, 1987), pp. 174-75.

As can be seen from the table, among blacks with high incomes (which is a very rough proxy for non-membership in the underclass communities), couple-headed households are by far the most common. That blacks have a lower percentage of couple-headed households and non-family households (which are mostly single persons) than whites at all income levels might be interpreted, as Farley and Allen have, that there is a cultural component in the pattern of extended families and flexible ties, or it could be interpreted as reflecting the less-than absolute coincidence between income and class or community membership. In either case, the Black Underclass family is, as I have stated, an ideal type, and it is not always possible to say whether a family, for example, is a conventional nuclear family or a sub-extended household within an extended family network. It is clear that most African Americans who have the economic means to do so conform to the general M-cluster pattern rather than to the Black Underclass pattern (Willie 1985; Heiss 1975).

Finally, it must be emphasized that, even though the Black Underclass adaptation to its deprived environment has resulted in a system considerably different from those of other M-cluster populations, this family ideal type still belongs firmly within the M-cluster, because it lacks the most important cohesive forces of the C-cluster systems: primarily management and transmission of property, and secondarily representation. It differs from the other M-cluster types examined here (the primary Euro-American type and the Japanese type) in that individuals in the underclass environment cannot depend either on themselves or on stable dyadic ties to meet the procuring and processing needs, and they cannot depend on being able to fulfill their socialization responsibilities in a stable parent-child relationship over the course of the child's life. They have thus evolved a system in which a large number of ties can be activated or inactivated depending on the particular situation.

The Japanese Alternative: Cultural Difference or Structural Lag?

In examining the transitions in the Japanese family from the pre-industrial society of the mid-19th century to the urban, industrial society of today, we find a curious fact: Japan has experienced only some of the transitions in the dyadic ties that make up the family. The demographic picture in Japan is roughly comparable to that elsewhere. In 1987 the crude birth rate was 11.0, infant mortality 5.0 per thousand, less than four percent of women were married before age twenty, and life expectancy at birth was 81.4 for women and 75.6 for men (United Nations 1990: *passim*). The total fertility rate, at 1.5 in 1992, was as low as that in Western Europe and lower than in the U.S. and Canada. Similarly, the decline of intergenerational ties has been, in some cases, startlingly rapid. But the transformation of conjugal ties has proceeded along completely different lines in Japan and in the West. The result is that Japan's family system today is radically different from that found in any of the comparably industrialized nations in North America and Europe. We can illustrate its ideal-type developmental cycle as shown in Figure 23-3.

We find the same kind of decline in the strength of intergenerational relations in Japan as we find in the Western industrialized countries. Japan's C-cluster system was based on a stem-family cycle, conceptualized as successive head couples managing an enduring estate. With the decline of the estate as manifested in urbanization and in the move from property to salary, something that became the norm in the years after World War II (Fuse 1984:2-3), along with the provisions of the 1947 constitution abolishing the formal position of household head and granting equal rights of inheritance to all sons and daughters (R.J. Smith 1978:53-55), much of the reason for the stem-family, which implies close property ties between elder and younger adult generations, gradually faded away. Between 1955 and 1980, households dependent entirely on wage labor for their income increased from 49 to 63 percent (Fuse 1984:2-3), and increased again to 72% in 1993 (Statistics Bureau 1995:56), while stem families with or without additional relatives, as a proportion of total households, declined from 36.5 to 17.9

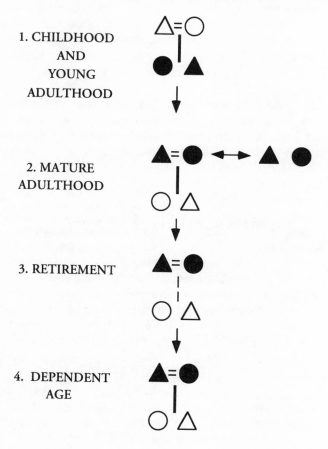

1. CHILDHOOD
   AND
   YOUNG
   ADULTHOOD

2. MATURE
   ADULTHOOD

3. RETIREMENT

4. DEPENDENT
   AGE

Figure 23-3: Stages in a Modern Japanese Developmental Cycle

percent and then to 12.7% in the early nineties (Statistics Bureau 1995:55). Even with such a decline in property-based interdependency, however, we would still expect a society with a stem-family tradition to retain a pattern of retired, and particularly dependent, elderly people continuing to live with their married children. This is the case, but even here the picture is changing. In 1970, 77% of those over 65 lived with their children, while 12% lived with their spouse only and only 6% lived alone. By 1985, only

65% lived with their children, while 22% lived with their spouse only, and 10% lived by themselves. Looked at from the other side, in 1960-64, 58% of eldest sons, who in the traditional system would have been household successors, lived with their parents; by 1980-82, the proportion had declined to 42% (Martin 1989:14-15). Even in those families where two adult generations have continued to co-reside, they tend to reduce the areas of their interdependency, to the point where residentially stem families have been characterized as "ideologically nuclearized," with separate quarters and separate budgets for the two couples living in the same apartment (Musselwhite n.d.:41).

Unlike the comparable situation in the Western countries, however, this weakening of ties between adult generations does not seem to be connected with a rise of individualism or the stress on self-fulfillment that is seen as so important in Western ideas of modernity. Japanese retain, in Smith's words, a "preference for acknowledgement of interdependence over expression of independence (1983:71)." But for the majority of Japanese men, who now work for corporations rather than family farms or businesses, much of the loyalty to the family has been displaced to the company or other organization (Rohlen 1974), and for the women married to these men, such loyalty and devotion has been displace from the household as corporation to their own children. One result of this process, in which young people, rather than becoming independent, displace their loyalty in different directions, is that there is no stage of single living in young adulthood as portrayed above for the Western countries. Both young men and young women continue to live with their parents until the age of marriage, which remains within a narrow range in the mid-twenties. Men by the time of marriage have already taken a job (likely to be permanent) with a company of some sort, while women are working at a temporary position they will expect to give up when their children are born (Brinton 1986:19-20). The 23% of Japanese households that are now single-persons (Statistics Bureau 1995:56) thus probably consists almost entirely of elderly widows and widowers, and of divorced adults.

It is in the configuration of conjugal ties, however, that the modern Japanese family system differs most from its Western counterparts. Whereas the Western pattern has moved from marriage as sex and division of labor to marriage as emotional companionship (of which sex is seen as a part), the Japanese system has retained, or in many cases even strengthened, the division of labor in marriage. For Japanese in the 1970s and 80s, marriage was assumed to be a stage in every life-cycle, and women were expected to be married between ages 22 and 25, or else risk hostile gossip (Lebra 1984:78-79). In fact, 70 percent of Japanese women in 1980 married between the ages of 20 and 25 (Brinton 1993:96-97). But whereas marriage in the traditional farming or small-business family involved a loose division of labor, with husband and wife sharing in many agricultural, farm management, or business tasks, the shift to wage-labor as the primary source of income has brought a rigidification of the division of labor, first pointed out by Ezra Vogel as early as 1963 (182), but continuing to the present day. Most Japanese companies, despite formal non-discrimination legislation passed in the late 1980s, still preserve a two-track employment system, in which men are expected to work from leaving school until retirement for the same organization, and are promoted or given seniority raises accordingly (Dore 1973:98-101) while women, who are expected to work for a few years and then stop working when their children are born, work almost entirely in low-prestige, low-paid jobs that involve little or no opportunity for advancement (Brinton 1993:ch. 4-5). From 1970 to 1993, in every industrial category tabulated by the Japanese government's Statistics Bureau, the total earnings of women remained right around 50% of the total earnings of men employed in the same industry (Statistics Bureau 1995:108-09).

In this system, procuring responsibilities are almost entirely thought to be in the hands of the male, despite the fact that many married women work for wages both before their first children are born and, increasingly in the 1980s, after their children are grown (Fuse 1984:9). In 1993, 74.5% of women aged 20-24, 58.7% aged 25-34, and 66.5% aged 35-44 were employed, showing that employment for all but a few years of adult life is now the norm for Japanese women, in spite of the extreme wage differential mentioned above.

As a predictable consequence of the idea that men hold the primary responsibility for procuring even when women work, women are thought to have almost exclusive responsibility for processing labor and for the socialization of children. In terms of processing, this is perhaps best summed up by Brinton, who states that "Most men readily admit that their cooking skills are limited to boiling water to make tea or instant noodles (1986:339);" boys who show any interest in cooking are often chastised by their fathers for paying too much attention to women's pursuits (Cynthia Harrell, personal communication). Even more striking to the Westerner is the amount of time, devotion, and responsibility expended by the Japanese mother on the socialization and education of her children. With fathers often out late socializing after work, and with extreme pressure to do well in school as a result of an educational system that almost entirely determines life chances (Rohlen 1983), the mother is in charge not only of the children's moral education, but in a very real sense of their academic education as well (Brinton 1993:92).

This kind of extreme division of labor in conjugal relationships is not, however, simply a continuation of a C-cluster pattern where marriage is predicated entirely on sex and division of labor, to the exclusion of emotion. Most young Japanese now feel that love is a major and necessary component of any marriage, and there is increasing feeling that families should spend time (that is to say, Sunday) together in outings and other recreational activities. But the ideal of love in marriage appears to be but another aspect of the Japanese desire to form interdependent relationships; it is not any kind of reflection of the Western idea of marital love as a means to fulfillment or actualization of the self.

We thus have a situation in Japan where vertical ties have undergone a double shift: weakening in the later phases of the life-cycle, with adult generations basically independent of one another, but remaining firm in childhood and early adulthood (which does not involve moving out, except to get married), and in some cases even strengthened by the crystallization of the mother-child unit in the virtual absence of the husband and father. Conjugal ties in this system are ideally based on love, but also contain a high proportion of interdependence in the division of procuring and processing labor.

Why should Japan, whose modernization in the material forces and relations of production is as far along or more so than the Western industrialized nations, have taken such a different path in its family organization? Two competing explanations present themselves:

First, we can attribute the family patterns to cultural differences. If individualism is the ideological core of modernity in the West, individualism has come from outside to Japan, and most Japanese people are uncomfortable with it. In a situation where creation of interdependence seems more desirable than assertion of independence, the Japanese have evolved a family system that has adjusted the structure of interdependency to the material and economic conditions of urban industrialism, but has not fundamentally altered the ethic of interdependency itself. The small size and influence of movements for women's equality, in the face of what seems to be almost universal resentment by Japanese women of their lot in life, is evidence of this. In this explanation, Japanese modernity in general, and the modern Japanese family system in particular, are on a different trajectory from those of the West.

The second explanation is that Japan is simply behind. Young and Willmott (1973) have posed a model of stages of modernization in England, in which the loose cooperation of the pre-industrial family farm or workshop was replaced in the first stage of industrialization by the kind of detached interdependency found nowadays in Japan: the matricentric household and the absent, wage-laboring man were seen as characteristic of an industrial-revolution pattern in England. It was only in the second stage that the family became its "symmetrical," fully modern self, in which both husband and wife were responsible for home and income alike, and the marital relationship itself became one of relative equals. If this formulation represents a universal sequence, then Japan is still in the first stage, and we can expect the Japanese family to become more like its Western counterparts in the next several decades.

It is impossible, given the present state of affairs, to decide between these two alternative explanations. As of 1995, however, even in the presence of a small feminist movement in Japan, the modernizing trends in the Japanese family are very different from those of Europe or "mainstream" North America.

The M-cluster family, as it is evolving in the late twentieth century, thus shows affinities with both its B-cluster and its C-cluster predecessors. We have become once again like our band-level forbears insofar as we have broken the bonds of property in the sense of a family estate that provides us with our physical means of subsistence and reproduction. Engels was right on this account—without property, the "monogamous family" characteristic of bourgeois 19th century Europe was changed radically, and people are no longer locked into its particular structures of gender and generation inequality. Dyadic bonds are more flexible, even optional, and both genders have at least the possibility (though not yet the equal chance) of assuming almost all public roles.

But at the same time, we are very distant from the B-cluster, in that we have retained the public sphere characteristics of the C-cluster, in particular the structures of social and economic inequality. The adjustive strategies of B-cluster family members have been replaced in the M-cluster by exclusive strategies in which family resources, like almost all other resources, are manipulated for social and economic advantage and prestige of the individual. This prestige is not based just on property, as classical Marxist theory would have it, but on a complex of markers that Bourdieu (1984) refers to as economic and cultural capital. In the life of most modern people, the family is merely a context in which the accumulation and retention of various kinds of prestige goods, tangible and intangible, is pursued by putatively autonomous individuals.

But there is a further difference between the M-cluster and all its predecessor clusters of societies. As mentioned in the beginning of this chapter, perhaps the most salient characteristic of modern life in general is the weakness of cultural prescriptions for all aspects of life. The modern consciousness is based on the assumption of individual freedom, which means the ability to criticize and to choose. It may be a question of individual political orientation whether we think there are actually more choices for modern individuals than for people in, for example, feudal Europe or pre-colonial Africa, but the ideology is unequivocally one of free choice and free expression. And one of the aspects of free choice and free expression is the "right" to express oneself on any issue, including issues related to the family. It is within the context of such freedom that there have sprung up in the

19th and 20th centuries a series of critiques of the dominant M-cluster model. It is to three of these critiques that I turn in Chapter 24.

Notes

1. I once overheard a locker-room conversation in which a sixtyish American volunteered that, "If they'd had Lean Cuisines when we were younger, there would have been no reason to get married."

2. The total marriage rate reflects the proportion of women in a particular cohort who would end up having married at least once if the rate in a particular year continues. It may exceed 1000 in certain years because individuals of different cohorts are marrying in the same year; conversely, at other times it may be artificially low because certain cohorts are postponing marriage at that time.

3. The perception that thirty seems to be a good time to begin thinking about children is pervasive among professionals in the United States in the early 1990s. This was graphically represented by a television commercial for a mortgage company, in which homey suburban images were backed by a gentle but educated-sounding female voice, saying "I'm turning thirty this year. I've got a responsible job; I've got a husband; it won't be long before I start thinking about having kids."

4. In late 1993, we received news that the opportunity to begin parenthood when one was already old would no longer be confined to males; reproductive technologists in England and Italy had brought about pregnancies in a 59- and a 62- year old woman, respectively.

24

Modernity and Critiques
of the Family

The Nature of Modern Critiques
of the Family

As mentioned in Chapter 21, modernity by definition is its own critique, and nowhere more so than in the theory and practice of the family. Like other spheres of life, the family in the still-incomplete transformation from C- to M- forms has experienced both a practical and a theoretical move away from the "thusness" or necessity of its C-cluster origins. It is now possible, as never before, to criticize, to design, to reform consciously, even to think about abolishing the family altogether. Insofar as it no longer seems inevitable that close relatives will cooperate in performing the eight kinds of family activities, two things become possible. First, one can design in theory and/or attempt to put into practice social arrangements that either eliminate some of the activities altogether or transfer them to groups other than the family. Second, one can blame the family (usually in the explicit guise of one or more of the activities it organizes) for one or another social injustice or restriction of individual freedom that ought to be eliminated, in the knowledge or at least the hope that an alternative form is possible. There have thus developed in the nineteenth and twentieth centuries, along with the "mainstream" trends and the culturally- or economically- determined alternatives, such as the Japanese and Black American Underclass systems, a series of consciously designed critiques and alternatives.

Modern critiques of the family are multifarious in their ideology, in their prescriptions for change, in the seriousness and the success of the attempts to implement them. But all of them originate in one or both of a pair of dissatisfactions with what the critics perceive as the existing family system. The first of these is the feminist dissatisfaction, the idea that as long as the current family system exists, it must involve, because it is fundamentally based on, structures of gender inequality.[1] Those who hold this dissatisfaction maintain that gender equality can only be achieved by abolishing (Firestone 1970) or severely modifying (Barrett and McIntosh 1982) existing family structures. The other dissatisfaction is the communalist dissatisfaction, the idea that the concentration of one or more activities in small groups, of which the family is by far the most common and pervasive, promotes selfishness or oppression of certain individuals or limitations on individual potential or even obstacles to social revolution.

At the same time, either feminist or communalist critiques can either be radical, in the sense that they see family structures themselves as inherently oppressive, and thus advocate the abolition of the family and its replacement by other social institutions, or they can be reformist or conditional, in the sense that they advocate changing or abolishing certain elements of the family that make it oppressive, but not eliminating it altogether.

Feminist Critiques

As Flax (1982) has pointed out, feminist critiques of the family are not all of a piece. She, in fact, divides them into three types. The first are the radical feminists, from Kate Millett to Shulamith Firestone, who see women's oppression as a result of the patriarchal power found in all societies, and see patriarchal power as embedded primarily in the male-female sexual pair. For these theorists, the family must be replaced by something else, either through a cultural revolution (Millett) or through abolition of the biological process of reproduction (Firestone).

Marxist feminists, on the other hand, see women's oppression as a result of the property structures particular to capitalism, and view the family, in the tradition of Engels, as the locus in which the property-holding male exercises power over the female. For these theorists (see especially Barrett and McIntosh 1982) the family is necessary as a locus of physical and emotional security as long as capitalist relations of production prevail, but at a cost of subordination and oppression of women as a category. The solution, of course, is social revolution, in which the abolition of private property and of social class will eliminate the dependence of the woman on the property-holding man.

Finally, Flax identifies the psychoanalytic feminists, such as Dinnerstein and Chodorow, who see the reproduction of gender inequality in the endlessly repeated experience of mother-child socialization and formation of affective bonds. The solution here is active and equal participation of males in the childrearing process, along with egalitarian participation of the genders in the public sphere (Flax 1982:247).

What all these feminist critiques have in common is the conviction that the family as presently constituted is oppressive of women, and must be changed. Where they differ is in identifying which family activities (division of procuring and processing labor for the radicals, management and transmission of property for the Marxists, socialization and emotional bonding for the psychoanalysts) are the primary loci of the family's oppression of women. And as a consequence, they also differ on the question of, as Flax puts it, "Does `the family' as such oppress women, or does the patriarchal (or capitalist) family oppress women?" (1982:251). Their position on this question, of course, has implications for the kinds of family reforms or revolutions they see as necessary to end oppression of women.

Communalist Critiques

Critiques based on communalism maintain that the family (or certain activities performed in and for the family) must be abolished or transferred to other groups in order to end various kinds of artificial limits on human potential, whether this potential is seen in religious terms, as with the Hutterites and other Anabaptists (Shenker 1986; Zablocki 1971) and the Oneida Perfectionists (Kanter 1972) or in secular terms, as with the 19th century utopian socialist colonies (Swan 1973) or the 20th century Kibbutzim (Shenker 1986).

As Abrams and McCulloch point out (1976:3), the radical ideal of communal living replacing the family is an old one in Western society, reaching back at least as far as Plato's Republic. And people, of course, sought to escape the confines of family life in all the great C-cluster civilizations, in ways ranging from the meditative monasticism of medieval Christianity and of Buddhism to the renouncer ideal in Hindu theory and practice. But a transformation of the communal ideal has accompanied the transition to M-cluster society. In the C-civilizations, the monastery or other intentional community (Shenker 1986:10-12) was usually an attempt to escape from the family, not to replace it. Monks and nuns in Christianity and Buddhism were and are prescriptively celibate, and monasteries do not reproduce themselves except by recruiting from outside. Their prevalence in medieval Europe was thus closely connected to the world-rejecting ideal of what Bellah has called "historic" religions (1972:43-45).

Modern builders of utopias and other communal forms critical of the family, however, do not seek to escape the world, and with it the family, as did their C-cluster predecessors, but rather to rebuild the world with an institution more humane, more capable of nurturing ideal human beings, than that flawed and restrictive institution they see in the family. The world for the modern communalists is not hopelessly flawed; only the family is, and with the abolition and replacement of the family, the world can be brought much closer to its real potential.

The distinction here is not one between religious and secular utopias. Starting with Hutterite colonies, begun in central Europe in the 16th century, and later spread to North America, where they flourish today, and with other radical Anabaptist communities such as the Moravian communal settlements in Pennsylvania late colonial times (Lindt 1969), religious utopians began to seek salvation in the world rather than beyond it. Many modern communes are religious, including the most famous of the American Utopias, the Oneida Community, which was founded on John Humphrey Noyes's idea of Christian Perfectionism (Kanter 1972:9-18), and extending to New Age settlements since the 1970s (Abrams and McCulloch 1976:83-92). There are, of course, numerous communitarian critiques of the family now practiced outside the setting of religious communities. But what distinguishes the M-from the C-cluster in a fundamental way here is that in modern society it is deemed possible to build a better world, whether on religious or secular foundations, while in the C-cluster, the world and the family were as one found them, and the only alternative was to renounce them both.[2]

The Relationship of Feminism to Communalism

In specific cases, the feminist and the communitarian dissatisfactions are sometimes separate, sometimes combined. Certain varieties of feminist critique, for example, see pairing of any sort, either heterosexual or homosexual, as destructive of human potential and therefore oppressive (Firestone 1970), and thus partake automatically of the communalist critique. Other feminisms are more directly concerned with particular structures of male-female relations, and thus see pairing as possible, even desirable, in certain situations, such as committed lesbian couples (Weston 1991, Pies 1990) or in some cases heterosexual couples with egalitarian relationships, once certain parameters have been altered (see Flax 1982). Similarly, certain primarily communalist critiques, notably the ideology of the early Kibbutzim (Shenker 1986; Spiro 1979), have incorporated feminist concerns, while others, particularly the religiously based communalisms such as Amana (Barthel 1984) and the Hutterites (Shenker 1986) have retained the sexual division of labor and even the implicit or explicit subordination of women in a context of replacing the family with communal forms.

What all the various modern critiques, whether feminist-inspired, communalist-inspired, or both, have in common with each other, however, is the conviction that it is the ways of organizing certain specific family activities that stand in the way of the egalitarian and/or communalist goal. It will thus help us make our analysis of critiques of the family parallel the general analysis of the history of family organization if we examine the specific critiques in terms of the specific family activities that they see as unjust and thereby in need of abolition or major reform. I will thus proceed activity-by-activity, in each case pointing out how critiques of that particular activity stem from a feminist, communalist, or feminist-communalist dissatisfaction.

Radical and Conditional Critiques and Family Activities

Procuring and Processing: *Eliminating the Sexual Division of Labor*

Some degree of sexual division of labor has been at the basis of all family systems up to and including the C-cluster, and while material modernization has opened up the possibility of severely reducing or eliminating gender roles in procuring and processing, evidence shows that such roles remain. So it seems natural that critics of the family, particularly feminist critics, would see part of the oppression of women as embodied in the ideal and practice of procuring by men and processing by women, as in Japan, or of procuring by men and women, and processing by women, as in the most recent trends in Europe and North America. This attack on the sexual division of labor has been mounted both in communalist critiques that have a feminist component to their ideology, and in non-communalist feminist critiques.

Communalist critiques with a feminist component are perhaps best exemplified by the early phases of the Kibbutz movement among Jewish settlers in Palestine. As Rabkin and Spiro characterize it, the early Kibbutz began with the intention of "destroying the bourgeois family and eliminating the traditional relationship between husband and wife and, more importantly, between parent and child (1975:469)." To this end, three measures were taken. First, procuring activities were removed from the family altogether—all procuring labor, which in the early days was almost entirely agricultural, was done communally. Second, as much processing as possible was communalized as well, with cooking and eating in collective kitchens and dining halls, laundry in a collective washroom (in the earliest days, Kibbutznikim did not even own their individual clothes, but turned in dirty shirts and pants to the laundry and exchanged them for clean ones in the same size) (Spiro 1955), and spartan accommodations that neither called for nor required much cleaning or decorating. Finally, in the early days, there was no differentiation in the procuring and processing tasks performed by men and by women (Spiro 1979:14).

In the evolution of the kibbutz from the pioneer days to the present, however, there has been considerable retreat on two of the three fronts. Procuring labor has remained resolutely collective, while expanding from subsistence agriculture to a mixed economy of food and cash crops, industrial manufacture, and operating tourist facilities (Rabkin and Spiro 1975:483-86). Various kibbutzim use different systems for allocation of personal shares of the collective income, but all shares are equal, based on the fact of kibbutz membership, and not on the amount or quality of work done, or on any personal connection to goods or property (Shenker 1986:113, 222).Processing labor, on the other hand, has partly reverted to the family unit. As accommodations have become comfortable, as restrictions on family ownership of durable consumer goods have gradually been lifted, as first hot-plates and then full-fledged stoves have been allowed in couples' living quarters, these quarters and their contents have become the object of care and upkeep, and a place to bake treats, serve snacks to guests, even have an occasional meal with the children away from the collective dining hall (Spiro 1979:27-34).

In addition, kibbutz history has seen a gradual flow of men into certain procuring occupations, particularly field agriculture, industry, and financial management, while women have flowed into the collective versions of "traditional" female tasks, such as childrearing, cooking, laundry, and garden agriculture (Shenker 1986:61; Spiro 1979:16-17).

The feminist critique embodied in the Kibbutz movement's original communalism has thus weakened, and it is the contention of at least some authors (Spiro 1979; Rabkin and Spiro 1975) that this movement of processing back into the family, as well as the re-establishment of a version of the previous sexual division of labor, has been done at the instigation of women, dissatisfied with their work roles in the early days of identical work roles for men and women. What remains today is an aspect of the communalist critique that give rise to the original feminism; the feminism itself is no longer embodied in an attempt to liberate women completely from "traditional family roles."

At least one utopian commune in the 19th-century United States also tried, though in a less thorough manner than the early kibbutzim, to implement sexual equality through partial elimination of the sexual division of labor. The Oneida community in upstate New York, which existed for several decades in mid-century, was based on the principles of Christian Perfectionism advocated by its founder and leader, John Humphrey Noyes (Kanter 1972:9), and one of these principles was that men and women were equally perfectible, so the community should seek, as far as possible, to do away with artificial distinctions between the sexes (Foster 1981:104-105). This involved collectivization of productive work (farming and light industry) similar to that seen in the Kibbutz, as well as the institution of the collective kitchen and dining hall (which seems to have invented, or perhaps introduced from China, the "lazy susan" round table now so familiar in Chinese restaurants) (Kanter 1972:9-10; Robertson 1970:84-85). Sexual division of labor was not entirely eliminated, however; for example most of the cooks were male and the waiters female in the dining operation (Robertson 1970:84-85); men put in more hours of factory work than did women (Robertson 1970:295-96); and women, but not men, were prone to knit or do needlework during community religious and business meetings (Noyes 1973:368).

There seems not, however, to have been a moving away from the revolutionary sexual division of labor during the lifetime of the Oneida Community, as there has been in the kibbutzim. This is perhaps due to the short lifetime of the commune (only 30 years in its fully communal state), or perhaps due to its small scale and the strong ideological commitment of its members. Because the community broke up and formed a joint-stock company in 1881, it is difficult to know whether there would have been a move back in the direction of traditional gender roles, or indeed whether the radicalism of the community contributed to the break-up itself (Kanter 1972:18).

Communes established in the 1960s and 1970s sometimes also formulated a critique of the sexual division of labor, albeit a rather unelaborated one. For example, members of two of the British "secular family communes" examined by Abrams and McCulloch in the early 1970s tried to share domestic labor without regard to gender, although they varied in the extent to which they were successful (Abrams and McCulloch 1976:58, 68, 75).

It should be pointed out, however, that many communes based on communalist critiques of the family, and on collectivization of many family activities, have not employed any feminist critique in their ideology or practice. For example, most of the religious communes of 19th and 20th century America, including the Hutterites (Shenker 1986), the less strict Moravian Bruderhof (Zablocki 1971:45-47; 131-39), and the Amana colonies of Iowa (Barthel 1984:27, 45-47, 53) preserved a division of labor where women did almost all the processing work, and where male and female roles in procuring labor were segregated. The same was true of the Fourierist phalanxes established in the nineteenth century, where collective labor was organized into "series," mostly gender-segregated (Guarneri 1991:205-208; Swan 1973:259-60), and of many of the "drop-out" rural communes of the 1960s and 1970s, where there was rarely a formal division of labor, but women tended to assume processing tasks, when they were done at all (Gardner 1978:55-57; Roberts 1971:49-50; Davidson 1973:348). It is thus evident that a communalist critique of the family may or may not imply an accompanying feminist critique.

The same is true in the other direction: feminist critiques of the division of labor may or may not imply communalist critiques. Some feminist critiques see exploitation of women as inevitable as long as procuring and processing are concentrated in a small, family-like unit containing pairing relationships, while other critiques do not contain or imply any desire to shift procuring and processing from the family to any larger unit, but rather to reform the division of labor within the family unit itself.

Those feminist critics who see "patriarchy" as the basic problem usually reject any kind of pair-based family as inherently exploitative of women. Firestone, for example, sees the freeing of women as "the ultimate revolution," one that will bring full self-determination, including economic independence, for both women and children (1970:234), through "the abolition of the labor force itself under a cybernetic socialism, the radical restructuring of the economy to make `work,' i.e. wage labor, no longer relevant (1970:235)." In this economy of the future, when even reproduction has been taken over by laboratory procedures, people will live either as single, non-reproducing beings, or in temporary, flexible households (not families) which contain no sexual division of labor and no permanent attachments between adults or between adults and children. Whatever chores (processing work) are still necessary will have been taken over by machines (1970:257-266).

Barrett and McIntosh (1982) take a slightly different tack. They accept some of the activities now associated with the family: "Affection, security, intimacy, sexual love, parenthood...we see as human needs, not pathological constructs (1982:132)." But the form in which these are now structured, (the bourgeois family) poisons the fulfillment of these needs because it is associated with the sexual division of labor and with private property. Therefore, the solution is to work toward collectivism in income maintenance and in the work of making meals and cleaning up, housekeeping, and caring for people (1982:134). This can be accomplished through various means, including communal living, shared childcare, shared housework, celibacy, non-parenthood, homosexuality that does not mirror heterosexual patterns, etc. What is unacceptable and oppressive is marriage of any sort, and socialists and feminists should neither marry nor attend weddings, with the possible exception of fake weddings staged to subvert national immigration laws (1982:142-43).

Certain lesbian feminist critics also adopt the position that any kind of family or permanent, family-like group will lead to the same kind of oppression as exists in the "traditional" family. For example, Ettorre (1980:59) states that "exclusivity is anti-woman," and that pairing relationships between lesbians are basically a result of "aping heterosexuals," and demonstrate the power of the dominant ideology. Thus even without a formal division of labor, much less a gender difference, any kind of long-term commitment leads to repression of individual potential.

Other lesbian feminists take a much different line, believing that the ordinary heterosexual division of labor is not necessarily reproduced in long-term, committed lesbian pairs, but that such pair relationships can be worked out on the basis of "negotiated-egalitarian reciprocity," with or without pooling of resources, and with a flexible assumption of processing duties when necessary (Sang 1984). In fact, there seems to have developed a trend toward "Families we Choose" among lesbians in the late 1980s in North America, requiring a less fundamental critique of the dangers of attachment, and believing that families, in the sense of couples or couples with offspring and/or other relatives attached, can be formed on a non-exploitative basis (Weston 1991:22).

Such critiques, which see the division of labor within the conventional family as oppressive, either to women or to people in general, but build on the possibility of families in which other functions are retained, but the division of labor is abolished, are a far cry from the more radical critiques that deem the family as such to be oppressive (Flax 251). They thus can set forth a feminist agenda independently of a communalist one.

Management and Transmission of Property: Domestic Slavery and Its Alternatives

Many modern critics of the family as an oppressive institution attempt to dig for root causes, and for a great number of these critics, the basis of oppression lies in the institution of private property, which they variously see as oppressing women (particularly if most or all property is controlled by men), as promoting a materialist consciousness that obstructs spirituality, as promoting selfishness instead of public spirit, or as strangling the potential for individual and community growth. Thus critics with widely differing ideologies, from "orthodox" Marxism to Marxist feminism to Anabaptism to utopian socialism have all begun their critiques with attacks on the family as a property-owing institution.

In fact, there is a great paradox embodied in the range of attacks on the family as a property-holding institution. On the one hand, there are those who criticize private property for promoting individualism instead of communalism, who see property as the basis of competition and striving, which needs to be eliminated if people are to return or progress (depending on the particular ideology) to sharing, collectivism, and work for the common good. On the other hand, we find a large number of critiques of family property as something that *retards the growth of the individual,* that keeps people enmeshed in a web of statuses and dependencies that limits their true potential. Both religious and secular ideologies have served as the basis for both kinds of critique.

The Collectivist Critique of Family Property. Of those who criticize family property-holding as promoting selfishness, many base their objections on religious grounds. The rejection of property and its economic imperatives reaches far back into C-cluster thinking, with vows of poverty taken by Buddhist and Christian monks and nuns, as well as Hindu renouncers. And indeed some of the practiced communitarian critiques of our own and recent times descend directly from radical Christian experiments originating in agrarian societies of Reformation Europe. The largest and longest-lived of the communitarian Christian movements, the Hutterites, assert that community of property re-creates the true Christian community of Christ and his disciples and of the early Church, in which everything was shared and was used for the betterment of the community as a whole, since God created everything for common use. To accept private property would be to accept the idea that one can gain at someone else's expense, which would mean that "the selfish and sinful nature in us will come to the fore (Shenker 1986:74-75)." Hence Hutterite colonies hold and work all property in common. The Bruderhof, likewise an Anabaptist communitarian group, emphasizes that the ego-renunciation required for successful communal living promotes acceptance of the Holy Spirit, and that a true Christian must thus deny the value of individual achievement as embodied in the accumulation of private property (Zablocki 1971:30-33).

On the other hand, one of the most militantly secular of modern critiques of the family, that embodied in the founding ideology of the Israeli kibbutz, is also anchored in a communalist ideal. While individual creativity is an important goal in the ideal society envisioned by Kibbutz ideology, the environment conducive to creativity can only be achieved through the institution of a communal society, in which no one has an institutional advantage over anyone else, and in which all are willing to subsume their individual desires voluntarily to the good of the cooperative (Shenker 1986:83-88). It is thus only through devotion to the collective that the individual can be part of a just society. Thus all invidious distinctions must be eliminated, and beginning with the individual and family control of property. The strict implementation of this principle at the beginning of the movement, which meant even collective ownership of clothing and furniture, has been relaxed over the decades until families now own a large number of consumer goods. But the basic principle of equal pay regardless of the nature or quality of work is still thought to preserve the ideal that material and spiritual being derive from the devotion to the collective (Shenker 1986:222).

The Individualist Critique of Family Property. As pervasive in the twentieth century as the collectivist critique of family property is a type of critique based on the opposite principle: that society ought to exist in order to create the conditions for the development of the individual, unfettered by conventional social arrangements that stifle expression, creativity, and truly meaningful achievement. The writings of Marx and Engels, for example, while they later formed the basis for the practice of a very mild sort of collectivism in the socialist interlude of the middle twentieth century, were originally directed toward creating a society where the conditions for true freedom existed. Marx's and Engels's famous poetic vision of a future where it was possible "to hunt in the morning, fish in the afternoon, rear cattle in the evening, criticize after dinner, just as I have a mind, without ever becoming hunter, fisherman, shepherd, or critic (Marx and Engels 1988:53)," sums up the essence of this individualistic ideal, which would only be possible once the property distinctions that made one person into a philosopher and another into a hunter had been abolished. Engels, in *The Origins of the Family, Private Property, and the State*, enunciated an application of this general idea to the condition of women in particular, when he stated that "the modern individual family is founded on the open or concealed domestic slavery of the wife... (1985:105)", and that she could only be free when property was taken away from the family and given to the collective. The express purpose here is to create an economy of public property in order to remove the fetters that private property has placed on the individual.

The utopian socialists, whom Engels excoriated so strongly for the impracticality of their programs, nevertheless held almost identical views about the stifling effects on the individual of family-held property. Charles Fourier, for example, went so far as to repudiate monogamy altogether in his writings, though the American Phalanxes, which put Fourierist principles into practice in the 19th century, implemented a modified version of this doctrine. They allowed marriages (as Engels would have in his own version of socialism) once private property was abolished, since the problem with the family in "Civilization" (Fourier's name for the bad society that had to be replaced by the higher form of "Association") was not the formation of marital pairs (see following section) but the subordination of the female in those pairs as long as they were embedded in the webs of private property and inequality that constituted Civilization (Guarneri 1991:142-43). The Phalanxes, however, were more tolerant of inequality between families than the Kibbutzim have been: whereas Kibbutzim pay all adult members equally, Fourierist Phalanxes implemented a system similar to the work-point systems of the China under Maoist collectivism, in which families were paid according to their members' specific labor contributions (Guarneri 1991:192-93; Swan 1973:260; for China see Parish and Whyte 1977:62-71; Chan, Madsen, and Unger 1984:90-93).

Objections to private property-holding might also come on religious grounds, as in the Oneida Community. The Christian Perfectionist beliefs of the Oneidans declared that every human was potentially perfectible, if the principles embodied in the doctrines of the Bible and the practice of the early Church were revived (Robertson 1970). To achieve perfection, Community members had to give up particular attachments to people and things, and this meant the communalization of all productive and consumer property, even to the extent of sharing the conventional "going away clothes" that community members wore to avoid public censure when they traveled into the wider world and had to give up the more practical costumes they wore around the Community (Kanter 1972:9-10).

Feminist Critiques of Property. The most pervasive critiques of the family as a property-holding group come, however, not from the advocates of a generalized individualism (as we have seen, family property can also be attacked on the grounds that it *promotes* individualism), but rather from advocates of feminism. These feminists argue that private property, controlled *de facto* by males in almost all "mainstream" C-cluster systems, inevitably relegates women to a specific and subordinate social position, which includes a processing role in the division of labor, unequal opportunities to advance in the public sphere, and vulnerability to physical and emotional abuse at the hands of male figures empowered by their control over the family property.

The Marxist-feminist position as articulated by Barrett and McIntosh (1982) is perhaps clearest on this point. Like all good Marxists, they have a functionalist cast to their thinking, admitting that what they see as functions of the family ("affection, security, intimacy, sexual love, parenthood") are innately desirable things. But, they say, women in capitalist systems have to enter into oppressive relationships of marriage and family in order to secure these goods for themselves. So the challenge for feminists is to create a society in which "the family is less necessary (1982:159)," where the collective provides for security and material needs, and these other desirable goods become available on a less coercive basis.

We thus see a wide variety of theories and practices critical of the M-cluster family as a property-holding corporation. This is perhaps ironic, in that the centrality of property has faded dramatically since the C-cluster. It is also noteworthy, however, that the greatest number of critiques of the family as a property-holding group came in the 19th century, a time when Western Europe and North America were in the midst of the transition from the property-based economy of the C-cluster into the salary-based economy of the M-cluster. Once individuals gained the possibility of economic independence, critiques tended to focus less on property itself and more on the oppressive nature of the division of labor (see above) and of cultural assumptions about permanent pairing relationships, to which we now turn.

Control of Sexuality: Is Pairing Tyrannical?

Long-term, paired social and emotional relationships have been another target of several different kinds of critics of the family. While some critics object to pairing itself, in any form, others only object to pairing under certain kinds of circumstances and constraints. To paraphrase the distinction (about the oppression of women) quoted above from Jane Flax, the question is whether pairing itself is inherently destructive of human potential, gender equality, or other desired ends (the radical critique), or whether it is oppressive only when people are forced by economic necessity or legal and moral sanctions to form and remain in stable pairs (the reformist critique). Let us look, in turn, at radical and reformist critiques of pairing relationships.

Radical Critiques of Pairing. Two of the earliest and most radical critiques of pairing relationships came in American religious communes of the nineteenth century, the Shakers and the Oneida community. For the Shakers, sexuality of any sort was indeed the root of all evil and corruption in the world—not only in religious matters, but also in economic, social, and political affairs as well. Only by renouncing all "carnal" desires...and by deciding to live a life of "virgin purity" could mankind be restored to God [Foster 1981:25]. Hence the Shakers eschewed sex, marriage, everything connected to lust or to attachment.

For the Christian perfectionists of Oneida, things were quite different. Noyes believed that it was attachments to particular others, or "stickiness" that got in the way of human perfection, but he and his followers never sought to deny sexuality or sexual love. Instead, they developed a system referred to as "complex marriage and male continence." Complex marriage meant that members of the community (which numbered about 200 people through most of its existence) were to have free sexual access, with consent, to all other members.[3] If members showed too much stickiness (to parents or children, as well as to sexual partners; see below) they became targets of formal group criticism meetings (Kanter 1972:15). As Noyes's granddaughter puts it, "The new Commandment [was] that we love one another, and that not by pairs, as in the world, but *en masse* (Robertson 1970:267)." In practice, complex marriage involved many members in a series of sexual liaisons carried on simultaneously, usually beginning in the teen years with "initiations" by older members of the opposite sex, and continuing into adulthood (Kanter 1972:12). "Male continence" seems to have been the practice of *coitus reservatus* (Foster 1981:64), used to prevent conception for more than twenty years at the beginning of the Community, but eventually partially supplanted by "stirpiculture" or eugenic breeding, planned and controlled by Noyes (Robertson 1970:270). Adult members each had their own individual rooms; younger members shared rooms with children of the same sex (Kanter 1972:11).

Other radical critiques of pairing come from a feminist angle. The radical feminist Shulamith Firestone, for example, has designed a society of the future in which people live either as individuals, with no regular sexual attachments (this lifestyle has precedents, she says, in the former lives of teaching nuns and cowboys, for example) or, for those who enjoy company or want to reproduce, in freeform households consisting of a group of anywhere up to ten or so people, adults and children of both sexes, who enter voluntarily into a short-term contract, and who all have equal legal rights and the freedom to engage in whatever sexual practices they mutually consent to, a return, she says, to our original "polymorphous perversity (1970:236; 257-65)." For Firestone, it is only in the elimination of all specific personal obligations, especially those of sexual and parental attachment, that liberation from the oppression of patriarchy can come.

Equally opposed to pairing are some of the lesbian-feminist critiques of the 1970s and 1980s. For example, the English lesbian writer E.M. Ettorre, in discussing the possible form of lesbian relationships, cautions that monogamous relationships between lesbian pairs too easily lead to "aping heterosexual society" (1980:57), and points out that many politically conscious lesbians choose multiple relationships, on the rationale that "exclusivity is anti-woman," that any kind of committed pairing relationship simply recreates the oppressive patriarchal structures from which lesbian feminists, like other feminists, need desperately to escape (1980:59-60).

Gay men have formulated and lived parallel critiques. The evolving gay morality of the 1970s, described by Dennis Altman in *The Homosexualization of America and the Americanization of the Homosexual*, attempted to build a community in which homosexual men lived most of their lives outside of exclusive relationships, in which by transcending monogamy they would transcend the vices of possessiveness and jealousy (1982:175), and in which communal living would provide an alternative for those unable to participate in the dominant family model of society (1982:166). But Altmann goes beyond the model of non-exclusive relationships as a gay alternative, and suggests that gay sexuality might provide a positive model for both homo-sexual and heterosexual people in a society in which commitment to single, exclusive partners seemed to be diminishing. Since the mid-1980s, such philosophy has gone into epidemiological decline with the rise of AIDS, a frightening environmental threat that has pushed many gay critics away from their former anti-pairing position.

Finally, we find radical critiques of pairing in a few of the "hippie com-munes" formed from the 1960s to the 1980s in the United States. At Harrod West, for example, a San Francisco group characterized by Ron Roberts as "erotic utopian," a much less formal but still Oneida-like system was fol-lowed, in which people rotated sexual partners several times a week, but were encouraged to have spontaneous sex as well (Roberts 1971:42). And Talsalsan, on the Illinois River in northernmost California, was originally founded as an "agrarian-based group marriage," though it did not last long in that form (Gardner 1978:171).

Conditional Critiques of Pairing. The other side of Flax's distinction is probably more heavily represented in critiques of the family than is the radical side. For most critics, whether they approach the problem from a Marxist, a feminist, or a homosexual perspective, or from some combina-tion of the three, rigorously fighting against attachments makes no more sense than rigorously fighting to form and keep them; the desired state of affairs is rather one in which couples are free to form and dissolve volun-tarily, in which there are no economic or legal constraints that either pre-vent people from coupling or keep them in couples when their best inter-ests lie in breaking up, and where intimate attachment to one partner does not necessarily preclude other kinds of close relationships.

Most Marxist critiques of the family, beginning with those of Engels him-self, have taken this kind of a stance. Engels, in fact, used the term "pairing marriage" for a form that he saw as characteristic of the era immediately before the institution of private property, when marital attachments were often close and enduring, but were strictly voluntary and easily dissolved, since they were not based on the economic and legal leverage of the man over the woman, as was bourgeois marriage in modern society. For Engels, as for modern Marxist-feminists such as Barrett and McIntosh (1982), it is not pairing that is the problem, but rather forced pairing under an eco-nomic and legal regime of gender inequality. The same position was taken by the Fourierists in the Phalanxes, and in the early years of the Kibbutz.

A similar position has recently become characteristic of both lesbian and gay male writings and practice. Flax's key question has been re-posed by Kath Weston in the lesbian context: "Are gay families inherently assimilationist, or do they represent a radical departure from more con-ventional understandings of kinship (1991:2)?" Leaving aside the "radi-cal" part (in my lexicon, they are not radical unless they reject the family

altogether), there seems to be a growing consensus that alternative structures can be built in which people can perform some of what are considered desirable activities of the family, such as sexuality, emotional security,
and sometimes shared child-rearing, without tying these to the inherently
oppressive activities of division of labor, management and transmission of
property, political representation, and enabling. One kind of building blocks
for such alternative structures are new kinds of sexual relationships (parent-child relationships will be discussed below).

Surveys of both lesbians and gay men have consistently shown that at
any given time, anywhere from a third to a half of gay males (Harry and
DeVall 1978:90; Berger 1982:129-30) and lesbians (Weston 1991:159; Raphael
and Robinson 1984:69) consider themselves to be in a relationship with a
primary partner at the time of interview. The problem thus becomes one of
determining what constitutes an egalitarian, non-exploitative relationship.
The negatively stereotyped "butch-fem" relationship between lesbians, for
example, is usually thought to be modeled after heterosexuality, and thus
inherently exploitative (Sang 1984:52-53). Gay and lesbian couples are also
often leery of property- or income-sharing, because of inequalities that might
potentially lead to power imbalances (Harry and DeVall 1978:80-82; Sang
1984:58-59). And perhaps most importantly, many critics consider it wrong
to demand sexual exclusivity even in relationships that are considered to
be primary and intimate on the emotional level. A relationship may in fact
be exclusive for a shorter or longer time, but it is considered wrong to demand exclusivity (Altman 1982:187; Sang 1984:60-62).

The conditional or reformist critique thus in the end rejects the more
radical idea that attachments in themselves are detrimental to either the
spiritual or the emotional development of the person. Instead, this critique
is one that openly welcomes the construction of structures very much like
what I have referred to as "families" in the previous chapters of this book.
They are small groups of people with either biological or ideological kinship, committed to at least medium-term sharing of certain family functions, particularly sexuality and emotional support. By avoiding certain
other obligations and entanglements, they hope to avoid the conflicts that
they see as being so destructive to people involved in "conventional" families.

Child Care and Socialization:
Attachment or Responsibility?

The last activity of the family that has come under attack by modern
critics is that of caring for and socializing children. Like other activities
discussed above, it has been attacked for different reasons. Those who feel

that family attachments get in the way of community commitment (as in the Kibbutz), of individual self-realization (as in Firestone's techno-feminist utopian vision), or of spiritual development (as in Oneida or the Bruderhof), see communal child-rearing as a way of breaking exclusivist attachments, sometimes as a parallel to the disallowal of couple-attachments. Others, usually with at least a partial feminist aspect to their ideology, see communal child rearing as a way to lift a large burden from mothers or other female relatives, in order to enable them to pursue personal development in other spheres. Still others find that primary parental responsibility for children is itself not a bad thing, if like alternative coupling it is situated in a context that is otherwise non-coercive and non-exploitative.

The Communalist Critique: Childrearing as the Creation of Attachments. In the same way that they view couples, many communalist critics of the family have viewed parent-child bonds as undesirable, because they create particular attachments between children and parents. The most radical realization of this critique came, as did so many other radical innovations, in the Oneida community, at least after stirpiculture replaced the strict rule of male continence. Here parent-child stickiness was thought to be as dangerous as stickiness between sexual couples (Kanter 1972:14). Mothers often felt emotionally close to their children, particularly when nursing them, but were always liable to accusations of a special love that got in the way of communal solidarity (Noyes 1973:370-71). For this reason, children past weaning were reared communally in the children's house, whose male and female directors the children called "mama" and "papa." They were allowed to see their natural parents once or twice a week, but could be taken away if they showed too close an attachment (Kanter 1972:13-14). Even at Oneida, however, surnames were assigned according to natural parentage, as witness Pierrepont Noyes, the author of the memoir "Growing Up in Oneida" (1973).

Other intentional communities have implemented communal childrearing in a less radical form. For both the American religious communities and such secular groups as the Fourierist phalanxes and the Zionist kibbutzim, the problem with parents raising their own children was not so much attachment *per se* as the degree to which rearing children got in the way of the parents' participation in the work of the community. It was to solve this problem that all these communities implemented rather similar systems in which children were cared for in collective nurseries, but still maintained various kinds of attachments to their natural parents. In the Bruderhof, for example, where children are reared in communal houses, they are still reported to be close to their parents and particularly to their grandparents (Zablocki 1971:122-26; 36-37). In the Kibbutzim, parents from the beginning always had the opportunity to see their children in the evening, and family attachments are expected to be close, unfettered as they are by the tensions of reward and punishment found in situations where the parents actually socialize their children (Rabkin and Spiro 1975:465; Shenker 1986:223-24). In fact, many kibbutznikim see the family as a refuge from the tensions of collective life and work (Shenker 1986:223-24), a sentiment similar to that of the Fourierist socialists, who felt that parents and children would be much closer if their relationship were not clouded by the demands of discipline (Guarneri 1991:143).

In these intentional communities, then, communal child-rearing is not necessarily seen as incompatible with strong family ties. Two aspects of recent social change in the Kibbutzim point this out graphically. The first is that, as reported by Rabkin and Spiro, the "sabra" generation, who grew up in the Kibbutzim and by the 1960s and 70s, were seeing their own children grow up in similar circumstances, seemed very comfortable with the idea and practice of communal child-rearing. The second is that despite the stability of the communal child-rearing system, the Kibbutz is becoming more and more family centered all the time, with the emergence of extended families a salient feature of the time when the grandchildren of the founders are reaching adulthood and having children of their own (Spiro 1979:41-42).

The Feminist Critique: Childrearing as an Aspect of the Sexual Division of Labor. The radical writer Shulamith Firestone sums up the more extreme form of the feminist critique of childrearing when she speaks of freeing women from "the tyranny of reproductive biology" by diffusing the responsibility of childbearing and childrearing to the society as a whole (1970:233). Firestone, in fact, sees the subordination and dependency of women and children as an outgrowth of something as basic as women's reproductive biology, which means that women will ultimately have to be replaced by some sort of laboratory reproduction if they are ever to be free of this burden (1970:235-36).

Firestone's work is a thought experiment as much as anything, but many other, more practical feminist critics have also seen the necessity to bear and care for children as a prime factor in the oppression of women. The Marxist feminists Michäle Barrett and Mary McIntosh, for example, do not see having and caring for children as demeaning in themselves, but only made demeaning and oppressive when they are undertaken in a context of the dependencies created by capitalism and property. Therefore the solution for these writers is not a Brave New World "Department of Hatcheries and Conditioning," but rather working toward collectivism in childcare along with collectivism in such other activities as procuring and processing (1982:133-34). Childrearing should not be the primary responsibility of the mother, but rather women and men should share childcare, and should do it the same way, and collective forms of child-rearing should be promoted actively (1982:145, 151-52). In addition, non-parenthood should be an accepted option for all people.

For both these critics, the feminist problem with child-rearing is not primarily one of drudgery and lack of career opportunities (though these do enter the picture), but rather the presumed dependency of women on men and children on women (and thus indirectly on men) in a situation where males hold power and property. This critique of dependency is also made in a slightly different fashion by radical lesbian critics such as E.M. Ettorre, who sees withdrawal from attachments to males as necessary for women to break through their own dependency. Lesbianism, then, in which women reject heterosexual relationships (but not necessarily economic and political relationships that involve males), is a way of escaping dependency; it also means at least the strong option to forego bearing and raising children (Ettorre 1980:31-32). Women should, in her view, maintain the choice to bear and raise children, but the childcare itself should be done in communal settings that do not use childcare as a way of subordinating women (1980:29).

The Conditional Critique: Creating New Kinds of Loving Family Environments. As with the other functions of the family discussed above, not all critics reject outright the idea of a family group whose adult members have responsibility for its children. Some critics, by contrast, try to envision and build family or family-like groups that still take care of their children, but do so outside what they see as the oppression and dependency of the mother-child bond attached to the powerful and economically dominant father.

This ideology has been put into practice most pervasively and consistently in the construction in North America in the 1980s and 1990s of "families we choose" (Weston 1991) by lesbian and, to a lesser extent, gay male parents. Homosexual people creating families have had to proceed by conscious choice, since there were few precedents and many obvious obstacles. They have thus both reasoned and documented their family practices to an extent not seen anywhere else, and this has been particularly true in the matter of obtaining and raising children. At each step of the process, ideological commitments to stay out of dependency have combined with practical considerations to create situations in which families of a sort raise children, but outside the conventional framework.

Lesbian mothers can obtain children by adoption, which was technically legal in 1990 in all but four states, but was often discouraged except for lesbians willing to downplay their sexual orientation and apply for children as single women of unspecified sexual preference. Joint adoptions by lesbian couples have been allowed in California, but are still very rare (Ricketts and Achtenberg 1990:102-108). Alternatively, they can bear children, either by having intercourse with a male explicitly for the purpose of conceiving, sometimes even in the presence of the non-bearing lesbian parent (Washburne 1987), or more commonly receiving artificial insemination from a known or anonymous donor (Pies 1990:145-46; Parber 1987:94-99; Weston 1991:167).[4] When the child is adopted or born, decisions must be made about responsibility for the child's care. One decision is whether or not to have a male involved (often but not necessarily the sperm donor), especially in the case of a boy child. Many but not all single or coupled lesbian mothers do choose to have a male involved; this usually means playing a kind of "uncle" role rather than being recognized as a parent (Zook and Hallenbeck 1987; Weston 1991:1972). Such practices potentially raise custody issues, however, and many lesbian parents choose to keep the donor anonymous (Hill 1987:112, 115).

The other important decision involves the respective roles of the birth mother and her lesbian partner, sometimes called the co-mother (Pollack and Vaughn 1987:13). For example, is the partner an aunt or special friend, or is she a second mother? How should she be addressed by the children? In some families, children call the two mothers Mama (or Mother or Mommy) Smith and Mama Jones, or Mama for the birth mother and Mama Jones for the co-mother, or Mama for the birth mother and Mutti or Kachan or something in some other language for the co-mother. Even Daddy Jones for the co-mother has been reported (Weston 1991:173).

More serious than the questions of terminology are those of rights and duties. Many lesbian couples with children report that the two parents are committed to ideological equality, sharing childrearing along with other household responsibilities, but that there is an explicitly or implicitly closer bond with the birth mother (Hill 1987:113, 119; Torotilla 1987:169). And there is the question of the custody of children in the event of the breakup of the union, especially if one or the other of the original partners takes another lover. Sometimes the coparent relationship continues (Torotilla 1987:171-73).

Such chosen families also occur with gay male couples as the core rather than lesbian couples; although there are no statistics, my impression is that they are less common, partly because many lesbians bear children in heterosexual relationships and then come out as active lesbians and are sometimes (though by no means always—see Lewin 1984) given custody of their children, while this happens less commonly with gay men. Also, there is no readily available practice for gay men equivalent to lesbians' becoming parents by artificial insemination. Still, gay men do form families with children by adoption or after divorce, and they face the same problems of rights and responsibilities for children as do lesbian parents. One study showed that gay fathers were both more likely to explain decisions to their children than straight fathers and more likely to set stricter limits on behavior (Bigner and Bozett 1990:155-175).

It should be emphasized that these chosen families are not necessarily best conceived as "lesbian families" or "gay families," but rather as families that contain one or more lesbian or gay sexual links as part of their structural core. They are not, after all, composed entirely of gays or lesbians—few gay or lesbian parents try to train their children into a particular sexual orientation; growing up with straight parents, they have seen that this does not usually work. In addition, other relatives may be included in these families; I personally know one family consisting of two lesbian professionals in a stable arrangement (including a sizable mortgage), together with the adopted son of one partner, the birth daughter of the other, and the widowed mother of the first.

Cases such as this one emphasize the nature of the conditional critique as exemplified by the gay and lesbian construction of alternative families. These arrangements are attempts to expand the definition and the ideal of the family as a place where children are raised and nurtured in a stable set of relationships with parents, and often with siblings and/or grandparents. What is at issue here is very different from what is at issue with some of the communalist and the more radical feminist critiques. These alternative constructions see the family as desirable, not as destructive. They may attempt to expand the acceptable definition of who can form a family and through what kinds of dyadic bonds, but they actively affirm the general notion of the family as a locus for child-rearing.

We can thus see, in the range of criticisms, counter-criticisms, and alternatives proposed by feminists and communalists, by radical and conditional critics, an affirmation of the assertion made at the beginning of Chapter 21, that the essence of modernity is its own critique. Those who call for a return to the absolutes of an imagined past (for a critique, see Coontz 1992), who in the name of "family values" demand a return to the singular certainty of a "traditional family," are calling for nothing less than the rejection of the modern condition altogether, something whose morals we can debate, but whose material basis we have no way of destroying and no desire to destroy. If we are to deal realistically with the "family crisis" that is now proclaimed to be upon us, we must do so within the parameters of the modern condition, which paradoxically includes not only debate and criticism, but the call for an end to debate and criticism and a return to an imagined certainty. In the concluding chapter, I present some thoughts about the practical challenges and possibilities.

Notes

1. The term 'patriarchy' has come, in recent years, to refer to social structures in

which females are subordinated to males in systematic ways (see Flax 1982 for a good review). But 'patriarchy' also has another, related but more restricted meaning of extended families ruled by senior-generation males—this is the sense in which Engels used the term in The Origins of the Family. I will avoid the term in its broader sense of male domination except in direct quotes and paraphrases of others' work.

2. A possible exception might be found in the Daoist theocracies of late 2nd-century China; unfortunately, although we know they experimented with sexual communism, we do not know enough about their family policies and practices to include them in a comparative discussion here (see Welch 1957:113-23).

3. As far as I can determine, this meant heterosexual relations only; the topic of homosexuality is not mentioned in the four sources on Oneida that I have consulted.

4. Some lesbian feminists are now using the term "alternative insemination (Weston 1991:167)," thinking that "artificial insemination" has a negative connotation. I don't assume natural is good and artificial is bad, but it does seem to me that one method occurs in nature while the other does not.

25

Conclusion

We have now traced the specific forms of the human family across the great transformations of human history, and placed the changes and debates of the present in the context of the range of variation that the human family has shown in the past. It remains to say something about the future, not the far-off times of science fiction or apocalyptic imagination, but the next few decades as the world becomes ever more closely linked by communications and the residual influence of C-cluster property structures continues to fade. What does the history of variation in the human family have to tell us about the current debates about the breakdown of the family and its impact on social order and social relations generally?

First, we need to decide whether some form or other of the family is necessary or inevitable. In the historical journey of the human family, from the rather strictly circumscribed B-forms to the culturally diverse variants of the A-, O-, and N- clusters and their equivalents in other parts of the world, to the concentrated household unit of the C-cluster, and finally (so far) to the looser aggregations of the modern family and its critiques, there run two important threads that may help us decide this question.

The first thread is that, at the widest level of generalization, the broad historical and evolutionary stages and transformations, it is activities that family members perform for each other that are the driving engine of family structure and process. For the B-cluster, the division of labor in mobile foraging was paramount, and could be seen as giving rise to the similarities in B-cluster families worldwide. In settled, pre-class societies, of whichthe A-, O-, and N- clusters are examples, all the family activites werepresent, but none was really determinative, and so we found the bewildering variety characteristic of the social organization of rank societies. When private property and the state came to prominence in the C-cluster, they became the primary drivers, concentrating many activities in a single kind of family unit, the classic household. Private property and the state did not invent the family, as Engels claimed, but they gave it its most concentrated form. Finally, in our modern era, family activities, reasons for family solidarity or even existence, are being stripped away, and family process once again has more alternatives, both in the mainstream life-cycle and in those of the conscious critiques.

None of this summary analysis is meant to deny the role of historical contingency and cultural particularity in the formation of various family systems; in fact the whole point of separate analyses for Africa, Oceania, and the Northwest Coast is that variation among these clusters is not functionally or environmentally driven. But it is striking that, despite cultural continuity across some of the great transformations, modern, urban Canadians and South Africans are coping with common questions about the loosening of the family, in the same way that the 19th and 20th-century family organizations of the !Kung and the Dogrib, are practically identical. What families organize for is different in the different clusters, and this is an important determinant of their family organization.

The second thread is that despite all this adaptationally-driven variation in structure and process, two kinds of relationships stand out as relatively constant throughout the entire evolutionary sequence: pair bonds and parent-child bonds. Nowhere do we find a society that is truly promiscuous, in the sense that single people have sex indiscriminately with other single people and do not form stable pair bonds. Certain communities, such as the US urban gay male community before the advent of AIDS, approached this ideal, but they achieved it only partially, and then only in the absence of reproduction. Likewise, nowhere do we find truly communal childrearing: even the Mbuti pygmies, the Oneida communitarians, and the pioneer kibbutznikim, who came closest, recognized parent-child bonds, and neither Oneida nor the kibbutz lasted very long in its near-communitarian state.

What this seems to say to us for the future is that although there is no particular form or cycle of the family that is natural, God-given, or inevitable, it still seems unavoidable that pair bonding and parent-child bonding are the irreducible minima of human social reproduction. Attempts to eliminate them have failed, at the same time as attempts to shape them into widely divergent forms have succeeded, from Marquesans to Nayars to lesbian families of choice. In every known historical instance where people have attempted to replace the family with some other form as a site for social reproduction, they have failed, and the basic building blocks of semi-permanent pair bonding and parent-child links have reasserted themselves. There is thus little reason to think that in the future we will ever see the withering away of the family.

But if the family seems inevitable in some form or other, we face our second important question: what form will it take? It is clearly not inevitable that it will take any form in particular. As we have seen from our close examination of variation within and between evolutionary stages, family variation is shaped by two kinds of factors: adaptation to the activities its members must perform, and historical/cultural traditions that people think of as right or comfortable. If we look at the near future, we should be able to delineate some of the possibilities for the family based on these factors.

First, it seems highly likely that the activities organized in and for the family, which have decreased so dramatically across the industrial transformation, will continue at their present low or minimal level. Procuring and processing will become even less problematic for salary-earners and pensioners, who will continue to be the great majority of any population. On the upper and lower fringes, to be sure, individual autonomy will be compromised respectively by property relations and by the need for sharing in poverty; achieving the liberal dream of a society of self-sufficient individuals would reduce these fringe groups to an even smaller percentage of the population than they occupy at present. Representation, management and transmission, and enabling will continue to be precluded for most people by the individualistic political and legal systems that continue to spread under the banners of democracy and human rights. In a sense, realization of a great part of Engels's dream is within sight, particularly if institutional gender biases, enormously reduced since the time Ruth Bader Ginsberg couldn't get a job in a law firm, continue to be worn away.

In Engels's dream, as in those of many liberals and feminists, family regulation of sexuality dies with the passing of property restrictions on individual behavior, and the only thing holding pairs together is mutual attraction, an aspect of what I have called the emotional activities of the family. The bonds of mutual attraction, however, are notoriously fragile and evanescent, and a full realization of the dream of human relations unencumbered by property thus implies a great fluidity of pair-bonding, of the sort that existed in many B-cluster family systems. The utopia of individual freedom and self-fulfilment thus coincides in its treatment of sex and pair-bonding with the utopia of public ownership and the elimination of private property.

Where all this fluid reverie comes up choking, of course, is on the final family activity—the care and socialization of children. Ever since Freud's *Civilization and its Discontents* we have realized that the safe and ordered society that is needed to facilitate many kinds of individual freedom and expression must come at the cost of suppression of certain other individual drives, particularly the penchant for violent solutions of conflicts that has driven so many, primarily male, humans across all the great transformations. Even when collective arrangements for childcare have been successful in meeting their instrumental goals, there has been a felt need for emotional connection in parent-child links, and a failure of social control of violence when this emotional connection has been weak. Thus the emotional and socialization activities appear to be the irreducible minimum for a family system even in an individualistic society, if that society is going to reproduce itself.

The problem here is that emotional bonds between pairs are so fluid and fragile, and that people pursuing these emotional bonds often do so at the cost of the emotional, and often the more practical, aspects of the parent-child bonds. There is no longer, as there was especially in the C-cluster, the stern pressure of property and political relations to hold families together in the absence of positive emotional ties, and there seems to be less of the alternative emotional and instructional support from other kin that sustained socialization in the B-cluster and some of the rank societies. To put it another way, we have no material means of ensuring that children will have parents, and we have less of a backup from other relatives if parents are not present.

It is thus totally natural (in the sense of evolutionarily inevitable) that the family has "broken down." It is also tragic (in the sense of morally inevitable). We are bound to have the family, but we are bound to have it not always work very well. It is the task not only of policymakers and bureaucrats, but of teachers and scholars as well, to try to nurture moral attitudes among the populace about the need to be responsible in creating the social and emotional environment for our children.

This must be done realistically. There is, in fact, no reason that having parents means having exactly two, or two of opposite sexes, much less two that happen to have gone through a wedding cermony. There is no reason that parents need be the producers of the egg and sperm from which the child grew. But the historical failure of the alternatives tells us that parents, in this wider, not exclusively biological, sense, will end up raising children. We have a historical imperative for emotional and socialization families, and a historical imperative for individual rights and freedom from the constraints of property. It is a difficult but absolutely imperative task to reconcile these in a realistic way. The debate about the family that is an inherent part of the modern family is also its, and our, only possible source of social salvation. We must have families and they will be flawed. The challenge is to live with this inevitable contradiction.

References

Abrahams, R. G. 1967. *The Political Organization of Unyamwezi*. Cambridge: Cambridge University Press.

Abrams, Philip and Andrew McCulloch, with Sheila Abrams and Pat Gore.1976. *Communes, Sociology, and Society*. Cambridge: Cambridge University Press.

Abu-Lughod, Lila. 1991. "Writing Against Culture," in Richard G. Fox, ed., *Recapturing Anthropology: Working in the Present*. Pp. 137-162. Santa Fe: School of American Research Press.

Ahern, Emily M. 1973. *The Cult of the Dead in a Chinese Village*. Stanford: Stanford University Press.

Ainsworth, Mary D. Salter. 1967. *Infancy in Uganda: Infant Care and Growth of Love*. Baltimore: Johns Hopkins University Press.

Alkire, William H. 1965. *Lamotrek Atoll and Inter-Island Socioeconomic Ties*. Illinois Studies in Anthropology No. 5. Urbana and London: University of Illinois Press.

___1974. "Land Tenure in the Woleai," in Henry P. Lundsgaarde, ed., *Land Tenure in Oceania*. Pp. 39-69. Honolulu: University Press of Hawaii.

___1978. *Coral Islanders*. Arlington Heights, IL: AHM Publishers.

Allen, Peter S. 1976. "Aspida: A Depopulated Maniot Community," in Ernestine Friedl and Muriel Dimen, eds., *Regional Variation in Greece and Cyprus*. Pp. 168-198. New York: New York Academy of Sciences.

Altman, Dennis. 1982. *The Homosexualization of America and the Americanization of the Homosexual*. New York: St. Martin's Press.

Amoss, Pamela T. 1978. *Coast Salish Spirit Dancing: The Survival of an Ancestral Religion*. Seattle and London: University of Washington Press.

___1993. "Hair of the Dog: Unravelling Pre-contact Coast Salish Social Stratification." *American Indian Linguistics and Ethnography in Honor of Laurence C. Thompson. Anthony Mattina and Timothy Montler*, eds., Pp. 3-35. Missoula, MT: University of Montana Occasional Papers in Linguistics No. 10.

Arensberg, Conrad and Solon T. Kimball. 1968. *Family and Community in Ireland*, 2nd Edition. Cambridge, Mass.: Harvard University Press.

Aswad, Barbara C. 1967. "Key and Peripheral Roles of Noble Women in a Middle Eastern Plains Village." *Anthropological Quarterly* 40, 3:139-152.

Bachu, Amara. 1993. Fertility of American Women, June 1992. U.S. *Bureau of the Census, Current Population Reports* P20-470. Washington, D.C.: U.S. Government Printing Office.

Baker, Hugh D. R. 1969. *Sheung Shui: A Chinese Lineage Village*. Stanford: Stanford University Press.

Balikci, Asen. 1970. *The Netsilik Eskimo*. Garden City, NY: Natural History Press.

Banfield, Edward. 1958. *The Moral Basis of a Backward Society*. Glencoe, Ill.: The Free Press.

Barnes, J. A. 1951. "The Fort Jameson Ngoni," in Elizabeth Colson and Max Gluckman, eds., *Seven Tribes of British Central Africa*. Pp. 194-252. London and New York: Oxford University Press.

Barrett, Michele, and Mary McIntosh. 1982. *The Anti-Social Family*. London:Verso/ NLB.

Barthel, Diane L. 1984. *Amana: From Pietist Sect to American Community*. Lincoln: University of Nebraska Press.

Basehart, Harry W. 1961. "Ashanti," in David M. Schneider and Kathleen Gough, eds. *Matrilineal Kinship*. Pp. 270-297. Berkeley and Los Angeles: University of California Press.

Beaglehole, Ernest and Pearl Beaglehole. 1938. *Ethnology of Pukapuka*. Bernice P. Bishop Museum Bulletin 150. Honolulu: The Museum.

Beardsley, Richard K., John W. Hall and Robert E. Ward. 1959. *Village Japan*. Chicago: University of Chicago Press

Becker, Gary S. 1991. *A Treatise on the Family*. (Enlarged Edition). Cambridge, Mass.: Harvard University Press

Beidelman, T. O. 1967. *The Matrilineal Peoples of Eastern Tanzania*. London: International African Institute.

Bellah, Robert N. 1972 (1964). "Religious Evolution." *American Sociological Review* 29: 358-74, Reprinted in William A. Lessa and Evon Z. Vogt, eds., *Reader in Comparative Religion*, Third Edition, Pp. 36-50.

Bellah, Robert N., Richard Madsen, William S. Sullivan, Ann Swidler, and Steven M. Tipton. 1985. *Habits of the Heart: Individualism and Commitment in American Life*. Berkeley and Los Angeles: University of California Press.

Benedict, Peter. 1976. "Aspects of the Domestic Cycle in a Turkish Provincial Town," in J. G. *Peristiany, ed., Mediterranean Family Structures*. Pp.219-241. Cambridge, England: Cambridge University Press.

Benedict, Ruth. 1934. *Patterns of Culture*. Boston and New York: Houghton Mifflin Company.

Benet, Sula, Ed. and Trans. 1970. *The Village of Variatino*. New York: Doubleday.

Berger, Raymond M. 1982. *Gay and Gray: The Older Homosexual Man*. Urbana: University of Illinois Press.

Berkner, Lutz K. 1976. "Inheritance, Land Tenure, and Peasant Family Structure: A German Regional Comparison," in Jack Goody, et al., eds., *Family and Inheritance*. Cambridge: Cambridge University Press.

Berman, Marshall. 1982. *All that is Solid Melts into Air: The Experience of Modernity*. New York: Simon and Schuster.

Bernard, H. Rusell. 1976. "Kalymnos, The Island of the Sponge Fishermen," in Ernestine Friedl and Muriel Dimen, eds., *Regional Variation in Greece and Cyprus*. Pp. 291-307. New York: New York Academy of Sciences.

Berndt, Catherine. 1970. "Digging Sticks and Spears, or the Two Sex Model," in Fay Gale, ed., *Women's Role in Aboriginal Society*. Pp. 39-48. Canberra: Australian Institute of Aboriginal Studies.

Berreman, Gerald. 1963. *Hindus of the Himalayas*. Berkeley and Los Angeles: University of California Press.

___1975. "Himalayan Polyandry and the Domestic Cycle." *American Ethnologist* 2.1:127-138.

Bierwert, Crisca. n.d. "The Sockeye Wife and Other Stories: An Analysis of the Interrelationship of Food, Luxury, and Sexual Liaison among the Halkomelem Salish." Unpublished paper.

___1986. Tracery in the Mistlines: Semiotic Readings of Sto:lo Culture. Unpublished Ph.D. Dissertation, University of Washington.

Bigner, Jerry J., and Frederick W. Bozett. 1990. "Parenting by Gay Fathers," in Frederick W. Bozett and Marvin B. Sussman. eds., *Homosexuality and Family Relations*. Pp. 155-175. New York: The Haworth Press.

Blackman, Margaret B. 1982. *During My Time: Florence Edenshaw Davidson, a Haida Woman*. Seattle and London: University of Washington Press.

Blurton-Jones, Nicholas. 1986. "Bushman Birth Spacing: A Test for Optimal Birth Intervals." *Ethology and Sociobiology* 7:91-105.

___1987. "Bushman Birth Spacing: Direct Tests of Some Simple Predictions," *Ethology and Sociobiology* 8:183-203.

Blustein, Jeffrey. 1979. "Child Rearing and Family Interests," in Onora O'Neill and William Ruddick, eds., *Having Children: Philosophical and Legal Reflections on Parenthood*. New York: Oxford University Press.

Boaz, Franz. 1940 [1920]. "The Social Organization of the Kwakiutl," in *Race, Language and Culture*. New York: The Macmillan Company.

Bohannan, Paul. 1954. *Tiv Farm and Settlement*. London: H. M. Stationery Office.

___1965. "The Tiv of Nigeria," in James L. Gibbs, Jr., ed. *Peoples of Africa*. Pp. 515-546. New York: Holt, Rinehart and Winston.

Boserup, Ester. 1970. *Woman's Role in Economic Development*. London: George Allen and Unwin.

Bott, Elizabeth 1957. *Family and Social Network*. London: Tavistock.

Bourdieu, Pierre. 1984. *Distinction: A Social Critique of the Judgment of Taste*. Cambridge, MA: Harvard University Press.

Brady, Ivan. 1974. "Land Tenure in the Ellice Islands: A Changing Profile," in Henry P. Lunsgaarde, ed., *Land Tenure in Oceania*. Pp. 130-177. Honolulu: University Press of Hawaii.

Brady, Ivan, ed. 1983. "Special Section: Speaking in the Name of the Real: Freeman and Mead on Samoa." *American Anthropologist* 85(4): 908-947.

Brandes, Stanley H. 1975. *Migration, Kinship, and Community*. New York: Academic Press.

___1980. "Like Wounded Stags; Male Sexual Ideology in an Andalusian Town," in Sherry B. Ortner and Harriet Whitehead, eds., *Sexual Meanings*. Pp. 216-239. Cambridge: Cambridge University Press.

Brinton, Mary C. 1986. "Women and the Economic Miracle: the Maintenance of Gender Differences in Education and Employment in Contemporary Japan." Unpublished Ph.D. dissertation, University of Washington.

___1993. *Women and the Economic Miracle: Gender and Work in Postwar Japan*. Berkeley and Los Angeles: University of California Press.

Bulatao, Rodolfo, Edward Bos, Patience W. Stephens, and My T. Vu. 1990. *World Population Projections*. 1989-90 Edition. Baltimore: Published for the World Bank by Johns Hopkins University Press.

Bureau of the Census. 1981. "Marital Status and Living Arrangement, March 1980," *Current Population Reports: Population Characteristics*, Series p-20, no. 365. Washington, D.C.: Bureau of the Census.

Burgess, Ernest R., Harvey J. Locke, and Mary Margaret Thomes. 1963. *The Family:*

From Institution to Companionship, 3rd Edition. New York: American Book Company.

Burrows, Edwin G. 1936. *Ethnology of Futuna*. Bernice P. Bishop Museum Bulletin 138. Honolulu: Bernice P. Bishop Museum.

____1937. *Ethnology of Uvea*. Bernice P. Bishop Museum Bulletin 145. Honolulu: The Museum.

Burrows, Edwin and Melford E. Spiro. 1957. *An Atoll Culture: Ethnography of Ifaluk in the Central Carolines*. Westport, Conn.: Greenwood Press.

Campbell, J. K. 1964. *Honour, Family, and Patronage*. Oxford: Oxford University Press.

____1965 "Honour and the Devil," in J. G. Peristiany, ed., *Honour and Shame*. Chicago: University of Chicago Press.

Carroll, Vern. 1970. "Adoption on Nukuoro," in Vern Carroll, ed., *Adoption in Eastern Oceania*. Pp. 121-157. Honolulu: University of Hawaii Press.

Cashdan, Elizabeth. 1983. "Territoriality among Human Foragers: Ecological Models and Applications to Four Bushman Groups," *Current Anthropology* 24:47-66.

Casselberry, Samuel E., and Nancy Vavavanes. 1976. "'Matrilocal' Greek Peasants and a Reconsideration of Residence Terminology." *American Ethnologist* 3.2: 215-226.

Caughey, John L. 1977. *Faanakkar: Cultural Values in a Micronesian Society*. Publications in Anthropology No. 2. Philadelphia: University of Pennsylvania.

Chagnon, Napoleon A. 1979. "Mate Competition, Favoring Close Kin, and Village Fissioning Among the Yanomamö Indians," in Napoleon A. Chagnon and William Irons, eds., *Evolutionary Biology and Human Social Behavior: An Anthropological Perspective*. Pp. 86-131. North Scituate, Mass.: Duxbury Press.

Chan, Anita, Richard Madsen, and Jonathan Unger. 1984. *Chen Village: The Recent History of a Peasant Community in Mao's China*. Berkeley and Los Angeles: University of California Press.

Chayanov, A.V. 1966. *The Theory of Peasant Economy*, Daniel Thorner, Basile Kerblay, and R.E.F. Smith, eds., Homewood, IL: The American Economic Association.

Clifford, James, and George E. Marcus (eds.). 1986. *Writing Culture: The Politics and Poetics of Ethnography*. Berkeley and Los Angeles: University of California Press.

Codere, Helen. 1950. *Fighting with Property: A Study of Kwakiutl Potlatching and Warfare, 1792-1930*. Seattle: University of Washington Press.

Cohen, Abner. 1965. *Arab Border Villages in Israel*. Manchester: University of Manchester Press.

Cohen, Myron L. 1968. "A Case Study of Chinese Family Economy and Development." *Journal of Asian and African Studies* 3, 3-4:159-170.

____1970. "Developmental Process in the Chinese Domestic Group," in Maurice Freedman, ed., *Family and Kinship in Chinese Society*. Stanford: Stanford University Press.

____1976. *House United, House Divided: The Chinese Family in Taiwan*. New York: Columbia University Press.

Cole, John W. and Eric R. Wolf. 1974. *The Hidden Frontier: Ecology and Ethnicity in an Alpine Valley*. New York: Academic Press.

Collier, Jane F. 1988. *Marriage and Inequality in Classless Societies*. Stanford: Stanford University Press.

Collier, Jane Fishburne, and Michelle Zmbialist Rosaldo. 1981. "Politics and Gender in Simple Societies," in Sherry B. Ortner and Harriet Whitehead, eds., *Sexual*

Meanings. Pp. 275-329. Cambridge: Cambridge University Press.

Collins, June McCormick. 1974. *Valley of the Spirits: The Upper Skagit Indians of Western Washington.* Seattle and London: University of Washington Press.

Colson, Elizabeth. 1953. *The Makah Indians: A Study of an Indian Tribe in Modern American Society.* Manchester: Manchester University Press.

___1958. *Marriage and the Family Among the Plateau Tonga of Northern Rhodesia.* Manchester: Manchester University Press.

___1960. *Social Organization of the Gwembe Tonga.* Manchester: Manchester University Press.

___1971. "The Impact of the Colonial Period on the Definition of Land Rights," in Victor W. Turner, ed., *Colonialsism in Africa,* Vol. III. Pp. 193-215. Cambridge: Cambridge University Press.

Cooper, J. P. 1976. "Patterns of Inheritance and Settlement by Great Landowners from the 15th to the 18th Centuries," in Jack Goody, et al., eds., *Family and Inheritance.* Pp. 192-327. Cambridge: Cambridge University Press.

Crocombe, R. G. 1964. *Land Tenure in the Cook Islands.* Melbourne and New York: Oxford University Press.

___1974. "An Approach to the Analysis of Land Tenure Systems," in Henry P. Lundsgaarde, ed., *Land Tenure in Oceania.* Pp. 1-17. Honolulu: Univeristy Press of Hawaii.

Cronin, Constance. 1970. *The Sting of Change.* Chicago: University of Chicago Press.

___1977. "Illusion and Reality in Sicily," in Alice Schlegel, ed., *Sexual Stratification.* Pp. 67-93. New York: Columbia University Press.

Cuisinier, Jean. 1976. "The Domestic Cycle in the Traditional Farm Organization in Tunisia," in J. G. Peristiany, ed., *Mediterranean Family Structures.* Pp. 137-155. Cambridge: Cambridge University Press.

Cunningham, Roger, William B. Stoebuck, Dale A. Whitman. 1993. *The Law of Property.* St Paul: West Publishing Company.

Czap, Peter. 1978. "Marriage and the Peasant Joint Family in the Era of Serfdom," in Donald L. Ransel, ed., *The Family in Imperial Russia.* Pp. 103-23. Champaign-Urbana: University of Illinois Press.

Damas, David. 1968. "The Diversity of Eskimo Societies," in Richard Lee and Irven DeVore, eds., *Man the Hunter.* Pp. 111-117. Chicago: Aldine.

___1969. "Characteristics of Central Eskimo Band Structure," in David Damas, ed., *Contributions to Anthropology: Band Societies.* Pp. 116-138. Ottawa: National Museums of Canada, Bulletin #228; Anthropological Series #84.

___1972. "The Copper Eskimo," in Marco Bicchieri, ed., *Hunters and Gatherers Today.* New York: Holt, Rinehart, and Winston, Pp. 3-50.

___1979. "Double Descent in the Eastern Carolines." *Journal of Polynesian Society* 88: 177-198.

Danielsson, Bengt. 1955. *Work and Life in Raroia: An Acculturation Study from the Tuamotu Group, French Oceania.* Stockholm: Saxon and Lindstrom.

Davidson, Sara. 1973 [1970]. "Open Land: Getting Back to the Communal Garden," *Harper's Magazine,* 240: 91-102. Reprinted in Rosabeth Moss Kanter, ed., *Communes,* Pp. 334-350.

Davis, Deborah. 1990. "Urban Job Mobility," in Deborah Davis and Ezra F. Vogel, eds., *Chinese Society on the Eve of Tiananmen.* Pp. 85-108. Cambridge, MA: Harvard University Press.

Davis, James C. 1975. *A Venetian Family and its Fortune, 1500-1900*. Philadelphia: American Philosophical Society.

Davis, J(ohn). 1973. *Land and Family in Pisticci*. London: Athlone Press.

_____1977. *People of the Mediterranean: An Essay in Comparative Social Anthropology*. London: Routeledge and Kegan Paul.

DeLaguna, Fredrica. 1972. *Under Mount St. Elias: The History and Culture of the Yakutat Tlingit*. Washington: Smithsonian Institution Press.

Denham, Woodrow W., Chad K. McDaniel, and John R. Atkins. 1979. "Aranda and Alyawara Kinship: A Quantitative Argument for a Double Helix Model." *American Ethnologist* 6: 1-24.

DeVos, George, and Hiroshi Wagatsuma. 1972. "Family Life and Delinquincy: Some Perspectives from Japanese Research," in William P. Lebra, ed., *Transnational Research in Mental Health*, Pp. 59-81. Honolulu: University Press of Hawai'i.

Diamond, Norma. 1968. *K'un Shen: A Taiwan Village*. New York: Holt, Rinehart, and Winston.

_____1975. "Women under Kuomintang Rule," *Modern China* 1, 1: 3-45.

Divale, William T., and Marvin Harris. 1976. "Population, Warfare and the Male Supremacist Complex." *American Anthropologist* 78: 521-538.

Doi, Takeo. 1973. *The Anatomy of Dependence*. Tokyo: Kodansha.

Donald, Leland, and Donald Mitchell. 1975. "Some Correlates of Local Group Size Among the Southern Kwakiutl." *Ethnology* 14: 325-346.

Dore, Ronald P. 1973. *British Factory, Japanese Factory*. Berkeley: University of California Press.

_____1978. *Shinohata*. London: Allen Lane.

Douglas, Mary 1963. *The Lele of the Kasai*. London: International African Institute.

Douglass, William. 1969. *Death in Murélaga*. Seattle: University of Washington Press.

_____1975. *Echalar and Murélaga*. New York: St. Martin's Press.

Draper, Patricia. 1975. "!Kung Women: Contrasts in Sexual Egalitarianism in Foraging and Sedentary Contexts," in Rayna Reiter, ed., *Toward an Anthropology of Women*. Pp. 77-109. New York: Monthly Review Press.

_____1976. "Social and Economic Constraints on Child Life," in Richard B. Lee and Irven DeVore, eds., *Kalahari Hunter-Gatherers*. Pp. 199-217. Cambridge, Mass: Harvard University Press.

Drucker, Philip. 1939a. "Rank, Wealth and Kinship in Northwest Coast Society." *American Anthropologist* 41: 55-65.

_____1939b. *Contributions to Alsea Ethnography*. University of California Publications in American Archaeology and Ethnology 35, 7: 81-102. Berkeley and Los Angeles: University of California Press.

_____1951. *The Northern and Central Nootkan Tribes*. Washington, U.S. Government Printing Office.

Drucker, Philip, and Robert F. Heizer. 1967. *To Make My Name Good: A Reexamination of the Southern Kwakiutl Potlatch*. Berkeley and Los Angeles: University of California Press.

Dubisch, Jill. 1976. "Ethnography of the Islands: Tinos," in Ernestine Friedl and Muriel Dimen, eds., *Regional Variation in Greece and Cyprus*. Pp. 314-327. New York: New York Academy of Sciences.

du Boulay, Juliet. 1974. *Portrait of a Greek Mountain Village*. Oxford: Oxford University Press.

Duff, Wilson. 1952. "The Upper Stalo Indians: An Introductory Ethnography." Unpublished M.A. Thesis, University of Washington.

Dyson-Hudson, Rada, and Eric Alden Smith. 1978. "Human Territoriality: An Evolutionary Reassessment." *American Anthropologist* 80: 21-41.

Edelman, Marian Wright. 1987. *Families in Peril: An Agenda for Social Change.* Cambridge. MA: Harvard University Press.

Edwards, G.E. 1985. *GDR Society and Social Institutions: Facts and Figures.* London and Basingstoke: Macmillan.

Edwards, Walter. 1987. "The Commercialized Wedding as Ritual: A Window on Social Values," *Journal of Japanese Studies* 13, 1: 51-78.

Elam, Yitzhak. 1973. *The Social and Sexual Roles of Hima Women: A Study of Nomadic Cattle Breeders in Nyabushozi County, Ankole, Uganda.* Manchester: Manchester University Press.

Ellis, William. 1829. *Polynesian Researches.* Volume II. London: Fisher, Son and Jackson.

Elmendorf, William Welcome. 1960. The Structure of Twana Culture. Monographic Supplement no. 2, Research Studies, Washington State University, Vol. XXVIII, No. 3, Supplement September 1960. Pullman: Washington State University.

Elster, Jon. 1983. *Explaining Technical Change.* Cambridge: Cambridge University Press.

Ember, Carol R. 1978. "Myths about Hunter-Gatherers." *Ethnology* XVII:439-448.

Engels, Fredrick. 1985 (1884). *The Origin of the Family, Private Property and the State.* Harmondsworth: Penguin.

English, Jane. 1979. "What Do Grown Children Owe Their Parents," in Onora O'Neill and William Ruddick, eds., *Having Children: Philosophical and Legal Reflections on Parenthood.* Pp. 115-122. New York: Oxford University Press.

Ettore, E.M. 1980. *Lesbians, Women, and Society.* London: Routledge and Kegan Paul.

Eustis, Nancy, Jay Greenberg, and Sharon Patten. 1984. *Long-term Care for Older Persons: A Policy Perspective.* Monterey, Calif.: Brooks/Cole.

Evans-Pritchard, E. E. 1951. *Kinship and Marriage Among the Nuer.* Oxford: Clarendon Press.

Fallers, Lloyd. 1956. *Bantu Bureacracy.* Chicago: University of Chicago Press.

___1957. "Some Determinants of Marriage Stability in Busoga." *Africa* 27:106-123.

Farley, Reynolds, and Walter R. Allen. 1987. *The Color Line and the Quality of Life in America.* New York: Russell Sage Foundation.

Farris, Catherine. 1993. "Work and Childcare in Taiwan: Changing Family Dynamics in a Chinese Society." *American Asian Review* 11, 3: 134-51.

Fei Hsiao-T'ung (Fei Xiaotong). 1939 *Peasant Life in China.* London: Routeledge and Kegan Paul.

Feinberg, Richard. 1979. "Kindred and Alliance on Anuta Island." *Journal of the Polynesian Society* 88:327-348.

____1981. *Anuta: Social Structure of Polynesian Island.* Honolulu: Institute for Polynesian Studies and Polynesian Cultural Center in Cooperation with the Danish National Museum.

Fel, Edit and Tamas Hofer. 1969. *Proper Peasants.* Chicago: Aldine.

Fernea, Elizabeth Warnock. 1965. *Guests of the Sheik.* New York: Doubleday.

Finney, Ben. 1966. "Resource Distribution and Social Structure in Tahiti." *Ethnology* 65: 80-86.

Firestone, Shulamith. 1970. *The Dialectic of Sex*. New York: William Morrow.

Firth, Raymond. 1959 (1929). *Economics of the New Zealand Maori*. Wellington, N.Z.: R.E. Owen, Government Printer.

_____1963 (1936). *We, the Tikopia: A Sociological Study of Kinship in Primitive Polynesia*. Boston: Beacon Press.

Fisher, J. L. 1957. "The Classification of Residence in Censuses." *American Anthropologist* 60: 508-517.

Flax, Jane. 1982. "The Family in Contemporary Feminist Thought: A Critical Review," in Jean Bethke Elshtain, ed., *The Family in Political Thought*. Amherst: University of Massachusetts Press.

Force, Roland W. and Maryanne Force. 1972. *Just One House: A Description and Analysis of Kinship in the Palau Islands*. Bernice P. Bishop Museum Bulletin 235. Honolulu: Bishop Museum Press.

Ford, Clellan. 1941. *Smoke from Their Fires: the Life of a Kwakiutl Chief*. New Haven: Yale University Press. Reprinted 1968, Hamden, CT.: The Shoe String Press.

Forde, Daryll. 1950. "Double Descent Among the Yako," in A. R. Radcliffe-Brown and Daryll Forde, eds. *African Systems of Kinship and Marriage*. Pp. 285-332. London and New York: Oxford University Press.

Fortes, Meyer. 1949a. "Time and Social Structure: An Ashanti Case Study," in Fred Eggan and Meyer Fortes, eds., *Social Structure: Essays Presented to A. R. Radcliffe-Brown*. London: Oxford University Press.

_____1949b. *The Web of Kinship Among the Tallensi*. London and New York: Oxford University Press.

_____1958. "Introduction," in Jack Goody, ed., *The Developmental Cycle in Domestic Groups*. Cambridge: Cambridge University Press.

_____1969. *Kinship and the Social Order: The Legacy of Lewis Henry Morgan*. Chicago: Aldine.

_____1970. *Time and Social Structure and Other Essays*. London: Althone Press; New York: Humanities Press.

Foster, Lawrence. 1981. *Religion and Sexuality: Three American Communal Experiments in the Nineteenth Century*. New York: Oxford University Press.

Fox, Robin. 1968. *Kinship and Marriage*. Harmondsworth: Penguin.

Freed, Stanley, and Ruth S. Freed. 1983. "The Domestic Cycle in India: Natural History of a Will-o-the-Wisp." *American Ethnologist* 10: 312-327.

Freedman, Maurice. 1958. *Lineage Organization in Southeastern China*. London: Athlone Press.

Freeman, Derek. 1983. *Margaret Mead and Samoa: The Making and Unmaking of an Anthropological Myth*. Cambridge, Mass.: Harvard University Press.

Freeman, Marsha A. 1995. "The Human Rights of Women in the Family: Issues and Recommendations for Implementation of the Women's Convention," in Peters and Wolper, eds, *Women's Rights Human Rights International Feminist Perspectives*. Pp. 149-175. New York: Routledge.

Freeman, Susan Tax. 1970. *Neighbors*. Chicago: University of Chicago Press.

Fried, Morton H. 1967. *The Evolution of Political Society: An Essay in Political Anthropology*. New York: Random House.

Friedl, Ernestine 1962. *Vasilika: Village in Modern Greece*. New York: Holt, Rinehart, and Winston.

Friedl, John. 1974. *Kippel: A Changing Village in the Alps.* New York: Holt, Rinehart, and Winston.

Fuller, C. J. 1976. *The Nayars Today.* Cambridge: Cambridge University Press.

Fuse, Akiko. 1984 "The Japanese Family in Transition," *The Japan Foundation Newsletter,* 12, 3-4, October and November.

Gamble, Sidney. 1954. *Ting Hsien: A North China Rural Community.* Stanford: Stanford University Press.

___1963. *North China Villages.* Berkeley and Los Angeles: University of California Press.

Game, Anne, and Rosemary Poole. 1983. "The Making of the Australian Family," in Ailsa Burns, Gail Bottomley, and Penny Jools, eds., *The Family in the Modern World: Australian Perspectives.* Pp. 80-102. Sydney: George Allen and Unwin.

Gardner, Hugh. 1978. *The Children of Prosperity: Thirteen Modern American Communes.* New York: St. Martin's Press.

Garfield, Viola E. 1939. *Tsimshian Clan and Society. University of Washington Publications in Anthropology* 7, 3: 167-340. Seattle: University of Washington Press.

Geddes, William H. 1977. "Social Individualisation on Tabiteuea Atoll." *Journal of the Polynesian Society* 86: 371-392.

Geertz, Clifford. 1965. "Religion as a Cultural System," in William Banton, ed., *Anthropological Approaches to the Study of Religion.* Pp. 1-46. London: Tavistock.

Geertz, Hildred. 1961. *The Javanese Family.* New York: The Free Press.

Gerritsen, J.C., E.W. Wolfensperger, and W.J.A. van der Heuvel. 1990. "Rural-Urban Differences in the Utilization of Care by the Elderly." *Journal of Cross-Cultural Gerontology* 5: 131-147.

Gerth, Hans, and C. Wright Mills. 1946. *From Max Weber: Essays in Sociology.* New York: Oxford University Press.

Gifford, Edward Winslow. 1929. *Tonga Society.* Bernice P. Bishop Museum Bulletin 61. Honolulu: Bishop Museum.

Gini, Corrado, and Elio Carranti. 1954. "The Family in Italy." *Marriage and Family Living.* Nov., Pp. 350-361.

Glasgow, Douglas G. 1980. *The Black Underclass: Poverty, Unemployment and Entrapment of Ghetto Youth.* San Francisco: Jossey-Bass.

Gluckman, Max. 1950. "Kinship and Marriage among the Lozi of Northern Rhodesia and the Zulu of Natal," in A.R. Radcliffe-Brown and Daryll Forde, eds., *African Systems of Kinship and Marriage.* Pp. 166-206. London and New York: Oxford University Press.

Gold, Thomas. 1990. "Urban Private Business and Social Change," in Deborah Davis and Ezra F. Vogel, eds., *Chinese Society on the Eve of Tiananmen.* Pp. 157-178. Cambridge, MA: Harvard University Press.

Goldman, Irving. 1970. *Ancient Polynesian Society.* Chicago: University of Chicago Press.

Goldschmidt, Walter. 1969. *Kambuya's Cattle: The Legacy of an African Herdsman.* Berkeley and Los Angeles: University of California Press.

Goldschmidt, Walter R., and Havold E. Driver. 1940. *The Hupa White Deerskin Dance.* University of California Publications in American Archaeology and Ethnology 135, 8: 103-142. Berkeley: University of California Press.

Goldstein, Melvyn C. 1971. "Stratification, Polyandry, and Family Structure in Central Tibet." *Southwestern Journal of Anthropology* 27: 64-74.

___1976. "Fraternal Polyandry and Fertility in a High Himalayan Valley in Nepal." *Human Ecology* 4, 3: 223-233.

Goodale, Jane C. 1971. *Tiwi Wives*. Seattle and London: University of Washington Press.

Goode William J. 1963. *World Revolution and Family Patterns*. New York: Free Press of Glencoe.

Goodenough, Ward H. 1951. *Property, Kin, and Community on Truk*. New Haven: Yale University Press.

___1955. "A Problem in Malayo-Polynesian Social Organization." *American Anthropologist* 57: 71-83.

___1956. "Residence Rules." *Southwestern Journal of Anthropology* 12: 22-37.

Goody, Esther N. 1973. *Contexts of Kinship: An Essay in the Family Sociology of the Gonja of Northern Ghana*. Cambridge: Cambridge University Press.

Goody, Jack. 1958. "The Fission of Domestic Groups among the LoDagaba," in Jack Goody, ed., *The Developmental Cycle in Domestic Groups*. Pp. 53-91. Cambridge: Cambridge University Press.

___1973a. "Bridewealth and Dowry in Africa and Eurasia," in Jack Goody and Stanley Tambiah, *Bridewealth and Dowry*. Pp. 1-58. Cambridge: Cambridge University Press.

___1973b. "Polygyny, Economy, and the Role of Women," in Jack Goody, ed., *The Character of Kinship*. Pp. 175-190. Cambridge: Cambridge University Press.

___1976. *Production and Reproduction*. Cambridge: Cambridge University Press.

___1990. *The Oriental, the Ancient, and the Primitive: Systems of Family and Marriage in the Pre-Industrial Societies of Eurasia*. Cambridge: Cambridge University Press.

Goubert, Pierre. 1977. "Family and Province: A Contribution to the Knowledge of Family Structure in Early Modern France." *Journal of Family History* 2, 3: 179-195.

Gough, Kathleen. 1961a. "Tiyyar: North Kerala," in David M. Schneider and Kathleen Gough, eds., *Matrilineal Kinship*. Pp. 405-414. Berkeley and Los Angeles: University of California Press.

___1961b. "Mappilla: North Kerala," in David M. Schneider and Kathleen Gough, eds., *Matrilineal Kinship*. Pp. 415-442. Berkeley and Los Angeles: University of California Press.

___1961c. "Nayar: North Kerala," in David M. Schneider and Kathleen Gough, eds., *Matrilineal Kinship*. Pp. 385-404. Berkeley and Los Angeles: University of California Press.

___1961d. "Nayar: Central Kerala," in David M. Schneider and Kathleen Gough, eds., *Matrilineal Kinship*. Pp. 298-384. Berkeley and Los Angeles: University of California Press.

___1961e. "Variation in Interpersonal Kinship Relations," in David M. Schneider and Kathleen Gough, eds., *Matrilineal Kinship*. Pp. 577-613. Berkeley and Los Angeles: University of California Press.

Gower Chapman, Charlotte. 1961. *Milocca: A Sicilian Village*. Cambridge, Mass.: Schenkman.

Graburn, Nelson H. H. 1969. "Eskimo Law in Light of Self and Group Interest." *Law and Society Review* IV: 45-60.

Gray, Francine du Plessix. 1990. "Soviet Women," *The New Yorker*, February19.

Gray, Robert F. 1964. "Sonjo Lineage Structure and Property," in Robert F. Gray and P. H. Gulliver, eds., *The Family Estate in Africa: Studies in the Role of Property in*

Family Structure and Lineage Continuity. Pp. 231-262. London: Routledge and Kegan Paul.

Guarneri, Carol J. 1991. *The Utopian Alternative: Fourierism in Nineteenth Century America.* Ithaca: Cornell University Press.

Guemple, Lee. 1979. *Inuit Adaptations.* Ottawa: National Museum of Canada.

Gulliver, P. H. 1955. *The Family Herds: A Study of Two Pastoral Tribes in East Africa.* London: Routledge and Kegan Paul.

___1964. "The Arusha Family," in Robert F. Gray and P. H. Gulliver, eds., *The Family Estate in Africa: Studies in the Role of Property in Family Structure and Lineage Continuity.* Pp. 197-229. London: Routledge and Kegan Paul.

Gunther, Erna. 1950. *Klallam Ethnography.* University of Washington Publications in Anthropology 1, 5: 173-314. Seattle: University of Washington Press.

Guyer, Jane I. 1984. "Naturalism in Models of African Production." *Man* 19:371-88.

___1991. "Female Farming in Anthropology and African History," in Micaela diLeonardo, ed., *Gender at the Crossroads of Knowledge: Feminist Anthropology in the Postmodern Era.* Pp. 257-77. Berkeley and Los Angeles: University of California Press.

Haeberlin, Hermann, and Erna Gunther. 1930. *The Indians of Puget Sound.* University of Washington Publications in Anthropology 4(1): 1-84. Seattle: University of Washington Press.

Halpern, Joel. 1972. "Town and Countryside in Serbia in the 19th Century," in Peter Laslett, ed., *Household and Family in Past Time.* Pp. 401-425. Cambridge: Cambridge University Press.

Halpern, Joel and Barbara Karewski Halpern. 1972. *A Serbian Village in Historical Perspective.* New York: Holt, Rinehart, and Winston.

Halpin, Marjorie. 1984. "The Structure of Tsimshian Totemism," in Jay Miller and Carol M. Eastman, eds., *The Tsimshian and Their Neighbors of the North Pacific Coast,* Pp. 16-35. Seattle and London: University of Washington Press.

Hammel, Eugene. 1972. "The Zadruga as Process," in Peter Laslett, ed., *Household and Family in Past Time.* Pp. 335-374. Cambridge: Cambridge University Press.

___1980. "Household Structure in 14th Century Macedonia." *Journal of Family History* 5: 242-273.

Hammel, Eugene and Peter Laslett. 1974. "Comparing Household Structure Over Time and Between Cultures." *Comparative Studies in Society and History* 16:73-109.

Handy, E. S. Craighill. 1923. *The Native Culture in the Marquesas.* Bernice P. Bishop Museum Bulletin 9. Honolulu: The Bernice P. Bishop Museum.

Handy, E. S. Craighill and Mary Kowena Pukui. 1978 (1958). *The Polynesian Family System in Ka'u, Hawaii.* Rutland, VT, and Tokyo: Tuttle.

Hanley, Susan B. 1985. "Family and Fertility in Four Tokugawa Villages," in Susan B. Hanley and Arthur P. Wolf, eds., *Family and Population in East Asian History.* Pp. 196-228. Stanford: Stanford University Press.

Hansen, Edward C. 1977. *Rural Catalonia Under the Franco Regime.* Cambridge: Cambridge University Press.

Hanson, F. Allan. 1970. *Rapan Lifeways: Society and History on a Polynesian Island.* Boston: Little, Brown.

Harrell, Stevan. 1982. *Ploughshare Village: Culture and Context in Taiwan.* Seattle and London: University of Washington Press.

Harrell, Stevan, and Sara A. Dickey. 1985. "Dowry Systems in Complex Societies." *Ethnology* 24: 105-120.

Harrell, Stevan and Thomas W. Pullum. 1995. "Marriage, Mortality, and the Developmental Cycle in Three Chinese Lineages," in Stevan Harrell, ed., *Chinese Historical Micro-Demography*. Pp. 141-162. Berkeley and Los Angeles: University of California Press.

Harris, Alfred, and Grace Harris. 1964. "Property and the Cycle of Domestic Groups," in *The Family Estate in Africa: Studies in the Role of Property in Family Structure and Lineage Continuity*. Robert F. Gray and P. H. Gulliver, eds., Pp. 17-53. London: Routledge and Kegan Paul.

Harry, Joseph, and William B. Devall. 1978. *The Social Organization of Gay Males*. New York: Praeger.

Hart, C. W. M. and Arnold R. Pilling. 1960. *The Tiwi of North Australia*. New York: Holt, Rinehart and Winston.

Harvey, David. 1989. *The Condition of Postmodernity*. Oxford: Basil Blackwell.

Hatanaka, Sachiko. 1971. "The Social Organization of a Polynesian Atoll." *Journal de la Société des Océanistes* 27: 250-264, 311-339.

___1972. "The Settlement and Population in Pukarua." Paper Presented to Pacific Atoll Population Conference. East-West Population Institute, Honolulu, December 27-30, 1972.

Hecht, Julia. 1977. "The Culture of Gender in Pukapuka: Male, Female, and the Mayakitanga 'Sacred Maid.'" *Journal of the Polynesian Society*, 86:183-206.

Heiss, Jerold. 1975. *The Case for the Black Family: A Sociological Inquiry*. New York: Columbia University Press.

Helm, June. 1968. "The Nature of Dogrib Socioterritorial Groups," in Richard B. Lee and Irven DeVore, eds., *Man the Hunter*. Chicago: Aldine.

___1972. "The Dogrib Indians," in M. G. Bicchieri, ed., *Hunters and Gatherers Today*. Pp. 51-89. New York: Holt, Rinehart and Winston.

Herdt, Gilbert. 1994. *Third Sex, Third Gender: Beyond Sexual Dimorphism in Culture and History*. New York: Zane Books.

Heuer, Berys N. 1969. "Maori Women in Traditional Family and Tribal Life." *Journal of the Polynesian Society* 78: 448-494.

HHS (U.S. Department of Health and Human Services). 1989. *Vital Statistics of the United States, 1987*: Volume I—Natality. Hyattsville, MD.

Hiatt, L. R. 1968. "Ownership and Use of Land Among the Australian Aborigines," in Richard B. Lee and Irven DeVore, eds., *Man the Hunter*. Pp. 99-102. Chicago: Aldine.

Hibbett Howard and Gen Itasaka. 1967. *Modern Japanese: A Basic Reader*, 2nd Edition. Cambridge, Mass.: Harvard University Press.

Hickey, Gerald Cannon. 1964. *Village in Vietnam*. New Haven: Yale University Press.

Hill, Kate. 1987. "Mothers by Insemination: Interviews," in Sandra Pollack and Jeanne Vaughn, eds., *Politics of the Heart: A Lesbian Parenting Anthology*. Pp. 111-119. Ithaca, NY: Firebrand Books.

Hiroa, Te Rangi (Buck, Sir Peter Henry). 1932a. *Ethnology of Tongareva*. Bernice P. Bishop Museum Bulletin 92. Honolulu: The Bernice P. Bishop Museum.

___1932b. *Ethnology of Manihiki and Rakahanga*. Bernice P. Bishop Museum Bulletin 99. Honolulu: The Bernice P. Bishop Museum.

___1934. *Mangaian Society*. Bernice P. Bishop Museum Bulletin 122. Honolulu: The Bernice P. Bishop Museum.

___1938. *Ethnology of Mangareva*. Bernice P. Bishop Museum Bulletin 157. Honolulu: The Bernice P. Bishop Museum.

Hochschild, Arlie. 1989. *The Second Shift: Working Parents and the Revolution at Home*. New York: Penguin.

Holleman, J. F. 1951. "Some 'Shona' Tribes of Southern Rhodesia," in Elizabeth Colson and Max Gluckman, eds., *Seven Tribes of British Central Africa*. Pp. 354-395. London and New York: Oxford University Press.

Homans, George C. 1941. *English Villagers of the 13th Century*. New York: Harper and Row.

Hughes, Diane Owen. 1977. "From Brideprice to Dowry in Western Europe." *Journal of Family History* 3, 3: 262-296.

Huntsman, Judith and Anthony Hooper. 1975. "Male and Female in Tokelau Culture." *Journal of Polynesian Society* 84: 415-430.

___1976. "The 'Desecration' of Tokelau Kinship." *Journal of the Polynesian Society* 85: 257-273.

Ishida Takeshi. 1971. *Japanese Society*. New York: Random House.

Jewitt, John Rogers. 1975. *Narrative of the Adventures and Sufferings of John R. Jewitt: While Held as a Captive of the Nootka Indians of Vancouver Island, 1803 to 1805*. Edited and annotated by Robert F. Heizer. Pomona, Calif.: Ballena Press.

Kaberry, Phyllis M. 1939. *Aboriginal Woman: Sacred and Profane*. Philadelphia: The Blakiston Company.

Kanter, Rosabeth Moss. 1972. *Commitment and Community: Communes and Utopiasin Sociological Perspective*. Cambridge, MA: Harvard University Press.

Keeling, Richard. 1992. *Cry for Luck: Sacred Song and Speech Among the Yurok, Hupa, and Karok Indians of Northwestern California*. Berkeley and Los Angeles: University of California Press.

Kenna, Margaret. 1976. "The Idiom of Family," in J. G. Peristiany, ed., *Mediterranean Family Structures*. Cambridge: Cambridge University Press. Pp. 347-362.

Kenyon, Susan M. 1980. *The Kyuquot Way: A Study of a West Coast (Nootkan) Community*. Ottawa: National Museums of Canada.

Kessinger, Tom G. 1974. *Vilyatpur 1848-1968: Social and Economic Change in a North Indian Village*. Berkeley and Los Angeles: University of California Press.

Keyes, Charles F. 1975. "Kin Groups in a Thai-Lao Community," in G.William Skinner and A. Thomas Kirsch, eds., *Change and Persistence in Thai Society*. Pp. 275-97. Ithaca: Cornell University Press.

___1976. *The Golden Peninsula*. New York: Macmillan.

Keyfitz, Nathan, and Wilhelm Flieger 1990. *World Population Growth and Aging*. Chicago and London: University of Chicago Press.

Kiernan, Kathleen. 1986. "Leaving Home: Living Arrangements of Young People in Six West-European Countries." *European Journal of Population* 2: 177-184.

Kirch, Patrick Vinton. 1984. *The Evolution of the Polynesian Chiefdoms*. Cambridge: Cambridge University Press.

Kirch, Patrick Vinton, and D. E. Yen. 1982. *Tikopia: The Prehistory and Ecology of a Polynesian Outlier*. Bernice P. Bishop Museum Bulletin 238. Honolulu: Bishop Museum Press.

Kiste, Robert C. 1974. *The Bikinians: A Study in Forced Migration.* Menlo Park, CA: Cummings.

Kiste, Robert C. and Michael A. Rynkiewich. 1976. "Incest and Exogamy: A Comparative Study of Two Marshall Island Populations." *Journal of Polynesian Society* 85: 209-226.

Kjellström, Rolf. 1973. *Eskimo Marriage.* Translated by Donald Burton. Stockholm: Nordiska Mussets.

Kolakowski, Leszek. 1985. "The Search for Community," in Hagihara Nobutoshi, Akira Iriye, Georges Nivat, and Philip Windsor, eds., *Experiencing the 20th Century.* Pp. 155-167. Tokyo: University of Tokyo Press.

Kondo, Dorinne K. 1990. *Crafting Selves: Power, Gender, and Discourses of Identity in a Japanese Workplace.* Chicago: University of Chicago Press.

Kopytoff, Igor. 1964. "Family and Lineage among the Suku of the Congo," in Robert F. Gray and P. H. Gulliver, eds., *The Family Estate in Africa: Studies in the Role of Property in Family Structure and Lineage Continuity.* Pp. 83-116. London: Routledge and Kegan Paul.

Kopytoff, Igor, and Suzanne Miers. 1977. "African 'Slavery' as an Institution of Marginality," in Suzanne Miers and Igor Kopytoff, eds., *Slavery in Africa: Historical and Anthropological Perspectives,* Pp. 3-81. Madison: University of Wisconsin Press.

Kornhauser, Wiliam. 1959. *The Politics of Mass Society.* Glencoe: The Free Press.

Krause, Aurel. 1956 [1878-9]. *The Tlingit Indians: Results of a Trip to the Northwest Coast of America and the Bering Straits.* Seattle: University of Washington Press.

Krige, Eileen Jensen. 1964. "Property, Cross-Cousin Marriage, and the Family Cycle Among the Lobedu," in Robert F. Gray and P. H. Gulliver, eds., *The Family Estate in Africa: Studies in the Role of Property in Family Structure and Lineage Continuity.* Pp. 155-195. London: Routledge and Kegan Paul.

Kroeber, A. L. 1925 *Handbook of the Indians of California.* Washington, U.S. Government Printing Office.

Kuper, Hilda. 1950. "Kinship among the Swazi," in A. R. Radcliffe-Brownand Daryll Forde, eds., *African Systems of Kinship and Marriage.* Pp. 86-110. London and New York: Oxford University Press.

Kyrk, Hazel. 1953. *The Family in the American Economy.* Chicago: University of Chicago Press.

LaFargue, Jane Peterson. 1981. Those You Can Count On: A Social Network Study of Family Organization in an Urban Black Population. Unpublished Ph.D. Dissertation, University of Washington.

Lancaster, C. S. 1976. "Women, Horticulture, and Society in Sub-Saharan Africa." *American Anthropologist* 78: 539-564.

Laslett, Peter. 1972. "Introduction: The History of the Family," in Peter Laslett, and Richard Wall, eds., *Household and Family in Past Time.* Pp. 1-89. Cambridge: Cambridge University Press.

____1978. "The Stem Family and Its Privileged Position," in K.W. Wachter, E. A. Hammel, and P. Laslett, eds., *Statistical Studies of Historical Social Structure.* Pp. 89-112. New York: Academic Press.

Leach, Edmund. 1957. *Rethinking Anthropology.* London: Athlone Press.

____1961. *Pul Eliya: A Village in Ceylon.* Cambridge: Cambridge University Press.

Leacock, Eleanor Burke. 1969. "The Montagnais-Naskapi Band," in David Damas, ed., *Contributions to Anthropology: Band Societies*. Ottawa: National Museums of Canada, Bulletin #228, Anthropological Series #84, Pp. 1-16.

___1972. "Introduction" to Frederick Engels, *The Origin of the Family, Private Property, and the State*. New York: International Publishers.

Lebra, Takie Sugiyama. 1984. *Japanese Women*. Honolulu: University of Hawaii Press.

Lee, Richard B. 1968. "What Hunters do for a Living, or How to Make Out on Scarce Resources," in Richard B. Lee and Irven DeVore, eds., *Man the Hunter*.

___1972. "The !Kung of Botswana," in M. C. Bicchieri, ed., *Hunters and Gatherers Today*. New York: Holt, Rinehart and Winston.

___1979. *The !Kung San*. Cambridge: Cambridge University Press.

LeMann, Nicholas. 1986. "The Origins of the Underclass." *The Atlantic Monthly* 257, 6: 31-55; 258, 1: 54-68

Le Roy Ladurie, Emmanuel. 1976. "Family Structure and Inheritance Customs in 16th Century France," in Jack Goody, et al., eds., *Family and Inheritance*. Pp. 37-70. Cambridge: Cambridge University Press.

Levine, Robert A. 1964. "The Gusii Family," in Robert F. Gray and P. H. Gulliver, eds., *The Family Estate in Africa: Studies in the Role of Property in Family Structure and Lineage Continuity*. Pp. 63-82. London: Routledge and Kegan Paul.

Lévi-Strauss, Claude. 1969. *The Elementary Structures of Kinship*. Translated by James Earle Brill and John Richard von Sturmer. Boston: Beacon Press.

Lewin, Ellen. 1984. "Lesbianism and Motherhood: Implications for Child Custody," in Trudy Darty and Sandee Potter, eds., *Women-Identified Women*. Palo Alto: Mayfield Publishing Company, Pp. 163-183.

Lewis, Henry T. 1971. *Ilocano Rice Farmers*. Honolulu: Univeristy of Hawaii Press.

Lewis, I. M. 1962. *Marriage and the Family in Northern Somali and Kampala*. East African Institute of Social Research.

Lieber, Michael D. 1968. The Nature of the Relationship Between Land Tenure and Kinship on Kapingamarangi Atoll. Ph.D. Dissertation. University of Pittsburgh.

___1974. "Land Tenure on Kapingamarangi," in Henry P. Lundsgaarde, ed., *Land Tenure in Oceania*. Pp. 70-99. Honolulu: University Press of Hawaii.

Liegle, Ludwig. 1970. *The Family's Role in Soviet Society*, trs. Susan Hecker. New York: Springer Publishing Company.

Lindt, Gillian. 1969. "Familiy Surrogates in Colonial America: The Moravian Experiment." *Journal of Marriage and the Family* 31: 651-57. Reprinted in Rosabeth Moss Kanter, ed., Communes, New York: Harper and Row, 1973, Pp. 308-317.

Lingenfelter, Sherwood Galen. 1975. *Yap: Political Leadership and Cultural Change in an Island Society*. Honolulu: University Press of Hawaii.

Linton, Ralph. 1940. "Marquesan Culture," in Abram Kardiner, ed., *The Individual and His Society*. Pp. 137-196. New York: Columbia University Press.

Lippit, Victor. 1978. "The Development of Underdevelopment in China." *Modern China* 4, 3: 251-328.

Lison-Tolosana, Carmelo. 1966. *Belmonte de los Caballeros*. Oxford: Oxford University Press.

___1971. Antropología Cultural de Galicia. Madrid: Siglo XXI de España Editores.

___1976. "The Ethics of Inheritance," in J. G. Peristiany, ed., *Mediterranean Family Structures*. Pp. 305-316. Cambridge: Cambridge University Press.

Lloyd, P. C.1965. "The Yoruba of Nigeria," in James L. Gibbs, Jr., ed., *Peoples of Africa*. Pp. 549-582. New York: Holt, Rinehart and Winston.

Lopatin, Ivan A. 1954. *Social Life and Religion of the Indians in Kitimat, British Columbia*. University of Southern California Social Science Series, No. 26. Los Angeles: The University of Southern California Press.

Lorimer, Frank. 1954. *Culture and Human Fertility*. Zurich: UNESCO.

Lundsgaarde, Henry P. and Martin G. Silverman. 1972. "Category and Group in Gilbertese Kinship: An Updating of Goodenough's Analysis." *Ethnology* 11: 95-110.

Lutz, Wolfgang. 1994. *The Future of World Population*. Population Bulletin 49, no. 1. Washington, D.C.: Population Reference Bureau, Inc.

Lyotard, Jean-Francois. 1984. *The Postmodern Condition: A Report on Knowledge*. Minneapolis: University of Minnesota Press.

MacGaffey, Wyatt. 1977. "Economic and Social Dimensions of Kongo Slavery," in Suzanne Miers and Igor Kopytoff, eds., *Slavery in Africa: Historical and Anthropological Perpsepctives*. Pp. 235-255. Madison: University of Wisconsin Press.

MacGregor, Gordon. 1937. *Ethnology of Tokelau Islands*. Bernice P. Bishop Museum Bulletin 146. Honolulu: Bishop Museum.

Malcolm, D. W. 1953. *Sukumaland: An African People and Their Country*. London and New York: Oxford University Press.

Malinowski, Bronislaw. 1955 (1927). *Sex and Repression in Savage Society*. London: Kegan Paul.

Marcus, George, and Michael M. J. Fischer. 1986. *Anthropology as Cultural Critique: An Experiemental Moment in the Human Sciences*. Chicago: University of Chicago Press.

Marshall, Lorna. 1976. *The !Kung of NyaeNyae*. Cambridge, Mass.: Harvard University Press.

Martin, Elmer P., and Joanne Mitchell Martin. 1978. *The Black Extended Family*. Chicago: University of Chicago Press.

Martin, Linda G. 1989. "The Graying of Japan," *Population Bulletin* 44, 2.

Marx, Emmanuel. 1967. *Bedouin of the Negev*. Manchester: University ofManchester Press.

Marx, Karl. 1970 (1859). *A Contribution to the Critique of Political Economy*. New York: International Publishers.

Marx, Karl, and Friedrich Engels. 1988 (1846). *The German Ideology*. NewYork: International Publishers.

Matley, William C., Jr., and Dwight L. Johnson. 1983. "America's Black Population, 1970 to 1982," *The Crisis* 90, 10:10-18.

McIlwraith, Thomas Forsyth. 1948. *The Bella Coola Indians*. Toronto: University of Toronto Press.

McKennan, Robert A. 1969. "Athapaskan Groupings and Social Organization in Central Alaska," in David Damas, ed., *Contributions to Anthropology: Band Societies*. Pp. 930115. Ottawa: National Museums of Canada.

Mead, Margaret. 1925. *Coming of Age in Samoa: A Psychological Study of Primitive Youth for Western Civilization*. New York: Blue Ribbon Books.

___1935. *Sex and Temperament in Three Primitive Socities*. New York:William Morrow and Co.

___1969 (1930). *Social Organization of Manu'a*. Bernice P. Bishop Museum Bulletin 76. Honolulu: Bishop Museum Press.

Meggitt, M. J. 1962. *Desert People*. Sydney: Angus and Robertson.

Mehta, Ved. 1979. *Mamaji*. New York and Oxford: Oxford University Press.

Metraux, Alfred. 1940. *Ethnology of Easter Island*. Bernice P. Bishop Museum Bulletin 160. Honolulu: Bishop Museum.

Milne, Carmen A. and Michael Dennis Steward. 1967. "The Inheritance of Land Rights in Laura," in Leonard Mason, ed., *The Laura Report: A Field Report of Training and Research in Majuro Atoll, Marshall Islands.*, Pp. 1-45. Honolulu: University of Hawaii.

Minge-Klevana, Wanda. 1980. "Does Labor Time Decrease with Industrialization? A Survey of Time and Allocation Studies." *Current Anthropology* 21: 279-292.

Mintz, Steven, and Susan Kellogg. 1988. *Domestic Revolutions: A Social History of American Family Life*. New York: Free Press.

Mitchell, B.R. 1976. *European Historical Statistics, 1750-1970*. New York: Columbia University Press.

Mitchell, J. C. 1951. "The Yao of Southern Nyasaland," in Elizabeth Colson and Max Gluckman, eds., *Seven Tribes of British Central Africa*. Pp. 292-353. London: Oxford University Press.

Mohsen, Safia K. 1967. "Aspects of the Legal Status of Women Among the Awlad 'Ali." *Anthropological Quarterly* 40: 153-66.

Moore, Melinda A. 1985. "A New Look at the Nayar Taravad." *Man* 20: 523-541.

Morgan, Lewis Henry. 1877. *Ancient Society*. New York: H. Holt.

Mumford, Lweis. 1961. *The City in History*. New York and London: Harcourt Brace Jovanovich.

Murdock, George Peter. 1936. *Rank and Potlatch Among the Haida*. Yale University Publications in Anthropology, No. 13. New Haven: Yale University Press.

Musselwhite, Diane. n.d. "Junior High Deviancy and the Creation of a Crisis: Social Drama in Contemporary Japan." Unpublished paper, University of Washington.

Myers, Fred R. 1982. "Always Ask: Resource Use and Land Ownership Among Pintupi Aborigines of the Australian Western Desert," in Nancy M. Williams and Eugene S. Hunn, eds., *Resource Managers*. Pp. 173-195. Boulder, CO: Westview Press.

Nakane, Chie. 1967. *Kinship and Economic Organization in Rural Japan*. London: Athlone.

Nason, James D. 1970. "Clan and Copra: Modernization on Etal Island, Eastern Caroline Islands." Ph.D. Dissertation. University of Washington.

———1981. "Aging in a Micronesian Community," in Pamela T. Amoss and Stevan Harrell, eds., *Other Ways of Growing Old: Anthropological Perspectives*. Pp. 155-173. Stanford, CA: Stanford University Press.

Nelson, Richard King. 1969. *Hunters of the Northern Ice*. Chicago: University of Chicago Press.

Netting, Robert McC. 1968. *Hill Farmers of Nigeria: Cultural Ecology of the Kofyar of the Jos Plateau*. Seattle: University of Washington Press.

Netting, Robert, Richard R. Wilk, Eric J. Arnould (eds.). 1984. *Households: Comparative Historical Studies of the Domestic Group*. Berkeley: University of California Press.

Naughton Barry. 1992. "Implications of the State Monopoly Over Industry and Its Relaxation," *Modern China* 18, 1: 14-41.

Newsweek. 1990. "The 21st Century Family." Washington, D.C.: Washington Post Company.

Noricks, Jay Smith. 1983. "Unrestricted Cognatic Descent and Corporateness on Niutao, a Polynesian Island of Tuvalu." *American Ethnologist* 10: 571-584.

Noyes, Pierrepont. 1973. "Growing Up in Oneida," in Rosabeth Moss Kanter,ed., *Communes*, Pp. 365-374.

Oberg, Kalervo. 1973. *The Social Economy of the Tlingit Indians*. Seattle and London: University of Washington Press.

O'Brien, John J. 1987. "The Three-Sector Nursing Home Industry." Unpublished Ph.D. Dissertation, Graduate School of Business, University of Washington.

Okonogi Keigo. 1978-9 "The Ajase Complex of the Japanese, parts 1 and 2," *Japan Echo* 5, 4: 88-105 and 6, 1: 104-118.

Oliver, Douglas L. 1974 *Ancient Tahitian Society*. Honolulu: University Press of Hawaii.

Olson, Ronald L. 1967 [1936]. *The Quinault Indians*. University of Washington Publications in Anthropology, Vol. VI, No. 1. Seattle and London: University of Washington Press.

___1940. "The Social Organization of the Haisla of British Columbia." *Anthropological Records*, Vol. 2, No. 5. Berkeley: University of California Press.

___1954. "Social Life of the Owikeno Kwakiutl." *Anthropological Records*, Vol.14, No. 3. Berkeley and Los Angeles: University of California Press.

___1955. "Notes on the Bella Bella Kwakiutl." *Anthropological Records*, Vol.14, No. 5. Berkeley and Los Angeles: University of California Press.

___1967. "Social Structure and Social Life of the Tlingit in Alaska." University of California Publications: *Anthropological Records*. Berkeley and Los Angeles: University of California Press.

Ortner, Sherry. 1981. "Gender and Sexuality in Hierarchical Societies: The Case of Polynesia and Some Comparative Implications," in Sherry B. Ortner and Harriet Whitehead, eds., *Sexual Meanings: The Cultural Construction of Gender and Sexuality*. Pp. 359-409. Cambridge and New York: Cambridge University Press.

Otterbein, Keith F. 1963. "Marquesan Polylandry." *Marriage and Family Living* 25: 155-159.

Ottino, Paul. 1967. "Early 'Ati of the Western Tuamotus," in Genevieve A.Highland, et. al, eds., *Polynesian Culture History: Essays in Honor of Kenneth P. Emory*. Pp. 451-481. Bernice P. Bishop Museum Special Publication 56. Honolulu: Bishop Museum Press.

___1970. "Adoption on Rangiroa Atoll, Tuamotu Archipelago," in Vern Caroll, ed., *Adoption in Eastern Oceania*, Pp. 88-118. Honolulu: University of Hawaii Press.

Parber, Pat 1987. "Gay Parenting, or, Look Out, Anita," in Sandra Pollackand Jeanne Vaughn, eds., *Politics of the Heart: A Lesbian Parenting Anthology*. Pp. 12-15. Ithaca, NY: Firebrand Books.

Parish, William and Martin King Whyte. 1977. *Village and Family in Contemporary China*. Chicago: University of Chicago Press.

Peacock, Nadine R. 1991. "Rethinking the Sexual Division of Labor: Reproduction and Women's Work Among the Efe," in Micaela di Leonardo, ed., *Gender at the Crossroads of Knowledge: Feminist Anthropology in the Postmodern Era*, Pp. 339-360. Berkeley and Los Angeles: University of California Press.

Peak, Lois. 1989. "Learning to Become Part of the Group: The Japanese Child's

Transition to Preschool Life," *Journal of Japanese Studies* 15, 1: 93-123.

Pearlin, Leonard J. 1974. *Class and Family Relations.* Boston: Little, Brown.

Peristiany, J. G. 1968. "Introduction to a Cyprus Highland Village," in J.G. Peristiany, ed., *Contributions to Mediterranean Sociology.* The Hague: Mouton.

Peters, Emrys Lloyd. 1965. "Aspects of the Family Among the Bedouin of Cyrenaica," in M. F. Nimkoff, ed., *Comparative Family Systems.* Pp. 123-46. Boston: Houghton Mifflin.

____1976. "Aspects of Affinity in a Maronite Village," in J. G. Peristiany, ed., *Mediterranean Family Structures.* Pp. 27-79. Cambridge: Cambridge University Press.

Peterson, Glenn. 1982. "Ponapean Matriliny: Production, Exchange, and the Ties that Bind." *American Ethnologist* 9: 129-144.

Peterson, Nicholas. 1970. "The Importance of Women in Determining the Composition of Residential Groups in Aboriginal Australia," in Fay Gale, ed., *Woman's Role in Aboriginal Society.* Pp. 9-16. Canberry: Australian Institute of Aboriginal Studies.

Picker, Jane. 1976. "Law and the Status of Women in the United States," in *Law and the Status of Women, Columbia Human Righs Law Review,* ed., Pp. 311-344. Centre for Social Development and Humanitarian Affairs, United Nations.

Pies, Cheri A. 1990. "Lesbians and the Choice to Parent," in Frederick W. Bozett and Marvin B. Sussman, eds., *Homosexuality and Family Relations.* Pp. 137-154. New York: The Haworth Press.

Piker, Steven. 1975. "The Post-Peasant Village in Central Plain Thai Society," in G. William Skinner and A. Thomas Kirsch, eds., *Change and Persistence in Thai Society.* Pp. 298-323. Ithaca: Cornell University Press.

Pilling, Arnold R. 1989. "Yurok Aristocracy and 'Great Houses.'" *American Indian Quarterly* 13, 4: 421-436.

Pitt-Rivers, Julian. 1961. *The People of the Sierra.* Chicago: University of Chicago Press.

Plakans, Andrejs. 1975. "Peasant Farmsteads and Households in the Baltic Littoral, 1797." *Comparative Studies in Society and History* 12: 2-35.

Pollock, Nancy J. 1974. "Landholding on Namu Atoll, Marshall Islands," in Henry P. Lundsgarrde, ed., *Land Tenure in Oceania.* Honolulu: University Press of Hawaii, Pp. 100-129.

Pollock, Sandra, and Jeanne Vaughn. 1987. "Introduction," in Sandra Pollock and Jeanne Vaughn, eds., *Politics of the Heart: A Lesbian Parenting Anthology.* Pp. 12-15. Ithaca, NY: Firebrand Books.

Porter, P. W. 1979. *Food and Development in the Semi-Arid Zone of East Africa.* Princeton, NJ: Maxwell School of Citizenship and Public Affairs.

Potter, Sulamith Heins. 1977. *Family Life in a Northern Thai Village.* Berkeley and Los Angeles: University of California Press.

Powell, Jay and Vickie Jensen. 1976. *Quileute: An Introduction to the Indians of La Push.* Seattle and London: University of Washington Press.

Rabkin Leslie Y., and Audrey G. Spiro. 1975. "Postscript: Children of the Kibbutz, 1974," in Melford E. Spiro, *Children of the Kibbutz: A Study in Child Training and Personality,* Pp. 463-499. Second edition. Cambridge, MA: Harvard University Press.

Radcliffe-Brown, A. R. 1924. "Mother's Brother in Southern Africa." *South Africa Journal of Science* 21: 542-555.

Rahman, Fazlur. 1979. *Islam.* 2nd Edition. Chicago: Univeristy of Chicago Press.

Rambo, A. Terry. 1991. "The Study of Cultural Evolution," in A. Terry Rambo and Kathleen Gillogly, eds., *Profiles in Cultural Evolution: Papers from a Conference in Honor of Elman R. Service.* Pp.23-109. Ann Arbor: Anthropological Papers, Museum of Anthropology, University of Michigan, no. 85.

Raphael, Sharon, and Mina Robinson. 1984. "The Older Lesbian: Love Relationships and Friendship Patterns," in Trudy Darty and Sandee Potter, eds., *Women-Identified Women.* Pp. 67-82. Palo Alto: Mayfield Publishing Company.

Rawlings, Steve W. 1984. *Household and Family Characteristics*, March 1983. Current Population Reports: Population Characteristics, Series 20, No. 388. Washington, D.C.: U.S. Bureau of the Census.

___1994. *Household and Family Characteristics*, March 1993. U.S. Bureau of the Census, Current Population Reports Pp.20-477. Washington, D.C.: U.S. Government Printing Office.

Ray, Verne Frederick. 1938. "Lower Chinook Ethnographic Notes." *University of Washington Publications in Anthropology* 7, 2: 29-165. Seattle: University of Washington Press.

Richards A. J. 1950. "Some Types of Family Structure amongst the Central Bantu," in A. R. Radcliffe-Brown and Daryll Forde, eds., *African Systems of Kinship and Marriage*, Pp. 207-251. London and New York: Oxford University Press.

___1964. "Authority Patterns in Traditional Buganda," in Lloyd A. Fallers, ed., *The King's Men: Leadership and Status in Buganda on the Eve of Independence.* Pp. 256-293. London and New York: Oxford University Press.

Richerson, Peter J., and Robert Boyd. 1992. "Cultural Inheritance and Evolutionary Ecology," in Eric Alden Smith and Bruce Winterhalder, eds., *Evolutionary Ecology and Human Behavior.* Pp. 61-92. New York: Aldine de Gruyter.

Ricketts, Wendell, and Roberta Achtenberg. 1990. "Adoption and Foster Parenting for Lesbians and Gay Men: Creating New Traditions in Family," in Frederick W. Bozett and Marvin B. Sussman. eds., *Homosexuality and Family Relations.* New York: The Haworth Press, Pp. 83-118.

Riesenberg, Saul H. 1968. *The Native Polity of Ponape.* Washington: Smithsonian Institution Press.

Rigby, Peter. 1969. *Cattle and Kinship Among the Gogo: A Semi-Pastoral Society of Central Tanzania.* Ithaca and London: Cornell University Press.

Roberts, Ron E. 1971. *The New Communes: Coming Together in America.* Englewood Cliffs, N.J.: Prentice-Hall.

Robertson, Constance Noyes. 1970. *Oneida Community: An Autobiography, 1851-1876.* Syracuse: Syracuse University Press.

Rogers, Edwards S. 1972. "The Mistassini Cree," in M. G. Bicchieri, ed., *Hunters and Gatherers Today.* Pp. 90-137. New York: Monthly Review Press.

Rogers, Garth. 1977. "'The Father's Sister is Black': A Consideration of Female Rank and Power in Tonga." *Journal of the Polynesian Society* 86: 157-182.

Rogers, Susan Carol and Sonya Solomon. 1983. "Inheritance and Social Organization Among Family Farmers." *American Ethnologist* 10: 529-550.

Rohlen, Thomas. 1974. *For Harmony and Strength: Japanese White Collar Organization in Anthropological Perspective.* Berkeley and Los Angeles: University of California Press.

___1983. *Japan's High Schools.* Berkeley and Los Angeles: University of California Press.

Roland, Alan. 1988. *In Search of Self in India and Japan: Toward a Cross-Cultural Psychiatry.* Princeton: Princeton University Press.

Rollier, Anne-Marie Dourlen. 1977. "Law and the Status of Women in France," in Columbia Human Righs Law Review, ed., *Law and the Status of Women: An International Symposium.* Pp. 51-68. Centre for Social Development and Humanitarian Affairs, United Nations.

Rosaldo, Michelle Zimbalist. 1974. "Woman, Culture, and Society: A Theoretical Overview," in Michelle Z. Rosaldo and Louise Lamphere, eds., *Woman, Culture, and Society.* Pp. 67-88. Stanford: Stanford University Press.

___1980. "The Use and Abuse of Anthropology." *Signs* 5, 3: 389-407.

Rose, Frederick G. G. 1960. *Classification of Kin, Age Structure, and Marriage Among the Groote Eylandt Aborigines: A Study in Method and a Theory of Australian Kinship.* Berlin: Akademische Verlag.

___1968. "Australian Marriage, Land-Owning Groups, and Initiations," in Richard B. Lee and Irven DeVore, eds., *Man the Hunter.* Pp. 200-208. Chicago: Aldine,

Rosenfeld, Henry. 1968. "The Contradiction between Property, Kinship, and Power as Reflected in the Marriage System of an Arab Village," in J. G. Peristiany, ed., *Contributions to Mediterranean Sociology,* Pp. 247-260. The Hague: Mouton.

Rosman, Abraham, and Paula G. Rubel. 1972. *Feasting with Mine Enemy: Rank and Exchange Among Northwest Coast Societies.* New York: Columbia University Press.

Rynkiewich, Michael A. 1976. "Adoption and Land Tenure Among the Arno Marshallese," in Ivan Brady, ed., *Transactions in Kinship.* Pp. 93-119. Honolulu: University Press of Hawaii.

Sahlins, Marshall D. 1957. "Differentiation by Adaptation in Polynesian Societies," in Alan Howard, ed., *Polynesia: Readings on a Culture Area.* Pp. 46-55. Scranton, London, and Toronto: Chandler P.C.

___1958. *Social Stratification in Polynesia.* Seattle: University of Washington Press.

___1961. "The Segmentary Lineage: An Organization of Predatory Expansion," *American Anthropologist* 63: 322-45.

___1972. *Stone Age Economics.* Chicago: Aldine.

___1976. *Culture and Practical Reason.* Chicago: University of Chicago Press.

Sahlins, Marshall D. and Elman R. Service. 1960. *Evolution and Culture.* Ann Arbor: University of Michgan Press.

Sanders, Irwin. 1949. *Balkan Village.* Lexington, KY: University of Kentucky Press.

Sang, Barbara 1984. "Lesbian Relationships: A Struggle Toward Partner Equality," in Trudy Darty and Sandee Potter, eds., *Women-Identified Women.* Pp. 51-65. Palo Alto: Mayfield Publishing Company.

Sangree, Walter H. 1965. "The Bantu Tiriki of Western Kenya," in James L.Gibbs, Jr., ed., *Peoples of Africa.* Pp. 43-79. New York: Holt, Rinehart and Winston.

Sauter, John, and Bruce Johnson 1974. *Tillamook Indians of the Oregon Coast.* Portland, Oregon: Binfords & Mort.

Scheper-Hughes, Nancy 1987. "Culture, Scarcity and Maternal Thinking: Mother Love and Child Death in Northeastern Brazil," in Nancy Scheper-Hughes, ed., *Child Survival.* Pp. 187-208. Dordrecht: D. Reidel.

Schmid, J. 1988. "Principles Emerging from Sociology for Definitions and Typologies of Household Structures," in Nico Keilman, Anton Kuijsten, and Ad Vossens, eds., *Modelling Household Formation and Dissolution.* Pp. 13-22. Oxford: Clarendon Press.

Schneider, Harold K. 1981. *The Africans*. Englewood Cliffs, NJ: PrenticeHall.

Schwarz, Karl. 1983. "Les Ménages en République Fédérale d'Allemagne, 1961-1971-1981. *Population* (Paris) 38: 565-584.

___1988. "Household Trends in Europe After World War II," in Nico Keilman, Anton Kuijsten, and Ad Vossen, eds., *Modelling Household Formation and Dissolution*. Pp.13-22. Oxford: Clarendon Press.

Schwartz, Theodore. 1983. "Anthropology: A Quaint Science." *American Anthropologist* 85, 4: 919-929.

Scott, Joseph W. 1986. "From Teenage Parenthood to Polygamy: Case Studies in Black Polygamous Family Formation." *Western Journal of Black Studies* 10, 4: 172-179.

Scott, Joseph W., and Albert Black. 1989. "Deep Structures of African American Family Life: Female and Male Kin Networks." *Western Journal of Black Studies* 13, 1: 17-24.

Service, Elman R. 1962. *Primitive Social Organization: An Evolutionary Perspective*. New York: Random House.

Shenker, Barry. 1986. *Intentional Communities*. London: Routledge and Kegan Paul.

Shih, Chuan-Kang. 1993. "The Yongning Moso: Sexual Union, Household Organization, Gender and Ethnicity in a Matrilineal Duolocal Society in Southwest China." Ph.D. Dissertation, Stanford University.

Shorter, Edward. 1975. *The Making of the Modern Family*. New York: Basic Books.

Shorter, M.G. 1972. *Chiefship in Western Tanzania: A Political History of the Kimbu*. Oxford: Clarendon Press.

Shostak, Marjorie. 1982. *Nisa: The Life and Words of a !Kung Woman*. New York: Vintage.

Silberbauer, George. 1981. *Hunter and Habitat in the Central Kalahari Desert*. Cambridge: Cambridge University Press.

Silverman, Sydel. 1968. "Agricultural Organization, Social Structure, and Values in Italy: Amoral Familism Reconsidered." *American Anthropologist* 70: 1-20.

___1975. *Three Bells of Civilization*. New York: Columbia University Press.

Sinha, D.P. 1972. "The Birhors," in M. G. Bicchieri, ed., *Hunters and Gatherers Today*. Pp. 371-403. New York: Holt, Rinehart, and Winston.

Siu, Helen F. 1993. "The Revival of Brideprice and Dowry in Rural Guangdong," in Deboarh Davis and Stevan Harrell, eds., *Chinese Families in the Post-Mao Era*. Pp. 165-188. Berkeley and Los Angeles: University of California Press.

Sjoberg, Gideon. 1960. *The Preindustrial City: Past and Present*. Glencoe: The Free Press.

Slobodin, Richard 1969. "Leadership and Participation in a Kutchin Trapping Party," in David Damas, ed., *Contributions to Anthropology: Band Societies*. Pp. 56-89. Ottawa: National Museums of Canada.

Smith, Eric Alden. 1991. *Inujjuamiut Foraging Strategies: Evolutionary Ecology of an Arctic Hunting Economy*. New York: Aldine de Gruyter.

Smith, Eric Alden, and S. Abigail Smith 1994. "Inuit Sex Ratio Variation: Population Control, Ethnographic Artifact, or Parental Manipulation?" *Current Anthropology* 35, 5: 595-623.

Smith, M. G. 1955. *The Economy of Hausa Communities of Zaria*. London: H.M. Stationery Office.

___1965. "The Hausa of Northern Nigeria," in James L. Gibbs, Jr., ed., *Peoples of*

Africa. Pp. 121-155. New York: Holt, Rinehart and Winston.

Smith, Marian W. 1940. *The Puyallup-Nisqually*. New York: Columbia University Press.

Smith, Robert J. 1975. *Ancestor Worship in Contemporary Japan*. Stanford: Stanford University Press.

___1978. *Kurusu: The Price of Progress in A Japanese Village, 1951-1975*. Stanford: Stanford University Press.

___1983. *Japanese Society: Tradition, Self, and the Social Order*. Cambridge: Cambridge University Press.

Sorensen, Clark Wesley. 1981. Household, Family, and Economy in a Korean Mountain Village. Unpublished Ph.D. Dissertation, University of Washington.

___1988. *Over the Mountains are Mountains: Korean Peasant Households and Their Adaptations to Rapid Industrialization*. Seattle and London: University of Washington Press.

Southwold, Martin. 1965. "The Ganda of Uganda," in James L. Gibbs, Jr.,ed., *Peoples of Africa*. Pp. 1-118. New York: Holt, Rinehart and Winston.

Spiro, Melford E. 1955. *Kibbutz: Venture in Utopia*. Cambridge: Harvard University Press.

___1977. *Kinship and Marriage in Burma*. Berkeley and Los Angeles: University of California Press.

___1979. *Gender and Culture: Kibbutz Women Revisited*. Durham: Duke University Press.

Spoehr, Alexander. 1949. *Majuro: A Village in the Marshall Islands*. Fieldiana: Anthropology Volume No. 39. Chicago: Natural History Museum.

Statistics Bureau, Management and Coordination Agency, Government of Japan. 1995. *Japan Statistical Yearbook, 1995*. Tokyo.

Stearns, Mary Lee. 1984. "Succession to Chiefship in Haida Society," in Jay Miller and Carol M. Eastman, eds. *The Tsimshian and Their Neighbors of the North Pacific Coast*. Seattle: University of Washington Press.

Stenning, Derrick J. 1958. "Household Viability Among the Pastoral Fulani," in Jack Goody, ed., *The Developmental Cycle in Domestic Groups*. Pp. 92-119. Cambridge: Cambridge University Press.

___1965. "The Pastoral Fulani of Northern Nigeria," in James L. Gibbs, Jr., ed., *Peoples of Africa*. Pp. 363-401. New York: Holt, Rinehart and Winston.

Sternlieb, George, and James W. Hughes. 1986. "Demographics and Housing in America." *Population Bulletin* 6, 1.

Steward, Julian H. 1938. *Basin-Plateau Aboriginal Sociopolitical Groups*. Washington, D.C.: U.S. Government Printing Office.

___1963. *Theory of Culture Change: The Methodology of Multilinear Evolution*. Urbana: University of Illinois Press.

Stirling, Paul. 1965. *Turkish Village*. London: Weidenfeld and Nicolson.

Stites, Richard W. n.d. "Women's Autonomy and the Stablility of Marriage in African Patrilinral Societies." Unpublished paper.

Sung, Lung-Sheng. 1981. "Property and Family division in Northern Taiwan," in Emily Martin Ahern and Hill Gates, eds., *The Anthropology of Taiwanese Society*. Pp. 361-378. Stanford: Stanford University Press.

Suttles, Wayne Prescott. 1951. Economic Life of the Coast Salish of Haro and Rosario Straits. Unpublished Ph.D. Dissertation, University of Washington.

___1955. *Katzie Ethnographic Notes*. Victoria, B.C., British Columbia Provincial Museum. Anthropology in British Columbia: Memoir No. 2.

___1958. "Private Knowledge, Morality, and Social Classes Among the Coast Salish." *American Anthropologist* 60: 497-507.

___1960. "Affinal Ties, Subsistence, and Prestige Among the Coast Salish." *American Anthropologist* (n.s.), 62: 296-305.

___1968. "Coping with Abundance: Subsistence on the Northwest Coast," in Richard B. Lee and Irven Devore, eds., *Man the Hunter*. Pp. 56-68. Chicago: Aldine Publishing Company.

Sutton, Peter and Bruce Rigsby. 1982. "People with 'Politicks': Management of Land and Personnel on Australia's Cape York Peninsula," in Nancy M. Williams and Eugene S. Hunn, eds., *Resource Managers*. Pp. 155-171. Boulder: Westview Press.

Swain, Norma Lippincott. 1979 [1975]. "The North American Phalanx," *Monmouth County Historical Bulletin*, 50-59; reprinted in Rosabeth Moss Kanter, ed., *Communes*, Pp. 257-263.

Swan, James G. 1870. *The Indians of Cape Flattery, at the Entrance to the Strait of Fuca, Washington Territory*. Smithsonian Institution.

Swanton, J. R. 1905. *Contributions to the Ethnology of the Haida*. Memoirs of the American Museum of Natural History, Vol. V, Part 1. New York: G. E. Stechert.

Synak, Bronan. 1989. "Formal Care for Elderly People in Poland." *Journal of Cross-Cultural Gerontology* 4: 107-127.

Tambiah, S. J. 1970. *Buddhism and the Spirit Cults in North-east Thailand*. Cambridge: Cambridge University Press.

___1972. "Dowry and Bridewealth and the Property Rights of Women in South Asia," in Jack Goody and S. J. Tambiah, *Bridewealth and Dowry*. Pp. 59-169. Cambridge: Cambridge University Press.

Tauxe, Caroline. 1992. "Family Cohesion and Capitalist Hegemony: Cultural Accommodation on the North Dakota Farm." *Dialectical Anthropology* 17, 3: 291-317.

Tentori, Tullio. 1976. "Social Class and Family in a South Italian Town—Matera," in J. G. Peristiany, ed., *Mediterranean Family Structures*. Pp. 273-286. Cambridge: Cambridge University Press.

Thomas, Elizabeth Marshall. 1958. *The Harmless People*. New York: Natural History Press.

Thomas, John Byron. 1980. "The Namonuito Solution to the 'Matrilineal Puzzle'." *American Ethnologist* 7: 172-177.

Tindale, Norman B. 1972 "The Pitjandjara," in M. G. Bicchieri, ed., *Hunters and Gatherers Today*. Pp. 217-268. New York: Holt, Rinehart and Winston.

Torotilla, Toni. 1987. "On a Creative Edge," in Sandra Pollock and Jeanne Vaughn, eds., *Politics of the Heart: A Lesbian Parenting Anthology*. Pp. 168-174. Ithaca, NY: Firebrand Books.

Tsurumi Kazuko. 1970. *Social Change and the Individual: Japan Before and After Defeat in World War II*. Princeton, NJ: Princeton University Press.

Turnbull, Colin M. 1961. *The Forest People*. New York: Simon and Schuster.

___1965a. Wayward Servants: *The Two Worlds of the African Pygmies*. Garden City, NY: Natural History Press.

___1965b. *The Mbuti Pygmies: An Ethnographic Survey*. New York: American Museum of Natural History, Anthropological Papers, Volume 50, part 3.

United Nations. 1988, 1990. *Demographic Yearbook 1986, 1988.* New York: United Nations.

Upham, Frank K. 1987. *Law and Social Change in Postwar Japan.* Cambridge, MA: Harvard University Press.

van de Kaa, Dirk J. 1987. "Europe's Second Demographic Revolution." *Population Bulletin* 42, 1.

van den Berghe, Pierre L. 1979. *Human Family Systems: An Evolutionary View.* New York: Elsevier.

van der Sprenkel, Sybille. 1962. *Legal Institutions in Manchu China.* London: Althlone Press.

Vaness, Dorothy. 1961. *Fatima and Her Sisters.* New York: John Day.

Van Horn, Susan Householder. 1988. *Women, Work, and Fertility, 1900-1986.* New York: New York University Press.

Vaughan, James Daniel. 1984. "Tsimshian Potlatch and Society," in Jay Miller and Carol M. Eastman, eds., *The Tsimshian and Their Neighbors of the North Pacific Coast.* Pp. 58-68. Seattle: University of Washington Press.

Vogel, Ezra F. 1963. *Japan's New Middle Class.* Berkeley and Los Angeles: University of California Press.

Wallace, Carolyn M. 1987. "Priesthood and Motherhood: Women and Men in the Church of Jesus Christ of Latter-Day Saints," in Caroline Bynum, Stevan Harrell, and Paula M. Richman, eds., *Gender and Religion: Essays on the Complexity of Symbols.* Pp. 117-140. Boston: Beacon Press.

Wang, Sung-Hsing. 1971. Pooling and Sharing in a Chinese Fishing Economy— Kuei Shan Tao. Ph.D. Dissertation, Tokyo University.

Ward, Barbara. 1966. "Chinese Fishermen in Hong Kong: Their Post-Peasant Economy," in Maurice Freedman, ed., *Social Organization, Essay Presented to Raymond Firth.* Chicago: Aldine Publishing Company.

Warner, W. Llloyd. 1958. *A Black Civilization* (revised edition). New York: Harper Torchbooks.

Washburne, Carolyn Kott. 1987. "Happy Birthday from Your Other Mom," in Sandra Pollack and Jeanne Vaughn, eds., *Politics of the Heart: A Lesbian Parenting Anthology.* Pp. 142-145. Ithaca, NY: Firebrand Books.

Watanabe, Hitoshi. 1968. "Subsistence Ecology of Northern Food Gatherers, with Special Reference to the Ainu," in Richard B. Lee and Irven DeVore, eds., *Man the Hunter.* Pp. 69-77. Chicago: Aldine.

Weiner, Annette B. 1985. "Inalienable Wealth." *American Ethnologist* 12:210-227.

Weiss, Kenneth. 1981. "Physiological Aspects of Human Aging," in Pamela T. Amoss and Stevan Harrell, eds., *Other Ways of Growing Old.* Pp. 25-58. Stanford: Stanford University Press.

Welch, Holmes. 1957. *Taoism: The Parting of the Way.* Boston: Beacon.

Wells, Robert V. 1982. *Revolutions in Americans' Lives. Contributions in Family Studies* #6. Westport, Connecticut and London: Greenwood Press.

Weng, Naiqun. 1993. "The Mother House," Ph.D. Dissertation, University of Rochester.

Weston, Kath. 1991. *Families We Choose: Lesbians, Gays, Kinship.* New York: Columbia University Press.

White, Isobel M. 1970. "Aboriginal Women's Status: A Paradox Resolved," in Fay Gale, ed., *Woman's Role in Aboriginal Society.* Pp. 21-29. Canberra: Australian Institute of Aboriginal Studies.

Williams, Nancy M. 1982. "A Boundary is to Cross: Observations of Yolngu Boundaries and Permission," in Nancy M. Williams and Eugene S. Hunn, eds., *Resource Managers*. Pp. 131-153. Boulder: Westview Press.

Willie, Charles Vert. 1985. *Black and White Families: A Study in Complementarity*. Bayside, NY; General Hall and Co.

Wilson, Monica. 1950. "Nyakyusa Kinship," in A.R. Radcliffe-Brown and Daryll Forde, eds. *African Systems in Kinship and Marriage*. Pp. 111-139. London and New York: Oxford University Press.

___1963 (1951). *Good Company: A Study of Nyakyusa Age-Villages*. Boston: Beacon Press.

Winans, Edgar V. 1974. "The Shambala Family," in Robert F. Gray and P. H. Gulliver, eds., *The Family Estate in Africa: Studies in the Role of Property in Family Structure and Lineage Continuity*. Pp. 35-61. London: Routledge and Kegan Paul.

Winner, Irene. 1971. *A Slovenian Village*. Providence, RI: Brown University Press.

Wittfogel, Karl August. 1957. *Oriental Despotism: A Comparative Study of Total Power*. New York: Vintage.

Wolf, Arthur P. 1970. "Chinese Kinship and Mourning Dress," in Maurice Freedman, ed., *Family and Kinship in Chinese Society*. Pp. 189-207. Stanford: Stanford University Press.

___1985. "Chinese Family Size: A Myth Revitalized," in Hsieh Jih-chang and Chuang Ying-chang, eds., *The Chinese Family and Its Ritual Behavior*. Pp. 30-49. Taipei: Academia Sincia.

Wolf, Arthur P. and Chieh-Shan Huang. 1980. *Marriage and Adoption in China*. Stanford: Stanford Univerity Press.

Wolf, Eric R. 1982. *Europe and the People Without History*. Berkeley and Los Angeles: University of California Press.

Wolf, Margery. 1972. *Women and the Family in Rural Taiwan*. Stanford: Stanford University Press.

Woodburn, James. 1968. "Stability and Flexibility in Hadza Residential Groupings," in Richard B. Lee and Irven DeVore, eds., *Man the Hunter*. Pp. 103-111. Chicago: Aldine.

Wrigley, C. C. 1964. "The Changing Economic Structure of Buganda," in *The King's Men: Leadership and Status in Buganda on the Eve of Independence*. London and New York: Oxford University Press.

Wrigley, E.A. 1969. *Population and History*. New York: McGraw Hill

Wrigley, E.A. and R.S. Schofield. 1981. *The Population History of England, 1541-1871*. London: Edward Arnold.

Yalman, Nur. 1967. *Under the Bo Tree*. Berkeley and Los Angeles: University of California Press.

Yanagisako, Sylvia Junko. 1979. "Family and Household," in Bernard J. Siegel, ed., *Annual Review of Anthropology* 8: 161-205.

Yang, C. K. 1959. *A Chinese Village in Early Communist Transition*. Cambridge, Mass.: MIT Press.

Yengoyan, Aram. 1968. "Demographic and Ecological Influences on Aboriginal Australian Marriage Sections," in Richard B. Lee and Irven DeVore, eds., *Man the Hunter*. Pp. 185-199. Chicago: Aldine.

Yim, Seong-Hi. 1961. Die Grundlage und die Entwicklung der Familie in Korea. Ph.D. Dissertation, Philosophischen Fakultät der Universität zu Köln.

Young, Michael, and Peter Willmott. 1957. *Family and Kinship in East London.* Harmondsworth: Penguin.

____1973. *The Symmetrical Family.* New York: Pantheon.

Zablocki, Benjamin. 1971. *The Joyful Community.* Baltimore: Penguin.

Zhao Xishun. 1985. "Zhuanye Hu Jiating Tedian Qianxi—Sichuan Sheng Nongmin Jiating Chouyang Diaocha Qingkuang" ("A Preliminary Analysis of Characteristics of Specialized Households—An Investigation of a Sample of Farm Households in Sichuan Province.") Shehui Kexue Yanjiu (Social Science Research).

Znaniecky, Florian. 1941. "The Changing Cultural Ideals of the Family." *Marriage and Family Living* 3: 58-62.

Zook, Nancy, and Rachel Hallenbeck. 1987. "Lesbian Coparenting: Creative Connections," in Sandra Pollack and Jeanne Vaughn, eds., *Politics of the Heart: A Lesbian Parenting Anthology.* Pp. 89-93. Ithaca, NY: Firebrand Books.

Index

About the Book and Author

This detailed study maps the variations in family systems throughout the world, focusing on the ways families interact with their societies. Tracing the developmental cycle of families in a wide range of times and places, Stevan Harrell shows how family members in different societies must cooperate to perform various activities and thus organize themselves in particular ways.

Within six major divisions, the book describes families in nomadic bands, traditional African societies, Polynesian and Micronesian societies, native societies of the Northwest, pre-industrial class societies, and modern industrial societies. Within each group, the author's copious examples demonstrate the variation from one family system to another. His case studies are clearly illustrated with a unique set of diagrams that allow comparison of complex groups and of family processes extending over a generation. Scholars and advanced students alike will find this ambitious book an invaluable resource.

Stevan Harrell is professor of anthropology at the University of Washington.